Encyclopedia of World Scriptures

ALSO BY MARY ELLEN SNODGRASS
AND FROM McFARLAND

Who's Who in the Middle Ages (2001)

A Multicultural Dictionary of Literary Terms (1999)

*Storytellers: A Biographical Dictionary of 120
English-Speaking Performers Worldwide* (1998)

Encyclopedia of World Scriptures

MARY ELLEN SNODGRASS

McFarland & Company, Inc., Publishers
Jefferson, North Carolina, and London

Library of Congress Cataloguing-in-Publication Data

Snodgrass, Mary Ellen.
Encyclopedia of world scriptures / Mary Ellen Snodgrass.
p.   cm.
Includes bibliographical references and index.
ISBN 0-7864-1005-1 (illustrated case binding : 50# alkaline paper) ∞
1. Sacred books—Encyclopedias.   I. Title.
BL70.S56   2001   291.8'2'03 — dc21   2001037057

British Library cataloguing data are available

Manufactured in the United States of America

*McFarland & Company, Inc., Publishers
Box 611, Jefferson, North Carolina 28640
www.mcfarlandpub.com*

For my friend Joan Lail, who walks with God

Acknowledgments

I would like to thank the following for their assistance: Wanda Rozzelle, reference librarian, Catawba County Library, Newton, North Carolina; Beth Bradshaw, reference librarian, Patrick Beaver Library, Hickory, North Carolina; Avis Gachet of Wonderland Books, Granite Falls, North Carolina; Burl Mc-Cuiston, reference librarian, Lenoir Rhyne College, Hickory, North Carolina; and Mark Schumacher, reference librarian, Jackson Library, University of North Carolina, Greensboro, North Carolina.

Table of Contents

Preface

The *Encyclopedia of World Scriptures* presents religious texts through history, description, citation, and analysis. Entries name works from the cities of Mecca, Jerusalem, Rome, Delphi, and Salt Lake City; from caves in Qumran and mountains in Japan; from the Indus Valley, East Asian mainland, American West and Great Lakes, ancient Egypt and Greece, eastern Mediterranean, Guatemala, and the separated Hebrew communities in Iberia and the German states. These entries demonstrate how the experiences of a young monk in a Zen monastery resonate with those of a Christian in North America, a Christian Scientist in Boston, and a Copt in Ethiopia; and how the Hindu prayers of the Granth echo the humility and thanksgiving found in Jesus' Sermon on the Mount, Joseph Smith's revelations from the angel Moroni, Deganawida's message of peace to the Mohawk, and the suppliant at the Delphic oracle singing the Hymn to Apollo.

To locate and identify the most important bodies of scripture, I have relied on a variety of source materials. For general reference, I anchored my work to primary sources plus classic reference works: *The Encyclopedia of Religion and Ethics, The Interpreter's Dictionary of the Bible, The Golden Bough, The Anchor Bible, The Penguin Atlas of Diasporas, Chronology of Native American History, Eerdmans' Handbook to the Bible,* Walter Abbott's *The Bible Reader,* the *New Catholic Encyclopedia, Encyclopedia Americana,* and *Encyclopædia Britannica.*

To control variances in identification, birth and death dates, locales, and events, I kept standard works on hand: *Zen Dictionary, A Dictionary of Buddhism, The Religions of Man, World Religions, The Encyclopedia of Judaism, The Penguin Dictionary of Religions, The Oxford Dictionary of World Religions, Encyclopedia of Mormonism, A Religious History of the American People, The Dictionary of Bible and Religion, The Oxford Annotated Bible, Harper's Bible Commentary, Encyclopedia of Japan, Eerdmans' Handbook of the World's Religions, The Sacred Writings of the World's Great Religions, Essential Sacred Writings from Around the World, Who's Who in Christianity,* and *Who's Who in Jewish History.*

I mined basic information from Karen Armstrong's *A History of God,* Swami Prabhupada's *Bhagavad-Gita as It Is,* Norman F. Cantor's *The Jewish Experience,* Gershom Scholem's *Kabbalah,* Venerable Bede's *History of the English Church and People,* Joseph Telushkin's *Jewish Literacy* and *Jewish Wisdom,* George Braziller's *Great Religions of Modern Man,* Warren Hollister's *Medieval Europe,* Kenneth K. S. Ch'en's *Buddhism,* William Montgomery Watt's *Companion to the Qur'an,* Joseph Strayer's *Dictionary of the Middle Ages,* Gerald L. Berry's *Religions of the World,* Hans Wolfgang Schumann's *Buddhism,* Thomas Hoover's *The Zen Experience,* and Edward Conze's *Buddhist Texts Through the Ages.*

For background material, I read from Joseph Epes Brown's *The Sacred Pipe,* Daniel Boorstin's *The Creators* and *The Discoverers,* Richard Cavendish's *Man, Myth and Magic,* Arvind Sharma's *Women in World Religions,* Geza Vermes' *The Complete Dead Sea Scrolls in English,* Patricia Crone and Michael Cook's *Hagarism: The Making of the Islamic World,* R. A. Nicholson's *Rumi: Poet and Mystic,* Siegfried Morenz's *Egyptian Religion,* Bruce Metzger's *The Apocrypha of the Old Testament,* John G. Neihardt's *When the Tree Flowered,* Marvin Meyer's *The Secret Teachings of Jesus,* Peter Powell's *Sweet Medicine,* Michael F. Steltenkamp's *The Sacred Vision,* and H. Michael Marquardt and Wesley P. Walters's *Inventing Mormonism: Tradition and the Historical Record.*

Of particular help were current religious publications and academic journals: *Americas, Earth Island Journal, Western American Literature, Islamic Herald, Catholic Historical Review, Moksha Journal, India Currents, Atlantic Monthly, Journal of the Royal Anthropological Institute, Journal of the American Oriental Society, Religious News Service, Twentieth-Century Literature, Journal of Asian*

Studies, Philosophy East and West, Harvard Theological Review, Christianity Today, Islam & Christian Muslim Relations, Parabola, Syracuse Journal, UNESCO, Journal of Ecclesiastical History, Hinduism Today, and *Bulletin of the Sri Ramakrishna Institute of Culture.*

I am indebted to numerous internet sites, particularly "Significant Events in Jewish and World History," "Tolerance in Islam," "The Catholic Encyclopedia," "Catholic Online Saints," "The Nyingma Lineage," "The Nyingma Tradition," Islamic Information Network, *Medieval Sourcebook* from Fordham University, Sikhs.Org, "Muslims Online," "The Nag Hammadi Library," "Native American Religion," *The Utah Encyclopedia*, "Purpose of Tsubaki America," and other sites mounted and maintained by the University of Chicago, Columbia University, Buddhanet, Jewishgates.org, University of Pennsylvania, Kabbalahsociety, University of Kentucky, Harvard University, University of Calgary, Library of Congress, University of Virginia, and Cornell.

In order to shape my research into a usable volume, I grouped facts under individual headings, then reframed the data and created time line and glossary. Most maddening to control and order was the variance of spellings in works that have flourished in multiple settings as religious ideas spread from nation to nation and continent to continent. For mastery of sacred geography, I value cartographer Raymond Barrett of Imagine Avenue in Hollywood, California, for his guidance in map drawing.

As an adjunct to self-directed reading, study, analysis, research, library reference, and lesson planning, this volume includes these study aids:

- a map that locates the germ of sacred revelation and writing in specific sites and general locales all over the globe.
- a brief glossary of crucial and recurrent terms. The *h*-based pronunciation system presents a simplified representation of sound without the intrusion of diacritical markings.
- a time line of datable events from the history of world scripture, from the beginnings of the I Ching in 2800 B.C.E. to publication of a child's version of the Popul Vuh in 1999. Entries on this time line emphasize sacred literature, religion, history, and human lives, especially those that reveal God's word through song, composition, translation, and publishing. To counterbalance traditional reli-

gions' bent toward patriarchy, I stress women's contributions wherever possible, including the *Women's Bible*, Mary Baker Eddy's astounding canon, and the stories and contributions of female Tantrists, the Pythia, Hafsa, Ruth, Izanami, Deborah, Chökyi, Mary Magdalene, Esther, Sarah, Ame no Uzzume no Mikoto, Hagar, the Virgin Mary, White Buffalo Calf Woman, Khadijah, Shiva, and Ayesha.

- an extensive bibliography of print and electronic sources, some containing original, searchable texts and commentary in Latin, Greek, Hebrew, Sanskrit, Aramaic, and modern foreign languages.

Significant to this volume is the comprehensive index with ample cross-referencing to assist researchers toward further study of print and electronic sources.

At the heart of this work is my intent to lessen confusion of identity and to make available biographies of the standard figures who have transmitted the events and writings of world religions—Confucius, Ezra, Paul, Black Elk, Deganawida, Lao-Tzu, Hiawatha, Muhammad, Arjuna, Krishna, Mormon, Rumi, Maimonides, Moses de Leon, Paul Wallace, O no Yasumaro, Joseph Smith, Nanak, and Luke—along with Essenes, Chinese emperors, Arab caliphs, Lakota shamans, lamas, the Longhouse Council, temple priests, soothsayers, and myriad translators who have made sacred works available in multiple languages. For maximum coverage, the entries delve into literary genres such as allegory, ghazal, and fable as well as evidence of genocide, syncretizers, religious wars, and modern redactors. The text considers, among others, painters and composers who have reset religious episodes as art, printers and writers of concordances, and famous people whose lives have mirrored sacred texts, such as Hans Christian Andersen, Johann Sebastian Bach, Ralph Waldo Emerson, Mary Baker Eddy, Mohandas Gandhi, Martin Luther, Percy Shelley, Enid Neihardt, Henry David Thoreau, Lucy Looks Twice, Johannes Brahms, Crazy Horse, and Martin Luther King, Jr.

The *Encyclopedia of World Scriptures* invites the reader, writer, historian, minister, worshiper, artist, teacher, librarian, researcher, or editor to sample a wide range of faiths, philosophies, and works and to contemplate the lives of earnest and intense men and women who, from prehistory to the present, have advanced our knowledge of the divine.

Introduction

From their earliest existence on earth, human beings have yearned to comprehend what they perceive as sacred—land, water, sky, and the inner landscape of mind and heart. Holy words, chants, liturgies, and narratives have enabled individuals to embrace and examine the mysteries of the universe. Bodies of liturgical composition survived through oral transmission for centuries until at last calligraphers could inscribe them in pictograph, symbol, and coded cipher or write them in words on stone stele, mural, scroll, parchment, and paper. Through repetitions of sacred speech and writing, couples enter holy wedlock, infants receive consecration and blessing, youths advance to adulthood, rulers dedicate temporal powers to God, cities pledge themselves to peace, and the dead pass from an earthly existence to the afterlife.

Of the many versions of global scriptures, this book is a reference to twenty-seven major works, the most sacred and influential writings of world history. The texts vary with the people: holy laws for Jews and Iroquois, funeral prescriptions from the Book of the Dead, ceremonies for Zoroastrians, Hindus, Greeks, Lakota, and Tibetan Buddhists. The literary genres include hero stories from the Quiché Popol Vuh and Japanese Kojiki, word puzzles from the koans of Zen Buddhism and the Ethiopian Book of the Dead, Christ lore from the Apocrypha and New Testament, matrices from the I Ching and Tantra, and numerology from the Jewish Kabbala. Style and intent vary widely; a vast gulf divides the rapture of Rumi's Mathnawi from the spare aphorism of Confucius's Analects, Muhammad's revelations in the Koran, and advice and comfort from Mary Baker Eddy's Christian Science writings.

Despite differences in style, purpose, and tone, all scriptures speak to human needs. The Tanakh promises Jews a messiah. The New Testament inspires Christians to world evangelism. The Tibetan Book of the Dead speaks to individuals letting go of the body and passing to an existence beyond life. Diviners of the future turn to the I Ching; Hindus and Buddhists consider the Tantra for everyday advice. The Avesta, like many sacred texts, speaks to proponents of one god; the Granth, to those serving the almighty; the Dhammapada, to the introspective ones who yearn to unite with God; *Black Elk Speaks* to Lakota worshipers communing with the Great Spirit through vision quest.

To understand how a faith began and took shape requires some knowledge of the rhythms and intensity of holy language, whether that language lists divine names in the Ethiopian Book of the Dead, draws mystic matrices in the Kabbala, intones hymns to Greek deities, or reveals long-hidden Essene texts from the Dead Sea Scrolls. Through the words of communities of the faithful, outsiders can experience the grace of the Koran and Homeric Hymns, the majesty of Rumi's Sufist verse and Egyptian tomb texts, the piety of Christian and Muslim hagiography, the creation myths in the Kojiki and Popol Vuh, and the reassurance of holy dialogues in the Bhagavad Gita and Vedas. From such experience comes understanding of otherness, movement across the divide that keeps "us" from knowing and accepting "them." By reading aloud the metaphors of the Tao-te Ching, ritual chants in the Avesta, history in the Book of Mormon, advice to youth in Proverbs and to new Christians in Paul's letters to the Corinthians, and law in *The White Roots of Peace*, the outsider may perhaps shed some reserve, narrow the space between himself and others, and share a oneness in the universality of holy word.

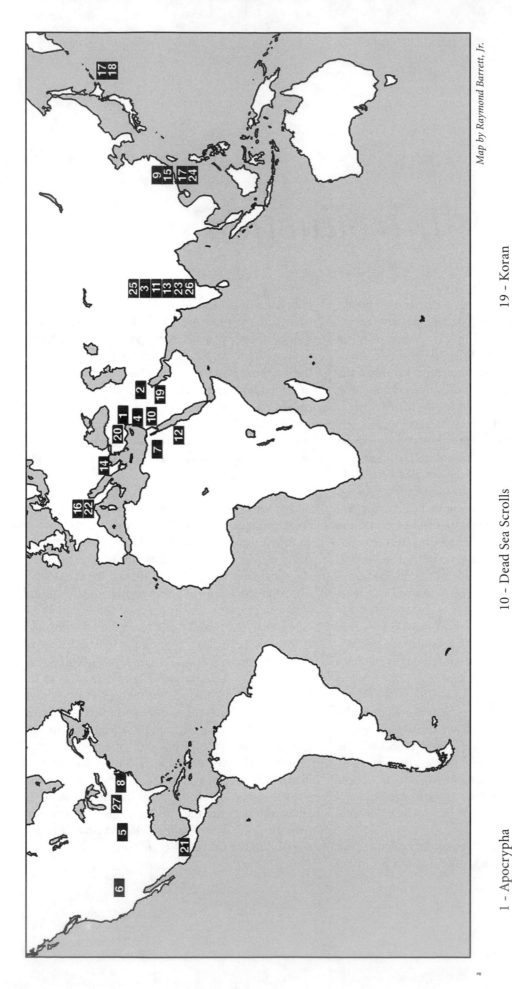

Map by Raymond Barrett, Jr.

1 - Apocrypha
2 - Avesta
3 - Bhagavad Gita
4 - Bible
5 - *Black Elk Speaks*
6 - Book of Mormon
7 - Book of the Dead (Egyptian)
8 - Christian Science writings
9 - Confucius's Analects
10 - Dead Sea Scrolls
11 - Dhammapada
12 - Ethiopian Book of the Dead
13 - Granth
14 - Homeric Hymns
15 - I Ching
16 - Kabbala
17 - Koan
18 - Kojiki
19 - Koran
20 - Mathnawi
21 - Popol Vuh
22 - Talmud
23 - Tantra
24 - Tao-te Ching
25 - Tibetan Book of the Dead
26 - Vedas
27 - *White Roots of Peace*

THE ENCYCLOPEDIA

Adi Granth *see* **Granth**

Analects of Confucius *see* **Confucius's Analects**

Apocrypha The literary term *apocrypha* derives from the Greek *apokryphos*, meaning "hidden or obscured things." The ambiguous term implies two actions—the priests' exclusion of apocryphal books from liturgical services attended by ordinary people and the reservation of more esoteric writings for an exclusive, sophisticated cadre of readers. In contrast to holy books, the Apocrypha are permeated with myth and legend. They contain a willful, human element not found in canonical text. Written anonymously or under obviously assumed identities, they inject disturbing details and extremes of scriptural interpretation. These radical texts dismayed selectors of canon work, who thought of themselves as guardians of the "true word," and caused them to push aside and demonize certain points of view later identified as non-orthodox, anti-orthodox, or gnostic. The styles, themes, and subject matter differ widely. Thus, theologians evaluate the texts individually, except in obvious cases of one writing influencing another.

The Apocrypha to the Old Testament consist of semi-sacred or quasi-sacred writings in various literary genres that appeared after the age of Ezra in the fifth century B.C.E. These post–Ezra works add details of Jewish history into the second century B.C.E. Numbering varies from fifteen books to a longer list that individualizes sections by subhead within books. To Roman Catholic and Orthodox worshipers, the term *Old Testament Apocrypha* carries an authority not recognized by Jews and Protestants, who value these appended works only as supplemental texts. Throughout the English-speaking world, pulpit Bibles in synagogues and Protestant churches dis-play the Old Testament Apocrypha in an addendum printed between Old and New Testaments, where Martin Luther placed them in 1534. In his opinion, they were unequal to sacred scripture, but were "useful and good to read" (Metzer 1965, viii).

The fifty-some New Testament Apocrypha and a sizable sheaf of fragments are less widely known and carry a tarnished image of made-up writings that have no bearing on scripture. Written from the second to the fourth centuries C.E., they lack godly inspiration and tend to replicate events and commentary found in the canon Gospels of Matthew, Mark, Luke, and John and Acts and in the signed writings of the patristic fathers of the church. These postcanon works share two qualities: anonymous or pseudepigraphic authorship and unsubstantiated or obviously false connections to Jesus or his family, apostles, patriarchs, or prophets. Their purpose is to fill in gaps in biblical accounts to satisfy the curiosity of people who wonder about Jesus' childhood and private life and who seek details of his disciples' ministries. The Apocrypha's colorful musings on scripture have served musicians, mosaicists, painters, and poets with artful poses and situations that reflect human suppositions about scripture and the divine.

The Apocrypha consist of a number of genres. Jewish noncanonical works fall into three categories: historical accounts of events not covered in the canon Bible; didactic texts intended to alter the ways of the wicked, blasphemous, and unfaithful; and, apocalyptic revelations of the end of time and the afterlife. New Testament apocryphal writings consist of narratives of Jesus' infancy and childhood, epistles, gospels, acts of the apostles, apocalypses, or agrapha, citations of Jesus not contained within the canon Bible.

The authorized Christian Bible derives from the Greek Bible of Alexandria, the scripture of Hellenized Jews. In the formative stages over the first and second centuries, varying opinions of the apostolic fathers prevailed concerning which writings deserved inclusion in the Bible and which belonged in a peripheral, non-sanctified collection. Among those in question are three major works: the Epistle to the Hebrews, which is not one of Paul's letters; the highly erotic Song of Solomon; and the Book of Revelation, which some scholars doubted because of its arcane imagery and historical implications. Others set aside because of uncertain origin are II Peter, II and III John, James, and Jude. In general, the decision as to what constituted the Holy Bible rested on whether public readings of these texts would enhance worship. In C.E. 170, the first authority, Melito, a Lydian bishop living in Sardis, deliberately separated spurious, theologically unsound writings from the canon Bible, God's hallowed word. In the next century, Origen, an Alexandrian theologian, certified only twenty-two books as the canon Old Testament. North African church councils in 393 and 397 supported a broader interpretation of scripture, which included apocryphal books.

The battle over inclusion and exclusion drew fire from the most learned, respected theological authorities. Jerome, the father of the Latin Bible, supplied the terms *ecclesiastical books* and *deuterocanonical books* to differentiate between holy books and a substratum of honored writings, which did not merit the designation of God-inspired scripture. His use of *Apocrypha* is intentionally pejorative as a warning that only divine writings should guide godly people. Similarly, Sidonius Apollinaris, a late fifth-century bishop from Lyons, France, divided authors into polar opposites: the *authentici* (genuine) Bible writers and the *disputatores* (discursive writers), who composed scriptural commentary, narrative, and dialogue.

Counter to Jerome and Sidonius was the opinion of Augustine of Hippo, a revered fifth-century theologian from Tagaste, Numidia, and author of *De Doctrina Christiana* (On Christian Doctrine; 397). He insisted that the Apocrypha remain in the Latin Vulgate. A century later, the Calabrian scholar Flavius Magnus Aurelius Cassiodorus proposed a system of designations that avoided the canon/noncanon labels. In place of extremes, he suggested four categories of authorship: *introductores* (originators), *expositores* (expounders), *magistri* (teachers), and *patres* (fathers of the church). However, his compromise did not prevail in the final classification of writings.

The Syriac canon Bible, the Peshitta, added to accepted scripture the nine most respected writings: Ecclesiasticus (or, the Wisdom of Jesus, the Son of Sirach); the Wisdom of Solomon; Baruch; the Letter of Jeremiah (sometimes listed as a chapter of Baruch); a dignified religious conclusion to the book of Esther (Esther 10:4–10);

and the final quartet, which forms a series of interpolations that expand the Book of Daniel: the Prayer of Azariah; the Song of the Three Young Men (or the Three Holy Children); Susanna; and Bel and the Dragon.

Ecclesiasticus

The Book of Ecclesiasticus (also Liber Ecclesiasticus; Church Book), one of the oldest apocryphal writings and the longest wisdom book, was composed in Hebrew around 180 B.C.E., probably in Jerusalem. It is the earliest Hebrew text that has survived under the title of its author, who was an *ecclesiasticus* (preacher). In the form of a liturgical text, Ecclesiasticus consists of two volumes divided into chapters 1–23 and 24–51. The anthology is a clever, cerebral compilation of maxims translated into Greek around 132 B.C.E. by Sira's grandson, Yeshua ben Eleazar, a pious student of the Torah and teacher of young men. Unlike other wisdom lore, the collected sapience focuses on the Torah as the consummate source of advice, the touchstone of probity.

Paralleling the Book of Proverbs, the collection begins with an assertion that wisdom comes from God, the author's guiding principle. Much of the advice is an elaboration on the Ten Commandments with injunctions against the seven deadly sins— impiety, pride, envy, avarice, violence, lust, and folly. Among the aphorisms is a popular truism, "The days of a good life are numbered, but a good name endures forever" (Meyer 1992, 183). Practical as well as ethical, such advice is accessible to almost any reader of apocryphal scripture.

Ecclesiasticus is valuable for preserving folksayings, ethics, and guides to courtesy and moral and religious behavior, particularly regarding the treatment of women, which the author details in chapter 9:1–9. The fastidious Sira disdains powerful women, loose women, singers, virgins, harlots, other men's wives, and voluptuous sirens of the streets. In chapter 26:13–18, he provides a picture of the ideal woman, a charming, modest wife, skilled at fattening up her husband and ordering a household.

Following commentary on the honorable physician, plowman, smithy, and potter, a paean to the working class in chapter 38:31–32, 34 urges:

All these rely upon their hands,
  and each is skillful in his own work.
Without them a city cannot be established,
  and men can neither sojourn nor live there...
They keep stable the fabric of the world,
  and their prayer is in the practice of their trade [Abbott 1969, 612].

The theme continues to the end, with chapter 51:30 reminding the reader to work without slacking and to expect a reward from God for diligence. The workaday attitude, tone, and pithy style suggest Benjamin Franklin's *Poor Richard's Almanack.*

Sira's text has influenced later writings. In 1636, Martin Rinkart, a pastor in Eilenburg, Saxony, composed "Nun Danket alle Gott" (Now Thank We All Our God) as a paraphrase of Ecclesiasticus 50:22–24, which asks a bounteous God:

Through all our life be near us,
With ever joyful hearts
  And blessed peace to cheer us;
And keep us in His Grace [*Hymnal of the United Church of Christ* 1974, 307].

The first line of chapter 44, "Let us now praise famous men," served novelist James Agee and photographer Walker Evans as the title of their 1941 photojournalistic treatise on southern laboring families during the depression.

Wisdom of Solomon

Composed anonymously in Alexandria around 50 B.C.E., the Wisdom of Solomon contrasts Jewish with Greek theology. The Greeks' pantheon of detached and self-absorbed gods had little in common with Yahweh, a jealous god who involved himself in the daily affairs of his people and demanded in return total fealty. Through extensive repetition of the word *wisdom*, the book warns Jews that adulteration by Hellenism threatens their survival as a culture and a people of God. The author cites idolatry and beast worship as examples of foolishness and ignorance. If Jews want to remain strong, he declares, they have to be Jews in the fullest sense of tradition and worship.

The author alludes frequently to the bondage of the Hebrews in Egypt and makes use of deft metaphors, including the common figure of Sophia (Wisdom) as a likely bride for the wise man. In an explanation of grace, the author employs an extended metaphor of a sea passage in chapter 14:1–4:

Again, one preparing to sail and about to voyage over raging
  waves
  calls upon a piece of wood more fragile
  than the ship which carries him.
For it was desire for gain that planned that vessel,
  and wisdom was the craftsman who built it;
  but it is thy providence, O Father, that steers its course,
  because thou hast given it a path in the sea,
  and a safe way through the waves,
  showing that thou canst save from every danger,
  so that even if a man lacks skill, he may put to sea [Abbott
    1969, 602].

A curious conclusion to this passage is a blessing for "the wood by which righteousness comes," a reference to

Noah's ark that prefigures the Christian image of the cross as the ultimate symbol of redemption through sacrifice.

The Wisdom of Solomon influenced a Unitarian minister, Edmund Hamilton Sears, of Wayland, Massachusetts, in his composition of a popular Christmas carol, "It Came Upon a Midnight Clear" (December 29, 1849). The text establishes midnight as the time when Mary gave birth to Jesus. The symbolic moment suggests a division of time between the Old World and the New and heralds a rising sun, an emblem of the second coming.

Baruch

Baruch (also I Baruch) is a three-stage Hebrew composition written in Babylon in the early first century B.C.E. Allegedly completed in Palestine during the Babylonian exile, it is the work of Baruch, Jeremiah's aide, who intended the text as a pious festival reading at the Temple of Jerusalem. After summarizing Jewish history, Baruch accuses Jews of suffering exile because they have neglected God and his laws. In recompense, Baruch demands that Jews confess their sins. He follows with a poem in chapters 3:9–5:9 that lauds God's gift of learning to his chosen people. The closing apostrophe to Jerusalem summons the abject to pride and promises that the faithful will reach glory when God again leads Israel.

Letter of Jeremiah

The Letter of Jeremiah is a 300 B.C.E. addendum to Baruch, supposedly written in Hebrew by the prophet Jeremiah to the exiled Jews in Babylon in 597 B.C.E. to stress the Jewish disdain for idol worship. In rambling, overblown rhetoric, the brief epistle presents ten warnings to the Jews about remaining true to God. The writer sticks to the issue of idolatry, noting in chapter 6:17, "For just as one's dish is useless when it is broken, so are the gods of the heathen, when they have been set up in the temples" (Metzger 1965, 206).

The epistle is not lacking in artistry. Clever conceits—the scarecrow in the cucumber bed and bird on the thorn bush — relieve the tedium of repeated adjurations to avoid the false gods of polytheists. Overall, it synopsizes theological concerns about appropriate behavior, church doctrine, and liturgy. Because the epistle derives from the period that separates the composition of the Old and New Testaments, it may have served as a model for the personal tone and style that permeates Christian epistles.

Esther

Esther, an expanded text that Jerome later pared down to the Hebrew original, is unique for its lack of prayers and reference to Yahweh. Additions to books 10–11 and 13–16 total 107 verses, most of which may have been the work of Lysimachus, an Egyptian Jew who translated the Hebrew text into Greek in 114 B.C.E. A pious prayer of Mordecai in book 13 calls on God, ruler of the universe, to save Israel. The text lists God's omniscience and omnipotence. Mordecai declares Yahweh the god of Abraham and the deliverer of Jews from Egypt.

The heroine, Esther, offers her own prayer after removing queenly garments and sprinkling dung and ash on her head. Her supplication reiterates God's choice of the Jews as a favored nation. She pleads for forgiveness for her people's sin of idolatry and begs deliverance from fear. Chapter 15 dramatizes Esther's courage in dressing in full array and appearing before the king, who moves from anger to concern after she faints in alarm at his fierce expression.

Shifting from the personal to the political, chapter 16 cites a letter from Artaxerxes to area kings and satraps exonerating Jews of evil doing and charging Haman with conspiracy. The king asks that magistrates post his letter for the public to read and to allow Jews to follow their own laws. He concludes with a promise of spears and flame against man and beast and bird if anyone defies the order.

Prayer of Azariah and Song of the Three Young Men

A brief two-stage liturgical hymn, the Prayer of Azariah and the Song of the Three Young Men appends traditional piety to the Book of Daniel. Added between verses 23 and 24 of chapter 3, the prayer arrives at a crucial point — where Abednego laments the destruction of the Temple at Jerusalem and declares the catastrophe a just penalty against Israel for its sins. The first half, which praises God and his creation, was probably the work of a Palestinian Jew writing in Hebrew. It summarizes Israel's historical plight in chapter 1:14–15:

> For we, O Lord, have become
> fewer than any nation,
> and are brought low this day in all
> the world because of our sins [Metzger 1965, 210].

The poet declares that there are no princes, prophets, or leaders to guide the Jews and that they are unable to call on God with burnt offerings because they lack incense and an altar. In place of the trappings of physical sacrifice, he offers a contrite heart and a humble spirit.

Beginning with verse 23, the second hymn tells of Abednego, also called Azariah, whom Nebuchadrezzar cast into the furnace with Shadrach and Meshach, and it concludes with their rescue by an angel. Spontaneously,

the three young men sing forty verses in unison to God's glory, with frequent mention of cosmic wonders, natural phenomena, and topography. The episode resurfaces in the Old English poem "Azarias" in the *Exeter Book* and in pious verse by Anne Bradstreet, William Blake, Christina Rossetti, and John Henry Newman.

Susanna

Susanna (also Susanna and the Elders) is a much-admired erotic encounter and exploit of Daniel, which authorities appended to the book after chapter 12. The plot describes a false accusation of adultery levied by two lecherous elders against Joakim's beautiful and refined wife, Susanna, whose emblematic name means "lily." The story stresses Joakim's wealth and honor among the Jews of Babylon. It unfolds with suitable details about a hot day and Susanna's decision to bathe in her garden. Ironically, the judges command her either to commit adultery with them or to face a charge of adultery, which they will concoct to defame her. She weighs the options and replies, "I choose not to do it and to fall into your hands, rather than to sin in the sight of the Lord" (Metzger 1965, 214).

From the beginning, Susanna's piety and grace outpace the behavior of her accusers. When she faces a death sentence, she prays simply, movingly for deliverance:

> O eternal God, who dost discern what is secret,
> who art aware of all things before they come to be,
> thou knowest that these men have borne false witness
> against me [Metzger 1965, 214].

God responds by rousing Daniel, a clever young man capable of outmaneuvering villainy. He questions her accusers and trips them up in their description of the tree under which the illicit sex act allegedly occurred. One identifies it as mastic, the other as an evergreen oak. Their conspiracy and false witness found out, the two appropriately face sawing in half with a sword, the execution the court had planned for Susanna. The story, which establishes Daniel's reputation, parallels Joseph's plight in the hands of Potiphar's scheming wife in Genesis 39 and his rise to a high position in the Egyptian court.

In the summer of 1748, English composer Georg Friedrich Handel captured the life of Susanna in an oratorio by the same name, which he performed the next February in Covent Garden's Theatre Royal. In a dramatic recitative in Act 3 between Daniel and the elders, he exclaims:

> Vain is deceit when justice holds the scale,
> The falsehood's flagrant by the vary'd tale.
> Susanna! from thy captive dungeon go,
> Thy fame is whiter than unsullied snow ["Handel's Oratorio Susanna"].

The story survives in a funerary fresco at Callistus's catacomb, in Annibale Carracci's etching "Susanna and the Elders," and in paintings by Artemisia Gentileschi, Giovanni Guercino, Rembrandt von Rijn, and Sir Peter Lely. The story also inspired Orlando di Lasso's chanson "Susanne un Jour" (Susanna One Day), sixty-seven plays, numerous poems, including the Middle English *The Pistil* [Epistle] *of Swete Susan*, and a mention in Robert Browning's *The Ring and the Book*.

Bel and the Dragon

The anonymous Bel and the Dragon are an unrelated pair of Semitic hero tales extolling Daniel and belittling the deities of Babylon. The text took shape in Palestine in the second century B.C.E. The first twenty-two verses explain how the prophet proves false the worship of a clay and bronze statue of the god Bel by spreading ash over the floor of a sealed chamber in the temple as visual evidence that seventy duplicitous priests and not the idol cross the floor to gobble gifts of flour, mutton, and wine. They manage to hide their impiety by entering the temple through a secret passage. As King Cyrus joins Daniel to examine the premises, Daniel, risking execution for blasphemy, laughs at the patterns of footsteps left by the priests and their wives and children. Cyrus gives Bel to Daniel, who destroys both idol and temple.

The second story, only twenty verses long, echoes elements from Daniel's episode in the lion's den. In this version, he vows to slay Babylon's dragon without resorting to sword or club. He kills the snake with cakes made from a boiled concoction of tar, fat, and hair. The cakes explode the snake much as Daniel explodes the practice of idol worship. The feat lands him in trouble with the people, who accuse Cyrus of becoming a Jew and force him to punish Daniel.

The story concludes with an interpolated fantasy. After Daniel survives six days in a cell with a hungry lion, the prophet Habakkuk obeys an angel's command to take his dinner from his home in Judea to feed to Daniel in Babylon. Daniel's response is a pious prayer, "Thou hast remembered me, O God, and hast not forsaken those who love thee" (Metzger 1965, 216). King Cyrus accepts Daniel's God as the Almighty. The story ends with poetic justice — Cyrus throws to the lions the people who conspired against Daniel.

In the C.E. 500s, according to the anonymous *Decretum Gelasianum de Libris Recipiendis et Non Recipiendis* (Gelasian Decree of Books to Be Accepted or Not Accepted, C.E. 382), church officials declared that five works of historical fiction — Tobit, Judith, I and II Maccabees, and I Esdras (also III Esdras, or Ezra) — should enlarge the Apocrypha.

Tobit

A popular oriental romance or novella about a father and son, Tobit was written in Hebrew or Aramaic before 175 B.C.E., perhaps in Palestine, Egypt, or Antioch. The anonymous author bases his work on folklore and sets the story on the Tigris River in Nineveh, capital of Assyria, during the reign of Shalmaneser in 722 B.C.E. The narrative features a Job like Tobit, who triumphs over multiple adversities through the intervention of the angel Raphael. He suffers blindness and loses his wealth, yet remains pious and altruistic. He merits the return of his sight by daring to bury a murdered Jew. A parallel plot rich with folklore tells of Sarah, a resident of Media, who prays for deliverance from Asmodeus, the demon who murdered seven husbands one by one shortly after each one's marriage to her. Divine providence requites both Tobit and Sarah. In advanced old age, Tobit summons his sons and grandsons, makes his testament about faith and charity, and dies at peace.

The King James version (1611) eloquently characterizes the Jewish concept of probity and charity in Tobit's instruction to his son Tobias in Tobit 4:15–16:

> Do that to no man which thou hatest: drink not wine to make thee drunken: neither let drunkenness go with thee in thy journey. Give of thy bread to the hungry, and of thy garments to them that are naked; and according to thine abundance give alms; and let not thine eye be envious, when thou givest alms [Komroff 1937, 80].

This type of character-building exhortation flourishes in scripture as the Golden Rule and figures in the Book of Common Prayer. The advice sequence reaches a literary height in the English Renaissance in William Shakespeare's tragedy *Hamlet* (ca. 1600) with Polonius's parting admonition to his son Laertes. The story recurs in art by Raphael, Perugino, Savoldo, di Bicci, Rembrandt, Strozzi, and Steen. A marriage scene from the story colors the windows of King's College Chapel, Cambridge, England.

Judith

A short fiction about a wily, seductive widow who rescues the Jews by murdering Holofernes, an Assyrian military leader besieging Palestine in the name of Nebuchadnezzar, the Book of Judith stands out among the Apocrypha as skillful feminist fiction. Written late in the second century B.C.E., the narrative exalts a resourceful woman of the unidentified town of Bethulia, who willingly confronts the general, lures him with her beauty, makes him drunk, and triumphs over his evil menace. The exploit begins with oratory that displays piety and knowledge of the Torah. Both a nationalistic triumph and a blow for womanhood, Judith, the widow of Manasseh, is a symbolic character whose name equates with "Jewess." One of the most remarkable heroines of ancient historical and religious lore, she speaks ably and confidently against the weak-willed Uzziah, who is willing to surrender to the Assyrians. He bows to her wisdom and yields the floor so she can outline her plan. She correctly predicts that the strategy will survive throughout history.

Before taking up a post at the city gate, Judith humbles herself in sackcloth and ashes and prays that God will allow her to use seduction as a weapon against Assyria. She decks herself in jewelry to gain Holofernes's attention. Her maid carries fruit, bread, oil, and wine as the two pass through the town gate. They engage an Assyrian patrol, to whom Judith promises to show a secret way of capturing the Judean hill country outside Jerusalem. Fearlessly, she approaches Holofernes's tent and convinces him of her sincerity. Because vanity prevents him from testing the story, Judith turns to advantage his weakness and vainglory.

The cat-and-mouse ruse extends four days, ending on a night's debauch that leaves Holofernes too drunk for sexual conquest. Her virtue safe, Judith reaches for his sword. At the climactic moment in Judith 13:7–8, 14, piety undergirds vengeance:

> She came close to his bed and took hold of the hair of his head, and said, "Give me strength this day, O Lord God of Israel!" And she struck his neck twice with all her might, and severed his head from his body....
>
> Then she said to [the men of the city] with a loud voice, "Praise God, O praise him! Praise God, who has not withdrawn his mercy from the house of Israel, but has destroyed our enemies by my hand this very night!" [Abbott 1969, 593].

Her cool retreat with the villain's head in a food bag concludes with a cry of victory at the gates of Bethulia.

The following action reveals much about the renowned Jewish heroine. When the eunuch Bagoas finds a headless corpse in the general's bed, consternation precedes a rout; the Jewish army capitalizes on an easy victory. The priest Joakim blesses and praises Judith; the people reward her with the villain's tent, beds, and trappings. Chapter 16 records her thanksgiving song and the procession to Jerusalem, followed by her rejection of suitors, a life of honor, and manumission of her courageous maid. The closing parallel is emblematic — Judith remains true to her dead husband's memory just as Israel remains loyal to the Lord.

Judith's assassination of Holofernes provided dramatic scenes for an Old English epic from the early tenth century and for painters Allori, Michelangelo, Botticelli, Titian, Cranach, Matteo di Giovanni, Caravaggio, Gentileschi, Donatello, and Vernet as well as German and Italian operas, tapestries, mosaics, page illuminations, and stained glass. She flourishes in citations in Geoffrey Chaucer's *Canterbury Tales* and in Martin Luther's *Preface to the Book of Judith* (1534), Friedrich Hebbel's tragedy *Judith* (1840), and Arnold Bennett's *Judith* (1919).

I and II Maccabees

The two books of Maccabees pose two versions of the heroic story of the zealot priest Mattathias of Modein and his five sons: John Gaddi, Simon Thassi, Eleazar Avaran, Jonathan Apphus, and Judah Maccabee (or Judas Maccabaeus), the famed Jewish guerrilla warrior. The text of I Maccabees appears to be the work of a Palestinian Jew writing in Hebrew. Dating to the mid- to late-second century B.C.E., it focuses on the post–Alexandrian era, the harsh rule of Antiochus IV in Egypt and Judea, and the Maccabean defiance of tyranny and pagan religion, a high point in Jewish history.

The story links to the Torah by comparing current warriors with Abraham, Joseph, Phineas, Joshua, Caleb, David, Elijah, and Daniel. After Mattathias's death in chapter 2, the text pictures Judah as one of the Hasmoneans, a family of willing warriors in I Maccabees 3:2–4:

> All his brothers and all who had joined his father helped him;
>   they gladly fought for Israel.
> He extended the glory of his people.
> Like a giant he put on his breastplate;
>   he girded on his armor of war and waged battles,
>   protecting the host by his sword [Abbott 1969, 621].

Thrilling combat against Apollonius enhances the concept of a godly he-man. Like his forebears, Judah achieves an initial win at the battle of Beth-horon, where he slays 800. The lopsided victory resurrects hope in the Hebrews, who are recovering from centuries of oppression and persecution.

After allying with Rome, the Jews fight against Nicanor, Gorgias, and Lysias. In the last half of chapter 4, the retreat of Lysias precedes the rededication of the Temple. Judah's fame inspires pleas for the defense of other pockets of Judaism, which were facing insurgents in Gilead and Galilee. The long campaign continues after Antiochus V replaces his father in 145 B.C.E. In chapter 6, Eleazar dies in battle; in the next engagement, Judah flees Nicanor, then outwits him on the road to Beth-horon. After allying with Rome, in chapter 9, he faces the Bacchides at Mount Azotus and dies on the field in 161 B.C.E.

In family tradition, Judah's brothers, Jonathan and Simon, take up the battle for freedom. Jonathan also loses his life in combat in 142 B.C.E. In chapter 14, the Jews assemble to honor the Hasmoneans. In 140 B.C.E., they decide to erect bronze tablets on Mount Zion extolling Simon. Chapter 16 concludes in 135 B.C.E. with the murder of Simon and his sons, Judah and Mattathias, and the rise to power of John Hyrcanus, priest and ethnarch.

The second Book of Maccabees contains more exaggeration, emotional name calling, and inflated arguments favoring the Jews over their oppressors. Composed in Greek from oral reports dating to the end of the second century B.C.E., it is the work of a North African, Jason of Cyrene, who may have witnessed the Hasmonean turmoil. Jason's history opens with a pious invocation and a letter to Aristobulus about the eight-day festival of Hanukkah. The narrative lauds the valor of Judas Maccabaeus and mourns the public parading and execution of women and the forced circumcision of their children. Jason remarks, "I urge those who read this book not to be depressed by such calamities" (Metzger 1965, 274).

The story particularizes a Seleucid atrocity in chapter 7, recounting the martyrdom of an unidentified mother and her seven sons. The episode reaches a melodramatic height in the King James version of a martial speech that Hannah's son delivers to King Antiochus in chapter 7:37–38:

> I, as my brethren, offer up my body and life for the laws of our fathers, beseeching God that he would speedily be merciful unto our nation; and that thou by torments and plagues mayest confess, that he alone is God; and that in me and my brethren the wrath of the Almighty, which is justly brought upon all our nation, may cease [Komroff 1937, 328].

Antiochus either cannot or will not comprehend the role model of eight people who refuse to capitulate to their captors and who remain loyal to God and his law.

II Maccabees returns to the valiant Hasmonean family and their struggles against Antiochus IV. The chronicle covers the king's death and the purification of the Temple, then launches into the next series of conflicts against Antiochus V. Near the end of chapter 14 and into chapter 15, the author enhances the advance of Judas Maccabaeus, "who was ever the chief defender of the citizens both in body and mind and who continued his love toward his countrymen all his life." Narratives detail the dismemberment of Nicanor, who lies on the battlefield in full armor (Komroff 1937, 349). Judah marches to Jerusalem to display Nicanor's tongueless head and amputated arm, losses he deserves for blaspheming God and menacing the Temple. After posting the head at the citadel, all agree to observe a festival on the thirteenth day of the month of Adar.

Judah's heroic story served the historian Josephus as a source for *Antiquities of the Jews* (94 C.E.) and Aelfric for a late tenth-century homily, *Passio Sanctorum Machabaeorum* (Passion of the Holy Maccabees). It was a source for poet Henry Wadsworth Longfellow in *New England Tragedies* (1868) and in the five-act poetic drama *Judas Maccabaeus*, published in his poetic works in 1891. Act 5 concludes melodramatically with Antiochus's dying words, which urge hearers to deliver royal robes, signet ring, crown, and scepter to his son, Antiochus Eupator. In 1948, Howard Fast's *My Glorious Brothers* reprised the valiant Judah as the first modern freedom fighter.

Musicians have set the high drama of Hasmonean family history as opera and oratorio. Russian pianist and composer Anton Rubinstein and librettist H. S. von Mosenthal recast the apocryphal book as an opera, *The Maccabees* (1875). Handel and librettist Thomas Morell honored the duke of Cumberland's victory over Jacobite Scots at the battle of Culloden with an oratorio, *Judas Maccabaeus* (1746). Handel's sequel, *Alexander Balus* (1747), is a history and martyrdom plot based on a political intrigue against Alexander and his brother Jonathan, leader of the Jews, against Demetrius, king of Syria.

I Esdras

A blended text, I Esdras provides an alternate reading of the Book of Ezra and appends historical material from II Chronicles and Nehemiah. The text of I Esdras may have reached completion late in the second century B.C.E. It covers three significant events: Josiah's Passover celebration in 621 B.C.E.; the succession of Jehoiakim, Jehoiachin, and Zedekiah; and, the destruction of the Temple in Jerusalem, Babylonian exile, the return of Jewish exiles, and the rebuilding of the temple.

A Persian touch to I Esdras belongs to the genre of court debate, a late-night disputation of Darius's guardsmen over the question of the greatest power, an episode foreign to the Septuagint. The speakers fantasize that the king will reward the wisest with a suit of clothes, a golden bed, and a promotion.

The debated powers range from the temporal to the esoteric. The first two watchers select wine and kings as the mightiest. The third guard, Zerubbabel (or Zorobabel), first chooses women, citing as proof the bearing and rearing of children, making fine clothes, wearing gorgeous jewelry, and loving their husbands. He alters his choice by selecting truth as the most powerful entity and concludes, "But truth endures and is strong for ever, and lives and prevails for ever and ever" (Meyer 1992, 8). Because Darius awakens and sides with the third argument, he aids in rebuilding the Temple by gathering cedar from outlying kingdoms and orders the return of Temple plate. Zerubbabel is so moved that he thanks God for blessing him with wisdom. The exiled Jews join him for a weeklong festival. The work concludes with a notable detail, a link between Zerubbabel and the house of David.

Late medieval and early Renaissance attitudes toward the Apocrypha grew more sectarian. In the tenth century, the authority on scripture was Athanasius (or Athenasius) the Athonite, a monastic from the Greek state of Trebizond on the Black Sea. In 963, Emperor Nicephorus Phocas assisted him in founding the Great Lavra (or Laura), a restrictive cloister on Mount Athos overlooking the Aegean Sea. As abbot, Athanasius built a respectable library. He sanctioned Christian texts and separated those read by Christians and Jews.

Into the Reformation, questions about which books did and did not belong in scripture occupied scholars throughout the Christian world. German editions were the first modern language texts to apply the term Apocrypha to questionable books. In 1526, Jacob van Liesveldt made a formal division between canon and Apocrypha. Martin Luther's German Bible of 1534 applied the word Apocrypha as a guide to readers. The translator comments: "Apocrypha: these are books which are not held equal to the sacred Scriptures and yet are useful and good for reading" (*New Catholic Encyclopedia*, 2:391). A shift back to acceptance occurred in 1546 at the Council of Trent. In 1563, the Church of England issued the Thirty-Nine Articles of Religion, which characterized apocryphal writing as edifying for readers.

The affirmation of canon and noncanon works continued beyond the English Renaissance. The publication of the Apocrypha between the Old and New Testaments of the King James Bible in 1611 provoked John Lightfoot, an English Hebraist, who declared in 1643 that the capricious placement might lead readers to the faulty conclusion that these noncanonical writings form an authoritative bridge between the two segments of scripture. More helpful to the Greek Orthodox reader was the 1672 Synod of Jerusalem, which affirmed only selected apocryphal books. From the Jacobean period onward, English printings in Britain and America moved toward exclusion of the Apocrypha as Protestants echoed the Jewish contention that only God-inspired works merited exaltation and the full devotion of his people. The Russian Orthodox church also capitulated to conservatism in the 1900s by sanctioning only orthodox scripture.

The theological warfare over accepted and unaccepted writings pertains to only a few texts that reflect on or add to the Bible. From uncertain sources come II Esdras (or Ezra), the Prayer of Manasseh, and the Story of Ahikar, three minor works of the Jewish Apocrypha.

II Esdras

II Esdras (also the Apocalypse of Ezra and *Esdras Propheta Secundus* [according to the Prophet Esdras] and erroneously identified as IV Esdras) dates to around C.E. 100, owing to a reference to three decades after Titus's destruction of the Temple, which occurred in C.E. 70. A grim narrative consisting of seven revelations, it demonstrates the root meaning of the Greek *apocalypsis* (unfolding or uncovering). II Esdras was the work of a glum Palestinian Jew composing in Hebrew or Aramaic, a blend of earlier material issued under the pseudonym of Ezra. Of significance to Christianity is the image of a Christ figure — a crown-bearing youth who rewards a crowd gathered before him on Mount Zion. The work is also a popular source of visions of the crucifixion, Good Friday warnings, an Easter antiphon, and a requiem for the dead.

The visions of Ezra follow numerology and the magical seven, the sum of two magic numbers, three and four. The first vision, set in the thirtieth year of the Babylonian captivity, describes Ezra as a troubled sleeper lying in bed and talking to God. The angel Uriel speaks for God by upbraiding Ezra for trying to simplify God's work. The second vision again pits Ezra against the angel in a reprise of Israel's sufferings. Uriel uses the image of birth to explain that all humanity cannot be born at one time. The metaphor implies that Ezra must patiently await the unfolding of human history.

Still troubled, Ezra experiences a third vision and asks why the Jews, God's chosen people, cannot possess the earth. Uriel sends Ezra to live off field flowers for seven days. In an interpolated folktale, he speaks with a woman who has lost her only son after thirty years of childlessness. Like Ezra, she despairs because her hopes go unfulfilled. The woman changes into the city of Zion in a transformation that shakes and disturbs Ezra. Uriel urges him to examine the city.

The fifth vision addresses the Jews' hatred of imperial Rome. Ezra experiences a complex pattern of symbols, but Uriel does not return to interpret. At this point, Ezra attains the role of prophet for his people. In the sixth vision, he predicts the messiah will be a man from the sea, a metaphysical being who climbs a mountain, breathes fire against God's enemies, and settles Israel's tribes in peace. In the final vision, Ezra enters a Mosaic setting where he hears a call from a bush. God assigns him forty days in which to comfort the Jews and to prepare to write scripture on tablets. Intoxicated by the holy spirit, he recites God's word to scribes, who fill ninety-four books. He issues twenty-four of the books for general use but retains seventy as secret information that will enable the people to survive earth's final days.

The Jewish apocalypse follows the evolving faith of Ezra. After his death, God vows to bring calamities against the unrighteous, whom he describes in agricultural terms:

Woe to those who are choked by their sins and overwhelmed by their iniquities, as a field is choked with underbrush and its path overwhelmed with thorns, so that no one can pass through! It is shut off and given up to be consumed by fire [Meyer 1992, 62].

He ends chapter 16 with a promise to deliver the Jews from tribulation. Christopher Columbus cited II Esdras 6:42 concerning the proportion of water to dry land as justification for crossing the Atlantic Ocean, which he erroneously assumed to be a short span separating Europe from Asia.

Prayer of Manasseh

The Prayer of Manasseh (or Manasses), a forty-two-line penitential psalm in Greek, demonstrates the individual's confession of sin. It appears to date to the first or second century B.C.E.; origin and language are unclear. The author speaks through Manasseh, king of Judah in the first half of the seventh century B.C.E. The dramatic situation is an appealing change of heart: the king is a wicked man petitioning God for forgiveness. In a deeply spiritual plea to a compassionate deity, he confesses sins that are more numerous than the sand in the sea.

With a facile metaphor, Manasseh bends his heart's knee in an act of contrition and humility and promises to continue begging God for mercy. The poem found little support with early church fathers but appealed to the eastern church. The ingenuous image of the heart's knee survives in "Balulalow," a Middle English lullaby to the Christ child, which Benjamin Britten anthologized in *A Ceremony of Carols* (1942) for harp and treble voices.

Story of Ahikar

An ancient model of secular wisdom literature, the Story of Ahikar appears to derive from Akkadian originals. The narrative spotlights Ahikar, Sennacherib's grand vizier, who longs for a child. The author uses a flimsy plot of unlawful imprisonment, rescue, and vengeance to salt the text with advice to the younger generation. To his ungrateful heir, Nadan, Ahikar offers a string of worthy but unrelated advice:

O my son! Be like a fruitful tree on the roadside,
  whose fruit is eaten by all who pass by,
  and the beasts of the desert rest under its shade
  and eat of its leaves.
O my son! Every sheep that wanders from its path
and its companions becomes food for the wolf [Barnstone
  1984, 185].

In an overblown model of poetic justice, Nadan swells up and explodes before going to hell. Ahikar muses, "For he who digs a pit for his brother shall fall into it."

The pseudepigrapha, varied noncanonical works written from 250 B.C.E. to C.E. 200 and strongly influenced by the Greeks, consist of numerous types and qualities of apocryphal writings written under pen names.

Letter of Aristeas

An apologia or propaganda piece, the Letter of Aristeas was composed at Alexandria around 130 B.C.E. during the reign of Ptolemy II Philadelphus. Contrived as an epistle to the Cypriot Philocrates, the text summarizes how the acquisitions librarian, Demetrius of Phaleron, requests an aide to copy volumes of Jewish law for the great academic library of Alexandria. Ptolemy dispatches Aristeas, an Egyptian courtier, to expedite the project. Aristeas persuades Ptolemy to manumit over 100,000 slaves as a gesture of magnanimity and honor to the Jewish god. When this exchange is complete, Ptolemy orders Demetrius to draft a letter to Eleazar, Jerusalem's high priest, concerning the addition to the library.

At the behest of Eleazar, seventy-two scribes copy Hellenized translations of the Hebrew Torah, known as the Septuagint. In an act of numerological tidiness, they finish the job in seventy-two days. The cultural exchange concludes with a week-long banquet at the Alexandrian court where translators politely exchange observations on royalty and, for their professional contributions, accept gifts—three costumes each, two talents of gold, a sideboard, a purple robe, a crown, a hundred lengths of linen, and gold bowls and plates. The letter's commentary on the theory and practice of translation as a literary task, the first of its kind in history, describes and evaluates the process of translation and warns about three common errors—transpositions, omissions, and additions.

III Maccabees

A farfetched persecution episode from around 150 B.C.E., III Maccabees establishes the endurance of a persecuted people against the power of an evil tyrant. The book relates the hardships of the Diaspora but has no connection with the Maccabean family. The story reprises the rebellion of Alexandrian Jews against taxation and their subsequent triumph over Ptolemy IV Philopator, whom God strikes mute for desecrating the Holy of Holies in the Jerusalem Temple. On his return to Egypt in chapter 2, he bars the faithful from houses of worship and initiates a census. Virtually slaves to Philopator, the Jews have one odious and unthinkable option — to worship the Greek god Dionysus.

In chapter 3, the Jews rebel and are rounded up and confined in Alexandria, obviously for extermination. Philopator uses the hippodrome as a prison corral, anticipating the Romans' use of the Circus Maximus as an arena in which they would slay Christians by a variety of means. Philopator's attempt to stampede 500 enraged elephants over them goes awry three times. First, he falls asleep; in the second instance, he forgets. The third execution falters after two angels turn the beasts against the Egyptian troops. Philopator liberates the captives, who erect a house of prayer and offer thanksgiving to God. After the execution of 300 renegade Jews, the faithful return home under the king's aegis.

IV Maccabees

Composed in learned Greek before C.E. 70, IV Maccabees is a two-part polemical sermon divided into eighteen chapters. It is the work of a Hellenized Jew who may have lived in Antioch. He addresses the first part of the discourse to Israelites and extols Mosaic law as a model of reason. The second segment describes the guile of the tyrant Antiochus IV Epiphanes.

The speaker glorifies the zealot priest Eleazar, who rejects pork with eloquent speeches. A highlight of the account is the torment and execution of the Maccabean martyrs—Eleazar, a mother, and her seven sons—and their exaltation of biblical law to the last. The mother stoically watches her children broken, flogged, and burned and deliberately hurls herself into the fire to avoid the touch of Antiochus's guards. The grotesque details and concluding lament prefigure Christian martyrologies, which have colored mosaics, statues, paintings, tapestries, hymns, oratorios, masses, and fiction.

Lives of the Prophets

The Lives of the Prophets is a biography series heavily larded with legend. It concerns the sixteen prophets, major and minor, and includes the life stories of Elijah, Elisha, Nathan, Abia, Joed, Azaria, and Zachariah.

Paralipomena of Jeremiah

The Paralipomena of Jeremiah (also the Remaining Words of Jeremiah and IV Baruch), written in Hebrew about C.E. 100, describes the prophet Jeremiah's task of concealing sacred vessels from the Temple shortly before the destruction of Jerusalem.

Life of Adam and Eve

The Life of Adam and Eve (or Apocalypse of Moses) is a body of Latin legends that embroider the original myth of the first couple with additional trials and woes plus prognostications about the rise of the Jews. The book concludes with angels burying Adam and Eve.

Apocalyptic works predicting the end of humankind comprise a colorful, imaginative category of addenda to scripture that particularize the curiosity of seekers about the afterlife.

Ascension of Isaiah

The Ascension of Isaiah (also the Ascension of Isaias) is an amalgam of literary traditions that describes two contrasting topics: King Manasses' order to Satan to halve Isaiah's body with a saw and Isaiah's prophecies concerning the hardships of the early apostles and followers, the Antichrist, and Christ's Second Coming. The Jewish original dates to the first century C.E. and the Christian interpolation a century later.

The didactic narration, directed to Hezekiah and Jasub, recounts the virgin birth, Jesus' infancy, treachery at the hands of the Jews, and Jesus' descent to hell. Isaiah swears Hezekiah to secrecy about matters that will not transpire until the end of time. The heroic prophet continues to recite scripture as his body is sawed apart.

III Baruch

III Baruch is a visionary melange of star lore. Written after C.E. 130, it opens on the destruction of Jerusalem and describes Baruch's introduction to a series of five heavens.

I Enoch

I Enoch (also Ethiopic Enoch, Liber Enoch, or Henoch) amasses a long-lived body of lore in Hebrew or Aramaic dating to 200 B.C.E. The book is an end-of-time composite of 108 chapters about Enoch, father of Methuselah, one of two Bible characters whom God enraptures into heaven. The rambling narrative covers fantastic journeys into outer space, reports of giants and tongues of fire, descriptions of Gehenna and paradise, and predictions about resurrection, punishment of the wicked in Sheol, and rewards to the just. Chapters 91–93 contain the Apocalypse of Ten Weeks, a capsule life story of the good man.

II Enoch

II Enoch (also the Book of the Secrets of Enoch and the Slavonic Henoch) offers another account of Enoch's visit to a series of ten heavens and hell. After God summons Enoch, he reveals the nature of creation, which passed from "nonexistence into existence, and from invisible into visible" (Barnstone 1984, 4). Enoch marvels at the sun and moon and returns to tell his children what God has imparted. He adds, "It is good to go morning, midday, and evening into the Lord's dwelling, for the glory of your creator" (Barnstone 1984, 8).

It is not surprising that Enoch's neighbors fail to understand how and why God took him into his confidence and revealed the workings of creation. After the angel Michael anoints and dresses Enoch in glorious raiment, Enoch obeys God's command to write 366 books containing cosmogonic elements, including works of sky, earth, and sea; the elements and thunder; sun, moon, and stars; seasons and divisions of time; the making of wine; an accounting of angels and their sons; human life and songs; and commandments and important additions to human knowledge.

IV Esdras

IV Esdras (sometimes misidentified as II Esdras) is an influential pre–Christian apocalypse that prophesies a mortal messiah, who will establish a limited reign of peace on earth. The work, a seven-stage vision written by a Jew around C.E. 95, never acquired the following necessary to elevate it to canon or liturgy but did find a place in the appendix of Jerome's Vulgate Bible. The text, paralleling Esdras's lament for Jerusalem and the Temple, mourns the oppression of Jews after Titus destroyed the Temple in C.E. 70.

Psalms of Solomon

A collection of eighteen hymns of thanksgiving and warning, the Psalms of Solomon were composed in Jerusalem in Hebrew in the Davidic style. Presumably written by one poet after 48 B.C.E., the songs contain themes of forgiveness, piety, altruism, virtue, and accountability for personal faults, and they indicate a belief in the resurrection of the body. The collection anticipates a mystic orator-messiah who will convert all people into sons of God. The style of conquest will require no weapons, only the sinless man's words.

Odes of Solomon

A separate collection of twenty-four hymns in Hebrew, Aramaic, or Syriac, the Odes of Solomon comprise the earliest Christian hymn book. References to gnosticism identify them as the work of a first-century or early second-century Hellenized Christian. Strongly Hebraic and mystical, the poems speak in the first person and concentrate on the themes of God's love, knowledge, and wisdom and allude to a messiah as the "anointed one." The style is antiphonal, with divisions for congregational response. The imagery is engaging, with such pictures as a cloven heart, the harp of the Holy Spirit, a singing dove, a flying chariot, and a groom's love for his bride.

Odes 8 and 19 contain an unusual conceit — the son as a lactating male with breasts full of milk, which nourished the virgin. Ode 19 begins:

A cup of milk was offered to me: and I drank it in the sweetness of the delight of the Lord.
The son is the cup and he who was milked is the father:
And the Holy Spirit milked him: because his breasts were full, and it was necessary for him that his milk should be sufficiently released;
And the Holy Spirit opened his bosom and mingled the milk from the two breasts of the Father and gave the mixture to the world without their knowing ["The Odes of Solomon Annotated"].

Assumption of Moses

The Assumption of Moses (also *Oratio Moysi* [Moses' Oration] and *Analepsis Mouseos*) was composed in Hebrew or Aramaic by a Palestinian Jew. The author, who may have belonged to the Essenes or another sect of zealots, receives mention in the epistle of Jude, but the part cited has not survived. Purportedly a body of prophecy that Moses asked Joshua to preserve, the work precedes Moses' death. The writings, which date to C.E. 30, affirm the laws of the Torah and outline Hebrew history, covering the Hasmonean monarchy and ending with the reign of Herod the Great. The book develops into an apocalypse of the messiah's return and reveals the chaos in nature that initiates a utopian era.

Jewish Sibylline Oracles

An overblown fifteen-book adaptation of Roman prophecy to Jewish situations, the Jewish Sibylline Oracles were composed in Alexandria in the second century B.C.E. The narrative anticipates the *Dies Irae* (Day of Wrath), a gloomy and forbidding segment of the mass for the dead, which became a well-known medieval hymn. Of the surviving twelve books, the focus is on the coming of a messiah who will end an era of shame, adultery, pedophilia, murder, and chaos. According to the oracles, the apocalypse will bring famine and murder, ravening birds, bloodied seas, and the wails of the damned. The order of heavenly constellations will interchange Virgo with Gemini and Pisces with Leo, and cause the death of the dog star from a sunburst. By the end of the cosmic cataclysms, the sky becomes starless.

Apocalypse of Baruch

The Apocalypse of Baruch (also called the Syriac Baruch or II Baruch), a pious, historically flawed vision drawn on IV Esdras, was composed around C.E. 115. It refers to a cataclysm that references Titus's conquest of Jerusalem in C.E. 70. Baruch, changed from Jeremiah's scribe to a prophet, interrogates God about the inequities suffered by Jerusalem and questions the purpose of the Jewish Diaspora. In despair, he asks why women should bear children, then bury them and why parents should name their children, only to lose them to slavery.

In the second section, the Vision of the Forest, the Vine, the Fountain, and the Cedar, God foresees the coming of a messiah to console the suffering Jews. In an uplifting coda, the angel Ramiel predicts a time of healing, justice, and the taming of animals, who will serve a small child. The image suggests the joyful idealism of Edward Hicks's *The Peaceable Kingdom* (1834).

Apocalypse of Abraham

Linked to IV Esdras and the Apocalypse of Baruch, the Apocalypse of Abraham summarizes the religious history of Abraham and his visions of heaven. The Hebrew patriarch, led by the angel Jael, enters heaven and foresees a gathering of the Twelve Tribes of Israel. Michael points out Abel, Adam and Eve's son, as the appointed judge, but God alone is the punisher of evil.

Book of Jannes and Mambres

The Book of Jannes and Mambres, referring to Egyptian magi whose spells reprised Moses' feats, is an obscure text mentioned in the Talmud.

Pseudepigrapha from the Dead Sea Scrolls include:

Book of Jubilees

The Book of Jubilees (also the Little Genesis), a nationalistic Hebrew pseudepigrapha from Palestine composed before 100 B.C.E., is a miniature Genesis that enlarges on the first two books of the Torah. The text derives from a revelation that Moses receives from the Angel of the Face. Although the tone is didactic and the purpose ham-handed, the presentation of Adam and Eve in Eden is appealingly lyric, especially the silencing of the beasts that had formerly "spoken to each other with one lip and one tongue" (Barnstone 1984, 13). The writer accuses his contemporaries of ignoring Moses' laws by neglecting tithes and kosher dietary restrictions and by fornicating and intermarrying with gentiles. The Dead Sea Scrolls, which contain the Qumran calendar, corroborate evidence of a 364-day solar calendar.

Testaments of the Twelve Patriarchs

The Testaments of the Twelve Patriarchs compiles the dying words of Jacob's twelve sons: Reuben, Simeon, Levi, Judah, Issachar, Zebulun, Dan, Naphtali, Gad, Asher, Joseph, and Benjamin. The text appears to have been written by a Jewish priest after 200 B.C.E., but contains obvious Christian interpolations. Each testament reveals personal regret and an appropriate didactic lesson. The collection, which resembles a sheaf of twelve sermons, closes on the expectation of a messiah from the Levites who will serve as high priest and civil magistrate. Under his eternal rule, sin will give way to righteousness. Heaven's gates will open to Jews and gentile converts, who will eat the fruit of the tree of life.

Additions to the pseudepigrapha derived from the discovery of the Dead Sea Scrolls in Qumran include Pesharim, the War Between the Sons of Light Against the Sons of Darkness, a manual of ordinances or manual of discipline, and Hodayot.

New Testament Apocrypha, consisting of gospels, acts of the apostles, epistles, and apocalypses as well as wedding hymns, epic and heroic verse, prophecy, and folk tales, relate to an extended holy family and Jesus' childhood, earthly and heavenly actions, and sayings to his disciples. The purpose of these early gospel writings was to supplement and illuminate aspects of Jesus' life and early ministry.

Thomas Gospel of the Infancy

Thomas Gospel of the Infancy (or the Infancy Gospel of Thomas), one of the first gospels of Jesus' childhood from around C.E. 150, is an incomplete text of Syriac nativity and childhood lore. It depicts future miraculous powers and knowledge during Jesus's first twelve years, the period omitted from canon gospels. The episode involving Jesus's modeling of twelve clay birds violates the Bible by claiming that the holy family are not Jews. Descriptions of Jesus as a miracle worker and willful, murderous brat are inconsistent with his adult behavior in the four canon gospels.

Protevangelium Jacobi

Protevangelium Jacobi (James's Original Gospel; also *Protevangelion Jacobi*, *Protoevangelium Jacobi*, and Infancy Gospel of James) is a narration composed in Greek by a gentile around C.E. 150. The author writes under the pseudonym of James, who was Jesus's brother or half brother, being either Mary's son or Joseph's child from a former marriage. The first-person narrative covers Mary's childhood in the home of her parents, Anne (or Anna) and Joachim, and her first appearance at the Temple. An introduction to the holy family starts with Mary's betrothal to Joseph, a widower with children, and proceeds to the virgin birth in a cave outside Bethlehem, the arrival of the magi, and multiple incidents of violence beginning with the murder of the innocents and of Zacharias (or Zachariah) and Herod's demise.

The Protevangelium creates an interesting minor character, Salome, the midwife who delivers Jesus and attests to Mary's virginity. Salome experiences fire on her hands and the visitation of an angel, who urges that she hold the infant, who will save her. By cuddling the babe, she is cured on contact with his holy flesh. The narration influenced Giotto's fresco showing Mary at the Temple with her parents and a picture of the marriage of Mary to Joseph.

Infancy Gospel of Pseudo-Matthew

The Infancy Gospel of Pseudo-Matthew (also the Book About the Origin of the Blessed Mary and the Childhood of the Savior, Gospel of St. Matthew, and *Liber de Infantiae Salvatoris* [Book of the Infant Savior]), a poetic summary of Jesus's birth, was composed in Latin around C.E. 800 and is apparently based on the Gospel of James. The narrative opens on Joseph's consternation at Mary's pregnancy and covers five miracles: the virgin birth, the infant Jesus's charming of predatory animals, the magical shortening of the trip to Egypt to one day, the collapse of idols before Jesus and Mary, and the conversion of Governor Afrodosius and the Egyptians. An appealing episode depicts Mary's request for palm fruit and the infant's command to the tree to bend down so his mother can gather fruit to refresh herself.

Latin Infancy Gospel: The Birth of Jesus

A medieval narrative based on the Gospel of James and the Infancy Gospel of Pseudo-Matthew, a Latin Infancy Gospel: The Birth of Jesus appears to belong to the second century C.E. It opens on a servant girl bearing a birthing chair for Zachel, the midwife, who follows Joseph to a cave to aid Mary in childbirth. Zachel marvels at the silence of wind, flowing water, the seas, and human voices as the characters in the drama await the birth of God. Mary produces an amazingly lightweight infant shining with a dewy splendor. His eyes flash like lightning.

Additional Apocrypha build on these Christ child stories and range further afield, particularly the Arabic Gospel of the Infancy, Armenian Gospel of the Infancy, *Historia de Conceptione Beatae Maria* (Story of the Conception of Blessed Mary), and the imitative gospels of the apostles Peter, Thomas, Matthias, Philip, Barnabas, Bartholomew, Judas Iscariot, Andrew, and John. New Testament gospels derive from Judeo-Christian sources.

Arabic Gospel of the Infancy

Derived in part from the Infancy Gospel of Thomas, Book of Joseph Caiaphas, the High Priest, Gospel of the Infancy, and the Perfect Gospel, the Arabic Gospel of the Infancy appears to be Syriac in origin. It covers the standard episodes of Jesus's birth and pious legends of childhood miracles, for example, the efficacy of his bath water against leprosy and the curative power of his clothing. A meeting with two thieves, Titus and Dumachus, prefigures the crucifixion of criminals at each side of Jesus's cross. Because Titus shelters the holy family, he later enters paradise before Jesus. Of particular interest is a brief morality tale, the Children Who Were Changed into Goats. After Jesus retrieves them from a furnace, they bow down and plead for mercy. He complies by transforming them back into children. The unprecedented occurrence suggests the suffering of individuals who neglect religious faith.

Secret Gospel of Mark

The Secret Gospel of Mark is a shred of Mark's gospel found in a letter from Clement of Alexandria, an Athenian theologian and principal of Alexandria's catechetical school. The noncanonical episodes from Jesus's life illustrate how the Gospel of Mark developed from unstable early editions formed of rumor, sayings, tales, parables, and eyewitness accounts. A primitive account of raising the dead prefigures Jesus's raising of Lazarus: "And straightaway, going in where the youth was, he stretched forth his hand and raised him, seizing his hand. But the youth, looking upon him, loved him and began to beseech him that he might be with him" (Barnstone 1984, 324).

Gospel of the Hebrews

The Gospel of the Hebrews (also Gospel According to the Hebrews), a fragmented 2,200-line text based on Jesus's life and displaying syncretism and gnosticism, is one of the most quoted of Judeo-Christian texts. Written in Egyptian tradition, it dates to around C.E. 100 and appears to have originated in Hebrew. Citations from the narrative color the writings of Cyril of Jerusalem, Origen, Clement, and Jerome, who quotes in *De Viris Illustribus* (On Famous Men) an appearance of the risen Christ to James:

And shortly thereafter the Lord said: Bring a table and bread! And immediately it is added: he took the bread blessed it and brake it and gave it to James the Just and said to him: My brother, eat your bread, for the Son of man is risen from among them that sleep [Barnstone 1984, 335].

The wording parallels the liturgy of the Christian Eucharist and alludes to the doctrines of salvation and resurrection.

Gospel of the Nazarenes

The Gospel of the Nazarenes (also Gospel of the Essenes), a Semitic Judeo-Christian text composed between C.E. 110 and 150 about a Syrian cult, exists in fragments. According to Epiphanius of Salamis, bishop of Constantia in the fourth century C.E., and the historian Jerome, the Nazarenes consulted a narrative that restated the canon Gospel of Matthew, which details the life and ministry of Christ.

Gospel of Bartholomew

Similar to the Gospel of Nicodemus, the Gospel of Bartholomew describes Jesus's sojourn in hell and the liberation of worthy souls as well as the nature of Beliar (Worthless), an alternate name for Satan. The image of Bartholomew holding down the sinuous beast depicts the conqueror with one foot on the creature's neck. Beliar narrates how he fell from the post of angel because of his disdain for Adam. Out of spite, he tempted and corrupted Eve and devoted his existence to dispatching devils to tempt and admonish humankind.

Gospel According to the Egyptians

The Gospel According to the Egyptians is a fragmented noncanonical text. It appears to be a gnostic work from the first half of the second century C.E. and contains a dialogue between Jesus and Salome.

Gospel of Nicodemus

The Gospel of Nicodemus, written in the third century C.E., offers a touchingly human exchange between Jesus and Bartholomew, who entreats, "My God, great Father and King; save, Lord, the sinners." Gently, Jesus replies that he can save the faithful, but not "boasters, drunkards, proud, merciless, idolaters, seducers to fornication, slanderers, teachers of falsehood, and doers of all the works of the devil" (Barnstone 1984, 358). A significant character in the narrative is Mary, who relates the angel's annunciation of her son's birth.

Gospel of the Ebionites

The Gospel of the Ebionites (or Gospel of the Twelve), a lost work of a Transjordan sect, appears to have been written in Greek in the second century C.E. It survived in

citations in the Panarion of Epiphanius, the didactic writer who was bishop of Salamis in 367. The text restates the canon gospels, for example, the calling of the disciples:

> As I passed the Lake of Tiberias, I chose John and James the sons of Zebedee, and Simon and Andrew and Thaddaeus and Simon the Zealot and Judas the Iscariot, and you, Matthew, I called as you sat at the receipt of custom, and you followed me. You, therefore, I will to be twelve apostles for a testimony unto Israel [Barnstone 1984, 337].

Pistis Sophia (Faith Wisdom)

Pistis Sophia, a Greek text by third-century Egyptian gnostics, pictures Jesus on earth twelve years after his death. He addresses his disciples and Mary Magdalene in the first three parts. The last section summarizes Christian concepts of baptism and the punishment and redemption of sin.

Dialogus Salvatorus (Savior's Dialogue)

Dialogus Salvatorus is a third-century gnostic conversation between Jesus and his apostles about creation.

A major addition to the world's knowledge of apocryphal books was the publication of texts comprising the Nag Hammadi library, a source of information on early Christianity. Muhammad 'Alí al-Sammán, an Arab laborer, discovered the cache of codices in December 1945 in the town of Nag Hammadi in upper Egypt near Thebes on the west shore of the Nile. He and his fellow workers were digging for *sabakh*, a rich soil they used as fertilizer, when they located an earthenware jar sealed with a bowl on top. Muhammad smashed the jar with his mattock. Among leatherbound papyrus books of fifty-two primary gnostic texts contained in the jar were priceless religious writings, which may have been deposited by monks from St. Pachomius Monastery in C.E. 390 to protect them from deliberate destruction during a church controversy over orthodoxy. Standing apart from the others were four books of scripture citing the words of Jesus.

Gospel of Thomas

The Gospel of Thomas, a Coptic anthology of 114 of Jesus's sayings, is attributed to Judas Thomas, Jesus's twin (also Didymos Judas Thomas). The aphorisms and analogies tease and edify the mind through ambiguity as well as puzzlement at lapses and gaps in the original manuscript. They open with a promise: "Whoever finds the interpretation of these sayings will not taste death" (Meyer 1984, 19). Some entries restate verses and teachings from the Gospels of Matthew, Mark, and Luke, for example, the parables of the sower, the lost sheep, and the mustard seed. The maxims contain everyday advice about self-protection, love, and self-criticism as well as provocative thought that suggests knowledge of cynic philosophy.

The Gospel of Thomas raised controversy by introducing alternate assumptions about orthodox Christian philosophy, for example, as it applies to the unforgivable sin. The orphic nature of these remarks discloses a whole new dimension of Jesus not found in the New Testament. In saying 106, he declares, "Whoever drinks from my mouth will be like me; I shall be that person, and what is hidden will be revealed to that one" (Meyer 1984, 37). In the style of Eastern theology, he advocates intuitive knowledge of the godliness contained in the human spirit.

The text concludes with a bold statement that the kingdom of God has already arrived. In Jesus's description, it is already spread upon the land, but humankind fails to see it. This work stirred much enthusiasm from post–Christian New Agers when some scholars hailed it as the missing fifth gospel.

Gospel of Philip

In the same enigmatic style found in the Gospel of Thomas, the Gospel of Philip is an incomplete text dating to C.E. 250. The author creates metaphors from sacraments, weddings, farming, husbandry, and slavery to reveal the nature of true enlightenment, which Philip the Evangelist describes as a light that never sets. The text opens with a denunciation of false information in the world concerning Father, Son, Holy Spirit, life, light, the virgin birth, baptism, resurrection, and the church and an explanation of Jesus's incarnation as the Christ and the sacraments of chrism and baptism. The author foresees the messiah as the reuniter of Adam and Eve. The surprising detail that sets the gospel apart from other Apocrypha is Jesus's kiss to Mary Magdalene, which raises jealousy in the apostles.

Book of Thomas the Contender

A fragmented text based on the canon gospels, the Book of Thomas the Contender records a conversation Matthias overhears between Jesus and Judas Thomas, his twin, after Jesus's ascension to heaven. Thomas is filled with curiosity about events beyond earthly life, "the things that are hidden" (Meyer 1984, 42). Jesus replies that these events are too difficult for earthly minds to comprehend and adds, "You are babies until you attain perfection" (Meyer 1984 43).

Jesus's instruction to his brother on heaven offers the obverse of the Beatitudes. Rather than the familiar "blessed are they," the series of lines begins "woe to you" and warns of false endeavors and misplaced faith. He exhorts, "Woe to you, for you have not learned the lesson" (Meyer 1984, 50). At the end of the exchange between the brothers, Jesus promises, "When you pray, you will find rest, for you have left pain and abuse behind" (Meyer 1984, 50). In shucking off suffering and passion, Jesus promises that the seeker will unite with the Almighty in eternal oneness.

Apocryphon of James

The Apocryphon of James (also the Secret Book of James and *Epistula Iacobi Apocrypha* [Apocryphal Letter of James]), an intimate reminiscence of Jesus's private conversations with his disciples, was composed around C.E. 150. Recovered in tatters, the untitled codex strings together bits of advice on how to emulate Jesus and attain salvation, for example, by hating hypocrisy and evil thoughts and through sobriety and satiety in the spirit. Bitterly, Jesus reminds his twelve followers that they have not suffered the worst of persecution — insult, false accusation, imprisonment, unjust condemnation, crucifixion, and burial. In gentler tones, he advises:

> So disdain death,
>   but care about life.
> Remember my cross and my death,
>   and you will live [Meyer 1984, 6].

Writings from the Nag Hammadi library offer additional views of Jesus and his personal relationship with the disciples.

Letter of Peter to Philip

The Letter of Peter to Philip is a mutilated text composed around C.E. 200 or slightly later. It describes a gathering of the apostles on the Mount of Olives and tells of the men's response to Jesus's voice. Peter prays that Jesus will enlighten his followers so they can work wonders. Jesus again appears to confer a benediction on them and urges them not to be afraid.

Acts of Peter and the Twelve Apostles

In a truncated allegory supplementing the gospels, the Acts of Peter and the Twelve Apostles tells of Jesus's offering of pearls to people living in a harbor town and his gift of a medicine pouch to John so his disciples can heal both body and spirit.

First Apocalypse of James

A badly preserved text, the First Apocalypse of James discloses Jesus's tenderness to James, who weeps at failed attempts to understand Jesus and his purpose.

Second Apocalypse of James

The Second Apocalypse of James, a second text riddled with lacunae, is set in Jerusalem at a speech recorded by the priest Mareim. James the Just expresses mixed terror and delight in Jesus's directives. The crowd grows so agitated that they stone James, who prays for salvation before expiring in a grave the mob made him dig.

One set of writings reflects on the feminine deity Sophia (Knowledge).

The Thunder, Perfect Mind

The Thunder, Perfect Mind is a mystical poem about a strong-voiced female deity, who some scholars call God the Mother and others connect with Athena and Isis lore. The Greek text, which may derive from second- or third-century Alexandria, presents a first-person speaker identifying herself in repeated strings of "I am" statements. Imagery suggests the paradoxical incarnations of the Buddha by describing knowledge as the first and last, wife and virgin, mother and daughter, and barren and prolific. Sophia scolds the Greeks for turning against wisdom and claims Egypt as a setting in which she has flourished. She promises the wise that they will avoid death.

Thought of Norea

The Thought of Norea offers a brief mystical invocation to Ennoia of the light from Norea, a divinity who speaks the words of life.

Sophia Jesu Christi

Sophia Jesu Christi (Wisdom of Jesus Christ), a Greek narrative from the third century, concerns Jesus's appearance to his apostles and seven female followers on a mountain in Galilee to reassure them about the afterlife. He speaks of himself, the Perfect One, in a string of parallels, "He is unchanging good. He is faultless. He is eternal. He is blessed" (Robinson 1990).

Exegesis on the Soul

The Exegesis on the Soul is an extended metaphor on the soul, a female entity alternately glimpsed as daughter, prostitute, parturient woman, mother, and widow. The author links the episode to the displacement of Helen of Troy, the Spartan queen of Homeric epic, whom Aphrodite betrayed by enticing her to leave Menelaus, her husband. The treatise closes by calling for sincere repentance.

A series of liturgical texts reprises some of the themes from the Gospel of Philip:

Discourse on the Eighth and Ninth

The Discourse on the Eighth and Ninth, an exchange between Father Trismegistus and Hermes, his son, includes a hymn and a prayer for understanding and wisdom. The father urges the son to record instruction in hieroglyphs on a turquoise stele. The selection closes with an oath that the reader of the holy book must swear to guard sacred wisdom.

Prayer of Thanksgiving

The Prayer of Thanksgiving is a brief exaltation of intellectual light, which precedes the eating of holy food that contains no blood.

A Valentinian Exposition

A mystic explanation of the passage of wisdom from God to his son, a Valentinian Exposition survives in badly flawed form. The text, a bridge between Christianity and gnosticism sometimes attributed to Heraklion, describes the pleroma, a metaphysical region permeated by God's presence. Ranging outward are lesser emanations. At the far edge resides Sophia, or Wisdom, whose sin is rejecting God. For humankind's duplication of her error there exists one possible salvation—knowledge and illumination of the spirit.

Less valuable are the Three Steles of Seth, a tripartite blessing and jubilation at the revelation of truth, and the Prayer of the Apostle Paul, a faith-born prayer of thanksgiving for godly gifts and redemption.

Departing from canonical accounts of creation and redemption are these gnostic writings.

Apocryphon of John

The Apocryphon of John (also the Secret Book of John) is a bizarre mystical revelation that accounts for Sophia, the feminine incarnation of Wisdom. Opening in a subdued mood, the introduction tells of John, brother of James and son of Zebedee, who enters the Temple and confronts the Pharisee Arimanios. He taunts John with accusations of negligence and closed-mindedness: "This Nazarene has deceived you badly, filled your ears with lies, closed your minds, and turned you away from the traditions of your parents," the standard charge that Jesus overturned Judaic customs and beliefs (Meyer 1984, 55).

In confusion, John wanders the desert to ponder why

God sent his son to earth. Jesus appears in the form of a youth who changes into an older man and servant. The multiform luminous figure of Jesus claims to be a divine triad:

I am with you always.
I am the Father,
I am the Mother,
I am the Child,
I am the incorruptible and the undefiled one [Meyer 1984, 56].

In textured myth, Jesus describes the nature of God, the invisible spirit, and immeasurable light.

The text ventures into an unprecedented cosmogony. Jesus explains how God created Barbelo, the divine mother, spirit of forethought, and the two produced a divine child, Ialdabaoth, who created four stars. Against the will of the father, the defiant Sophia produced a child and repented of her rebellion. After God forgives her, humankind takes shape as Adam and Eve. The revelation closes with a hymn to the savior, who returns to heaven. At his disappearance, John bears the mysterious information to the other apostles. Similarly creative is the Hypostasis of the Archons, a variant creation myth depicting Adam's temptation and fall.

On the Origin of the World

On the Origin of the World (also the Untitled Text), a second variant creation myth, refutes the statement in Genesis 1 that the cosmos was preceded by nothingness. A compilation of gnostic lore, the book is a treatise revealing a syncretic myth of creation. Similar in mystic form and style to the Apocryphon of John, the text recounts the creation of the demiurge Ialdabaoth, son of Sophia, the feminine form of Wisdom. A subversion of Genesis occurs in the declaration that the first father lied when he declared, "I am God. No one else exists before me" (Barnstone 1984, 68).

The creation of Adam is a gynocentric twist on orthodox Eden lore: because he arises from the mud a soulless being, Sophia sends Eve, called Zoë, or Life, to complete the creation of man. He opens his eyes and greets her as "'mother of the living' because you are the one who gave me life" (Barnstone 1984, 70). Because of the first couple's disobedience in eating from the Tree of Knowledge, the world lapses into "a distraction and an ignorance and a stupor." The segment concludes that humankind lived in error until the "appearance of the true man" (Barnstone 1984, 73). The book ends with a summary of gnostic thought concerning the triumph of light over darkness.

Apocalypse of Adam

The Apocalypse of Adam is a gnostic text set in the year 700 when Adam teaches his son Seth about the coming events, including Noah's generation and thirteen successive kingdoms. The revelation opens with three men who approach Adam and bid him exit the sleep of death. God greets Adam and reveals rain that destroys all flesh for its faithlessness. From Noah's family comes a new generation of earthlings. The creation myth concludes with a series of thirteen kingdoms and the promise of a redeemer, all of which Seth passes on to his children.

Paraphrase of Shem

A non–Christian or pre–Christian codex from Nag Hammadi, the Paraphrase of Shem is a revelation experienced by Shem of the redeemer Derdekeas, the son and image of perfect light, another name for the Creator, who he identifies as Elorchaios. After being taken up to heaven, Shem's spirit detaches from his sleeping body. He witnesses three forms of power — light, darkness, and spirit. Derdekeas pities Shem's plight. To rescue him from darkness, Derdekeas takes the form of a beast and battles the evil force in hell. He warns Shem to recognize the goodness of light and to avoid darkness, which is unclean. Derdekeas stresses that humankind must rely on heaven for protection and promises that Shem will understand more in death, when the mind separates from the body.

A collection of gnostic observations and commentaries reflects on the nature of the soul.

Gospel of Truth

Perhaps written by Valentinus, the Egyptian gnostic, before C.E. 175, the Gospel of Truth is a sermon in Greek glorifying the revelation of truth through God's son, Jesus. Rich in hope, the speaker promises a mystic union with God:

And they do not go down to Hades. They have neither envy nor moaning, nor is death in them. But they rest in him who rests, without wearying themselves or becoming involved in the search for truth. But, they, indeed, are the truth, and the Father is in them, and they are in the Father, since they are perfect, inseparable from him who is truly good [Grant 1961].

A compelling aspect of this gospel is the repeated quotation of passages from the New Testament. It offers no new insights into Jesus's life but reinterprets materials from the canon gospels.

Second Treatise of the Great Seth

A blend of Christian and gnostic philosophy, The Second Treatise of the Great Seth contains Jesus's declaration that he is the son of man, one among other humans, who is despised for the sake of humanity. He reflects on Ennoias, or Hell, and reveals the role of Sophia, or Wisdom, his sister, in preparing the way for the messiah. Identifying himself as the son of man, Christ declares himself incorruptible and ineffable. He accounts for the human qualities of Adam, Abraham, Isaac, Jacob, David, Solomon, the twelve prophets, and Moses as a contrast to his uniqueness as the source of goodness, who has dwelled in God's bosom from the beginning of time.

Teachings of Silvanus

The Teachings of Silvanus is a series of warnings and instructions encouraging mature, virtuous actions. To rid the unknowing of sin, the teacher urges his pupil to embrace wisdom and faith in God and to accept Jesus. The speaker incorporates the Greek admonition to "know thyself."

Testimony of Truth

A patchy text, the Testimony of Truth urges that readers go beyond the shallow title of Christian to learn more about Jesus's promise of eternal life. The speaker rejects the idea of resurrection of the body. Integral to the text is a reexamination of foreknowledge as it applies to God's injunction that Adam avoid the fruit of the tree at the center of the garden.

Less valuable are the Treatise on the Resurrection, composed in a one-on-one setting where the speaker instructs Rheginos on salvation from death, which Jesus swallowed up; and Eugnostos the Blessed, similar in literary style to the Wisdom of Jesus Christ, which extols the Lord of the universe and Sophia, the female incarnation of Knowledge.

Fictitious episodes of the holy family and John the Baptist fill in gaps in biblical accounts of Jesus' life.

De Transitu Beatae Mariae Virginis

De Transitu Beatae Mariae Virginis (On the Assumption of the Blessed Virgin Mary; also, the *Dormitio Mariae* [Mary's Sleep], *Transitus Mariae* [Assumption of Mary], and *Evangelium Joannis* [Gospel of John]), listed in the *Decretum Gelasianum*, relates the final days, death, and entombment of Mary before she rises into heaven from Jerusalem to be greeted by Jesus and a host of an-gels. Composed in Greek before the fourth century, the popular legend recurs in Syriac, Coptic, Armenian, and Arabic versions. It opens with a subtitle: "The Account of St. John the Theologian of the Falling Asleep of the Holy Mother of God."

A supernatural element of the deathbed scene is the reassembly of the apostles from various locales, including the afterlife for those who had already died. Another quaint touch is the loss of two hands by an impious Jew who touched Mary's corpse and the apostles' restoration of the hands. The book influenced such medieval and Renaissance art as *The Death of the Virgin*, painted by the Sienese master Duccio de Buoninsegna, and *The Madonna in Glory*, a sixteenth-century work by Dossi Dossi.

Evangelium de Nativitate Mariae

A fictional summary of Mary's birth, childhood, marriage, and motherhood of Jesus, the *Evangelium de Nativitate Mariae* (News of Mary's Birth) was written around 800. It provided Marian lore for the *Legenda Aurea* (Golden Legends), a collection of saints' lives by the thirteenth-century Genoese archbishop James (or Jacob) of Voragine.

History of Joseph the Carpenter

A fourth-century Greek story, the History of Joseph the Carpenter was composed in Egypt to venerate St. Joseph. In the narrative, Jesus reveals family history to the disciples on the Mount of Olives. They recorded the events on a scroll and placed it in the library at Jerusalem. Chapters 1–11 are birth stories encompassing Jesus's conception, birth, and infancy. The remaining twenty-one segments relate the last years of Joseph's life and Jesus's confrontation with Death, a personified being who gently removes Joseph's spirit. The angels Michael and Gabriel receive it, wrap it in silk, and waft it to heaven. Jesus, content that Joseph is well cared for, returns to the corpse to complete the burial ritual and to convey sympathy to his mother and siblings.

Gospel of Nicodemus

A skillful, dramatic fourth- or fifth-century compilation of passion gospel, the Gospel of Nicodemus consists of the Acts of Pilate and Christ's Descent into Hell, the legendary harrowing of hell, reported by the sons of the priest Simeon. Opening on an eyewitness account by Ananias, officer of the guard, the work enlarges on Jesus's trial before Pilate, the crucifixion and burial, resurrection, and sojourn in hell, where Jesus defeats Hades himself, the personification of death. Significant to the text is praise of good Jews—Nicodemus and Joseph of Arimathea, who provided a tomb and winding cloths for Jesus's corpse—and chastisement of bad Jews for failing to recognize and acclaim the true messiah. At the conclusion, Jesus frees souls in hell and apprehends Satan.

Gospel of Gamaliel

The Gospel of Gamaliel (or Laments of Mary), a fifth- or sixth-century fragment, is a Coptic tale based on the Gospel of John and influenced by the *Acta Pilati* (Acts of Pilate) found in the Gospel of Nicodemus. The text relates Pilate's investigation of Jesus's alleged resurrection and his subsequent conversion from skepticism to belief that Jesus rose from the dead.

Gospel of Peter

A Greek parchment composed around C.E. 125 and based on the four canon gospels, the Gospel of Peter relates Jesus's suffering, death, burial, and resurrection. Among its additions to the Bible account are references to a throne upon which unbelievers placed Jesus to mock him.

Minor works of this group include the Life of St. John the Baptist, a fictional account of the evangelist's early years, wanderings in the desert, and demise; *Narratio de Praeciso Joannis Baptistae Capite* (Story of John the Baptist's Decapitation), a post–fifth-century compilation filling in the gaps of the life of Elizabeth and Zachariah, her flight with John, and John's arrest, incarceration, and dramatic death; the Lament of the Virgin, a fifth-century Egyptian narration of Mary's grief for her crucified son and his subsequent appearance to her; and the History of the Blessed Virgin Mary, a fifth-century Syrian legend derived from Jesus's infancy lore and Mariana.

A separate section of the Apocrypha covers the earthly adventures of the disciples and fleshes out biographies with folk tradition and obvious fictions.

Acts of Peter

The Acts of Peter (also *Actus Petri cum Simone* [Act of Peter with Simon] and Circuits of St. Peter), a Palestinian narrative from around C.E. 190, contains the *Quo Vadis* legend, Peter's cruelty to his crippled daughter, Peter's farewell sermon, and his crucifixion. At the height of his suffering, Peter extols Christ:

> You are my father; you are my mother. You are my brother. You are friend. You are servant. You are housekeeper. You are the All, and the All is in you. You are being, and there is nothing that is, except you [Barnstone 1984, 443].

The text concludes with Marcellus's preservation of the corpse with milk, wine, mastic, myrrh, aloe, and spices and an anecdote about Emperor Nero, whom Peter chastised for persecuting Christians. A high point in the work is the competition between Peter and the sorcerer Simon Magus in the Roman Forum. Peter overcomes Simon while the magus flies through the air. He plummets to earth and dies of a head injury.

Acts of Paul

A popular three-part fiction written by a church elder from Asia Minor before C.E. 198, the Acts of Paul contains the *Acta Pauli et Theclae* (Acts of Paul and Thecla), a Greek romance about an Iconian aristocrat, whom Paul converts with sermons on chastity. She gives up her intended husband, cuts her hair, garbs herself like a man, and renounces the world to follow Paul. Her ministry takes her from Iconium in Turkey southeast to Seleucia in Syria. On the way, she encounters wild beasts that refuse to harm her. Her courage influenced an undated limestone relief of Thecla defying wild beasts.

Also included is the Letter of Paul to the Corinthians (or Third Epistle to the Corinthians), prefaced by commentary from the Corinthian elders; and *Martyrium Pauli* (Paul's Martyrdom). This work offers a physical description of Paul as short and bow-legged and mentions his eyebrows joining above a hooked nose. The section recounts his match with a lion at the Ephesian amphitheater, beast lore similar to Androcles and the Lion, which Aulus Gellius recorded in *Noctes Atticae* (Attic Nights, C.E. 180). The address to Onesiphorus of Iconium includes Paul's reprise of the Beatitudes with additional blessings on ascetics and virgins. The most unusual episode is the evangelism of Thecla, the unique female apostle, who baptizes herself and others.

Acts of Peter and Paul

A merger of the Acts of Peter and Acts of Paul, the Acts of Peter and Paul begins with Paul's embarkation from Miletus and his secret landing in Italy. Because Jews misidentify his companion at Puteoli and behead him, the sea engulfs the port. After Peter welcomes Paul to Rome, the two begin a successful crusade. The apostles match the magic of Simon Magus at Nero's throne. Simon shatters his body by attempting to soar over the Via Sacra and collapsing on the stony thoroughfare.

The text lapses into mayhem as Nero plots to destroy the missionaries. Paul is decapitated; Peter, after telling the *Quo Vadis* episode, is crucified in the inverse position to Jesus's crucifixion. Peter lies in a tomb later called the Vatican; Paul's remains occupy a grave on the outskirts of Ostia, Rome's seaport.

Acts of Andrew

The Acts of Andrew, an early third-century work attributed to Leucius Charinus, supposedly John's disciple, dramatizes the martyrdom of Andrew at the order of Aegeates, proconsul of Patrae, an Achaian harbor. The narrative contains stand-alone episodes— Andrew's miracles during his trek from Pontus to Greece, Andrew and Matthias among cannibals, Andrew's crucifixion, and the Story of Peter and Andrew. A touch of melodrama occurs immediately after Andrew's death because his estranged wife, Maximilla, claims the body and buries it. Aegeates is so distraught at her defection that he rises in the middle of the night and leaps to his death from a great height. Seventeenth-century Calabrian artist Mattia Preti painted Andrew being tied on an X-shaped cross by a mob gathered before an ornate Corinthian temple.

Acts of Thaddeus

The Acts of Thaddeus (also Teaching of Adda, the Apostle), based on the Syriac *Doctrina Addai* (Doctrine of Thaddeus) and a fictional correspondence between Jesus and Abgar V of Edessa, is attributed to Labubna, son of Senaak, around C.E. 400. Following the resurrection, Thaddeus achieves Jesus's intent to heal Abgar and Christianize Edessa. The text indicates that Abgar's ambassador commissions a painting of Jesus.

Acts of John

An imaginative gnostic romance from around C.E. 180, the Acts of John names Leucius Charinus as John's traveling companion. The text is one of the oldest that Manichaeans anthologized in a five-part Apocryphal Acts of the Apostles. It contains accounts of John's missions from Miletus to Ephesus, the collapse of the Temple of Artemis on its priest, a hymn of Christ and circle dance of the apostles, and the Eucharist for the dead. John restores motion to Cleopatra, the paralyzed wife of Lycomedes. In chapters 26–29, at Lycomedes' request, an artist paints John's portrait. Chapters 111–115 recount John's request that Verus call men to dig a trench and John's lyric prayer before he stretches out in the bottom and joyfully gives up his life.

Acts of Thomas

The Acts of Thomas (also Acta S. Thomas), composed early in the third century, is the sole extant text of the acts of the five apostles. Christ's disciples— Simon Peter; his brother Andrew; James and John, sons of Zebedee; Philip and Bartholomew; Thomas and Matthew the publican; James, son of Alphaeus; Simon the Canaanean; and Judas, the brother of James— separate after dividing the mission field into five parts and assigning India to Jesus's brother, Judas Thomas the Twin. The text contains the nuptial verse the Song of the Bride, the Manichaean allegory Hymn of the Soul (also Hymn of the Pearl), the bursting of a gall-choked serpent, and details of Thomas's mission to India, his miracles, and death. The bridal song bears the tone and style of the Song of Solomon:

The maiden is the daughter of light.
Upon her stands and rests the majestic effulgence of kings.
Delightful is the sight of her,
  radiant with shining beauty.
Her garments are like spring flowers,
  and a scent of sweet fragrance is diffused from them [Barnstone 1984, 467].

The poem concludes piously rather than carnally with glory to God the father.

Acts of Matthew

The Acts of Matthew, a sixth-century Abyssinian text, is replete with legends. Most memorable is the Latin *Passio Sancti Matthaei* (Passion of St. Matthew), which describes the apostle's martyrdom in Abyssinia. The drama served J. S. Bach for his oratorio *St. Matthew Passion*, a classic choral masterpiece, which debuted in Leipzig on April 15 — Good Friday —1728.

Apocryphal epistles written by early Christian missionaries include six examples from Paul, Barnabas, Titus, and the eleven of Jesus's disciples surviving after Judas's death.

Epistle of St. Paul to the Laodiceans (also Pseudo-Epistle to the Laodiceans) may be another name for Paul's letter to the Ephesians, a widely circulated letter. The fake epistle fills in the gap left by a lost missive.

Correspondence of Paul and Seneca (also Pseudo-Correspondence of Paul and Seneca) is a fictitious exchange of fourteen Latin letters— eight from Seneca and six from Paul —composed around C.E. 380. They imply that the Stoic philosopher Seneca upbraids Paul for his lackluster rhetorical style.

The Third Epistle of St. Paul to the Corinthians is a reply to the people of Corinth concerning the gnostic heresies of Kleobius and Simon, who refuted Jesus' resurrection and God's creation of the world.

Epistle of the Apostles (or Testament of Our Lord in Galilee), an eastern Mediterranean work completed around C.E. 150, claims to be a message of the eleven surviving apostles to all Christian churches. Its summary of Jesus' life, resurrection, and ascension reflects the influence of other apocryphal works.

Epistle of Barnabas, an anti–Jewish essay, was composed around C.E. 140, perhaps by an Alexandrian Christian. The text instructs the reader on the failure of Jews to understand the Torah.

Epistle of Titus, Disciple of Paul, *de dispositione sanctimonii* (on the management of a holy life), is a Latin sermon exhorting ascetics to remain pure.

Apocryphal apocalypse is a subgenre of revelations of the end of time and the afterlife, replete with numerology, misogyny, and prevailing notions of sin and recompense.

Apocalypse of Peter

The Apocalypse of Peter is a Greek vision of the resurrected Jesus who returns to the Mount of Olives to warn his followers of the Antichrist and the punishments of sinners. For example, people who bore false witness must chew their tongues and spout flames from their mouths. Composed around C.E. 150, the text is the earliest guided tour of hell and is led by Jesus himself. There are no devils in charge, only the angels Uriel and Ezriel, who administer suitable punishments.

The narrative draws on Homeric and Virgilian styles of reporting visits to the afterlife. The author embroiders the recompense of those who worship pagan idols, murder, blaspheme, fornicate, prostitute themselves, and abort unborn children. Peter's voyeuristic tour of the underworld goes to extremes of sadism and scatology — hanging, casting into a pit, burning, choking in excrement, eyes burned out, entrails devoured by worms, lips excised, bodies stung by asps, and torture with hot irons. A primitive piece of psychological control, the text goes to the extremes of cruelty to terrify Christians and keep them in line.

Apocalypse of Paul

The Apocalypse of Paul (also *Visio Pauli* [Paul's Vision]) was written in Greek around C.E. 388 and found at his house in Tarsus. The work is the latest tour of the underworld and one of the most detailed of early tours of metaphysical kingdoms. It characterizes rivers of fire, pits of blood and snow, avenging angels bearing torture devices, worms, and fearful beasts. Critics determine its popularity in part from copies translated into Syrian, Coptic, and Ethiopic. In the vision, Jesus appears to Paul as a small child and directs his disciple to the heavens.

Passing from the seventh to the tenth heaven in mystic flight, Paul greets the apostles.

The book describes Paul's witness to God's system of dispatching angels and Paul's view of a heavenly city of gold and the punishments awaiting corrupt priests, which was a primary source for Dante Alighieri's *Inferno*. Paul encounters prophets, patriarchs, Enoch, and Adam and witnesses a *refrigerium*, a respite from torment. At the end of Paul's vision, Adam urges him to take courage from the knowledge that he had repented and received mercy from a compassionate God. Restored to normalcy, Paul obeys a compulsion to write his experience on a scroll and conceal it under the wall of his house.

Apocalypse of Thomas

A brief revelation from Jesus to Thomas, the Apocalypse of Thomas concerns the end-time, which concludes after seven days of portents. Possibly composed in Greek, the text parallels the canon Book of Revelation in its obsession with numbered days and hours and the power of the Almighty against satanic evil. In straightforward warning, Jesus refers to himself as the Son of God the father. He warns of five signs of the end-time, which will fulfill prophecies concerning the redemption of humankind — kingly power, hunger, pestilence, enslavement, and earthly distress. A reign of seven days of terror will conclude on the eighth day with a sweet heavenly voice, a vision of God's chariots in the clouds, and a chorus of angels welcoming the elect to heaven.

Christian Sibyllines

The Christian Sibyllines is a body of end-time prophecies based on the Jewish Sibyllines of Alexandria. Beginning around C.E. 150, the Christian prophecies feature female seers and restructured narratives to give them a Christian slant. In book 6, the Hymn to Christ, the singer speaks of Jesus's baptism in the Jordan River and his wise teachings, walking on water, healing, resurrecting the dead, and banishing suffering. The deity who stretches one bag of bread to feed all men is a member of the house of David. In an apostrophe to the holy cross, the singer exults,

O tree most blessed, on which God was stretched out,
Earth shall not have you, but you shall see a heavenly home
When your fiery eye, O God, shall flash like lightning [Barnstone 1984, 561].

Minor examples of the genre include the Apocalypse of St. John the Apostle, a Greek vision composed after 400 detailing John's visit with the ascended Jesus on Mount Thabor to explain the last judgment, heaven and hell, the Antichrist, and resurrection; the Apocalypse of John, a brief Greek conversation on ethical matters between Jesus and John, composed in Cyprus between C.E. 500 and 700; Mysteries of the Virgin Apostle St. John, a Greek text narrating John's rise into heaven on angels' wings to glimpse Eden, Adam's punishment, and elements of cosmology; *Apocalypsis Beatae Mariae Virginis de Poenis* (The Vision of the Blessed Virgin Mary Concerning Punishments), a ninth-century Greek tale of Mary's intercession for those tormented in hell; and *Visio Mariae Virginis* (The Vision of the Virgin Mary), a post–seventh-century creation that has Mary rising to a third level of heaven and her witness to the damnation of corrupt clergy.

See also Book of Mormon; Dead Sea Scrolls.

SOURCES: Abbott 1969, Alexander and Alexander 1982, The Apocrypha n.d., Armstrong 1993, Augustine 1981, Barnstone 1984, Bogan 1984, Boorstin 1983, 1992, Bowder 1980, Broderick 1987, Burke 1984, Cavendish 1970, Clifton 1992, Cohn-Sherbok 1998, Comay and Cohn-Sherbok 1995, Cooper 1996, Cunningham 1998, Curtius 1953, Delehaye 1955, Fine 1994, Foss 1997, Gabel and Wheeler 1990, George 1995, Gilson 1983, Goldstein 1976, 1983, Grant 1961, Groothuis 1991, "Handel's Oratorio Susanna," Hastings 1951, Holmes 1988, *Hymnal of the United Church of Christ* 1974, Jeffrey 1992, Johnson 1968, Kieckhefer 1989, Komroff 1937, Larue 1968, Lawless 1987, Magnusson 1990, Mays 1988, McGuire 1996, Metzger 1965, Metzger and Coogan 1993, Meyer 1984, 1992, Miller 1994, "The Nag Hammadi Library" 1998, *New Catholic Encyclopedia* 1967, O'Daly 1987, "The Odes of Solomon Annotated," Pagels 1989, Palmer 1992, Rice 1965, Robinson 1990, Snodgrass 1995, 1999, Telushkin 1991, Thompson 1975, Turner 1991, Turner 1993, Vermes 1998.

Aranyakas *see* Vedas

Avesta The Avesta, meaning Injunction, Knowledge, or Foundation, is the sacred scripture of Zoroastrianism, or the Good Religion, the work of a Persian prophet called Zoroaster, Zarathustra, or Zara-ushtra (Camel Driver). At present a dying sect, it is one of the world's most ancient living faiths and the first to preach universality, or acceptance of all converts. Drawing on a thousand years of oral traditions, the Avesta is the earliest example of Iranian thought and poetry and a forerunner of monotheistic scripture. The Roman encyclopedist Pliny the Elder spoke of Zoroaster's writings as encompassing two million verses.

The Zoroastrian code of ethics offers equal status to men and women and encourages prosperity through herding and planting, marrying, and producing children. The philosophy of Zoroastrianism, also called Mazdaism, syncretizes ancient tradition and anticipates the theology

A miniature Khurda Avesta. (Courtesy the UNESCO Parzor Project.)

of Greeks, Jews, and early Christians, who may have profited from Zoroaster's thinking on God, the war between Asha and Druj (truth and falsehood), the character of Satan, and resurrection and its implications for human destiny. The concepts of the prophet also influenced the naming of the hero Sorastro in Mozart's opera *The Magic Flute* (1791) and the title of philosopher Friedrich Wilhelm Nietzsche's *Also Sprach Zarathustra* (1885).

Zoroaster, a *zaotar* (priest) of the Spitama family, was part of a pastoral tribe around 628–551 B.C.E. A member of the knight class, he was the son of Pourushaspa and lived on the Drja, a river unknown in history. Contemporaries described his home as the mythical Aryana Vaejah near the current borders of Iran, Afghanistan, and Turkmenistan. Historians corrected that misinformation by declaring him a native of Rhages, a suburb of Tehran, in Media.

Zoroaster is the only one of the world's great religious prophets to belong to the priesthood. His name reached the West through the magi, a respected hereditary class of male dream interpreters, royal consultants, diviners, and chaplains from western Iran, who came to Greece in 400 B.C.E. and transmitted Zoroastrianism to the West. Classical authors erroneously characterized him as a Persian or a Mede magician until around 300 B.C.E., when Hecataeus of Abdera revealed that Zathraustes, the Greek spelling of his name, was an Aryan prophet, social reformer, composer of *manthras* (sacred words or prayers) and possibly a priest of a deity named Ahura Mazda (also Auramazda, Ormazd, or Ormuzd), the Wise Lord, or Lord Wisdom.

The prophet received sacred revelations around

600–590 B.C.E. and evolved a monotheistic faith. According to tradition, after entering a cave on Mount Sabalan, he experienced a vision of Ahura Mazda's seven faces, which represent eternal light, omniscient wisdom, righteousness, power, piety, benevolence, and eternal life. The revelation signaled the beginning of Zoroaster's ministry. To prepare him, the Wise Lord taught him to distinguish between truth and falsehood. The lesson developed into a powerful Middle Eastern faith.

Like Judaism, Christianity, and Islam, Zoroastrianism is a positive, uplifting belief system. The prophet advocated turning thoughts, words, and deeds against lies and injustice. For daily life, he taught thrift, friendship, and love. To Zoroaster, truth and free will formed the core of a personal faith that places deity and humankind, both male and female, on an equal basis. His text departs from the earlier Indo-Iranian concepts of good and evil spirits, whom worshipers placated with offerings. Offering more hope to these puppet figures manipulated by vengeful gods, Zoroaster anticipated a messiah, the reclamation of souls in paradise, and a new world populated by the virtuous.

The prophet moved steadily toward building a base of followers. He converted his cousin Maidyoimanha (or Metyoma) as the first *ashavan* (follower). Other disciples known by name are Jamaspa, vizier under the Kavi monarch Vishtaspa (later called Gashtasp or Hystaspes) and husband of Zoroaster's youngest daughter, and Fashaoshtra, Jamaspa's brother. Although Zoroaster rose in position through his son-in-law, he faced hostility from royals, priests, and scholars, who rejected his religion as an enemy of an entrenched tribal polytheism dating into prehistory. He appears to have lived during the conquest by Cyrus the Great, who annexed Aryan land for Persia in 559 B.C.E. The loss of independence was a blow to Zoroaster, who was a friend and supporter of Vishtaspa, namesake of the father of Darius and king of Chorasmia, an area south of the Aral Sea. It was Vishtaspa who received the Avesta, composed in gold script, into the archives of Stakhra, the ancient name of Persepolis. A back-up copy, written in twelve chapters on gilt tablets, remained in the treasury of the fire temple at Samarkand.

The outcome of the prophet and king's friendship came about in 588 B.C.E., when the prophet converted his friend and monarch to the new faith. Their close relationship lasted through religious wars against Arjataspa, king of the Hyaonas, and preceded the conversion of the entire royal family and their retainers. In his royal quarters, Zoroaster took three wives and sired a large family.

Unfortunately, the fall of the king cost the prophet a privileged place at court. In his late seventies, Zoroaster was martyred by the Hyaonas. According to legend, he was performing a ceremony at the Temple of the Sacred Fire when invaders stabbed him to death, slaughtered his priests, and burned the Avesta.

Historically, Zoroastrianism emerged at the height of struggle between nomadism and agrarianism, shortly after the Aryan migration from central Asia to the Middle East. In the prophet's allegorical explanation of the virtue of farming, husbandry, and civilized society, he names Ahura Mazda as the supreme deity and maker of the cosmos. As the source of light and darkness, he gave humankind nature, law, and moral order. He sired a pan-

Name	Meaning	Province	Festival
Vohu Manah	Perfect Divine Mind, Vision, Love	cattle	– – –
Asha Vahishta	Righteousness, Order, Plan of Grace, Excellent Truth	fire	New Day
Khshathra	Dominion, Divine Noble Government, Realm of God, Anticipated Kingdom	sky, metal	Midspring
Armaiti	Piety, Holy Character, Proper Mind, Devotion	earth	Corn Harvest
Haurvatat	Wholesomeness, Completeness, Health of Mind and Body	water	Midsummer
Ameretat	Immortality, Life in Heaven, Anti-Death	plants	Homecoming

[Clark 1998, 28]

theon of six archangels, whom later scripture calls by name.

These six divinities comprise a fighting force, which Ahura Mazda mustered against evil. In the battleground that is earth, deities and humankind are to pursue the same excellence of character through high ethical goals as a means of attaining an idyllic afterlife.

The preexisting cosmology was a complicated struggle between opposing forces. Because spirits were free to choose good or evil, they produced Ahriman (or Angra Mainyu, the Evil Spirit), prince of evil, and the daevas, his earthly minions. These evildoers are a thinly veiled equivalent of desert nomads, whom Zoroaster calls the Druj, the Kingdom of the Lie. In the view of the more civilized Persians, the Druj's contribution to humanity was a multilayered curse — waste, enmity, hatred, plunder, and ruin — the standard results of war in ancient times. Their weapons were serpents, locusts, whirlwinds, floods, epidemics, and vermin, all adversaries of piety, compassion, forbearance, and peace.

According to Zoroastrianism, it is the duty of humankind to select either the kingdom of Ahura Mazda or that of Ahriman, whom Ahura Mazda countered by reciting the twenty-one-word Ahuna Vairya (or Ahunvar), Zoroastrianism's most hallowed prayer, which immobilized Ahriman for three millennia. Ahriman revived through the ministrations of the Primal Woman, but could not win the final battle. He seduced the first human couple and undermined creation, which he enriched with gifts of fire, earth, water, plants, cattle, and metal. His seventh gift was humankind. The perversion of perfect beings cost future earthlings their immortality, but left a five-part mortality composed of *ahu* (life), *daena* (religion), *baodah* (knowledge), *urvan* (soul), and *fravashi* (previous souls of heroes or ancestral spirits).

After the arrival of Zoroaster on earth, Ahriman lost his power and began to fight Ahura Mazda on equal ground. Zoroastrians believe that Ahura Mazda reigns supreme over evil and, in three millennia, will obliterate Ahriman's wicked realm. The followers of evil will earn everlasting misery; to the faithful belongs perpetual reward for goodness. Symbolizing that future date when goodness will reign is the uniform of Zoroastrian priests—the *sadre* or *sudre*, a white cotton tabard, cinched with a *kusti*, the ceremonial cord formed of seventy-two lamb's-wool threads and wrapped three times about the waist. The first Persian holy men donned this simple outfit as an armor of truth following a ceremonial *navjote* (initiation), which all children undergo as their introduction to the faith.

In the aftermath of Zoroaster's reform, his life passed from history into legend because little remained to substantiate his actual teachings. According to folk tradition, he was sired by Gosurvan, the sacred bull; nature embraced the sacred offspring at his birth, when he burst into laughter. A demon that reached for the babe in his crib saw his own hand wither; another demon tried in vain to stampede cattle into his path. Wolves refused to harm him and led him to a ewe to suckle. The prophet Jeremiah supposedly tutored the boy and protected his impressionable mind from evil. At his assumption of manhood at age fifteen, he wore the sacred girdle of religion and worked among the needy, aged, and sick.

Disciples upheld Zoroaster as the consummate farmer, artisan, soldier, priest, warrior, and healer. He allegedly preached widely, established hallowed hearths, and fought a sacred war. At his death, a rainbow appeared in the sky as a token of the prophet's continued support of the human struggle for right. Zoroastrians claimed all the Avesta as the prophet's original writing and anticipated his rebirth in the form of three sons, born a thousand years apart at periods of extensive moral degeneracy. The last, named Astvat-ereta (Justice), would bear the title of Saoshyans or Sashoyant (the Savior). Beyond his role as diviner, the Greeks admired Zoroaster's philosophy and exalted him as a mathematician, astrologer, and mage and as one of the founders of the secret science of alchemy. He held a demonized position among the anti–Hellenic Jews and Christians, who damned him for black magic and heresy.

Over the centuries, Zoroastrianism survived a series of unorthodox or quasi-orthodox shifts in emphasis. Late in the sixth century B.C.E., the worship of Ahura Mazda passed to Darius. He chose to convert to Zoroastrianism as a means of stabilizing his empire, but in a gesture toward polytheism, reduced Ahura Mazda's entities to minor deities. Darius declared, "Ahura Mazda brought me help because I was not wicked, nor was I a liar, nor was I a tyrant. I have ruled according to righteousness" (Berry 1956, 37). Darius's successor, Xerxes, ended the worship of hostile deities in Babylon and replaced them with Ahura Mazda, whom seekers worshiped at a growing number of fire temples, including the Naqsh-i-Rustam near Persepolis, a square tower topped with a dentate edge, which survives in ruins.

In the mid–fourth century B.C.E. under Artaxerxes I, priests evolved a world-year calendar, a significant religious innovation. As described by Peter Clark in *Zoroastrianiam: An Introduction to an Ancient Faith*:

> Since the Zoroastrian calendar is solar rather than lunar, it contains 360 days, and so five Gatha Days are also celebrated, bringing the total to 365. Each 30-day period or month thus enables the tradition to acknowledge, on a regularly recurring basis, one of thirty divine beings per day, twelve of which are also celebrated with their own "month" [Clark 1998, 119].

Under Artaxerxes II and III, inscriptions characterized a trinity—Ahura Mazda, Mithra, and Anahita (or Anahit)—all of whom derive from the prophet's teachings.

The original Avestan anthology did not survive the campaign of Alexander the Great, who wanted to form one kingdom by merging Greece and Persia. To that end, he burned Persepolis in 330 B.C.E., slaughtered priests, conquered Samarkand, and suppressed local cultures under pervasive Hellenism. Reduced from 12,000 cowhides to a fourth its original size, the surviving codex comprises cosmogony, law, ritual, invocations, and the wisdom of Zoroaster. Magian priests rose to power late in the fourth century B.C.E. and monopolized court religion. Around 90 B.C.E., the Zoroastrian calendar appeared at Nisa in modern Turkmenistan. In the Syrian district of Commagene around 50 B.C.E., gods carried Greek names plus Iranian surnames—Zeus Oromazdes, Apollo Mithra, Helios Hermes, and Artagnes Herakles Ares.

The period contemporaneous with the rise of Christianity quelled fervid Zoroastrianism. From around C.E. 50 to 225, the fire cult vanished during the eclipse of Iranian religion. Only fragments of the lost Avestan verses survived in Greek, Persian, and Syriac. Redactors attempted to reconstruct and enlarge the lost parts in the first century C.E. The surviving Avesta is the work of the Sasanian kings, the dynasty that arose in the third century C.E., at the end of the ancient era, when Zoroastrianism became the state religion and the sacred fire, Ahura Mazda's son, once more burned on altars. The milieu of the reemergence of Zoroastrianism and Mazdaism as world religions and the writing of Avestan scripture was a time of chaos and shifting loyalties. After Ardashir I, a priest and proponent of the faith, established his throne in Persis, he annexed Mesene in southern Mesopotamia, which the modern world knows as Iran. He overwhelmed the Parthians, a west Iranian tribe, in C.E. 224 and killed their last king, Artabanus V, at the battle of Hormuz.

Safe on his throne, Ardashir, the great civilizer of Persia, founded the Sasanide dynasty and had himself proclaimed King of Kings. To reestablish the empire and centralize religious power, he commissioned the theologian Tansar (or Tosar) to collect Zoroaster's sacred writings and establish a canon. Under Shapur in C.E. 226, Tansar restored the native faith, which spread from Iran to the south and west. After making a capital at Ctesiphon on the banks of the Tigris twenty miles southeast of Baghdad, Ardashir attempted to vanquish Hatra in northwest Iraq. In C.E. 232, the intervention of Emperor Severus Alexander and his Roman legions ended Sasanian ambitions. Three years later, when Severus died, the Persians invaded neighboring lands, annexing Nisibis and Harran in southeastern Turkey by C.E. 238 and Hatra two years later. Tansar rose to the position of *magupat* of Ormazd (chief magian of Ahura Mazda).

Ardashir's son Shapur (or Shahpuhr) I led Persian troops against the Roman army of Gordian III in C.E. 243 and lost Harran and Nisibis in a one-sided battle near Resaina. Shapur regrouped at Anbar and won. He pressed on into northern Syria and Anatolia. His campaign peaked in C.E. 259, when he captured Emperor Valerian at Edessa. Shapur lost to the Palmyran king, Septimius Odaenathus (or Odainath), who seized the throne and the cities of Harran and Nisibis. Northern Mesopotamia returned to Roman control in C.E. 273, when Emperor Aurelian conquered Palmyra.

During a peaceful interlude after the imprisonment and death of Mani, founder of Manichaenism, Bahram II chose Karter (or Kartir), the Zoroastrian high priest, as judge and savior of the soul of Bahram. Late in the third century, the power struggle between Persia and Rome resumed. In C.E. 297, Roman troops captured Narses I and fortified Nisibis as a Roman outpost controlling territory between the Euphrates and Tigris rivers. Shapur II, under whom the more recent parts of the Avesta were written, renewed the struggle from C.E. 337 to 350. He appointed the high priest Aturpat (also Adarbad Maraspand) as prime minister to standardize the Avesta. To trounce sectarians and heretics, Aturpat submitted to trial by ordeal and survived having metal poured on his chest. In 363, Jovian ceded Persian land to the Sasanians.

In the fifth century, the survival of Zoroastrianism continued to hinge on placement of power. Around C.E. 420, Bahram V appointed a *magupatan magupat* (supreme magus). Under Qobad (or Kavadh) I, at the beginning of the sixth century, the threat of an extreme form of communism under the Mazdaites caused an upheaval that unseated the king in favor of his brother Jamaspa. Within two years, Qobad returned and disbanded those favoring total egalitarianism. His son Khosrow (also Khosrau, Khusru, or Chosroes) I, a champion of the faith, around C.E. 530 promoted Mazdaism as the state faith by restoring order, defining orthodoxy, collecting and standardizing parts of the Avesta, and consolidating a Zoroastrian church.

After the faithful achieved a canon text, the resulting Avesta consisted of old and new writings: one *nask* (section) in ancient Zend and subsequent parts written in a script that evolved into the Aramaic alphabet.

Yasna

Composed in simple language, Yasna (Worship or Sacrifice) is the heart of liturgy and the most sacred and life-affirming ritual. The lyrics are revelations from Ahura Mazda that caused Zoroaster to end sacrifice to dark forces, which was an impetus to excessive drunkenness and sacrifice of cattle. In supplanting orgiastic cult worship with a symbolic offering, he elevated the cult of fire, the mystic fluid of life, honored by priests at the Temple of Fire.

Yasna advocates a public gift of *haoma* (alcoholic drink), a hallowed liquor and healing potion made from juice pressed from twigs of the ephedra plant, a leafless desert bush marked by nodes, and blended with milk and aromatic additives. Ahura Mazda's priests presented the sacred drink along with water and milk before the holy fire while reciting scripture from the Avesta. Priests nurture the temple fire and periodically feed it embers from community fires, a symbol of regeneration.

Believed to be composed by Zoroaster or at least dating to Indo-Iranian times, the Yasna collection consists of seventy-two *haiti* (chapters), which are symbolized in the seventy-two strands forming the sacred cord. Some of the chapters including 5 and 37, 18 and 47, as well as 63, 64, 66, and 67, replicate other sections as a means of increasing the number of chapters to the sacred number seventy-two:

Introit	Introduction to the worship of Ahura Mazda and holy fire
Yasnas 1–27	Invocation to Ahura Mazda and lesser divinities
	3–8 holy vows to follow sacred ritual and offerings, ending with a prayer

(continued on p. 30)

(continued from p. 29)		
	9–11	Hom Yasht (or Homast Yasht), sacred ritual revering haoma
	12	Zoroastrian Creed
Invocations and dedication of sacrifices		
	13	a sacred formula
	14–15	beginning of the Staota Yesnya
	16	invocation to the day spirit
	17	divisions of day and year and types of fire
	19–21	commentary on the three most hallowed prayers
	22–27	Homast Yasht, ritual for the second ceremonial preparation of Haoma
Yasnas 28–53	The five Gathas and the Yasna Haptanghaiti, the most revered section of the Avesta, appear to summarize the teachings of Zoroaster.	
	28–34	Ahunavaiti Gatha, a series of hymns to Ahura Mazda
	35–42	Yasna Haptanghaiti, a series of short prayers to the Bountiful Immortals
	43–46	Ushtavaiti Gatha, a collection of divine songs in heavy parallel style
	47–50	Spentamainyush Gatha, spiritual songs marked by the personal concerns of Zoroaster
	51	Vohukhshathra Gatha, a song praising creation and justice
	52	three-verse prayer expressing piety
	53	Vahishtoishti Gatha, a call for reward to the good and ruin to the evil
Yasnas 54–72	The conclusion of the Gathas and the calls for blessing from Sraosha, personification of obedience and prayer and protector of the soul from death and judgment in the afterlife, a parallel to the Egyptian Book of the Dead.	
	54	Airyaman Ishya
	55	summary of the Gathas
	56–57	introduction and the Srosh Yasht
	58	praise of prayer
	59–60	blessing of the house
	61	formula for exorcism
	62	propitiation of sacred fire
	63–64	Ab-zor, or offering to the water
	65	praise to Anahita, goddess of waters
	66–68	consecration of holy water
	69–72	concluding invocations

The badly preserved introit, which is unnumbered, states Zoroastrian beliefs in a first-person list of promises to worship Ahura Mazda, oppose daevas, accept doctrine, and propitiate and praise fire. To promote ethical behavior, the speaker declares in verses 4–5:

I praise good thoughts, good words, and good deeds and
  those that are to be thought, spoken, and done.
I do accept all good thoughts, good words, and good deeds.
I do renounce all evil thoughts, evil words, and evil deeds.
I proffer to you, O Amesha Spentas, sacrifice and prayer, with
  thought, with word, with deed, with [my] being, with the
  very life of my body ["Avesta—Zoroastrian Archives"].

The Hom Yasht dedicates the worshiper to *haoma*, the sacred plant that took the place of blood sacrifice and elevated Zoroastrianism above less-civilized worship. In Yasna 10:4–5, the speaker extols nature:

This wide earth do I praise, expanded far [with paths], the
  productive,
  the full bearing, thy mother, holy plant!
Yea, I praise the lands where thou dost grow, sweet-scented,
  swiftly spreading, the good growth of the Lord.
O Haoma, thou growest on the mountains, apart on many
  paths,
  and there still may'st thou flourish.
The springs of righteousness most verily thou art,
  [and the fountains of the ritual find their source in thee]!
Grow [then] because I pray to thee on all thy stems and
  branches,
  in all thy shoots [and tendrils] increase thou through my
  word! ["Avesta—Zoroastrian Archives"].

Chapter 12 states at length from first-person perspective the intent of the follower of Ahura Mazda. In verses 1–4, each devotee pledges:

I declare myself a Mazda-worshipper, a supporter of
  Zarathushtra,
  hostile to the Daevas, fond of Ahura's teaching,
  a praiser of the Amesha Spentas,
  a worshipper of the Amesha Spentas.
I ascribe all good to Ahura Mazda, and all the best, ... whose
  is the light,
  may whose blissful areas be filled with light.
I choose the good Spenta Armaiti for myself; let her be
  mine....
I want freedom of movement and freedom of dwelling
  for those with homesteads,
  to those who dwell upon this earth with their cattle....
I reject the authority of the Daevas, the wicked, no-good,
  lawless,
  evil-knowing, the most druj-like of beings, the foulest of beings,
  the most damaging of beings....
  I reject any who harm beings.
I reject them with my thoughts, words, and deeds.
I reject them publicly ["Avesta—Zoroastrian Archives"].

The lengthy litany concludes with high praise to Ahura Mazda: "This is to render Him who is of all the greatest, our lord and master."

Gathas

The most ancient and holiest part of the Yasna, the Gathas (Songs or Psalms), written in the Gatha-Avestan dialect, are intensely personal devotional outpourings. Like the Vedas, they take the form of an octosyllabic metrical chant or poetic hymn devoid of the repetition found in other parts of the Avesta. These inspired utterances composed in a complex poetic style are rich in allusion.

They consist of varied types of songs, dialogues with deities, meditations, and prophetic anthems. As described by Roni Khan, Zoroastrian scholar of India:

> they present the most dazzling metaphysical revelations of transcendental divinity, breathtaking cosmology and supreme ethics, all at the highest esoteric and philosophical levels, and are replete with technical terms and expressions, spiritual metaphors, and layer upon layer of mystical meaning [Khan 1995].

The Gathas were composed in varying meters in Zend, an eastern Iranian language related to Sanskrit and used only by priests. The enigmatic and virtually untranslatable fountainhead of Zoroastrianism, they appear to be the prophet's most sublime versifications on good and evil, a perpetual warfare that the god Ahura Mazda must win as a preface to the establishment of a heavenly kingdom.

The most frequently recited Gathas are the four main and most potent of Zoroastrian prayers, which Ahura Mazda recited at the dawn of creation.

• Ahuna Vairya (or Ahunavar), the first prayer a child learns, outlines the right way to live. Recorded in Yasna 27:13, it states:

> As the Ahu is excellent, so is the Ratu [one who rules] from [his] sanctity, a creator of mental goodness, and of life's actions done for Mazda; and the kingdom (is) for Ahura, which to the poor may offer a nurturer ["Avesta — Zoroastrian Archives"].

• Airyema Ishyou (or Airyaman Ishya) is a blessing for weddings that also assures the submission of house, village, tribe, and province and restores the dead on the day of resurrection. Stated in Yasna 54:1, it reads:

> Let the Airyaman, the desired friend and peersman, draw near for grace to the men and to the women who are taught of Zarathushtra, for the joyful grace of the good mind, whereby the conscience may attain its wished-for recompense. I pray for the sacred reward of the ritual order which is [likewise so much] to be desired; and may Ahura Mazda grant it, [or cause it to increase] ["Avesta — Zoroastrian Archives"].

• Ashem Vohu sustains and guides the universe toward purity and spiritual perfection. Recorded in Yasna 27:14, it rejoices, "Holiness [Asha] is the best of all good: it is also happiness. Happy the man who is holy with perfect holiness!" ("Avesta — Zoroastrian Archives")

• Yenhe Hatam, a prayer of dedication, stated in Yasna 4:26 and described in Yasna 21, reads, "Those beings, male and female, whom Lord Mazda knows the best for worship according to truth, we worship them all" ("Avesta — Zoroastrian Archives").

The allusive lyrics of the Gathas relate thoughts, words, and deeds to the afterlife, when the Wise Lord re-wards goodness. The worthy pass over Cinvat, the Bridge of the Requiter, before entering eternal bliss. At the end of life on earth, the Wise Lord will destroy evil doers and resurrect the dead. Historical figures and places named in the Gathas remain a mystery.

Derived from an agrarian era, Yasna 33 offers a subdued litany of praise anthems interlaced with pastoral imagery of the herder similar to the metaphors and motifs of the psalms of David. Verses 1–4 foresee an idyllic state of justice:

> According as it is with the laws that belong to the present life,
>   so shall the judge act with most just deed
>   towards the man of the lie and the man of the right,
>   and him whose false things and good things balance [in equal measure].
> Whoso worketh ill for the liar by word or thought or hands,
>   or converts his dependent to the good —
>   such men meet the will of Ahura Mazda to his satisfaction.
> Whose is most good to the righteous man,
>   be he noble or member of the community or the brotherhood, Ahura —
>   or with diligence cares for the cattle,
>   he shall be hereafter in the pasture of right and good thought ["Avesta — Zoroastrian Archives"].

The theme of the triumph of good over evil permeates the work and worship of the simple peasant, whose faithful husbandry of animals parallels the protection of Ahura Mazda over all creation.

In the personal, one-on-one questions of worshiper to deity, Zoroaster questions Ahura Mazda. Similar to the cry of David to Yahweh, Yasna 50:1–4 is a call-and-response from earthling to God:

> Can my soul count on any one for help?
> Who is there found for my herd,
>   who for myself a protector, indeed,
>   at my call other than the right and thyself.
> O Mazda Ahura, and the best thought?
> How, O Mazda, should one desire the luck-bringing cattle,
>   one who would fain it would come to him with the pasture?
> They that live uprightly according to the right
>   among the many that look upon the sun,
>   those whom they stand in judgment,
> I will settle in the dwellings of the wise.
> So this [reward] shall come to him through the right,
>   O Mazda, [this reward] which by the dominion and good thought
>   he promised....
> I will worship you with praise, O Mazda Ahura,
>   joined with right and best thought and dominion,
>   that they, desired of pious men,
>   may stand as Judges on the path of the obedient
>   unto the House of Song ["Avesta — Zoroastrian Archives"].

This affirmation of the questioning individual attests to the appeal of Zoroastrianism to people of lowly station, who achieve right thinking through worship and ethical behavior as dictated by Ahura Mazda. Those who met the standards of Ahura Mazda advanced at death to the House of Song, or heaven; those who failed resided in hell, the House of Lies.

Visperad

Less important to the collection is the Visperad (also Visp-rat or Vispered [All the Lords or Patrons]), a supplemental series of encomia to Zoroastrian priests and invocations and honor to gods and saints to be recited on solemn occasions. The text lists:

Visperad 1–2	Introduction
Visperad 3	Roll call that precedes the haoma ritual
Visperad 4–6	Sacrificial liturgy
Visperad 7	Worship of spirits by name
Visperad 8	Invocation to Ahura Mazda
Visperad 9–12	Offering liturgy
Visperad 13–14	Statements of belief
Visperad 15	Call to worship that declares: "Hold your feet in readiness, and your two hands, and your understandings, O ye Zarathushtrian Mazdayasnians! for the well-doing of lawful deeds in accordance with the sacred order, and for the avoidance of the unlawful and evil deeds which are contrary to the ritual. Let the good deeds for the furtherance of husbandry be done here ["Avesta—Zoroastrian Archives"].
Visperad 16	Praise to fire
Visperad 17	A single statement: "And we strive after the good thoughts, words, and deeds inculcated in the Yasna Haptanghaiti. A blessing is the right [called] the best, [there is] weal; [there is] weal for this [man] when toward righteousness best [there is] right" ["Avesta—Zoroastrian Archives"].
Visperad 18–20	Acknowledgment of the god and saints.
Visperad 21–24	A statement of the congregation's purpose in worship, which concludes, "And we sacrifice to that reward, health, healing, furtherance, and increase, and to that victory which is within the two, the Ahuna-vairya and the Airyema-ishyo, through the memorized recital of the good thoughts, words, and deeds [which they enjoin]" ["Avesta—Zoroastrian Archives"].

Vendidad

The only complete section of the Avesta, the Vendidad (or Videvdat [Law Rejecting the Daevas]), reached completion between 141 B.C.E. and C.E. 224. It is a strongly Parthian text containing a lengthy night ritual repelling demons, notably, the allegorical figures of Wrath, Greed, Lying, and Procrastination. With this verbal charm, priests repel evils by reading the entire Vendidad from midnight to 7:00 A.M. The text lists twenty-two *fargards* (sections) of

ritual and civil codes governing ceremonies, penalties for infractions, medical treatments, and purification rituals.

Fargard 1	Sixteen perfect lands created by Ahura Mazda and sixteen plagues created by Ahriman
Fargard 2	Myths of Yima, the Golden Age, and Yima's survival of a terrible winter and subsequent flood. According to verse 33, he lives through the catastrophe in the style of Noah and the Ark: "And Yima made a Vara, long as a riding-ground on every side of the square. There he brought the seeds of sheep and oxen, of men, of dogs, of birds, and of red blazing fires. He made a Vara, long as a riding-ground on every side of the square, to be an abode for men; a Vara, long as a riding-ground on every side of the square, for oxen and sheep ["Avesta—Zoroastrian Archives"].
Fargard 3	Earthly pleasures and trials, lauding agriculture and warning that rotting corpses defile the land
Fargard 4	Contracts, assault and other offenses, and punishments
Fargards 5–12	Purity laws that result from contact with corpses and methods of cleansing the earth, particularly Barashnum, the nine-night lustration ceremony. This section covers specifics of custom and belief:
8	Funerals, purification, illicit sex
9	Barashnum, the nine-night lustration ceremony, which cleanses the land
10	Formulas recited during cleansing
11	Special formulas for cleansing the house
12	Upaman, the ritual cleansing after a death in the family
Fargards 13–15	Summary of the ritual reverence for the dog, a treasured beast in the early pastoral age.
13	Paean to the dog
14	Atoning for murdering a sacred dog
15	Atoning for sins
Fargard 16	Purity laws regarding menstruation and intercourse with a menstruating woman
Fargard 17	Disposing of hair and nails, which can summon demons
Fargards 18–19	Combating evil
18	Differentiating between pious and impious priests and revering the rooster, which summons the worshiper to early morning prayer. Verse 21 calls directly to the pious: "Up! arise, thou husbandman! Put on thy kusti [girdle] on thy clothes, wash thy hands, take wood, bring it unto me, and let me burn bright with the clean wood, carried by thy well-washed hands" ["Avesta—Zoroastrian Archives"].
19	Zoroaster's temptation and the soul's destiny after death. In verse 7, he retorts to the impulse to do evil: "No! never will I renounce the good religion of the worshippers of Mazda, either for body or life, though they should tear away the breath!" ["Avesta—Zoroastrian Archives"].

(continued from p. 32)

Fargards 20–22	Medical matters	
	20	Thrita, the first healer, who in verse 7 orders, "To thee, O Sickness, I say avaunt! to thee, O Death, I say avaunt! to thee, O Pain, I say avaunt! to thee, O Fever, I say avaunt! to thee, O Evil Eye, I say avaunt! to thee" ["Avesta—Zoroastrian Archives"].
	21	Four praise hymns
	22	Angra Mainyu's creation of 99,999 diseases, which the manthra of Ahura Mazda counters.

The first *fargard*, which demonstrates a formulaic and highly repetitive style that mimics an oratorio, narrates how Ahura Mazda regards the earth. The second section summarizes the creation of fire, the source of life, and the story of the first man and first earthly ruler, Yima, the Adamic good shepherd and Noah figure, whom Ahura Mazda chose to rescue creation from a catastrophic winter and flood. After refusing to preach, Yima declares in verse 5:

Yes! I will make thy world increase, I will make thy world grow.
Yes! I will nourish, and rule, and watch over thy world.
There shall be, while I am king, neither cold wind nor hot wind, neither disease nor death [Darmesteter 1898].

Yima flourishes on earth for 900 years and fills the land with flocks and herds. In verses 36–37, he embellishes nature:

There he brought the seeds of every kind of tree, of the highest of size and
 sweetest of odour on this earth;
 there he brought the seeds of every kind of fruit,
 the best of savour and sweetest of odour.
All those seeds he brought, two of every kind,
 to be kept inexhaustible there....
And there were no humpbacked, none bulged forward there;
 no impotent, no lunatic; no one malicious, no liar;
 no one spiteful, none jealous;
 no one with decayed tooth, no leprous to be pent up,
 nor any of the brands wherewith [Ahriman] stamps the
 bodies of mortals [Darmesteter 1898].

The Yima section ends with the first man's direct questions to Ahura Mazda, which reaffirm the Creator's omnipotence and omnipresence at the beginning of human habitation of the earth.

Yashts

The twenty-one mythic anthems known as *Yashts* (or *Yasts* [Offering Chants or Anthems]) are composed of minor scriptural verses, mythic hymns, and prayers, some composed in Achaemenid, the ancient Persian language. They reflect an Aryan polytheism of twenty-one deities whom Zoroaster disclaimed, in particular, the goddess of the waters; Mithra (or Mithras), an Indo-Iranian god of truth and light; the star deity Tishtrya; and souls of the virtuous. The paeans begin with a formulaic homage to Ahura Mazda. Yasht 1 is dedicated to the Wise Lord; Yasht 10 to Mithra.

The final verses, 62–63, of the apocalyptic Zand-i Vohuman Yasht anticipate a peaceful era after good overthrows evil and religion is saved from annihilation:

Afterwards, desolation and adversity depart from this world,
 while I make a beginning of the millennium.
Then Soshyant makes the creatures again pure,
 and the resurrection and future existence occur.
May the end be in peace, pleasure, and joy, by the will of God
 [yazdano]!
 so may it be!
 even more so may it be! ["Avesta—Zoroastrian Archives"].

The spirit of this conclusion replicates in miniature the thrust of Zoroastrianism and its belief in the universal struggle of right over evil.

Fragments

Fragmented texts include the Aogemadaeca, a treatise recommending resignation to mortality. Composed in Pahlavi and surviving in Parsi, it takes the form of a sermon that declares in verses 1–2:

I come, I accept, I resign;
I come into this world,
I accept evil,
I resign myself to death ["Avesta—Zoroastrian Archives"].

The last of the 111 verses calls for reward for the righteous and a suitable afterlife for those who yield willingly to death. In addition to this text, the fragments include the Hadhoxt Nask (Section of Sayings), which describes the soul's fate after death; the Arin-i Paighambar Zartusht, which honors Zoroaster and blesses kings; the Nirangistan, three chapters of ritual prescription; and the Frahang i-Oim, a glossary of Avesta-Pahlavi terms.

Khurda Avesta

Composed of extensions to liturgy that date to the reemergence of paganism, the Khurda Avesta (also Khordeh or Khorda Avesta; Small, Abridged, or Younger Avesta), compromises Zoroastrian monotheism. The text opens on a pseudo-original introduction claiming that it derives from Ahura Mazda's revelation to Zoroaster. Segments include fragments and minor scripture for use by both priests and laity, in particular, the Niyayeshes (or

Nyaishes; Litanies) and the four Afringanas (Benedictions). The Kwarshed Niyayesh (Litany to the Sun) begins with obeisance to the most high:

> In the name of God. I praise and invoke the creator Ormazd, the radiant, glorious, omniscient, maker, lord of lords, king over all kings, watchful, creator of the universe, giver of daily bread, powerful, strong, eternal, forgiver, merciful, loving, mighty, wise, holy, and nourisher. May [his] just kingdom be imperishable. May the majesty and glory of Ormazd, the beneficent lord, increase. [Hither] may come the immortal, radiant, swift-horsed Sun. Of all sins ... I repent ["Avesta — Zoroastrian Archives"].

The remaining nineteen verses laud the sun for purifying the earth, free-flowing waters, wells, seas, and "water that is standing."

Less sacred are the Afringan-i Dahman, which honors the dead who were faithful Zoroastrians; the Afringan-i Gatha, a recitation for the last five days of the year, when souls return to earth to visit the living; the Afringan-i Gahanbar, which instructs the laity on participating in six annual festivals; and the Afringan-i Rapithwin, a recitation to welcome and conclude summer.

A special duad within the Khurda Avesta is the two Sirozas (or Sirozahs), which list the gods presiding over the thirty days of a month and provide liturgy for the thirtieth day after a death. Verse 30 of the second Siroza concludes with typically repetitive mantric form:

> We sacrifice unto the water, made by Mazda and holy;
>   we sacrifice unto the golden and tall Haoma;
>   we sacrifice unto the enlivening Haoma,
>   who makes the world grow;
>   we sacrifice unto Haoma, who keeps death far away;
>   we sacrifice unto the pious and good Blessing;
>   we sacrifice unto the awful, powerful, cursing thought of the
>   wise, a God
>   we sacrifice unto all the holy Gods of the heavenly world;
>   we sacrifice unto all the holy Gods of the material world.
> I praise, I invoke, I meditate upon, and we sacrifice
>   unto the good, strong, beneficent Fravashis of the holy ones
>   ["Avesta — Zoroastrian Archives"].

The style suggests a sonorous hymn or doxology preceding sacrifice. Its contribution to worship appears to be the sound and rhythm of its chanting or singing.

Central to Zoroastrian spirituality are the five *Gahs* (Prayers), which cover sunrise to noon, noon to midafternoon, midafternoon to sunset, sunset to midnight, and midnight to dawn. These formal devotions require cleansing of the face and extremities and untying of the sacred cord before facing the light to recite the appropriate prayer. The Khurda Avesta also offers mealtime and ablution blessings, aubades, denunciations, pleas for mercy, hymns to angels, exorcisms, and glimpses of the end-time, a bloodbath against evil when the dead will revive at the command of a savior conceived by Zoroaster's seed in a virgin.

History challenged the survival of the Avesta. War with Byzantium from 572 to 591 ended with a twofold blow to Zoroastrianism: Khosrow II, married to a Christian, retained the throne; and the Byzantines regained parts of northern Mesopotamia.

In 602, Persian forces again seized northern Mesopotamia along with Syria, Palestine, Egypt, and Anatolia. The Byzantine emperor, Heraclius, ended Sasanian rule in Media in 615 and destroyed the royal compound in 628. After three centuries of sporadic loss and reconquest plus epidemics and heavy flooding of the Tigris and Euphrates rivers, Mesopotamia lay in ruins. The brief resurgence of Persian hopes under Yazdegerd III ended during the rise of Muslim Arabs, who defeated Persian armies at al-Qadisiyah in 635. Under the influence of Islam, language, script, and the Zoroastrian faith changed considerably, especially after Muslims destroyed temples and scriptures. Eleventh-century Turkish depradations and Mongol invasions of the twelfth century further eradicated original scriptures. Henceforth, Zoroastrians survived in the shadows of the southeast between Yazd and Kerman as a targeted minority. Early in the twenty-first century, they thrive only in Fars in southwest Iran.

The mid- to late Middle Ages transformed the canon Avesta. In the C.E. 800s, an anonymous compendium known as the Dinkart preserved Zoroastrian religion by summarizing in the Pahlavi dialect all twenty-one *nasks* (or *nosks*; books) of the Avesta that were extant in the Sasanian empire. The text reveals the Avesta's encyclopedic nature and its collection of history, eschatology and the savior to come, liturgy, ritual and priestly duty, exegesis, guides to virtue and piety, military law, property and inheritance, and Persian cosmogony, astrology, and astronomy. The books fall under three headings of seven books each: gasan, the moral and spiritual teachings; datik, the codes of law and prescriptions; and hatak-mansarik or hadha-manthra, a blended text covering morality and law. Also in the ninth century, a supplemental Pahlavi text, the Greater Bundahishen, united mythology from three traditional sources. The text offers a thorough explanation of the Zarathushtrian heavenly court and apocalyptic vision, the modified world-year calendar, and an ancient creation story. This source describes Ahura Mazda more fully than the Avesta. In the 900s, Zoroastrianism found a refuge in Gujarat in western India, where followers emigrated. However, it was not until 1477 that Iranian and Indian Zoroastrians united.

The Avesta survives in copies found in European collections. One, dated 1323, is housed at the Bodleian Library at Oxford University. Serious study of Zoroastrian scripture began with Thomas Hyde, professor of Hebrew and director of the Bodleian Library. Drawing on Parsi sources, he published *Historia Religionis Veterum Persarum* (History of the Religion of the Ancient Persians; 1700), his most celebrated oriental study. In 1762, Hyde's critic, scholar Abraham Hyacinthe Anquetil du Perron, a master of Hebrew, Persian, and Arabic, introduced Eastern philosophy and language to Europe by bringing copies of the Avesta from India to France. He also found ancient Iranian scripture by Zoroaster at the Royal Library in Paris and collected around 200 sacred manuscripts.

Despite the dismissal of Sir William Jones, who declared the Avesta a counterfeit scripture, Anquetil du Perron completed a translation into French in 1771 as *Zend-Avesta, Ouvrage de Zoroastre* (The Interpretation of the Avesta, the Work of Zoroaster). His working method differed from Hyde's: Rather than translate texts, he joined the military so he could interview priests during his service in India. On his release from the army, he learned modern Persian and induced holy men to instruct him in Avestan. He produced articles and lectures on Middle Eastern religions and published *Législation Orientale* (1778), *Historical and Geographical Research on India* (1786), *India in Rapport with Europe* (1798), and his last contribution, *Upanishada* (Secrets Never to Be Revealed; 1804).

The Avesta continued to flourish in compendia of world scripture and received more scholarly attention in the nineteenth century. Currently, Zoroastrians read from the Kurda Avesta, a prayer book intended for lay worshipers. Available for in-depth study is the Zand-Avesta (or Zend-Avesta [Interpretation of the Injunction]), a title often erroneously applied to the Avesta.

Zoroastrianism flourishes as Parsiism in India, as Gabarism or Zardoshtism in Iran, and in the Americas, Australia, and Great Britain in the Pahlavi language as Daena Mazdayasni (The Good Religion of the Worshipers of Mazda). As described by Roni Khan in the *Jam-e-Jamshed Weekly*, published in Bombay, in 1995, the faith is a "complete spiritual system with the four inseparable and integrated components of Hakikat, Marefat, Tarikat and Shariat" (Khan 1995). He summarizes these essentials as:

- Hakikat, philosophical exposition of universal truths
- Marefat, channels or agencies for spiritual communion
- Tarikat, ritualized spiritual discipline
- Shariat, religious rules and injunctions

SOURCES: "Achaemenid Royal Inscriptions" 1998, Alexander and Alexander 1982, "Avesta — Zoroastrian Archives," Ballou 1944, Berry 1956, Bowker 1997, Braden 1954, Clark 1998, Darmesteter 1898, Dhabar 1932, Eliade 1967, Frost 1972, Frye 1993, Gentz 1973, Hastings 1951, Hinnells 1984, Khan 1995, *New Catholic Encyclopedia* 1967, Senior 1985, Shariari 1998, Smith 1995.

Bandlet of Rightness see *Ethiopian Book of the Dead*

Bardo Thodol see *Tibetan Book of the Dead*

Bhagavad Gita　A lucid Sanskrit masterpiece written around 200 B.C.E., the Bhagavad Gita (or Bhagavadgita; Song of Lord or the Blessed One, Song Divine, or Celestial Song) has been called the Hindu's book of bedside reading. It supports India's great religious civilization with readable counsel on matters of conscience. Also known as Gitopanisad, Bhagavadgitopanisad, or simply Gita, the poem is the bible of Hinduism, the secret doctrine disclosed by the Blessed One. The first and most representative exposition of the Bhagavatan philosophy, it is a compact scripture written by a single anonymous author.

A revered moral and theistic scripture, among the faithful, the Gita equates in value and holiness with the Upanishads and the Brahma sutras. The text derives from a Hindu sect, the Bhagavata (the Lord's Devotee), an early Hindu brotherhood pledged to devotion and uncomplicated worship of one god, identified as Vishnu, Vasudeva, Krishna, Hari, or Narayana. Originating before Christianity among the Yadava of the Mathura area of northern India, Bhagavatism spread via tribal migration to the west and north.

Not a sacred revelation, the text is both civil war narrative and symphonic poem — joyous and serene in its contemplation of God, majestic and vital in its commentary on human motivation. It functions as book 6, a later segment of the collection of narratives that make up the Mahabharata (Great Epic of the Bharata Dynasty), are Indian epic and, at 100,000 verses, the world's longest poem. On its own, the Gita is composed of eighteen chapters and 700 verses, which have become India's messianic gospel and the revered jewel of Hindu scripture. Its focus is human liberation from the law of karma, a self-perpetuating system that either reincarnates the soul or releases it, based on the consequences of good and bad actions in the past life. The poem proposes a forbearance that produces spiritual vision and promises bliss in place of repetitive lives bound in petty struggles.

At the background of the Gita lies dynastic treachery within the Kuru family when King Dhritarashtra's hundred sons plot against the five Pandava sons of Pandu and Kunti. The Pandava brothers are pious heroes, whom the envious king tries to kill in a deliberate palace fire. Undetected, the brothers flee to the forest and live in poverty like holy Brahmans. During their self-exile, Arjuna, the youngest son, wins Princess Draupadi in a test of strength by stringing a bow and hitting a target. When the brothers return to the forest with Arjuna's bride, they obey their mother's command to share the princess equally.

The Pandavas, now allied by marriage to the princess's family, make peace with King Dhritarashtra and accept the lesser half of his kingdom, a wasteland on the Jamuna River in Bangladesh. They clear land, erect a city, and crown as monarch Yudhisthira, the oldest and worthiest of the five Pandavas. Unaware of a plot against him, he enters a rigged dice game with the cheat Sakuni and loses all to Prince Duryodhana, King Dhritarashtra's greedy son. Enslaved and maltreated, the Pandava brothers appeal to the king, who forces the evil prince to set them free. A second rigged dice match again exiles the brothers to the forest under the stipulation that they live one year out of thirteen in the city without being recognized. To retrieve his brothers from death as a result of drinking from a magic lake, King Yudhisthira answers questions about duty and virtue. His words form a Hindu creed:

- Truth is the way to heaven.
- Happiness is the result of right conduct.
- Self-discipline is the supreme escape from grief.
- Humility is the basis of love.
- True religion is the example set by saints.

These statements, particularly the final line, prefigure Arjuna's actions in the Gita.

The Gita is the outgrowth of chaos. The Mahabharata War erupts after Prince Duryodhana again refuses to share territory with the Pandava princes. Area monarchs take sides until the conflict spreads over all India. They call on Krishna, the founder of the monotheistic Bhagavata religion, who allows them to enlist his kinsmen or himself. Duryodhana and the hundred sons of King Dhritarashtra choose the relatives; the warrior prince Arjuna, captain of the Pandavan forces, selects his cousin Krishna as charioteer, a significant partner to the archer, who must draw near the enemy to shoot accurately. The war ends with the overthrow of King Dhritarashtra's hundred sons and the rise of the Pandavas over all India, with King Yudhisthira on the throne for thirty-six years.

The action of the Bhagavad Gita occurs at an emotional height on the plain of Kurukshetra before the war begins. The narrative takes the form of a stylized dialogue between Arjuna and Krishna, who advance to no-man's-land between the battle lines to view forces standing in readiness on each side. The prince pauses at the sight of his comrades and kin poised for conflict and considers the outcomes of a war that his side is likely to win. Despairing in anticipation of carnage, he drops his bow to the ground. At a moral crossroads, he succumbs to the weight of futility and questions the meaning of life. Krishna restores a more practical point of view by admonishing him to perform the duty of a nobleman and soldier by trusting in God and abandoning any hope of triumph or personal enrichment.

Because Krishna debates from a weak premise of chivalric responsibility, he lifts the exchange to a metaphysical level. Significant to this battlefield relationship is Krishna's revelation that he is not Arjuna's cousin and friend, but an avatar, an earthly incarnation of the god Vishnu, the first such example of god-in-flesh in Hinduism. He allows Arjuna a singular experience for a mortal — a glimpse of Vishnu's divine self. The scripture pursues a broad study of godly nature and the human understanding of God's impartiality. At its height, the text summarizes India's religious thought and history on the subjects of creation, self-discipline, duty, and perfection. The characterization of God ranges from the initial view of Krishna as a personal deity to a broad definition of transcendence.

In the epic convention of *in medias res* (in the middle of things), chapter 1 reveals the escalating spirit of conflict that precedes the Mahabharata War. King Dhritarashtra, stricken blind, depends on his charioteer Sanjaya, a clairvoyant, for a verbal description of the scene. In the allegorical role of the interpreter, Sanjaya reports the exchange between Arjuna and Krishna. Arjuna declares:

My limbs are weakened,
My mouth is parching,
My body trembles,
My hair stands upright,
My skin seems burning,
The bow Gandiva
Slips from my hand [Prabhavananda and Isherwood 1951, 31].

Overcome by omens of evil, he grows faint at the thought of slaying teachers, grandfathers, uncles, and cousins. He demands, "How could we dare spill the blood that unites us?" (Prabhavananda and Isherwood 1951, 33). He would rather die in battle than slaughter such a dear and worthy company.

The dialectic takes a post–Buddhist turn by abandoning pacifism and defending the way of the warrior. In the second chapter, Krishna responds, "What is this weakness? It is beneath you" (Prabhavananda and Isherwood 1951, 35). He urges Arjuna to develop serenity and to realize that people must die and that destiny is changeless. He declares that all bodies are shed and the souls reincarnated like new garments. With a mentor's touch, he exhorts, "Die, and you win heaven. Conquer, and you enjoy the earth. Stand up now, son of Kunti, and resolve to fight.... Do this and you cannot commit any sin" (Prabhavananda and Isherwood 1951, 39).

Arjuna pursues his argument for nonaggression in chapter 3 by asking how Krishna can goad him to perform terrible deeds. The charioteer replies that Arjuna must embrace sacrifice or else reduce his life to nothing. To differentiate between human limitations and godly powers, Krishna begins revealing his divine self. He declares that he remembers all his past lives, but Arjuna is limited to the current existence:

I am the birthless, the deathless,
Lord of all that breathes.
I seem to be born:
It is only seeming ...
In every age I come back
To deliver the holy,
To destroy the sin of the sinner,
To establish rightness [Prabhavananda and Isherwood 1951,
    50].

This declaration of many holy forms allies Krishna with Buddha and Jesus, both earthly divinities sprung from a supreme godhead.

In explanation of destiny, Krishna claims that he created the four-caste system, which impels Arjuna toward full sainthood by performing duties demanded by his social group. Krishna urges him to find Brahman, the high god, by mastering the senses and doing the work expected of a soldier. Such warring against evil will restore social order to India. With dual imagery referring both to combat and an internal war against self, he commands:

Where is your sword
Discrimination?
Draw it and slash
Delusion to pieces [Prabhavananda and Isherwood 1951, 56].

The delusions that inhibit Arjuna — fear of death and desire for victory — are the twin outcomes of war. Krishna's philosophy negates both fear and desire as subjective motivations, which are unworthy of a holy man's concern. To reach oneness with God, Arjuna must shuck off battlefield reality and reach inside himself for pure spirituality, the ultimate reality.

The Gita's philosophy of the holy life takes shape in the next six chapters. The fifth chapter debates the worth of action as opposed to the renunciation of action, a central issue that has sparked perennial controversy among analysts of the Gita. Chapter 6 is a classic explication of yoga or meditation, from which the worshiper climbs upward to unite with Brahman. The acquisition of yoga comes from daily practice:

- Daily harmonize the soul in a quiet place.
- Hope for nothing; wish nothing.
- Sit on a skin or on grass and purify the soul in silence before God.
- Without moving, look inward between the eyebrows.
- Abandon fear and ingather peace and holiness.
- Extend harmony to balance of diet and rest.
- Flee restlessness by becoming one with God.

In the seventh chapter, Krishna urges Arjuna to devote himself wholeheartedly to the divine. He declares, "I know all beings, Arjuna: past, present and to come. But no one knows me. All living creatures are led astray as soon as they are born, by the delusion that this relative world is real" (Prabhavananda and Isherwood 1951, 73). The best way to escape the fear of age and death is to take refuge in Krishna.

With this reference to Krishna, the poem stimulates curiosity about the form and nature of God. In chapter 8, Arjuna asks for a description of Brahman. Krishna summarizes his being as the immutable creative energy that causes all living things to form and move. He commands Arjuna to meditate:

When a man leaves his body and departs, he must close all the doors of the senses. Let him hold the mind firmly within the shrine of the heart, and fix the life-force between the eyebrows. Then let him take refuge in steady concentration, uttering the sacred syllable *om* and meditating upon me [Prabhavananda and Isherwood 1951, 76].

He promises Arjuna that the faithful find release from the cycle of *samsara* (rebirth) and dissolve into "the sleeping germ of life" (Prabhavananda and Isherwood 1951, 77). In this imperishable form, the soul moves beyond the actions taught by the Vedas, which call for reading scripture, sacrificing, living austerely, and offering charity.

The Gita advances to pure mysticism in chapter 9, in which Krishna speaks a mesmerizing self-revelation:

I am the sire of the world, and this world's mother and
    grandsire,
I am he who awards to each the fruit of his action:
I make all things clean, I am *om*, I am absolute knowledge....
I am the cosmos revealed [Prabhavananda and Isherwood
    1951, 82].

In exchange for total faith, adoration, offerings, and prostrations, in lines 31–34, Krishna promises salvation. He declares that the pious will achieve eternal life, a core belief that links Hinduism with Christianity, Zoroastrianism, and Islam.

The tenth chapter, the poem's height, extends God's manifestation to Arjuna as "knowledge, that brilliant lamp, dispelling its darkness" (Prabhavananda and Isherwood 1951, 87). Arjuna accepts Krishna as God and asks for instruction. Krishna agrees to reveal his many forms—Atman, Vishnu, Sama Veda, Shiva, Brihaspati the priest, Skanda the warrior chief, Bhrigu the seer, Narada the sage, Chitraratha the musician, horse and fig tree, thunderbolt and serpent, giant and time, lion and eagle, king of all men, wind and water, beginning, middle, and end. He concludes, "Know only that I exist, and that one atom of myself sustains the universe" (Prabhavananda and Isherwood 1951, 90).

Chapter 11 reveals Arjuna in a different mood. Relieved of pre-battle jitters, he is calm in the mystic and sublime knowledge of the Almighty. Krishna allows him divine sight, a sign that compares with Moses's confrontation with God at the burning bush and Muhammad's first glimpse of Allah. Describing this epiphany to his blind master, Sanjaya is overcome by a radiance greater than a thousand suns. The revelation, a popular subject for Indian iconography, amazes Arjuna, who perceives the infinite, a sight denied to other humans. Krishna uses this moment to urge Arjuna back into armor to "win kingdom, wealth and glory" (Prabhavananda and Isherwood 1951, 94). Arjuna realizes that he has been treating Krishna as an everyday friend and comrade, a fellow mortal. To restore their original relationship, Krishna returns to human form, with which Arjuna can identify.

The twelfth chapter discusses worship of the unmanifest God. To those devoted to Krishna, he promises:

I shall save them
From mortal sorrow
And all the waves
Of life's deathly ocean [Prabhavananda and Isherwood 1951, 98].

In the thirteenth chapter, Krishna reveals himself as knower of all. He urges Arjuna to be upright, humble, obedient, clean, and steadfast. Freed from self, whatever the battle's outcome, he can never be a slave.

In the fourteenth chapter, Krishna continues mentoring by revealing the height of wisdom and promising everlasting truth and joy. The fifteenth chapter begins with the allegory of the fig tree, which puts forth leaves that transmute into the Vedas. He bids Arjuna to sharpen his ax in Brahman and cut down the tree in triumph over ignorance. In the sixteenth chapter, Krishna reveals human duality—the divine and demonic tendencies that cause humans to be good or evil. Chapter 17 explains how people can put on a semblance of faith by following the scriptures but remain selfishly attached to material results.

The Gita carefully controls the crescendo of the opening chapters to a climax and a steady decrescendo to the original discussion between two comrades. In the final chapter, Krishna declares that he instructs Arjuna because his friend is dear to him. Krishna explains that the godly accept duty because they have no stake in the outcome. He adds:

The leader's duty,
Ordained in nature,
Is to be bold
Unflinching and fearless,
Subtle of skill
And open-handed,
Great-hearted in battle,
A resolute ruler [Prabhavananda and Isherwood 1951, 126].

In Arjuna's last comment, he promises to abandon delusions and to end all doubt by surrendering himself to Brahman. Reconciled to duty, he does the charioteer's bidding.

A handbook of prophecy and spiritual discipline, the Bhagavad Gita displays the creative synthesis of its time, which saw the emergence of the ideal of karma. While not an authoritative text, the poem is a sacred source uniting transcendentalism, mystic monism, and Krishna theism. Unique to the poem is the equality of all seekers of either gender or any caste. All share in Krishna's love and grace.

To accommodate action, devotion, and self-knowledge of *yajña* (personal sacrifice), the Gita promotes the individual's surrender to Brahman. As aids to piety, the text advocates meditation and resolution. Neither for nor against war, it stresses the interdependence of duty and *dharma* (universal order). Thus, Arjuna's performance of responsibility to his caste and fellow soldiers becomes a reverent gift to Brahman. By maintaining an objective view of perfection and valuing the universe as a symbol of Brahman, the seeker can escape base motives and achieve deeds revealing an otherworldly purpose.

For centuries, the Bhagavad Gita has challenged theologians. The Indian philosopher and saint Shankara (also Sankara, Sankaracarya, or Shankaracharya; Master Shankara) wrote the earliest commentary on the Gita around C.E. 750. The son of Shivaguru, a pious father who worshiped the goddess Shakti, Shankara was a native of the southwest coastal village of Kalai in the Malabar district. When his father died, he disobeyed his mother to become an ascetic and study under Govinda. Later, Shankara traveled India to learn multiple creeds of various intellectuals and to visit ordinary Hindus, who were free of the sybarism found in cities.

Shankara was a proponent of the Vedantic or scripture-based Hinduism. To develop his ideas, he founded monasteries at Sringeri, Dwarka, Puri, and Badrinath that revived Hindu thought and propagated his teachings. He valued the Upanishads as India's most sacred literature and interpreted the Hindu doctrine of *advaita* (monism or unified godhood) by revealing the merger of the individual soul with the god Brahman. To achieve oneness, the worldly spirit relinquishes its hold on physical phenomena and removes emotional contaminants.

At age fourteen, the prodigy and saint Jñanadeva (also Jñanashvar or Jñaneshvara) of Marathi composed another classic exegesis on the Gita, the *Bhavartha-dipika* (Lamp of Simple Explanation; 1296). Jñanadeva viewed the Gita not as a philosophy to be explained, but a miracle of God's love to be glorified. The poet Eknath enlarged and popularized Jñanadeva's philosophy around 1600.

Translated into over a dozen languages, the Bhagavad Gita is a particular favorite of Christians, who perceive Krishna as the loving, nurturing Hindu messiah, the source of eternal salvation found in the Gospel of John. The poem has found admirers in all cultures, in particular, New England's nineteenth-century transcendentalists. Their chief theologian and essayist, Ralph Waldo Emerson, became one of the first Americans to own the Gita and the first to advocate study of the scriptures of India. He remarked in volume 10 of *The Journals and Miscellaneous Notebooks of Ralph Waldo Emerson* (1914) in an entry dated October 1, 1848:

> I owed a magnificent day to the *Bhagavad Gita*. It was the first of books; it was as if an empire spoke to us, nothing small or unworthy, but large, serene, consistent, the voice of an old intelligence which in another age and climate had pondered and thus disposed of the same questions which exercise us [Prabhupada 1981, cover].

Emerson loaned his copy of the Gita to poet John Greenleaf Whittier, who was intrigued enough to study Eastern philosophy. Another poet and contemporary, Walt Whitman, received a copy of the poem for Christmas in 1875 and incorporated its mysticism into his verse.

Emerson's friend, essayist and activist Henry David Thoreau, exalted the Gita above the literature of his time, which he characterized from personal experience in "The Pond in Winter" from *Walden* (1854):

> In the morning I bathe my intellect in the stupendous and cosmogonal philosophy of the *Bhagvat Geeta*, since whose composition years of the gods have elapsed, and in comparison with which our modern world and its literature seem puny and trivial; and I doubt if that philosophy is not to be referred to a previous state of existence, so remote is its sublimity from our conceptions [Thoreau 1982, 324–325].

An English contemporary, utopian novelist Aldous Huxley, author of *Brave New World* (1932), proclaimed the work's universal appeal as a clear and comprehensive summary of spiritual thought, valuable for all times to all readers.

Into the twentieth century, the Gita retained its popularity with American and European Indologists. It ordered the thinking of freedom fighter Martin Luther King, Jr., and influenced the reverent lines of T. S. Eliot's *The Waste Land* (1922), a profound and controversial elegy that became the most analyzed poem of the modern era. In admiration of the Gita, Eliot rated it second only to Dante's *Divina Commedia*. The freedom fighter Mohandas K. Gandhi first read the book during his second year of law school in London in 1888. A model pacifist, he interpreted the poem's prowar stance as a peerless allegory of the soul's struggle against evil. In an article for the August 6, 1925, issue of his weekly magazine, *Young India*, he wrote:

> When doubts haunt me, when disappointments stare me in the face, and I see not one ray of hope on the horizon … I turn to the *Bhagavad Gita*, and find a verse to comfort me; and I immediately begin to smile in the midst of overwhelming sorrow [Fischer 1954, n.p.].

His secretary, Mahadev Desai, testified that Gandhi consciously emulated the Gita on a daily basis as a spiritual resource and model of the yogi of action or karma yogi, the Indian term for a saintly Hindu. In Gandhi's definition, which reasserts Krishna's commands, the karma yogi refrains from jealousy, egotism, and selfishness to become a "fount of mercy … who treats alike cold and heat, happiness and misery, who is ever forgiving, who is always contented, whose resolutions are firm" (Fischer 1954, n.p.).

By merging with God, the karma yogi arouses no fear in others because he is pure, desireless, unaffected by winning or losing, and detached from criticism. Impervious to worldly judgments, the true seeker of God chooses silence and uses solitude as an opportunity to discipline reason. To accusations that Hindu renunciation produces indifference and passivity, Gandhi rebutted that actions that derive from disinterest in the outcome produce the most successful results because the doer has nothing to lose. He justifies the claim that the karma yogi achieves self-control because the source of the yogi's strength is inner peace rather than ambition. Motivated by abstinence and self-denial, the yogi's only aim is *samadhi*, full consciousness of God. To reach that goal, Gandhi recited the Bhagavad Gita at home and in temple several times per month.

An influential American social critic and spiritual philosopher of the 1960s, Thomas Merton, a Trappist monk at the Abbey of Gethsemani in Trappist, Kentucky, praised the Bhagavad Gita for its lofty ethics and timely comments on issues the world faced during the arms race of the Cold War. After he expanded his concerns to pacifism, non–Christian spirituality, and Zen Buddhism, he began corresponding with leading world thinkers. He declared the Gita

> a salutary reminder that our highly activistic and one-sided culture is faced with a crisis that may end in self-destruction because it lacks the inner depth of an authentic metaphysical consciousness. Without such depth, our moral and political protestations are just so much verbiage [Prabhupada 1981, 1].

Late in the twentieth century, the Gita continued to generate interest. In 1997, Krishna Software Inc. released *The Gita as It Is*, an interactive, multimedia CD-ROM. Appealing for its music and full-screen, color video imaging, it offers a translation of scripture plus the "Disciplic Succession" from Krishna to Swami Prabhupada. The electronic format maintains the centrist Hindu embrace of devotion as the highest of human ideals.

SOURCES: Agarwal 1996, Alexander and Alexander 1982, Ballou 1944, Berry 1954, "Bhagavad Gita" 1998, "Bhagavad Gita: The Kingdom of God," Bhaskarananda 1994, Bouquet 1954, Bowker 1997, Braden 1954, Burger 1998, Eliade 1967, Fischer 1954, Frost 1972, Gentz 1973, "The Gita as It Is" 1997, "The Great Transcendentalist, Henry David Thoreau," Hastings 1951, Hinnells 1984, *New Catholic Encyclopedia* 1967, Prabhavananda and Isherwood 1951, Prabhupada 1981, Smith 1958, Smith 1995, Snodgrass 2001, Thoreau 1982, *World Literature* 1998, *World Religions* 1998.

Bible

A significant spiritual touchstone to much of the world, the Bible is a landmark in world scripture. The word *bible* is a general term for scripture. When capitalized as Bible, it denotes the sacred writings revered by Jews and Christians based on God's covenants with his chosen people. The text amasses genres ranging from riddles and weddings songs to oracle, prayer, dirge, and lament. Specific pieces include Deborah's war cry and the victory celebration at the fall of Jericho, Nathan's fable and Jesus's parables, litanies and lyric verse from the psalms, oratory, folk tale, and the short story of Ruth's courtship of Boaz, the legend of Goliath, Paul's letters to the new churches, the allegory of the vineyard, the saga of David and his family, confession and erotic verse in the Song of Songs, the biography of Jesus, Jewish history, Mosaic law codes, Isaiah's prophecy, and Solomon's maxims, intended as a guide to ethical behavior.

The Bible takes its name from the Greek *biblos*, a reference to the papyrus pages that preceded vellum, and from the derivative Latin term *biblia*, a similar term denoting books. More than a mere "book," it provides the basis of prayers, hymns, liturgy, and worship assemblies and continues to influence ethics and secular law, the media, oratory, art, literature, drama, and architecture.

It has remained at the forefront of scholarly and literary endeavors and exists in some 1,250 languages and dialects.

In tribal tradition, the written version of law solidified for a community the civilizing structures that affirmed all aspects of life. The traditional body of sacred myth, history, prophecy, songs, meditation, and thanksgiving was the source of cult and ritual, but had no clear-cut list of accepted works or ordering system. Over a long period of time, the neophyte churches at Alexandria, Antioch, Corinth, Rome, and Thessalonica shared texts composed by Jesus's apostles, creating at each location a treasury of writings, which were the forerunners of the canon Bible.

Canon, the term indicating an authorized body of writings, derives from the Greek word *kanon*, meaning a rod or ruler, a metaphor for a standard of measure. Theologically, *canon* applies to right doctrine derived from any element of church literature that guides faith and practice. As described in the *De Vita Contemplativa* (On the Contemplative Life) of Judaeus Philo, a first-century C.E. Jewish philosopher among the Alexandrian literati, Bible writers composed through a divine possession — a religious ecstasy that allowed God to speak from a higher sphere through an earthly human instrument.

See also Bible: Old Testament; Bible: New Testament.

Bible: Old Testament

A tripartite collection, the Old Testament was originally composed of twenty-seven books divided into three parts: the Torah or Pentateuch, the Nevi'im or Prophets, and the Ketuvim or Hagiography. Jews refer to these three divisions by a single acronym TaNaKh (also TNK or Tanak), a normative text that embodies the essence of Judaism — ethics and law or Torah along with history, institutions and traditions, wisdom, instruction, theology, and philosophy of daily life. Tanakh reflects the evolution of Jewish faith from the monotheism of one godly man, Abraham of Ur, a nomadic *Habiru* (also *Abiru* or *Apiru*) chieftain who arrived in Canaan around the end of the twentieth century B.C.E. and settled in Hebron.

To Protestants, the Old Testament is a body of thirty-nine books revered in a separate order from the Judaic collection of holy books. It was originally composed primarily in Hebrew with small segments of Genesis, Jeremiah, Ezra, and Daniel in Aramaic, the universal language that replaced Hebrew in the Middle East. Transmitted by generations of scribes, the Old Testament centers on the evolution of monotheism as the foundation of the Judeo-Christian theology. The writing of the Old Testament began in 1200 B.C.E. and continued to 100 B.C.E. In C.E. 170, Melito, a Lydian bishop living in Sardis and writing in Greek, coined the term *Old Testament* to differentiate between narration about the early Jews and the biography of Jesus and works of his followers, whose acts prefigured the establishment of Christianity.

The Old Testament's treasured scrolls traverse biblical geography. The Book of Deuteronomy was a Temple treasure in Jerusalem dating to 621 B.C.E. By 609 B.C.E., the grouping of Deuteronomy with Joshua, Judges, Samuel, and Kings approached the present ordering.

In 458 B.C.E., Moses's laws, which Ezra transported from Babylon, became the soul of Judaism, the landmark civilizing agent that set the Hebrews apart from their contemporaries as "people of the law," a model of monotheistic godliness and probity.

The remaining books of Isaiah, Jeremiah, Ezekiel, and the Twelve entered the compilation of Jewish scripture after the Exile. Late in the completion of the Old Testament, ben Sirach produced Ecclesiasticus, written about 180 B.C.E. In a preface to the book, his grandson commented on the three-stage scripture, but left open the possibility of later additions to God's holy word. The canon closed officially after the destruction of the Temple in C.E. 70, when the Jews realized they had to defend their culture against the aggressive rise of Christianity as they had once before closed ranks against Hellenism.

Around C.E. 100, the Hebrew apologist and priest Josephus Flavius, vindicator of the faith, corroborated the three separate categories of Hebrew scripture in Book 1 of *Contra Apion* (Against Apion), a commentary on Jewish custom and practice. He was qualified to make this distinction because he was Jewish by birth until he fell into Roman hands in C.E. 67, accepted elevated status as a Roman citizen and prophet, and, under a commission from the emperors Vespasian and Titus, composed *The Jewish War* (C.E. 77), followed by *Jewish Antiquities* (C.E. 93).

In reference to the canon Torah, Josephus declared that there are twenty-two books esteemed by Jews. Of their attachment to the inviolable word of God, he explained:

> It becomes natural to all Jews, immediately and from their own birth, to esteem those books to contain divine doctrines, and to persist in them, and, if occasion be, willingly to die for them. For it is no new thing for our captives, many of them in number and frequently in time, to be seen to endure racks and deaths of all kinds upon the theatres, that they may not be obliged to say one word against our laws, and the records that contain them [*Against Apion* 1:8 in *Josephus: Complete Works*, 609].

He states that the holy text is of divine origin and authority and can never be more nor less in length. His reckoning characterizes the first five books as the laws and traditions of Moses. The next thirteen he categorizes as books of the prophets who lived between Moses and Ar-

taxerxes I. The last four Josephus lumps together as books of hymns and aphorisms.

A century later, a Talmud declaration slightly altered the accounting from that of Josephus. It declared the number of canon books of the Torah to be twenty-four by separating Ruth from Judges and Jeremiah from Lamentations as separate entities.

Books of Moses	The Twelve	Writings
Genesis	Hosea	Psalms
Exodus	Joel	Proverbs
Leviticus	Amos	Job
Numbers	Obadiah	Song of Songs
Deuteronomy	Jonah	Ruth
Prophets	Micah	Lamentations
	Nahum	Ecclesiastes
Joshua	Habakkuk	Esther
Judges	Zephaniah	Daniel
Samuel	Haggai	Ezra
Kings	Zechariah	Nehemiah
Isaiah	Malachi	Chronicles
Jeremiah		
Ezekiel		

Laws of Moses

The first segment of Hebrew scripture to take a fixed order and importance was the Torah or Laws of Moses, also known as the Pentateuch, which was canonized about 400 B.C.E. Coverage in the Torah is largely chronological, beginning with creation and the primeval patriarchs:

1950 B.C.E.	Abram and Sarai's arrival in Palestine from Ur
1800 B.C.E.	Joseph's sojourn in Egypt and the enslavement of the Israelites
1250 B.C.E.	Moses's leadership of the Hebrews from Egypt
1210 B.C.E.	Joshua's emergence as a military leader
1120 B.C.E.	Influence of the Judges
1020 B.C.E.	Saul's emergence as a warrior-monarch
1000 B.C.E.	Pivotal reign of David, the shepherd king
965–922 B.C.E.	Solomon's succession and rule
722 B.C.E.	Amos's service as prophet

The text reveals Hebrew history through oppression and servitude, redemption, and the construction of the Tabernacle in Exodus. Legalism takes over in Leviticus, which outlines ritual sacrifice, purification, offerings and tithes, and priestly duties. Numbers summarizes the end of the Jewish tenure in Sinai and follows the Hebrew children through the desert of Paran. Deuteronomy details specific laws derived from the Mosaic tradition. The composite of

Every Jewish synagogue contains a handwriten scroll of the Torah on parchment and wrapped in a protective cover. (Photospin.)

these five books is the most sacred writing of Judaism, and an individual assessment of the books of the Torah establishes its value to a people who, then and now, revere history, piety, and civil order.

GENESIS

The Book of Genesis distills Judean, Ephraimite, and priestly oral traditions to focus on one family and one man, Abraham, and the covenant he receives from God. The book opens and closes outside the realm of everyday reality — from a chaotic universe in primeval history and advancing over generations of Israel's fathers to the death of Joseph, interpreter of dreams.

The title derives from the Greek *gignesthei* for "to be born" and from *genesis*, "a beginning." The book relates the derivation of the human family from one God, the sole Creator, who deliberately and painstakingly places the first beings on earth and gives them the power to do good or evil. The first chapters contain two accounts of the creation of the cosmos and of the first human inhabitants of earth, Adam and Eve, caretakers of the garden of Eden.

The narrative of the introduction, chapters 1–11, is richly symbolic. The separation of light from dark on day one, earth from sky on day two, land from water on day three, and heavenly bodies on day four is a necessary prologue to the creation of grass, herbs, and trees. After God regulates time, in Genesis 1:20–22, he creates living animals in the waters and sky on day five. The emergence of humankind on day six appears in Genesis 1:26, when man takes shape "in our image."

The evocative wording of Adam's creation in Genesis 2:7 describes how Yahweh formed man (*adam*) from dust (*'adamah*), an ineffable linkage of humankind with earth. The affection God feels for Adam appears in Genesis 2:18, when he observes:

> It is not good that the man
> should be alone;
> I will make him an helpmeet
> for him.

The verse prefaces the creation of all living beings, fish, fowl, and plant, including Eve, Adam's companion, whom God conceives as "bone of my bones, and flesh of my flesh" (Genesis 2:23).

The suffering inflicted on the first couple derives from the sin of disobedience after Eve falls under the spell of the wily serpent, who God robs of its legs and forces to crawl on its belly. In chapter 3, in anger for the eating of fruit from the forbidden tree, God punishes Adam and Eve, the prototypical man and woman, with multiple curses, requiring woman to war against man and to suffer pain in childbirth. As described by American writer and editor E. L. Doctorow, this theme locks the remaining women of Genesis into "an exclusively biological destiny as childbearers." He explains:

> Theirs is a nomadic society that to survive must be fruitful — and the movable tent kingdoms in which they live may be unquestioningly paternalistic, but the modern reader cannot help but notice with relief how much grumbling they do [Doctorow 1999, xi].

Adam is forced to wrest his living from the soil and to battle thorns and thistles. Emblem names continue in chapter 4 with the first children and first murderer and victim, Cain (Smith) and Abel (Breath). The result of their crime is the break-up of the family unit, with Cain, mystically marked by God in Genesis 3:15, traveling into the land of Nod east of Eden.

Paralleling the Roman concepts of an age of gold followed by successive devaluation in later ages, the downward spiral of human history begins in chapter 5 and reaches a terrible conclusion in chapters 6–8 in the Flood that washes away earth's corruption. Set in the Bronze Age, the story reflects a classic literary motif dating to Mesopotamia and Sumer. The only person who finds favor with God is Noah, a righteous, blameless man, who "found grace in the eyes of the Lord" (Genesis 6:8). As is true with other humans whom God favors, Noah must follow detailed commands, beginning in chapter 7 with the building of an ark, a shelter from destruction. The image of the protective boat prefigures Jesus's selection of fishermen as apostles and the use of "nave" from the Latin *navis* (ship) as the architectural name for the congregational section of a church.

The carnage is profoundly thorough. In Genesis 7:22, "All in whose nostrils was the breath of life, of all that was in the dry land, died." As though suspended in a microcosm, Noah and his family and the animals they shelter on the ark live above the watery chaos. Their departure bears the simplicity of creation:

> Every beast, every creeping thing,
>   and every fowl,
>   and whatsoever creepeth upon the earth,
>   after their kinds,
>   went forth out of the ark [Genesis 8:19].

In chapter 9, God restores creation, reconstitutes humankind, and establishes a new covenant relationship with Noah by promising in Genesis 9:11 never again to submerge the earth in water. His token of promise is the rainbow, a prominent emblem in world scripture.

After the mythic stories of the Flood and a long genealogy comes another season of human error in chapter 11. God's punishment this time is the Tower of Babel, which separates humankind into identifiable nations and language families. In Genesis 11:27, the narrative departs from mythic history to launch into storytelling with the cycle of Abram and Sarai of Ur, a pair of migrant outlanders, whom God leads to Haran in Canaan.

From the outset, Abram is an innovative rebel, Mesopotamian journeyman who defies the pagan idols made by his father, Terah. In the place of these multiple deities, Abram extols the one God, called Elohim (God) or Yahweh (Lord), with whom he shares a one-on-one relationship. An epiphany, Genesis 12:1–3, states Yahweh's promise to Abram that he will found a great nation and receive a divine blessing that will extend into the future to all of earth's families. It is this covenant that establishes the race known to history as the chosen people.

After promising to reward Abram in Genesis 15, God renames the couple Abraham (Father of Many People) and Sarah (Princess) in Genesis 17:5, 15. Although Abraham has already sired a son, Ishmael, by his servant Hagar, the blessing of a son to the aged Sarah delights the patriarch, who chuckles that his ninety-year-old wife is at last pregnant. The response prefigures their choice of Isaac (laughter) as a worthy name. The episode concludes with circumcision for all males in Abraham's household.

Chapters 18–19 return to the demanding deity who wipes out the sinful cities of Sodom and Gomorrah, which probably sank under the waters of the Dead Sea. Just as catastrophe overcame people in Noah's time, the fall of the twin cities is dreadful to behold. God calls down fire and brimstone and wipes out buildings and inhabitants. In the wake of destruction, Abraham rises the next morning to look out on a landscape as murky "as the smoke of a furnace" (Genesis 19:28). In chapter 21, Isaac is born, and Sarah, jealous of Hagar's boy, casts her and the boy into the desert. In Genesis 21:18, God protects the wanderers and promises of Ishmael, "I will make him a great nation," a prophecy of the Muslims, who claim Ishmael as their progenitor.

The remainder of the Book of Genesis tells of the lives and journeys of the three patriarchs—the aged Abraham, his son Isaac, and grandson Jacob, father of twelve sons, called the Twelve Tribes of Israel—and the Bible mothers, Sarah, her servant Hagar, Isaac's wife, Rebekah, and Jacob's wives, Rachel and Leah, and his servant women, Bilhah and Zilpah. Genesis excites the imagination with multiple human dramas, including mourning for Sarah's death (Genesis 23), Isaac's betrothal to Rebekah (Genesis 24), Abraham's dignified demise (Genesis 25:1–11), Rebekah's twin sons, Esau and Jacob (Genesis 25:25–26), Jacob's complicity with his mother and the trickery of his aged father (Genesis 27:5–10), the theft of his twin brother Esau's birthright and their standoff before Jacob flees into exile (Genesis 27:30–45), Jacob's vision of a heavenly ladder mounted by angels and God's promise to remain with him (Genesis 28:12–15), the establishment of Bethel as sacred ground (Genesis 28:18–22), and Jacob's fourteen-year service in Haran to his duplicitous kinsman Laban as bride price for Laban's daughters, Leah and Rachel (Genesis 29:14–20). The statement of distrust between Jacob and Laban, son-in-law and father-in-law, called the Mizpah Benediction, has lost its original caginess in later recitations of Genesis 31:49: "The Lord watch between me and thee when we are absent one from another."

Jacob's return home and his reconciliation with his twin brother precede a wrestling match with an angel in chapter 32, an obscure entanglement that suggests a symbolic interpretation of Jacob's long years of deceit and clever, self-serving calculation. As a result of this ongoing spirit of suspicion and mistrust, Jacob breeds dissent in his own household by showing favoritism to Rachel's son Joseph, the mystic clairvoyant and, in Genesis 37:3, recipient of a coat of many colors. In vengeance against Jacob's pet, the brothers sell Joseph at Dothan to a caravan of Ishmaelite traders bound across the Sinai peninsula for Egypt. The route prefigures the return of the Hebrews from bondage in the Book of Exodus.

In chapter 39, Joseph manages to impress Potiphar, captain of Pharaoh's guard, and rises to the post of overseer. He falls into the lustful grasp of Potiphar's wife and in verse 20, lands in prison. Even there, God's favor restores Joseph to power as an interpreter of dreams. As a reward for predicting prosperity followed by famine, in Genesis 41:41, Pharaoh makes Joseph the grand vizier of Egypt:

> And Pharaoh took off his ring from his hand,
>   and put it upon Joseph's hand,
>   and arrayed him in vestures of fine linen,
>   and put a gold chain about his neck [Genesis 41:42].

Final events in the Joseph cycle include vengeance on his ten older brothers in chapter 42 and a reunion of brothers, youngest brother, Benjamin, and aged father, Jacob. The emotional easing of hard feelings causes Joseph to "[kiss] all his brethren, and [weep] upon them" (Genesis 45:15).

After the family resettles in Egypt, in Genesis 48:1, Jacob on his deathbed blesses two grandsons, Manasseh and Ephraim, born in Egypt. One by one, he addresses individual farewells tailored to suit each of his twelve sons, founders of the Twelve Tribes of Israel:

- To Reuben, the firstborn, he comments on pride and power, instability and corruption.
- To Simeon and Levi, he warns of cruelty and dependence on the sword, by which "in their anger they slay men, and in their wantonness they hamstring oxen" (Genesis 49:6).
- For Judah, "the lion's whelp," the old father foresees at length praise, sovereignty over enemies, and a sure hand on the scepter that rules an obedient people (Genesis 49:9).
- In brief, he depicts Zebulun as a shore dweller along the perimeter of Sidon.
- An ambiguous description of Issachar witnesses his willingness to work like "a strong ass, crouching between the sheepfolds" (Genesis 49:14). Jacob predicts that his son will endure servitude at hard labor.
- Jacob sees Dan as a judge under questionable circumstances, which he describes metaphorically as "serpent in the way, a viper by the path that bites the horse's heels so that the rider falls backward" (Genesis 49:17).

- The eighth son, Gad, the father predicts will be a hard-handed desert raider.
- As Jacob views Asher, he will luxuriate among dainties and wealth.
- Naphtali, the free spirit, Jacob depicts as "a hind let loose" (Genesis 49:21).
- Joseph, Jacob's golden child, is the family's "fruitful bough," whom "the Rock of Israel" has blessed.
- Benjamin, the youngest, receives the final line in the deathbed farewell, a portentous vision of "a ravenous wolf, in the morning devouring the prey, and at evening dividing the spoil" (Genesis 49:27).

The reconciliation of the house of Jacob and unparalleled success for an expatriate ends with Jacob's death at age 110, which precedes the Egyptian enslavement of the Hebrews.

EXODUS

Derived from the Greek *exodos* for "departure," the Book of Exodus is a Hebrew fable—the story of Moses's rescue from abandonment by a princess is interwoven with the resurgence of a vital, enduring, captive people. The setting focuses on two locales—the royal court of Egypt's nineteenth dynasty on the banks of the Nile River and the Hebrew encampment at the base of Mount Sinai. The action covers motivation and method as the Hebrews emancipate themselves from Pharaoh's slave quarters and make their way northeast to the Promised Land, where they forge a nation. Along the way, God's chosen people, cut off from exterior events and people and immersed in their unique identity and displacement, survive a nomadic, borderless self-exile.

The epic narrative opens long after the days of Joseph and reveals the travail of the Hebrews in Egypt under Egyptian overlords, who "made their lives bitter with hard bondage" (Exodus 1:14). The departure requires a leader, Moses, whom Pharaoh's daughter rescues in chapter 2 in his infancy from a basket floating in the Nile. Heavy symbolism suggests that Moses is able to float in his tiny ark on the very life blood of Egypt. In a biblical rags-to-riches account, he grows up in the royal household, ostensibly as an Egyptian. In chapter 2:11, he lives like a young lord until he witnesses the brutality of overseers against Hebrew drones. The scenario welds him solidly with his own people. After killing the supervisor, Moses realizes that he cannot hide the implications of his spontaneous intervention. The act of second-degree murder links him irrevocably to the fate of the priest-nation that gave him life.

In an unexpected episode, Moses greets God face-to-face in a burning bush and removes his sandals as a gesture of reverence. In Exodus 3:6, God establishes a tie with the Hebrew people by proclaiming himself "the God of thy father, the God of Abraham, the God of Isaac, and the God of Jacob." At Moses's request for identification, the narrative enlarges the picture of God contained in Genesis. For the first time, Yahweh describes himself, choosing in Exodus 3:14 a brusque reply—the Hebrew *ehyeh asher ehyeh* (I am that I am)—as a suitable explanation of deity, God promises to remain with Moses during a trying period of self-liberation. Although Moses quibbles that he is no leader and no speaker, the instructions are direct: reveal God's command to the Hebrew elders and prepare to assault Egypt.

The drama of Exodus is unique in world scripture. Chapter 5 begins a seven-chapter battle against Pharaoh requiring no weapons, no face-to-face combat. After the ten plagues of Egypt—bloodied Nile waters, frogs, gnats, beetles, a livestock epidemic, boils, hail, locusts, darkness, and the last, the Angel of Death snatching firstborn sons—Moses wins the contest. Before the last confrontation, the Hebrews share the first Passover meal and, sheltered in Yahweh's care, survive unharmed. God declares the tense meal a national memorial and commands, "Ye shall keep it a feast by an ordinance for ever" (Exodus 12:14).

At the end of chapter 12, the Hebrews launch a successful peasant uprising preceding a great northern migration under commander Moses, who packs in his gear the bones of Joseph. A gripping rescue story in chapter 14 depicts the Egyptian Pharaoh as a capricious slaver who changes his mind and pursues the departing Hebrew horde to the Sea of Reeds. The waters part for Moses's people, then, in Exodus 14:28, engulf the army. Chapter 15 resounds with the song of the Israelites, who exult:

> Who is like unto thee, O Lord,
>   among the gods?
> Who is like thee,
>   glorious in holiness,
>   fearful in praises,
>   doing wonders? [Exodus 15:11].

The Hebrews trek to the Sinai Desert, where they bond with their God, who feeds them manna, a miraculous food rained down from the sky.

Subsequent episodes incorporate God's covenant with Moses on Mount Sinai and the issuance of the Ten Commandments, a decalogue intended for all people. In Exodus 20:3, the ten open with a strong admonition of loyalty, "Thou shalt have no other gods before me," and continue with commands to make no idols nor take the name of God in vain. The last seven commands are straightforward:

Remember the sabbath day to keep it holy (Exodus 20:8).

Honor thy father and thy mother.
Thou shalt not kill.
Thou shalt not commit adultery.
Thou shalt not steal.
Thou shalt not bear false witness against thy neighbor.
Thou shalt not covet (Exodus 20:12–17).

In the aftermath, Exodus records the rise of the Hebrews into an Israelite nation. Although they grumble, backslide, and regroup, they stay on the move.

Crucial to Israel's survival as a people is the first commandment, Yahweh's demand that they forgo idol worship and remain true to him, an order they frequently violate through interaction with alien tribes. In chapter 25, Yahweh gives explicit instructions about building an ark of the Tabernacle, a permanent ceremonial housing for the stone tablets bearing the Ten Commandments. Curtained off within the Holy of Holies, the decalogue survives under a constant light and the guardianship of Moses's brother Aaron and his sons, whom God delegates as the nation's priests. Moses initiates a census and a standard offering to God.

In chapter 32, the people weaken and, led by the priest Aaron, make a golden calf. Moses, astonished at their audacity, admonishes them:

Ye have sinned a great sin:
  and now I will go up unto the Lord;
  peradventure I shall make an atonement for your sin [Exodus 32:30].

He announces the crime outright to God, who promises to blot the name of sinners from his book. God sends an angel to guide Moses and turns back to plague the people.

After Moses prays for forgiveness, God rewards him in Exodus 33:11 by appearing "face to face, as a man speaketh unto his friend." In chapter 35, Moses's carpenters begin building a Tabernacle and, in chapter 39, make priestly vestments of blue, purple, and red. Aaron and his sons receive holy chrismation, a token of investiture as God's representatives. In Exodus 40:34, a cloud appears and God's glory fills the tent. The phenomena of cloud and fire, as ineffable as Yahweh himself, guide the march. Thus, the Tabernacle remains in the people's sight throughout their trek north.

LEVITICUS

Once called Torath Kohanim (Law of the Priests), the Book of Leviticus is a rule book that continues the discussion of priestly tradition begun in Exodus 25–31, 35–40. Leviticus describes Israel's sanctity as Yahweh's chosen people and outlines the liturgical style of their worship. It follows a tight plan:

chapters 1–7, laws governing sacrifice
chapters 8–10, consecration of priests
chapters 11–15, laws separating clean from unclean
chapter 16, ritual for the Day of Atonement
chapters 17–26, laws governing everyday religiosity
chapter 27, a collection of sacred vows

The title, which derives from "concerning the Levites," sets up the pattern of ritual worship that separates the Israelites from other nomadic peoples. Unlike desert tribes, the Hebrews perform cultic duties that require neither magic nor idols.

The book opens with detailed descriptions of sacrificing animals, which the worshiper burns to send pleasing smoke up to God. Throughout chapters 1–7, the text emphasizes the purpose of sacrifice as a dual token of dedication and request for forgiveness. Acts of contrition, repentance, and restitution must precede the ritual cleansing of sin. After the dedication of Aaron and his son, food laws permit the eating of cud-chewing animals, fish, some birds, and locusts. Forbidden are scavengers, pigs, vermin, and shellfish. In Leviticus 11:44, Yahweh summarizes the concept of sacrifice to a sacred deity:

For I am the Lord your God:
ye shall therefore sanctify yourselves,
and ye shall be holy;
for I am holy.

This section on purity concludes with washing away sexual contaminants. In chapter 13, Moses and Aaron receive instructions on how to keep the body free of leprosy. Ancient rituals involving the slaying of a scapegoat, cleansing meat of blood, and avoiding sexual abominations precede a list of religious ethics in chapter 19, which elaborate on the Ten Commandments. Chapter 20 lists capital crimes.

The next chapters regulate the priesthood and a series of festal commemorations binding the Hebrews in a cyclical calendar. Chapter 23 establishes Jewish holidays, including:

- Shabbat (the Sabbath) on the seventh day of the week from Friday evening to Saturday evening
- Pesach (Passover) in spring, an eight-day celebration of God's freeing of the Hebrews from servitude in Egypt
- Thanksgiving for first fruits in April at the end of the barley harvest
- Shavuoth (also Shavu'ot; Pentecost) in June, a harvest festival that celebrates Moses's return from Mount Sinai bearing the Ten Commandments

- the first of three in the fall, the Feast of Trumpets, or Rosh Hashanah (also Ro'sh h-Shanah), the first two days of the Jewish New Year and the beginning of ten days of atonement
- Yom Kippur (Day of Atonement), the holiest, most solemn holiday, a period of fasting, prayer, and penitence that ends the ten high holy days and ushers in the Jewish New Year
- Succoth (also Sukkot; Feast of Tabernacles), an eight-day commemoration of the four decades the Hebrews wandered the desert under Moses's leadership

One of the most frequently cited injunctions appears in Leviticus 24:20, a restatement of the law of Hammurabi, which demands no more revenge than the original evil — an eye for an eye, a tooth for a tooth.

The text unfolds requirements for God's people and concludes in chapter 25 with a command to observe the *yoval*, or jubilee. Of this holy calendar, novelist David Grossman asks:

What did the children of Israel feel about God having inscribed them in the historical consciousness of generations to come, while they themselves were but the dust of men, bewildered and frightened? Did they know they were only one step on the road to another, more exalted existence? [Grossman 1999, x].

The result of these fervent rituals is a long line of celebrants wending their way through the twelve-month cycle as though each new generation of Jews follows Moses by faith and feet to God's promised reward of redemption and reclamation.

NUMBERS

The Book of Numbers, named for the numbering of the children of Israel, details the organization and leadership of the Hebrew people. Originally called "In the Wilderness," the text follows the Hebrews on their long sojourn in the desert:

chapters 1–10:10, departure from the Sinai
chapters 10:11–21:13, arrival at Kadesh, where they remain for thirty-five years
chapters 21:14–36:13, continuing over Transjordan toward eastern Canaan and concluding at an encampment on the plains of Moab

The events cover a period of thirty-eight years of wandering before the host of ex-slaves crosses the Sinai peninsula and reaches Canaan, the Promised Land. In chapter 1, the people undergo a patriarchal form of census, a tribal evaluation which includes a head count of each male twenty years old and above. Enacted by Moses and Aaron, the census denotes tribes and heads of households. The separation of people by clan under group standards suggests the marching order of an army.

In chapter 3, the leading family, the Levites, God's firstborn, become the chosen performers of Tabernacle duties, a task that still falls to the Cohen or Cohn families. To the Kohathites passes responsibility for shepherding sacred vessels; the Gershonites transport Tabernacle drapery; the Merarites superintend the frame, supports, pegs, and guy ropes. In chapter 6, a fifth group, the Nazirites, accept consecration as servants of God and agree to abstain from strong drink, keep their hair long, and avoid contact with corpses. Numbers 6:23–26 contains the Aaronic benediction, one of the most beloved scriptural blessings, which Aaron bestows on the Israelites:

> The Lord bless thee, and keep thee:
> The Lord make his face shine upon thee,
>   and be gracious unto thee:
> The Lord lift up his countenance upon thee,
>   and give thee peace.

Priestly injunctions include God's call for two silver trumpets as tokens of assembly and alarm and as announcements of war and festivity.

Shadowed by a protective cloud, the Hebrews move on from Sinai to Kadesh, carrying their ark with them. Unity weakens in chapters 11–14, causing Miriam and Aaron to question Moses's decision making. He selects seventy elders to keep order, but his own household suffers dissension and Miriam contracts leprosy, which God cures after a seven-day quarantine. After reconnaissance officers return with a report, the Israelites reject eyewitness data and put their trust in outlandish rumor. In Numbers 14:4, they consider ousting Moses, choosing a captain, and returning to Egypt. As they prepare to stone him, Moses intercedes with an angry God and pleads for the mutineers. In Numbers 14:19, he prays, "Pardon, I beseech thee, the iniquity of this people." At dawn, a chastened company assembles on the mountaintop to repent.

After the death of Miriam in Numbers 20:1, Moses himself falls away from obedience by striking a rock with his rod. For failure to comply exactly with divine command, God forbids him to enter the Promised Land. In chapters 22–24, Balaam the diviner begins to prophesy what lies ahead, including a mystic symbol: "There shall come a star out of Jacob, and a scepter shall rise out of Israel" (Numbers 24:17), a hint at a Jewish messiah or savior who would lead the Hebrews. In Numbers 27:12–23, Moses obeys the command to appoint Joshua as the shepherd of the people. The ceremonial laying on of hands

serves as a model that has remained significant in worship to the present. In chapter 33, the march continues toward Moab.

DEUTERONOMY

Found on a temple scroll which the high priest Hilkiah, father of the prophet Jeremiah, discovered in 621 B.C.E., the Book of Deuteronomy influenced the Hebrews during a period of Assyrian control, a nadir of their history when Baal and Moloch worship replaced duty to the god of Moses. The book takes its name from the Latin *Deuteronomian* (Second Law). Originally, it was part of the Hebrew Mishneh Torah (Repetition of the Torah) and served Jews as one of their most uplifting statements of purpose. The fifth and final book of the Torah, Deuteronomy is an extended oration containing rules governing the Israelites' relationship with God and each other. The historical moment on the threshold of Canaan, the Promised Land, gives Moses an opportunity to exhort his followers to renew the covenant.

The text falls into five identifiable segments of varying length forming beginning, middle, and end. Chapter 1:1–5 introduces the work. In chapters 1–4:40, Moses's historical prologue summarizes the people's trek through the wilderness. In chapter 3:23, he makes a personal plea for permission to enter Canaan, but God angrily rebukes him. All that he allows Moses is a view of Israel's greatness from the peak of Mount Pisgah across the Jordan River. In the remainder of chapters 4–26, Moses offers sermons on the laws that Yahweh has issued to his chosen people. Moses reminds his followers of the laws and ordinances that bind them under God's guidance. Chapters 27–30 summarize curses and blessings, and the remaining four chapters conclude with matters of succession and formal readings of the law. Chapter 33 is Moses's benediction to the Twelve Tribes. Chapter 34 describes his death and the passing of rule to Joshua.

Supreme among the Hebrews' memories is the covenant with Yahweh to keep him uppermost in their hearts and to abstain from worshiping foreign gods. In the second exhortation, in chapter 5, the text repeats the Ten Commandments. The command of Deuteronomy 6:4, "Hear, O Israel: The Lord our God is one Lord," is the Jewish watchword, an invocation called in Hebrew the Sh'ma (Hear). In compliance with the rest of the chapter, orthodox Jews, who lack personal copies of the scripture, must memorize and recite the verse twice daily. To perpetuate God's law, they teach it to their children and bind the words on their hands and foreheads and to doorways and gateposts. Scriptural command to remember the law inspired the creation of ritual ornaments: tephillen (phylacteries), folded leather straps containing scripture to be worn by pious Jews, and the mezzuzah, a wood or metal container for the doorpost, which holds the Sh'ma on a tiny scroll.

Less onerous than Moses's more strident commands is a humanistic discourse. In Deuteronomy 10:12, he urges followers to fear God and admonishes them

> to walk in all his ways,
> and to love him,
> and to serve the Lord thy god
> with all thy heart and with all thy soul.

The reminder of this loving guide to the wanderers in the desert personalizes the relationship between Yahweh and his people.

In Chapter 12, Moses establishes a duty that resonates throughout Jewish history — the need to tear down foreign altars and raise up a specific place for God's habitation. This charge precedes the creation of a permanent, centralized temple, a symbol of a settled people who have abandoned nomadic ways. Chapter 14 calls for a tithe every third year as a just return to a generous deity and a protection of orphans and widows. Essential to the community is the manumission of slaves, the forgiveness of debts every seventh year, observation of three ritual feasts, rules for war, and the establishment of a system of civil laws and courts, one of the pinnacles of civilization. Chapter 26:5–10 appends a confession of faith:

> When we cried unto the Lord God of our fathers,
>   the Lord heard our voice, and looked on our affliction,
>   and our labor and our oppression:
>   and the Lord brought us forth out of Egypt
> with a mighty hand,
>   and with an outstretched arm,
>   and with great terribleness,
>   and with signs, and with wonders.

The imagery of this majestic summary of the Exodus depicts an essentially incorporeal deity who stretches forth arm and hand, as though Yahweh had guided them to Canaan with a father's tenderness.

In the final segment, Moses, in his last days, charges Joshua and the priests with their tasks and pronounces a benediction over the people. He intones:

> Happy art thou, O Israel:
>   who is like unto thee,
> O people saved by the Lord,
>   the shield of thy help,
>   and who is the sword of thy excellency! [Deuteronomy 33:29].

At Yahweh's command, Moses prepares himself to sleep among the patriarchs. Upon his death in the land of Moab, the Israelites bury him in the valley in an un-marked grave. After a thirty-day mourning period for their savior, the Israelites follow Joshua. They continue to treasure Moses as one of a kind, unlike any for the signs and the wonders he performed in Egypt. The verses of Deuteronomy 34 conclude Simchas Torah (Rejoicing of the Torah), a religious holiday that ends the reading of the Pentateuch and celebrates a return to Genesis 1 in an un-ending cycle that binds God's people to scripture.

According to German biblical scholar Julius Wellhausen, the addition of Joshua to the Torah's five volumes completes the Hexateuch, an overview of the founding of Israel and its acquisition of the Promised Land, with the conquest of Canaan and reaffirmation of God's covenant with Abraham.

JOSHUA

The Book of Joshua is conquest literature, the beginning of some of the most violent chapters of early Hebrew history. The text appears to compile invasion lore dating to 1440–1200 B.C.E. and to express the evolution of Israel as a unified nation. Chapters 1–6 cover the crossing of the Jordan River and the capture of Jericho. Chapters 7–8 are a summary of the Hebrew armies' advance from the Jordan Valley to the uplands to seize Ai, east of Bethel. Chapter 10 relates confrontations with Canaanite chiefs and triumph over the South. Chapter 11 is the crushing of Canaanite control of Palestine. Chapter 12 is a testimony to Joshua's skill. Chapters 13–23 cover the division of property to the tribes, and chapter 24 details Israel's covenant with God.

For continuity, the opening chapter reflects on the examples set by Abraham, Isaac, and Jacob and on the collective hardships suffered by the children of Israel. The summary prefaces a war on Canaan's dissolute people, the worshipers of Baal and Asherah. The text describes distasteful ritual acts of divination, human mutilation and sacrifice, and sexual depravity. The leader, Joshua or Yeshua, bears the name that becomes Jesus in Latin. Thus, the echo of the great Hebrew savior recurs in Christian lore.

The book opens immediately after Moses's death, as Joshua, an Egyptian-born Israelite, pledges his loyalty to the Hebrew people. He exhorts them to be strong and courageous so that they may inherit Canaan. Immediately, he begins operating like a military commander in anticipation of seizing the land beyond the Jordan River and, in a suspenseful episode in chapter 2, dispatches two secret agents to Jericho. They locate Rahab, a sympathetic woman who hides them on her roof until they spy out the land. In anticipation of an easy capture, the two proclaim, "Truly the Lord hath delivered into our hands all the land" (Joshua 2:24).

Leading the way the next morning, when the Israelites cross the Jordan River, is the ark of the covenant, borne by twelve men representing each of the Twelve Tribes of Israel. The advance is a pinnacle of Joshua's command marked by God's grace:

> And the Lord said unto Joshua,
> This day will I begin to magnify thee
>   in the sight of all Israel,
>   that they may know that,
>   as I was with Moses,
>   so I will be with thee [Joshua 3:7].

Because males were not circumcised during the long journey through the wilderness, Joshua calls for a revival of the ritual, followed by a period of healing. The ceremony reunites the people in covenant relationship with God. As the wanderers begin their metamorphosis into settlers, manna ceases to fall from the sky; the people begin to live off the rich land.

In Joshua 5:13–14, the commander, like Moses, undergoes a mystical experience with an unidentified swordsman known only as "the captain of the Lord's host." After abasing himself as Moses did before the burning bush, Joshua studies how to seize Jericho, an ancient city dating to 8,000 B.C.E., and comes up with a feat of psychological warfare that historians and archaeologists still ponder. Applying numerology, he has his band silently encircle the city with the ark for six consecutive days. At dawn on the seventh day, at the blowing of the ceremonial ram's horn, the people march around seven times and raise such a shout that the city collapses. The event concludes with mass annihilation of the citizens and livestock of Jericho, which the captors burn. According to Joshua 6:25, only Rahab and her family survive. The city's capture establishes the godliness and might of Joshua, a necessary passing of sovereignty from Moses to his replacement.

Just as Moses faced tests of faith, Joshua survives the faltering of the Hebrews at Ai. The testing of each man for loyalty proves Achan a holdout and sinner for rifling Ai for booty. Justice is swift—the people gather Achan and his family, confiscate their goods, and stone them to death. At a crucial moment, Joshua raises an altar at Mount Ebal and, in Joshua 8:32–35, reinscribes the Ten Commandments, which he reads aloud, including "the blessings and cursings."

Warfare consumes Joshua's energies with a campaign southwest to Gibeon and cities beyond. In chapter 11 a parallel campaign takes his troops north to Hazor. As Joshua's story draws to a close in chapters 13–19, he apportions property and goods to the deserving and settles minor squabbles. At the height of anticipation, in Joshua 18:1, the Israelites assemble at Shiloh and erect a tabernacle.

In chapter 23:14, Joshua makes a graceful exit speech. He affirms God's might, warns of future "snares and traps," and declares,

> Not one thing hath failed
>   of all the good things
>   which the Lord your god spake
>   concerning you;
>   all are come to pass unto you;
>   and not one thing hath failed thereof.

He reminds the people of their duty to God and sets up a ritual stone under an oak. After renewing the covenant at Shechem, the people bury his remains in Ephraim north of Mount Ga'ash.

Prophets

Next to the Pentateuch or Hexateuch, depending on the point of view, Jews revere the Nevi'im, or Prophets, canonized around 200 B.C.E. An addendum to Israel's founding, the original books of prophecy order the establishment of a monarchy and the interaction of kings with divine seers, who mediated between earthly events and God's intent. Individual texts comprising the Prophets are the histories known as Joshua (see previous section), Judges, Samuel, and Kings plus the predictive writings of Isaiah, Jeremiah, Ezekiel, and twelve minor prophets—Hosea, Joel, Amos, Obadiah, Jonah, Micah, Nahum, Habakkuk, Zephaniah, Haggai, Zechariah, and Malachi. Judges continues the legalism of the Torah with a philosophical assessment of history and the importance of the judges Deborah, Gideon, and Jephthah. The work concludes with the fall of Samson. The Book of Samuel reveals the importance of Samuel and Saul to Israel and introduces David, the first sovereign to unite a desert people under one capital city, Jerusalem. The Book of Kings establishes the chronology of Solomon's reign. The drama of Hebrew history reaches a climax with the divided monarchy and the rise of the prophets Elijah and Elisha before the collapse of Israel and Judah. The prophecies of Isaiah, Jeremiah, and Ezekiel revive hope among the Hebrews. The lesser prophecies corroborate a brighter outlook.

JUDGES

The Book of Judges, an original title taken from the Hebrew Shofetim, follows the development of the Hebrew nation from 1220 to 1050 B.C.E. as it evolves leadership following the deaths of Moses and Joshua. The Hebrews, strengthened by Joshua's military command, continue to ward off attackers. No longer desert wanderers, they adapt to agrarian living and weather intertribal strife.

Outstanding among the twelve judges are five: Ehud, Deborah, Gideon, Jephthah, and Samson. The author, living about the time of David, redacts patriotic hero lore and cites a favorite episode, Deborah's song.

During the Iron Age, the pattern of disloyalty to Yahweh is a constant. No sooner is Joshua buried than the people forsake their God and grovel before Baal, whom worshipers honor with prostitution, orgies, and human sacrifice. The Hebrews' disloyalty results in military failures as the retribution of an angry God. In chapter 3, the first major figure, Othniel, defeats Israel's Mesopotamian enemies around 1200; a successor, Ehud of Benjamin, overcomes Eglon of Moab's desert alliance with Amalekites and Ammonites around 1170 B.C.E. Twenty years later, Shamgar continues the pattern against the Philistines, a coastal nation that had perennially jockeyed for power over inland peoples.

Breaking a pattern of male judges over the Israelites is Deborah, who comes to power with her field commander, Barak, around 1125 B.C.E. In perhaps the oldest biblical hymn, Judges 5, Deborah sings a martial air. She simplifies the conquest in Judges 5:20–21 with thanks to nature:

> They fought from heaven;
>   the stars in their courses
>   fought against Sisera.
> The river of Kishon swept them away,
>   that ancient river, the river Kishon.
> O my soul, thou hast trodden down strength.

Verses 24–31 introduce an encomium to Jael, a blessed woman who murders Sisera with one blow of a mallet to his head. In Judges 5:31, Deborah exults, "So let all thine enemies perish, O Lord!"

In chapter 6, Gideon rises to fame around 1100 B.C.E.

by crushing the Midianite stranglehold on Israel. He asks God for a sign of blessing by leaving a fleece on the ground overnight. The next day, according to Judges 6:37–38, he squeezes enough dewdrops to fill a bowl. The heavenly aegis aids Gideon in selecting 10,000 fearless soldiers and in rejecting 2,200 cowards. In a second test of manhood, found in chapter 7, he leads candidates to water and chooses only those 300 who cannily sip from their cupped hands while keeping watch for attackers. That night, his select company divides into three units, sneaks up on the enemy camp, blows trumpets, and breaks jars covering torches. With a shout, Gideon's host disperses the Midianites. The slaughter concludes in Judges 7:24 with the execution of two princes, Oreb and Zeeb.

After Gideon comes the usurper Abimelech, Gideon's overly ambitious son by a concubine. In chapter 9, the speaker Jotham stands on a mountaintop to present the people an illustrative fable about the trees and brambles. In Judges 9:16, his bold exemplum denounces Abimelech by name as a power-mad tyrant. Like the bramble, the unstable ruler is capable of bursting into wildfire and devouring all in its path. Jotham's prophecy comes true within three years, when Abimelech's corrupt rule produces mass revolt.

After a brief summary of the reigns of Tola and Jair, chapters 10–12 tell of Jephthah, the judge who overcomes the Ammonites around 1170 B.C.E., but vows to sacrifice to God the first person who greets him. Even though the first celebrant of triumph is his daughter, he carries out his pledge and sacrifices her in Judges 11:39. The event precedes civil strife with the Ephraimites, whom Jephthah's Gileadites ferret out of the neighborhood by having them pronounce "shibboleth." In Judges 12:6, those who cannot form a *sh* sound are slain on the banks of the Jordan. Chapter 12 concludes with brief histories of Ibzan, Elon, and Abdon.

Set around 1070 B.C.E., the story of Samson, son of Manoah and his barren wife, is an appealing warrior tale, which begins in chapter 13. The focus is a likable but promiscuous strongman who commits bold, self-serving acts of strength and daring. The fourteenth chapter contains a riddle in verse 14:

> Out of the eater [a lion's carcass]
>   came something to eat [honey].
> Out of the strong came something sweet.

Because his Philistine wife wheedles the answer to the riddle and divulges it to his enemies, Samson recognizes her disloyalty. He kills thirty and relegates his adulterous wife to his friend. Out of anger, Samson sets fire to torches tied to foxes' tails and destroys Philistine fields. When they learn the cause of his anger, they burn the faithless wife and her father. In Judges 15:16, Samson retaliates by slaying the Philistines with the jawbone of an ass. The episode concludes with a sign of God's approval: "God clave a hollow place that was in the jaw, and there came water thereout" (Judges 15:19).

Samson's misadventures conclude with a prominent scriptural account of a fool for love. After Delilah learns that he acquires strength from his hair, she betrays him three times. Foolishly, he divulges the real source of his strength. After a Philistine shaves off Samson's hair, God deserts him. The Philistines rip out his eyes and set him to turning a mill wheel in Gaza. By the time that Samson's hair grows back, the people have forgotten his great strength. While they worship the bestial god Dagon, Samson calls upon Yahweh:

> O Lord God,
> remember me, I pray thee,
> and strengthen me, I pray thee,
> only this once, O God,
> that I may be at once avenged of the Philistines
> for my two eyes [Judges 16:28].

With God's help, he pulls down the temple pillars, killing 3,000 tormentors and himself. This popular tale figures in a closet drama, *Samson Agonistes*, by the English epicist John Milton, in Georg Friedrich Handel's oratorio *Samson*, and in Camille Saint-Saëns's opera *Samson and Delilah*.

SAMUEL

The prophet Samuel, a major figure during the rise of kings Saul and David and Israel's last judge, served at Shiloh and influenced the shrines at Bethel, Gilgal, and Mizpah. The Book of Samuel prefaces events occurring between 1050 and 960 B.C.E. Attributed to the prophets Samuel, Nathan, and Gad, the book may have been authored by the priest Abiathar, who preceded Samuel at the shrine of Shiloh, or by Ahimaaz, a son of Zadok. The text, divided into I and II Samuel in 1516, appears to be a court document based on two major sources of archival material.

The biography of Samuel begins with the familiar convention of the barren woman praying for a child, a parallel to the yearning of Sarai and a forerunner of Elizabeth's childlessness before she and Zechariah conceive John the Baptist. The poignant scene in I Samuel 1:11 depicts Hannah's desperation in a prayer to God:

> O Lord of hosts, if thou wilt indeed look
> on the affliction of thine handmaid,
> and remember me,
> and not forget thine handmaid,
> but wilt give unto thine handmaid a man child,
> then I will give him unto the Lord
> all the days of his life.

She is so wrapped up in prayer at the temple in Shiloh that the priest Eli thinks she is drunk. When he realizes her heartache, he promises an end to her childlessness. Hannah keeps her vow by dedicating her weanling son to God. Her song of thanksgiving in I Samuel 2:1–10 prefigures the Magnificat of Luke 1:46–55, a standard scenario in which the Virgin Mary honors God for choosing her to bear a heavenly child.

Samuel serves Eli during a time of travail and public humiliation for the adulteries of his sons, Hophni and Phinehas, who are inappropriate successors. When Samuel is near the age of twelve, Eli experiences a nighttime revelation from God. Old and nearly blind, the former priest surmises that the boy is God's elect and commands:

> Go, lie down: and it shall be,
> if he call thee,
> that thou shalt say,
> Speak, Lord;
> for thy servant heareth [I Samuel 3:9].

When Samuel reaches adulthood, in chapter 4, Eli and his family die at the disastrous battle of Shiloh, where Dagon-worshiping Philistines capture the ark. In chapter 6, after a series of disasters, they load it on a cart and return it.

In advanced old age, Samuel appoints Joel and Abiah as judges and predicts the coming of a grasping, tyrannous king. In response to the people's demand for a monarch, in chapters 9–10, Samuel secretly anoints Saul, son of Kish, at Ramah. Saul is a tall, handsome prospect later confirmed prince of Israel at Mizpah, but he fails as a leader in chapters 13–14. After a protracted power struggle with Samuel in chapter 15, Saul disobeys God by neglecting to execute King Agag of the Amalekites and by keeping their livestock for sacrifice. Samuel warns:

> For rebellion is as the sin of witchcraft,
> and stubbornness is as iniquity and idolatry.
> Because thou hast rejected the word of the Lord,
> he hath also rejected thee from being king [I Samuel 15:23].

Because Saul tears Samuel's priestly garment, the old man predicts that God will wrest Israel from the king. Samuel rebukes the king by calling for Agag and hacking him to pieces.

In chapter 16, the political situation takes a new turn. At God's command, Samuel goes to Bethlehem to anoint David, the eighth son of Jesse and a tanned, pretty-eyed shepherd lad known for skill at the lyre. He comes into Saul's court as a court harper, soothes the king's foul moods, and rises to the post of armor bearer. The great episode in the boyhood of David is the slaying of Goliath of Gath in chapter 17, an interpolated event that may derive from earlier heroic literature. The boy's careful choice and delivery of one of five smooth stones elevates him from singer to slayer of a giant. With suitable savagery, David lops off the giant's head, causing a Philistine rout.

A favorite model of friendship arises from chapter 18, in which Saul's son Jonathan befriends David. The boy warrior's rise climaxes in danger in verse 7 as Israelite women sing, "Saul hath slain his thousands, and David his ten thousands." The king's jealousy results in a murder plot. By offering his daughter Michal in marriage in exchange for the deaths of a hundred Philistines, Saul hopes to rid himself of David. The lad's success results in a second plot, in which Saul dispatches Jonathan to kill David. Jonathan betrays his father and sends his friend away. Michal also outwits her father and helps David flee. An outlaw, he escapes to the cave of Adullam and retreats to the hill country of Ziph at Horesh. In chapter 24, David spares the king's life at a cave at Engedi.

In chapter 28, Saul's desperation produces an odd biblical event — a summoning of Samuel from the dead by the Witch of Endor, whom Saul pardons in advance for sorcery. The ghost of Samuel predicts death the next day for Saul and his sons. The experience so unnerves the king that the sorceress makes him rest and eat to regain strength. The savage end of the Israelites under Philistine swords and Saul's battlefield suicide and dismemberment in chapter 31 conclude the first half of the Book of Samuel in one of the Old Testament's bloodiest crescendos.

The rise of David in the remainder of the text begins with a majestic lament for the king and his son. In the King James version of II Samuel 1:23, David applies ancient battlefield hyperbole in the cry,

> Saul and Jonathan were lovely and pleasant in their lives,
>   and in their death they were not divided:
>   they were swifter than eagles,
>   they were stronger than lions.

The soulful encomium foreshadows David's despair at the slaughter of another prince, his rebellious son, Absalom.

Crowned king at Hebron, David swiftly becomes the prototype of the crafty warrior-king, who consolidates his power by seizing prime territory and overthrowing rivals. In chapter 6, he dances before the ark after its recovery from the enemy. The jubilant processional includes "all manner of instruments made of fir wood, even on harps, and on psalteries, and on timbrels, and on cornets, and on cymbals" (II Samuel 6:5). Immediately, he discusses with his prophet Nathan a permanent temple. In II Samuel 7:8–16, God appears to Nathan and promises great things for David's reign. Chapter 8 establishes his cabinet, including Zadok the priest; chapter 9 depicts David making a gesture to the past dynasty by welcoming a royal cripple, Mephibosheth, out of love for his father, Jonathan.

The multilayered love story of David and Bathsheba is a human lapse in the biography of an otherwise blameless king and servant of God. The author of II Samuel 11–12 suggests that the king walks his rooftop by night and accidentally spies a beautiful matron at her bath. As is typical of patriarchal writing, no explanation of Bathsheba's behavior or motivation enlightens the brief account of their initial love affair. After illicit sexual relations, David realizes that he must account for their illegitimate child by sentencing her husband, the faithful soldier Uriah, to die in battle. The letter to Joab, David's field commander, reveals David's cold-blooded will:

> Set ye Uriah in the forefront of the hottest battle,
>   and retire ye from him,
>   that he may be smitten, and die [II Samuel 11:15].

The setup goes smoothly. After Bathsheba mourns Uriah, she and King David unite legally.

Chapter 12 contains a significant confrontation between king and prophet pitting earthly power against heavenly control as Nathan blames David for his crimes of adultery and murder. The accusation takes the form of a fable-within-history — a verbal mousetrap about the rich man with many sheep and the poor man with only one pet ewe lamb. Referring indirectly to David's despoilment of a presumably decent woman, the story grabs the king's attention and causes him to burst out with a spontaneous, heartfelt condemnation of the killer of the poor man's lamb. With a dramatic thrust home, Nathan declares, "Thou art the man."

After prophesying that David's kingdom and family will live under the sword, Nathan predicts that the king will not die, but his illegitimate child will perish soon after birth as God's punishment. The seven-day illness distracts the king:

> David therefore besought God for the child;
>   and David fasted,
>   and went, and lay all night upon the earth [II Samuel 12:16].

The servants so fear the king's malaise that they hesitate to report the infant's death. After God forgives David, he presents a heavenly sign in the conception and birth of Solomon, David and Bathsheba's second son and Israel's wise monarch.

Late in David's reign, Nathan's prophecy of domestic strife comes true in incest, sedition, violence, and death within the royal household. In II Samuel 13:1–14, his son Amnon grows so sick with unnatural passion for his sister Tamar that he tricks, then rapes her. The episode depicts Amnon's abnormal feelings as twisted into loathing and Tamar's response as deviant seduction of her brother. Violence takes Amnon and his brothers Adonijah and the would-be usurper Absalom. The favorite, the handsome Absalom flees Joab and the king's forces, but inadvertently tangles his hair on an oak bough. Against orders, Joab's men swiftly slaughter him. Although victory sustains the kingdom, David's cry in II Samuel 18:33 is the keening of a distraught father:

> O my son Absalom,
>   my son, my son Absalom!
>   would God I had died for thee,
>   O Absalom, my son, my son!

Again in II Samuel 19:4, David cries unconsolably until Joab reminds him that the people expect him to rejoice at the victory over rebellion. David's wits return; he sits at the gate and greets his subjects. In II Samuel 22:2–51, he sings one of his most popular anthems, which begins, "The Lord is my rock and my fortress and my deliverer."

Poetry concludes the book with the king's deathbed proclamation, a convention of scriptural leave taking. In II Samuel 23:1–4, David, "the sweet psalmist of Israel," declares,

> He that ruleth over men must be just,
>   ruling in the fear of God.
> And he shall be as the light of the morning,
>   when the sun riseth,
>   even a morning without clouds;
>   as the tender grass springing out of the earth
>   by clear shining after rain.

Ironic in its idealism, the description of the perfect ruler is in no way a summary of David's reign.

KINGS

The book of Kings, set about 970–586 B.C.E. and completed before 536 B.C.E., builds on two lost histories, the Book of the Acts of Solomon and the Book of Chronicles of the Kings of Judah. Traditionally attributed in part to the prophet Jeremiah, who edited the rest, Kings is actually the compilation of an unknown author. It outlines Solomon's reign, the moral stature of later monarchs, and the fall of the united kingdom, which split into Israel's amalgam of ten tribes to the north and Judah's two tribes to the south. At the end of an era, Assyria's capture of Israel and Babylon's capture of Judah precipitate a subdued mood among the Israelites.

Like the Book of Exodus, I Kings opens on a royal power struggle. The priest Nathan acts quickly to override the claim of Adonijah, the elderly King David's oldest son. The king holds a formal ceremony at Gihon to name his and Bathsheba's son to succeed to the throne. In his words, "Assuredly Solomon thy son shall reign after me and he shall sit upon my throne in my stead; even so will I certainly do this day" (I Kings 1:30). The ritual in-

cludes anointing by Nathan and the priest Zadok and the blowing of the trumpet, followed by public announcement of the succession. Chapter 2 divulges the harsh work of a king in David's final act and King Solomon's initial housecleaning—banishment of the priest Abiathar and execution of Joab, Shimei, and Solomon's brother Adonijah.

As he did in the Pentateuch, God continues to take a personal interest in Hebrew history. He appears to Solomon in a dream in chapter 3 and promises wisdom and great wealth. God adds in verse 14:

> And if thou wilt walk in my ways,
>   to keep my statutes and my commandments,
>   as thy father David did walk,
>   then I will lengthen thy days.

Solomon's emergence as a wise judge colors chapter 3:16–28, the famous incident of the two mothers claiming the same infant. The king prospered from such clever court action and from his 1,005 songs and 3,000 proverbs. The author credits God for elevating Solomon and for giving him "wisdom and understanding exceeding much, and largeness of heart, even as the sand that is on the seashore" (I Kings 4:29).

Solomon's building projects amaze his contemporaries, but royal corruption begins the downfall of the Davidic line. In chapters 6–8, over a period of seven and a half years, Solomon constructs a temple $60 \times 20 \times 30$ cubits and adorns it with carved cedar and an overlay of gold. At the center, he places the ark and celebrates with a feast, the first celebration of Succoth. In chapter 10, his fame lures the queen of Sheba and others, who present him with precious metals, ivory, spices, ornate clothing, and livestock. After placing foreign wives in the royal harem in chapter 11, he falls into idolatry by allowing them to spend public funds on statues of alien gods. In verse 7, he goes so far as to worship "Molech, the abomination of the children of Ammon." In anger, God vows to seize the kingdom from Solomon's son Jeroboam, who flees to Egypt to escape his father's wrath, then returns in chapter 12 to claim the birthright from his brother Rehoboam.

The princes' conflict divides Solomon's kingdom. In chapter 13:2–3, an unnamed prophet foretells the birth and accession of Josiah and predicts the destruction of the altar. A prophecy by Ahijah at Shiloh assures Jeroboam that he must pay for his evil with the death of his son. Rehoboam rules next in Judah, where paganism continues to thrive "on every high hill and under every green tree" (I Kings 14:23). Books 15–16 briefly recap the kings of Israel and Judah, beginning with Abijam, followed by Asa in Judah and by Nadab, Baasha, Elah, Zimri, and Omri in Israel.

In I Kings 16:29, Omri's successor, Ahab of Israel, marries Jezebel, a Samaritan Baal worshiper and the Old Testament's most notorious seductress. Pagan worship causes the wonder worker Elijah the Tishbite to prophesy a drought. After a period of withdrawal in chapter 18, during which Jezebel ousts God's prophets, Elijah confronts the king and upbraids him for sacrilege. Before the people, the priest sets up a trial at Mount Carmel that pits him in public competition against the 450 priests of Baal. The trial concludes with God setting fire to wet wood on the altar. After Elijah prays:

Then the fire of the Lord fell,
  and consumed the burnt sacrifice,
  and the wood, and the stones, and the dust,
  and licked up the water that was in the trench [I Kings 18:38].

He seizes the foiled alien priests and slays them. Jezebel angrily forces the prophet to flee. God nurtures him for forty days in the wilderness; afterward, Elijah anoints Jehu as the new king of Israel and selects his own successor, Elisha.

The second Book of Kings, chapter 2, depicts a spectacular end to Elijah. As he passes on the prophet's mantle, a chariot of fire whirls him away into heaven. Because Elisha performs miracles in chapters 4–6, climaxing in the cleansing of Naaman the leper and the floating of an iron axhead, the people accept Elisha as Elijah's successor. Elisha prophesies the kingship of Hazael, who grows so eager to rule that he suffocates his predecessor. As the political situation worsens under Jehu, Jehoahaz, and Jehoash, Elisha sickens with mortal illness. Joash grows distraught and cries out, "O my father, my father, the chariot of Israel, and the horsemen thereof" (II Kings 13:14). Elisha commands Joash, the King of Israel, to strike the ground with arrows. Because the king strikes three times, Elisha predicts that he will defeat Syria three times, but will not triumph in the end. The capture of Samaria in 720 B.C.E. results in a Hebrew diaspora. The dispersed Jews are later known as the Ten Lost Tribes of Israel.

Israel's loss reignites the religious zeal of Judah. Led by the prophet Isaiah, in chapter 18, the people survive the assault of the Assyrian king Sennacherib. After the slaughter of 185,000 Assyrians, Sennacherib retreats to Nineveh. According to II Kings 21, the triumph is short-lived, for King Manasseh of Judah chooses to cultivate an alliance with Assyria. During his long reign of fifty-five years, he so adulterates the local culture with idolatry and sacrilege that he weakens the Hebrews' moral fiber. In chapters 22–23, his grandson Josiah attempts reform. A high point of his reign is the high priest Hilkiah's discovery of a book of law in the Temple in II Kings 22:8. Josiah reads the book and mourns Judah's decline. He causes Hilkiah to cleanse the Temple of Baal worship and commands the

people to celebrate the Passover, but his efforts to reclaim Judah are too little, too late. In II Kings 23:29, Josiah dies in battle at Megiddo, the town later anathematized as Armageddon.

Downfall is swift and humbling. In chapter 24:11–12, Nebuchadnezzar seizes Jerusalem, King Jehoiachin, his family, and the palace staff. The Babylonians loot the Temple, hack apart golden vessels, and kidnap thousands of the cream of Hebrew manhood and artisanship. King Zedekiah tries to hold out during a subsequent siege at Jerusalem, but the enemy bests him, kills his son, and blinds the king before marching him to Babylon. Chapter 25 concludes with a pardon for Jehoiachin, a small concession in a grim chapter of Hebrew history.

ISAIAH

No oracle has so captured the Judeo-Christian imagination as does the collection of sixty-six chapters of vivid, eloquent prophecy from Isaiah. A wise nobleman, son of Amoz (or Amos), husband of a prophetess, he was chief political and judicial counselor to the crown. Citybred, he grew up in Jerusalem observing the examples of prophets Amos, Hosea, and Micah. He may also have been a priest.

A champion of social justice, Isaiah came to power in Judah in 740 B.C.E. and remained the royal adviser of four kings— Uzziah, Jotham, Ahaz, and Hezekiah, under whom Isaiah initiated reform. A powerful charismatic, he proclaimed maledictions, sermons, and prophecies that his disciples later recorded on scrolls. His themes covered moral laxity, greed, graft, insincere religious ritual, and oppression of the poor. According to folk tradition, Manasseh executed Isaiah by severing his torso with a cross-cut saw sometime after 687 B.C.E. (see Apocrypha).

The Book of Isaiah, which appears to be the writing of several contributors, falls into three segments:

Chapters 1–39, Isaiah's contribution, recount Judah's history from 740 to 701 B.C.E. during his four decades of service.

Chapters 40–55 cover the period of captivity in Babylon, from 587 to 548 B.C.E.

The final eleven chapters, set from 538 to 400 B.C.E., express the emotions of the Hebrews on their trek from exile to their ancestral home in Palestine.

The prophet's themes are standard scriptural fare — stiff warnings about alien influence and idolatry and reminders of the first commandment of Moses, which requires total allegiance to God.

The book opens in medias res, with the prophet's taxing job of aiding a sinful, iniquitous people. Chapter 1 enjoins worshipers to stop making a mockery of Temple sacrifice and, in verse 4, to cease forsaking the "holy one of Israel." After hinting that Judah may fall in a catastrophe similar to that of Sodom and Gomorrah, the prophet orders the people to cleanse themselves and to rehabilitate their degraded character. Chapter 2 contains a vision of a savior who will teach and judge the people. In obedience, the chastened followers will reshape weapons into useful agricultural tools—swords into plowshares and spears into pruning hooks. Isaiah follows with outrage at the shamelessness of Zion, which he depicts as a flashy, perfumed hussy. He creates an agrarian parable in chapter 5, which cries woe to the besotted wastrel.

In chapter 6, Isaiah reflects on his career's beginnings and the interactive vision of God's glory that draws him into prophecy. In verse 3, he hears seraphim calling out, "Holy, holy, holy is the Lord of hosts; the whole earth is full of his glory," the source of a standard Christian invocation and processional. Stricken with his inadequacy, he laments unclean lips, which a seraphim purifies with a burning coal. In response to God's summons, in verse 8, Isaiah replies, "Here am I! Send me." Christian recruiters use his spontaneous wholeheartedness to exhort youth contemplating religious service.

Isaiah serves Ahaz in 735 B.C.E. when the king ponders a course of action as stronger nations loom and threaten to consume Judah. To Isaiah's advice to remain strong of heart against Assyria, Ahaz demands a heavenly sign. Under protest, the prophet complies and envisions a young mother giving birth to a son named Immanuel, literally "God with us." Christians interpret his vision as an Advent lesson anticipating Mary's conception of Jesus. An extensive passage in Isaiah 9:2–7 appears to predict Christ, a "great light" shining on people who walk in darkness. A major segment of Advent liturgy comes from verses 6–7:

> For unto us a child is born,
>   to us a son is given:
>   and the government shall be upon his shoulder,
>   and his name will be called
> Wonderful, counselor, the mighty god,
>   the everlasting father, the prince of peace.
> Of the increase of his government and of peace
>   there shall be no end …
>   from henceforth even forever.

The prophecy of a Davidic hero-rescuer continues in chapter 11, the source of a utopian vision that has inspired preachers, musicians, and artists. A notable image of the peaceable kingdom foresees shy animals cohabitating with predators and a little child leading them. The image may have colored the Roman poet Virgil's fourth Eclogue (37 B.C.E.), in which he prophesies a golden era of goodwill ushered in by the birth of a holy child.

Rooted in the present, Isaiah continues to inveigh against alliance with Assyria. In the style of his father, Ahaz, Hezekiah makes the same mistake of ignoring the prophet. Meanwhile, Isaiah works himself into paroxysm with warnings about foreign nations—Babylon, Assyria, Philistia, Moab, Damascus, Ethiopia, Egypt—and commits them to writing for a heedless people who reject his foresight. Fortunately for the king, Isaiah foresees safety for Jerusalem from Assyrian attack.

A second voice takes up the book of Isaiah in chapter 40, the consolation to Jews for their long period of exile in Babylon. The text reverberates with keen images of departure from the wilderness, the short life of grass, and majestic words of the Almighty. The omen of a "voice crying in the wilderness" suggests to Christians the ministry of John the Baptist, Jesus's cousin and forerunner who baptized him in the River Jordan. Chapter 45 prophesies that the Persian king Cyrus will liberate the Jews. In ringing oratory, the prophet summons the exiles home to Judah. The image of the suffering servant in chapter 53:4–5 again suggests Jesus's role as the crucified martyr "wounded for transgressions" and "bruised for our iniquities." Like the scapegoat, the unnamed suppliant accepts chastisement and redeems wandering sheep by accepting "the iniquity of us all."

The final stave of the Book of Isaiah, composed by a third author, appears to parrot Ezra and Nehemiah's injunction to Hebrew males to divorce foreign, idol-worshiping wives. In a hint of Jesus's welcome to all comers, Isaiah counters royal orders in chapter 56:6 with an invitation to foreigners to convert to Judaism and "join themselves to the Lord, to minister to him, to love the name of the Lord, and to be his servants." Ardently, in chapter 60:1, the prophet urges Hebrews to cast off their dolor and "Arise, shine; for thy light is come, and the glory of the Lord has risen upon you." Another meaningful passage in this anthem foretells of camel drivers bearing the "wealth of nations," specifically gold and frankincense, two of the gifts of the magi to the Christ Child in the Book of Matthew. The apocalypse that concludes the book in chapters 65–66 foresees joy in Jerusalem as the returning exiles rebuild the city, replant vineyards, and bear blessed offspring once more.

Jeremiah

Some one hundred years after Isaiah's tenure, Jeremiah, son of the high priest Hilkiah and descendant of the priest Abiathar, rises to the post of prophet in Jerusalem during a golden age of seers Habakkuk, Zephaniah, Daniel, and Ezekiel. Less tactful than his predecessor, Jeremiah is a loner and zealot who annoys fellow prophets, priests, and commoners with a jarring, unrelenting outcry.

His book is lengthy and filled with historical events that place him in the white heat of political and social upheaval. Surprisingly, he and his grimly realistic prophecy survived.

From 626 to 586 B.C.E., under King Josiah, Jeremiah denounces the Assyrian tyranny that replaces worship of Yahweh with idols of Baal, Moloch's fire ritual, and Mesopotamian astrology. In 621 B.C.E., during Jeremiah's tenure, his father recovers the Book of Deuteronomy from the Temple and reads aloud the laws that Hebrews are violating wholesale. Jeremiah assists King Josiah in launching cultural reform to restore a love and reverence for Yahweh. The people, newly invigorated, abandon superstition, smash idols, and raze alien worship centers.

The renewal of monotheism and obedience to Mosaic law ends abruptly in 609 B.C.E., when Egyptian forces kill King Josiah in battle at Megiddo. His subjects read into his defeat the comeuppance of angry Assyrian gods. Resumption of idolatry, forced labor, and perpetual wars under King Jehoiakim reave the people of direction. Jeremiah upholds the faith, exhorting hearers to a change of heart and behavior, but the times do not support his effort. Frustrated, he grows strident and shrill and angers priests and officials by supporting Nebuchadrezzar of Babylon over the Egyptians, whom Jerusalem courted. In 598 B.C.E., the oracles come true in the fall of Judah to Babylon, the dismantling of the Temple, and the abduction of 7,000 families into exile. Branded a turncoat and imprisoned for desertion, Jeremiah continues to urge King Zedekiah to shift allegiance.

After the murder of the royal princes and blinding and enslavement of the king, Jeremiah's tenure ends in fiasco in 586 B.C.E. A failed cabal forces him to accompany rebels to Egypt. Legend describes him preaching to Jewish refugees, who repudiate his advice and stone him to death. His book, one of the most mournful and grim, gives rise to the terms *jeremiad* for a protracted lamentation or harangue and *jeremiah* for a monomaniac attuned perpetually to incipient doom.

The text opens with a straightforward introduction of Jeremiah's religious calling at his home in Anathoth outside Jerusalem. Still immature, he replies in Jeremiah 1:6, "Ah, Lord God! Behold, I do not know how to speak, for I am only a youth." Reassured that God will provide inspiration, the boy prophet begins exhorting the wicked for falling away from the God who led their forebears out of bondage in Egypt. True to scripture, he predicts that their punishment will be bitter.

Chapter 4 resorts to martial imagery to warn Judah that invasion and looting await. In Jeremiah 4:23, the prophet launches a series of parallel visions. He looks out on waste, darkness, trembling mountains, and a deserted city in ruins. Repeatedly, he blames the faithless for their folly and senseless abandonment of God. At a moment of crisis, chapter 7 pictures Jeremiah at the gates of the Temple charging hearers to enter and renew their vows to God. In reference to spiritual decline, Jeremiah 8:22 asks, "Is there no balm in Gilead?" a reference to a source of healing ointment. The harangue closes in chapter 9 with Jeremiah weeping over the eventual fate of his fellow Jews.

Undismayed, Jeremiah perseveres against violations of Mosaic law. In chapter 10, he repudiates astrology as superstition and labels Assyrian customs false. In a direct attack on idolatry, in Jeremiah 10:8, he shouts, "They are both stupid and foolish; the instruction of idols is but wood!" He pursues the attack with claims that they embrace delusion and worthlessness. When Jerusalem enters a period of drought in chapter 14, God ignores the people's cry for water. Instead of recognizing divine chastisement, they despise the prophet for remaining loyal to an unresponsive God.

In chapter 16, the prophet declares that God instructed him to remain celibate because there will be no time to establish a home and children. In verse 13, an irate God promises to hurl idolaters out of the land to a place of exile, "and there you shall serve other gods day and night, for I will show you no favor." Like the potter in chapter 18, he can choose to remold a wayward people rather than leave them in their current contrary state. In chapter 19, he presents the parable of the shattered jug as a warning of irreparable damage when invaders end their tenure in Jerusalem.

As in the case of Moses and Isaiah, Jeremiah chafes at a difficult task. Into chapter 20, the role of spokesman for God weighs heavy. Jeremiah resents being pilloried by ungrateful Hebrews, but recognizes that a prophet has no choice but to follow God's command. Chapter 24 pictures the wayward as bad figs as the time of the Babylonian invasion draws nigh. A clash with Hananiah reduces Jeremiah further in public estimation, but he refuses to give up.

After the exile to Babylon, in chapter 29, Jeremiah sends a letter urging them to rebuild a pious Hebrew community on foreign soil. His advice in verse 7 is sensible, "See the welfare of the city where I have sent you into exile, and pray to the Lord on its behalf, for in its welfare you will find your welfare." He predicts that the Hebrews' travail will last for seventy years and challenges them to avoid diviners and remain true to God. Chapter 30 records a hopeful vision in which God promises Jeremiah in verse 18 to "restore the fortunes of the tents of Jacob" and to rebuild the city of Jerusalem. The next chapter offers a new beginning through a renewed covenant relationship with God.

Jeremiah offers an intimate glimpse of his life and methods. In chapter 32, he purchases land in Judah as though declaring hope for the future. In chapter 36, after the king burns his prophecy, Jeremiah selects Baruch to take dictation on a new scroll. This period of industry comes to a halt in the next chapter, in which a sentry arrests Jeremiah at the Benjamin Gate.

Beaten and incarcerated for his political opinions, the prophet serves King Zedekiah in secret and warns that defeat at the hands of Babylon is imminent. The king removes Jeremiah from the dungeon and places him in the guardhouse on a ration of one loaf of bread a day. Plotters intercede and cast him into a nearby well, where he sinks in mud until an Ethiopian rescues him. Jeremiah's fate worsens after Nebuchadrezzar seizes Jerusalem. Aged and unable to ward off doom, he falls into the hands of plotters who force him into flight to Egypt. Still outspoken about worship of foreign gods, in chapters 43–44, he exhorts Jews to abandon Egyptian idolatry, then lapses into silence.

EZEKIEL

The Book of Ezekiel, a homogeneous text written by a native prophet and priest of Jerusalem and a contemporary of Jeremiah, derives from the tenure of a prophet among Jewish exiles in Tel-abib. In episodes set from around 593 to 571 B.C.E., at age thirty, he begins prophesying in the reign of Jehoiachin and protests a rebellion against Babylonian subjugation. In his view, his people have to endure enslavement as punishment for faithlessness.

Ezekiel, melodramatic and skilled at moving crowds, sticks doggedly to his task. In chapters 1–24, he urges the Jews to repent; the next eight chapters prophesy the menace of aliens. In chapters 33–39, he uplifts spirits with the promise of an end of their travail in Babylon. The last nine chapters envision the resurgence of Jerusalem. The prophet appears to have died on foreign soil under the rule of Nebuchadrezzar.

More mystic than poet, Ezekiel opens chapter 1 with the onset of visions by the Chebar River. Among gaping Chaldeans, he details the occasion when he looked up at a whirlwind enfolding fire and beheld strange winged creatures. Explicit about shape and likeness, he observes and describes a fiery wheel and falls face down as a voice begins to address him. Chapter 2 states God's message to his toiling people. In chapter 3, the Lord makes Ezekiel Israel's watchman to warn the wicked to abandon wrongdoing. Like a classroom teacher, he either sketches on a tile or forms a clay model of the siege at Jerusalem in chapter 4 and, falling on the ground, acts out Israel's waywardness and doom. In chapter 5:5, he completes his playacting with a message from God, "This is Jerusalem."

Ezekiel is clever. In chapter 8, he envisions the faulty worship practices that defile the Temple, but the people refuse to heed him. He reenacts the role of the exile. In chapters 13–14, he scolds Hebrews for relying on seers and magicians and accuses them of replacing God with idols. Chapter 15 presents the parable of the vine, a common representation of Israel, which has become worthless. Ezekiel follows with the allegory of the adulteress, which depicts Israel as the reclaimed orphan who turns away from God to flirt with heathens.

Ezekiel abandons stories and recounts history in chapter 20, which indicates that the Hebrews are about to suffer a second exile, a parallel to their sojourn in Egypt. A more damning allegory in chapter 23 compares the sisters Oholah and Oholibah, representing Samaria and Jerusalem. Like loose women, they chase after foreigners and deserve the fate that awaits them. So involved is Ezekiel in his task that in chapter 24, he has no opportunity to withdraw and mourn the death of his wife.

Subsequent visions compel Ezekiel to batter the rebellious Hebrews. God instructs him to warn that sinners will die. In chapter 34, the prophet repeats the prophecy of Isaiah that a Davidic savior will arise to lead them like a herdsman guiding sheep. God promises to baptize the people to cleanse them of idolatry. Ezekiel makes his most vivid word picture in chapter 37, in which he foresees a valley of dry bones and the rejuvenation of Israel from the breath of God, which will reclothe the skeletons in living tissue and lead them like warriors. Ezekiel concludes the text with new regulations for the resurrected Temple.

The Twelve

The presentation of the twelve minor prophets may derive from the Temple scribes' convenient grouping of these books on single papyri. Listed out of chronological order, the prophets actually fall historically into three time periods:

eighth century B.C.E.	Amos, Hosea, Micah
seventh century B.C.E.	Zephaniah, Nahum, Habakkuk
539–333 B.C.E.	Haggai, Zechariah, Obadiah, Malachi, Joel

Jonah, the only truly unplaceable figure, appears to belong to the Hellenistic period, which extended from 332 B.C.E. into the second century B.C.E.

These twelve prophets illustrate a generalization of the role of prophet from guide of the chosen race to spokesman to all the earth. Their warnings about vice and cruelty apply universally. To the Jews, the prophets warn of disloyalty, idolatry, self-absorption, and insincerity. To root out hypocrisy, God's spokesmen predict a day of judgment when enemies of the Hebrews will suffer for their brutality and the Jews, refined of earlier faults, will establish a new era of peace and faith. To prevent mass punishment, the prophets implore the wicked to repent and convert to Judaism. To that end, these men set a moral example, spoke God's messages, performed noteworthy deeds, and interpreted events as divine symbols.

HOSEA

Listed first of the Twelve, Hosea, an Ephraimite, comes to power in the northern half of the divided kingdom around 743 B.C.E. during Uzziah's last years and serves four decades in Israel under kings Jotham, Ahaz, Hezekiah, and Jeroboam II. Although Jerusalem and its Temple seem secure, Hosea doubts that Israel's status quo will last. He knows of the predictions of the prophet Amos to the south and, out of love, warns his people that infractions of the Mosaic laws and subservience to foreign gods endanger the Jews. He scolds them for hypocrisy and disobedience and begs for their repentance to a loving, compassionate God.

The text begins with God's command that Hosea commit a symbolic act — to marry a harlot, symbolizing the faithlessness of the people to God. After Hosea weds Gomer and sires Jezreel, God prophesies the collapse of Israel in the valley of Jezreel. Two more children carry emblematic names — a daughter is called Loruhamah (Not Pitied) and a son, Loammi (Not My People). Chapter 2 speaks in richly symbolic language a formulaic statement of divorce and proclaims the Jews' disloyalty. Verse 13 states their crime: "And I will punish her for the feast days of the Baals when she burned incense to them … and forgot me." The Lord promises in verse 18 that, on the day the people denounce Baal, "I will abolish the bow, the sword, and war from the land; and I will make you lie down in safety." This messianic era will renew covenant life with God and cause the earth to flourish once more.

The terse declarations of the prophet pound the Jews for iniquity, which he typifies as whoring and falsehood, a continuation of the marriage motif. In chapters 5 and 6, he accuses them of running hot and cold, righteous when they want relief from suffering, and indifferent when they have no need of divine intervention. Sin becomes a bad habit and will once more enslave them to overlords, as it did in the time of Moses.

Hypocrisy is the thrust of the prophet's complaint. Israel, Hosea proclaims in 10:1, "is an empty vine." Chapter 11 reminds Ephraimites that God is like a loving father who taught them to walk and carried them in his arms. In chapter 13, Hosea declares that God, unlike idols, never changes. The Lord's generosity shines in 14:4, where he promises to heal and love them. The beneficent image of dew on the lily and the deep-rooted olive tree concludes the book with reconciliation and a promise of God's abiding love.

JOEL

The brief Book of Joel, son of Pethuel, is the work of an insider. As cultic prophet at the Temple of Jerusalem, he supervises priestly duties. The text, which offers little historical or biographical data, appears to derive from 400 to 350 B.C.E. Joel's grimly catastrophic warning is standard Catholic scripture for Ash Wednesday and synagogue reading for the period that separates Rosh Hashanah, the Jewish New Year, and Yom Kippur, the Day of Atonement.

The impetus to chapter 1 is a swarm of locusts and Joel's disgust with wine bibbers. With overflowing emotion, in Joel 1:15 he mourns, "Alas for the day!" Chapter 2 is a surreal transformation of invasive insects into attacking troops. The prophet foresees a trumpet call for Zion, a day of judgment for the wicked and mercy for the godly. He depicts renewal in terms of abundant staples — grain, wine, and oil — and promises longevity and reverence for the holy city of Jerusalem and vengeance against Zion's enemies.

AMOS

A herder and arborist from the desert town of Tekoa, twelve miles south of Jerusalem, Amos begins a brilliant career of writing and preaching in the northern kingdom around 750 B.C.E. during the reigns of Uzziah in Judah and Jeroboam II in Israel. Amos's mission takes him to the idolaters of Samaria and Bethel. He informs Jews that God will extend no favors to the chosen race and pioneers the concept of religious ethics by crusading for social justice. His doom-laden prophecy in chapter 1 envisions God's wrath as a roar from Zion. In a strict verse pattern, he outlines the results of sin in Damascus, Tyre, Edom, Judah, Israel, and Moab.

Amos offers no choice to sinners. Hunting and stalking metaphors create a fearful atmosphere in chapter 3; grain, vineyard, and fig images color chapter 4. Amos 5:2 laments:

> The virgin of Israel is fallen;
>   she shall no more rise:
>   she is forsaken upon her land;
>   there is none to raise her up.

In Amos 5:22–23, the prophet warns that going through the motions of burning offerings will not redeem the people, nor will the singing of hymns.

The duality of Amos's prophecies emerges in the final chapters. In Amos 5:27, fate condemns the people to "captivity beyond Damascus." In chapter 7, the text contains a confrontation between the temporal monarch and God's spokesman in which Amos refuses to back down. The priest Amaziah reports to Jeroboam that Amos foresees death for the king and exile for Jerusalem. With a domestic image from Amos 9:9, God promises to "shake the house of Israel among all the nations as one shakes with a sieve." In the last three verses, Amos 9:13–15, the prophet speaks of a time of sweet wine and rebuilding, when God will replant the Jews "and they shall never again be plucked up."

OBADIAH

The prophet Obadiah produced a single book of twenty-one verses, the shortest in the Tanakh, which offers only hints of a link to history. Some of his predictions suit the period after 587 B.C.E., when Babylon captured Jerusalem. Their convergence on themes circulating at the time suggest that he may have voiced popular texts rather than produce original oracles.

In Obadiah 1:10, the prophet foresees a general uprising against the proud nation of Edom "for the violence done to your brother Jacob." The rhythm and style of Obadiah's chastisement turns on a series of "you should nots" for gloating, rejoicing in human misery, boasting, and breaching the people's gate to loot and hinder refugees. In verse 15, Obadiah warns that the Lord's day is at hand and that transgressors will not escape a fitting comeuppance. The houses of Jacob, Esau, and Joseph will suffer, but Mount Zion and Mount Esau will remain safe.

JONAH

The book of Jonah is a didactic hero story or parable similar to the tales of Daniel. The trial by ordeal that befalls the prophet Jonah, son of Amittai, may have occurred during the forty-year rule of Jeroboam II, from 783 to 743 B.C.E. Other possibilities place it in the sixth century or in the time of the exiles' return from Babylon, which would make Jonah a contemporary of the reformer Ezra and the builder Nehemiah. The emphasis on repentance and reconciliation with God in Jonah's story amplifies a picture of the Almighty as a beneficent, forgiving father.

The ordeal begins with Jonah's refusal to minister to the iniquitous citizens of Nineveh, who he does not want God to redeem. Assuming that he can escape God's jurisdiction, Jonah flees the assignment, takes sea passage out of Joppa, and heads for Tarshish. When God assails the ship with high winds and waves, the sailors cast lots to discover who is at fault for their peril. When divination points to Jonah, he explains that he is a Hebrew. The quaking crew takes his suggestion and throws him overboard. Instantly, the seas calm.

The underwater adventure begins in Jonah 1:17, when a great fish swallows the prophet. After three days in its innards, he prays that he has suffered near drowning in a place as terrifying as Sheol, the forerunner of hell. Recanting waywardness, in Jonah 2:7 he confesses, "When my soul fainted with me, I remembered the Lord; and my prayer came to thee." Instantly, God causes the fish to disgorge Jonah onto dry land. For Christians, the three-day trial followed by release from the fish compares with Jesus's burial and resurrection.

Chapter 3 recounts Jonah's second chance to go to Nineveh, where he terrifies the people with his warning of imminent overthrow. Their sincere repentance impresses God in Jonah 3:10, causing him to relent and spare the Ninevites, even though they are heathens. Jonah's anger at God causes him to retreat to a shelter outside the city gates. God withers the vine that shades the prophet and explains why he pitied the 120,000 Ninevites.

MICAH

In Judah during the reigns of Jotham, Ahaz, and Hezekiah from 740 to 693 B.C.E., Micah, a peasant from the hamlet of Moresheth, flourishes contemporaneously with the great prophet Isaiah in Jerusalem and with the lesser prophets Amos and Hosea in Israel. A simple outlander from the Philistine border, he expresses dismay at local corruption and greed that widens the gap between haves and have-nots. In the span of seven chapters, he warns of God's displeasure, but reassures the people of a benevolent messianic era to come. His prophecy serves as the annual synagogue reading for the sabbath that falls between Rosh Hashanah and Yom Kippur.

In the opening verses, Micah warns the house of Israel of its flaws and promises to hack and burn the idols of Samaria. In Micah 1:16, he urges adults to shave their heads in mourning over the fate of younger generations, who will dwell in exile. Chapter 2 condemns class disparity. In his vision, the upper classes tear flesh from the poor. Micah decries well-fed priests, men of prestige and means who lead the people astray by ignoring the plight of the hungry. He predicts in 3:6, "The sun shall go down over the prophets, and the day shall be black over them." This eclipse of seers will shame diviners, who will have no remedy for the prophets' distress.

The prophet's vision in chapter 4 foretells the rise of God's people to the mountaintops. In verse 5, Micah foresees all people walking with God, a merciful deity who will retrieve the refugee, the exiled, and the afflicted. Chapter 5 predicts a time of war against Assyria and presages the rise of a king from Bethlehem, a jubilant reign when Jacob's offspring will sweeten gentiles like dew on grass.

The picture is only briefly rosy. In chapter 6, Micah commands the people to worship God sincerely and stop using rich sacrifices and incense as substitutes. He predicts doom to enemy strongholds, witches, and soothsayers. With self-assurance, he declares in Micah 7:7, "I will look unto the Lord; I will wait for the god of my salvation: my god will hear me." In the final verses, the prophet addresses God, asking him for nurturance, pardon, compassion, and the kind of mercy that he once offered Abraham.

NAHUM

The three-chapter prophecy of Nahum the Elkoshite, an unknown prophet from an obscure place, foretells the dreadful collapse of Nineveh, Assyria's capital city, in 612 B.C.E. under Medean and Babylonian attack. An outspoken defender of God's justice, the prophet warns that God is jealous and avenging and that his wrath is all-consuming. In graphic detail, Nahum pictures mighty men red with carnage and chariots aflame in the city streets. The palace will dissolve and looters will strip it of silver and gold. Like a medieval Hellmouth, the pictorial representation of judgment day, chapter 3:3 speaks of a chaotic melange of "horsemen charging, flashing sword and glittering spear, hosts of slain, heaps of corpses, dead bodies without end — they stumble over the bodies!" The witnesses to Assyria's collapse will hear the news and applaud the end of "unceasing evil."

HABAKKUK

Also only three chapters in length, the Book of Habakkuk appears to fit around 608–598 B.C.E., making it contemporaneous with the prophecies of Jeremiah. The unusual name of Habakkuk is Assyrian rather than Hebrew. His work appears to be adulterated with the interpolation of chapter 3, an annual synagogue reading on Shavuoth. His prophecy reveals an answer to a common question about the allotment of victory. To questions about the prosperity of evil while the righteous suffer, the prophet concludes that disparity is an illusion, an injustice of the moment. Ultimately, the faithful will reap the justice they deserve.

Chapter 1 depicts Habakkuk crying to God for succor and complaining that "the wicked doth compass about the righteous, therefore wrong judgment proceedeth." In verse 6, he singles out the Chaldeans as a "bitter and hasty nation." In chapter 2, God reassures the prophet that the enemy will not triumph over the people who have been dehumanized and abased. He commands Habakkuk to inscribe plainly on tablets his vision of an inevitable time of justice. The purpose of prophetic writing is the spiritual uplift of the righteous.

Habakkuk particularizes the faults of his own day. In Habakkuk 2:19, he denounces idol makers, who craft "wooden things" and "dumb stone." The chapter conclu-

sion is a familiar invocation in church and synagogue: "The Lord is in his holy temple: let all the earth keep silence before him." The final stave strikes terror in the reader at the dreaded slaughter. As a result, fig and vine fail, olive tree and wheatfield yield nothing, and fold and stable lie empty of livestock. In the face of desolation, Habakkuk rejoices in God, who will rescue the faithful from carnage.

ZEPHANIAH

The three-chapter Book of Zephaniah, also called Sophonias, reprises the dream of the messianic era, when Zion will flourish once more and humankind will live in harmony and serenity. A remnant of the beginning of Josiah's rule in 638 B.C.E., the book places Zephaniah in the time of Jeremiah, a greater speaker and more influential prophet. Zephaniah himself is of royal lineage, tracing his ancestry back to King Hezekiah in the time of the great prophet Isaiah.

The Book of Zephaniah repeats dire warnings of downfall for the Jews' enemies. In Zephaniah 1:12, the seer predicts that God will search Jerusalem by candlelight to punish evil aliens. The outstanding prognostication in Zephaniah 1:15–18 is translated by St. Jerome in the Vulgate as *Dies irae, dies illa* (Day of wrath, that day), the text of a major medieval hymn. The verse served painters as a subject for Hellmouth and provided Wolfgang Amadeus Mozart with a fierce, unrelenting chorus for his *Requiem*. The dirge, building on repetitions of "day," predicts total darkness as clouds of dust obscure events. Only the trumpet call and battle cry rise above chaos.

To reassure his people, Zephaniah urges them in chapter 2 to stick together, call on God, and seek righteousness and humility. The prophet predicts that destruction of coastal powers will leave lands for shepherds to inhabit and pasturage for flocks. The last chapter warns that the disreputable city is ripe for waste. Zephaniah 3:14 launches into a praise anthem, calling for rejoicing and celebration for the reunion of Jews, the favored people who God will restore and raise from poverty.

HAGGAI

Haggai, the post-exilic Judean prophet, arises around 520 B.C.E., in the time of the governor Zerubbabel and the high priest Joshua. Haggai concerns himself with the problems inherent in repatriation — the resettling of the land and restoration of the Temple. Apathy and discouragement overtake the Jews, bringing the work to a halt and requiring the stimulus of the prophets Haggai and Zechariah, whose job it is to nurture and promote the people's spirituality.

In the first of two chapters, Haggai reasserts religious

priorities. He reminds the returnees of the Temple's former glory, which few experienced firsthand, and assures the former expatriates that God attends them still. In Haggai 2:7, God promises to once more "fill this house with glory." In the final revelation, Haggai 2:22–23, God warns Zerubbabel, heir of the David dynasty, that he will destroy heathen kingdoms and raise up his servant "as a signet," an authorized emblem of majesty and might.

ZECHARIAH

The Book of Zechariah, also called Zacharias, is the height of post-exilic prophecy. In the time of Haggai, the exiled priest Zechariah, a scion of a priestly family, returns to Jerusalem with his clan in 536 B.C.E. and experiences eight nocturnal visions. After a long period of inaction on restoring the Temple, he joins Haggai in inspiring self-confidence. Zechariah believes that the reconstruction is a requirement of a golden era. His vivid imagery influences the apocalyptic figures of New Testament writers.

In chapter 1, Zechariah blames the exiled Jews for arousing God to anger by their wickedness. A vision of four mounted patrols standing under myrtle trees leads the prophet to conclude that peace is stable and Jerusalem on the way to prosperity once more. Zechariah also envisions a man with a measuring line and Joshua standing between Satan and God's angel. In chapter 4, Zechariah talks with an angel and witnesses a menorah, the eight-branch candelabrum, fed by a pair of olive trees, which may represent Zerubbabel and Joshua, the priests who support the people in their worship. The menorah becomes the symbol of Hanukkah, a festival that promises the survival of the Jewish people.

Visions continue to overwhelm Zechariah in subsequent chapters. In chapter 5, he sees a flying scroll; in chapter 6, four chariots ranging out from two brass mountains suggest that God is actively patrolling the earth. The sharp alteration of tone and style in chapter 9 suggests a second, more optimistic author. The speaker breaks into a joyous anthem to Zion that predicts a triumphant king. He sings in Zechariah 9:16 of "the flock of his people," who shall adorn God's crown like jewels. Chapter 14, which serves as scriptural reading for the Jewish feast of Succoth, foresees an unending day when the Jews will observe God striking down the enemy with plague and strife.

MALACHI

The last of the Twelve, Malachi (My Messenger) is an anonymous author, possibly publishing under a pseudonym. The prophet, who issues his oracles sometime after 460 B.C.E., faces the disillusionment that follows the construction of the new Temple. The people, who take literally the prophecies of triumph for the Jews, decry their state and grow offhand, even resentful of the requirements of worship. Malachi leads them to reaffirm faith through ceremony and a change of heart. He instructs them by composing a formal dialectic. Beginning with a single truth, he counters with a question, thus leading them gradually to a renewed perspective of their role as God's children. This didactic method later enters religious instruction as catechism.

Like his forebears, Malachi is a stickler for regulations. Chapter 1 questions the dishonor of priests who profane temple sacrifices with imperfect animals. Chapter 2 warns that insincere worship will provoke a curse from God. Beginning in verse 10, Malachi warns of the dangers of divorcing older wives and marrying young aliens. He promises that there will come a day of cleansing and absolute justice.

The next chapter lists the judgment of God against sorcerers, adulterers, falsifiers, and oppressors. He warns backsliders in verse 16 that he keeps account of individual faults in a "book of remembrance." Chapter 4 promises a day in which God will burn the wicked like chaff in an oven. He orders all to obey Mosaic law and promises to send Elijah before judgment day to "turn the heart of the fathers to the children and the heart of the children to their fathers." To Christians, the prophecy refers directly to John the Baptist, the herald of Jesus, the true messiah.

Writings

The final segment of Hebraic scripture, the Ketuvim or Kethubim (Writings) is also hagiographa, writings about saints or venerated heroes. It consists of the wisdom or didactic literature found in Psalms, Proverbs, and Job. Less authoritative than the Laws and Prophets, this collection, written between 750 and 250 B.C.E., deals with the nature of good and evil. It includes five history scrolls—Song of Songs, Ruth, Lamentations, Ecclesiastes, and Esther—plus the books of Daniel, Ezra, Nehemiah, and Chronicles, which depart from devotional writings to purely nationalistic or patriotic texts. Because the Ketuvim lacks a definitive subtitle equal to the Torah and Prophets, its ranking among the completed canon suggests ambivalence as to the sanctity of these later works, particularly the amorous nature of the Song of Songs, the wisdom lore collected in Proverbs, and the historical commentary in Esther and Ecclesiastes.

PSALMS

The Hebrew hymnal originally called Tehillim (Praises), the Book of Psalms supplies the Temple of Zerubbabel with performance lyrics and ritual responses. It provides varied genres for public and private devotion — early religious songs, laments, processionals, encomia, doxologies intended for antiphonal chanting, call and response, meditations, and thanksgiving hymns to be accompanied by strings, flute, and percussion instruments. The volume falls into five identifiable sections: 1–41, 42–72, 73–89, 90–106, and 107–150. The concluding psalm summarizes the style and purpose of hymn singing. Because the poems remain true to human emotion, the collection is one of the most widely read and memorized compendia of world scripture.

The sources of the Book of Psalms are a complex issue. Although King David did not compose all the songs, he wrote and/or collected many of them and is mentioned in seventy-three psalms. Others postdate his reign. Much of the anthology permeates the New Testament, in particular, the words and imagery of Jesus, and has served as a source of inspiration for art, drama, oratorio, songs, hymns, chorales, and adapted verse forms.

The style, motivation, and mood for the writings vary. The opening psalm honors the godly person and applies to the lives of the patriarchs, prophets, and Job. It coordinates with Psalm 11, a doxology; Psalm 15, a testimony to righteousness; Psalm 26, the prayer of the just; Psalm 89, a fifty-two-verse paean to the steadfast love of God; and with Psalms 90–92, songs that describe the facets of God's beneficence. Others on the topic of righteousness, especially Psalms 26, 27, and 116, list the attributes of the godly, notably integrity, loyalty, piety, and peace. A contrasting poem, Psalm 52, pictures the sinner.

The second psalm is a ceremonial hymn suitable for an anointing or crowning. To the future ruler, the psalmist advises in verses 10–11:

> Be wise now therefore, O ye kings:
>   be instructed, ye judges of the earth.
> Serve the Lord with fear,
>   and rejoice with trembling.

This motif, classed as a royal psalm, recurs in Psalms 21, 72, and 110. Similarly, Psalm 45 honors a royal wedding and exalts the warrior-king as a mighty, majestic ruler.

One class of psalms, notably 3, 7, 12, 13, 22, 25, 51, 55, 59, 61, 64, 70–71, 86, 109, 120, 123, and 140–143, cries out for succor and reclamation from loneliness, need, doubt, and terror. In childlike simplicity, Psalm 3:5 pictures David's trust in God: "I laid me down and slept; I awaked; for the Lord sustained me." It follows with the plea in verse 7, "Arise, O Lord; save me, O my God."

Psalm 51:20 specifically requests, "Create in me a clean heart, O God, and renew a right spirit within me," a favorite Bible verse of Sunday school teachers. Of similar import is Psalm 130, which opens with a *de profundis* (out of the depths), a graphic representation of the soul's humble state. The resounding hope and promise of redemption makes this a standard funeral passage and an element of the Catholic mass for the dead.

Psalms 4 and 5 are companion pieces intoned before sleep and upon awakening. The speaker considers sacrifices and trust important elements of daily life and upon retiring for rest. Psalm 4:8 declares, "I will both lay me down in peace, and sleep: for thou, Lord, only makest me dwell in safety." The pious sleeper arises and attunes the self anew to God, calling in Psalm 5:3,

> My voice shalt thou hear in the morning, O Lord;
>   in the morning will I direct my prayer unto thee,
>   and will look up.

The penitential psalms, beginning with Psalm 6, include 32, 38, 51, 102, 139, 143, and 151. With awareness of human frailty, in Psalm 6:2, the speaker admits:

> Have mercy upon me, O Lord;
>   for I am weak:
> O Lord, heal me;
>   for my bones are vexed.

Johannes Brahms reprised the description of human frailty and self-loathing from Psalm 39:6 in the *German Requiem*, which declares, "Verily mankind walketh in a vain show and his best state is altogether vanity." The Catholic church bases the doctrine of Original Sin in part on Psalm 51:5, which states, "Behold, I was shapen in iniquity; and in sin did my mother conceive me."

The eighth, nineteenth, and thirty-third psalms rejoice in God's rule of nature and honor his creation of humankind. The structure of Psalm 8 exemplifies the use of a repeated chorus in verses 1 and 9: "O Lord our Lord, how excellent is thy name in all the earth!" Similarly, Psalms 29 and 104 resound with praise for God's control of the earth, ocean, mountains, skies, and waters. Psalm 104:31 exclaims, "May the glory of the Lord endure forever; may the Lord be glad in his works!"

Acrostics mark the ends of lines in Psalms 9, 25, 34, 37, 111, 112, and 145, an example of the energetic, optimistic praise anthem. Another of the acrostic psalms, 119, is the longest biblical chapter, extending to 176 verses.

Psalm 10 displays the complex relationship between the trusting servant and the Lord. The poet acknowledges God's greatness, but questions how he can allow the wicked to prosper, a pervasive theme of Old Testament prophets. Graphic illustrations of the clever deceiver and the insidious murderer, like a skulking lion, crouched to spring on the unwary, precede a bold command in verse 12:

> Arise, O Lord;
>   O God, lift up thine hand:
>   forget not the humble.

Similarly, the psalmist cries out in panic in Psalm 22 that God abandons him, then reverts to stout praise. He demands vengeance in Psalm 28, begs for mercy in Psalm 31, and confesses sins in Psalm 32. Additional testimony to the hardships of the faithful occurs in Psalms 77 and 88.

Psalm 14 and its restatement, Psalm 53, are wisdom poems reminding the doubter that atheism is an abomination. Likewise, Psalm 36 depicts the sin of the self-deceiver and exalts God for protecting his own. Psalm 37 instructs the seeker in the steadfastness of the Almighty; Psalm 46:10 offers advice to the noisy denyer of deity to "Be still and know that I am God." A somber meditation on death in Psalm 49:17 warns that no one carries away glory after death. The next hymn urges:

> Call upon me in the day of trouble:
>   I will deliver thee,
>   and thou shalt glorify me [Psalm 50:15].

Additional philosophic musings color Psalms 8 and 90.

The psalmist offers a testimonial to trust in God in Psalm 16. In verse 11, he anticipates that

> [God] wilt show me the path of life:
>   in thy presence is fullness of joy:
>   at thy right hand there are pleasures for evermore.

The companion piece, Psalm 17, asks for guidance on the issue of vengeance. In verse 15, the speaker promises to observe God's actions. He declares, "I shall be satisfied, when I awake, with thy likeness." Other joyous personal affirmations of trust include Psalms 34, 40, 46, 56–58, 62–63, 73, 91, 116, 124, 129, and 131.

Psalms of singing and thanksgiving dot the collection, particularly 18, 30, 47, 48, 65–67, 85, 95–108, 111–113, 135, 136, 138, and 146–150. A war hymn, Psalm 18, pictures God as the mystical deliverer similar to Zeus or Poseidon—a mythic earth shaker, who expels smoke from his nostrils and fire from his mouth before flying with the wind to his dark lair, thundering into the heavens, and raining hailstones and embers on the ungodly. In joy at rescue, the psalmist exults in verse 46,

> The Lord liveth;
>   and blessed be my rock;
>   and let the God of my salvation be exalted.

Psalm 20:7 contrasts heathen and righteous warriors:

> Some trust in chariots,
>   and some in horses:
>   but we will remember the name of the Lord our God.

The most cited of the hymns, Psalm 23, is a common memory project for children and a favorite recitation at sickbeds and funerals. Prefiguring the New Testament concept of the Good Shepherd, it pictures salvation from the point of view of the lonely herder, who views God as a shepherd and guide of weak, dependent beings. Rising from green pastures are the terrors of the valley of death, a likely place for brigands to set upon the lone protector or for predators to leap on hapless sheep. The end of verse 4 is an unexpected shift from discussion of God's characteristics to direct address, "for thou art with me." The speaker enumerates the rewards to the blessed and pictures an eternal resting place in God's house.

Praise is the subject of Psalm 24, a processional antiphony suggesting David's rejoicing on the return of the ark to Jerusalem, and of Psalm 132, a commemoration of David's triumph. Praise also resounds in 9, 29, 33, 75, 92, 93, 95–100, 113–119, and 136, collectively known as theocratic psalms for their study of God's role in government.

Psalms 120–134 contain processional elements, which suggest their use for marches or pilgrimages. The favorite of this cycle, Psalm 121, promises in verse 1 to look up to the hills for aid; verse 7 prefigures the hereafter in the declaration, "The Lord shall preserve thee from all evil: he shall preserve thy soul."

Psalm 30 notes new strength after illness. Psalm 38 begs for forgiveness and admits in verse 7, "my loins are filled with a loathsome disease: and there is no soundness in my flesh." The metaphors point to psychosomatic illness resulting from an unsound conscience, a motif also powerful in Psalm 41:8. A greater testament of faith in Psalm 139 professes God's assurance, even to the backslider and sinner, and concludes, "When I awake, I am still with thee." A severe state of emotional distress in Psalm 69 raises a hint of emergency. Verse 21 anticipates Jesus's crucifixion with images of inappropriate food and drink: "They gave me gall for my meat; and in my thirst they gave me vinegar to drink."

A model of the warrior's faith, Psalm 35 employs martial images to express joy in salvation. Likewise, Psalm 44:6–7 declares:

> For I will not trust in my bow,
>   neither shall my sword save me.
> But thou hast saved us from our enemies,
>   and hast put them to shame that hated us.

Additional martial imagery permeates Psalms 60, 68, 76, 144.

Psalms 42, 43, and 91 state a longing for home. More

mournful is Psalm 137, which opens with a reminder of the Babylonian exile, where "we sat down, yes, we wept, when we remembered Zion."

A direct connection with history occurs in Psalm 74, a lament for the Temple's destruction. In verses 6–7, the psalmist witnesses how "they break down the carved wood thereof at once with axes and hammers" and mourns the desecration of God's house. A more general summary of history occurs in Psalm 78, which opens on Jacob's revelation, and in Psalms 79–81, 83, 87, 89, 114, 115, and 137, which contemplate the hardships of God's chosen people. Psalms 133 and 134 single out the unified nation of Zion and the Temple guard.

Psalm 83 focuses on the nature of justice and pleads in verses 3–4:

> Defend the poor and fatherless:
>   do justice to the afflicted and needy.
> Deliver the poor and needy:
>   rid them out of the hand of the wicked.

Similarly, Psalms 94 and 109 testify to God's justice, mercy, and comfort to the afflicted.

Psalm 84, opening with "How lovely is thy dwelling place," is often the featured recitation or anthem at the dedication of a worship center. The words appear in one of the frequently excerpted anthems from Johannes Brahms's *German Requiem*.

Psalm 109 displays the psalmist's penchant for parallel construction. A similar psalm, 150, concludes the collection with parallel images of music making in praise of the Lord. It ends with an upbeat call — "Let everything that breathes praise the Lord! Praise the Lord!" Such repeated elements are a familiar teaching strategy, a method that the preacher or evangelist relies on to impress upon an audience a simple but crucial theme.

PROVERBS

A companion to Psalms, the Book of Proverbs is a compact library of 900 aphorisms, admonitions, and exhortations in nine anthological collections that serve as a single textbook on wisdom. The title names a literary form that serves as classroom fodder for the teacher of the young. In the words of novelist Charles Johnson, Proverbs is "that richly detailed, many-splendored map ... a two-millennium-old blue-print for the staggering challenge of living a truly *civilized* life" (Johnson 1999, vii–viii). He continues: "Culture, we realize after reading *Proverbs*, is an on-going project. We are not born with culture. Or wisdom. And both are but *one* generation deep."

Just as David receives credit for composing and anthologizing the Psalms, his son Solomon, the wise judge, is extolled as the expounder of the Bible's chief wisdom book. However, internal evidence suggests that the book reflects events and themes extending over eight centuries, concluding in 180 B.C.E. The backbone of this cycle of oral teachings is pragmatism — wisdom grounded in good sense and in prevailing attitudes toward justice, morality, character, and right thinking.

The author of the first collection, addressing remarks to "my son," extends no opportunity for equivocation. The litany of terse axioms of truth and righteousness forces the reader to choose good conduct over evil, reason over folly. The reward for a wise choice is happiness and a mature satisfaction that all works out for the best. To the foolish, the recompense for imprudence is discontent, a foul reputation, destruction of family, even an early grave.

The groupings that form the whole are identifiable by purpose, several by geographic source, one by the author's gender, and three by author or editor's name. Collection 1, Proverbs 1:1–9:18, is an introduction to the anthology that pictures wisdom as the owner of a house built on seven columns, which are chapters 2–7, broken down into seven units of twenty-two verses each. Collection 2, Proverbs 10:1–22:16, is a mass of 375 proverbs of Solomon composed in antithetic form for presentation at the royal court at Jerusalem. Collection 3, Proverbs 22:17–24:22, is a compilation of strophes composed with the direct, personal tone of a mentor to a neophyte, perhaps drawn from a reading of the Egyptian compendium *The Teaching of Amenemope* (ca. 1300 B.C.E.) edited at Abydos. Collection 4, Proverbs 24:23–34, is a short list from an unidentifiable ethicist. Collection 5, Proverbs 25:1–29:27, is a second Solomonic text by King Hezekiah of Judah, a religious reformer of the early seventh century B.C.E. Collection 6, Proverbs 30:1–14, is a short segment from an unknown Arabic source. Collection 7, Proverbs 30:15–33, is an independent text from an ancient source that organizes thoughts by an internal enumeration made by an unknown, Agur, son of Jakeh of Massa, an Arabian tribe. Collection 8, Proverbs 31:1–9, is a rare inclusion of a woman's advice to her son, Lamuel, marked by the Aramaisms of an Ishmaelite tribe from northern Arabia. Collection 9, Proverbs 31:10–31, is an acrostic poem of twenty-two verses beginning with the letters of the Hebrew alphabet.

Chapter 1 opens with an all-encompassing statement of didactic purpose and grounds the list of advice with verse 7, "The fear of the Lord is the beginning of knowledge," an assertion that reflects the attitude of Moses and the prophets toward human imperfection. Subsequent stand-alone verses spool out into a series of commands from parent to son or paternalistic instructor to pupil. Although the philosophy is overt, the imagery often resorts to subtle pairings, for example, Proverbs 3:15–18, which describes wisdom as the Greek Sophia, a personified feminine attribute worth desiring, pursuing, and embracing.

The source of much sage advice is folk wisdom, derived from hard-learned lessons, as is the case with Proverbs 3:28–32, a series of verses affirming neighborliness and choice of friends. Similarly homespun, Proverbs 5 contrasts the danger of promiscuity and the reward of a wholesome marital relationship. In a simplistic warning about adultery, verse 15 advises, "Drink waters out of thine own cistern, and running waters out of thine own well." Verse 20, which advocates avoiding strange women, suggests the Hebrew abhorrence of consorting with alien, idol-worshiping prostitutes.

Like Aesop's fable about the thrifty ant and the sluggard grasshopper, Proverbs 6:6–11 promotes hard work and anticipation of future needs. A series of character-building verses in Proverbs 6:16–19 enumerates common faults—haughtiness, violence, deceit, falsehood, and fractiousness. Chapter 8 repeats the vision of Sophia as a woman who calls out to men. In verses 18–21, she proclaims:

> Riches and honor are with me,
>   enduring wealth and prosperity.
> My fruit is better than gold, even fine gold,
>   and my yield than choice silver.
> I walk in the way of righteousness,
>   In the paths of justice,
>   endowing with wealth those who love me,
>   and filling their treasuries.

Verses 22–31 declare that wisdom existed before creation, when Sophia guided God in the creation of the earth, heavens, and seas. The final verses contrast life urges with the death urge, which results from disobedience to God and violation of conscience.

Chapters 10–22, identified as proverbs originated by Solomon, express separate adages intended to apply to specific needs. For example, Proverbs 13:20 warns the wise not to select fools for companions. On another topic, Proverbs 14:30 advocates serenity over ungoverned passion. One of the most cited verses, Proverbs 16:18, states, "Pride goeth before destruction and an haughty spirit before a fall." Chapter 20 classifies wine as a mocker and disdains deceit, gossip, and disrespect of parents. When the wise apply the sum of these, they acquire a strength of character that encompasses all aspects of outlook, deportment, and decision making.

The style of Proverbs displays poetic sophistication. For example, chapter 23:29 allies six rhetorical questions about troubles preceding a single cause, indulgence in wine. The author admonishes the tippler in verses 33–34:

> Your eyes will see strange things,
>   and your mind utter perverse things.
> You will be like one who lies down
>   in the midst of the seas,
>   like one who lies on the top of a mast.

Other verses create word pictures of honey in the comb, gray hairs, roaring lion, limbs cloaked in rags, and a savory meal laced with herbs.

The schoolmaster's delivery relaxes in chapters 25–29 after an introduction establishing them as a collection of Solomon's proverbs made by Hezekiah. One salient bit of advice concerns treatment of an enemy. The text of Proverbs 25:22 urges offering the foe food and drink, a surprise treat that will "heap coals of fire upon his head." Subsequent verses reject boasting and extol friendship. Chapter 30 incorporates adages concerning family life and humility, a compilation of the unidentified Agur.

Contrasting earlier diatribes against wily, unprincipled females, the lyric picture of the virtuous woman in Proverbs 31:10–31 sets up the paradigm of the ideal wife. The key to her success is a combination of thrift, hard work, persistence, and strength. She is the multitalented farm wife who handles property effectively, plants fruit for the future, and puts her hand to the perennial fiber work of women, symbolized by the distaff and spindle. The virtues that set her above others include charity, wise teachings, and kindness. For these qualities, in verse 28, she earns the title of "blessed" from husband and offspring.

JOB

A revered morality tale of trial by torment, the Book of Job presents one man's test of faith. Set in patriarchal times among a pastoral people, the account, drawn in part from Mesopotamian folklore, is traditionally attributed to Moses. Because of irregularities in the text and obvious interpolations of prologue, epilogue, and speeches, the final book appears to be of much later composition. Scholars suggest 400 B.C.E. for the finished framework story, which has inspired authors Mark Twain and H. G. Wells, the poet Robert Frost, and dramatist Archibald MacLeish, author of the morality play *J. B.*

The story is both uplifting and troubling. Chapter 1 introduces Job of Uz with standard hyperbole. Above the example of his contemporaries, he is a righteous, godly man devoid of faults. His ample livestock and stable of servants make him a great man in the east, a wealthy sheikh, and the father of ten children. When Satan, the universal trickster, appears in heaven in verse 6, he challenges God to test Job's faith. The response is a problematic shift in precedent — God allows Satan to control Job's future.

Job's troubles drop on him in the span of a day. They begin in verse 13, when enemies kill his servants and steal his plow animals, his sheep burn in a mysterious fire from heaven, Chaldeans raid his camels, and only one messenger survives to bear news of each episode. While he stands before Job, a fourth messenger reports that the house collapsed on Job's eldest son's family. Job begins a series of ceremonial mournings, followed by worship and praise of God. The statement of his belief in verse 21 characterizes his humility: "Naked I came from my mother's womb and naked shall I return; the Lord gave, and the Lord has taken away; blessed be the name of the Lord." The words recur in history and literature to mark personal losses and catastrophes.

After a second confrontation between Satan and God, Job contracts sores. His disloyal wife rails at him. His friends Eliphaz, Bildad, and Zophar comfort him for a week without speaking a word. In chapter 3, Job breaks the silence to lament that he was ever born. He ponders the afterlife in Sheol and concludes, "I was not in safety, neither had I rest, neither was I quiet; yet trouble came" (Job 3:26). Three rounds of debate flesh out the text. Chapter 4 applies the deuteronomic formula and its corollary — evil befalls those who deserve it and prosperity is a sign of goodness. Eliphaz suggests that Job rejoice in the punishment of the wicked and reflect on God's gifts to his family. Job replies that God has singled him out for suffering. In Job 7:21, he begs for an end to the trials and vows, "For now shall I sleep in the dust; and thou shalt seek me in the morning, but I shall not be."

The debate continues with discussions of God's attitude toward the good and the wicked. Zophar, who believes that only the evil suffer, remains convinced that Job is concealing some vile fault or shortcoming. Job's elegiac response is philosophic:

> Man that is born of woman is of few days,
>   and full of trouble.
> He comes forth like a flower,
>   and is cut down;
>   he fleeth also as a shadow,
>   and continueth not [Job 14:1–2].

As adamant as Zophar, Job holds to a belief that God will vindicate him.

A second round of arguments begins in chapter 15, with Job declaring his faith in God. After the third round, beginning in chapter 22, Job presents a lengthy discourse in chapters 26–31. Chapter 26:12–13 offers a lyric summary of God's creation, when

> He divideth the sea with his power,
>   and by his understanding
>   he smiteth through the proud.
> By his spirit he hath garnished the heavens;
>   his hand hath formed the crooked serpent.

In Job's estimation, God is beyond human understanding. Chapter 28:12–28 is a paean to wisdom, a treasure more precious than gold or silver, coral or pearls. The poem concludes with the wisdom of the Book of Proverbs, that wisdom begins with "the fear of the Lord." After Elihu enters the discussion in chapter 32, he alters the men's thinking toward a new direction, that suffering cleanses and refines the spirit. In Elihu's words in Job 37:21, "And now men see not the bright light which is in the clouds: but the wind passeth, and cleanseth them."

The interruption of the whirlwind in chapter 38 imposes God's will on Job in a mystic discourse composed of rhetorical questions about creation:

> Where was thou when I laid the foundations of the Earth?
>   declare, if thou has understanding.
> Who hath laid the measure thereof, if thou knowest?
>   or who hath stretched the line upon it?
> Whereupon are the foundations thereof fastened?
>   or who laid the corner stone thereof [Job 38:4–6].

Healed of his affliction, Job repents of his doubts in Job 42:1–6. God rebukes Eliphaz, Bildad, and Zophar for false counsel and doubles Job's fortunes. The reestablishment of Job's family concludes with a suitable death for the elderly believer after a long, eventful life.

SONG OF SONGS

Read annually at Pesach (Passover), the book entitled Song of Songs, alternately known as the Song of Solomon or Canticle of Canticles, takes the form of a pastoral prothelamium, a skillfully worded wedding hymn honoring Solomon's marriage to one of many wives. Suited to successive readings during week-long nuptials, the carnal, mystic nature of its poesy and the frankness of its male-female attraction disturbs puritanical rabbis and ministers, who prefer to think of the writing as an allegory of God's covenantal love for the Jews or, in the case of Christian apologists, God's alliance with Holy Mother Church. Attempts at literal understanding have moved church legalists to ban extraorthodox interpretations.

The enigmatic narrative binding the passion-charged utterances describes a female herder, tanned and comely, who loves a Shulamite shepherd. According to chapter 1:6, because her brothers intrude and force her from lea to vineyard, she languishes without her beloved. In chapter 2:2, the monarch, enthralled by her stunning beauty, calls the shepherdess a "lily among thorns" and entices her with his prestige and wealth. Bereft of her sweetheart, in chapter 3:1, she suffers sleepless nights and fruitlessly calls to him from her bed. Court women, no doubt jealous of her pure loveliness, accuse the shepherdess of betraying true love. Because she lives in visions and imagined dialogue with her shepherd love, the king must send her back to the pasture to the lowly male who is his rival. The chapter closes with a grand display of Solomon's wealth and might, which occupy a sphere far removed from the country girl and her love.

Parallel encomia in chapters 4 and 5 depict love from opposite points of view — man for maid and she for him. Unabashedly physical and promising an evening tryst, the passages substitute rich oriental imagery for anatomical terms. In chapter 4:16, an apostrophe to the wind asks it to "blow upon my garden, that the spices thereof may flow out. Let my beloved come to his garden, and eat his pleasant fruits," a honeyed reference to their anticipated lovemaking. In chapter 5, the dream filters in and out, leaving the dreamer unsatisfied. To Solomon's harem, the shepherdess presents an idealized picture of the man for whom she yearns. In desolation, the shepherd begs his Shulamite dove to return.

Court drama reaches its height in the dialogue of chapter 7:1–9, where the king, with embroidered endearments, presses the maid for intimacy. In verse 10, she steadfastly declares, "I am my beloved's and his desire is for me." Imagery turns to architecture, a safe retreat from carnality. Her brothers, who have worried that their little sister might give up being a stoic wall and become a compliant door, threaten to immure her in chapter 8:8–9. With justification, she exults in chapter 8:10, "I was a wall, and my breasts were like towers." Content that she weathers a trying time, she brings her lover peace.

Ruth

A serene hero story, the Book of Ruth is a favorite short idyll. The quiet grace of the narrative is an effective break from the pulsing brutality and blatant nationalism of previous war stories. It follows the Book of Judges chronologically and shifts from pro–Israel literature to a gentle story of love and loyalty, a masterful biography that dates to 1100 B.C.E. Composed like a protest novel, the poetic story of Ruth selects as a heroine a Moabite woman born among detested aliens. Chapter 1 covers the exposition of Ruth's marriage to a Hebrew, her widowhood, and her decision to live in Judah with Naomi, her mother-in-law. Chapters 2:1–4:12 reveal the courtship of Boaz. Chapters 4:13–22 explore the family's link to King David. Historians place the composition in the post-exilic period and express its purpose as a balance to the decrees of Ezra and Nehemiah that Hebrews spurn pagan maids and marry within their culture and faith.

The story, read annually in June at the Jewish festival of Pentecost, begins in travail with a famine, which causes Elimelech and Naomi to travel from Bethlehem to Moab in Syria. Their sons marry local women — Ruth and Orpah. After the death of Naomi's husband and sons, she returns to Judah with her daughters-in-law. The most memorable line of chapter 1 is Ruth's profession of devotion in verses 16–17:

> Intreat me not to leave thee,
>   or to return from following after thee:
>   for whither thou goest, I will go,
>   and whither thou lodgest I will lodge;
>   thy people shall be my people,
>   and thy god my god.
> Where thou diest, will I die,
>   and there will I be buried:
>   the Lord do so to me, and more also,
>   if ought but death part thee and me.

This winsome pledge of faith until death has undergone a transformation into a vow of bride and groom pledged at the altar.

The return of the unprotected women to Judah places them at the mercy of a patriarchal society, which countenances gleaning as a method of feeding the poor. Naomi sends Ruth to scavenge grain in the barley fields. Deliberately, Ruth chooses the land of Boaz, Naomi's elderly kinsman by marriage. Boaz learns of her plight and declares,

> The Lord recompense thy work,
>   and a full reward be given thee
> of the Lord God of Israel,
>   under whose wings thou art come to trust [Ruth 2:12].

The chemistry between Boaz and Ruth results in a marital bond. After clearing the union with relatives according to custom in chapter 4, Boaz marries Ruth, the mother of Obed, grandmother of Jesse, and great-grandmother of David. The tie to Bethlehem and David is fortuitous to Christians, whose messiah was born to the house of David.

Lamentations

Read annually in synagogues at the Fast of the Ninth of Av (or Ab) in August, the Lamentations of Jeremiah is a five-book elegy attributed to the prophet upon the destruction of Jerusalem in 586 B.C.E. The poignant text bears little resemblance to the prophet Jeremiah's oratory and characteristic sentence structure, particularly the imaginative use of acrostics in the first four chapters, which display the twenty-two letters of the Hebrew alphabet. A more likely author would be a contemporary who lived through the same chaotic era. The focus is suffering and an unanswered plea for God's intercession and forgiveness of his people's waywardness.

The first book bewails the desolation of Jerusalem, which the speaker likens to a widow and vassal. The Judean exile and subsequent enslavement precipitated invasion of the sanctuary, famine, and despair. The speaker urges:

Look, O Lord, and see!
With whom hast thou dealt thus?
Should women eat their offspring,
  the children of their tender care?
Should priest and prophet be slain
  in the sanctuary of the Lord? [Lamentations 2:20].

The author cries out from personal grief and wails, "My soul is bereft of peace, I have forgotten what happiness is" (Lamentations 3:17).

The drama of a people overrun by insurgents parallels Virgil's descriptions of the fall of Troy to the Greeks in the *Aeneid*. Lamentations 4:15 expresses the people's urgency to "depart, depart, touch not." The text closes with a plea to God to pity Judah's humiliation and the loss of its heritage to strangers. The multiple horrors of rape, torture, enforced child labor, and harassment of elders overwhelms the Jews with sorrow and longing for Mount Zion, now the lair of jackals. Their only hope lies in restoration to God's care.

ECCLESIASTES

Read annually at the Jewish Festival of Tabernacles in September, Ecclesiastes earns the dubious distinction of being the Bible's most somber wisdom lore. Attributed to the wise Solomon, Jerusalem's judicial king, it takes its title from the Greek translation of the Hebrew *qoheleth* (preacher). Its diction and Persian terms place it after 300 B.C.E. In the first two verses of chapter 1, the first-person exhorter, identifying himself as David's son, warns, "Vanity of vanities. All is vanity." Emphasis on the cycles of nature contrasts with the brief human lifespan. The author mourns a sorry state that perpetuates humanity's inherent mistakes.

Speaking in rhythmic parallels, the third chapter, usually referred to as "To Everything There Is a Season," is often excerpted as a poem about balance within the human condition. It moves from abstraction to concrete image with

a time to seek, a time to lose;
a time to keep, a time to cast away;
a time to rend, and a time to sew [Ecclesiastes 3:6–7].

The times for birthing and dying, planting and harvest, killing and curing, and razing and construction cover the expanse of earthly activities. The humanistic touches of contrasting actions — embracing, seeking, possessing, tearing, repairing, speaking, and remaining silent — conclude in verse 8 with two antitheses, love and hate and war and peace.

Like the speaker of Proverbs, the wise voice of Ecclesiastes directs the young to make the most of pre-adulthood. Chapters 5–6 warn of the inconstancy of money

and business success. The prophet advises the worker to live for satisfaction rather than hope of security. He moves into existential philosophy in chapters 7–9 with a reminder that death is a part of life and that brevity of life compels each person to enjoy life while it lasts, an anticipation of the Roman concept of *carpe diem* (sieze the day), as stated in book II of Horace's *Odes* (23 B.C.E.).

Following two loosely constructed chapters of pragmatic adages on various aspects of wisdom and folly, a coda, chapter 12, instructs the neophyte to revere the Creator from childhood on. A recreation of mourning rises to one of the most lyric passages on death:

The almond tree blossoms,
  the grasshopper drags itself along and desire fails;
  because man goes to his eternal home,
  and the mourners go about the streets;
  before the silver cord is snapped,
  or the golden bowl is broken,
  or the pitcher is broken at the fountain,
  or the wheel broken at the cistern,
  and the dust returns to the earth as it was,
  and the spirit returns to God who gave it [Ecclesiastes 12:5–8].

Verse 9 describes the preacher's task as modeling prudence, teaching knowledge, and carefully collecting and studying wise sayings as models for behavior.

ESTHER

The legend of Esther, read annually in March at the Jewish festival of Purim, is alternately referred to as the Megillah, a singular form of the Hebrew for "scroll." According to Esther 10:2, the story derives from the Book of Chronicles of the Kings of Media and Persia. Public reading of this complex Cinderella story has become a traditional audience participation event, with cheers for the heroine and *greggers* (noisemakers) sounding at the mention of the tyrannic Jew-killer, Haman, to expunge his name from history. Spirited recitations preface folk festivals, joyous fairs, skits, dress-up balls, and gift giving. Artists and musicians have enlarged on Esther's importance with portraits and arias, including Georg Friedrich Handel's oratorio *Esther*.

The historical Esther became queen of Persia in 480 B.C.E. during the Babylonian captivity and, supported by her uncle Mordecai, triumphed over a villainous anti–Semite. The composition of her story appears to coincide with the oppressive rule of the Syrian autocrat Antiochus IV Epiphanes from 175 to 163 B.C.E. or of the Roman empire. Esther's story opens in the final days of the reign of King Ahasureus at Shushan, where public outcry forces the king to dethrone and divorce Queen Vashti for disobeying his summons. After a royal study of maidens in outlying provinces, Esther, an orphan reared by Morde-cai, catches the king's eye and favor. In Esther 2:17, the author states that, because "the king loved Esther above all the women," she earns his favor above all the virgins he examines. He crowns her in Vashti's place. His largess spills over to the region as he "[grants] a remission of taxes to the provinces, and [gives] gifts with royal liberality" (Esther 2:18).

The haughty courtier Haman is a festering malcontent. He despises the proud bearing of Mordecai, who had gone unheralded and unrewarded for saving Ahasureus from an assassination plot. In chapter 3, Haman decides to defame all Jews to turn the king against their foreign ways. To sweeten the plan, he offers 10,000 silver talents to the treasury. At the king's consent, Haman posts letters that Jews must die on the twelfth of the month of Adar. The result concludes verse 15 with a contrast of high with low: "And the king and Haman sat down to drink; but the city Shushan was perplexed."

In chapter 4, Mordecai and the Jewish community grieve for the coming slaughter. When Esther learns of the planned annihilation of her people, she fasts and dresses with care before entering the king's inner court, a dangerous mission for one who has no appointment for an audience. The sudden appearance does not anger the king:

> And it was so, when the king saw Esther the queen
>   standing in the court,
>   that she obtained favour in his sight:
>   and the king held out to Esther the golden scepter
>   that was in his hand.
> So Esther drew near
>   and touched the top of the scepter [Esther 5:2].

Past the first hurdle, she invites Haman and the king to a wine-tasting banquet, followed by a second night of feasting. Between feasts, in Esther 5:14, Haman orders the building of a gallows on which to hang Mordecai.

Chance plays a key role in Esther's destiny. By coincidence, Ahasureus reads the state chronicle, which indicates the intervention of Mordecai against two potential regicides. This fortuitous perusal of history produces an unexpected twist in Haman's plans: The king orders him to honor Mordecai with royal dress, a crown, and a public procession on horseback. At the second banquet in Esther 7:3, the queen begs:

> If I have found favour in thy sight, O king,
>   and if it please the king,
>   let my life be given me at my petition,
>   and my people at my request.

She declares her people sold "to be destroyed, to be slain, and to be annihilated" and names Haman as the plotter of genocide (Esther 7:4).

The story ends with Ahasureus's protection of his wife. The king withdraws to ponder Haman's wickedness. On returning, he sees the villain fawning over Esther and asks, "Will he force the queen also before me in the house?" (Esther 7:8). In retaliation for Haman's impropriety to the royal wife, Ahasureus immediately orders a bit of poetic justice — hanging on Haman's own gallows. The story ends with the Jews slaying 500 of their enemies and, with the king's permission, Haman's ten sons. The Jews celebrate last-minute salvation on the fourteenth of Adar, now declared a religious holiday to be commemorated henceforth by all Jews.

DANIEL

An early apocalypse, the romanticized hero story of Daniel (or Dan'el) and his three companions begins with six chapters of biography and continues in chapters 7–12 with his adventures following four dream visions. Composed in Aramaic and evolved from several sources, the Daniel cycle characterizes him as a nobleman among the exiles from Judah. A royal counselor in Babylon as Joseph was in Egypt, in 605 B.C.E., Daniel advises Belshazzar, successor of Nebuchadnezzar, and continues as statesman and minister under Darius and Cyrus. The series inspired courage during the reign of Antiochus IV Epiphanes, a Syrian tyrant, during the second century B.C.E., when foreign influence prevailed on the Hebrews to forgo scriptural dietary laws.

A favorite episode of Daniel lore begins in his youth in chapter 2 with the troubling dreams of Nebuchadnezzar. At the failure of Chaldean astrologers and soothsayers to interpret the dream, the king has them executed. Daniel reports a vision to him and describes the particulars of the dream of a huge statue:

> The head of this image was of fine gold,
>   its breast and arms of silver,
>   its belly and thighs of bronze,
>   its legs of iron,
>   its feet partly of iron and partly of clay [Daniel 2:32–33].

He interprets the dream politically as a succession of four Mediterranean empires (Babylonian, Persian, Greek, and Roman), concluding with a divided kingdom. Amazed at the specificity of Daniel's interpretation, Nebuchadnezzar abases himself before Daniel and, in verse 47, proclaims Israel's God a "revealer of mysteries." In payment, the king names Daniel a provincial ruler and prefect of scholars and appoints Shadrach, Meshach, and Abednego as court officials.

Chapter 3, the story of Daniel and the fiery furnace, is a favorite among artists and in anthologies of Bible stories for children. It begins with Nebuchadnezzar's golden image on the plain of Dura and a proclamation that forces all within hearing distance of ritual music to fall down and worship. Some Chaldeans complain that the newly appointed Jewish court officials ignore the command. When the king questions the trio, they declare God sufficient against any furnace. In a touch of hyperbole common to hero stories, the king stokes the furnace seven times hotter than usual and has the abstainers bound and cast into the flames. The furnace tenders die from the heat, but the three Jewish youths survive along with a mysterious fourth man, possibly the angel Gabriel. A clutch of rulers, magistrates, and royal counselors gather to gape at the men. In wonder, the king himself ventures near the glowing furnace door and calls out:

> Shadrach, Meshach, and Abednego,
>   servants of the Most High God,
>   come forth, and come here! [Daniel 3:26].

The drama ends with Nebuchadnezzar exempting from the edict all worshipers of the Jewish God.

After a scenario in which Nebuchadnezzar suffers insanity, a separate episode in chapter 5 tells of a royal banquet of 539 B.C.E. featuring a terrible blasphemy — heathens and their concubines dining from consecrated vessels of gold and silver robbed from the Temple at Jerusalem. Before the startled Belshazzar, a disembodied male hand writes, "mene mene tekel upharsin" on the wall. The king promises royal purple, a chain of gold, and a share of the kingdom to any of his enchanters and astrologers who can interpret the writing. As one would anticipate in a hero story, the interpreters fail. When Daniel is escorted before the king, he correctly translates the Aramaic terms to mean "number, number, weigh, and divide" and predicts that Babylon will fall to the Medes and Persians. That night, Persian insurgents slay Belshazzar, and Darius seizes his realm.

The great test of Israel's God comes in chapter 6, in which Daniel's prestige raises jealousy among Darius's satraps. They trick the king into issuing an interdiction against propitiating any God for thirty days. When Daniel continues openly worshiping God three times a day, the plotters report him to Darius. The king has Daniel sealed in the lions' den. After a sleepless night, he finds Daniel alive. In verse 22, Daniel explains:

> My god sent his angel and shut the lions' mouths,
>   and they have not hurt me,
>   because I was found blameless before him;
>   and also before you, O king, I have done no wrong.

After his release, Darius orders the governors and their families cast to the lions, which quickly reduce them to bone fragments. Verse 26 bursts into a praise anthem acknowledging "the living god, enduring forever."

The Book of Daniel closes with four visions aswirl with mythic and real animals and numerology. Chapters 10–11 depict Daniel ending a fast and envisioning a glorious figure:

> His body was like beryl,
>   his face like flaming torches,
>   his arms and legs like the gleam of burnished bronze,
>   and the sound of his words like the noise of a multitude
>   [Daniel 10:6].

The figure is the antithesis of the statue with clay feet. Christians connect the divine being with Christ.

The foreshadowing of Christian philosophy permeates the last of the text. Daniel 12:2–3 introduces a shift in religious tenets by predicting resurrection of the dead:

> And many of those who sleep in the dust of the earth shall
>   awake,
>   some to everlasting life,
>   and some to shame and everlasting contempt.
> And those who are wise
>   shall shine like the brightness of the firmament;
>   and those who turn many to righteousness,
>   like the stars for ever and ever.

The celestial phrasing anticipates the concept of heaven and hell and an apocalypse, for which Daniel's words await, sealed in his book.

EZRA

Ezra is the book of an intellectual giant who was dispatched to Judah in 458 B.C.E. He was a descendant of Aaron and a follower of the prophet Jeremiah. Ezra's roles as a religious zealot, reformer, theologian, and canonizer of Israelite scripture precede his transformation of Judaism into a state religion. The resurgence of Israel begins under Cyrus, the Persian monarch who came under Jeremiah's influence. Cyrus determines to reestablish the Temple at Jerusalem and to manumit the Jews with money, goods, and pack animals to facilitate their return. He proclaims in Ezra 1:3:

> Who is there among you of all the people?
>   his god be with him,
>   and let him go up to Jerusalem,
>   which is in Judah,
>   and build the house of the Lord God of Israel,
>   he is the God who is in Jerusalem.

Led by the chieftains of the houses of Judah and Benjamin along with priests and Levites, the people, enumerated by clan in chapter 2, return to Jerusalem bearing the holy vessels that Nebuchadnezzar's forces looted.

Chapter 3 details the painstaking reestablishment of temple ritual and the reconstruction of a foundation. In verse 12, recalling the first Temple, the elder Levites and chief priest weep and shout for joy. In chapter 4, Samaritans hinder the rebuilding into the reign of Darius. Restored to progress by the prophets Haggai and Zechariah in chapter 5, builders Zerubbabel and Jeshua get back to work and proclaim:

> We are the servants of the God of heaven unto wrath,
>   he gave them into the hand of Nebuchadnezzar
>   the king of Babylon, the Chaldean,
>   who destroyed this house,
>   and carried the people away into Babylon [Ezra 5:12].

They complete the project during Darius's sixth year on the throne of Persia, around 515 B.C.E. In celebration, at the end of chapter 6, the Jews observe the Passover, a historical landmark among their many deliverances from oppression.

In chapter 7, many years later under the aegis of King Artaxerxes, Ezra departs with a huge party of followers on a pilgrimage to Israel to study and disseminate Jewish law, which becomes state law. In chapter 9, he masterminds an ousting of foreign wives, who had brought God's punishment for breaking the commandments. Ezra prays:

> O Lord God of Israel, thou art righteous:
>   for we remain yet escaped, as it is the day:
>   behold, we are before thee in our trespasses:
>   for we cannot stand before thee because of this [Ezra 9:15].

Ezra's public repudiation of intermarriage with aliens and the children born to pagan women reinstates spiritual purity among the Jews.

Nehemiah

The Book of Nehemiah is a state history that the church leader Origen dubbed the "second Book of Ezra" around C.E. 250. The text draws on archival material for its composition, apparently completed around 424 B.C.E. After Nehemiah comes to power twenty years earlier, he leads the Jews in reforming Jerusalem's walls and resurrecting its civic greatness. Speaking in the first person of the depleted state of David's capital city, in Nehemiah 1:3, he weeps that "the wall of Jersalem also is broken down, and the gates thereof are burned with fire." After a period of fasting and prayer, he convinces Artaxerxes to allow a secret survey of the city. At chapter's end, Nehemiah encourages:

> The God of heaven, he will prosper us;
>   therefore we his servants will arise and build:
>   but ye have no portion, nor right nor memorial, in
>   Jerusalem [Nehemiah 2:20].

His differentiation between Jews and non–Jews recurs in modern times as a slogan hurled during Middle Eastern confrontations between Israelis and Palestinians.

The core of Nehemiah's text is a tribute to dedication to task, a theme that has buoyed Israel since its nationalization in 1948. In chapters 4–6, working day and night, armed laborers and their servants continue the project under threat of attack. In chapter 5, Nehemiah inveighs against usury and, in verse 13, calls on God to

> shake out every man from his house and from his labor
>   that performeth not his promise.
> So may he be shaken out and emptied.

In fifty-two days, the faithful finish the job, impressing detractors with the power of God and his followers.

The festal atmosphere of the book rises to a stately crescendo. In chapter 8, Nehemiah, the governor of Jerusalem, gathers the people at the Water Gate, where the priest Ezra climbs a wooden pulpit and reads from the Torah each morning. A team of interpreters explains holy law to the populace. In verse 14, they reinstitute the festival of Succoth, the Feast of Booths, after the example of Moses. The Levite priests join Nehemiah in a renewal of the covenant and, in chapter 12, a dedication of the city walls. The people return to pious observances, including a thanksgiving for first fruits, respect for the sabbath, and collection of tithes to support the Temple. Through a lottery, officials determine which Jews will inhabit and defend the holy city.

Chronicles

Called in Hebrew *Dibre Hayammim* (Events of the Times), the Book of Chronicles takes its current name from the Latin of Jerome's Vulgate heading *Liber Chronicorum* (Book of Chronicles). Although tradition states that Ezra and Nehemiah compiled the text around 450 B.C.E., shortly before Aramaic replaced Hebrew as the common language, the book appears to be the work of a priest. He restated archival material around 300 B.C.E., drawing on the Book of the Kings of Israel and Judah, Chronicles of Samuel the Seer, Chronicles of Nathan the Prophet, Commentary on the Book of Kings, and Chronicles of Gad the Seer.

The historical events summarized in Chronicles reprise David's dynasty as a pinnacle of Jewish history. To prove that Jews are God's chosen people, chapter 1 lists the Hebrew lineage from Adam and the patriarchs and concludes with the kings of Edom. Chapters 2–8 summarize the lineage of the Twelve Tribes of Israel: Leah's sons, Reuben, Simeon, Levi, Judah, Issachar, and Zebulun; the slave girl Bilhah's sons, Dan and Naphtali; Rachel's sons, Joseph and Benjamin; the servant Zilpah's sons, Gad and Asher.

The passage emphasizes the genealogies of Benjamin and Judah. Chapter 2:3–55 states the offspring of Judah. Chapters 3–4 align David's descendants, with chapter 4 returning to the royal line of Judah and concluding with Simeon's line in verses 24–43. Chapter 5 states the sons of Reuben, Israel's firstborn, followed by Gad's sons and Aaron's family. Levi's genealogy continues the listing in chapter 6 with strands of the families of Issachar, Asher, Naphtali, Levi, and Zebulun. Issachar's genealogy occupies chapter 7:1–5, with Benjamin's family line appearing in verses 6–12, Naphtali's in verses 13–29, and Asher's in verses 30–40. Benjamin's prolific line fills chapter 8.

The chronicler departs from abstractions to stress the particulars of a hard-won authority. Chapters 10–29 reprise David's rule after the deaths of Jonathan and his brothers Abinadab and Malchishua in battle against the Philistines and Saul's subsequent suicide by falling on his sword. The grisly dismemberment of Saul's remains serves as a warning, stated in I Chronicles 10:13:

> So Saul died for his transgression
>   which he committed against the Lord,
>   even against the word of the Lord,
>   which he kept not.

In contrast, David retrieves the ark and composes psalms honoring God and recalling Abraham's covenant with Yahweh. In chapter 17, the author recounts David's building of a permanent house for the ark, Israel's detailed census, and duties of the Levite priests. The narrative ends with the king's fervent prayer blessing God. I Chronicles 29 concludes with David passing succession to his son Solomon, whose name derives from the Hebrew for "peace." In verse 10, David prays, "Blessed be thou, Lord God of Israel our father, for ever and ever."

By ignoring ignoble events in the northern half of the divided kingdom, the chronicler magnifies the high points of Jewish history. Book 2 enlarges on Solomon's reign and the building of the Temple. In chapter 1:7, God appears to Solomon, causing him to pray for wisdom to judge the people. In verses 11–12, God makes a unique covenant with the king:

> Because this was in thine heart,
>   and thou hast not asked for riches, wealth, nor honour,
>   nor the life of thine enemies,
>   neither yet asked long life;
>   but has asked wisdom and knowledge for thyself,
>   that thou mayest judge my people…
> I will give thee riches, and wealth,
>   and honour,
>   such as none of the kings have had
>   that have been before thee,
>   neither shall there any after thee have the like.

The glories of the Temple and the king's wealth merit a visit from the queen of Sheba. In chapter 9, Solomon's brilliance and the splendor of his entourage so bedazzle the African visitor that she blesses his God, who obviously loves Israel. The chronicler glories in the great treasure that Solomon acquires, a return to the concept that God blesses the righteous with wealth.

Second Chronicles 10–36 summarize the reigns of Judah's kings. This section features Rehoboam's tenure, when the Davidic kingdom divides into Israel and Judah. The people's anger at Rehoboam forces him to mount his chariot and flee to Jerusalem. After war under the rule of King Abijah come the godly works of Asa and his son Jehoshaphat, a warrior-king who reappoints judges in Jerusalem from among the Levites. The didactic text stresses the power of God in repeatedly defending followers from attack. The chronicler summarizes in chapters 21–36 with these events:

chapter 21, King Jehoram's loss of control over Edom and Libnah and the institution of idolatry.

chapters 22–23, King Ahaziah's death during Jehu's purge and Athaliah's seizure of the throne, ostensibly for his infant son, Joash, the true heir.

chapter 24, Joash's benevolent reign and repair of the Temple before his moral deterioration and assassination.

chapter 25, Amaziah's defeat of Edom and establishment of heathen gods.

chapter 26, Uzziah's extension of territory to the Red Sea and his assumption of the role of priest. He falls to a sad state after contracting leprosy, a sign of inner defilement.

chapter 27, Jotham's temporal power, the annexation of Ammon, and the continued worship of alien gods.

chapter 28, the coming of God's punishment under Ahaz, a godless king.

chapters 29–32, Hezekiah's reform of Temple worship and sacrifices and the joyous celebration of the Passover, which had lapsed during Solomon's reign. Before his death, Hezekiah fends off Sennacherib's invasion and dies with honor.

chapter 33, Manasseh, the worst of Judah's monarchs, defiles the Temple and initiates human sacrifice. Although he experiences a conversion, it comes too late. His servants kill him in his quarters.

chapters 34–35, Josiah, Judah's reformer, restores the Passover once more. He falls in ill-advised combat against King Necho of Egypt.

chapter 36, Jehoahaz gives up his throne to Jehoiakim, the tool of the Egyptian crown.

After Nebuchadnezzar kidnaps him to Babylon and loots the Temple, Prince Jehoiachin rules fourteen weeks before abdicating in favor of his brother Zedekiah, during whose reign the kingdom falls to its lowest state after Nebuchadnezzar's invasion and burning of the Temple. The book ends in verses 22–23 with Cyrus's manumission of the Hebrews to rebuild the Temple, a statement that links directly to the opening lines of the Book of Ezra.

Chronology

The Torah, written between 1200 and 100 B.C.E., characterizes the rise of the Hebrews from a loose body of nomadic shepherds to a highly structured civilization. Significant events in the lives of Jews frame biblical history.

ca. 1950	Abram and Sarai arrive in Palestine.
ca. 1800	Joseph begins his sojourn in Egypt and the Israelites enter 550 years of enslavement.
1300–1100 B.C.E.	The feudal system gives way to monarchy.
1250 B.C.E.	Moses guides the Hebrew slaves from Egypt in a national resettlement known as the Exodus.
ca. 1210 B.C.E.	Joshua rises to greatness.
1200 B.C.E.	The Hebrews invade Canaan.
ca. 1120 B.C.E.	The Judges begin their rule.
1025–930 B.C.E.	The Hebrews establish a united monarchy.
ca. 1020 B.C.E.	Saul rises to greatness.
1000 B.C.E.	David is formally anointed as future king of Hebron.
993 B.C.E.	David ends tribalism by uniting the Hebrew clans and making Jerusalem a neutral capital.
960 B.C.E.	After putting down the rebellion of his son Absalom, David anoints Solomon as his successor and dies within the year.
950 B.C.E.	A Judean writer organizes historic events into a Hebrew epic.
931 B.C.E.	Rehoboam succeeds Solomon and initiates such bad government that he divides the kingdom his grandfather built.
930–722 B.C.E.	Subsequent changes affect the monarchy of northern Israel, concluding with Samaria's fall to Sargon II.
by 750 B.C.E.	A writer from Ephraim in northern Israel proposes an alternate version to the Judah text.
732 B.C.E.	Hoshea, Israel's last king, begins a ten-year rule.
722 B.C.E.	Judah enters a tenuous 140-year period.
716–687 B.C.E.	Hezekiah fortifies Jerusalem against Assyrian invaders.
622 B.C.E.	Josiah discovers a scroll of the law and institutes religious reform.
621 B.C.E.	The Book of Deuteronomy enters Temple use in Jerusalem after Hilkiah discovers it.
588 B.C.E.	Chaldeans under Nebuchadnezzar capture Jerusalem and raze the Temple.
586–538 B.C.E.	Babylonians rule the Jews.
538 B.C.E.	Medes and Persians under Cyrus rule the Jews as a commonwealth and return exiles to their Palestinian homeland.
515 B.C.E.	During Darius's reign, Zerubbabel rebuilds the Temple.
480 B.C.E.	Esther reigns as queen of Persia.
458 B.C.E.	Ezra is dispatched to Judah.
443 B.C.E.	Nehemiah and his work gangs rebuild Jerusalem's gates and walls.
397 B.C.E.	Malachi composes prophecy.
332 B.C.E.	Israel acquires Hellenistic kings.
246 B.C.E.	Ptolemy II Philadelphus initiates a translation of Hebrew scripture into the Greek Septuagint at Alexandria.
200 B.C.E.	Prophets enters the Hebrew canon.
167 B.C.E.	Antiochus Epiphanes outrages the Jews by dedicating the Temple to Zeus Olympius.
164 B.C.E.	Under Judah Maccabee, the Jews recover and purify the Temple and celebrate the first Hanukkah.
104 B.C.E.	Aristobulus becomes the first Hasmonean king.
63 B.C.E.	Israel suffers under Roman rule after Pompey colonizes Syria. Roman legions violate the Temple at Jerusalem.
30 B.C.E.	Augustus initiates the Roman Peace, which lasts until 180 C.E., uniting the Mediterranean world.
37 B.C.E.	Herod the Great supplants the Hasmonean dynasty.
ca. 4 B.C.E.	Mary gives birth to Jesus. Herod the Great dies.

Translation

The Torah originated in Hebrew, the traditional language of Jews. A small portion existed in Aramaic. When

Aramaic became the language of the eastern Mediterranean under Persian control, religious worthies had the Torah converted to Aramaic (also called Syriac from the northern Aramaic dialect). These versions, called Targumin or Targums (Translations), survived the original Torah scrolls, which were lost in the upheavals of antiquity. In 400 B.C.E., scholars completed a Samaritan Targum. After the conquests of Alexander the Great, Greek permeated the eastern Mediterranean. When the Greek language superseded Aramaic around 250 B.C.E., in the time of Ptolemy II Philadelphus, experts convened at Alexandria, Egypt, to make a new translation, the Greek Septuagint, abbreviated as the LXX. The tedious task of coordinating seventy-two scholars—six from each of the Twelve Tribes of Israel—extended the job until 150 B.C.E. Subsequent versions by Aquila, a Pontine Jew, and Symmachus, a translator of Hebrew into Greek, display questionable grammar and rhetoric. A Palestinian text of the period rendered into Greek by Theodotion of Ephesus presents a mechanical word-for-word recension.

A trend toward orthodoxy sent Palestinian and Babylonian Talmudic scholars back to the Torah's original Hebrew about C.E. 500. Locating and reworking the Hebrew text as a scriptural authority for the Jewish faith required centuries of toil at textural criticism. The method of examining oral traditions contained in the Masora required meticulous study of ancient Hebrew idiom and pronunciation. The resulting Masoretic Torah (or Hebrew Torah) received overwhelming acceptance in the 900s. Handwritten copies flourished in synagogues and libraries until printers issued the first paper copies after Johann Gutenberg invented movable type.

The Renaissance encouraged translations from ancient texts to modern European languages. In Lublin in 1616, Polish writer Jacob ben Isaac Ashkenazi converted Hebrew scripture into the Yiddish *Tz'enah u-Re'na*. Moses Mendelssohn's editions in High German anticipated the complete text of Gotthold Salomon in 1837. Isaac Leeser, a Sephardic rabbi who immigrated to Philadelphia, became the first translator to render a Jewish text in English. He issued a five-volume Hebrew and English version in 1845, which offered both texts on facing pages. He reduced the cumbrous translation to the *Twenty-Four Books of the Holy Scripture*, an English-only scripture issued in 1853 and embraced by English-speaking Jews as the standard version.

In the twentieth century, Abraham Harkavy revised Leeser's scripture by replacing obsolete diction and updating spelling. The following year, the Jewish Publication Society employed the cooperative model for a major project: they used the King James Bible and the British and American revised texts for the *Holy Scriptures According to the Masoretic Text*, edited by Max L. Margolis and published in 1917. A major twentieth-century rendering by philosopher Martin Buber and Franz Rosenzweig appeared in 1937 in Berlin and underwent revision in 1962. Also published in 1962 was the Jewish Publication Society's Torah, which employs bold typefaces and simplified language. For rhetorical structure, editors relied on the mid–tenth-century Arabic version of Gaon Saadye (or Saadiah) ben-Joseph, an Egyptian scholar who published a Hebrew dictionary. In 1985, a fresh vernacular Hebrew Bible, *Tanakh: The Holy Scriptures*, balanced idiomatic English with meticulous scholarship.

SOURCES: Alexander and Alexander 1982, Anderson 1966, Armstrong 1993, Asimov 1981, Bonchek 1996, Bono 1999, Cohn-Sherbok 1998, Comay 1974, Curtius 1953, Doctorow 1999, Eckstrom 1995, Frazier 1999, Gentz 1973, Grossman 1999, Johnson 1999, *Josephus: Complete Works* 1960, Larue 1968, Lessing 1999, May and Metzger 1962, Mays 1988, Metzger and Coogan 1993, *New Catholic Encyclopedia* 1967, Price 1925, Snodgrass 1998, Wigoder 1989.

Bible: New Testament Comprising the more influential books for the Christian faith, the New Testament was the work of Greek composers writing in *koine*, the pervasive vernacular language of eastern Mediterranean peasants. The text was originally known as the Euangelion (Evangel) and the Apostolos (Apostles), a clear division between the biography of Jesus and the acts of his apostles after his death and resurrection. First named around C.E. 200 by the Roman centurion Quintus Tertullian of Carthage, the New Testament collects early Christian history, beginning with the Synoptic Gospels, a four-sided view of the life and career of Jesus by four eyewitnesses—Matthew, Mark, Luke, and John.

Compilation of the New Testament was an exercise in negotiation. The only way the early church leaders could establish authorized versions of God's holy scripture as opposed to pious writings was to assemble holy works into categories, with canon or sacred works coming before all others for their sanctity and godly inspiration. In the middle of the second century, St. Justin the Martyr referred to the memoirs of the four evangelists—Matthew, Mark, Luke, and John—as *gospels*, meaning "good news." Around C.E. 188, Irenaeus espoused a tetramorph, the Quadriform Gospel revealed by God, which was favored by Hippolytus, Tertullian, Clement the Roman, Valentinus, and Titian.

Within decades, the four gospels topped a longer list of authorized books. Late in the second century, the Muratorian catalogue listed scrolls suitable for use in church. This canon added Paul's thirteen epistles, but excluded Hebrews, James, and III John and possibly I and II Peter. The Palestinian authority Eusebius, bishop of Caesarea, referred to a *homologoumena*, the universally agreed-upon sacred texts, which included the gospels, Paul's letters, Acts, and the disputed books of Hebrews, I Peter, and I John. Eusebius separated the remaining sacred writings into two classes—the questionable books of James, Jude, II Peter, II John, and III John; and the spurious works that imitated or violated traditional doctrine. Among these he listed Revelation as spurious. His definitive classifications prevailed over the next century.

The accepted list grew to twenty-seven books by the fourth century, when the Protestant canon took shape. It appeared in print as the New Testament in C.E. 367, when Athanasius, bishop of Alexandria, issued his *Epistula Festalis* (Festival Letter) designating the list as truly inspired wellsprings of salvation. Missing were the books of Barnabas, the Didache (ca. C.E. 110), and the Shepherd of Hermas (ca. C.E. 125), which never recovered status among church fathers. By C.E. 400, the canon received unofficial acceptance. It was generally approved in C.E. 525, when

Dionysius Exiguus set the birth of Jesus in December as C.E. 1, the opening of the Christian calendar. However, the list did not reach a vote for a millennium, until the Council of Trent in 1546, when the Protestant Reformation forced Roman Catholics to delineate their beliefs.

In the Christian canon, the arrangement opens with law and instruction contained in the five books of the Torah, which account for the importance of the Hebrews as God's chosen people and their beginnings and wanderings before settling in the Promised Land. To Roman Catholics and the Eastern Orthodox, the total extends to seven additional books known to Protestants as the Apocrypha and excluded from most Bibles or included as addenda. The largest of canon lists is the Ethiopic version. The smallest is the Samaritan Bible, containing only five books. Of these canon works, the Roman Catholic Bible maintains an idiosyncratic spelling.

Divisions of the Bible

Roman Catholic	Protestant	Eastern Orthodox	Ethiopic	Syriac (Nestorian)	Samaritan
Law and Instruction	*Law and Instruction*	*Law and Instruction*	*Law and Instruction*	*Law and Instruction*	*Law and Instruction*
Genesis	Genesis	Genesis	Genesis	Genesis	Genesis
Exodus	Exodus	Exodus	Exodus	Exodus	Exodus
Leviticus	Leviticus	Leviticus	Leviticus	Leviticus	Leviticus
Numbers	Numbers	Numbers			Numbers
Deuteronomy	Deuteronomy	Deuteronomy	Deuteronomy	Deuteronomy	Deuteronomy
Histories	*Histories*	*Histories*	*Histories*	*Histories*	
			Enoch	—	
			Jubilees	—	
Josue	Joshua	Joshua	Joshua	Joshua	
Judges	Judges	Judges	Judges	Judges	
Ruth	Ruth	—	Ruth	Ruth	
I Samuel	I Samuel	Samuel	I Samuel	I Samuel	
II Samuel	II Samuel	—	II Samuel	II Samuel	
I Kings	I Kings	Kings	I Kings	I Kings	
II Kings	II Kings	—	II Kings	II Kings	
I Chronicles	I Chronicles	Chronicles	I Chronicles	I Chronicles	
II Chronicles	II Chronicles	—	II Chronicles	II Chronicles	
I Esdras	Ezra	I Esdras	Ezra	Ezra	
II Esdras	—	II Esdras	—	—	
Nehemiah	Nehemiah	—	Nehemiah	Nehemiah	
			III Ezra	—	
			IV Ezra	IV Ezra	
Tobias	—	Tobit	Tobit	Tobit	
Judith	—	Judith	Judith	Judith	
Esther (and addenda)	Esther	Esther (and addenda)	Esther (and addenda)	—	
—	—	Wisdom of Solomon	—	—	
I Maccabees	—	I Maccabees	I Maccabees	I Maccabees	
II Maccabees	—	II Maccabees	II Maccabees	II Maccabees	
—	—	—	III Maccabees	III Maccabees	
—	—	—	—	IV Maccabees	
Wisdom Books	*Wisdom Books*	*Wisdom Books*	*Wisdom Books*	*Wisdom Books*	
Job	Job	Job	Job	Job	
Psalms	Psalms	Psalms	Psalms (plus Psalm 151)	Psalms	

Divisions of the Bible

Roman Catholic	Protestant	Eastern Orthodox	Ethiopic	Syriac (Nestorian)	Samaritan
Wisdom Books	*Wisdom Books*	*Wisdom Books*	*Wisdom Books*	*Wisdom Books*	
—	—	—	—	Psalms 152–155	
Proverbs	Proverbs	Proverbs	Proverbs (1–24)	Proverbs	
—	—	—	Täagsas (Proverbs 25–31)	—	
—	—	—	—	I Esdras	
—	—	—	Wisdom of Solomon	Wisdom of Solomon	
Ecclesiastes	Ecclesiastes	Ecclesiastes	Ecclesiastes	Ecclesiastes	
Song of Songs	Song of Solomon	Song of Songs	Song of Solomon	Song of Solomon	
Ecclesiasticus (or Sirach)	—	Wisdom of Sirach	Ecclesiasticus	Book of Sirach	
—	—	—	—	Epistle of Jeremiah	
—	—	—	—	Epistle of Baruch	
—	—	—	—	Baruch	
—	—	—	—	II Baruch	
—	—	—	—	Bel and the Dragon	
—	—	—	—	Susanna	
—	—	—	—	Josephus	
Prophecy	*Prophecy*	*Prophecy*	*Prophecy*	*Prophecy*	
Isaiah	Isaiah	Isaiah	Isaiah	Isaiah	
Jeremias	Jeremiah	Jeremiah	Jeremias	Jeremiah	
Lamentations	Lamentations	—	Lamentations	Lamentations	
Baruch	—	Baruch	Baruch (with Letter of Jeremiah as chap. 6)	—	
Letter of Jeremiah	—	—	—	—	
Ezechiel	Ezekiel	Ezekiel	Ezekiel	Ezekiel	
Daniel	Daniel	Daniel	Daniel	Daniel	
Osee	Hosea	Hosea	Hosea	Hosea	
Joel	Joel	Joel	Joel	Joel	
Amos	Amos	Amos	Amos	Amos	
Abdias	Obadiah	Obadiah	Obadiah	Obadiah	
Jonas	Jonah	Jonah	Jonah	Jonah	
Micheas	Micah	Micah	Micah	Micah	
Nahum	Nahum	Nahum	Nahum	Nahum	
Habaccuck	Habakkuk	Habakkuk	Habakkuk	Habakkuk	
Sophonias	Zephaniah	Zephaniah	Zephaniah	Zephaniah	
Aggeus	Haggai	Haggai	Haggai	Haggai	
Zacharias	Zechariah	Zechariah	Zechariah	Zechariah	
Malachias	Malachi	Malachi	Malachi	Malachi	
Gospels	*Gospels*	*Gospels*	*Gospels*	*Gospels*	
Matthew	Matthew	Matthew	Matthew	Matthew	
Mark	Mark	Mark	Mark	Mark	
Luke	Luke	Luke	Luke	Luke	
John	John	John	John	John	
Acts	Acts	Acts	Acts	Acts	
Epistles	*Epistles*	*Epistles*	*Epistles*	*Epistles*	
Romans	Romans	Epistles of Paul	Romans	Romans	
I Corinthians	I Corinthians	—	I Corinthians	I Corinthians	
II Corinthians	II Corinthians	—	II Corinthians	II Corinthians	
Galatians	Galatians	—	Galatians	Galatians	
Ephesians	Ephesians	—	Ephesians	Ephesians	
Philippians	Philippians	—	Philippians	Philippians	
Colossians	Colossians	—	Colossians	Colossians	
I Thessalonians	I Thessalonians	—	I Thessalonians	I Thessalonians	
II Thessalonians	II Thessalonians	—	II Thessalonians	II Thessalonians	

Divisions of the Bible

Roman Catholic	Protestant	Eastern Orthodox	Ethiopic	Syriac (Nestorian)	Samaritan
Epistles	*Epistles*	*Epistles*	*Epistles*	*Epistles*	
I Timothy	I Timothy	—	I Timothy	I Timothy	
II Timothy	II Timothy	—	II Timothy	II Timothy	
Titus	Titus	—	Titus	Titus	
Philemon	Philemon	—	Philemon	Philemon	
Hebrews	Hebrews	Hebrews	Hebrews	Hebrews	
James	James	—	James	James	
I Peter	I Peter	Peter	I Peter	I Peter	
II Peter	II Peter	—	II Peter	II Peter	
I John	I John	John	I John	I John	
II John	II John	—	II John	II John	
III John	III John	—	III John	III John	
Jude	Jude	Jude	Jude	Jude	
Apocalypse	*Apocalypse*	*Apocalypse*	*Apocalypse*	*Apocalypse*	
Revelation	Revelation	Revelation	Revelation	Revelation	
		Apocrypha			
		Bel and the Dragon			
		Prayer of Azariah			
		Song of the Three			
		Young Men			
			Church Order		
			Sinodos		
			Book of the		
			Covenant		
			Clement		
			Didascalia		

Thus, Roman Catholics acknowledge forty-seven books in the Old Testament and twenty-seven in the New Testament for a total of seventy-four. The Protestant Bible contains sixty-six books — thirty-nine in the Old Testament and twenty-seven in the New. Less easily defined is the range of canonical books in the Eastern Orthodox church, which structures the list differently and embraces more of the Apocrypha as inspired. The content of the Ethiopic Bible totals eighty-three books.

Matthew

Drawn from the writings of Mark and apparently composed by a publican — a tax accountant or customs agent — around C.E. 80, Matthew, the opening book of the New Testament, may have been the work of an anonymous writer using Matthew's collection of Jesus's words as a source. The text probably originated in Aramaic and soon appeared in a Greek version. The fullest of the gospels, it offers a thorough biography of Jesus and collects his sermons and sayings into five divisions, preserving for all time the Sermon on the Mount, the heart of Christian teaching. In response to the Jewish belief in a promised messiah, Matthew accepts Jesus as Jewish royalty, the chosen savior, and establishes the founding of the

Christian church on God's covenants with Israel. Underlying the doctrinal importance of Jesus is a grand humanistic metaphor summarized by novelist Francisco Goldman: "those who suffer and those who show love for those who suffer are joined through suffering and grace to Jesus Christ" (Goldman 1999, xv).

The first chapter clarifies Jesus's emergence from Abraham's line and the resulting Davidic dynasty, a genealogical link between Old Testament patriarchs and Jesus. As a scion of King David, unifier of Israel, Jesus deserves the right of succession, which covers fourteen generations. The family tree passes through men of the stature of Abraham, Isaac, and Jacob and, in verses 5–6, his genealogy is traced from the matriarch Ruth, wife of Boaz and grandmother of David, who was husband of Bathsheba, mother of the wise King Solomon. The genealogy makes a brief stop in verse 11 to note the abduction of Hebrews to Babylon, one of the hallmarks of Jewish history. Verse 12 continues with the post-exilic period.

In Matthew 1:16, the patriarchal line takes an inexplicable turn with the listing of Joseph, husband of Mary, Jesus's mother. In view of Jesus's divine conception by the Holy Spirit, Matthew gives no justification for the linkage to a human father. The chapter indicates that Jesus acquired a title, Christos or Christ, the Greek translation of the Hebrew *moshiah* (messiah). The Greek abbreviation of the title took the form of the Greek letter *chi* usually superimposed over rho and called the *chi rho*. An abbreviation of Jesus, Greek for the Hebrew *Yeshua* (Joshua), also enters Christian symbolism and art as three letters, IHS, a shortening of the Greek spelling of Iesous. (Note that the Greek letter *eta* takes the shape of the letter H.) (The letters duplicate the English letters X and P.)

Matthew 1:18–25 summarizes the conception and birth of Jesus, a contribution to Christian worship that links the text to the seasons of Advent and Christmas. The author comments that Joseph, a just but troubled man, chooses to marry his pregnant fiancée, to whom he is legally bound. His compassion protects her from the terrible death by stoning that awaits immoral women. The angel who sways his decision predicts the birth of a boy named Jesus, whom the prophet Isaiah had foretold in Isaiah 7:14 as a virgin's son with the symbolic name of Immanuel, meaning "God with us." The final verse specifies that Mary remains untouched by human intercourse until after she gives birth. The verse implies that Jesus grows up in a normal family blessed by subsequent children.

Unique to Matthew's gospel is the visitation of sages, an unidentified party of wise men who know of the birth from their interpretation of star patterns. They follow one bright star westward to Bethlehem. The astral event fulfills the prophecy of Numbers 24:17, which predicts a star out of Jacob. Tradition, based on the three gifts to the Christ child, assumes that there were three magi. Legend assigns them Caucasian, Negroid, and Asian features and names them Caspar (or Gaspar), Melchior, and Balthasar. Matthew mentions none of these details. The gifts have also taken on emblematic meaning: gold for royalty, frankincense for godhood, and myrrh, a burial ointment, prefiguring a human demise.

The pleasant idyll ends in a flurry of activity after King Herod, alerted by the sages, determines to rid his rule of rivalry from a purported princeling and heir to Herod's throne. His massacre of the innocents, a poignant subject in Christian art and music, costs the lives of many male toddlers. Matthew appends a link to Genesis in verse 18 with the image of the sorrowing mother Rachel, the Old Testament matriarch:

> In Rama was there a voice heard,
>   lamentation, and weeping, and great mourning,
>   Rachel weeping for her children,
>   and would not be comforted,
>   because they are not.

Mass terrorism forces the holy family to flee to Egypt, a reverse of the Exodus in Moses's time. Upon the king's death, the family still feels unsafe in Archelaus's Judean kingdom, yet manages to repatriate themselves in Nazareth.

Matthew's omission of Jesus's childhood and early manhood precipitated a tradition of folktales about the boy growing up in the carpentry shop and apocryphal accounts offering magical and prophetic episodes that prefigure the messiah's ministry and resurrection. The text moves directly to Jesus's manhood during the wilderness preaching of John the Baptist, the son of Elizabeth, Mary's maternal aunt. John, the last in the Old Testament prophet tradition, admonishes Judaeans to repent and "Prepare ye the way of the Lord" (Matthew 3:3). Anticipation of a new world order and the numinous baptism of Jesus in the Jordan River humbles and energizes John, who accepts the advice of his cousin Jesus to "fulfill all righteousness" (Matthew 3:15).

After the temptation by the devil and the call to preach, in chapter 4, Jesus gathers disciples, the usual teaching method of Eastern gurus. The company begins with Simon Peter and his brother Andrew, fishermen whose vocation provides one of the Bible's most resilient images—the netting of converts. The group grows with the addition of brothers James and John, sons of Zebedee. With these four supporters, Jesus begins preaching, healing, and bearing his message and establishing a reputation about Galilee and Syria.

The most beloved of biblical oratory, the Sermon on the Mount, fills chapters 5–7. The physical description of a mountain is both practical and emblematic: the orator can better address a milling body from above them; also, Jesus models the dignity and example of Moses the lawgiver, who received and disseminated God's message from Mount Sinai. Jesus's teaching begins with the Beatitudes (Matthew 5:3–12), a series of parallel statements urging meek, gentle behavior among the righteous. The eleventh verse speaks to the crowd:

> Blessed are ye,
>   when men shall revile you, and persecute you
>   and shall say all manner of evil against you
>   falsely for my sake.

The sermon moves into rich metaphor, likening Christians to the salt of the earth and the light of the world.

Jesus works at reconciling his ministry with orthodox Judaism. Verse 17 answers questions gnawing at pious Jews. The newcomer declares that he has no wish to override prophecy. Rather, his ministry is a fulfillment of Isaiah's prediction of a messiah. Jesus's injunction against evil thoughts, spite, and grudges includes a warning about bearing a hate-filled heart into the Tabernacle and about lusting for women. He dramatizes the danger of a hidden agenda with images of ripping out an offending eye and of lopping off an offensive hand. Verses 39–40 introduce a revolutionary mindset, turning the other cheek to attackers. Jesus restates the idea of offering good for evil in verse 44:

I say unto you,
Love your enemies,
  bless them that curse you,
  and pray for them which despitefully use you,
  and persecute you.

In the harsh rivalries and Roman usurpations of the eastern Mediterranean, the concept of doing good to enemies challenges a political reality that dates into prehistory.

Chapter 6 turns the attention of the Jews toward their public display of piety. He warns of two empty, self-serving gestures—alms giving and praying on street corners. He provides a teaching model of prayer in Matthew 6:9–13, commonly known in Latin as the Paternoster (Our Father) and in English as the Lord's Prayer. Patterned after the Kaddish, the Jewish doxology, the text magnifies God and looks beyond earth to a heavenly kingdom. It also reflects the silent Hebrew *Amidah* (Standing Prayer), the *Shmoneh Esreh* (Eighteen Benedictions), which petitions for forgiveness and asks for guidance.

Jesus redirects righteousness from earth to heaven. Unlike the strident prophets of the Old Testament, he gently advises, "For where your treasure is, there will your heart be also" (Matthew 6:21). The unfolding of imagery in verses 24–30 is an oft-cited model of faith. Poets and orators return to the metaphors of "the lilies of the field," which surpass Solomon's glorious raiment in grace and effortless luminance. The final verses summarize the thought that seekers should look to righteousness rather than to earthly wealth and that worry over the morrow is a waste of energy.

Chapter 7 opens on a less subtle command that the righteous should not judge others. Jesus balances this directive with a generous promise stated in three parallel images of petition:

Ask, and it shall be given you:
  seek, and ye shall find;
  knock, and it shall be opened unto you [Matthew 7:7].

Although he repeatedly refers to Old Testament law, his rules are "thou shalts" rather than "thou shalt nots." He summarizes with the Golden Rule, "All things whatsoever ye would that men should do to you, do ye even so to them" (Matthew 7:12). The image of the righteous building upon rock ends a remarkable lecture, which leaves hearers astonished at his authority.

Wonder working, a convention of the Old Testament, continues in the New. Chapters 8–9 contain a series of ten miracles that Matthew has collected from word of mouth. Jesus heals a leper and a paraplegic in Capernaum, lessens the fever of Peter's mother-in-law, saves his apostles from a storm at sea, and exorcises devils at Gadarenes, southeast of the Sea of Galilee. The result is instant notoriety and a whole city turning out. The cures

continue with a man rid of palsy, a woman saved from hemorrhage, the raising of a girl from the dead, and restoration of sight in two blind men. In reference to his busy ministry, Jesus wishes for more disciples.

By chapter 10, the list of apostles has grown threefold with the addition of Philip, Bartholomew, Thomas, Matthew the publican, James the son of Alphaeus, Thaddeus, Simon, and Judas Iscariot, whom the writer identifies as a traitor. Jesus advises disciples on what to do and what to expect from a lifetime of service. He states in the form of paradox: "He that findeth his life shall lose it: and he that loseth his life for my sake shall find it" (Matthew 10:39). After a prayer of thanks to God in Matthew 11:25–26, he calls followers from the laboring class to end their toil and accept his charge. He promises, "my yoke is easy and my burden is light."

Confrontations with Pharisees, a hypercritical Jewish sect, continue opportunities for Jesus to dispel Judaic legalism in favor of mercy and humanism. Chapter 13 contains the first of Jesus's parables, a teaching model about the sower and an application of its symbols to the responses of the hearers of the gospel. In summary, he compares God's kingdom to buried treasure, pearls, and a fishing net. On return to his homeland, he encounters disdain, which prompts him in verse 57 to characterize the prophet as a man without honor in his own country.

Throughout the next chapters, Jesus continues to perform mighty works, causing Herod to wonder if John the Baptist has arisen from the dead. Chapter 14 reveals the bizarre manner of John's death—decapitated by Herod to please Herodias's daughter, who asks to dance with the head on a platter. The loss causes Jesus to withdraw and mourn, but the surge of followers brings him back to ministry and healing. He feeds them in verses 19–20 on five loaves and two fish, producing a miracle that causes the food to expand to satisfy the hunger of a crowd of 4,000. Like God's bounty, the meal ends with twelve baskets of leftovers. A second miracle, walking on a roiling sea and lifting the doubts of Peter, precedes an episode of healing in the Galilean city of Gennesaret, a new territory to serve.

Plagued by quibbling, nit-picking Pharisees and Sadducees, Jesus reaches a height in Matthew 16:16, when Peter identifies him for the first time as "the Christ, the Son of the living God." To reward his disciple, Jesus makes a play on his name, Petros, which sounds like *petra* (rock). Jesus's statement, which Catholics revere in the Latin version as the Petrine Supremacy, encircles the dome of St. Peter's Basilica in Rome in script framed in gold: *Tu es petrus, et super hanc petram aedificabo ecclesiam meam* (Thou art Peter, and upon this rock I will build my church), a justification for the popes, all of whom take the title of vicar of Christ. Alarmed at a prophecy of death and resurrection, Peter tries to alter Jesus's fate. Jesus rebukes him as an incarnation of Satan and declares that obedience to God's plan is the preface to life eternal.

That latter portion of Matthew completes the transformation of the Nazarite carpenter into deity. In chapter 17, Peter, James, and John witness an effulgent transfiguration of Jesus's face and garment and a voice from heaven identifying Jesus as "my beloved Son, in whom I am well pleased" (Matthew 17:5). Jesus indicates that the messiah is no longer expected, but present. In Matthew 18:3, he issues another revolutionary dictum: that his followers must "become as little children" if they intend to enter God's kingdom. He presents the parable of the talents, which is unique to Matthew's gospel. Chapter 19 continues the motif of Pharasaic challenge and clever reply, including in verses 18–19, a restatement of five Mosaic commands and a sixth, "Thou shalt love thy neighbor as thyself."

Matthew's version of Jesus's arrest, torture, condemnation, and crucifixion begins in Matthew 20:18–19 with a prediction of the series of humiliations that awaits him. In chapter 21, he reaches the pinnacle of Judaism, the Temple at Jerusalem, where he drives out money changers and heals the blind and lame. On departing the Temple in chapter 24, he foresees its total destruction, which the Romans accomplished in C.E. 70. His passionate monologue continues, rising to visions of heaven and the transcendent example of charity toward the lowly. To questioners, Jesus declares, "Inasmuch as ye have done it unto one of the least of these my brethren, ye have done it unto me" (Matthew 25:40).

In Matthew 26:1–16, the author summarizes the events following the Passover in Jerusalem, where chief priests, scribes, and elders led by high priest Caiaphas conspire to kill Jesus, one of a long line of upstarts claiming to be the messiah. For thirty pieces of silver, Judas Iscariot betrays his master to the chief priests. The gracious Passover meal of Matthew 26:26–28 serves Christians as the liturgy for communion. In anticipation of the Second Coming, he promises:

> I tell you I shall not drink again of this fruit of the vine
> until that day when I drink it anew with you
> in my father's kingdom [Matthew 26:29].

After prayers on the Mount of Olives, Jesus encounters an armed mob led by the Temple hierarchy. On his arrest, Peter withdraws. His triple denial of Jesus precedes the crowing of the cock, a famous Christian symbol of faintheartedness that marks many artistic images of Peter.

Before Pontius Pilate, the Roman procurator, the next morning, Jesus faces condemnation. In anguish, Judas Iscariot hangs himself in grief at his betrayal. For two millennia, Christian anti–Semites excuse their preju-

dice by translating his name as "the Jew." In Matthew 27:26, as Barabbas the thief goes free, Jesus suffers mockery and torment before bearing his cross to Golgotha. The best known of Christian images, the crucifixion beneath an impertinent inscription proclaiming "King of the Jews" reaches a distressing nadir when Christ calls on God for reassurance. Matthew connects Jesus's death with a natural cataclysm — an earthquake that splits rocks and rips the Temple veil top to bottom. Graves open, casting up the remains of saints, which walk the streets. Jesus's mother and two women watch from a distance. Joseph of Arimathea receives the body and entombs it in a hewn rock cavity obstructed with a boulder. The envious Pharisees urge Pilate to seal and guard the chamber lest the apostles steal the remains and falsify a resurrection.

Chapter 28 ends the Easter liturgy with a post-sabbath miracle. Mary Magdalene and another Mary witness an empty tomb guarded by a lambent angel. In verse 9, Jesus appears and spreads the message that he has fulfilled his prophecy to live again. In his charge to the apostles, Jesus dispatches them to teach and baptize all nations and assures, "Lo, I am with you always" (Matthew 28:20).

Mark

Written around C.E. 70, the Book of Mark, only sixteen chapters in length, is the oldest, leanest, and most realistic of the apostles' writings. Christian tradition assigns the writing to John Mark, a member of Jerusalem's first Christian community, and places composition in Rome at the end of Peter's pulpit career. The book's unique contributions are seven lines — Mark 3:17, 5:41, 7:11, 7:34, 10:46, 14:36, 15:34 — rendered in Jesus's own Aramaic speech. A source for both Matthew and Luke, the text may derive from Peter's sermons and possibly identifies the author as Peter's disciple or a companion of Paul on his first mission. The gospel may have been valued by the other three gospel authors as a prototype.

Mark appears not to know of the virgin birth or the other wonders of Jesus's birth. Chapter 1 begins with Jesus's baptism and a vivid portrayal of John the Baptist in verse 6 as a crudely dressed man of the wild girded in camel's hair and animal skin for a loincloth. After calling disciples, Jesus begins a vigorous campaign from town to town, preaching, casting out devils, and healing. In chapter 3, he counters the pious, who rebuke the healer for restoring a man's withered hand on the sabbath. In verse 6, Mark depicts the Pharisees snatching up this evidence of impiety and moving rapidly to treachery. In verse 17, Jesus invests his twelve followers with similar powers of healing. In chapter 4, at a seaside setting, he delivers the parables of the sower, the wheat and weeds, and the mustard seed before calming the Sea of Galilee from a great windstorm. To display his mastery of nature to his disciples, he speaks to the waters, "Peace, be still" (Mark 4:39). Chapter 5 completes the journey with healing on the opposite shore and a riveting resurrection of a dead girl.

Matthew's concept of the prophet without honor in his own land recurs in Mark. Chapter 6 follows Jesus and his apostles to Nazareth, where local people ask of a hometown boy:

> Is not this the carpenter, the son of Mary,
>   the brother of James, and Joses,
>   and of Juda, and Simon,
>   and are not his sisters here with us? [Mark 6:3].

Still focused on ministry, Jesus dispatches his disciples two by two. Herod identifies his skill with that of John the Baptist, others with Elijah and the prophets. The wonders continue with the feeding of the multitudes, walking on water, and throngs of petitioners.

In chapter 7, the Pharisees from Jerusalem condemn the miracle worker's disciples for eating with unclean hands. Jesus challenges their hypocrisy with a challenge to orthodoxy: "These people honoreth me with their lips, but their heart is far from me" (Mark 7:6). In chapter 9, his paradox rebukes the disciples for jostling for first place:

> If any man desire to be first,
>   the same shall be last of all,
>   and servant of all [Mark 9:35].

On the way to Jerusalem, he debates with the Pharisees the ethics of divorce and commands, "What therefore God hath joined together, let not man put asunder" (Mark 10:9).

Confrontation with meticulous Jews continues. After arriving in Jerusalem to celebrate the Passover, Jesus undergoes more test questions from the Pharisees and instructs them to love God and love their neighbor. He makes an audacious summation of duty: "There is none other commandment greater than these" (Mark 12:31). To commoners, he warns of scribes, who love posturing in public and praying at length. By way of contrast to the self-important, in Mark 12:42–44, he relates the parable of the widow's mite. In chapter 13, he warns disciples of violence and widespread hatred in coming days. He reassures them, "Heaven and earth shall pass away: but my words shall not pass away" (Mark 13:31).

Legalism fuels the confrontation with the Jewish hierarchy. Chapters 14–16 recount betrayal, arrest, and questions before an assembly of chief priests, elders, and scribes. Jesus refuses to answer preliminary questions, but, to identification as Son of God, he predicts, "Ye shall see the son of man sitting on the right hand of power, and coming in the clouds of heaven" (Mark 14:62). The drama of Jesus's death compels a centurion to declare him God's son. Appearances to apostles, a charge to baptize nations, and reception into heaven end the book. An addendum of twelve verses rounds out a truncated text, which halts abruptly at Mark 16:8. The writing is literate, the commentary undergirded with knowledge of the other gospels and the Book of Acts.

Luke

A fuller biography of Jesus written around C.E. 90, the Book of Luke references Mark's gospel, but supplies unique information about Jesus's infancy and boyhood and details of his final journey to Jerusalem. Tradition identifies Luke as the good doctor, whom Paul mentions in II Timothy as the "dear physician." Luke is Mark's friend, an appealing humanist whom Dante extolled as "*il scriba della gentilezza di Cristo*" (the scribe of the kindness of Christ) (Cahill 1999, xvi). Luke's profession may have disposed him to a humanitarianism and egalitarianism toward women and the underclass not found in the gospels of Matthew, Mark, and John. Unlike the other New Testament writers, he was the only gentile, a variance of point of view that enriches the four gospels with a reliable, accurate memoir devoid of attempts to corroborate Jesus's life and ministry with Old Testament prophecy.

Speaking like an educated man, maybe even a scholar, Luke opens chapter 1 with a discussion of source materials from eyewitness accounts. He addresses his manuscript to Theophilus, an unidentified Roman. The name, meaning "lover of God," may be a token of all godly people. Prefaced by the late-in-life conception of John the Baptist to Elizabeth and Zachariah, the lines beginning with Luke 1:26 link the birth of Jesus's forerunner to Mary. In the overview of author Thomas Cahill, "Luke's writing is full of fruit and offspring, wombs and promises of miraculous births. We are about to experience a cosmic explosion of fecundity. Fulfillment is at hand, so reality itself is pregnant" (Cahill 1999, xv).

A favorite in Catholic liturgy and art are verses 28–38, the angel's annunciation to Mary of her role in the birth of God in human form. From verses 46–55 come the liturgical and musical tradition known as the magnificat, a poetic exaltation predicting Jesus's greatness. Elizabeth's adherence to heavenly command causes her to break tradition and name her son John. Zachariah, who had been mute since his son's conception, corroborates his wife's choice of name, then breaks into spontaneous speech, praise of God, and prophecy that his son will "guide our feet into the way of peace" (Luke 2:79).

Chapter 2 is so familiar to Christians that even small children recognize the passage beginning, "And it came to pass." Opening on the onerous Roman census, a preface to taxation, the account depicts Joseph as a dutiful citizen transporting his wife, heavily pregnant, from Nazareth to Bethlehem. Artists augment the scene with images of Mary, her faced lined with the early stages of labor, and Joseph anxiously scanning the road ahead. In the crush of civic enrollment, the holy family finds no space in an inn and opts for a manger. The touching scene, which allies Jesus with the agricultural and herding classes, serves art and Christmas decor as the first crèche (crib), alternately situated in a three-walled shed, barn, or cave. Simultaneous with his birth is the celestial dispatch of the first visitors, a company of shepherds, who leave their flocks and follow the angels' direction to worship the holy child swaddled in strips of cloth and sleeping in the manger.

The shepherds' amazement grows when the angel voices blossom into a heavenly host singing the most familiar Christmas message:

> Glory to God in the highest,
>   and on earth peace,
>   good will toward men [Luke 2:14].

The line is the first yuletide carol and a mainstay of the Gloria, a jubilant segment of the mass. When the shepherds arrive, their wonder sends them out into the countryside spreading the news. Thus, Luke ennobles them as the first spokesmen of the gospel.

According to the strictures of Jewish family life, Mary must be purified from the taint of childbirth, a law applied to the defilement of any body effluvium, and the boy child must be circumcised at the Temple along with a parental sacrifice of doves or pigeons. Luke describes a unique character, Simeon, whom God had promised to see the Christ. The pious man's testimony is a useful literary and cultural tool, which gives Luke an opportunity to glorify Jesus as "light to lighten the Gentiles, and the glory of thy people Israel" (Luke 2:32). The widow Anna, a Temple volunteer, also recognizes the divinity of the child and thanks God that Israel will at last be redeemed.

After ritual circumcision, Jesus returns with his family twelve times on annual pilgrimages to Jerusalem to celebrate the Passover. At age twelve, Luke depicts a familiar scene — the consternation of parents looking for a wandering child. After three days of searching, they return to the Temple and find him disputing the law with the learned. In the child's sharp retort to his elders, he demands: "How is it that you sought me? Did you not know that I must be in my father's house?" (Luke 2:49). The evidence of a child prodigy accords with epic and mythic texts identifying wise children as the forerunners of great sages. For the next eighteen years, Jesus lives quietly in Nazareth, saying nothing about his role as Son of God. Only his mother seems capable of storing up his wisdom and anticipating the greatness foretold by the angel at the boy's conception.

Chapter 3 opens on the bustle and self-importance associated with Roman colonizers of Palestine. John the Baptist, the fulfillment of Isaiac prophecy, develops into the "voice of one crying in the wilderness" (Luke 3:4). After setting publicans and mercenaries straight about injustice, John promises a mightier voice, who "shall baptize you with the Holy Ghost and with fire" (Luke 3:16). As John disappears into Herod's dungeon, Jesus, at age thirty, begins his ministry. At this point in the narrative, Luke pauses to present Jesus's pedigree, beginning with Joseph and working back through David and Boaz, Judah, Jacob, Isaac, Abraham, and his father and grandfather all the way to Adam, the universal ancestor.

Jesus is ready for his messianic role in chapter 4 as a result of baptism in the Jordan River, the watercourse that halves Palestine from north to south much as Jesus's ministry divides Jews and Christians. Luke follows the events recorded in Mark, detailing temptation, healing, preaching, and reading from scripture in sabbath services. A hostile confrontation in the synagogue at Nazareth places Jesus in a precarious position. In Luke 4:29, a mob readies for violence:

> And they rose up and put him out of the city,
>   and led him to the brow of the hill
>   on which their city was built,
>   that they might throw him down headlong.

Without counteraction or comment, he peacefully moves along toward Capernaum. His choice of nonviolence prefigures world peacemakers like Mohandas Gandhi, Martin Luther King, Jr., and Cesar Chavez.

Luke covers the recruitment of fishermen, miraculous healing of cripples and lepers, and the harassment of Pharisees, who hope to catch the self-proclaimed messiah in some fault or misapplication of Torah. In chapter 6, he instructs his twelve followers in an abridged version of the Sermon on the Mount, beginning with the Beatitudes in verses 20–26. Luke's incomparable style reduces revolutionary teaching to simple precepts:

> Judge not, and ye shall not be judged:
>   condemn not, and ye shall not be condemned:
>   forgive, and ye shall be forgiven.
> Give, and it shall be given unto you [Luke 6:37–38].

His models are equally simple — the blind leading the blind, the brother removing a mote from his fellow's eye, and the good tree bringing forth rotten fruit. In simple summary, he sends a message to John declaring:

> How that the blind see, the lame walk,
>   the lepers are cleansed, the deaf hear,
>   the dead are raised,
>   to the poor the gospel is preached [Luke 7:22].

A question about loving neighbors launches him into his most beloved parable, the Good Samaritan, a text in Luke 10:30–36 that is a favorite of children and their teachers. The author also introduces Jesus's amiable relationship with Mary and Martha, siblings at Bethany who quarrel about household duties as opposed to listening to preaching.

In the protracted debate with the Pharisees, Jesus wearies of their posturing and hypocrisy. In Luke 11:44, he compares them to unmarked graves, a threat to Jews, who must avoid contact with the dead to remain pure. In thundering cries of "Woe unto you," he calls them parlous lawyers:

> For ye have taken away the key of knowledge:
>   ye entered not in yourselves,
>   and them that were entering in ye hindered [Luke 11:52].

The constant battle with provokers builds tension into chapters 12–13, as he answers questions about inheritance and delivers the parable of the rich fool. He returns to the elements of the Sermon on the Mount, declaring that trust in God is all that is necessary.

In Luke 13:34, Jesus prefigures the coming crucifixion by mourning the fate of Jerusalem's prophets:

> O Jerusalem, Jerusalem, which killest the prophets,
>   and stonest them that are sent unto thee;
>   how often would I have gathered thy children together,
>   as a hen doth gather her brood under her wings,
>   and ye would not?

He narrates the parables of the lost sheep, lost coin, the banquet, and the lengthy account of the prodigal son, a story of sibling rivalry and youthful profligacy that concludes with rejoicing, "for this thy brother was dead, and is alive again: and was lost, and is found" (Luke 15:32).

Unlike Matthew, Luke covers less religious quibbling and more real-life quandaries, which Jesus analyzes in analogies drawn from the Old Testament. In chapter 16, he speaks of the larcenous manager, the story of the rich man and Lazarus, and the duties and responsibilities of disciples. The return of the one leper out of ten in Luke 17:15 offers Jesus an opportunity to stress gratitude. To a Pharisee, he expresses the difference between the coming of God's kingdom on earth and the emergence of God in the human spirit. Jesus enlarges on the sinful era preceding the Flood and the destruction of Sodom by warning that the messiah's arrival will find people unready.

The disciples misinterpret Jesus's prophecy in Luke 18:31–33 of mockery, scourging, and death. In Jericho, he encounters Zacchaeus, chief publican, and launches the parable of the talents. Outside Jerusalem, Jesus weeps and mutters,

> Would that even today
>   you knew the things that make for peace!
> But now they are hid from your eyes [Luke 19:42].

The group's entrance into the holy capital and appearance at the Temple offer officials another opportunity to accept Jesus, but they plot to kill him because of his popularity with the peasantry. The perusal of validity continues in chapter 20 with the officials questioning his authority. He replies with the parable of the vineyard, which predicts the crushing of those who reject God's cornerstone. In a charge to the disciples in chapter 21, he warns of the pitfalls that await them.

After Peter and John prepare the Passover meal in the upper room, Jesus goes to the Mount of Olives to pray. His arrest and mockery end chapter 22. Upon his appearance before Pilate, the governor remarks, "I find no fault in this man" (Luke 23:4). A second hearing before Herod concludes with Pilate's attempt to please the Jewish mob by sentencing Jesus to crucifixion. At Calvary, he prays, "Father, forgive them: for they know not what they do" (Luke 23:34).

The cruel death, which scientists describe as slow suffocation from shock and a loss of blood and muscle tone, ends with complaint of thirst and a final cry to God, "Father, into thy hands I commend my spirit" (Luke 23:46). Upon Jesus's resurrection and return to earth to walk among the disciples, Jesus urges the disciples to touch him, feed him fish and honeycomb, and hear the prophecy that his death and resurrection fulfill. He leads them to Bethany, where he confers his blessing and ascends to heaven.

John

Composed contemporaneously with or slightly after the Book of Luke, John's writing comes from the end of the first century C.E. The work of "God's eagle," the mystic depicted in Ezekiel's vision, the book is more spiritual than historic. One of the "sons of thunder," John, the beloved disciple, who calls himself one of Jesus's twelve, has a number of possible identities: he is James ben Zebedee's brother and may have been a son of Salome, Mary's sister, or a disciple of John the Baptist. Because of John's close association with Jesus, he, along with Peter and James, attends the master at Gethsemane and witnesses the transfiguration. As Jesus weakens on the cross, he commends Mary to John's care, a transference of responsibility that distinguishes John for love and concern.

The overall image of Jesus in the Book of John points to a solitary figure unique in majesty and grandeur, yet approachable as a companion, friend, and counselor. For imagery, John resorts to a simplified vocabulary, choosing words drawn from eating, herding, and parts of the house. To end the questions of orthodox Jews about the messiah, John introduces Jesus in chapter 1 as "the word," a lingual connection to the Tanakh, the indisputable word of God. In verse 6, John identifies himself as a witness of "the light," a gift to the world of illumination. Of Jesus's birth, he states, "The word was made flesh, and dwelt among us" (John 1:14). He expresses the difference between Moses and Jesus in verse 17, which extends Mosaic law to "grace and truth." In contrast to Torah, grace denotes the gift that the receiver does not have to deserve, the gift freely given out of compassion for suffering humanity.

John introduces biography in John 1:15 with the preaching of John the Baptist, who typifies Jesus as "the lamb of God" (John 1:29), a metaphor that dominates early Christian mosaics, sacred vessels, tapestries, stained glass, Christmas ornaments, and headstones, and the requiem masses of Johann Sebastian Bach, Wolfgang Amadeus Mozart, and Gabriel Fauré. To the questions of Levites, the Baptist stated that he was not Christ, but the prophet preparing his path. After selecting apostles, Jesus attends a wedding in Cana, an event unique to John's gospel. The episode depicts Jesus's relationship with his mother at the scene of the first miracle, changing water to wine, a proof to the disciples that he is capable of wonders.

John's gospel moves rapidly to Jesus's sojourn in Jerusalem and the launching of his ministry. An unusual encounter takes place at night, when Nicodemus, a Jewish ruler, seeks the newcomer prophet under cover of darkness. Nicodemus's questions are typical of literal-minded scholars, but steeped in confusion:

> Rabbi, we know that you are a teacher come from God;
>   for no one can do these signs that you do,
>   unless God is with him [John 3:2].

In John 3:5–7, Jesus carefully explains the term "born again," a section of gospel frequently cited by fundamentalists concerning salvation. Another familiar passage to Christians is John 3:16, the declaration that God sent his son to earth out of love and that he redeems all believers. In John's opinion, "He that believeth on the son hath everlasting life" (John 3:36).

A one-on-one encounter at Samaria has Jesus talking with a Samaritan woman, whom he petitions for a drink. Her hesitance to aid a Jew leads him to remark on the subject of refreshment. Earthly water slakes a human thirst, which will recur. He concludes:

> But whosoever drinketh of the water
>   that I shall give him
>   shall never thirst;
>   but the water that I shall give him
>   shall be in him a well of water
>   springing up into everlasting life [John 4:14].

He makes so deep an impression on her that she returns to the city to send others to meet "the Christ."

John reprises the details of Jesus's healing the crippled man at Bethesda, feeding the multitudes, and walking on water. In chapter 7, Jesus avoids Jewry because of danger from plotters. At the Feast of the Tabernacles, he returns to the Temple to witness to his purpose, but fails to convince all hearers. At the Pharisees' accusation of an adulteress, Jesus manages to walk the fine line between obeying the law and transcending it. He refuses to be drawn into the mob that would stone the woman, but grants them permission with a single injunction, "He that is without sin among you, let him first cast a stone at her" (John 8:7). With simple kindness, he commands the sinner to go free, but sin no more, then condemns her captors as sons of the devil, who prefer murder to compassion. The book ends with Jesus hiding and retreating from the Temple as the Pharisees gather stones to throw at him.

In chapter 10, John enlarges on the image of the Good Shepherd, who "[lays] down his life for the sheep" (John 10:15). A more powerful picture comes from chapter 11, the resurrection of Lazarus, John's contribution to the gospels. To Martha, Lazarus's sister, Jesus states a godly purpose that has become standard funeral liturgy:

> I am the resurrection and the life:
>   he that believeth in me,
>   though he were dead,
>   yet shall he live.
> And whosoever liveth and believeth in me
>   shall never die [John 11:25–26].

His friends' grief is so powerful that Jesus, too, weeps. In a dramatic reversal of death, he calls forth Lazarus, who walks from the tomb still clad in a winding sheet and face covering. The miracle sways so many to believe that the Jewish hierarchy moves quickly toward a death plot.

The story has a coda, the anointing at Bethany. In John 12:1–8, Jesus and Lazarus share a supper served by Martha. Mary, out of deep gratitude for her brother's restored life, takes ointment, the type used for dressing bodies for burial, and massages it into Jesus's feet, wiping the excess with her hair. Judas declares the offering frivolous. He declares the dressing worth 300 denarii, which would make a sizable donation to the poor. Jesus reminds him that Mary is honoring her lord while she has the chance:

> Let her alone, let her keep it for the day of my burial.
> The poor you always have with you,
>   but you do not always have me [John 12:7–8].

Ironically, the description of the poor often surfaces as justification for hard-heartedness toward the needy.

Chapter 12 reaches the commanding moment of

Jesus's triumphal entry into Jerusalem. At the conclusion of the Passover meal, Jesus leaves the table and, as an example of service, takes basin and towel to wash his apostles' feet. On Maundy Thursday, the pope and his bishops perpetuate the model, an ancient ritual that is *mandatum* (commanded). The warm moment of love and brotherhood ends with identification of the traitor, to whom Jesus hands a morsel dipped in broth. The disciples have no suspicion of Judas and suppose that Jesus dispatches him with coins to give the poor. In art, Judas is often seen hurrying to the door, apart from the remaining eleven disciples, whom artists tend to group in a tight brotherhood.

At one of his final intimate moments with his disciples, Jesus gives them a new commandment, a restatement of Mosaic law in a single verse: "That ye love one another; as I have loved you" (John 13:34). Jesus considers loving compassion the true outward sign of a Christian. Into chapter 14, the atmosphere grows heavy with concern. In verse 1 of an emotional love letter, Jesus calms his apostles, urging, "Let not your heart be troubled." The resonant verses of this book elevate John in the estimation of the godly, who recite at funerals:

> In my father's house are many mansions:
>   if it were not so,
>   I would have told you.
> I go to prepare a place for you.
> And if I go and prepare a place for you,
>   I will come again,
>   and receive you unto myself:
>   that where I am,
>   there ye may be also [John 14:2–3].

Jesus advises that the only way to reach God is through the earthly Son, the incarnation of God. In distressing times, these comforting words touch the empty places in the human spirit, promising peace with the command, "Let not your heart be troubled" (John 14:27).

The personal message from the Book of John encourages love, sacrifice, and tender parting. A pervasive theme in art comes from chapter 15, in which Jesus uses vineyard imagery to express the fruitfulness of love. In John 16:5, Jesus explains, "Now I go my way to him that sent me" and predicts that the "comforter," a reference to the Holy Spirit, will come to take Jesus's place on earth. Like the travail and anguish of childbirth, suffering gives place to joy in the infant's safe delivery, a metaphor for redemption. Without interruption by the actions or words of others, Jesus continues his farewell address in chapter 17 with an eloquent prayer to the Father denoting completion of an earthly assignment. He requests union with humanity, who will "be with me where I am; that they may behold my glory" (John 17:24), a sign of God's love that began before the creation of earth.

Chapter 18 returns to the drama of a final walk in the garden where Judas expects the arresting officers to find Jesus. Peter swiftly retaliates against a servant, Malchus, and slices off his ear. Jesus upbraids his apostle:

> Put your sword into its sheath;
>   shall I not drink the cup
>   which the father has given me? [John 18:11].

The interrogation proceeds as Peter, standing outside, denies association with Jesus three times—to a woman at the door, to officers warming their hands at a fire, and to Malchus. At the third denial, Peter hears the cock crow.

John particularizes the scourging, crowning with thorns, and cries of the mob that conclude Jesus's torment with dramatic counterpoint. In John 19:23–24, soldiers cast lots for his seamless coat. Adjacent to the cross, Jesus's mother, Mary Magdalene, and Mary, wife of Cleophas, observe the horror of a scene typified in art and music as *Stabat Mater* (The Mother Was Standing). Tenderly, Jesus consigns his mother to John. The brief comments of a dying man survive in "I thirst" and "It is finished" (John 19:28, 30). In addition to the punishments of torn hands and sagging torso, John records the breaking of a thief's legs and the piercing of Jesus's side, a wound that recurs in fresco and oil drawings as well as myriad carved crucifixes.

John augments the mystery and majesty of the risen Christ with three salutations wishing peace on the disciples and with the doubts of Thomas. To satisfy his disciple's skepticism, Jesus bids him:

> Reach hither thy finger,
>   and behold my hands:
>   and reach hither thy hand,
>   and thrust it into my side:
>   and be not faithless, but believing [John 20:27].

In the last two verses of the chapter, John explains that he writes of these events and words of Jesus to convince readers that he was the Son of God.

An epilogue appended to Jesus's reappearance describes the apostles returning to their work as fishermen. In Galilee on the Sea of Tiberias, five work at casting their nets. The mysterious presence of Jesus at dawn takes on symbolic significance after he urges them to cast their net to the right of the boat. Peter, who recognizes the Lord, hurries to shore, where the men share a simple shoreman's breakfast of bread and fish. Countering Peter's three denials, Jesus asks three times whether Peter loves him. The author, or possibly an editor, indicates that Jesus loves John, the disciple who survives to "[testify] of these things" (John 21:24), which he declares would fill more books than exist on earth.

Acts

The fifth New Testament book originated before Paul's decapitation during Nero's persecution around C.E. 67. Covering thirty-three years, it sketches in the gap between Jesus's resurrection in C.E. 30 through Paul's imprisonment in C.E. 63. Central to the text is the controversy over orthodox Judaism and the establishment of the Christian church, which spread outward from Palestine to Syria, Turkey, Cyprus, Greece, and the rest of the Roman empire. The author may have been Luke, a native of Antioch or Philippi. He probably intended the work to supplement his gospel with eyewitness accounts of the apostles' good works and interviews with Paul, Barnabas, James, and Philip. The author directed the writing project of the books of Luke and Acts to Theophilus as a confirmation of fact and refutation of rumor and outright fabrication.

Possibly writing from a travel diary, the author orders his work spatially, beginning with a formal introduction common to the era and moving directly to Jesus's departure from earth. At the master's command, the apostles wait in Jerusalem. Like children anticipating a treat, they look forward to the restoration of Israel, but Jesus offers no clue to a fixed date. While awaiting the descent of the Holy Spirit and missions to Judea, Samaria, and other parts of the earth, they gather in the upper room with Jesus's family and female followers and cast lots for a twelfth man, Matthias, to take Judas's place.

In chapter 2, the apostles are celebrating the Jewish feast of Shevuoth when they undergo a supernatural experience — wind, forked flames, and the ability to speak foreign languages. Christian hymnologists recreate this apotheosis in the words of *Veni Creator Spiritus* (Come, Creator Spirit). The Holy Spirit singles out Peter, who prophesies visions, dreams, and wonders and declares Jesus alive in heaven at God's side. In a stirring sermon, Peter directs the company to repent and be baptized. The converts, similar to the Essenes of Qumran, form a brotherhood dedicated to prayer, fellowship, and communal meals, the forerunners of the Eucharist. In the final verse, the writer expresses the single purpose of mission: "And the Lord added to the church daily such as should be saved" (Acts 2:47).

Peter's first cure of a lame man generates public controversy, which climaxes in chapter 4 with the Sadducees' arrest of John and Peter, who refuse to be muzzled. They acquire a valuable convert, Joseph Barnabas, a Levite who becomes Paul's companion in the mission field. After others pool resources, the assembly witnesses the sudden deaths of Ananias and Sapphira, who are guilty of retaining proceeds from their sale of property. Signs and wonders before a gathering at Solomon's Portico ignite more jealousy among the Sadducees, who arrest the apostles. During the night an angel frees the men to continue their work. On the advice of the Pharisee Gamaliel, the council releases the apostles. A tense atmosphere in Jerusalem erupts into outrage and the stoning of Stephen, the first Christian martyr.

The author humanizes the early Christian mission by depicting real danger, the resulting persecution of apostles, and the flight of converts for their lives. In chapter 8, the apostles bury Stephen. Meanwhile, Saul, the future Paul, one of Stephen's opponents, hinders the Christian campaign:

But Saul laid waste the church, and entering house after
   house,
 he dragged off men and women
 and committed them to prison [Acts 8:3].

Perhaps in search of safer territory, Peter and John move from Samaria to Gaza, preaching and proselytizing as they travel.

In chapter 9, the conversion of Saul reprises the drama of Pentecost: light from heaven strikes him and a voice asks why he persecutes Christ. After three days of blindness in Damascus, a parallel to Jesus's three days in the tomb, Saul amazes Jews by changing his allegiance from Jewish orthodoxy to belief in the messiah. The geography of Christian witness moves on from Jerusalem to Lydda, Joppa, and Caesarea on the coast. In chapter 10, Peter receives a vision of earthly animals, a perplexing dream that overrides a Levitican injunction against eating unclean animals, including serpents. The experience enlarges the widening schism between orthodox Judaism and the development of a new faith and spreads controversy over all of Peter's mission.

As the mission advances, Christians continue to walk a fine line between safety and peril. Chapters 11–13 move from Damascus to Antioch and Cyprus. On the perilous journey through hostile Roman territory, Herod executes James with a sword and, to please Jewish authorities, imprisons Peter, whom angels liberate. He arrives at the home of John Mark's mother, creating a stir among the devout. God's grisly comeuppance to Herod proves the power of the message, which Barnabas, Paul, Mark, and John continue to spread. With persecutors at their heels, Paul and Barnabas move on to Iconium. In council in chapter 15, the new Christians make a momentous decision to suspend circumcision as a requirement for conversion of males. Pharisees, ever sticklers for each element of the law, declare: "It is necessary to circumcise them, and to charge them to keep the law of Moses" (Acts 15:5).

Christianity moves into Philippi, the first European mission, in chapter 16, where Paul meets Timothy. Paired with the author, Paul leaves Beroea and enters Athens, a metropolis and intellectual center, and disdains idol worship. On the Areopagus, a podium outside the Parthenon, he boldly refutes worship of an unknown god and declares:

God that made the world and all things therein,
  seeing that he is lord of heaven and earth,
  dwelleth not in temples made with hands;
  neither is worshiped with men's hands,
  as though he needed any thing,
  seeing he giveth to all life, and breath, and all things [Acts 17:24–25].

The mixed reception confronts Paul with doubters and potential converts. To lend credence to the mission's success, the author continues to name converts, citing Dionysius the Areopagite and Damaris. The journey continues southwest to Corinth, where the great preacher reunites with Silas and Timothy. By night, the Holy Spirit continues to support Paul, promising, "I am with thee, and no man shall set on thee to hurt thee" (Acts 18:10).

On his return to Antioch, Paul sets out a third time for the port city of Ephesus, one of his successful forays extolling the Way, his term for Christianity. While he preaches, he also composes his first letter to the Corinthians. The impetus of Christianity runs counter to the worship of Diana, patron goddess of the city, but because Paul makes no attack on her worship, the town clerk urges rioters to give a fair hearing. In chapter 20, Paul chooses to move on to Macedonia and by ship to Assos, Chios, Samos, and Miletus before returning to Jerusalem for Pentecost. Chapter 21 details the itinerary as his party approaches Phoenicia and Syria and lands at Tyre. When Paul runs afoul of Jews from the holy city, he exclaims, "I am ready not to be bound only, but also to die at Jerusalem for the name of the Lord Jesus" (Acts 21:13). To a centurion threatening lashing, Paul declares himself a Roman citizen, a legal status conferring civil rights. After pleading innocence before the sanhedrin, procurator Antonius Felix; his successor, Porcius Festus; and King Agrippa, Paul intends to take his case to Nero, the emperor at Rome.

Traveling with prisoners in chapter 27, Paul continues toward Italy by way of Sidon and Lycia, encountering a deadly storm off the island of Cauda southwest of Crete, and he is shipwrecked off Malta. A profound, composed spokesman for the new faith, he declares to crew and passengers that God intends for him to arrive safely at Rome to appear before Caesar. He quotes an angel that appeared the previous night:

Do not be afraid, Paul;
  you must stand before Caesar;
  and lo, God has granted you all who sail with you [Acts 27:24].

Rome is the focus in chapter 28, in which Paul cites Isaiah 6:9–10, a reminder that Jews have historically not listened to prophecy. Under benign custody for two years, he flourishes among the Jews of Rome, teaching and evangelizing.

In addition to the Gospels and Acts, the Epistles or letters, dating from around C.E. 46–93, detail profound, brotherly correspondence between Paul and neophyte churches—at Rome, Corinth, Galatia, Ephesus, Philippi, Colossae, and Thessalonica—and summarize the pastoral letters to Timothy and Titus, Paul's epistle to Philemon, and the undesignated letter to the Hebrews. The Epistles occupy twenty-one of twenty-seven books and take up a third of the New Testament. In both informal and wide audience formats, they promulgate good advice to new Christians concerning conduct and faith. Canonists appear to have arranged them in order of importance rather than by style or date.

Romans

While on a return visit to Corinth before his arrest in Jerusalem, Paul communicates with one body of Roman Christians in a formal essay explaining the nature of faith. The letter has appealed to the giants of Christianity—theologian Augustine, reformer Martin Luther, allegorist John Bunyan, and John Wesley, founder of Methodism. Dispatched around C.E. 54–57, the epistle opens in Greek style with an identification of the evangelist as "servant of Jesus Christ, called to be an apostle" (Romans 1:1) and anticipates his first visit to the capital in which he claims citizenship. Paul greets Romans as "beloved of God, called to be saints" and confers a standard Christian benediction, "Grace to you and peace from God our father, and the Lord Jesus Christ" (Romans 1:7). After polite overtures, he states exactly who he is and what he believes.

The text bears the evangelist's longest statement and most profound advice. With pulpit vigor, he launches forth in chapter 2 with a sermon opener: "Therefore thou art inexcusable, O man" (Romans 2:1). He declares that the world needs upgrading, particularly the Jews, whom he acknowledges in chapter 3 as receivers of God's prophecy. He concludes that all humanity is heir to God's righteousness, which individuals must access through faith. Through detailed disputation, he cites the example of Abraham, the Old Testament paragon of uprightness and receiver of God's covenant.

In chapter 5, Paul summarizes the joy of Christianity, a new faith that sees Jesus's execution as a redemptive death freeing all people. He puzzles over the negative attitude of fellow Jews, who acknowledge the coming messiah, yet look upon Jesus as a threat to the laws of Moses. In Romans 7:22–23, Paul identifies both the intellectual love of law and the sinful nature to which humanity is heir. He concludes with a pointed rhetorical question: "Who shall separate us from the love of Christ? shall tribulation, or distress, or persecution, or famine, or nakedness, or peril, or sword?" (Romans 8:35). In Romans 10:12, Paul boldly asserts a revolutionary thought — that there is no separate salvation for Jew and Greek, "for the same lord over all is rich unto all that call upon him." Thus, the Jews have no right to think of themselves as the chosen any more than other humans.

To rescue his treatise from anti–Hebrew tirade, in chapter 11, Paul retrenches by reminding the Romans that he, too, is a Jew, a descendant of father Abraham and a scion of Benjamin's tribe. To those Jews who harden their hearts against the messiah, Paul advises them to penetrate the mystery of Christ's execution and resurrection. In an oversimplification of the Beatitudes from the Sermon on the Mount, he advocates Jesus's teaching concerning vengeance:

Bless them which persecute you;
  bless, and curse not.
Rejoice with them that do rejoice,
  and weep with them that weep.
Be of the same mind one toward another [Romans 12:14–16].

In chapter 13, Paul urges adherence to the Ten Commandments, but demands that people not judge each other so punctiliously by the letter of the law that they hinder or block a fellow seeker. After stating his hope to preach in Spain, he closes formally in Romans 16:33 with "amen," meaning "so be it." An appended chapter salutes Christians by name, including his associate Timothy. Paul identifies certain residences as safehouses and declares that he has entrusted his missive to Phoebe, a member of the church at Cenchrea, a seaport near Corinth.

I Corinthians

After his mission to Corinth, Paul had returned to Ephesus. He heard of dissension at the church at Corinth when he wrote the first Book of Corinthians advising new Christians on how to function in an idolatrous, immoral setting. The letter, written around C.E. 53, shortly before the epistle to the Romans, treats specific questions and divisiveness in a multicultural church blessed with members of different races and religious backgrounds, including Aphroditism and Judaism. He moves from formal salutation and benediction to a challenge that "there are contentions among you" (I Corinthians 1:11). In reply to rumors and a delegation of members, he answers questions about cliquishness, incest, litigation, freedom versus license, and unruly behavior. He covers marriage versus celibacy, divorce and mixed marriage between pagan and convert, idolatry, autonomy of women, and the meaning of resurrection of the dead.

Paul opens chapter 2 with a disclaimer that he is no model of oratory or intellect. Rather, he speaks through revelation from God. In a first-person example, he calms early church jitters, admonishing the members at Corinth to avoid taking problems to secular courts. In reference to the carnality for which Corinth is known, he urges flight from fornication for "your body is the temple of the Holy Spirt" (I Corinthians 6:19). He commands that women adopt the custom of covering their hair when they worship, unlike harbor prostitutes, who flaunt loose hair as a symbol of loose morals. After a long list of picky details, chapter 12 ends with sensible advice: "Covet earnestly the best gifts."

Chapter 13, one of the most lyric of religious canticles, stands out from Paul's weightier harangues for its beneficence and joy in Christian love. His opening line suggests the continual battering he has undergone from the Jewish hierarchy. Noting the difference between the loving and the litigious, he says of himself:

Though I speak with the tongues of men and of angels
  and have not charity,
I am become as sounding brass,
  or a tinkling cymbal [I Corinthians 13:1].

A clever put-down to pompous interpreters of the law, the words accuse no one but Paul. Verse 4 begins the poetic analysis of charity, the long-suffering, kind, and modest virtue that is courteous and unassuming. In an outburst of parallels he adds, "Beareth all things, believeth all things, hopeth all things, endureth all things" (I Corinthians 13:7).

Paul's paean to charity digs deeper and finds more qualities to extol. Charity is unfailing, he declares. With a backward glance at Judaism's tradition of prophecy, he looks ahead to "that which is perfect," the messiah whom Temple officials reject (I Corinthians 13:10). To these denyers of the promised one, he states that their vision is obscure, "through a glass, darkly" (I Corinthians 13:12). The true joy of the Christ, he says, is personal involvement, which generously bestows love.

Chapter 14 continues Paul's complaint that new Christians are still acting like contentious Jews. In verse 26, he accuses them of coming together for worship, but breaking into individual doctrines, revelations, and interpretations. He prefers silence and speaking to self and God, the two-way communication of prayer. In a focused chapter, he reminds them at length of the centrality of resurrection to Jesus's life and ministry. Paul's delineation of life after death remains unequaled in modern verse:

Behold, I shew you a mystery.
We shall not all sleep,
  but we shall all be changed,
  in a moment, in the twinkling of an eye,
  at the last trumpet:
  for the trumpet shall sound,
  and the dead shall be raised incorruptible,
  and we shall be changed [I Corinthians 15:52–53].

He dares death to flaunt its sting, the grave to proclaim a victory. Paul concludes, "Your labour is not in vain in the Lord" (I Corinthians 15:58). Departing from his task as inspirer of those struggling to found a faith, he drops his mantle and speaks congenially on local matters and of his and Timothy's itineraries. He conveys the holy kiss of the brethren. The final line names the scribes who finished the job of dictation.

II Corinthians

Less easily dated, Paul's follow-up letter, dispatched from Macedonia some months after I Corinthians, may be one of a regular series of communications, the rest of which have not survived. Most certainly, there has been a sharply critical exchange that has provoked anguish among beloved followers. Thus, the reader hears only one side of a situation that presses Paul to the limits of patience and understanding. Like arriving in the middle of a movie, the reader can only guess the charges and failings the apostle must deal with long distance and in writing rather than face to face as they map out the new faith.

The text of II Corinthians, composed around c.e. 54, seems contemporaneous with Galatians and Romans and some months after I Corinthians and Philippians. It indicates that Paul encountered life-threatening adversity in Asia and that he is willing to put himself in jeopardy to spread the gospel. Eager to know how the congregation at Corinth is faring, he had tried to cross paths with Titus on the Troad, a point of land in Asia Minor at the entrance to the Dardanelles. To his delight, in Macedonia, Paul encounters Titus and learns that church infighting is lessening. To assure stability in Corinth, he plans another pastoral call on the congregation.

Paul never strays far from his mission. In II Corinthians 9:11, he promises that Christians will be "enriched in every thing to all bountifulness, which causeth through us thanksgiving to God." In chapter 11, he declares them wedded to Christ and pours out the onus of mission as it spreads far from headquarters. Still defensive after criticisms of his performance as preacher and organizer, he warns:

Let no man think me a fool;
  if otherwise, yet as a fool receive me,
  that I may boast myself a little [II Corinthians 11:16].

To charges that he is not a true apostle because he has no personal knowledge of Jesus, he defends his position with divine backing. He claims that God spoke to him to acknowledge "My grace is sufficient for thee, for my strength is made perfect in weakness" (II Corinthians 12:9).

In the final analysis, Jesus's life becomes the model for new Christians. Like a fond but high-minded parent, Paul instructs the Corinthian Christians to test their behavior and determine if they are emulating Christ. He closes the admonition with simplified commands to be perfect, mutually comforting, and peace loving. As tangible proof of brotherhood, he reminds them to bestow the saintly kiss as evidence of union.

Galatians

Probably composed around c.e. 54–55 after Paul completed his first and second missions, the letter from Rome to the churches in Galatia traveled farther east than any of his other seven epistles. It is a momentous occasion, a crisis that requires prompt, unequivocal answers before his new churches crumble. By way of scrutinizing the ticklish question of conversion, Paul clarifies the parameters of Christianity. He determines that non–Jews can move directly into Christianity without first passing the test of Judaism. He firmly declares repentance and faith in Christ the only requirements for salvation. Thus, Paul issues a veritable Declaration of Independence from Judaism. His bold answer sweeps aside centuries of loyalty to Mosaic law, circumcision, sacrifice at the Temple altar, and ritual observance and establishes that Christianity is indeed a viable religion.

The text emphasizes that Paul is a divine emissary speaking for Christ. After the formal salutation, he bursts out, "I marvel that ye are so soon removed from him that called you" (Galatians 1:6) and rails at the notion of rival preachers, the Judaizers who subvert their constancy. Beginning with verse 13, he delivers a brief autobiography of his own conversion from a persecutor of Christians to a believer. Under the influence of Peter and James, Jesus's brothers, Paul has become an example of godliness. He outlines his association with colleagues Barnabas and Titus and builds up to a grand statement of Christ's universality:

There is neither Jew nor Greek,
  there is neither bond nor free,
  there is neither male nor female:
  for ye are all one in Christ Jesus [Galatians 3:28].

Immediately, he turns back to his roots and adds that Christ's children are the promised seed of Abraham and heirs to the covenant with the God of the Torah.

In chapter 6, Paul stresses that each Christian must stand upon individual merit. With Old Testament gravity, he thunders:

> Be not deceived;
> God is not mocked:
> for whatsoever a man soweth,
> that shall he also reap [Galatians 6:7].

So worked up is the preacher that he takes the pen from his secretary in Galatians 6:11 and writes in his own hand a strong restatement that circumcision is a minor outward show of the law, but faith marks the whole body as belonging to Christ.

Ephesians

The first of the captivity letters, the Book of Ephesians, like Colossians, Philippians, and Philemon, appears to be an encyclical or circular epistle, i.e., Paul's message from prison distributed to a consortium of churches. Because the letter derives from Ephesus on the Mediterranean coast of modern Turkey, it carries a name designating the Ephesians as the receivers. Composed at the Mamartine Prison adjacent to the Roman Forum around C.E. 62 and written contemporaneously with the books of Colossians and Philemon, the body of the letter speaks to the issue of unity among gentile and Jewish converts.

With a touch of nostalgia that he is confined from his usual energetic travels, Paul exudes contentment in the blessing of faith in Christ and declares, "We should be holy and without blame before him" (Ephesians 1:4). The distillation of years of meditation has refined Paul's view of Christianity and compels him to unceasing thankfulness and anticipation of reunion with the savior. In chapter 2, Paul marvels at God's mercy in resurrecting humanity to live forever in a heavenly abode. The letter exults that people who were once "strangers and foreigners" are now "fellow citizens with the saints, and of the household of God" (Ephesians 2:19).

Chapter 3 identifies his circumstance as a prisoner because he has violated Jewish superiority by declaring gentiles their equal. In verse 14, he prays that Christ may enter hearts and replace bickering with love. Stressing unanimity of faith and purpose, he commends them to "one Lord, one faith, one baptism, one god and father of all" (Ephesians 4:5–6). Even though some nations receive apostles and others evangelists, pastors, and teachers, no one has reason for vanity, for each Christian has the same value before God. Paul's purpose is a matter of survival. Using a controlling metaphor drawn from the helmeted Roman guards who operate the prison, he exhorts,

> Put on the whole armor of God,
> that ye may be able to stand
> against the wiles of the devil [Ephesians 6:11].

He closes by dispatching Tychicus, "beloved brother and faithful minister in the lord," as intermediary and bearer of peace and love (Ephesians 6:21).

Philippians

More bread-and-butter note than instructional missive, Paul's four-chapter letter from prison to the Roman colony at Philippi thanks his friends for a donation. Speaking for his companion Timothy, he prefaces his sojourn. Paul may have composed the note at Caesarea or Ephesus around C.E. 53 near the issuance of I Corinthians, or possibly sent it a decade later from Rome's Mamartine Prison. The text addresses a single church on the European coast of the Aegean Sea.

Unlike the smoldering letters to quarreling congregations, this text reveals a more contemplative author, who has had time in prison to gentle his thoughts about the beginnings of a "good work" (Philippians 1:6). As before in notes from his cell, he thinks of himself as Christ's prisoner rather than as an inmate in a manmade lockup. So sure is he of eternal life that he asserts, "For to me to live is Christ, and to die is gain" (Philippians 1:21). As though reteaching the example set by Jesus, he reminds his readers, "He humbled himself, and became obedient unto death, even the death of the cross" (Philippians 2:8).

To Paul, Christians are a unique family. Baying about are the Judaizers, whom he reviles as "dogs" that work evil and insist on circumcision as proof of godliness (Philippians 3:2). Overcome by loneliness and frustration at inactivity, Paul admits that he weeps at the thought of Christ's enemies who would destroy rather than build up God's kingdom. With forbearance, he promises, "The lord is at hand" (Philippians 4:5). He exhorts all to pray and confers a noble benediction, "The peace of God, which passeth all understanding, shall keep your hearts and minds through Christ Jesus" (Philippians 4:7).

Significant to Paul's ministry is his intent to stay humble. He acknowledges that he, too, has been admonished and asserts that he can function both as pastor and prisoner. With the wisdom of experience, he declares, "I can do all things through Christ which strengtheneth me" (Philippians 4:13). In closing, he thanks the Philippians for being the only church to send money, which they have posted more than once. Their parcel, carried by Epaphroditus, contained a fragrance, possibly potpourri or sweet oil.

Colossians

The tenor and themes of this four-chapter letter to the Christians of Colossae suggest that Paul may have posted a similar note or circular letter from prison to other congregations. Dating is uncertain. It may be a prison letter sent from Rome around C.E. 61. The occasion appears to converge with the letters to the Ephesians and Philemon and targets one church in Asia Minor a hundred miles inland from Ephesus.

Paul has learned from his emissary, Epaphras, that rival preachers are undermining the new church. In his usual style, he opens with a salutation and thanks to God. His spirits lift from evidence of God's work among Christians. Paul intervenes and alerts backsliders "lest any man should beguile you with enticing words" (Colossians 2:4). In reference to ritual, he orders, "Let no man therefore judge you in meat, or in drink, or in respect of an holy day, or of the new moon, or of the Sabbath days" (Colossians 2:16).

Counter to a growing syncretic element at Colossae, Paul rejects mind-centered doctrines and reminds his fellow Christians that their faith must focus on Christ. As a guide, chapter 3 instructs Colossians to break with the old life and restructure their thinking. He queries:

> if ye be dead with Christ from the rudiments of the world,
>   why, as though living in the world,
>   are ye subject to ordinances?
> Touch not; taste not; handle not [Colossians 2:20–21].

As in the Book of Galatians, Paul stresses the universality of Christianity, a religion centered in heaven rather than in the strictures of legalistic, earthbound faiths. Of the people who make up society, he explains:

> There is neither Greek nor Jew,
>   circumcision nor uncircumcision,
>   barbarian, Scythian,
>   bond nor free:
>   but Christ is all, and in all [Colossians 3:11].

He belts out his usual cheery homily: "Whatsoever ye do, do it heartily, as to the Lord, and not unto men" (Colossians 3:23).

A concern of Christianity is the abomination of slavery. In the final chapter, Paul overturns the authority of the slave master by reminding Christians that they have a heavenly master. He states his indebtedness to a group of Christians he acknowledges by name: Tychicus, Onesimus, Aristarchus, Mark, Justus, Epaphras, Luke, Demus, and Nympha, a woman who maintains a body of worshipers at her home. The list forms an historical link to the early church and the men and women who remain loyal to the faith during Paul's incarceration. He urges that the congregants share letters with the church at Laodicea in Turkey. The epilogue refers to Tychicus and Onesimus, Paul's messengers, his only link with the outside world while he awaits trial in Rome.

I Thessalonians

Perhaps the earliest of Paul's letters, the five-chapter first Book of Thessalonians derives from a sojourn Paul, Silas (or Silvanus), and Timothy make at Thessalonica, capital of Macedonia and a thriving Aegean harbor town. They arrive around C.E. 50, after a mob thrusts them from Philippi. The times are distressing. Subsequent to the founding of a congregation and three successive sabbath sermons from Paul, Jason and other followers were jailed. To keep peace and lessen persecution by Jews, Paul's company departs to Beroea. After he settles at Athens and moves on to Corinth, he dispatches Timothy back north to learn of the Thessalonians' fate.

The letter represents Paul's reflections over his teaching and mission. Mature and confident, he speaks to one church. Writing from Corinth, he thanks God that Christianity has taken hold in Thessalonica as a seedbed for missions throughout Macedonia and south to Achaia. In I Thessalonians 2:9, he acknowledges that the missionary's work is a life of affliction and adversity, though he brightens in chapter 3 after receiving encouraging news from the Thessalonians.

Paul's mind is ever attuned to unclean and impious behavior. Chapter 4 returns to his instructions, particularly about resurrection. In I Thessalonians 4:13–18, he implores members not to grieve for the sleeper because Christ has assured a new life in heaven. Moving toward a close, he calls new Christians "the children of light," a term that separates them from the people of darkness, who pious Jews anticipated fighting on judgment day (I Thessalonians 5:5). In verse 8, he returns to martial metaphors of armor and helmet. Like soldiers going into battle, he urges them to think like comrades. As though hesitating to end his letter, he adds a comprehensive code of piety:

> Rejoice evermore.
> Pray without ceasing.
> In everything give thanks....
> Quench not the spirit.
> Despise not prophesyings.
> Prove all things;
>   hold fast to that which is good.
> Abstain from all appearance of evil [I Thessalonians 5:16–21].

As an assurance of brotherly behavior, he reminds them again about bestowing the holy kiss on fellow Christians and charges them to share their letters with other churches.

II Thessalonians

Written a year later, the sequel letter to the first Thessalonians, dispatched from Athens, is only three chapters in length. It exhorts new Christians in hard times, when Jews lob charges of heresy. In the midst of tribulation, he bids them take comfort in the Second Coming, when Christ will immolate those who disobey the gospel in consummate ruin. In chapter 2, Paul attacks the question of when Christ will return to earth by reminding them in verse 3 that rebellion and lawlessness will precede the end of time. His reference to a "man of sin" allies with the apocalyptic vision of the Antichrist, a symbolic being obsessed with subverting goodness and seizing control of earth. Paul balances damnation to the wicked with blessings on the Thessalonians, whom "God hath from the beginning chosen" (II Thessalonians 2:13). Such language attests to Paul's background as a Jew and to his belief that God selects the best of humanity, just as he chose Abraham, Noah, David, and Elijah.

As always, Paul asks for prayers and deliverance. He promises that Christ will keep safe his followers. In an extended benediction, he commands Thessalonian Christians to avoid disorderly people and to behave in accord with his example. Specifically, he upbraids idlers and busybodies. According to his advice, Christians must earn their keep like all sensible people. To assure authenticity, Paul adds to the scribe's page a line in his own handwriting.

I Timothy

The first of the pastoral letters, I Timothy relates to Timothy of Lystra, Paul's beloved colleague, some advice on congregational organization and pulpit duties. The letter writer, who may or may not have been Paul, appears to speak from the wisdom of old age and may have dispatched the note from Laodicea around C.E. 64, about the time of its sequel and the Book of Titus. Another possibility is that a disciple may be speaking pseudonymously, completing a letter that Paul left in outline or note form. Whatever the situation, the fire of the earlier letters appears banked into a steady warmth of Christian love and contentment.

The text summarizes the task of leading a new church. It addresses issues of worship, such as asceticism and celibacy, qualifications of bishops and deacons, and attitudes toward specific members, i.e., widows, elders, and slaves. A subdued opening confers blessing from Paul, who may be writing in his last months when his vigor is gone. The speaker refers to speculators and quibblers, but gives few particulars about those who "have wandered away into vain discussion" (I Timothy 1:6). Verse 18 lovingly addresses Timothy as "my son" and impels him to fight the good fight, a continuation of Paul's military imagery. The fatherly tone may derive from Paul's decline, as he reflects on Timothy's faithfulness as

confidant and delegate in times when Paul could not be in two places at once.

The second chapter requests that monarchs and authority figures grant Christians "a quiet and peaceable life in all godliness and honesty" (I Timothy 2:2). With self-assurance, the writer declares that all serve one god and that Christ is the mediator between humankind and God. Without the feistiness of earlier letters, he seeks quiet tolerance for prayer and the modesty of Christian women. One of the disturbing statements to women is his specific request that women be quiet and submissive and that they not take control.

The writer's advice to pastors and church officials is to distance themselves from godlessness and mythology and to devote themselves to teaching and duty. Chapter 3 lists the qualities of a temperate, family-minded man capable of welcoming guests, maintaining sobriety, and administering personal affairs before accepting the challenge of a church. Ministers should devote themselves to studying scripture, preaching, and teaching. The writer offers no model of the pulpit prodigy; rather, he concentrates on day-to-day attention to task, thus preferring the simple parson to the flash-in-the-pan evangelist.

Chapter 5 reestablishes honor to elders and singles out the ideal widow as worthy of support, especially

if she have brought up children,
if she have lodged strangers,
if she have washed the saints' feet,
if she have relieved the afflicted,
if she have diligently followed every good work [I Timothy 5:10].

The last chapter speaks to all members and warns against the proud, disputatious malcontent who corrupts the mind.

The author falls into a series of adages that have survived as sage advice. He reduces all to a simple formula: "We brought nothing into this world, and it is certain we can carry nothing out" (I Timothy 6:7). To this he adds, "For the love of money is the root of all evil" (I Timothy 6:10), an adage that is often misquoted. Upmost in his mind is an adjuration to Timothy to forget putting on pompous airs and to strive for good works.

II Timothy

Without self-pity or regret, Paul, or the writer assuming his identity, takes the role of veteran spokesman for the faith and passes on to the second generation a daunting task. From a prison cell, he addresses Timothy once more as though he were a beloved son and mentions prayers and longing directed at him for his sincerity. Paul wishes to touch Timothy's head, thus conferring blessing through the ancient rite of laying on of hands.

This four-chapter letter of fatherly advice urges the receiver to be the stoic soldier and to accept the suffering that comes with the role of Christian. The text turns to a poetic parallelism in II Timothy 2:11–13:

If we be dead with him, we shall also live with him.
If we suffer, we shall also reign with him:
  if we deny him, he also will deny us.
If we believe not, yet he abideth faithful:
  he cannot deny himself.

Paul prepares Timothy for the perilous times that will precede Christ's return to earth. Before the end-time, there will be persecution, evil men, imposters, and deceivers. In II Timothy 2:15, Paul urges:

Study to shew thyself approved unto God,
  a workman that needeth not to be ashamed,
  rightly dividing the word of truth.

This image of the clear-eyed loyalist contrasts with the next verse, which speaks of profane and vain babblers, whom Paul considers ungodly.

As a bolster to the faithful Timothy, Paul recommends scripture, God's inspired word, which "is profitable for doctrine, for reproof, for correction, for instruction in righteousness" (II Timothy 3:16). He charges Timothy with the task of preaching, rebuking, and exhorting, the three-part role of a good minister. In anticipation of execution at the hands of the Romans, the aged missionary foresees a crown honoring his own righteousness. In the absence of supporters, he has stood alone in the docket of Nero's tribunal, but continues to rely on God.

The epistle stresses Paul's acceptance of human limitations. He closes with explicit instructions that Timothy reunite with his mentor, who has only Luke to rely on. Paul asks that Timothy bring Mark and a stout mantle, books, and parchments. He names his followers and indicates who is still in the mission field, who has defected, and who is unable to go on. With his time growing short, Paul prays that the Lord be with Timothy.

Titus

Contemporaneous with the two letters to Timothy, Paul's three-chapter note to Titus, dispatched around C.E. 64, speaks to a trusted Christian who he has relied on to settle crises in distant churches. While Titus resides amid dishonest Cretans, Paul instructs him to rely on scripture. Against such a background, he directs Titus to take strength from his faith.

Chapters 2–3 summarize the best of Christian behavior as opposed to the worst examples among Cretans. Paul names worthy traits in the elder, older woman,

young men, and slaves as the ideal set before the teacher. He concludes, "These things speak, and exhort, and rebuke with all authority. Let no man despise thee" (Titus 2:15). Paul is exacting: he expects hard work, kind words, harmony, gentleness, and courtesy. The model for human perfection is Jesus, who made humanity "heirs according to the hope of eternal life" (Titus 3:7).

Athough old and feeble, Paul is still demanding. In the last lines, he expects Titus to perform good works and to avoid the tedious quibbles, genealogy, and legal puzzles that absorb the Jews. Paul wants to meet Titus at Nicopolis, a port on the west coast of Greece where Paul intends to spend the winter. In a brief, friendly sign-off, he bids farewell and sends his greetings to fellow Christians.

Philemon

A brief note from Paul composed around C.E. 62, the letter to Philemon, a Colossian in Phrygia, is an example of personal correspondence to a generous Christian. The subject is unpleasant for an egalitarian missionary: Paul has encountered Onesimus, Philemon's slave who has run away to Rome, met Paul, and converted. Central to the letter is Paul's preparation for the meeting of two of his converts, master and recalcitrant slave. Onesimus can rightfully expect flogging, branding, or the slicing off of an ear. Note that Onesimus is guilty of robbing Philemon of his own person, which a slave cannot own.

From his cell in a Roman prison, Paul greets Philemon as well as other "fellow soldiers" who meet for worship at Philemon's house. Without attacking slavery as a social evil, Paul pleads for lenience, for he has come to value Onesimus ("my child") as one who "might have ministered unto me" (Philemon 1:13). Paul challenges Philemon to rise above the master mindset and to cherish Onesimus as "a brother beloved, specially to me" (Philemon 1:16). In Christly fashion, Paul accepts Onesimus's wrongdoing as a personal burden, much as the Good Samaritan took responsibility for the wounded man's debts. Paul, out of faith in Philemon, expects him to render even more mercy than requested.

A short personal addition asks for lodging. Obviously, Paul hopes to regain his freedom and continue island hopping and city-to-city work, which might include observation of Philemon's forgiveness of Onesimus. Paul names his Christian friends and salutes Philemon with the standard "grace of our Lord Jesus Christ" (Philemon 1:25).

Hebrews

Linked to Rome, the epistle to the Hebrews is the Bible's most thorough, precise disputation. The text lacks a specific address or salutation and may have been sent around C.E. 66. Its topic is the assurance of nostalgic Jews that Christianity supersedes orthodox Judaism. Because the writer knows Timothy, the letter appears to derive from the tight group of confreres whom Paul mentions by name in his missives. The style is refined Greek from a skilled teacher and student of the Septuagint, most likely a Hellenized Jew. The recipients are probably a cell of converted Jews who have weathered their share of adversity from their orthodox brethren. The writer suspects that they need a strong exhortation to remain true to Christianity.

Speaking in the plural "we" rather than an accusatory "you," the writer opens full throttle in defense of Christ, the promised messiah, who was deity in human form. The author notes that angels serve the Lord, but deserve no worship. The text inserts an unthinkable statement from God to angels:

> For unto which of the angels said he at any time,
>   Thou art my son,
>   this day have I begotten thee?
> And again, I will be to him a father,
>   and he shall be to me a son? [Hebrews 1:5].

To establish Jesus in terms a Jew can appreciate, the writer compares him to high priests and to Moses, giant of the Exodus, but only a man, no more than a tool of God. Just as Aaron, Moses's brother, served the people as high priest and spokesman for God, Jesus came to earth to welcome humankind into God's abiding love, a gift that the godly cannot refuse.

To keep the Hebrews from abandoning their new faith, in chapter 5, the writer attacks weak-kneed rebellion. The long harangue cites argument after argument and culminates in chapter 10 with a warning that rejection would surely doom the flagging Christians. The argument continues with warnings of tragic loss. Just as the Israelites shirked their duty to God, Christians risk losing the Promised Land by allowing their faith to waver. The writer contrasts Israelites with Christians:

He that despised Moses' law died without mercy
  under two or three witnesses.
Of how much sorer punishment, suppose ye,
  shall he be thought worthy,
  who had trotted under foot the Son of God? [Hebrews
  10:28–29].

To create a picture of faith in readers' minds, in chapter 11, the writer piles up evidence in the actions of Abel, Enoch, Noah, Abraham, Isaac, Jacob, Joseph, Moses, Joshua, the Judges, David, Daniel, Elijah, Jeremiah, Isaiah, and Zechariah — a brief summary of the entire Old Testament. The writer concludes:

> These all died in faith,
>   not having received the promises,
>   but having seen them afar off,
>   and were persuaded of them,
>   and embraced them,
>   and confessed that they were strangers
>   and pilgrims on the earth [Hebrews 11:13].

The future demands of the Hebrews a break with the earthbound sacrifices and an acceptance of Jesus, the one true sacrifice.

In conclusion, the writer bids the Hebrews to display loving hospitality, "for thereby some have entertained angels unawares" (Hebrews 13:1). He urges visits to prisoners and compassion toward persecuted Christians, and he extols honor to marriage vows. As a watchword for the future, he declares, "Jesus Christ the same yesterday, and today, and forever" (Hebrews 13:8). The author's benediction survives in current use verbatim from the first century:

Now the god of peace,
  that brought again from the dead our Lord Jesus,
  that great shepherd of the sheep,
  through the blood of the everlasting covenant,
  make you perfect in every good work to do his will,
  working in you that which is well-pleasing in his sight
  [Hebrews 13:20–21].

A personal postscript declares that Timothy has gained his freedom and conveys salutations from Italian Christians.

From the Pauline epistles and the anonymous Book of Hebrews, the New Testament canon continues with the books of James, Peter, John, and Jude, known as general epistles. The twenty-seven-book compendium concludes with Revelation, also called the Apocalypse, John's cryptic vision of a conclusive battle between good and evil and the return of Jesus to judge earth's people.

James

Scholars attribute the book of James to James the Lesser, possibly a nephew of Mary and therefore Jesus's cousin, who is close enough to be called a brother. A "catholic" or pragmatic epistle composed either around C.E. 44 or before C.E. 70, his writing reads like an old-time pulpit text. He speaks formally to all Christians rather than to an individual or particular church. Sermon-style, the five-chapter harangue treats the significant change that converted Jews experience when they move from a legalistic faith bound by the Pentateuch, which is a strict code of behavior for all aspects of life. To those who grasp their freedom too liberally, James reminds them that a true Christian must display by actions a decency and principle that derives from faith.

James's discourse opens with a blessing and moves smoothly from point to point in the manner of a persuasive essay. As though leaning from a podium, he warns:

> Do not err, my beloved brethren.
> Every good gift and every perfect gift
>   is from above,
>   and cometh down from the Father of lights,
>   with whom is no variableness,
>   neither shadow of turning [James 1:16–17].

That said, James turns on lazy or shallow Christians in verse 22 and exhorts them to action by consoling orphans and widows and remaining pure from worldly influence.

James the preacher does not neglect specifics. Chapter 2 rejects partiality and informs the reader that Christianity overrides class barriers. He declares:

> But if ye have respect to persons,
>   ye commit sin,
>   and are convinced of the law as transgressors [James 2:9].

Chapter 3 treats the problem of uncontrolled speech:

> And the tongue is a fire,
>   a world of iniquity:
>   so is the tongue among our members,
>   that it defileth the whole body,
>   and setteth on fire the course of nature;
>   and it is set on fire of hell [James 3:6].

This hard-edged, epigrammatic advice was a favorite of Puritans, who admired scripture that was easily excerpted and that pulled from on high the lofty, the supercilious, and those who maligned humble Christians.

In summary, James states that the wise Christian avoids these pitfalls and resides in a patient, loving concern for humankind. Unlike clever manipulators, Christians should retreat from affluence and self-centered goals to a prayerful communion with God. James closes with simple answers to a list of human situations:

> Is any among you afflicted:
>   let him pray.
> Is any merry?
>   let him sing psalms.
> Is any sick among you?
>   let him call for the elders of the church
>   and let them pray over him [James 5:13–14].

Prayer, he reiterates, is an answer to quandary. Just as it saved Elijah, it is the Christian's bulwark.

I Peter

An uplifting epistle from Rome, the four-chapter Book of I Peter addresses churches in northern Asia Minor and supports new Christians during multiple local persecutions. Dispatched around C.E. 63, a year before his execution in Rome at the hand of Emperor Nero, the letter is the work of Andrew's brother, an admired Galilean. The two fishermen from Capernaum were Jesus's beloved converts. From day labor, Simon Peter advanced to apostle, fell from grace by denying his Lord, then rebounded to lead cells of Christians with the help of Silas and John Mark.

Peter anticipates hardship for Christians and dispenses hope and solace. He insists that tests of faith should gladden the faithful, whose hope in reunion with Christ is a reward too precious to lose sight of. Peter's advice in chapters 2–3 is thoughtful and easily applicable to daily life. He contends that Christians must think of themselves as newborns and God's elect:

> Ye are a chosen generation,
>   a royal priesthood,
>   an holy nation,
>   a peculiar people [I Peter 2:9].

They must accept the fact that they stand out from non–Christians, much as the Jews held themselves apart from pagan nomads.

With the end-time in mind, Peter speaks of adherence to governmental authorities, slave masters, and spouses as a necessity. To women in particular, he urges chastity, submission, and modest attire after the style of Sarah, Abraham's wife. To husbands, he urges consideration and honor to wives. Peter's succinct conclusion reminds readers to be unified, compassionate, humble, and patient in times of distress. He negates vengeance with a simple rule:

> Not rendering evil for evil
>   or railing for railing:
>   but contrariwise blessing;
>   knowing that ye are thereunto called,
>   that ye should inherit a blessing [I Peter 3:9].

Speaking as an elder, he promotes long-suffering and hospitality to all in the style of "the chief shepherd" (I Peter 5:4). Before Peter entrusts his letter to Silas, he shares with readers the greetings of Mark and an unnamed woman, who passes along her salutation.

II Peter

The sequel letter, addressed to the recipients of I Peter, summarizes threats to the neophyte church, but offers no clues as to a historical period. It speaks of Paul's letters as though they have been anthologized and revered by Christians like earlier scripture. Thus, this three-chapter missive must date after Paul's death. Because the style, tone, and diction differ from the first letter, scholars assume that the book of II Peter may be the writing of a pseudonymous disciple, perhaps writing after Peter's death. The text indicates that Peter has little time left.

The author reiterates James's message that the genuine follower of Christ manifests a change of heart through actions. Unlike false, self-serving teachers, who inherit the same godly wrath that destroyed the earth in Noah's time and incinerated Sodom and Gomorrah, the Christian must be deep down devoted to goodness. In chapter 3, Peter exults in the Second Coming:

> Wherefore, beloved, seeing that ye look for such things,
>   be diligent that ye may be found of him in peace,
>   without spot, and blameless.
> And account that the long-suffering of our Lord is salvation
>   [II Peter 3:14–15].

He exhorts Christians to remain steadfast and grow in grace and knowledge of the Lord.

I John

The most recent of New Testament books, I John and its two sequels, the work of the gospel writer John, appear to date to around 90 C.E., when Christianity had established itself throughout the Roman empire over a half century of missions. The elder John, retired to Ephesus, is alert to unorthodox tenets of gnosticism, a mind-based philosophy that denied Jesus's humanity. To a loving, devout preacher like John, this anathema requires immediate refutation through encyclical letters to the churches. However urgent the need, his gentle delivery never rises to the fire of James or the vigor of Paul.

John selects light as an apt metaphor for God's word and darkness as the antithesis, an image of sin and self-delusion. He pinpoints the multiple meanings of light as truth, intact and pure, and declares, "The darkness is past, and the true light now shineth" (I John 2:8). John insists that, to grow in the light, Christians must obey God by embracing humanity for all its faults and abandoning hatred. They must also avoid the Antichrist, the embodiment of evil subversion. An exponent of love, John uses chapters 3–4 to define Christian love as displayed in God's sacrifice of his son. As though addressing children, the fatherly preacher makes numerous points about good behavior, repeating the word *love* until it echoes through the passages with affirmation.

II John

Addressed to a specific "elect sister" and her children, the second letter of John reiterates the message of the first missive. He continues to embrace Christians as naive and innocent of evil. In thirteen verses, he takes hope from those who follow truth and instructs the woman "that we love one another" (II John 1:5). He alerts her to the Antichrist. His close tells much about the writer. John would rather speak person to person than write letters. Thus, he relishes a future meeting.

III John

Equally brief, the elder at Ephesus challenges an interloper, a maverick elder named Diotrephes, whose egotism and discourtesy are disrupting a congregation, traditionally identified as the church at Pergamum in Asia Minor. John characterizes this upstart as one "who loveth to have the preeminence among them" (III John 1:9). His message to the unidentified Gaius is to overcome the chaotic element and leave Diotrephes to John, who will put a stop to his surliness. The upshot of John's third letter is the importance of hospitality to itinerant preachers and church leaders who nourish the flame of Christianity while stamping out controversy. As in John's second letter, he prefers talking to writing and looks forward to a meeting with Gaius.

Jude

A short communication, the Book of Jude refers to the heresy mentioned in II Peter. Both Jude and James appear to have been Jesus's brothers. The letter, dating around C.E. 79, reprises the information contained in II Peter, in particular, the danger of false teaching by superior, self-important men seeking to overturn church authority. Jude cites the example of the citizens of Sodom and Gomorrah and bemoans speakers of evil:

> Woe unto them!
>   for they have gone in the way of Cain,
>   and ran greedily after the error of Balaam for reward,
>   and perished in the gainsaying of Core [Jude 1:11].

Jude waxes lyrical on the subject, comparing such false teachers to clouds blown about by wind, blighted trees, foam-edged waves of the sea, and wandering stars. For a touch of grace, he confers a benediction in the name of "him that is able to keep you from falling" (Jude 1:24), a familiar blessing conferred on Protestant congregations.

Revelation

The Bible's most puzzling apocalypse, derived from the Greek *apocalypsis* (unfolding or uncovering), the Book of Revelation reveals allegorical visions of divine justice and retribution. Christ's return is pictured as a triumphal reentry into the world of humankind. Composed by John the Divine from a penal colony on Patmos

Island, southwest of Ephesus, the book is prison literature issued from a period of exile around C.E. 95, near the end of the reign of Domitian. The exact identity of John leaves open a possible connection with the gospel and epistle writer John, but he lacks the fire to have produced so vivid a dreamscape, obviously penned by a passionate theist. The whirling images of phantasms, plagues, and mythic beasts and citations from many parts of the Bible have served authors, singers, evangelists, and artists with profound and imaginative subjects.

Without condemning outright the Roman empire or opening himself to arrest for sedition, the author, drunk on Old Testament prophecy, depicts a historic power struggle that exalts Christ as cosmic Lord. The montage that flashes past lacks the control of mundane logic or chronology. Like a dream, the details plunge the reader into an extraterrestrial world view anchored in chapter 1 to the seven churches of Asia Minor: Ephesus, Smyrna, Pergamum, Thyatira, Sardis, Philadelphia, and Laodicea. From the outset, John bestows blessings that move beyond time that was, is, and will be. As though transcending time constraints, the visionary Jesus sees himself as "alpha and omega," the beginning and end of the Greek alphabet (Revelation 1:8, 11).

A pattern of sevens—candles, candlesticks, stars—confines the subject to the churches, which contain their own seeds of destruction. The voice condemns such abominations as the seductress Jezebel and warns in chapter 3:

Be watchful, and strengthen the things which remain,
  that are ready to die:
  for I have not found thy works perfect before God [Revelation 3:2].

The overriding tone of condemnation and rebuke, like a musical motif, soars from grand and terrible lines that depict Christ in the act of judging and casting out the unrighteous. Of the Laodiceans, the voice advises, "Buy of me gold tried in the fire," a reference to steadfast, loyal members who have survived an era of persecution [Revelation 3:18].

In chapters 4–11, the tone shifts from lordly seat of justice to John's own two eyes, which see into heaven. The image bears a strong resemblance to the *skene* of the Greek theater. Bright rainbow colors around the throne and a company of twenty-four elders precede more sevens—lamps and spirits of God—and many-eyed beasts in the form of a lion, calf, man, and eagle. This encircling chorus sings out an Old Testament anthem to God:

Holy, holy, holy,
  Lord God Almighty,
  which was, and is, and is to come [Revelation 4:8].

John looks upon a sealed book and weeps because no being is worthy to open it, only Christ, whom he envisions as a slain lamb wreathed in sevens and capable of opening all seven seals. The freeing of the text produces silence, a symbol of the end-time relieved by the heavy skirmishes on earth that plague humanity. This lengthy throne-room scene concludes with the appearance of the ark, played about with lightning, thunder, voices, an earthquake, and hail. Significant to John's dream is a realization of God's covenant with Abraham, who is indeed father to a grand multitude "from all nations, and kindreds, and people, and tongues" (Revelation 7:9).

The symbols of the second half of Revelation enhance an anticipation of the Second Coming. John sees a woman in labor, a reflection of the difficult birth of the Christian church, an image that philosopher Mary Baker Eddy interpreted as a revelation of her own birth and the founding of Christian Science. Persecuted by a dragon, the church retreats to the wilderness to replenish its strength. The dragon follows, tormenting the church's offspring "which keep the commandments of God, and have the testimony of Jesus Christ" (Revelation 12:17). Subsequent images of powerful, wicked beings suggest the travails of Christians in the Roman empire, beset by cruelty, oppression, and emperor worship.

The scene shifts in chapter 14 to a pastoral image of the lamb atop Mount Zion ringed about by harpers, choristers, and the "first fruits unto God," indicating the early Christians (Revelation 14:4). From heaven comes a benediction that resounds in liturgical music:

Blessed are the dead which die in the Lord from henceforth:
Yea, saith the spirit,
  that they may rest from their labours;
  and their works do follow them [Revelation 14:13].

The purification of earth and the overthrow of evil result in exultant anthems, rituals, and the reception of Christ's bride, "arrayed in fine linen, clean and white" (Revelation 19:8).

The high point of John's dream is in chapters 21–22, the revelation of a new heaven and earth, a vision of God's face, and the writing of his name on foreheads:

And there shall be no night there;
  and they need no candle,
  neither light of the sun;
  for the Lord God giveth them light:
  and they shall reign for ever and ever [Revelation 22:5].

This climactic point of the vision reassures John, as does the promise, "Behold, I come quickly" (Revelation 22:7). As a reaffirmation of the Jews, Jesus declares himself once more the progeny of David's line, "the bright and morning star" (Revelation 22:16). A third time, Jesus promises to return quickly. John can only murmur, "Even so, come, Lord Jesus" (Revelation 22:20).

Bible: Translations

One of the hardships of spreading Christianity was the need for versions of scripture in languages other than Aramaic or the Greek Septuagint version of the Torah. Of great value was the scholarship of Origen of Alexandria, Egypt, an early third-century student of Rabbi Hillel, who composed the Hexapla (Six-Part Book; ca. 235), a multi-columnar arrangement of Hebrew text and five Greek translations, notably the Septuagint and versions by Aquila, Symmachus, and Theodotion. Later translations into Old Latin (or Italia), Coptic, Ethiopic, and Gothic preceded the work of polemicist and scholar St. Jerome, the father of biblical science and translator of the Vulgate Bible. Born Eusebius Hieronymus around 340 in Stridon near Aquilea, Dalmatia, he came from an aristocratic family. Named for his father, he received a quality education in Rome while reading law and the classics under rhetorician Aelius Donatus. After Bishop Liberius baptized Jerome in 365, Jerome took holy orders and journeyed through Gaul and Antioch. On his last stop, he suffered a high fever and experienced a vision of God's judgment. Jerome recuperated at a Syrian hermitage, where he faced the difficult choice of giving up classical literature to devote himself to biblical scholarship.

From fluency in Greek and Hebrew, Jerome quickly recovered his self-confidence while studying under Gregory of Nazianzus, bishop of Constantinople. When he completed training, he began work as a scriptural bibliographer and translator by issuing Latin versions of the chronicle of Eusebius of Caesarea and Origen's sermons. Jerome worked for Paulinus and as Pope Damasus's secretary in Rome, then launched a monumental project, translating scripture into common or vulgar Latin. The work occupied him from 383 to 405, the height of his career.

Jerome's devotion to teaching the Bible put him in contact with Paula, Marcella, and Eustochium, notable Roman missionaries who admired him for his dedication to translating the Bible into a readable language. Others found him less approachable and spread the word that Jerome was prickly and at times explosive when he considered himself the final authority on scholarly matters. To rein in his bad temper, in 382, he settled into the post of adviser in a Bethlehem monastery and aided Paula in opening four religious houses. The rest of his life, he studied Origen's textural criticism at the library in Caesarea and worked doggedly at translating the Bible. From the opening lines to the end, the results bear the sonorous grace of a master:

In principio creavit Deus caelum et terram.
Terra autem erat inanis et vacua,
    et tenebrae erant super faciem abyssi,
    et spiritus Dei ferebatur super aquas.
Dixit Deus: Fiat lux. Et facta est lux.
Et vidit Deus lucem quod esset bona
    et divisit lucem a tenebris.
Appellavitque lucem diem et tenebras noctem.
Factumque est vespere et mane, dies unus [*Biblia Sacra*, Genesis 1:5].

In the beginning God created sky and land. And the land was vacant and empty, and there were shadows above the face of the deep, and the spirit of God was borne above the waters.

God said: Let there be light. And light was made. And God saw that the light was good and divided light from shadows. He called the light day and the shadows night. From evening and morning was made day one.

Jerome also produced the *Psalterium Romanum* (Roman Psalter) and scriptural commentary as well as correspondence and biographies of St. Paula, St. Eustochium, and St. Fabiola. He compiled *De Viris Illustribus* (On Illustrious Men), a series of biographies of Malchus, Paul the Hermit, and Hilary. At age sixty-five, Jerome completed the Vulgate, which served Christendom until the Reformation and formed the groundwork for translations into Arabic, Spanish, Georgian, and English.

According to Mar Eshai Shimun, the head of the Holy Apostolic and Catholic Church of the East, the Syriac Peshitta (or Peshito) derives from Aramaic scriptures obtained from the apostles themselves. Composed in Jesus's own language, the sixty-six canon books survive unchanged and unrevised from the original scrolls. The Peshitta remains the preference of Christians from the eastern Mediterranean to India. The modern English translation by George M. Lamsa results from his immigration to the United States during World War I, when he dedicated himself to biblical scholarship. An Assyrian from Kurdistan who grew up with the Aramaic language and Semitic tradition, he founded the Aramaic Bible Society in 1943. The original Aramaic books of Moses (C.E. 464), housed in the British Museum, comprise the world's oldest dated Bible manuscript.

As assistance to congregations unschooled in Latin, translations flourished late in the Middle Ages and throughout the Renaissance. Around C.E. 670, an unschooled Yorkshire shepherd named Caedmon experienced a vision of creation. He entered the monastery at Whitby and, under the mentorship of the Venerable Bede, paraphrased Genesis, the first of a series of Bible poems in Anglo-Saxon verse. Only a fragment of his work survives.

Aldhelm, a West Saxon teacher and versifier, translated the Psalms from Latin to Old English around C.E.

700. Contemporaneous with his work is the Lindisfarne Gospels, a colorful illuminated masterpiece of interlinear translation, and Latin manuscripts known as the Rushworth Gospels.

The Venerable Bede translated the Gospel of John into Anglo-Saxon or Old English before 735; he died in the act of dictating a revision to a scribe. An anonymous translation of the gospels into Gothic derived from the monastery of Fulda in Hesse in 830.

In 863, the brothers Cyril and Methodius from Thessalonica translated part of the Bible into Slavonic; their work is the foundation of Slavonic literature as well as of Russian Orthodox worship. Cyril, the librarian of the Hagia Sophia in Constantinople, created the Cyrillic alphabet; his less scholarly brother, who outlived him by sixteen years, evangelized the Slavs of Moravia.

Late in the ninth century, Alfred the Great, a philosopher king and reconqueror of southern England from the Danes, earned the name of Father of English prose for producing an Anglo-Saxon Psalter, translations of Acts and some Psalms, and a version of the Ten Commandments and Mosaic laws, which he appended to his own law codes as a preface.

Around 1005, the Old English prose master Aelfric Grammaticus, an early linguist trained under Aethelwold at Winchester and appointed abbot of Eynsham, paraphrased Genesis, Exodus, Leviticus, Numbers, Deuteronomy, Joshua, and Judges. He intended the composite, known as Aelfric's Heptateuch, as an aid to his priests.

In 1244, Dominican cardinal Hugh of Saint-Cher (also Hugo de Sancto Caro), author of a concordance to the Vulgate, became the first to divide the Bible into chapters, although other sources claim that the innovation was the idea of Stephen Langton, archbishop of Canterbury until 1228. Before 1350, William of Shoreham completed a prose rendering of the Psalms.

Basing his work on Jerome's Vulgate, John Wycliffe, dubbed the Morning Star of the Reformation, worked with a staff of Oxford scholars to publish a vernacular Middle English Bible in 1382 (Abbott 1969, 958). His version displays the orthography and grammar of the pre–Renaissance era:

> Sothely as a man goynge fer in pilgrimage, cleide his seruauntis, and bitoke to hem his goodis; And to oon he gaue fyue talentis, forsothe to an other two, but to an other oon, to eche after his owne vertu; and went forth anoon [McArthur 1992, 1122].

Unsettling to modern readers is the use of the letter *u* for the *v* sound in "fyue" and "seruauntis," the obsolete adverbs "sothely" and "anoon," and the obsolete participial form of "bitoke" for "took."

Wycliffe's followers, called Lollards, disseminated his scripture to commoners. Of his hand-lettered originals, 180 survive, most from the second version issued by Wycliffe's secretary, John Purvey. Wycliffe's turns of phrase survive in the Christian admonition "strait is the gate and narewe is the waye" and in "of the people, by the people, and for the people," a series of parallel phrases that Abraham Lincoln worked into the Gettysburg Address (Abbott 1969, 959).

By 1400, the Bible had found its way into seven Asian and five African languages, including Sinhalese, High Malaysian, and Formosan. One of the most beautiful translations, *Très Riches Heures du Duc de Berry* (The Very Rich Hours of the Duke of Berry; 1489), is a masterwork among medieval illuminated manuscripts. Duke Jean commissioned it in 1413 from the Limbourg brothers, skilled painters who worked at the task until the duke's death in 1416. Jean Colombe took up the project in 1485 on behalf of Duc Charles I de Savoie and finished the work in four years.

In 1455–1456, Johann Gutenberg published the first machine-produced Bible, the three-volume Mazarin Bible in Latin, from his office in Mainz, Germany. A collector's item in elegant Gothic type on vellum, it holds an honored place in collections in the U.S. Library of Congress, California's Huntington Library, Harvard University, Yale University, London's British Library, and the Bibliothèque Nationale in Paris.

In early March 1516, humanist Desiderius Erasmus issued a New Testament in an updated Latin translation. He followed with a German translation of both Old and New Testaments in 1534 and a revision published as the Zurich Latin Bible in 1543. His work, the first printed edition of Greek manuscripts, served German Christians and formed the basis of Old Norwegian, Swedish, Icelandic, and Dutch translations.

In 1517, during the fertile period introduced by Spanish monarchs Ferdinand and Isabella, Archbishop Francisco Ximénez (or Jiménez) de Cisneros, founder of the University of Alcalá de Henares and proselytizer of the Moors, led the commission that published the first Polyglot Bible (also Alcalá Polyglot or Complutesian, a Latinate synonym). Dedicated to its sponsor, Pope Leo X, it took fifteen years and an investment of £25,000 to complete. The multicolumnar text offers Hebrew, Greek, and Latin versions of the Old Testament and a Greek and Latin comparative of the New Testament. The scholarly work influenced subsequent biblical scholarship.

In 1528, Santes Pagninus divided the Old Testament chapters into verses, while in 1534, Martin Luther began a series of Bible editions that reached eleven revisions by his death in 1546. He pioneered the return to Greek and Hebrew texts, the first instance of reliance on primary sources in Western Europe. Of his choice of original documents, he proclaimed, "They are the sheaf in which the sword of the spirit is encased. They are the box in which this jewel is carried" (Abbott 1969, 959). Among the scholars who influenced him were French Hebraic scholar Nicolas de Lyre and Rabbi Shlomo ben-Isaac, popularly known as Rashi, the eleventh-century Talmudic scholar whose long-lived religious manual was the first printed in Hebrew.

In 1535, William Tyndale produced a more scholarly New Testament and portions of the Old Testament, based on "new learning" from Hebrew and Greek texts and on Erasmus's Latin translation rather than Jerome's Latin Vulgate. To assist his work, followers had begun smuggling the text into England as waste paper in 1526. The finished Bible was a milestone — the first whole text in Renaissance English. After suffering bitter opposition and charges of perverting scriptural intent, Tyndale was martyred at the stake in October 1536. He did not live to see the last segments printed. Later translators used his valuable work as a foundation for subsequent English versions.

Tyndale's contemporary, Miles Coverdale, a Church of Scotland moralist, worked under commission from Henry VIII to produce a vernacular translation unadulterated by German Lutheranism. The Coverdale Bible (1535) went through two revisions. His psalter was an element of the Book of Common Prayer (1549), an official liturgy issued in 1662.

In 1539, attorney Richard Taverner revised the Matthew Bible, which John Rogers had published two years earlier under the pseudonym Thomas Matthew, by synthesizing the work of Tyndale and Coverdale.

In a Paris office, Coverdale reworked the Matthew Bible as the Great Bible, the first authorized Bible, so named for its immense size. Issued in April 1539, it became the first printed in London. Oliver Cromwell sanctioned the Great Bible by placing it on all English pulpits.

Robert Estienne, a printer in Paris, became the first to separate the French New Testament chapters into verses in 1551.

A milestone in biblical scholarship written by exiles from the papist Queen Mary I, the Geneva Bible (1560), with Protestant annotations, was a conservative text revered for accuracy. Translated by William Whittingham and his team, it was the first English Bible to number verses and chapters. Dubbed the Breeches Bible because it referred to the loincloths of Adam and Eve as "breeches," the Geneva Bible was the work of a consortium headed by John Knox, bishop of Exeter, and Miles Coverdale and influenced by John Calvin. It excluded the Apocrypha as a fringe or suspect body of writings. The finished text reached print in England in 1576 and rose to prominence during the reign of Elizabeth I, who sanctioned its placement in every church. The Geneva Bible

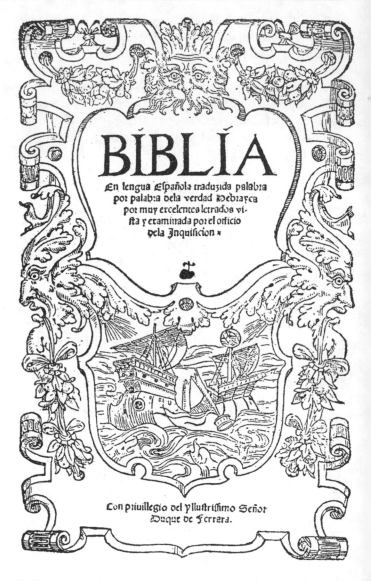

Title page of Abraham Usque's Spanish Bible printed (1553) at Ferrara.

was the personal scripture of William Shakespeare, the Puritans, Scottish Covenanters, the Pilgrims who settled New England, and John Bunyan, author of *Pilgrim's Progress*.

Bishops of the Church of England counteracted the popular Geneva Bible with their own version, the Bishop's Bible, a copy of the Great Bible. Issued in 1568, it was the first to carry the imprimatur of the English church.

Jerome's Latin Bible was the basis for the Rheims-Douai Bible, which a Greek and Hebrew scholar, Gregory Martin, and his team of translators published as a New Testament in 1582. After delays to seek funds, they printed it with the Old Testament in 1610. This version, corrected and updated in 1772 by theology professor Richard Challoner, served the Catholic world well into the twentieth century.

In 1593 at a secret printing firm in Kralice-upon-Oslava, Moravian pietists became the first Protestant sect to publish a modern language Old and New Testament as well as a hymnal in the vernacular. Translated from original Hebrew, Aramaic, and Greek texts, the six-volume Kralice (or Kralitz) Bible offers scripture in Czech. In 1627, the anti–Hussite backlash launched persecutions against Moravians and collected their hymnals and Bibles, which dissenting women baked into loaves of bread.

A literary height of translation in English occurred in 1611, when James I of England, the former James VI of Scotland, assembled fifty-four scholars into six companies to produce an authorized version. Among them were Lancelot Andrewes, John Hardinge, John Harmer, John Reynolds, Henry Saville, Miles Smith, and Robert Spalding. The work began after the king's receipt of the Millenary Petition, a request for a new translation of the Bible signed by 750 reformers of the Church of England. He assigned his staff to produce a version "as consonant as can be to the original Hebrew and Greek ... and only to be used in all churches of England" (McArthur 1992, 120).

Working separately at Oxford, Cambridge, and Westminster, the companies drew on Tyndale's translations, the Bishop's Bible, and the Rheims-Douai. To express their working hypothesis, they explained in the preface:

> An other thing we thinke good to admonish thee of [gentle Reader] that wee haue not tyed our selues to an vniformitie of phrasing, or to an identitie of words, as some peraduenture would wish that we had done, because they obserue, that some learned men some where, haue beene as exact as they could that way.... Thus to minse the matter, wee thought to savour more of curiositie then wisedome, and that rather it should breed scorne in the Atheist, then bring profite to the godly Reader. For is the kingdome of God become words or syllables? why should wee be in bondage to them if we may be free, vse one precisely when wee may vse another no lesse fit, as commodiously? [Crystal 1995, 64].

They also took a stand on another canon matter: Between Old and New Testaments, the translators appended the Apocrypha, although later printings omitted noncanonical writings. Readers and theologians revere the finished work into current times as the King James Bible (or KJB), also referred to as the Authorized Version (or AV).

Composed at the height of Jacobean English, the text supplanted all other versions for poetic beauty and the absence of ponderous scholarship. An example, Psalm 139:7–12, displays an agility with tone, cadence, and metaphor:

> Whither shall I go from thy spirit?
>   or whither shall I flee from thy presence?
> If I ascend up into heaven, thou art there:
>   if I make my bed in hell, behold, thou art there.
> If I take the wings of the morning,
>   and dwell in the uttermost parts of the sea;

> Even there shall thy hand lead me,
>   and thy right hand shall hold me.
> If I say, surely the darkness shall cover me;
>   even the night shall be light about me.
> Yea, the darkness hideth not from thee;
>   but the night shineth as the day:
>   the darkness and the light are both alike to thee.

The text also provided the English language with resilient phrases: my brother's keeper, in the twinkling of an eye, filthy lucre, a thorn in the flesh, the patience of Job, at their wit's end, a man after his own heart, to spy out the land, signs of the times, all things to all men, fight the good fight, a lamb to slaughter, the blind lead the blind, suffer fools gladly, my name is legion, and physician, heal thyself.

The King James version of the Apocrypha incorporates the drama of Jewish history in the assertion of Mattathias concerning pagan sacrifice as it is recorded in Maccabees 1:19–22:

> Though all the nations that are under the king's dominion obey him and fall away every one from the religion of their fathers, and give consent to his commandments: yet will I and my sons and my brethren walk in the covenant of our fathers. God forbid that we should forsake the law and the ordinances. We will not hearken to the king's words, to go from our religion, either on the right hand, or the left.

The resonance of biblical English was a hallmark of the early seventeenth century and echoed the lingual grace and majesty of playwrights Christopher Marlowe and William Shakespeare.

Milestones in biblical scholarship continued throughout the late Renaissance and into the current age. In 1613, the Bible was available in Japanese, the work of M. Barreto, a Jesuit priest. A copy remains in the Vatican Library. Puritan missionary John Eliot produced a Native American version for Massachusetts Indians in 1661. In 1715, German missionary Bartholomäus Ziegenbalg, aided by Johann Ernst Gründler, issued a Bible in Tamil, the first printed in a language of India. It spread Christianity throughout southern and southeastern Asia as well as parts of Africa.

In 1755, a worthy translation, New Testament with Explanatory Notes, derived from a field missionary to the Indians of Savannah, Georgia, John Wesley, the father of Methodism, who wanted to supply a readable version to ordinary Christians.

New World publisher Robert Aitken issued the King James Bible in 1782 from a Philadelphia printing house. David Macrae, a Scotch Presbyterian Bible authority, published a translated text in 1799. His unique method placed alternate wording in parentheses following key or unclear passages, for example, the metaphoric references to the failure of human faculties in advanced age as described in Ecclesiastes 12:1–7.

As of 1800, there were seventy-one published translations of the Bible, including additional Asian versions compiled by Baptist missionary William Carey. As an adjunct of nineteenth-century evangelism, in 1804, the British and Foreign Bible Society, founded by Thomas Charles, distributed inexpensive vernacular scriptural texts to peoples worldwide. In 1816, a parallel organization, the American Bible Society, spread scripture from its New York headquarters across the Atlantic seaboard and west to the frontier.

Aided by William Milne, missionary Robert Morrison, father of Christian outreach to China, concluded a triumph for Christianity in 1823 with his publication of a Chinese Bible in Canton. Oceania received a Bible in 1829 in the languages of Java and Tahiti. As of 1833, the Chippewa had a version of the New Testament. By 1834, Adoniram Judson, an evangelist from Malden, Massachusetts, had paralleled the Oceanic Bible with a Burmese text. For his innovation, he is honored with a stained glass window in the First Baptist Church of Washington, D.C. A coup for missionaries to the Sandwich Islands was a Hawaiian New Testament in 1835. In 1850, Samuel Adjai Crowther produced the epistle to the Romans in Yoruba for the evangelizing of western Nigeria.

In 1853, Rabbi Isaac Leeser, an American educator, published the standard American Jewish Bible. It remained the authorized version until the beginning of the twentieth century when the Jewish Publication Society of America met the demands of Reformed Jews for a new text, which was issued in 1917 and based on the Masoretic original.

James Evans, missionary to the Cree, produced a syllabary in which to codify a version in the language of Plains Indians in 1862. An Eskimo Bible reached print in Labrador in 1871. The Dakota Bible was completed in 1879.

A meticulously revised Protestant Bible (or English Revised Version, referred to as the RV), compiled and updated by a conservative convocation of the province of Canterbury, appeared in 1885. Over a decade of work in the United Kingdom and the United States, translators attempted a return to original Hebrew and Greek, but the RV never achieved the popularity of the King James Bible. American scholars countered with their own revision, the American Standard Version (or ASV), in 1901. Its grandeur and cadencing reflect the continued dominance of the King James version, as found in the Psalms:

O Jehovah, our Lord, how excellent is thy name in all the
  earth,
 who hast set thy glory upon the heavens!
Out of the mouth of babes and sucklings hast thou established strength,

because of thine adversaries,
 that thou mightest still the enemy and the avenger.
When I consider thy heavens, the work of thy fingers,
 the moon and the stars, which thou hast ordained;
 what is man, that thou art mindful of him?
And the son of man, that thou visitest him? [Psalm 8:1–4;
 "The Unbound Bible"].

Elizabeth Cady Stanton, one of the masterminds of the first Woman's Rights Convention held in Seneca Falls, New York, in 1848, organized a committee of five women to compile the Woman's Bible, a bestselling anthology of essays and commentary on the Bible. Cady Stanton, the major author of the work, intended the compendium as a guide to women who had felt degraded and discounted. The work was a necessity to the uplifting of women from second-class citizenship to full participation in democracy, the objective of the National Woman Suffrage Association.

Additional idiomatic translations of the early twentieth century brought the Bible closer to the people. They include Richard Francis Weymouth's New Testament in Modern Speech (1903), James Moffatt's energized New Translation of the Bible (1913), and Edgar J. Goodspeed and J. M. Powis Smith's Complete Bible: An American Translation (1927). Weymouth's version of the Gospel of John states:

Let not your hearts be troubled. Trust in God: trust in me
  also.
In my Father's house there are many resting-places.
Were it otherwise, I would have told you;
 for I am going to make ready a place for you.
And if I go and make ready a place for you,
I will return and take you to be with me,
 that where I am you also may be [John 14:2–4; "The Unbound Bible"].

The simple vocabulary and phrasing reassure readers who need extra help in understanding and applying scripture to everyday situations.

In 1912, Baptists ended sixty-two years of agitation for a Bible that replaces references to baptism with "immerse" or "immersion." Their sectarian propaganda resulted in the Bible: An Improved Edition Based in Part on the Bible Union Version.

The first female translator, Helen Barrett Montgomery, issued her work in two volumes as the Centenary Translation of the New Testament (1924) in celebration of the American Baptist Publication Society centennial. Her version reset the text from verses into paragraphs introduced by subtitles.

Bible scholarship underwent upheaval in the 1940s with the discovery of the Nag Hammadi Library and the Dead Sea Scrolls, which offered ancient copies that added new writings and established the authenticity of questionable passages.

In 1949, Ronald Knox produced the Holy Bible, an upgraded Roman Catholic scripture based on Jerome's Vulgate. But it was not until 1950 that a Swahili version made scripture available in a major African tongue.

Anonymous Jehovah's Witnesses published New World Translation of the Christian Greek Scriptures (1950) and New World Translation of the Hebrew Scriptures (1953), products circulated by the Watch Tower Bible and Tract Society.

Published on September 30, 1952, the Revised Standard Version (RSV) resulted from the collaboration of thirty-two scholars. Nonetheless, it provoked controversy as various denominations abandoned the familiar King James Bible for up-to-date language and clarity. An example of straightforward prose presentation comes from I Kings 2:2–5, referred to as the last words of David to Solomon, his son and heir:

> I am about to go the way of all the earth. Be strong, and show yourself a man, and keep the charge of the Lord your God, walking in his ways and keeping his statutes, his commandments, his ordinances, and his testimonies, as it is written in the law of Moses, that you may prosper in all that you do and wherever you turn; that the Lord may establish his word which he spoke concerning me, saying, "If your sons take heed to their way, to walk before me in faithfulness with all their heart and with all their soul, there shall not fail you a man on the throne of Israel."

The RSV has flourished in part because of its authorization by the National Council of Churches of Christ in the United States.

A more popular version issued in 1958 and revised in 1972 is the New Testament in Modern English by J. B. Phillips, a minister from Swanage, Dorsett, and a survivor of the Blitz. With genuine sympathy for the modern Christian, he returned passages to numbered paragraph form and obscurities into conversational idiom. In an example from the gospels, Jesus addresses his apostles and his heavenly Father in prose:

> Then Jesus came with the disciples to a place called Gethsemane and said to them, "Sit down here while I go over there and pray." Then he took with him Peter and the two sons of Zebedee and began to be in terrible pain and agony of mind. "My heart is breaking with a death-like grief," he told them, "stay here and keep watch with me." Then he walked on a little way and fell on his face and prayed, "My Father, if it is possible let this cup pass from me — yet it must not be what I want, but what you want" [Phillips, Matthew 26, p. 57].

He concluded the text with a brief index of people and places and a handful of notes on scribes, Pharisees, Sadducees, and the interpolation of the episode of the female adulterer in John 7:53 and 8:11.

The Jerusalem Bible in 1966 offered a scholarly translation derived from textual recensions of the Roman Catholic School of Biblical Studies to *La Bible de Jérusalem* (1961), a French translation by Dominicans for L'École Biblique (The Bible School). A subsequent edition offers prefatory essays by Jewish, Catholic, and Protestant theologians.

Sponsored by the Bishops' Committee of the Confraternity of Christian Doctrine, the New American Bible of 1970, a Roman Catholic edition based on the Septuagint, Dead Sea Scrolls, and other ancient texts, presented scripture in precise English. That same year, British churches and Bible societies sponsored The New English Bible (NEB), a scholarly undertaking that employed recent historical, textual, and linguistic findings. The simplicity of this version undergirds a new reading of the Sermon on the Mount:

> How blest are those who know that they are poor;
>   the kingdom of Heaven is theirs.
> How blest are the sorrowful;
>   they shall find consolation.
> How blest are those of a gentle spirit;
>   they shall have the earth for their possession [Matthew 5:3–5].

A major fault of this version is its loss of flow, the reduction of diction to the lowest common denominator.

The Bible had reached 250 lingual groups by the 1970s, with significant portions of scripture available in 1,300 languages. As an aid to family devotions, Kenneth Taylor issued the Living Bible (1971), a conversational conservative effort aimed at the average reader.

A surprise bestseller was The Good News Bible, a product of the American Bible Society translated in 1976 by R. G. Bratcher's consortium. Its vigorous prose attests to changes in English:

> At that time the Kingdom of heaven will be like this. Once there was a man who was about to go on a journey; he called his servants and put them in charge of his property. He gave to each one according to his ability: to one he gave five thousand gold coins, to another he gave two thousand, and to another he gave one thousand. Then he left on his journey [McArthur 1992, 122–123].

Another cooperative effort, the New International Version (NIV), involved evangelical scholars in an effort to emulate the dignity of the early English Bible. In 1989, the Revised English Bible (REB) corrected the speculative scholarship and inconsistent language of the NEB of 1970 and also removed sexist language that denigrated women. Also in 1989, editors of the New Jerusalem Bible reworked a 1966 translation based on French scholarship.

Into the twenty-first century, an ongoing project, the Anchor Bible, appeared in stand-alone volumes prepared by Jewish, Catholic, and Protestant scholars from the United States, Israel, Italy, and Scandinavia. In addition, this scripture encircled the globe in 143 languages:

Ainu	Gilbertese	Nama
Albanian	Giryama	Ngoni
Amharic	Gogo	Nguna
Aneityum	Gondi	Nias
Arabic	Grebo	Nyanja
Arawâk	Gujarati	Pahri
Armenian	Haida	Palityan
Batak	Hausa	Pangasinan
Beaver Indian	Igbira	Panjabi
Bengali	Igbo	Pasto
Bondei	Japanese	Persian
Breton	Javanese	Ponape
Bulgarian	Kabyle	Samoan
Bullom	Kaguru	Sangir
Burmese	Kannada	Sanskrit
Chaga	Karen	Santali
Cherokee	Kashmiri	Seneca
Chinese, Canto-	Khasi	Shilha
nese	Korean	Sindhi
Chinese, Foo-	Kurdish	Sinhala
chow	Kusaie	Slavey
Chinese, Hakka	Kwagutl	Slavonic
Chinese, Hang-	Lahnda	Soso
chow	Lao	Sotho
Chinese, High	Lepsha	Sukuma
Wenli	Lifu	Swahili
Chinese, Kuoyö	Luda	Syriac
Chinese, Low	Magi	Tahitian
Wenli	Malagasy	Tamil
Chipewyan	Malay	Taveta
Choctaw	Malekula	Telugu
Cree	Maori	Temne
Dakota	Marathi	Tongan
Efik	Mbundu	Torres Island
Eskimo	Mende	Turkish
Estonian	Micmac	Umön
Ethiopic	Mohawk	Urdu
Fang	Mongo	Xhosa
Formosan	Mongolian	Yao
Gallinya	Motu	Yoruba
Ganda	Mundari	Zulu
Garo	Muskogee	Zya
Georgian	Myènè	

SOURCES: Abbott 1969, Alexander and Alexander 1982, Armstrong 1993, Baugh 1948, 1957, *Biblia Sacra* 1957, "Biblical Canons," Bowder 1980, Bradley 1995, Broderick 1987, Bryant 1967, Buttrick 1962, Cantor 1993, 1994, 1996, Coates 1999, Cohn-Sherbok 1998, Comay and Cohn-Sherbok 1995, Crystal 1995, Cunningham 1998, Curtius 1953, Dolan 1968, "Early Bilingual Lexica," Eckstrom 1995, Farmer 1992, Freedman 1992, Goring 1994, Greenspan 1994, Harpur 1995, Hastings 1951, Heffernan 1988, Hodges 1999, Hollister 1994, Holmes 1988, *Holy Bible* 1986, Hunt 1991, Jackson 1969, Kee, Young and Froehlich 1965, Kemp 1976, Lamsa n.d., Leyser 1995, Lopez 1967, Mantinband 1956, May and Metzger 1962, McArthur 1992, McCall 1979, McCrum et al. 1986, McMurtry 1989, Metzger and Coogan 1993, *New Catholic Encyclopedia* 1967, *The New English Bible* 1961, Noss and Noss 1984, Orr 1925, Parker 1994, Phillips 1972, Raby 1953, 1959, "Rashi's Commentary on the Talmud," Reeves 1995, Rice 1965, Snodgrass 2001, Stowe 1992, Szarmach 1998, "The Unbound Bible," Webster 1924.

Black Elk Speaks *Black Elk Speaks: The Life Story of a Holy Man of the Oglala Sioux* (1932), a classic elegy of American religious literature, is an intriguing Native American memoir that has been labeled history, psychology, anecdotal autobiography, and scripture. The *hanbleceya* (visions) of *Black Elk Speaks* are a transcription of revelations from *Tunkashila* (the Creator) to Nick Black Elk, a revered shaman and social visionary of the Oglalas, one of seven subgroups of the Western Teton residing in South Dakota, Nebraska, Montana, and Wyoming. *Black Elk Speaks* begins a sacred tetralogy, which systematizes Lakota worship and culture in three subsequent works: *The Sacred Pipe* (1948); *When the Tree Flowered: The Story of Eagle Voice, a Sioux Indian* (1951), published in 1953 by Andrew Melrose of London as *Eagle Voice: An Authentic Tale of the Sioux Indians*; and *The Sixth Grandfather: Black Elk's Teachings Given to John G. Neihardt* (1984).

As described by Salley McCluskey of Northern Illinois University at an annual meeting of the Western Literature Association in October 1971 at Red Cloud, Nebraska, Nick Black Elk was not a saint or the usual Western hero, but a fully developed human character: "His faith, his fears, his rage, and his humanity unite, making him a complex human being who walked real roads, saw real clouds, smelled real winds, and tasted real meat" (McCluskey 1972, 232).

From 1905, commissioners from Washington, D.C., expressed an interest in Lakota shamanic tradition, which was then transmitted solely by word and example to the next generation of practitioners. They made a second study in 1908 to determine if the Lakota were practicing witchcraft or propitiating a nature god. Their quest remained partially unfulfilled until 1932, when Lakota scripture reached print in the reminiscences of Black Elk, America's most studied Indian. By the late 1940s, his first-person story was available in French, German, and Italian to a white audience still seeking details of the Lakotas' archetypal faith.

Just as Jesus's teachings survive through his disciples' memories and as Socrates' words live on through his students' writings, Black Elk's visions passed into book form through an outsider's work. The holy man dictated his autobiography to Nebraska poet laureate and historian John Gneisenau Neihardt, literary columnist for the *St. Louis Post-Dispatch*. This work serves Native America as a rare scripture in written form from a culture dominated by oral tradition. To obtain details of *chanunpa* (sacred pipe) religion and the Ghost Dance, over several interviews, Neihardt sought material for *Song of the Messiah*, the final volume of his epic narrative, *A Cycle of the West* (1915–1941). He chose Black Elk as spokesman for native rites because an employee of the Pine Ridge Agency had suggested the aged mystic as an "unreconstituted

Indian" who had previously turned away a journalist researching the life of Crazy Horse (McCluskey 1972, 235).

The meeting of poet with shaman produced an unusually close spiritual affinity. Black Elk had foreseen the visit and welcomed Neihardt as a man worthy to be entrusted with Oglala scripture. Neihardt, who had lived among Indians and shared their pantheism, reported his own childhood dream of flying in space and hearing voices, an experience that duplicated Black Elk's dynamic vision and suggested a mystic bond between teller and recorder. In October 1930, Neihardt secured funding from New York publisher William Morrow to advance the research into a biography. Neihardt wrote to Black Elk on November 6 to justify the task, not as a money-making scheme, but "to tell the things that you and your friends know ... [in] an honest and a loving book" (DeMallie 1984, 29).

In April 1931, Neihardt traveled with his son, Sigurd, and daughters, Hilda and Enid, from their home in Branson, Missouri, to the holy man's home in Manderson, South Dakota, and began work. To welcome his visitors, Black Elk had erected guest quarters consisting of a privy and a white duck tipi painted with a flaming rainbow — the leaping, flickering entrance to the six grandfathers' tipi in his vision. He also invited elders Fire Thunder, Standing Bear, Chase in the Morning, and Holy Black Tail Deer to corroborate details. In addition, other Lakota came, remained at a respectful distance, and joined in the meals that family members prepared.

To bridge the gulf created by two cultures speaking two tongues, Neihardt arranged a four-step transmission. First, the sixty-nine-year-old prophet spoke his Sioux language to his son, lecturer Benjamin Black Elk, educated for two years at the Indian school in Carlisle, Pennsylvania. Ben translated from the Lakota dialect for stenographer Enid Neihardt, who passed transcribed notes to her father for editing and publication. Interviews required eighteen days; the total work occupied four months. Neihardt considered naming it "The Tree That Never Bloomed" in token of Black Elk's famous earth prayer:

Grandfather, Great Spirit,
  once more behold me on earth and lean to hear my feeble
    voice.
You lived first, and you are older than all need, older than all
    prayer.
All things belong to you — the two-legged, the four-legged,
  the wings of the air, and all green things that live.
You have set the powers of the four quarters of the earth
  to cross each other.
You have made me cross the good road and road of difficul-
    ties,
  and where they cross, the place is holy.
Day in, day out, forevermore, you are the life of things.

Hey! Lean to hear my feeble voice.
At the center of the sacred hoop
You have said that I should make the tree to bloom.

With tears running, O Great Spirit, my Grandfather,
With running eyes I must say
The tree has never bloomed.

Here I stand, and the tree is withered.
Again, I recall the great vision you gave me.

It may be that some little root of the sacred tree still lives.
Nourish it then
  that it may leaf and bloom
  and fill with singing birds!

Hear me, that the people may once again
  find the good road and the shielding tree ["Black Elk, Holy
    Man of the Oglala Sioux"].

Mona Neihardt, the poet's wife, proposed a nonjudgmental title, *Black Elk Speaks*. In gratitude for his work, Black Elk adopted Neihardt, named him Flaming Rainbow, and allowed him to remain at Pine Ridge to complete his epic.

Although the book was not monetarily successful, its publication elevated Black Elk to the height of Native American theologian. The original transcript, housed in the Neihardt archives at the University of Missouri, came under scrutiny by historians and theologians in midcentury. In 1980, during a renaissance of traditional native religion, Raymond J. DeMallie reconstructed Enid Neihardt's notes from the interviews, including previously unpublished material. Four years later, he published *The Sixth Grandfather*, a more exact edition of notes and interviews.

Preliminaries for *Black Elk Speaks* offered Black Elk a second chance at vision and fulfillment. He said to Flying Hawk, the village interpreter, "I can feel in this man beside me a strong desire to know the things of the Other World. He has been sent to learn what I know, and I will teach him" (Neihardt 1979, xvii). To prepare himself to communicate sacred truths usually limited to Oglalas, the aged seer donned a sacred morning star, a painted rawhide amulet attached to an eagle feather and a strip of buffalo hair, which he tied about his neck just as his own father had worn it. He later presented Neihardt with the ornament, which symbolized a desire for enlightenment, high thinking, and earthly wealth. Neihardt reciprocated by distributing cigarettes.

For the first time in decades, the old prophet climbed Harney Peak, the highest point in the Black Hills, and addressed his people's God. Instead of traditional red body paint, he dressed in a loincloth and modest red long johns. In a gesture to transcendent truths from the past, he appended a dedication:

What is good in this book is given back
  to the six grandfathers
  and to the great men of my people [Neihardt 1979, v].

The volume was only the beginning. In 1944, Neihardt returned to gather material for *When the Tree Flowered*, which he published in 1951. Meanwhile, Joseph Epes Brown's sequel volume of native scripture, *The Sacred Pipe*, particularized Black Elk's earnest belief in and practice of the seven rites of the Oglala.

Black Elk's biography characterizes the evolution of priesthood. In the tradition of his second cousin Crazy Horse, Black Elk was an Oglala Lakota medicine man and *yuwipi* (metaphysician) of the Big Road band and lived in the *Paha Sapa* (Black Hills) during an era of entrenched resistance to usurpation of tribal land by white squatters, pioneers, missionaries, and the military. The fourth generation to carry the name Black Elk, he was born Hehaka (or Hchaka) Sapa to White Cow Sees and the elder Black Elk, a holy man like his brothers, in December 1863 (or 1862) on the Little Powder River, Wyoming. When he was three, his father suffered a broken leg at the Fetterman massacre at Fort Phil Kearney in Dakota Territory, where Arapaho, Cheyenne, and Sioux formed a war coalition to halt erection of an army fortress on sacred land.

The boy grew up acting out famous Sioux wars with his brothers and cousins and learning tracking, native weaponry, and horsemanship. He studied sacred lore under the mentorship of Whirlwind Chaser, Black Road, and Elk Head, keeper of the sacred pipe and educator in spiritual heritage and history. Black Elk lived an unremarkable childhood until 1872, when prophetic dreams and power visions of two men flying down from a cloud called him to be a *wichashu wakon* (priest) on a lifetime mission to revive tribal faith.

As a subject of Chief Red Cloud, Black Elk took on a heavy onus: he promised to restore his people's optimism in the face of massive inundation by *wasichus* (whites). In supplication to *Wakan Tanka* (the Great Spirit), he asked for divine inspiration. The revelation he received introduced him to the sacred circle, a symbol of a native utopia. To wrest direction from visitations with his six grandfathers, who represented north, south, east, west, up, and down, he retreated to the wild to glimpse skyriders wielding flaming spears and to escape his body in transmigrations to heaven. Among the faces he saw was his own visage in old age; he looked down from a mountain peak at the sacred hoop, broken beyond repair, and the holy tree bereft of birds. These startling supernatural experiences he kept secret to spare his parents.

Four years after Black Elk began the dream states, he collapsed from an inexplicable loss of muscle tone. A trance robbed him of contact with the world while he heeded the call of the spirits. To their "younger brother," they promised the aid of a cleansing wind to heal the body and affirm the soul of the Oglala Lakota. After twelve days in a coma, he awoke within a vivid aura. He fasted,

prayed, and retreated to the netherworld to receive augury and tribal history taught by Black Road, Whirlwind Chaser, and Elk Head. By 1876, the promise proved true when he developed the power to heal.

On June 25–26 of that year, Black Elk fought the intrusive *wasichus* (whites) at the battle of the Little Bighorn, where five troops of white cavalrymen died in a well-executed massacre. He tried to commit his first scalping as his reward for combat and found the skin too tough. Even though he survived, he suffered anxiety attacks and waves of terror of the Thunder Beings, whose lethal thunderbolts he fled from lodge to lodge. In 1880, he confessed to Black Road, a medicine man, the source of his anguish and learned to interpret supernatural visitation as a psychic experience. From Fort Buford, North Dakota, Black Elk and his male kin followed Crazy Horse until his death, then pledged loyalty to Sitting Bull, with whom they made an expedition to Canada. The exodus placed them in jeopardy from hunger, exposure, and cold. Black Elk records his hands frozen to his rifle and chafed by the act of ripping them free from cold metal. Swathed in freshly skinned buffalo hides, he, his father, and one other man huddled by a fire all night. They turned at the sound of whimpering to find a "party of porcupines" cowering on the outer rim of the fire (McCluskey 1972, 234). Out of pity, the men left the small animals unharmed. In the spring of 1881, Black Elk displayed his vision by enacting the Horse Dance for his family and refugees at Fort Keogh, Montana. He repeated the dance and performed buffalo and elk rites to establish his power as a healer.

The Lakota settled at Pine Ridge Reservation, South Dakota, in 1886. Counselees who visited Black Elk's tent to seek comfort and glimpses of the future could see all too well that the future of migratory bison was ending as hunters gunned down whole herds, stripped them of horns, tongues, and hides, and abandoned the carcasses to prairie predators. To the Sioux, the ongoing desecration of nature proved that whites had no soul. Despairing at the loss of free-ranging buffalo, the focus of their social order and religion, they attempted to farm to supplement government handouts.

As trans–Mississippi westering ended the free movement of Indians across the Plains, the Sioux coped with fences, agriculture, forts, and overland migration as gold seekers rushed to strip the land of its riches. Black Elk abandoned his warrior upbringing and, under the childhood name of Kahnigapi (Choice), traveled with a dance troupe to Omaha, Chicago, and Europe to study the white world. As a performer in Buffalo Bill Cody's Wild West Show, in 1886, during Queen Victoria's Jubilee, he earned $25 a month plus board and expenses.

After a debut at Madison Square Garden in New York City, Black Elk entertained the court of the queen, whom he renamed Grandmother England. During the tour, he learned some English. From Manchester, he wrote in Lakota to his people:

> I know the white men's customs well. One custom is very good. Whoever believes in God will find good ways—that is what I mean. And many of the ways the white men follow are hard to endure. Whoever has no country will die in the wilderness [DeMallie 1984, 8–9].

His letter appeared in the March 1888 edition of *Iapi Oaye* (Word Carrier), published in Santee, Nebraska.

After becoming separated from Buffalo Bill's entourage, Black Elk and two fellow Lakota traveled France, Germany, and Italy on a two-year tour. In December 1889, he posted a second letter to his people in which he cited Paul's famous statement on charity from I Corinthians 13. Black Elk displayed an interest in Christianity and curiosity about the Holy Land, a distant place "where they killed Jesus," an arid land where only camels can survive (DeMallie 1983, 10). This religious education was the work of Buffalo Bill, who paid a Christian teacher to accompany the troupe and "upgrade" Indian morality.

Before his return, Black Elk suffered ill health and lodged with a French family until late in 1889, when he was well enough to cross the sea once more and travel west to the Dakotas. At Pine Ridge, he discovered that his sister and brother were dead, his mother was tending her dying husband, and the once healthy tribe was languishing from drought and famine. The desperate situation called for Black Elk to reassume his role as physician. For cash, he worked at a reservation store and continued studying the sacred tree, hoop of the people, and other spiritual matters.

At this period of Black Elk's quest, a great alteration seized the Oglala with the arrival of Wovoka (Cutter; also Wanekia or Jack Wilson), the Paiute holy man who had experienced mystic transport in 1889 and launched an Indian "messiah craze" (McCluskey 1972, 235). On his return from Europe, Black Elk learned of Wovoka's prophecy that another world was arriving in a whirlwind from the West. The cataclysm would kill off the moribund elements and restore grass and meat in a great Sioux renaissance. The dead would return to earth in their former vigor and the buffalo would once again thrive. Black Elk questioned Wovoka's vision, but dropped his skepticism as Teton and Yankton Sioux retreated to the Badlands and, along Wounded Knee Creek, sang and pulsated in long nights of the Ghost Dance, a ritual in costume said to make them impervious to bullets. With uplifted faces painted red, they passed the sacred pipe and danced around the tree of life.

On December 29, 1890, two weeks after Sitting Bull's assassination at Standing Rock Reservation, U.S. cavalry launched a sneak attack on Big Foot's village at Wounded Knee Creek in southwestern South Dakota. Black Elk suffered a slash to the midriff in the backlash that brought whites en masse against the Ghost Dance. His uncle stanched the wound with pieces of blanket. Black Elk refused treatment and demanded a leg up on his horse to face death fearlessly, but the uncle reminded him that he was worth more to the Oglala as a guide and healer than as a martyr.

The event destroyed the Lakota faith in Wovoka's prophecy. At the end of his book, Black Elk grieved over the freezing remains of women and children, coated with mud. Christian missionaries were quick to point out that God willed the massacre to punish Lakota paganism; Indians, on the other hand, gave up religion entirely. Burdened with personal weakness, failure, and the death of his father that same year, Black Elk declared defunct the dream of a supernatural return of Indian spirits. As Charles Eastman, a Sioux doctor, examined the corpses recovered from the blizzard and placed in a makeshift morgue, Black Elk despaired for Sioux culture and the free and plentiful Plains tradition. As a prisoner of war, he experienced an enervating hopelessness.

Weighted with the tragic onus of unfulfilled promise, Black Elk cried out to the six powers of the world for succor in the eclipse of Native Americans. He married Katie War Bonnet in 1893 and returned to Indian ways. Katie bore their son Never Showed Off, also called William, in 1893, followed two years later by Good Voice Star, called Johnny. Her elder son died in 1897; in 1899, she gave birth to Benjamin. During hard times after the Lakota ceded more than half the reservation, Black Elk saw a surge in white intrusions. All he could do for his people was support his family and offer his services as healer, herbalist, and performer of the *yuwipi* ceremony, a conjuring ritual. These contributions brought him the anger of Jesuit missionaries and increased bitterness toward meddlesome whites, who suppressed native faith and traditional authority figures.

Disillusioned by mounting violence on the Plains and grieved by Katie's death, Black Elk repudiated his shamanship and, in 1904, converted to Catholicism and joined the St. Joseph Society in Manderson, a new source of respect and influence. As newly baptized Nicholas Black Elk, he continued to counsel and pray with his people and enhanced his meager living by earning $5 a month as a catechist. He wrote letters to the *Sinasapa Wocekiye Taeyanpaha* (Catholic Herald) from 1907 to 1912, attended Catholic gatherings, and raised funds in New York, Boston, Chicago, Washington, D.C., and Omaha. He joined missions to Wind River Reservation in Wyoming in 1908 to convert the Arapaho and did similar work on the Winnebago Reservation in Nebraska and among the Sisseton.

In 1906, Black Elk fathered a daughter, Lucy Looks Twice, with his second wife, Anna Brings White (or Brings White Horses). Black Elk's fortunes fluctuated in the ensuing years with the death of Good Voice Star in 1909, the birth of Nick Jr. in 1914, and the departure of Ben to the Carlisle Indian School, an acculturation academy in Pennsylvania, in 1915. During this period, Black Elk lost much of his vision and sought treatment for chronic tuberculosis at Hot Springs. At the beginning of World War I, perhaps to spare Ben from the military, Black Elk requested the boy's return to assist with farming and livestock.

The last half of Black Elk's life brought rewards denied him in the beginning of his ministry. He rejoiced in the opportunity to complete his life's mission through Neihardt's writing. With sacred purpose he prayed:

> Oh hear me, grandfathers, and help us, that our generation
>   in the future will live and walk the good road
>   with the flowering stick to success.
> Also, the pipe of peace we will offer it
>   as we walk the good road to success.
> Hear me, and hear our plea [DeMallie 1984, 46].

In tribute to his chronicler, Black Elk arranged a formal adoption of Neihardt, renamed Peta Wigmunke (Flaming Rainbow), on May 15, 1931, and received his daughters into the tribe—Enid as Sagye Wakan Yuha Mani Win (She Walks with Her Sacred Stick) and Hilda as Anpo Wicahpi Win (Daybreak Star Woman). The ceremony was necessary to complete the requisite family exchange limited to father and son. Because Ben had soiled his heart with too much whiteness, Black Elk chose his adopted white son to receive the sacred mysteries and take charge of the sacred pipe and symbolic shield. The rite was a mix of sober responsibility, friendship, and Lakota fun. According to Hilda Neihardt's memoir, *Black Elk and Flaming Rainbow* (1995), all joined in the playing of hoop and spear, a skill game resembling pitching horseshoes, which Cherokees call *chungke*. Festivities concluded the next day with dancing and a traditional feast of soup, cooked by traditional stone boiling, and a sweet fruit pudding.

For the first time to Indians and whites, the text of *Black Elk Speaks* reveals the seer's mighty vision, his oneness with the divine, and a sense of his mission as reformer and rescuer of the Sioux. At the eclipse of native autonomy, he aims to restore and nourish the nation to new life, which will allow it to flourish once more like a tree in bloom. To return Lakota sanctity, he intends to make the people walk a sacred path in tune with heavenly powers. To renew ties with the past and create interrelation in the present, he means to help the Oglala reenter the sacred hoop and relocate the red road they once trod. His medium is Neihardt, who clarified in a 1971 interview that he and Black Elk were collaborators, with the seer being the chief participant in completing a religious obligation.

Black Elk's interviews, reframed in print by Neihardt, come across as straightforward memories interlaced with mystic communion with many levels of earth and the supernatural. Chapter 1 opens with a sincere welcome to Neihardt and the introduction of the sacred pipe, which he offers to heavenly powers and shares with his guest. Black Elk's prayer flows as naturally as conversation:

> Grandfather, Great Spirit, you have been always,
>   and before you no one has been.
> There is no other one to pray to but you.
> You yourself, everything that you see,
>   everything has been made by you [Neihardt 1979, 5].

The priest concludes by calling to the four quarters and declaring his kinship with creation.

In the second chapter, Black Elk introduces autobiographical material and a tradition of prophecy dating to Drinks Water's warning of massive changes to the native lifestyle. Fire Thunder and Standing Bear augment Oglala history with their own memories. Chapter 3, "The Great Vision," is a long narrative detailing the voices that call to Black Elk in boyhood. A great apocalypse of a talking bay horse and groups of twelve beautiful black horses, sorrels, and buckskins dancing around precedes a visit to a tipi of grandfathers, who he describes as "older than men can ever be—old like hills, like stars" (Neihardt 1979, 25). The boy accepts a magical cup of water, a powerful herb, a peace pipe, and a budding branch. Black Elk, the fourth of a family of shamans, receives the power to kill and to quicken. The sixth grandfather warns that the boy will need power to survive a time of great earthly troubles.

Black Elk performs a ritual planting of the branch at the center of the nation's sacred hoop. The vision continues with grand spectacle and with a tragic era of hunger and loss of holiness. Black Elk knows all—that his people will sicken, that the bison die out, and that rapid gunfire and smoke will envelop Lakota territory. With an unusual maturity, he declares, "I saw more than I can tell and I understood more than I saw; for I was seeing in a sacred manner the shapes of all things in the spirit, and the shape of all shapes as they must live together like one being" (Neihardt 1979, 43). He envisions the rejuvenation of his people and his own demise. The chapter closes with a hymn from the sun and his return to his body, prone in a faint.

Because of the power of his vision, Black Elk does not recover completely, but retains a divine nimbus. He returns to normal activities—hunting, pranks, courting a girl, joining the Sun Dance, and, in chapter 9, triumphing at the battle of the Little Bighorn. In the grip of pervasive fear in chapter 13, he takes the advice of his uncle Black Road, an elderly shaman, who urges him to perform what is demanded of him or suffer bad consequences. In chapter 15, "The Dog Vision," in the midst of boyhood memories of the Horse Dance, the elderly narrator lapses into regret that he once cured many, "but my nation I could not help" (Neihardt 1979, 180).

In chapter 17, Black Elk elucidates the importance of the circle to the Oglala. He disdains life in square cabins, which violate "the Power of the World [which] always works in circles, and everything tries to be round" (Neihardt 1979, 194). He substantiates his claim by listing the round sky, earth, stars, wind whirls, birds' nests, moon, and tipis. After locating a sacred herb with a long root, he cures his first patient, the son of Cuts-to-Pieces, with prayers, a cup of water, and application of a purifying northern wind. Success draws many patients to Black Elk, who was then nineteen.

The beginning of despair grips Black Elk in chapter 19 after three years of work as a healer. Against family advice, he takes a train and joins Omahas and Pawnees in a wild west show. Separation from the Plains strips him of vision. He remarks, "I felt dead and my people seemed lost and I thought I might never find them again" (Neihardt 1979, 217). The battle against encroaching whites seems hopeless as the Sioux abandon the Earth Mother and endure incarceration on reservations. The transatlantic journey is so terrifying that Black Elk, overcome with seasickness, dresses himself for death and sings the death song. The trip broadens his knowledge, but leaves him homesick. In Paris, he experiences a vision of the Missouri River that lasts three days. On his return to Pine Ridge, he recognizes the scene as the one he had experienced in France.

Chapter 21 returns to the plight of the Oglala and Black Elk's resumption of healing powers. Filled with hope that his world vision will come true, he dresses for the Sun Dance in chapter 22 and experiences a swinging sensation. He makes a sincere prayer to the Great Spirit and weeps for the renewal of earth. A vivid vision of a beautiful young man fails to buoy Black Elk against the worst troubles of his life — the death of Crazy Horse and the cavalry attack on Wounded Knee, which he describes as a hopeless slaughter. To assure Neihardt's understanding, Black Elk took him to the creekside site and pointed out events of the one-sided battle. According to the text, the site of mayhem fills him with longing for vengeance.

Black Elk chooses a poignant, dramatic moment as the end of his narrative. In combat against cavalrymen in the Badlands, he has the sensation of being his people's *wanekia* (savior), like Wovoka. The impression fades, leaving him saddened by the mass murder of innocent people. In bloody mud covered with snow, he sees his people's dream die. In old age, he concludes, "You see me now a pitiful old man who has done nothing, for the nation's hoop is broken and scattered. There is no center any longer, and the sacred tree is dead" (Neihardt 1979, 270).

Throughout his priesthood, Black Elk does not delude himself that restoration will be an easy fix. He differentiates between the death of an individual and the demise of a people, a calamity of dismaying proportions but one that a realist must endure. Although he does not doubt his commission nor the heavenly promise he received in youth, he never trusts his capability. In old age, as physical and psychic power desert his withered frame, he takes heart from the visits of Neihardt, a white man offering a second chance to complete God's task. At the completion of the telling, the seer declares that narration has passed the power from him to Neihardt, his spiritual son.

Publication of Neihardt's work brought enthusiastic applause from the Bureau of Indian Affairs, but outrage from the Jesuit priests at Holy Rosary Mission, where Black Elk had long served as catechist. According to author and native expert Vine Deloria, Jr., *Black Elk Speaks* slowly built a faithful following for its authentic expression of Plains religious tenets. When the white world began suffering its own decimation in the 1960s from industrialization, pollution, and overdevelopment, individual seekers turned to the Oglala shaman for reaffirmation. His book served as a source of New Age spiritualism and a touchstone against which evolving faiths were compared. To young native Americans who never experienced free-roaming buffalo and the circling eagle, the text is Lakota scripture, an American Indian bible extending insight, identity, guidance, and spiritual substance, which had dwindled with the death of tribalism.

At age eighty-four, Black Elk was blind and crippled when he granted audience to Joseph Epes Brown at a cabin outside Manderson, South Dakota, to teach the seven sacred rites of the Lakota. With the aid of his bilingual son, Benjamin Black Elk; Ben's wife, Ellen Black Elk; and a friend, Little Warrior, for six years, the two worked at the sessions that would produce *The Sacred Pipe*, issued before Black Elk's death on August 19, 1950, at Pine Ridge Reservation. Over an Assiniboin pipe, the aged seer had looked inward and foresaw Brown's arrival. Black Elk mourned the loss of peace between neighbors and spurned Christian predictions of peace on earth. Chapter 1 describes the native communion through the sacred pipe, a *lela wakan* (very sacred) gift which a mystic female messenger, later identified as White Buffalo Cow Woman, offered to Chief Standing Hollow Horn. Ethnologist J. L. Smith dates the event in 1798.

The sacred teaching begins in a consecrated lodge, symbolically constructed with the twenty-eight poles and wall coverings of several tipis. Its shape represents the universe. In Black Elk's simple telling, "The people were, of course, all very excited as they waited in the great lodge for the coming of the holy woman, and everybody was wondering where this mysterious woman came from and what it was that she wished to say" (Brown 1989, 4). The pipe she offered Standing Hollow Horn was holy and thus restricted from the eyes of the impure. Decked with twelve feathers of the *wanbli galeshka* (spotted eagle) to represent all birds, the pipe consists of a red stone bowl dug from Mother Earth. As she explains, "This earth which he has given to you is red, and the two-legged who live upon the earth are red; and the Great Spirit has also given to you a red day, and a red road" (Brown 1989, 7).

Sheathed in a ceremonial cover, the pipe holds an honored place in the seven-part ritual that climaxes in invocation to Grandfather, the Sioux designation of the Creator. It symbolizes a promise of eternal life to the Lakota and of love for neighbors. To assure holiness, White Buffalo Cow Woman, walking sunwise or clockwise as she speaks, calls for a righteous priest: "He who keeps the soul of a person must be a good and pure man, and he should use the pipe so that all the people, with the soul, will together send their voices to *Wakan-Tanka*" (Brown 1989, 8–9). At the completion of her instruction, she shifts her shape to a white buffalo, then to a black buffalo that disappears over a hill.

In chapter 2, Black Elk alternates explanations of soul keeping with the prayers and gestures of Hollow Horn before he begins the smoking of the pipe of ritual tobacco, *kinnikinnik*, which is a dried inner bark of red alder or red dogwood. Because of its bitterness, the user blends twist tobacco and fragrant roots or herbs mixed in ritual proportions. As ethnologist Francis La Flesche explains in "War Ceremony and Peace Ceremony of the Osage Indians" (1939), the pipe becomes a body. References to its parts name a neck, mouth, sides, hollow, and windpipe.

In chapter 3, Black Elk explains the purification ritual, which takes place in the *onikare* (sweat lodge), a temporary domed dwelling shaped of willow lathes. As a symbol of the universe, it encompasses a world inhabited by birds and four-legged animals as well as humankind. It faces east and contains an eternal fire. Before cleansing, the seekers burn sweet grass and smudge body, feet, head, hands, and the pipe as a means of consecration. Worshipers welcome intrusions by curious children, whom adults consider pure of heart. The completed ceremony ends with thanksgiving for Wakinyan-Tanka (Thunderbird), a profoundly important deity symbolized by the thunderbolt, which cleanses earth of pollutants.

In the next chapter, Black Elk details the Hanble-cheyapi (Crying for a Vision, or Lament) ritual, a purification rite that antedates veneration of the sacred pipe. He specifies that only the worthy receive great visions that strengthen the health and welfare of the Lakota. The seeker of a vision consults a *wichasha wakan* (holy man) for guidance in communicating with the powers of nature. When Crazy Horse cultivated vision, he communicated with the rock, shadow, badger, day, spotted eagle, and a prancing horse, for which he was named. Afterward, he bore on his person some tangible connection with each power to maintain its potency.

Visions bolster the spirit for combat or an ordeal, such as the Sun Dance. They also curry favor with *Wakan Tanka* to heal a relative, offer thanks for a gift, or establish unity with nature and cognizance of a universal source of all being. Male seekers climb to an isolated mountaintop; women purify themselves, then climb a hill for a ceremony lasting from one to four days. Males dress in buffalo robe, breechcloth, and moccasins and carry a pipe. Within a willow lodge, both men and women initiate a quest by placing their feet on the earth to ground the quest on sacred turf. They make an offering of tobacco. Prayers to the Great Spirit in the west, the giant of the north, the sun in the east, and the sacred winds to the south conclude with a prayer to Galeshka (Spotted Eagle), the winged being who circles the earth and observes life below.

The vision quest requires intervention of the holy man, who directs placement and use of the sacred pipe and chants to the powers above:

> They are sending a voice to me.
> From the place where the sun goes down.
> Our grandfather is sending a voice to me [Brown 1989, 55].

The singing prefaces the sprinkling of water on hot rocks to make steam. From the lodge, the seeker traverses a sacred path and, while departing alone to an elevated spot, cries out to the Great Spirit for mercy. The lengthy quest requires fasting, sleeping on a bed of sage, and anticipation of meaningful dreams. The divinity these seekers experience becomes a protective force, much like the Christian concept of a guardian angel, and helps them cultivate a pure heart.

In chapter 5, Black Elk explains the annual Wiwanyag Wachipi (Sun Dance), a summer prayer and worship ceremony that began long after the receipt of the sacred pipe. The ritual dismayed Jesuits, who interpreted it as an anti–Christian parody of Christ's crucifixion. To lessen violent clashes of natives and whites, the U.S. government, claiming that the ritual was barbaric and inhumane, repressed it as early as 1879 and banned it completely on April 10, 1883. Thus, the proscription halted Black Elk's professional practice through his most productive years.

The ban survived for forty-nine years; body piercing remained forbidden until 1952.

Black Elk names the mythic Kablaya as the first Sun Dancer and describes a spontaneous vision that caused Kablaya and others to rise, drop their robes, and dance with arms raised skyward to the sun, which they honored as light of the world. According to Kablaya's instructions, the mystic dance requires tobacco, *kinnikinnik*, sweet grass, knife and ax, rabbit pelts, eagle feathers, red and blue paint, celestial shapes cut in rawhide, wing bone whistles, drums, otter skin necklaces, and the tallow, calf hide, and skull of a buffalo. Kablaya indicated to five singers the focus of the dance: "The sacred pipe [which is] always at the center of the hoop of our nation" (Brown 1989, 69).

Because of its intensity, the ritual piqued interest in the outside world. Although whites tend to think of it as a toughening of braves through torture, the dance reenacts creation to safeguard the tribe and propitiates the Great Spirit for cures. In a circular lodge symbolizing the universe, the Holy of Holies is the cottonwood pole supporting the roof at center and representing the Milky Way. Here, dancers take on a unique significance: "When you stand at the center of the sacred hoop, you will be the people, and you will be as the pipe, stretching from heaven to earth. The weak will lean upon you, and for all the people you will be a support" (Brown 1989, 74). Under the supervision of medicine men and elders, participants communicate with divinity to secure blessing and continuity. After the ceremony, they abandon the lodge to nature.

In the original Sun Dance, participating males stripped chest and feet, braided their hair, and donned a special apron. After adorning themselves in red, black, and blue paint, celestial symbols, and powdered sage, they blew eagle bone whistles. Throughout the ritual they suffered physical torment by abstaining from drinking fluids, gazing directly at the sun, slicing pieces of flesh as offerings, and attaching thongs radiating from the center pole to skewers piercing the torso. At the height of ecstasy, celebrants pulled outward, ripping off hunks of flesh.

With the rising of the first star, participants prayed and began a vigorous all-night shuffle to hymns sung and chanted by a choir. The pattern altered the second day, when solo and duo dances began before dawn and advanced to lines of performers praying to the sun, drumming, and blessing the sick. The Sun Dance reached its pinnacle on the third day with distribution of pipes, healing, and visions. Before the end of the dance on the fourth day, the facilitator offered water to the earth, steam from hot rocks, and drinks to participants.

A peacemaking ritual, Hunkapi (the Making of Relatives), is the subject of chapter 6. Black Elk claims that the Lakota originated holy adoption of former enemies as a response to the vision of Matohoshila, or Bear Boy, discoverer of corn. To establish peace with the Ree or Arikara, a Caddoan tribe related to the Pawnee, the Lakota instituted a ceremonial union with a visiting Ree as an example of oneness with other Indians. Like the Sun Dance, the sacred gathering requires certain natural and handmade items as ritual equipment — pipe and tobacco, four stalks of corn with ears and one without, sticks to make a drying rack, red and blue paint, eagle feathers, knife, and buffalo skull, bladder, and meat. To purify celebrants and site, the holy man makes a fire of sweet grass and initiates prayers and gestures to unite the two tribes. The complicated ceremony concludes with singing, chanting, and drumming in the presence of both Ree and Lakota, who share a communal feast.

Chapter 7 explains a female-centered ritual — the Ishna Ta Awi Cha Lowan (Preparing a Girl for Womanhood), which acknowledges menarche. The rite dates to the vision of Slow Buffalo, who saw a mother buffalo cleansing her calf. He became a holy man and promoted the womanhood ceremony as a benefit to Lakota youth. At the request of Feather on Head, he initiated his first budding female, White Buffalo Cow Woman Appears, daughter of Feather on Head. The initiation requires a cup and water, sweet grass, sage, cherries, pipe and tobacco, *kinnikinnik*, knife and hatchet, red and blue paint, and a buffalo skull.

Black Elk states that young virgins learn from tribal training how to honor the lunar influence on their bodies and how to train children within the sacred Lakota traditions. The initiate pairs with an older woman, who tutors her in womanly skills, such as the making of moccasins and other garments. After smudging, a ritual cleansing with the smoke of sweet grass, and sipping consecrated water, the girl receives her commission to "go forth among your people in a holy manner" (Brown 1989, 125). The priest orders her to be humble and fruitful and to walk a sacred path, which requires receiving and nurturing orphans. The investiture concludes with feasting and a giveaway, a tribal redistribution of wealth through the exchange of gifts.

Black Elk concludes *The Sacred Pipe* with a description of Tapa Wanka Yap (Throwing of the Ball), a sacred game that constitutes the last of the seven sacred rituals. The structure of the game represents human life. The ball, painted to represent the cosmos, is an emblem of luck, which passes from team to team and allows individuals to score. The rules derive from a vision of Waskan Mani (Moves Walking) and the application of High Hollow Horn, who laid out the game course. On a holy day, celebrants dress in fine clothes and paint their faces. The game reassures the Lakota, who welcome consecration at a sacred rite. Black Elk concludes his text with a sobering thought that some people no longer scramble for the ball. He realizes that the end of native domination is near. He prays that the ball will return to the center and bring with it his people to their traditions.

The third installment of Black Elk's career, *When the Tree Flowered*, resulted from John Neihardt's return to work for the Bureau of Indian Affairs after the completion of his epic work. Near the end of World War II, he accepted an assignment to gather information for an Oglala cultural history. With the aid of daughter Hilda, he interviewed three Oglala males from November 27 to December 11, 1944. Hilda typed her transcription directly on the page without passing through shorthand notes. He spent four days with ninety-three-year-old Eagle Elk, a skilled buffalo hunter, warrior, and participant in the Sun Dance. For seven days in December, Neihardt returned to Black Elk to learn the bulk of Sioux history from early times to the arrival of whites. His text covers adventure and combat stories, the Ohunkakan (winter-telling myth), origins of the knife, bow and arrow, and fire making, and the naming of relatives, directions, and animals. Black Elk summarizes the Sioux diaspora, taming of wild dogs, creation of the horse culture, systemization of government, and the holy man Wood Cup's prophecy of the end of the Sioux lifestyle. Neihardt's last interview was with Andrew Knife, who related the wooing of Red Hail.

Unlike the faithful rendering of Neihardt's first volume, *When the Tree Flowered*, composed in novel form, creates a chronological plot related by the fictional narrator Eagle Voice, a composite of Black Elk and Eagle Elk. The rhetorical method allows Neihardt more control of the collected materials. The merger of voices produces a character who internalizes his grandfather's ancient oral lore and who recalls the major events of the era: the Fetterman massacre, battle of the Little Bighorn, and the massacre at Wounded Knee. Thus, the scope of Eagle Voice's story produces continuity in a history that allies pre–Columbian Plains traditions with the settlement of the American West.

Chapter 1 opens in a one-room log cabin, where the elder speaker sits cross-legged in blankets and welcomes a white friend who is truly sympathetic to Lakota ways. He begins "before the hoop of our people was broken" (Neihardt 1951, 2). Covering elements of native life from prehistory, he relates details of communal birthing, the training of young girls in womanly skills of sewing with a bone needle, and making tipi covers from hide and stretching them over poles. Before Red Cloud leads the Oglala in war, Eagle Voice, then age eight, plays soldier-and-Indian games on Duck River near Fort Laramie when he encounters Tashina Wan-blee (Her Eagle Robe), whom he intends to marry.

Eagle Voice halts to tell of Wooden Cup's vision of the coming of a strange people and the depletion of bison. The narrator returns to his story by recalling talks between Red Cloud and white officials and the killing of a hundred soldiers on Peno Creek, a reference to the Fetterman massacre at Fort Philip Kearny in 1866. Eagle Voice recalls his father's partial recovery from an arrow in the hip, which inhibited him from an even stride but did not halt his riding and fighting.

The description of the death of Eagle Voice's father in chapter 4 typifies the work of family members and friends in preparing a corpse. Five adults wash the body and paint it red. After braiding the deceased man's hair and tying on an eagle feather for "spirit power," they paint his face with a new moon symbol. Dressed in buckskin and tied in a buffalo robe, he goes to the spirit land. A cortege accompanies a pony drag to a scaffold, where mourners sacrifice the animal. After the grandfather's prayer to the Great Spirit, Eagle Voice has a vision of a unified people and ample buffalo. Kind villagers bathe and feed the family to prepare them for four days of mourning and prayer.

During the family's departure from the village, the grandfather tells of the seven *teoshpaiay* (bands), seven council fires, and the Oglala. Eagle Voice recalls a buffalo hunt on the Rosebud River in chapter 6 and the decline of Red Cloud's reputation in chapter 7, where he appears to be "a *Wasichu* with a forked tongue like all the others" (Neihardt 1951, 44). Blue Spotted Horse initiates Eagle Voice into the vision quest. The boy, then thirteen, prays the ancient prayer:

> Grandfather, Great Mysterious One! You have been always, and before you nothing has been. There is nothing to pray to but you. The star nations all over the heavens are yours, and yours are the grasses of the earth. You are older than all need, older than all pain and prayer. Day in, day out, you are the life of things [Neihardt 1951, 52].

Blue Spotted Horse, the boy's mentor, predicts that he will survive many battles and count many coups without harm, but will not see the sacred hoop of all people under a flowering tree.

Led by Crazy Horse in chapter 9, Eagle Voice joins a war party at Greasy Grass Valley. In chapter 15, he tells of the Sun Dance, held under the *chun wakon* (sacred tree), which supplies the pole at the center of the dance. While dancing and gazing at the sun, he feels "white-hot knives" in his eyes and retreats into darkness (Neihardt 1951, 120). Drumbeats and singing waft him away into the night, where he envisions a wide green land. Attendants rub him with sacred sage and paint him with sacred blue and yellow paint. On the third day, when he earns the name Eagle Voice, the speaker bears a bison skull tied to his back and a thong piercing his chest. Lost in vision and pain, he merges with the morning star. At the end of the dance, he continues to throb and receives from Chagla a quirt as a token of the power he received from the ritual.

Chapter 21 moves beyond congenial grandfather tales to the break-up of the sacred hoop. In Eagle Voice's description:

> We were living on a big island, and the *wasichus* were like great waters washing all around it, nibbling off the edges, and it was getting smaller, smaller, smaller. It is very small now. The people have lost the sacred hoop, the good red road, the flowering tree [Neihardt 1951, 202].

At age seventeen, he witnesses the alliance of Cheyenne, Arapaho, Miniconjou, Sans Arc, Hunkpapa, Oglala, Santee, Yankton, and Brûlé and recalls how Sitting Bull foresaw victory at the Little Bighorn in a rain of soldiers' corpses. At the end of the battle, which occurred June 25–26, 1876, Eagle Voice is overcome with memories and weeping. In chapter 29, he recalls Wounded Knee, site of the shameful massacre of noncombatants led by U.S. cavalrymen on December 29, 1890. They charged the village and slaughtered women and children with the "wagon-guns-that-shoot-twice [Hotchkiss guns]" (Neihardt 1951, 247). He concludes with a romantic touch: reunion with Tashina and, at her death, burial of his protective quirt between her breasts.

Black Elk's health declined rapidly in the winter of 1933 following a wagon accident that broke two of his ribs. The close shave with death caused him to convert formally to Catholicism on January 26, 1934, when he stated a belief in the church's seven sacraments and their superiority to the Sun Dance and Ghost Dance. That same year, he declared that all his children and grandchildren belonged to the "black-gown church," which he considered not a replacement, but an alternate interpretation of the "great mystery" (Johansen and Grinde 1998, 37). In the spring of 1935, however, he gave a public demonstration of Lakota spirituality, which included a prayer to the six grandfathers and shamanic healing. His death in 1950 coincided with a meteor shower over Pine Ridge, a convergence that he had predicted.

Black Elk left his photographs to the Smithsonian Institution in Washington, D.C., where they remain at the National Anthropological Archives. His daughter, Lucy Looks Twice, was inconsolable until friends urged her to read *Black Elk Speaks* for the first time. She was so moved that the book changed her life. She became a Lakota pipe carrier. In Bancroft, Nebraska, in August 1977, she joined Hilda Neihardt Petri on Neihardt Day for a public recitation of another version of Black Elk's prayer in Lakota and English:

Grandfather, Great Mysterious One, you have been always, and before you nothing has been.
There is nothing to pray to but you.
The star nations all over the universe are yours, and yours are the grasses of the earth.
Day in, day out, you are the life of things.
You are older than all need, older than all pain and prayer.
Grandfather, all over the world the faces of living ones are alike.
In tenderness they have come up out of the ground. Look upon your children with children in their arms, that they may face the winds and walk the Good Road to the Day of Quiet.
Teach me to walk the soft earth, a relative to all that live.
Sweeten my heart, and fill me with light. Give me the strength to understand and the eyes to see.
Help me, for without you, I am nothing.
Hetchetu aloh! [Neihardt 1995, 121].

In 1993, Michael F. Steltenkamp, a Jesuit anthropologist, published a definitive biography, *Black Elk: Holy Man of the Oglala*, which he based on observations by the old man's only surviving child, Lucy Looks Twice; her mother, Anna Brings White; and an Oglala pipe carrier. The text adds details of Black Elk's ministry to the Arapaho, Winnebago, and Omaha.

DeMallie's *The Sixth Grandfather* recaps the life, interviews, and writings about Black Elk. Published in 1984, DeMallie's version opens with a positive foreword by Hilda Neihardt Petri, who lauds the scholarship of the author as an anthropologist and Western historian intent on truth. The need for a fourth volume derives from issues of what Black Elk said, what his Lakota words meant, and how Neihardt went about determining both. DeMallie's preface justifies the title, the designation that Black Elk chose for himself as the "down" entity, a spiritual representative of earth and humankind as opposed to the spirits of north, south, east, west, and the upper sphere. The author refutes application of Black Elk's narratives as an anthropological study of Lakota culture, psychological analysis of the native personality, or philosophical understanding of tribal religion. Rather, DeMallie interprets Neihardt's work as the next stage in Black Elk's ministry and a vehicle for the sixth grandfather's mission. The text precedes a concordance that indexes material from the original interviews by page in the first two volumes.

After a detailed biography of the Lakota seer in part 1, part 2 recreates the 1931 interviews and particularizes material Neihardt added from his research to flesh out details of Crazy Horse's influence, the Sun Dance, battle of the Little Bighorn, and the death of Crazy Horse. DeMallie emphasizes the circle as the supreme symbol of Lakota spirituality and characterizes the vision quest as an act of humility. Through discussion of the Ghost Dance, herbalism, and the Bear Medicine Ceremony, he stresses the original religiosity of Black Elk and his receipt of sacred power from the six grandfathers. Overall is an emphasis on ecumenicity, the respect for native and white faiths that permeated Black Elk's last thirty-five years following his (conversion) to Catholicism. By reinterpreting native elements, Black Elk was able to syncretize Christ and salvation as alternate symbols to his belief in the sacred tree and hoop.

To reiterate Black Elk's dog vision without Neihardt's ethnocentric restatement, DeMallie separates its elements into eleven identifiable symbols:

- rising into clouds with two men depicts Black Elk as responding to his western grandfather and to oneness with all six grandsires
- witnessing the horses of four directions, which the bay horse points out
- following the bay to the grandfathers' cloud tipi, where the western grandfather sings first of the Thunder-Being nation, followed by the northern grandfather's song of the White Geese nation
- walking the black sacred road from west to east and overcoming the spirit in the water, a reenactment of cosmic war between sky and water powers
- walking the red sacred road from south to north, a complex event that confers the power of the sacred days
- receiving a healing herb of the north and seeing the sacred tree at the center of the nation's hoop
- killing a flaming dog and receiving the healing herb of the west, which cures the black horse
- reaching earth's center and receiving the daybreak star herb, events that establish the vision's universalism
- receiving the soldier weed of destruction, a military episode that Neihardt omitted because it violated the spirit of universalism
- returning to the six grandfathers, where Black Elk glimpses a vision of earthly unity in a cup of water and swallows a small blue man with a bow and arrow
- following the spotted eagle home

The dog vision committed Black Elk to perform the Heyoka ceremony, a vision of thunder and direct communication with spirits who guard warriors, and revealed natural forces conferred for *wakan* (holy) power to make the seer an intercessor for the Lakota.

Part 3 duplicates the 1944 interviews, which depart from the history and significance of the first encounters. At age eighty-one, Black Elk had had adequate time to reflect on Lakota history and culture from the perspective of years of acculturation to white society. One of his lengthy memories includes a summary of four ways of divining the future:

- in a coma induced by the Sun Dance
- by maintaining a vigil on a hill
- by decoding mysterious petroglyphs that appear on rocks at the Little Bighorn
- by studying the visions that occur in the hours preceding death

These details of his priesthood account for his stature among Native Americans.

SOURCES: Adamson 1987, Alsberg 1949, "Battle of Wounded Me" 1994, Bellafante 1995, Black Elk and Lyon 1990, "Black Elk, Holy Man of the Oglala Sioux," "Black Elk's Prayer," "Black Elk: The Family Speaks," Brooke 1989, Brown, Dee, 1970, Brown, John Epes, 1989, Buchanan 1999, Cantor 1993, Champagne 1994, 1998, Collier 1947, Cummings 1993, DeMallie 1984, Deur 1972, Dobie 1996, Grinnell 1971, Harrod 1987, Heinerman 1989, Holler 1995, Johansen and Grinde 1998, "Keepers of the Sacred Traditions of Pipemakers," Ketchum 1957, *Lakota: Seeking the Great Spirit* 1994, Lehn 1980, Maynor and McLeod 1999, McCluskey 1972, Milne 1995, Neihardt, Hilda, 1995, Neihardt, John G., 1951, 1979, Patterson and Snodgrass 1994, Powell 1969, Powers 1977, Skafte 1997, Smith 1995, Snodgrass 1995, 1997, 2001, "A Statement from Dr. Arvol Looking Horse," Steiger 1974, Steinmetz 1998, Steltenkamp 1993, Vogel 1998, Waldman 1990, Weddell, Wiget 1996.

Book of Mormon

The Book of Mormon (1830) is one of four sources of scripture for members of the Church of Jesus Christ of Latter Day Saints, a millennarist sect that also reveres the Bible, Doctrine and Covenants, and the *Pearl of Great Price*. Composed in holy idiom drawn from the Elizabethan English of the King James Bible, the Book of Mormon resembles its predecessor in five aspects: a patriarchal point of view, stress on genealogy, citation of the words of Jesus, grim prophecies, and repetitive battle motifs.

The work is an ancient history set in North America, which explains how God transferred his chosen people from Palestine to the New World. The book takes its title from Mormon, the ancient North American prophet who preserved a record of events dating over a thousand years, from 600 B.C.E. to C.E. 421. A team of twenty-three recorders contributed to the history, which is currently available in twenty-four languages and Braille.

The book was the work of Joseph "Jo" Smith, Jr., a prophet of Jehovah and the founder of Mormonism. A native of Sharon, Vermont, he was born on December 23, 1805, to farmer, storekeeper, and root harvester Joseph Smith, Sr., and Lucy Mack Smith, a clairvoyant. At the height of an American revivalist movement, when Joseph was ten, the family moved along the Erie Canal to Palmyra, New York. There, he experienced the emotional stimulus to repent and accept Jesus. The intense religious phenomenon was a response to the Methodism of English evangelists Charles and John Wesley and was developed by circuit-riding preachers and at camp meetings, all-day assemblies climaxing in mass baptism. The movement, known as the Great Awakening, sparked a second crusade, the Second Awakening, which spread from Presbyterians to Baptists and Methodists.

Amid this soul-stirring furor, Smith attended religious gatherings, but took issue with the variant Protestant faiths that jostled for control of the populace. In 1819, he suffered a religious depression that preceded a vision at his home near Sacred Grove. He remarks in the *Pearl of Great Price*, "It was the first time in my life that I had made such an attempt, for amidst all my anxieties I had never as yet made the attempt to pray vocally" (Hastings 1951, 11:85). Nearly twenty years later, he recalled seeing two sacred beings, who ordered him to avoid local sects.

On September 21, 1823, the angel Moroni commanded Smith to do God's work and hinted that he would encounter a book composed on gold plates and bound by three rings. To interpret it, he should access a decoding

THE

BOOK OF MORMON:

AN ACCOUNT WRITTEN BY THE HAND OF MOR-
MON, UPON PLATES TAKEN FROM
THE PLATES OF NEPHI.

Wherefore it is an abridgment of the Record of the People of Nephi; and also of the Lamanites; written to the Lamanites, which are a remnant of the House of Israel; and also to Jew and Gentile; written by way of commandment, and also by the spirit of Prophesy and of Revelation. Written, and sealed up, and hid up unto the LORD, that they might not be destroyed; to come forth by the gift and power of GOD, unto the interpretation thereof; sealed by the hand of Moroni, and hid up unto the LORD, to come forth in due time by the way of Gentile; the interpretation thereof by the gift of GOD; an abridgment taken from the Book of Ether.

Also, which is a Record of the People of Jared, which were scattered at the time the LORD confounded the language of the people when they were building a tower to get to Heaven; which is to shew unto the remnant of the House of Israel how great things the LORD hath done for their fathers; and that they may know the covenants of the LORD, that they are not cast off forever; and also to the convincing of the Jew and Gentile that JESUS is the CHRIST, the ETERNAL GOD, manifesting Himself unto all nations. And now if there be fault, it be the mistake of men; wherefore condemn not the things of GOD, that ye may be found spotless at the judgment seat of CHRIST.

BY JOSEPH SMITH, JUNIOR,
AUTHOR AND PROPRIETOR.

PALMYRA:

PRINTED BY E. B. GRANDIN, FOR THE AUTHOR.

1830.

Title page of the first edition of the Book of Mormon.

device contained on two transparent stones. The text would enlighten the world on the history of early settlers of the New World who had sailed from Palestine via the Pacific Ocean. Immediately, Smith found the plates in a stone receptacle under a rock at Cumorah Hill outside Manchester in Ontario County, New York, where they had lain for fourteen centuries. Under orders, he waited four years before taking any action on the vision. During this period, an unscrupulous realtor cheated his family of their acreage. They sank from farm owners to tenants. Smith responded to perpetual poverty with fruitless treasure hunts in local Indian mounds.

According to Smith, the angel Moroni (also identified as Nephi) presented him with a copy of the Book of Mormon on September 22, 1827. The text was inscribed on gold-toned metal plates around 6" × 7" and rendered in a reformed Egyptian language. To translate this celestial message, Smith followed divine instructions to apply a decoding device consisting of two stones in a silver bow, which adorned a breastplate. It was not until 1833 that he identified these magical stones as the Urim and Thummim, which appear in the canon Bible in Exodus 28:30, Leviticus 8:8, Ezra 2:63, Nehemiah 7:65, Deuteronomy 33:8, Numbers 27:21, and I Samuel 28:6, but are not named in the Book of Mormon. Local people pressured him to reveal his divine plates, but he chose to take them to Susquehanna County, Pennsylvania.

Working behind a curtain to conceal the sacred plates from the curious, Smith began translating and reciting these passages to Emma Hale, his wife, on April 12, 1828. He shifted the burden of writing to farmer and money lender Martin Harris in Manchester, New York. Three witnesses and Emma described his working method: dropping his "peek-stone" into his hat, he plunged his face into the inner rim and rested his elbows on his knees. Out of visual range of the golden plates, he glimpsed words in bright Roman script, which appeared in sequence on parchment.

After misplacing the original 116 pages of transcription, Smith ceased work for a year. With the assistance of scribe Oliver Cowdery, he resumed the project on April 7, 1829, and received ordination as an apostle of John the Baptist. When Smith and his aides finished their labors three months later, Moroni reclaimed the metal plates, which disappeared from the earth. With funding from Martin Harris, in March 1830 in Palmyra, New York, E. B. Grandin, publisher of the *Wayne Sentinel*, printed 5,000 copies of the book's 306,000 words in 590 pages. The original handwritten text no longer survives.

Much as Virgil's *Aeneid* provided upstart Romans with a respected genealogy and a historical tie with the Trojan War, Smith's Book of Mormon satisfied an American hunger for a chronicle linking the New World to the sacred history of Palestine. The first Mormon newspaper, the *Evening and Morning Star*, excerpted passages to establish doctrinal purity and exalted them above questionable modern translations of the canon Bible. To further establish the Mormon faith, Smith authored the Book of Commandments, which he enlarged into Doctrine and Covenants (1835), a collection of predictions and interpretations. This volume contains a revelation of February 1831, which set up a church receiving center for properties:

> And the residue shall be kept to administer to him who has not, that every man may receive accordingly as he stands in need: and the residue shall be kept in my storehouse, to administer to the poor and needy, as shall be appointed by the elders of the church and the bishop; and for the purpose of purchasing lands, and the building up of the New Jerusalem, which is hereafter to be revealed [Hastings 1951, 11:87].

The autobiographical *Pearl of Great Price* (1851), a sixty-page text, was published posthumously after Smith's murder. It contains the *Book of Moses* and the *Book of Abraham*, a speculative, noncanonical text purportedly composed on papyrus while Abraham lived in Egypt. The *Pearl of Great Price* concludes with the Articles of Faith of the Church of Jesus Christ of Latter Day Saints.

Immediately, Smith launched the Mormon church, claiming that it reinstated an ancient Christian faith devoid of Protestant doctrinal adulteration. On April 6, 1830, he allied family and friends in Fayette, New York, into the first congregation, led by Oliver Cowdery as elder and apostle and Smith as "Prophet, Seer, and Revelator" (Hastings 1951, 11:84). In November, Sidney Rigdon, a skilled and dynamic leader, joined the assembly and partnered with Smith in several unsuccessful business ventures. The sect grew during an expansionist period in the United States. To maintain its tenets, Smith remained in control as patriarch and organizer. In 1831, he led followers to establish a temple in Kirtland, Ohio, and continued southwest to a commune, the United Order of Enoch, in Jackson County, Missouri.

Detractors grew in number as the Mormon population threatened the gentile political majority. Critics labeled the Book of Mormon Smith's "Golden Bible." In 1832, after he exhorted Mormons to sell their property and prepare for the end of time, a mob assaulted him and Rigdon. Smith countered by organizing the secret society of Danites, his own band of vigilantes. He issued a revelation of August 6, 1833, which authorized Mormons to fight back. A general upheaval within the ranks in 1836 cost him followers. The core band ridiculed the dissenter Martin Harris and excommunicated David Whitimer, an antipolygamist. In 1838, Rigdon issued a Fourth of July speech predicting a cataclysmic war between Mormons and gentiles. By October, the state of Missouri had exhausted its patience and declared Mormons enemies to be expelled or exterminated.

After locals ousted Smith's ecclesiastical oligarchy, in 1839, he and 15,000 Mormons retreated to Commerce, Illinois, his new headquarters, which the Illinois legislature had chartered. He renamed the town Nauvoo, commanded a local militia called the Nauvoo League, and served as mayor of over 20,000 citizens in the largest municipality in the state. In vain, he called on President Martin Van Buren to help Mormons reclaim losses of property and begged redress from Senator Henry Clay. Smith's political involvement reached such lengths that, in February 1844, he launched a short-lived run for the U.S. presidency.

Smith lost primacy as skeptics, fearing that the Mormons endangered Missouri's rights as a slave state, discredited his heavenly visions. A majority of critics opposed the doctrine of polygamy, which he published on July 12, 1843, as *Revelation on the Eternity of the Marriage Covenant, including Plurality of Wives*. Within the text, the Lord justifies the practice of multiple wives for Abraham, Isaac, Jacob, Moses, David, and Solomon. In section 132, the Lord declares:

> As pertaining to the law of the priesthood: If any man espouse a virgin, and desire to espouse another, and the first give her consent; and if he espouse the second, and they are virgins, and have vowed to no other man, then is he justified; he cannot commit adultery, for they are given unto him; for he cannot commit adultery with that that belongeth unto him and to no one else [Hastings 1951, 11:83].

Orson Pratt had previously systematized polygamy in *Treatise on the Regeneration and Eternal Duration of Matter* (1840), which claims that celestial marriage places a heavenly seal on polygamy, which duplicates on earth the reunion in heaven of a man with all the wives who predeceased him. Moving decidedly toward civil disobedience, Pratt declared the matter an ecclesiastical concern outside of the jurisdiction of earthly governance.

The antipolygamy backlash began with arson, night riding, and rowdyism and crystallized on June 7, 1844, with attacks printed in the *Nauvoo Expositor*, a single-issue journal published by R. D. Foster, William Law, and Wilson Law. Smith countered by destroying the press and ousting the editor for his anti–Mormonism and rebuke of men marrying multiple wives. Joseph Smith and his brother Hyrum organized a retreat to the Rocky Mountains. Under state protection, they were jailed for treason in Carthage, Illinois. On June 27, rioters led by Thomas Ford forced their way to the cellblock and shot both men.

Loss of leadership disoriented and temporarily derailed the Mormon community. A schism resulted in three splinter sects:

- the majority band led by Brigham Young, successor to the prophet Smith and head of the Council of the Twelve Apostles
- a failed dissident body led by the propolygamist J. J. Strang, which dissolved after his death in 1856
- the dissident Reorganized Church of Jesus Christ of Latter Day Saints or "Young Josephites," an antipolygamist group led by Joseph Smith, III, oldest surviving son of Joseph Smith and Emma Hale's nine children.

This third sect headquartered in Lamoni, Iowa, and flourished in Iowa and Illinois.

From 1846 to 1847, the most loyal Mormons, unified under persecution and martyrdom, followed Brigham Young on the nation's great Mormon diaspora. After his reconnaissance agents searched California and Oregon for likely locations, he led the Mormon hegira to the Great Salt Lake Valley, far to the west, where state and federal law had no jurisdiction. According to section 136 of Doctrine and Covenants, a specific revelation commanded:

> The word and will of the Lord concerning the camp of Israel in their journeyings to the west: let all the people of the Church of Jesus Christ of Latter Day Saints, and those who journey with them, be organized into companies, with a covenant and promise to keep all the commandments and statutes of the Lord our god [Hastings 1951, 11:89].

In obedience to divine will, the first group of 1,553 Mormons left on July 4, 1847, from Elk Horn River and traveled over 1,100 miles to sparsely populated land in Utah. By 1869, some 80,000 Mormons had made the trek on horseback or by handcart or wagon; after the completion of the transcontinental railroad, latecomers traveled by train.

To establish a self-sustaining religious commonwealth, the Utah Mormons colonized the desolate land around the Great Salt Lake. Working zealously, they tamed the desert through irrigation, laid out land parcels, and built a modern city based on scientific principles. Because Young refused to abandon polygamy, the U.S. government denied a request for statehood in 1849; the following year, Utah became a territory governed by Young. When Mormons instigated the Mountain Meadows massacre against gentile travelers from Arkansas and Missouri in 1857, President James Buchanan sent cavalry to suppress the militants. The expedition failed, but managed to undermine Mormon control.

With the acceptance of Mormonism into American religious faith came the authorization of Smith's writings and the promulgation of the thirteen Articles of Faith, which predict that Israel's Ten Tribes will be restored and that "Zion will be built upon this continent," after which Christ will reign on earth in "paradisiac glory" (Berry 1956, 123). The completed Book of Mormon, which complements the two testaments of the canon Bible, tells of the daily lives, leadership, work, and combat of opposing colonies in the New World. Its preface declares:

> Written, and sealed up, and hid up unto the Lord, that they might not be destroyed; to come forth by the gift and power of God unto the interpretation thereof; sealed by the hand of Moroni, and hid up unto the Lord, to come forth in due time by the way of Gentile; the interpretation thereof the gift of God [Hastings 1951, 11:85].

In Smith's words, Christ "planted the gospel here in all its fullness and richness, and power, and blessing" in the same tradition found in the eastern Mediterranean. Smith explains the variance in America's Hebrew history as a natural consequence of being cut off from the parent Hebrew culture (Hastings 1951, 11:85). In assessing the motivation for Smith's style and scope, one outspoken critic, J. Jastrow, writing in the *Psychological Review* of January 1903, maligned the book as a product of a diseased mind during an abnormal state of dissociation.

The text opens on the emigration of Lehi, a Hebrew, from Jerusalem, while Ishmael, another righteous man, proceeds to South America. Leading his family and that of Ishmael, Lehi sets out. His sons, Nephi and Laman, split their following into two colonies. The Nephites, God's chosen people, succeed; the Lamanites, forerunners of American Indians, lose faith and never rise above a nomadic existence. A parallel exodus from Jerusalem brings the Mulekites to North America, where they join the Nephites. A fourth party, the Jaredites, is an earlier migration contemporaneous with the Tower of Babel, a history known to the Nephites. The Nephites receive Jesus, who returns to earth to educate them. Around C.E. 400, the Lamanites overwhelm the Nephites and destroy their culture, leaving only the prophet Mormon and his son Moroni alive.

The table of contents lists fifteen units. The first six — Nephi I and II, Jacob, Enos, Jarom, and Omni — are translations from the smaller plates of Nephi. Following the Words of Mormon, a brief explanation of this sestet and introduction to the remaining books, are the last eight — Mosiah, Alma, Helaman, Nephi III and IV, Mormon, Ether, and Moroni. The octet abridges the writings of Mormon and his son Moroni, who summarize Jesus's teachings. In all, twenty-three recorders participated in writing the Mormon scriptural history.

Nephi I

The first of Nephi's four books records the words of his father, the prophet Lehi, who journeys from Jerusalem around 600–570 B.C.E. with his wife, Sariah, and their four sons, Laman, Lemuel, Sam, and Nephi. The book opens with Nephi's statement that he was educated in the Jewish tradition and writes in an Egyptian language. He chronicles the events of the first year of Zedekiah's reign, when prophets declare that Jerusalem must repent or fall to ruin. God reveals to Lehi a fiery pillar on a rock. The prophet returns home and experiences a vision of God enthroned among angels. For Nephi's zealotry, the Jews mock him and make attempts on his life.

As Lehi wanders the wilderness along the Red Sea, Nephi, his most obedient and pious son, supersedes his brothers. Of the lesser sons, the Lord promises to "curse them even with a sore curse, and they shall have no power over thy seed except they shall rebel against me also" (I Nephi 2:23). Like Jacob's sons conspiring against Joseph, the brothers attack Nephi, whom an angel rescues. To secure the writings of Moses and the prophets contained on sacred plates, Nephi kills his brother Laman. In chapter 8, Lehi has a vision of the tree of life. He predicts the Babylonian captivity of the Jews in chapter 10 and foretells the coming of a savior and a forerunner who will baptize the messiah. The vision continues with the messiah's ministry and crucifixion.

The brothers marry the daughters of Ishmael. Under the power of God, in chapters 17–18, Nephi makes iron tools and, with the Lord's assistance, builds a ship in the land of Bountiful, where they settle in 592 B.C.E. Before departure, Lehi sires Jacob and Joseph. At the end of chapter 18, after multiple hardships at sea and strife with his brothers, Nephi's company arrives at the Promised Land, the first name assigned to the Americas. There he finds fertile soil, forests, domesticated animals, and rich ores. Nephi makes metal plates and records his clan's history.

Nephi II

Nephi's second book, which covers events from 570 to 545 B.C.E., begins with the last prophecies of Lehi. He declares that "there shall none come into this land save they shall be brought by the hand of the Lord" (II Nephi 1:6). In chapter 3, Lehi declares his son Joseph a descendant of the prophet Joseph, whose brothers sold him into bondage in Egypt in the canonical book of Exodus. After Lehi's death in chapter 4, Nephi honors him in verses 16–35 with a prayerful song filled with grief at his father's passing and the strife that destroys the family unit. He pleads:

O Lord, wilt thou redeem my soul?
Wilt thou deliver me out of the hands of mine enemies?
Wilt thou make me that I may shake at the appearance of sin?
May be the gates of hell be shut continually before me,
  because that my heart is broken and my spirit is contrite!
  [II Nephi 4:31].

Ultimately, the brothers separate into two factions, Nephites and Lamanites. Nephi maintains the brass plates, teaches the people building skills, and constructs a temple. He consecrates his younger brothers, Jacob and Joseph, as priests and teachers.

Thirty years after their passage from Jerusalem, Nephi records what the Lord commands. In a lengthy parallel list, chapter 9 predicts woes to liars, murderers, adulterers, idol worshipers, and the unredeemed. At a climactic point in Judaic history, he prophesies the birth of Jesus: "There shall come forth a rod out of the stem of Jesse, and a branch shall grow out of his roots" (II Nephi 21:1), a restatement of Isaiah's prophecy of a messiah. In chapters 26–27, Nephi writes of Jesus's Second Coming to the Nephites, his "beloved brethren" (II Nephi 26:1), and of the appearance of a sacred book of divine revelation. In his closing words in chapter 33, Nephi declares,

I glory in plainness;
  I glory in truth;
  I glory in my Jesus,
  for he hath redeemed my soul from hell [II Nephi 33:6].

The parallel construction continues with Nephi's love for his people, the Jews, and the gentiles.

Jacob

Set between 544 and 421 B.C.E., Jacob's book tells of his teachings and those of his brother Joseph. After the death of Nephi, the people take the names of the brothers and of Zoram and Ishmael. To the people obsessed with rich ores, Jacob denounces greed, pride, and polygamy or concubinage. Chapter 5 contains the allegory of the decayed olive tree and the grafting of wild shoots, which parallels the future destruction of the wicked:

But behold, this time it hath brought forth much fruit,
  and there is none of it which is good.
And behold, there are all kinds of bad fruit;
  and it profiteth me nothing,
  notwithstanding all our labor;
  and now it grieveth me that I should love this tree [Jacob 5:32].

Jacob inveighs against the unbeliever in chapter 6, when he exhorts, "Know ye not that if ye will do these things, that the power of the redemption and the resurrection, which is in Christ, will bring you to stand with shame and awful guilt before the bar of God?" (Jacob 6:9).

Chapter 7 begins the story of Sherem, a learned man equipped by the devil with charisma and oratory. He demands that Jacob provide a sign of the Holy Spirit. God strikes Sherem, who fears he has "committed the unpardonable sin" for lying to God and denying Christ (Jacob

7:19). After Sherem's death, peace returns to the people, who study scripture and ignore wicked words. The book concludes with Jacob's deathbed farewell and passage of the plates to Enos.

Enos

In a lyric one-chapter book, Enos, son of Jacob, continues the historic events from 544 to 421 B.C.E. Enos declares that he was hunting when he recalled his father's words:

> And my soul hungered; and I kneeled down before my Maker, and I cried unto him in mighty prayer and supplication for mine own soul; and all the day long did I cry unto him; yea, and when the night came I did still raise my voice high that it reached the heavens [Enos 1:4].

The Lord addresses Enos and promises to preserve the sacred records. Enos declares that the Nephites try to restore the Lamanites to righteousness, but they cling to hatred and evil because "they became wild, and ferocious, and a blood-thirsty people, full of idolatry and filthiness" (Enos 1:20). The description of living in tents, wearing breechcloths, shaving their heads, and hunting with bow and ax fits the lifestyle of prehistoric Native Americans, who contrast the bucolic agrarianism of the Nephites.

Jarom

A second short book, the writings of Jarom continue the family tradition of chronicling events of Nephite history. He summarizes that "two hundred years had passed away, and the people of Nephi had waxed strong in the land" (Jarom 1:5). He attributes their survival to respect for Mosaic law, honoring the sabbath, refraining from blasphemy, and obeying strict laws. This period witnesses progress in mining, woodworking, metalcraft, tool making, and weaponry to protect them from the Lamanites.

Omni

The one-chapter book of Omni, Jarom's son, records migrations and battles of immigrants from 361 to 130 B.C.E. from the point of view of Amaron, Chemish, Abinadom, and Amaleki, who records the Babylonian captivity during the reign of Mosiah, ruler of Zarahemia contemporaneously with the reign of Zedekiah of Judah. The text tells of Mosiah's receipt of an engraved stone from God and of a tower where "the Lord confounded the language of the people" (Omni 1:22). In old age, Omni, who is childless, delivers the plates to King Benjamin.

Words of Mormon

This brief book, composed around C.E. 385, narrates the next stage in the transmission of history. Opening on the near total destruction of the Nephites, Mormon, an eyewitness to chaos, adds the Nephite writings to his own chronicle. He concludes with a brief life of King Benjamin, a holy man, peacemaker, and stout ruler who had established the church at Zarahemla in 125 B.C.E. He fought lengthy battles with the Lamanites "until they had driven them out of all the lands of their inheritance" (Mormon 1:14). He restores holy men to power and applies all his strength and skill to keeping the peace.

Mosiah

This book narrates events from 124 to 91 B.C.E. Once King Benjamin establishes order, he educates his sons Mosiah, Helorum, and Helaman in the family tradition and teaches them to summarize events on the brass plates. In Mosiah 1:18, in 124 B.C.E., Mosiah takes his father's place on the throne. Freed of responsibility, Benjamin builds a tower in chapter 2 so he can address the people concerning the mysteries of God. The exhortation continues to the beginning of chapter 4. At his direction, the people repent; in Mosiah 6:5, Benjamin dies, leaving the kingdom in capable hands. Mosiah learns of the land of Lehi-Nephi through a prisoner, Limhi, son of Noah and grandson of Zeniff of the land of Zarahemla. Alma rises to importance in chapters 17–18 as a teacher and preacher.

Through a clever plan, the Lamanites become drunk and lose control of their slaves, who flee to King Mosiah. Alma, risen to high priest, suffers persecution in chapter 24. In accordance with Mosiah's wish, around 147 B.C.E., Alma founds the Church of God:

> And they were called the people of God.
> And the Lord did pour out his spirit upon them,
>   and they were blessed, and prospered in the land [Mosiah 25:24].

In chapter 28, Mosiah translates the twenty-four Jaredite plates. In the last book, Mosiah and Alma the Elder die.

Alma

Composed by Alma the Younger, founder of the Nephite republic in 91 B.C.E., this lengthy narration chronicles the acts of the Nephites from 91 to 51 B.C.E. Under the rule of judges, Amlici sows discord by grasping at the throne and dying in battle against Alma the Younger. In chapters 5–6, Alma educates his people in the ways of righteousness and restores the church. In chapter 14, he falls into rebel hands and endures hunger and thirst in prison, where he lies naked and bound with cords. He cries out:

How long shall we suffer these great afflictions, O Lord?
O Lord, give us strength according to our faith
  which is in Christ, even unto deliverance [Alma 14:26].

When the cords break, the people flee from a phenomenal sign of holiness.

In chapter 22, Alma characterizes the mission journeys of elders and priests. Chapters 36–37 synopsize testimony to his son Helaman about a remarkable conversion brought on by an angel, which strikes him to earth just as an angel wrestled with Jacob in Genesis. For three days, Alma is paralyzed and mute. In summation, he exults,

Yea, I say unto you my son,
  that there could be nothing so exquisite
  and so bitter as were my pains.
Yea, and again I say unto you, my son,
  that on the other hand,
  there can be nothing so exquisite and sweet as was my joy [Alma 36:21].

The vision of God and his angels restores Alma to strength and initiates a lifetime of service to the Almighty bringing souls to repent and advocating rebirth in God. Alma hands over the scriptural plates of Nephi to Helaman.

Alma continues issuing commandments and speaks wisdom that parallels the Book of Proverbs in the Old Testament. He warns his son Shiblon of the harlot Isabel. To his son Corianton, Alma exhorts him to avoid vanity and foolishness and selects him as a preacher of God's word. When war begins, Moroni leads armies against the Lamanites. In chapter 45, Alma prophesies that the Nephites shall lose. Speaking for God, he declares:

Cursed shall be the land, year, this land,
  unto every nation, kindred, tongue, and people, unto destruction,
  which do wickedly, when they are fully ripe;
  and as I have said so shall it be;
  for this is the cursing and the blessing of God upon the land,
  for the Lord cannot look upon sin
  with the least degree of allowance [Alma 45:16].

Moroni continues fortifying the Nephite lands, yet, in chapter 53, dissension among the people weakens the Nephite defense and allows the Lamanites to win.

In chapter 56, Helaman writes to Moroni an eyewitness account of war with the Lamanites. He declares that 2,000 young soldiers fought admirably and exults:

To my great joy, there had not one soul of them fallen to the earth;
  yea, and they had fought as if with the strength of God;

yea, never were men known to have fought
  with such miraculous strength;
  and with such mighty power did they fall upon the Lamanites,
  that they did frighten them, and for this cause
  did the Lamanites deliver themselves up as prisoners of war [Alma 56:56].

After this miracle, the era of bloodshed concludes in the twenty-ninth year of the judges, when the Lamanites, suffering massive losses, retreat to their own land. After Moroni's death, record keeping passes to Helaman, son of Helaman.

Helaman

This text covers a half century from 52 to 2 B.C.E. In subsequent wars and contention, Helaman records events preceding the arrival of Christ. In chapter 4, dissenters unite with the Lamanites in the fifty-fourth year of the judges. The Nephites, fearful of destruction, see that their laws had become corrupted,

and that they had become a wicked people,
  insomuch that they were wicked even like unto the Lamanites.
And because of their iniquity the church had begun to dwindle;
  and they began to disbelieve in the spirit of prophecy
  and in the spirit of revelation,
  and the judgments of God did stare them in the face [Helaman 4:22–23].

Under the exhortation of Nephi and Lehi, the people listen to fiery sermons. A series of heavenly phenomena and voices terrorizes 300 listeners. In the sixty-second year of the judges, a temporary peace reigns until Satan stirs up the Nephite hearts to join forces with robbers. Because of this secret league, the Nephites are ripe for destruction.

In chapter 10, God designates Nephi as prophet. While he ponders the sins of his people, he hears a celestial voice saying:

Blessed art thou, Nephi, for those things which thou hast done;
  for I have beheld how thou hast with unwearingness declared the word,
  which I have given unto thee, unto this people [Helaman 10:4].

To redeem the Nephites, Nephi prays for a famine. The people repent briefly, but are unable to maintain goodness. Nephi realizes that many will fall to endless misery on judgment day.

The prophet Samuel the Lamanite arises in chapter 13. He predicts a star as a sign of Christ's coming:

Therefore, there shall be one day and a night and a day,
  as if it were one day and there were no night;
  and this shall be unto you for a sign [Helaman 14:4].

Nephi baptizes Samuel's converts. Those who doubt strike Samuel with stones and arrows. He escapes to his own people to preach and prophesy. In the ninetieth year of the judges' reign, Satan still holds many hearts.

Nephi III

Patterned after the New Testament Gospels of Matthew, Mark, Luke, and John and containing citations similar to those in the Bible, this book is central to the Book of Mormon. It begins with a crescendo in earthly corruption as the opening chapters continue the history of the Nephite apostasy. Chapter 8 depicts monumental destruction to North America over a period of three hours at the same time as Jesus's crucifixion. Cities sink and burn; buildings collapse or vanish in a whirlwind. A cloak of darkness descends and hovers for three days. In this period,

there could be no light, because of the darkness,
neither candles, neither torches;
neither could there be fire kindled with their fine and exceed-
  ingly dry wood,
so that there could not be any light at all [III Nephi 8:21].

Fearful voices howl and weep, regretting that they did not repent while there was time.

Apocalypse and chastisement consume the narration. In chapters 9–10, Christ's voice calls out "Wo, wo, wo unto this people" (III Nephi 9:2) and chastises survivors from above. He warns:

O ye people of these great cities which have fallen,
  who are descendants of Jacob, yea,
  who are the house of Israel,
  how oft have I gathered you
  as a hen gathereth her chickens under her wings,
  and have nourished you [III Nephi 10:4].

In chapter 11, Jesus, clad in a white robe, descends to the city of Bountiful and asks the people to touch his torn hands and feet as proof that he has been sacrificed for earthly sinners.

In a restatement of the Sermon on the Mount in the Gospel of Matthew, chapter 12 repeats the Beatitudes and Jesus's exhortation to "be perfect even as I, or your Father who is in heaven is perfect" (III Nephi 12:48). As a model of prayer, Jesus offers the Lord's Prayer in III Nephi 13:9–13; he heals the sick and blesses children. In chapter 15, he commissions twelve apostles to minister to the Nephites; in chapter 18, he institutes the sacrament of communion. After ascending into heaven in chapter 19,

he leaves twelve disciples to minister to the Nephites. On his return, he warns of the destruction of sinners. At his Second Coming, the wayward will burn like stubble. The events that witnesses observe are unspeakable, too sacred to be written.

Nephi IV

This single-chapter book, composed by Nephi, a disciple of Jesus, continues the acts of the Nephites from C.E. 34 to 321. The disciples form the Church of Christ and rebuild the great city of Zarahemla:

And there were great and marvelous works
  wrought by the disciples of Jesus,
  insomuch that they did heal the sick,
  and raise the dead,
  and cause the lame to walk,
  and the blind to receive their sight,
  and the deaf to hear;
  and all manner of miracles did they work among the chil-
    dren of men;
  and in nothing did they work miracles save it were in the
    name of Jesus [IV Nephi 1:5].

The Nephites grow strong, but again fall into evil ways. In anticipation of retribution, Ammaron hides the sacred records.

Mormon

Composed by the prophet Mormon, commander in chief of the Nephite army, this text covers Nephite history from 322 to 401 C.E. At age ten, Mormon, a descendant of Nephi, accepts the task of record keeper of Nephi's plates. When war resumes between Nephites and Lamanites, Mormon is incapable of preaching to the ungodly. At age sixteen, he leads the army, which defeats 50,000 with a host of 30,000. At the end of chapter 4, the Lamanites overwhelm their enemies, slaughtering them before idols. Returning to his job as chronicler, Mormon predicts that the people "shall be scattered, and shall become a dark, a filthy, and a loathsome people, beyond description of that which ever hath been amongst us" (Mormon 5:15).

When the Nephites make a stand at Cumorah, the aged Mormon conceals the records in the hill, saving a few plates for his son Moroni. Carnage so overwhelms him that he cries:

O ye fair ones, how could ye have departed from the ways of
  the Lord!
O ye fair ones, how could ye have rejected that Jesus,
who stood with open arms to receive you! [Mormon 6:17].

He warns those who are spared destruction that they, members of the house of Israel, should repent and be saved. Moroni takes over the writing in chapter 8 and prepares to hide the plates in the earth. He blesses the man who brings to light the metal plates, which contain God's word.

Ether

The first book chronologically, Ether records the wanderings of the Jaredites, who emigrated from Babylon in 2200 B.C.E. Introduced by Moroni, the book opens on a genealogy and a call to God from Jared, a righteous leader. The Lord instructs him to

> Go to and gather together thy flocks,
>   both male and female of every kind;
>   and also of the seed of the earth of every kind;
>   and thy families [Ether 1:41].

The chapter concludes with a covenant like that between Jehovah and Abraham in Genesis, promising the founding of a great nation.

After the preparation of barges for the exodus to a promised land in chapter 3, to Jared's brother, Jesus reveals his finger touching stone tablets. The chapter predicts the use of two stones to explain a hidden language to be revealed "in mine own due time unto the children of men" (Ether 3:27). According to Moroni, Ether tells of a New Jerusalem, which

> shall be a new heaven and a new earth;
> and they shall be like unto the old save the old have passed
>   away,
> and all things have become new [Ether 13:9].

For their wickedness, the Jaredites die in battle at Ramah.

Moroni

The writings of Mormon's son Moroni to the Lamanites summarize the prophet's life and works from C.E. 401 to 421. In keeping with the tone of the entire Book of Mormon, these final lines lean toward a clear dichotomy of good and evil. The work delineates the choice of disciples, ordination of priests and teachers, and observation of sacramental bread and wine. Chapter 6 explains the conditions of baptism.

In chapter 7, Moroni speaks of Mormon's vision of faith, hope, and charity, a phrase that reprises Paul's writing in I Corinthians 13. In an elongated benediction to the faithful, Moroni declares:

> Wherefore all things which are good, cometh of God;
>   and that which is evil, cometh of the devil;
>   for the devil is an enemy unto God,
>   and fighteth against him continually,
>   and inviteth and enticeth to sin,
>   and to do that which is evil continually [Moroni 7:12].

In his final exhortation, Moroni urges his hearers to cherish Christ's gifts and to remember that the Lord is "the same yesterday, today, and forever, and that all these gifts of which I have spoken, which are spiritual, never will be done away, even as long as the world shall stand" (Moroni 10:19).

SOURCES: Alsberg 1949, Anderson 1993, Berry 1956, "The Book of Abraham Revisited," Book of Mormon 1981, Bouquet 1954, Braden 1954, Demke 2000, Frost 1972, Goeringer 1998, Gregory 1994, Gutjahr 1998, Hartshorn 1966, Hastings 1951, Hinnels 1984, Kaltenbach 1999, Marquardt and Walters 1998, McConkie and Millet 1987, "Mormonism — No. II" 1859, Mutrux 1982, Reynolds and Sjodahl 1955, Smith 1995, "Translation or Divination?" 1999, Walters 1999, Whittaker 1992, Wood 1958, *World Religions* 1998.

Book of the Dead *see* Egyptian Book of the Dead; Ethiopian Book of the Dead; Tibetan Book of the Dead

Christian Science Writings

A self-taught philosopher and metaphysician, the Reverend Mary Morse Baker Eddy, author of a body of Christian Science writings, holds a unique distinction: she is the first and only American female to found a religion. Inferring doctrine from experiences with spinal deformity, she originated a form of metaphysical healing known as Christian Science, forerunner of the Church of Christ, Scientist. Prosaic, yet profound, her writing takes varied forms— questions and answers, exhortations, allegories, verses, refutations, anecdotes, letters, and the more familiar aphorisms and exegeses of the Bible. In all, she rarely strays from the central message that wholeness comes from godliness. In her words, "Christian Science exterminates the drug, and rests on mind alone as the curative principle, acknowledging that the divine mind has all power" (Eddy 1934, 157).

A bright and idealistic child of Calvinist parents, Eddy cultivated a personal relationship with God in girlhood. She was born in Bow, New Hampshire, on July 16, 1821, the last of the six children of farmer and attorney Mark and Abigail Ambrose Baker. She grew up loved and coddled by siblings and a paternal grandmother, but lived in awe of her rigid father, the town representative at the court of common pleas, who spoke authoritatively and espoused harsh beliefs in predestination. In 1831, before the family moved to Sanbornton Bridge near Swampscott, Massachusetts, she joined the Congregational church.

Eddy lived in a prison of mind and body. Neurosis and semi-invalidism limited her access to school. She taught herself through private reading and conversations with an older brother, Albert, who was studying philosophy at Dartmouth College. To escape daily suffering, she developed a gift for clairvoyance and focused on celestial voices urging her to rise above suffering through patience. At age twelve, she cured herself of back pain.

A decade later, Eddy married a neighboring builder, Colonel George Washington "Wash" Glover, eleven years her senior, and traveled south by rail and ship to their home in Charleston, South Carolina. Although she flourished from writing reviews for the newspaper and verse for the *Floral Wreath*, a ladies' magazine, the racism common to the South dismayed her. Outbursts against brutality in one of the East Coast's prime slave markets produced rifts with her in-laws. After six months of marriage, the couple traveled to Wilmington, North Carolina, where her husband died suddenly from yellow fever. After manumitting his slaves, in July, she retreated to New Hampshire; two months later, she gave birth to a son, George Jr., called Georgy. Because pregnancy and childbirth exacerbated Eddy's chronic spinal pain, she passed the baby to the care of a foster mother and lived estranged from him for most of his youth.

Eddy's life remained in flux. After marrying itinerant dentist and homeopathic physician Daniel Patterson of Franklin, New Hampshire, in 1853, she moved to North Groton to be near Georgy, but was too frail to manage the wayward, impulsive boy. In his teens, he joined the Union Army and sustained a severe wound in April 1862 at the battle of Shiloh. Her husband, who served the New Hampshire governor

Mary Baker Eddy, discoverer of Christian Science, author of *Science and Health with Key to the Scriptures*, and founder of the Church of Christ, Scientist. (Photograph by Calvin Frye. Copyright for this photograph is owned by the First Church of Christ, Scientist, in Boston, Massachusetts, U.S.A.)

as a civilian courier during the Civil War, was captured on a mission to Washington, D.C., and held in Libby Prison, from which he escaped. Weary of a sickly wife, he pursued other women and deserted her in 1866. After seven years, she obtained a divorce.

Along with painful separations, the war years brought Eddy her most useful ally. In the fall of 1862, she made friends with mesmerist and amateur psychotherapist Dr. Phineas Parkhurst Quimby of Portland, Maine, a proponent of neo-gnosticism. From him she learned the curative power of faith. Like the heavenly voices she heard in childhood, the value of kindness and positive thinking

altered her immersion in self. After Quimby's death, she plunged once more into depression and, in February 1866, injured herself badly: a concussion and an incurable spinal dislocation resulted from a fall on ice one evening at the corner of Market and Oxford streets in Lynn, Massachusetts.

Disenchanted with standard medicine, homeopathy, hydropathy, mesmerism, and medical charlatanism, Eddy concluded that she could heal herself through Christian faith, prayer, and reinterpretation of scripture. After three days of intense pain, she recovered spontaneously from reading Christ's cure of the palsied man in Matthew 9:1–8.

In 1866, she evolved a faith she called Christ Science, modeled on Christ's power to regenerate and heal the sick and influenced by the philosophy of Georg Hegel, Emersonian transcendentalism, neo-Platonism, Swedenborgianism, spiritualism, and hypnosis.

To prepare herself to follow Quimby as teacher and healer, Eddy spent three years studying the New Testament and settled in Lynn in 1875 to undertake her mission in partnership with Richard Kennedy. Her residence became the Christian Scientists' Home and, on June 6, the location of the sect's first service. Her sober, unemotional outreach grew in opposition to orthodox dogma and evangelical revivalism. Because of its fairness to women, the group drew large numbers of urban females from educated, moneyed backgrounds.

The focus of Eddy's contribution to world scripture is the Christian Science textbook first called *Science and Health*, then *Science and Health with Key to the Scriptures*. She believed the message was divinely inspired as a guide to seekers of truth. As she states in chapter 6, God related to her that

> matter possesses neither sensation nor life; that human experiences show the falsity of all material things; and that immortal cravings, "the price of learning love," establish the truism that the only sufferer is mortal mind, for the divine mind cannot suffer [Eddy 1994, 334].

Composed of fourteen chapters, the text moves formlessly, repetitiously over numerous topics:

1. Prayer
2. Atonement and Eucharist
3. Marriage
4. Christian Science Versus Spiritualism
5. Animal Magnetism Unmasked
6. Science, Theology, Medicine
7. Physiology
8. Footsteps of Truth
9. Creation
10. Science of Being
11. Some Objections Answered
12. Christian Science Practice
13. Teaching Christian Science
14. Recapitulation

Following a glossary and exegeses on the books of Genesis and Revelation, she concludes with the eighteenth chapter, entitled "Fruitage." The style is simple, earnest; the diction is straightforward and uncomplicated. Eddy issued the first edition in 1875 and extended the original in 1890, 1894, 1901, 1903, and 1906. Posthumous upgrades appeared in 1917 and 1934. After the Bible, the chief Christian Scientist text, *Science and Health*, along with

hymns and prayer, remains the source of weekly lessons and sermons and midweek testimonial meetings.

Eddy's writings war on ignorance by explaining how the individual can apply Christ's transforming power to personal ills. She believed that the key to health was an understanding of the influence of the divine mind on the body. As she explains in "Advantage of Mind-Healing" from her *Miscellaneous Writings*:

> *First:* It does away with material medicine, and recognizes the fact that the antidote for sickness, as well as for sin, may be found in God, the divine mind.
>
> *Second:* It is more effectual than drugs, and cures where they fail, because it is this divine antidote, and metaphysics is above physics.
>
> *Third:* Persons who have been healed by Christian Science are not only cured of their belief in disease, but they are at the same time improved morally. The body is governed by mind, and mortal mind must be corrected in order to make the body harmonious [Eddy 1924, 255–256].

Her text supports sensible health practices, immunization, quarantine from contagion, as well as dental and optometric care. The guidebook also countenances nursing care, midwifery and obstetrics, and rest at sanitariums, but discourages reliance on doctors, surgeons, and psychiatrists. For other medical needs, Eddy recommends that the sick rely on Christian Science practitioners, acknowledged healers and advisers trained by the sect.

To perpetuate her philosophy, Eddy founded the Christian Scientist Association in 1876. After wedding a convert and former student, Asa Gilbert Eddy, in 1879, she led fifteen followers in chartering a mother church, Boston's First Church of Christ, Scientist. Because other Christians rejected her concept of spiritual healing, she officially founded a separate and distinct faith in 1892. She supplied the sect with its constitution and by-laws, named a board of directors, and led the ministry personally on a declining basis from 1895 until her death in 1910. From her understanding of the teachings of Christ and St. Paul, she created doctrine based on God's love, biblical revelation, and spiritual support.

Eddy's theological tenets bypass Judeo-Christian materialism, predestinarianism, and millennialism and laud the ability to heal the ailing body and spirit through faith. According to her thinking, divine order offers wholeness on earth. This tenet refutes the standard Protestant belief that perfection of self comes through death and the afterlife. To achieve earthly healing, Eddy taught that suffering Christians need to pray and affirm Christ's power. She characterized sin, sickness, error, disease, death, and evil as destructive imaginary constructs, as affirmed by John 8:32, "Ye shall know the truth, and the truth shall make you free." In reference to this and other exact citations from the Bible, she declared:

The Scriptures are very sacred. Our aim must be to have them understood spiritually, for only by this understanding can truth be gained. The true theory of the universe, including man, is not in material history, but in spiritual development. Inspired thought relinquishes a material, sensual, and mortal theory of the universe, and adopts the spiritual and immortal [Eddy 1994, 547].

According to this doctrine, by avoiding sin and uniting with God, the Christian Scientist could know physical rejuvenation as God's will.

Christian Science writings base much of their advice on the mind's war against disease and psychosomatic ills. In chapter 7, Eddy declares: "Mind is all that feels, acts, or impedes action. Ignorant of this, or shrinking from its implied responsibility, the healing effort is made on the wrong side, and thus the conscious control over the body is lost" (Eddy 1994, 166). To realign the mind in concert with God, her teaching advises the sufferer to master sin, disease, and death and achieve harmony and immortality through right thinking.

Eddy earned a mix of scorn and admiration for applying idealism and monism to Christianity. Another revolutionary aspect of her philosophy is denial of Christ's divinity and acclamation of his example of earthly beneficence. She names the resurrection as evidence of a power that overrides mortality. She exhorts Christian Scientists to enact a daily regimen of prayer, radical scriptural reinterpretation, and intense self-analysis. To achieve health, she urges individual seekers to repent, humble the self, abandon materialism, live cleanly and calmly, and wait upon God.

To promote radical Christian education, in 1879, Eddy established Massachusetts Metaphysical College, which was officially chartered in 1881. She served on the faculty for eight years, training mostly women in the practice of spiritual healing. Under her guidance, the staff established a family of publications—the monthly *Christian Science Journal*, founded in 1883; the *Christian Science Quarterly*, established in 1890; the weekly *Christian Science Sentinel*, begun in 1898; the quarterly *Christian Science Bible Lessons*; and the monthly and quarterly *Herald of Christian Science*. By 1890, the nucleus of Christian Science had spread to twenty churches, ninety Christian Science branch societies, and some 250 practitioners. That same year, Christian Science teaching centers grew to thirty-three; the journal reached 10,000 households, libraries, and institutions.

Eddy's editorials, addresses, verse hymns, and sermons, later bound into a volume of miscellaneous writings, offer a straightforward explanation of faith in a deity who is neither male nor female. One poem, "Mother's New Year Gift to the Little Children," urges youngsters to pray to a mother-father for protection and guidance. The second verse, addressed to "the Big Children," asks salvation from the "Father-Mother good" (Eddy 1924, 400). Similarly, in a lecture delivered at Tremont Temple on March 16, 1885, she declared her trust in a personal God, who takes on characteristics projected from her own bias:

> I believe in God as the supreme being. I know not what the person of omnipotence and omnipresence is, or what the infinite includes; therefore, I worship that of which I can conceive, first, as a loving father and mother; then, as thought ascends the scale of being to diviner consciousness, God becomes to me, as to the apostle who declared it, "God is Love" [I John 4:16] [Eddy 1924, 96].

Her description of a supernal parent deity prefigures late twentieth-century alterations of patriarchal language, which describe God as a nurturing mother or parent of unspecified gender.

Another example of a citation of biblical sources within her writings occurs in an address to the National Convention in Chicago on June 13, 1888. In midtext, she develops the idea that truth destroys error:

> Nothing appears to the physical senses but their own subjective state of thought. The senses join issue with error, and pity what has no right either to be pitied or to exist, and what does not exist in science. Destroy the thought of sin, sickness, death, and you destroy their existence [Eddy 1924, 105].

At the conclusion of this generalization, she quotes Galatians 6:7, in which Paul, in agricultural imagery, explains to a distant congregation, "Whatsoever a man soweth, that shall he also reap."

Eddy's outlook retained much of her family's strict Calvinistic moralizing. In a lecture to her "beloved students" at the Massachusetts Metaphysical College, in 1893, she stresses obedience, a favorite tenet of her father. At the height of the talk, she inserts a parable built on imagery from an example in Matthew 25: "The neophyte is inclined to be too fast or too slow: he works somewhat in the dark; and, sometimes out of season, he would replenish his lamp at the midnight hour and borrow oil of the more provident watcher" (Eddy 1924, 117). She defines the Almighty as a fount of illumination who lights the path of the obedient follower. In a strong gesture, she departs from puritanic castigation and declares, "Be of good cheer; the warfare with one's self is grand; it gives one plenty of employment, and the divine principle worketh with you" (Eddy 1924, 118).

Eddy's message to the annual meeting of the mother church in 1896 displays a maternalism in her greeting to "beloved brethren, children, and grandchildren" (Eddy 1924, 125). Along with claims of the sect's progress and receipt of blessings from God, she incorporates a call for communion with the Almighty and urges "that Christian

Scientists, here and elsewhere, pray daily for themselves; not verbally, nor on bended knee, but mentally, meekly, and importunately" (Eddy 1924, 127). The text justifies constant petitions to "the divine Father-Mother God" and anticipates the blessings of health and holiness and a river of divine pleasure. Her advice includes a call for loving others and performance of good deeds.

In an undated letter to the First Church of Christ, Scientist, in Scranton, Pennsylvania, Eddy speaks at length on the nature of God. She calls the supreme deity universal, "defined by no dogma, appropriated by no sect" (Eddy 1924, 150). Grounded in the infinite principle of life, truth, and love, he is guardian, guide, sustainer, and keeper. Of his power, she exults:

> God is a consuming fire. He separates the dross from the gold, purifies the human character, through the furnace of affliction. Those who bear fruit he purgeth, that they may bear more fruit. Through the sacred law, he speaketh to the unfruitful in tones of Sinai: and, in the gospel, he saith of the barren fig-tree, "Cut it down; why cumbereth it the ground?" [Luke 13:7].

She characterizes God as both father and mother, minister and great physician, and she urges her followers to acquaint themselves fully with all divine attributes.

Concerning the nature of Christ, Eddy delivered a Christmas sermon at Chickering Hall in Boston on the Sunday before Christmas in 1888. To illustrate the prophecy of Christ's birth, she opened with an Old Testament reading of Isaiah 9:6 and recounted the three-year ministry attested to in the gospel. In her reckoning, Christ assumed a "dazzling, God-crowned summit" and prepared to "stem the tide of Judaism" (Eddy 1924, 162). At the peak of her theme of Christ's significance, she departs from discourse to question and answer:

> Is he deformed?
> He is wholly symmetrical; the one altogether lovely.
>
> Is the babe a son, or daughter?
> Both son and daughter: even the compound idea of all that resembles God.
>
> How much does he weigh?
> His substance outweighs the material world.
>
> How old is he?
> Of his days there is no beginning and no ending.
>
> What is his name?
> Christ Science [Eddy 1924, 167].

The question-and-answer format continues with details of Christ's family, estate, and works, particularly healing the sick. Her commission to the congregation stirs them to emulate Christ: "Go, and tell what things ye shall see and hear: how the blind, spiritually and physically, receive sight; how the lame, those halting between two opinions

or hobbling on crutches, walk" (Eddy 1924, 168). The segment concludes with the dead "buried in dogmas and physical ailments."

At length in an undated Bible lesson based on the Gospel of John, Eddy encourages individuals to become offspring of God. She declares the divine birthright to be spiritual rather than material. Intent on a message of liberation, she declares, "Man is free born: he is neither the slave of sense, nor a silly ambler to the so-called pleasures and pains of self-conscious matter" (Eddy 1924, 183). She insists that the last chapter of the Gospel of Mark commands that followers go forth to lay hands on the sick and make them well. Thus, all Christians are "properly called Scientists who follow the commands of our lord and his Christ, truth" (Eddy 1924, 193).

These reinterpretations of Christ's ministry drew large numbers of Christians who had lost interest in standard pulpit fare. On October 19, 1893, Eddy gave up the frame structure in Oconto, Wisconsin, and commissioned the Boston sanctuary. Before its dedication the next year, she restructured church administration and issued *The Manual of the Mother Church* (1895), a handbook of democratic government, management, and growth. The text centered worship on the healing presence that early Christians once experienced. Against the grain of New England Protestantism, Christian Scientists ignored hostile locals and derision from the popular press and launched an innovative worship style. Without written liturgy, sacraments, preachers, or missionaries, Eddy's followers organized a system of health practice bolstered by the sect's Boston-based publishing house, which has issued to date over 60,000 testimonies of cures and has revived interest in Christian healing in other denominations. For establishing gender equity in American religion, in 1995, Eddy was named to the National Women's Hall of Fame.

In addition to doctrinal literature, in January 1897, Eddy contributed a preface to a collection of writings covering 1883–1896. It anthologizes her contributions to the sect's publications, some published under her maiden name and some under pseudonyms. Her tendency toward romanticism and the rhetoric of the King James Bible echoes in the preface:

> There is an old age of the heart, and a youth that never grows old; a love that is a boy, and a psyche who is ever a girl. The fleeting freshness of youth, however, is not the evergreen of soul; the coloring glory of perpetual bloom; the spiritual glow and grandeur of a consecrated life wherein dwelleth peace, sacred and sincere in trial or in triumph [Eddy 1924, ix].

She expresses in an essay dated 1883 the natural human aversion toward metaphysical therapy:

That man is the idea of infinite mind, always perfect in God, in truth, life, and love, is something not easily accepted, weighed down as is mortal thought with material beliefs. That which never existed, can seem solid substance to this thought. It is much easier for people to believe that the body affects the mind, than that the mind affects the body [Eddy 1924, 5].

For justification, the essay entitled "One Cause and Effect" calls on the Ten Commandments, the Sermon on the Mount, and the Book of Revelation in testimony to the idea of tapping the kingdom of God within the individual spirit. She declares, "There is no life, truth, intelligence, nor substance in matter. All is infinite mind and its infinite manifestation, for God is All-in-all" (Eddy 1924, 21).

In 1908, Eddy made her greatest contribution to American thought by founding the *Christian Science Monitor*, a current events daily now internationally respected for objectivity. Before she died of renal failure and pneumonia at Chestnut Hills outside Boston on December 3, 1910, she stabilized the sect, which continued to spread the concept of spiritual healing worldwide. She was buried at Mount Auburn Cemetery in Cambridge. Her legacy included properties and $2 million for perpetuation of Christian Science. For her empathy and control over human ills, some of her followers declared her divine, a notion she denounced.

In addition to guided instruction, Christian Scientists began setting up neighborhood and college campus free reading rooms and promoting public education through the Board of Lectureship. Open to all visitors seeking information on illness, spirituality, and emotional growth, these centers offer the Bible and Eddy's prolific writings, including sermons, verses, and essays found in *The Science of Man* (1876), *Christian Healing* (1886), *The People's Idea of God* (1886), *Unity of Good* (1887), *Retrospection and Introspection* (1891), *No and Yes* (1891), *Pulpit and Press* (1891), *Rudimental Divine Science* (1891), *Christ and Christmas* (1893), *Poems* (1894), *The First Church of Christ, Scientist* (1896), and *Christian Science versus Pantheism* (1898). Christian Science scripture and writings are available for on-site study or purchase in French, Norwegian, Swedish, Danish, Dutch, Spanish, Portuguese, Italian, Indonesian, Japanese, Greek, and Braille.

SOURCES: Ahlstrom 1972, Alexander and Alexander 1982, *American Decades* 1998, Berry 1956, *Biography Resource Center* 1999, Bouquet 1954, Bowker 1997, Braden 1954, Broderick 1958, Carpenter and Carpenter 1985, *Contemporary Heroes and Heroines* 1998, Dakin 1990, Eddy 1924, 1934, 1994, *Encyclopedia of World Biography* 1998, "The First Church of Christ, Scientist" 1999, Frost 1972, Gentz 1973, John 1962, Kunitz & Haycraft 1938, Melton 1992, Mutrux 1982, *New Catholic Encyclopedia* 1967, *Notable Asian Americans* 1995, Powell 1950, Rice 1982, Sharma 1987, Sherr and Kazickas 1976, Singer and Lalich 1995, Smaus 1966, Smith 1989, Smith 1995, Snodgrass 1993, *World Religions* 1998, Zeinert 1997, Zweig 1990.

Confucius's Analects

To the Chinese, Confucianism, the structured state cult of Confucius, is called the *Jü-kiao* (School of the Learned). The philosophy at its foundation is the work of a passionate, upright mentor of the young, who was China's distinguished adherent of the self-made individual through *wen* (culture), *hsüeh* (learning), and *jen* (humanity). Known by the Latinized name Confucius, conferred by Catholic missionaries in the seventeenth century, in China, he bore the honorific K'ung Fu-tsu (Grand Master) and was a peripatetic teacher-philosopher, political theorist, and founder of China's first private college. To students, he expounded five beliefs:

- Humankind is basically good.
- No deity controls the individual.
- Unbounded by fate, individuals are free to choose.
- The best choice of action toward a fellow human is to refrain from actions that the individual would not want done to him.
- Moral behavior acquires no reward or spiritual affirmation.

So prestigious did Confucius become that, today, the Chinese revere the area of his birth as holy turf.

Much of the accepted data about Confucius comes from a portion of the *Shiki* (also *Shih Chi* or *Shi-chi* [Historical Annals]; ca. 185 B.C.E.) by Szema (or Ssu-ma) Ch'ien, China's first historian. Born to a poor but respected lineage on September 28, 551 B.C.E., during China's feudal era in Ch'ü-fu, Lu province (modern Shandong), Confucius was a descendant of a Sung king. The son of Ho and his mistress, Yen Chentsai, he was the youngest of eleven and bore the nickname Ch'iu (Hill) for a bulge on his forehead. His birth name, Chung-ni (Second Mount Ni), indicates that an older brother was the original Mount Ni of the family.

Confucius was left fatherless and penniless at age three, but, under his mother's care, he grew into a well-favored and long-limbed man. Most contemporaries remembered him less for brilliance than for courtesy and gentlemanly demeanor. In childhood, he amused himself by playacting at formal ritual, one of the passions of his life. At age fifteen, he determined to become a scholar and paid regular visits to the Grand Temple of the duke of Chou, a model of propriety and ritual piety. Confucius married at nineteen and established a family, about whom he said little. By his twenties, he was already attracting pupils.

Unlike the leaders of other world faiths, Confucius

was neither prophet nor divine, but he gave heaven its due and warned that sins against heaven left the sinner with no direction in which to pray. To prepare himself for a worthy life, he gained knowledge and wisdom in a mundane but deliberate fashion and treasured well-thumbed manuscripts edged in marginalia. In an earnest concern for propriety, he traveled to the capital city of Chou to question the state philosopher and archivist, Lao-tzu, on ritual. In place of the prevailing spiritualism, he made a universal moral force his religion and repudiated concerns about ghosts and the afterlife in favor of the study of humanity. His evasion caused historians to rank him among skeptics and agnostics but not among atheists.

While supervising herding and grain storage and keeping accounts on an estate, Confucius taught himself. At the right moment, imbued with self-confidence, he rose to the position of courtier in the household of Baron Chi. Quality instructors elevated Confucius's knowledge of the six arts, which they expanded to include classics and poetry, ritual and etiquette, history, music, archery, charioteering, calligraphy, and math. By 520, he had already made a reputation as a sage and had elevated teaching to a respected profession and a mission he passionately pursued all his adult life. Simultaneously, he participated in government as the obligation of a community-spirited citizen. He advanced from minor posts to magistrate, assistant minister of public works, ambassador for King Lu, and state chief justice.

Both wise and affable, Confucius could also be self-ennobling, blunt, and unsparing of the crass or wicked. Because he made his living among spoiled aristocrats, he grew to hate hereditary fiefdoms, where the affluent few lorded over the disenfranchised with displays of fine fashion, dining, and amusement. At the age of fifty, he abandoned his appointment and rid China of its self-indulgence and utilitarian education by reinstating public worship and festivals and by revitalizing the values of self, family, and community that had undergirded the golden age. To age sixty-three, he traveled his home province and the feudal states of Wei, Ch'en, Ch'u, and Ts'ai before returning to Wei to become the nation's first professional teacher. He opened an academy to train *chün-tzu* (superior individuals) as China's ethical vanguard. Because he believed in human equality, he accepted eager learners, whether peasant youth or knight cadet, and trained them for statecraft with coursework in the classics, history, rhetoric and debate, math, ritual, and music. Simultaneously, he attended to the practical need for bowmanship and riding and to the grooming of the inner man to live at ease with himself and his place in history.

To reform China and rid it of flatterers and preferment seekers, Confucius had to strip the young of conceit, prejudice, and self-absorption, the hallmarks of the rul-

ing class. In place of arrogance, he taught values—good manners, charity, ethics, spiritual excellence, and respect for elders. He created a paradigm of morality that began with good and true and ranged upward in stages of beautiful, great, wise, and spiritual. His reverence for the humanities appears in the Analects 8:8, in which he lauds poetry for arousing the mind, ritual for regulating character, and music for polish and harmony.

Among Confucius's seventy-two star students were notables in the professions:

- the talented, garrulous, but hypercritical Tzu-kung (or Tsekung), the first disciple, who hovered six years by the master's tomb and later became an ambassador. In his early years, Confucius accused him of being too clever.
- the loyalist Tseng-tzu (also Tsengtse or Tseng Ts'an), the youngest disciple, tutor to Confucius's grandson Tsesze (or K'ung chi), and the most valuable of the master's interpreters
- the learned litterateur, Tzu-hsia (or Tsehsia), who became a respected teacher and minor sage
- a lieutenant and secretary to Baron K'ang Chi, Jan Ch'iu (also Jan Yu or Tzu-lu), a pragmatist, affectionately known as Yet Yen, who accompanied the master on his wanderings from state to state. Confucius eventually expelled Jan from his school, perhaps because the youth was too literal-minded and lacked the required lust for learning.
- the diplomat Tseyu, affectionately known as Yen Yen, who may have recorded the Third Discourse
- the extrovert, Tselu (or Tzulu), a devil's advocate, who challenged the master and criticized his conduct but accompanied him on his wanderings
- the introverted mystic Yen Hui (also Yen Huei or Yen Yüan), a back-alley stripling older than the other students, who also attended Confucius on his wanderings. Yen became the master's pick for embodying the principles of inner worth, loyalty, and reverence for life.

An unofficial pupil was Confucius's only son, K'ung Li (or Poyu). One student questioned the boy and learned that he received the same education at home that students received in the master's school. The answer satisfied members of the academy that Confucius was even-handed with all who sought his teaching.

In teaching these young men, Confucius transmitted rather than originated Chinese wisdom. He had a nestorian devotion to history and was notably well-rounded, admitted gaps in his learning, and liked to sing, play stringed instruments, and joke. His mien was unassuming, congenial, and anything but ponderous or saintly. Of himself, he said, "I am a man who forgets to eat when he is enthusiastic about something, who forgets all his worries when he is happy, and who is not aware that old age is coming on" (Yutang 1938, 25). In another admission, he ruefully agreed with a viewer who compared him to a wandering stray dog, an image that epitomizes his frustration in seeking a platform on which to stand while reinventing Chinese society.

Confucius's idealistic venture cost him home and steady income and exposed him to perils. He retired in 483 B.C.E., after the deaths of his son and Yen Hui, whom he mourned with cries to heaven. Settled once more in his home district, he compiled the *Book of Songs*, a text of traditional aphorisms selected to combat evil and advance courtesy and proper behavior in all aspects of human interaction. The purpose of his compendium, as delineated by book 18, verse 6, was the introduction of the Tao (the Way) as a replacement for a bureaucratic state in which the humble suffered tyranny, torment, and capricious execution.

Confucius anticipated that the Tao would initiate a serene haven where humankind would live as a unified family. In his utopia, benevolence and peace would eradicate evil and violence and lead his people to the Great Unity, a preface to heaven. To prepare his readers for an edenic environment, he emphasized honesty, dignity, and respect for truth and groomed the Tao mind, a godly consciousness that became second nature. He died without realizing the power of his ideals, which promoted harmony, balance, and divine love and wisdom.

At Confucius's funeral at the K'unglin cemetery on the Su River in Ch'ufu in 479 B.C.E., he received the filial love of former students and ceremonial honor equivalent to his station as Grand Master K'ung, patron saint of education. Around his tomb sprang up the hamlet of K'ungli (K'ung's Village). At the Temple of Confucius, archivists stored his garments, stringed instruments, books, and carriages, and the devout venerated the master with sacrifices. His temples spread over China's 2,000 counties, where schoolchildren continue to recite homilies in class, and citizens treasure Confucianisms as bits of sage advice. September 10, the traditional date of his death, became China's national Teacher's Day.

In ensuing centuries, disciples Mencius (also Meng k'o or Mengste) and Hsün-tzu compiled the *Lun-yü*, or Analects of Confucius, a compendium of 497 verses in twenty chapters extolling character over wealth, prestige, and power. Confucius's Analects are China's revered scripture and monopolized the learning of his day. Issued by second-generation followers, the text orders his oral and written instruction in the succinct, pithy style later categorized as Confucian. The written version of his dialogues illustrates the communal memory of his students, to whom he stood at center, imparting a living tradition of self-improvement and right thinking. He revealed much about his self-knowledge and delights, his aims and doubts, and a binding commitment to lifelong learning and national reform.

Essential to Confucius's character building was a golden rule: "Do not do unto others what you would not want others to do unto you!" (Analects 15:23). From this core belief in consideration and fairness evolved a holistic philosophy of humanism, which requires sharing of self and wealth to uplift others. During a mass book burning under Shih Huang Ti of the Ch'in dynasty in 213 B.C.E., Confucians, like the rescuers in Isaac Asimov's *Fahrenheit 451*, memorized passages to preserve them for future generations. One of Confucius's relatives concealed his writings in the walls of his home. Upon their recovery, people named the house Lu-pi (Wall of Lu).

Some 250 years after his death, Confucians disagreed on the master's legacy and split into eight variant schools. The most authentic Confucian, Mencius, the early third-century B.C.E. intellectual and social critic, recognized that Confucius's ideal state had yet to materialize. In a chaotic period that saw the demise of feudalism and the rise of the state, power still flowed from money and prestige. Confucians rejected hegemony and, outside politics, pursued a social consciousness that championed ordinary Chinese. Like Plato, Mencius foresaw a new class of learned officials and philosopher-kings who would oversee social welfare while remaining untainted by the proceeds from agriculture, industry, and commerce. To attend to matters of reform, each scholar-official would sensitize rulers to the needs of humanity and to the dangers of affluence and corruption.

Because of his tactless didacticism, overt hostility, and skill at annoying and antagonizing officials, Mencius retired from his futile efforts to reform government. To demonstrate Confucian ideals, he wrote seven books containing 260 chapters of his version of Confucian philosophy. His writings exposed the flaws of the two prevailing philosophies, collectivism and individualism, and extolled right thinking and benevolence as the true grounding of patriots. According to his populist scheme, the people owe allegiance to government and the ruling class. In the event that authority figures lose their sense of public service, it is the duty of the people to overthrow and supplant unjust rulers, a form of civil disobedience later extolled by Henry David Thoreau and Mohandas Gandhi.

Mencius's contemporary, the scholar Hsün-tzu of Chi-hsia, the state capital of the eastern province of Ch'i, transformed Confucian ideals into a realistic study of the human condition, with special reference to ritual and authority. A skilled empiricist and pragmatist, he mercilessly critiqued the prevailing intellectualism, including that of his rival, Mencius. To rid Confucianism of naivete, he replaced optimism with a realistic social and political outlook that took into account inborn human flaws.

Revered for 300 years, Hsün-tzu preserved the master's insistence on self-cultivation as the basis of social progress. He characterized education as a lifelong acquisition of knowledge, skill, experience, insight, and wisdom. Like Confucius, he favored a skeptical view of human nature, which falls into error by gratifying the will. To offset evil in society, he advocated clearly codified laws and the restoration of ritual and authority. To instill morality, he proposed socializing the mind in a communal pattern to assure survival, harmony, and well-being. His vision of a grand educational superstructure required harnessing society's worthies and governors for nationwide training in classics, debate, manners, law, and public duty. In the wake of this ideology, China came under an authoritarianism that precipitated the Ch'in dictatorship administered by two of his students.

After the downfall of legalism, control of China fell to the Western Han (206 B.C.E.–C.E. 25), during which total subjugation to an emperor gave place to the Huang-Lao mode of reconciliation and noninterference, a convergence of the rule of Emperor Huang-ti and the mysticism of Lao-tzu, Confucius's contemporary and the founder of Taoism. The slow but steady growth of Confucianism within government agencies took hold under noble statesmen and their staffs. Under Emperor Wu Ti, fifth ruler of the Han dynasty, around 136 B.C.E., prime minister Kung-sun Hung established Confucianism as the state cult and the master's Analects as a state-mandated textbook. Within a progressive government education program, five scholars taught fifty male pupils selected as the student body of the first state university. Within eighty-five years, enrollment grew 600 percent and supplied all levels of government with Confucian-trained public servants. Confucianism took on the trappings of a highly structured imperial religion in C.E. 58; by C.E. 175, a state-approved version of the Analects was inscribed on stone tablets as scripture and erected at the capital.

Unlike Judeo-Christian scripture, canonization of the Confucian bible was an open process welcoming scholarly addition, reinterpretation, and countertradition. To accommodate state control, Wu Ti appointed scholars, led by chief minister Tung Chung-Shu, to compile the *Wu Ching* [*Five Classics*] (136 B.C.E.), a five-volume authoritative curriculum that serves as China's first book of scripture.

I Ching

The metaphysical basis of the *Five Classics* preserved the original language of the I Ching (also the *Yih-King* or *Yiking* [Classic of Changes]), a favorite manuscript that Confucius read so often that he had to replace its thong binders three times. He declared that, to rid himself of grave faults, he would like to live another half century to study the I Ching. The work is a long-lived Chinese handbook of magic and prognostication. A body of glosses known as the Ten Wings explains divination through the octogram, numerology, musical tones, geometric matrices, and ethical applications.

At the core of I Ching philosophy is the balance of yin and yang, the first representing the dark, weighty, female passivity and the latter the light, effulgent, male energies. These vital, interrelated powers parallel universal dynamism and transform *ch'i* (matter) into the five elements — metal, wood, water, fire, and earth — the building blocks of the universe. In explanation of a golden mean, Confucius applied the yin-yang concept to his search for the superior man:

> The great man is he who is in harmony,
>   in his attributes, with heaven and earth;
>   in his brightness, with the sun and moon;
>   in his orderly procedure, with the four seasons;
>   and in his relation to what is fortunate and what is calamitous [Bouquet 1954, 162].

Shu Ching (or Shuking; Classic of History)

The oldest work of China's classics, the Shu Ching (also *Shang Shu*; Official History), subtitled *The Book of History,* is a fifty-eight-chapter sheaf of historic documents and royal proclamations dated 2357–627 B.C.E. and composed in archaic Chinese during the nation's golden age. The book originated as a compilation of one hundred books detailing the history of wise and wicked rulers, whom the gods either supported or opposed. Some books were lost by Confucius's time; others vanished after his era. The surviving book is divided into thirty-three chapters that fall into four chronological ages:

- Chapters 1–5, the deeds and accomplishments of emperors Yao and Shun
- Chapters 6–9, the semi-legendary Hsia dynasty, ca. 2205–ca. 1766 B.C.E.
- Chapters 10–16, the Shang dynasty and the years 1765–1122 B.C.E.
- Chapters 17–33, the Chou dynasty from 1121 to 771 B.C.E.

Revered as scripture primarily because of its age, the Shu Ching offers political grounding in kingship and humane or virtuous governance through moral persuasion and education.

Reading much like Leviticus, Numbers, and Deuteronomy, the legalistic books of the Torah, the Shu Ching honors both good conduct and the arts. In reference to caution, the text warns the monarch:

Do not fail to observe the laws and ordinances.
Do not find your enjoyment in idleness.
Do not go to excess in pleasure.
In your employment of men of worth, let none come between
   you and them.
Put away evil without hesitation....
Study that all your purposes may be with the light of reason
   [Frost 1972, 93].

The passage continues its list of strictures by urging support of what is right and compliance with the will of the people.

Chapter 5 takes a religious stance in declaring that heaven loves commoners and that the king must honor this divine mindset. Subsequent advice to the wary monarch begins with a warning that evil precipitates disorder in the state, which leads to ruin. To avoid disrupting tranquility, the monarch should think through all actions, earn his merit, promote harmony among neighbors, and "be a fence to the royal house," an ambiguous image that suggests both support structure and shield from the outside world (Frost 1972, 97). For smooth operations at court, the text advocates appointment of upright ministers rather than flatterers.

Shih Ching (or Shiking)

China's first poetry anthology, the Shih Ching (Classic of Poetry), also called the *Book of Songs* or *Book of Odes*, contains 305 songs, ballads, stately odes, folk songs, court verses, temple liturgies, and hymns that date from 1766 to 586 B.C.E. The compendium, edited by Confucius (ca. 475 B.C.E.), models the lyrical style and spontaneous diction suited to numerous folk occasions. The songs are intended for chanting or singing to the accompaniment of stringed instruments; the cadence is primarily tetrameter. Topics cover the range of human activities — romance, planting, sports, ambition and disappointment, festivals, royalty, warfare. A 400-line epic cycle attests to the thousand-year rise of the Chou kingdom; related cycles summarize Chou campaigns and wars.

The *Kwo Fang*, the first of four divisions, contains fifteen books and 160 titles relating to the temple and altar. Stylistic details include repetition, touches of nature, and the conventions of the lament and triumphal anthem. The opening ode, "The Na," a sacrificial ode of Shang extolling "the descendant of Thang," speaks of drumming, bells, and soothing music, accompanied by flutes in a harmonious blend. Like David's psalms, the anthem swells with delight in orderly ceremonial dances before state visitors. In a gesture to the past, the author lauds the decorum of his ancestors:

The former men set us the example; —
   how to be mild and humble from morning to night,
   and to be reverent in discharging the service [Frost 1972,
   99].

The concluding lines ask that the receiver accept fall and winter sacrifices as honors to Thang's descendant.

Part 2, the *Hsiao Ya*, a smaller collection of the kingdom's minor odes, fills eight books with seventy-four pieces and six titles. More elegaic than the *Kwo Fang*, the stanzas speak of a sorrowing heart, divination by reeds and turtle shell, and the dreams of herders. Ode 5 comments on hard fate: "The way of heaven is hard and difficult," a parallel to the Old Testament verse, "Man is born unto trouble, as the sparks fly up" (Job 5:7). Confucius's concluding comment offers a reason for earthly sorrow, "This man does not conform" (Frost 1972, 101).

The major odes of the kingdom in part 3, the *Ta Ya*, fill three books with thirty-one poems yielding insight into the role of illustrious and virtuous men in the destiny of the state. The ideal governor inherits the rewards of right thinking:

He orders rightly the people, orders rightly the officers,
   and receives high dignity from heaven,
   which protects and helps him, and confirms his appointment,
   by repeated acts of renewal from heaven [Frost 1972, 101].

The text's political focus illustrates Confucius's influence on the state cult. Although he barely touches on religion, his faith in a divine power is the source of a belief that humankind has an obligation to goodness and order.

Ode 10 cites the opposite of reward for order by declaring that heaven sends calamity to peasants who are indifferent or out of tune with propriety. By speaking harmonious, gentle, and kind words, they can restore unity. To the noble he is addressing, Confucius warns that contemptuous indifference and derision are an outrage to the humble philosopher. He reminds, "The ancients had a saying: 'Consult the gatherers of grass and firewood.'"

In the second stanza, Confucius explains his concept of the orderly state. In the first line, he declares that the good are a fence. He extends the idea of protection with states as screens, families as buttresses, and the royal family as a fortified wall. The purpose of these social bulwarks is to shield the king from solitude and despair. His final stanza proclaims heaven's anger an appropriate comeuppance to the idle, jeering people of earth. With respect for heaven, he declares that God sees clearly the errant, self-gratifying humanity below.

Lessons from the states in part 4, the *Sung*, fill three books with forty poems in a variety of moods. The pervasive dignity and calm in "The Zhai Fan" describe a woman performing ritual for her prince. After gathering wood from the wild, she dons a headdress and reverently enters the temple before dawn to worship. Still serene and imbued with the aura of godliness, she returns to her dwelling.

One of Confucius's swelling anthems, "The Ko Shang," captures an elegaic truth about the long wait for earthly renewal. A subtle pair of introductory stanzas are the same except for the alteration of two words. In the first, morning glory vines cover the wasteland as the seeker declares that he lives alone. In the second stanza, the same vines drape tombs, leaving the seeker to rest alone. Like a wistful mourner, the speaker regrets the loss of an admirable leader and anticipates long days and seasons—a century of waiting to reunite with a great man.

Li Chi

A manuscript of China's social foundations, the Li Chi (or *Liki* [Record of Rites] ca. 475 B.C.E.), a Chinese equivalent of Leviticus and the Roman Hesiod's *Works and Days*, is the writing of Confucius. It illustrates communal trust and cooperation among farmers, crafters, merchants, and scholars through duty and ritual appropriate to the Chou dynasty. The text presents a rigidly ordered view of the universe. Like Genesis, the writer sees time as a division of light and dark, sun and moon. The four seasons display the five elements in a harmony that establishes earthly rhythm. To these elements, nature affords exactly measured additives—five harmonic tones, five flavors, twelve articles of diet, and five basic colors. From the early Chinese sages comes a profound statement about nature and humankind:

They felt it necessary to find the origin of all things in heaven
  and earth;
  to make the two forces of nature the commencement of all;
  to use the four seasons as the handle of their arrangements;
  to adopt the sun and stars as the recorders of time,
  the moon as the measurer of work to be done [Ballou 1944, 493].

The ordering of earthly actions advances to rules of behavior and righteousness, the cultivation of human emotion, and the domestication of animals. The passage concludes that heaven offers all things to humankind for rightful use.

Advancing to human makeup, the text names seven emotions: joy, anger, sadness, fear, love, dislike, and preference. Because they lurk in the subconscious, emotions cannot be quantified. These unlearned responses underlie appropriate behavior to parents and siblings, mates, elders, and children. Similarly, innate feelings cause people to desire food and sexual pleasure and to avoid the four trials—death, exile, poverty, and suffering.

Central to the foundations of ceremony is the foundation of the state on militarism, a necessity for survival against Mongol raids from the north. As males have their state-centered work to do, so do women, who society relegates to the home. The ideal wife is one displaying contentment at the fireside with her worldly experience limited to the view through the crack of the door. To maintain womanly decency, the text commands that girls remain indoors from age ten onward. While boys learn to read, write, count, and fight, young women study weaving, observe the sacrifices from a distance, and practice pleasant speech and seemly manners.

In summary of daily offices of courtesy and ceremony, the text outlines the particulars of obligation. Men are to arise at dawn, wash, cleanse their mouths, comb and arrange their hair, dress neatly, and equip themselves with the tools they will need for the day. At the same time, women should arise, make similar ablutions, dress modestly, and serve their in-laws, a prescription found in the actions of O-lan, the female protagonist in Pearl Buck's classic novel *The Good Earth*. The ritual acts of pouring water for their elders, offering a towel, and bringing anything that is needed must proceed pleasantly, willingly.

In chapter 9, while attending the winter sacrifice, Confucius walks the city gate and mourns for the decadence of the province of Lu. To Jan Ch'iu, his companion and pupil, he justifies despair that people no longer follow the Great Way. When governors practice morality, he declares, good men serve in public office and base their lives on love and faith. In Confucius's time, however, the province has declined:

Each regards as parents only his own parents, as sons only his
  sons;
  goods and labour are employed for selfish ends.
Hereditary offices and titles are granted for ritual law
  while walls and moats must provide security [Eliade 1967, 566].

He regrets that righteous behavior arises from self-serving motives rather than a dedication to the commonweal.

Ch'un-ch'iu (Spring and Autumn Annals)

Confucius's annotated chronicle, the Ch'un-ch'iu, was China's first chronological history. Covering government under two heads of state in the province of Lu from 722 to 481 B.C.E., it maintains a month-by-month record of archival and historical data, such as lunar eclipses, comet showers, and droughts. Like the Native American winter counts, the book promoted a national identity and self-knowledge and served as a paradigm to dynastic historians of the empire. This culmination of China's classical learning incorporated Confucianism along with strands of Taoism, Tung Chung-shu's mysticism, yin-yang cosmology, shamanism, geomancy, and prognostication.

A radical return to old school Confucianism as a common creed typified the last years of the Western Han era, but this conservative trend did not last. A new version of Confucianism, the *Fa-yen* (Model Sayings) of Yang Hsiung (ca. C.E. 10), emulated the master's style in a body of apothegms as Confucian scholasticism evolved away from peasant culture to the elitist realm of the ivory tower. Still, the Analects continued to thrive in school curricula, government handbooks, and day-to-day parlance. By the close of the Han dynasty, the state university was enrolling 30,000 students while public classrooms continued the ritual of sacrificing to the master.

Around C.E. 150, the deterioration of bureaucracy from bungled tax collection and inept rule precipitated the fall of the Eastern Han. In protest of factions and eunuch-led hegemony, the state's university erupted in mass rebellion as peasant life declined to near serfdom. In C.E. 169, the court ruling to incarcerate and execute thousands of protesters made peasant life unbearable. The alliance of students, farmers, Taoist faith healers, the military, and Confucian scholars ended the Han dynasty, China's first empire, opening the way to barbarian opportunists from Mongolia. Three centuries of chaos threatened Confucianism as Taoism and Buddhism rose in popularity.

Not until China stabilized early in the seventh century did Confucianism return to authority. Issuance of an authorized *Wu Ching*, codification of laws, and restoration of ritual restored confidence in traditional ideals, which were once more the basis of state examinations. During the T'ang dynasty, domination by Buddhism and Taoism paralleled publication of two significant doctrines—*Chungyung* (Doctrine of the Mean) and *I-chuan* (The Great Commentary of the Classic of Changes)—which influenced Buddhists and Taoists. Imbued with rural mores, peasants continued to honor Confucianism. Simultaneously, bedrock values permeated officialdom and local politics.

The 800s produced an uneven adherence to scripture. An early ninth-century social critic, Han Yü, denigrated Buddhism by reigniting scholarly discourse on the Confucian Tao. In rebuttal, a worthy literary contribution, Li Ao's essay, "Returning to Nature" (ca. 840), resonated with Confucian principles. To assure the perpetuation of ancient ideals, the emperor Wen Tsung commissioned a library in stone of the Thirteen Classics: *Chou-li* (Rites of Chou); *I'li* (Book of Etiquette); *Li Chi* (Record of Rites); three books of ritual; Confucius's Ch'un-ch'iu and three commentaries on it—the *Tso-chuan, Ku-liang-chuan,* and *Kung-yang-chuan*; Confucius's Analects; *Hsiao-ching* (or *Hsiao King*; Classic of Filial Piety); and *Erh-ya* (also *Erya*), a philosophical dictionary. Some 350 years later, Emperor Kuang Tsung added Mencius's writings to this collection.

During six centuries of the evolution of Chinese Buddhism from its Indian beginnings, a boomerang effect returned newcomer religious leaders to Confucianism to cannibalize his Analects and rediscover his precepts. An unease following the fall of the T'ang dynasty restored China to a common heritage as a force of stabilization and spiritual resource. From the tenth to the thirteenth centuries, the Sung dynasty flourished in culture and economy by developing cities and markets through technology and shipping, enlarging communication networks with advances in printing, and popularizing drama, literature, and traditional Confucianism. As the peasantry produced an educated middle class, the Chinese began to attain some of Confucius's humanistic and political aspirations.

Integral to the twelfth-century Confucian renaissance was Chu Hsi (or Chicius), a theologian and educator who reconstituted tradition by reinterpreting scripture and recasting its tenets into neo–Confucianism. His publication of *The Four Books* (or *Ssu-shu*), a treasury of sayings of and writings about Confucius, served education and government as a new handbook of Chinese ethics. The books, sometimes called the *Catechism of the Confucian Teaching*, demonstrate the development of Confucius's writings through the time of Mencius.

Tahsueh (or Ta Hsueh; The Great Learning)

The *Tahsueh*, originally "Ethics and Politics" or chapter 42 from the Li Chi, is the first lesson that Chinese schoolchildren learn. A gateway to virtue, the essay describes the education of upper-class intellectuals to prepare them for rule. In his identifiable rhetoric, Confucius orders the perfection of a nation from the top down:

To order the nation, regulate the family;
To regulate the family, cultivate the personal life;
To cultivate the personal life, cleanse the heart;
To cleanse the heart, clarify the will; and
To clarify the will, achieve true knowledge.

Thus, the text leads to Confucius's strongest belief, that education is the only path for a nation to follow on the way to greatness. After summarizing these stages individually, in chapter 7, Confucius moves beyond China by relating national health to world peace.

Chungyung

The *Chungyung* (Central Harmony or Doctrine of the Mean), originally chapter 31 of the Li Chi, is traditionally attributed to Confucius's grandson Tsesze, who also composed chapters 32–33 of the Li Chi. The doctrine states the pillar of Confucianism, the golden mean or middle way, a tenet shared by the ancient Greeks and Romans and summarized in the Latin adage *Nihil nimis* (Nothing in excess) (Bartlett 1992, 115). According to the Chinese version, "Let the states of equilibrium and harmony exist in perfection," a utopian balance that will nourish all things (Ballou 1944, 511). At the summit of the author's sentiments on temperance, as earth's energies produce currents and transformations, things in harmony remain neutral, causing no injury or collision.

The preface explains the nature of innate gifts and establishes that the fulfillment of self benefits the universe. Chapters 2–4 develop the idea of morality as the key ingredient to world order. On the issue of self-perfection, Confucius urges, "Whenever there is shortcoming, never fail to strive for improvement" (Yutang 1938, 110). In the discussion of particular examples of enlightened rulers in chapter 5, he explains the continuity of human existence:

To gather in the same places where our fathers before us have
   gathered;
   to perform the same ceremonies which they before us have
   performed;
   to play the same music which they before us have played;
   to pay respect to those whom they honored;
   to love those who were dear to them — in fact,
   to serve those now dead as if they were living,
   and now departed as if they were still with us:
   this is the highest achievement of true filial piety [Yutang
   1938, 115].

He concludes the chapter on devotion to ancestry with a paragraph explaining why temple sacrifices serve God.

Chapter 6 advances to ethics and politics and applies the concepts of morality to the ruler. Confucius determines that the first requirement of governance is regulation of the self. The best of men should display wisdom, compassion, and courage, virtues that may be inborn or developed through education. Daily affairs should be goverened by a nine-point checklist:

- controlling personal conduct
- honoring the worthy
- cherishing and attending relatives
- respecting state officials
- identifying with public concerns
- shepherding the peasantry
- supporting the arts
- nurturing outsiders
- promoting the welfare of the empire

This passion directed outward rids the ruler of self-absorption at the same time that it draws all classes into an integrated society.

Being true to the self is the topic of chapters 7–8, a loosely organized series of homilies preceding a eulogy to Confucius. The general precepts of moral consciousness contain a brief summary of the master's career: he taught truths that originated in China's past and adopted and perfected social and religious laws that harmonized with divine order. A general description of moral nature, the passage ends with praise for the self-educated man:

How simple and self-contained his true manhood!
How unfathomable the depth of his mind!
Who can understand such a nature except he who is gifted
   with the most perfect intelligence and endowed
   with the highest divine qualities of character,
   and who has reached in his moral development the level of
   the gods? [Yutang 1938, 131].

In the epilogue, the author cites from the *Book of Songs* descriptions of morality that stress its unobtrusive nature. Neither ostentatious nor overbearing, the evidence of ethics should be "light as hair" (Yutang 1938, 134).

Lun-yü (Confucius's Analects)

The core Confucian bible, the Analects reads like a book of quotations and discourses studied and collected perhaps a half century after the master's death. Just as human concerns present themselves in no particular order, the entries on personal and moral matters are unclassified, unedited, and random. Each epigram requires study and thought and forces the reader to dip slowly into the text over a period of months and years rather than wolfing down the contents at a single sitting.

The meandering nature of the Analects orders stand-alone units of wisdom alongside exchanges between master and pupil or outsiders. Some epigrams, such as those found in Chapter 5, read like mottos: "I select a good person and follow his example" (Yutang 1938, 164). Others are straightfoward pronouncements, e. g. "I prefer vulgar people to snobs" (Yutang 1938, 181). Some, like the rhetorical questions "Can I deceive God?" and "Does heaven talk?" leave ample space for individual interpretation (Yutang 1938, 175, 173). Others display piquant touches of wit, as in "Respect the heavenly and earthly spirits and keep them at a distance" (Yutang 1938, 168). These complexities of style and presentation as well as frequent contradictions account for the difficulty of subsequent generations to reduce Confucianism to a simple formula.

Group dynamics and dialogues between master and pupil are the impetus for longer entries, for example, in this truncated exchange:

Confucius said: "There are three things about the superior man that I
have not been able to attain.

The true man has no worries;

the wise man has no perplexities;

and the brave man has no fear."

Tsekung said, "But, Master, you are exactly describing yourself" [Yutang 1938, 162].

Some dramatic recreations are longer and more revealing. For example, in book 3, in asking the boys about their ambitions, Confucius questions each in turn and makes no comment on their aspirations. When he comes to Tseng Hsi, the boy self-consciously bangs down his stringed instrument and blurts out that his aims differ from the rest. With some gentle persuasion, Confucius elicits from Tseng an unassuming peasant fantasy about accompanying bathers to the River Ch'i, resting in a spring breeze in the Wuyi woods, then singing with the group on the way home. To this idyll, Confucius replies, "You are the man after my own heart" (Yutang 1938, 171).

The editors of the Analects stress the human quirks of the master, such as his disdain for red and blue, his pickiness about food, and his tendency to indulge liberally in wine, but never to overeat. The editors make no comment on the Confucian style, but capture his preferences for repetition, male-centered commentary, parallelism, antithesis, and cause-and-effect statements. His skillful turn of phrase dominates a comment on wealth: "It is easy to be rich and not haughty; it is difficult to be poor and not grumble" (Yutang 1938, 181). In many of these observations, Confucius separates behaviors by extremes—foolish and wise, poor and rich, proud and humble, evil and good, but never male and female. His most cited adage, called the Golden Rule, advises, "Do not do unto others what you do not want others to do unto you," a negative version of Jesus's dictum: "All things whatsoever ye would that men should do to you, do ye even so to them" (Matthew 7:12).

Central to the Analects are the elements of humanism and the revelation of the true man, Confucius's ideal. In chapter 7, he declares, "A true man is very slow to talk" (Yutang 1938, 190). The summation of these descriptors gives the impression of the motivated, self-controlled individual who knows himself well, but acquires wisdom more from observing others than from studying his own tastes and foibles. Many of these statements of the well-rounded man contain adjectives and phrases that advocate elements of character, such as broad-minded, liberal, firm, "not a partisan," understands, and "blames himself" (Yutang 1938, 191). Unlike the goody-goody, whom he calls a thief of virtue, Confucius's ideal man feels shame that his words are better than his actions.

Equally clear are the men who Confucius despises. Chapter 8 lists the impulsive, bad-tempered, deceitful, and improper. At Sze's insistence, the master personalizes the list by singling out spies, hypocrites, poseurs, babblers, and grovelers. In a rare mention of women, he lumps them and the uneducated into the same generalization and declares, "When you are familiar with them, they become cheeky, and when you ignore them, they resent it" (Yutang 1938, 197).

In chapters 8–9 of the First Discourse, Confucius particularizes the role of morality in government and education. In an extreme of idealism, he declares, "There should be no lawsuits" (Yutang 1983, 198). In one of his more lyrical similes, he likens the sovereign to Polaris, "which remains in its place and the other stars revolve around it" (Yutang 1938, 199). Less poetic are his three requirements for good government: enough to eat, a sufficient army, and confidence in rulers. He then reverses priorities to state that the moral leader puts the people's trust above food and weaponry. A final pronouncement on youth concerns their study: First, they should learn respect for family and society, then conduct themselves lovingly and faithfully, and finally, associate with kind people. Confucius concludes, "If after learning all this, they still have energy left, let them read books" (Yutang 1938, 204).

In Confucius's discourse on education, he is candid rather than nostalgic about the past, which is the model for the present. His lengthy preface explains why a curriculum must be well-rounded. His organizational method calls for extended definition, as with the qualification of *li*, the principle of social order. In his summary paragraphs, he notes that *li* "prevents the rise of moral or social chaos as a dam prevents flood" (Yutang 1938, 214). Essential to maintaining order is respect for ceremonies, especially marriage, the village wine feast, funerals, sacrificial rites, and diplomatic visits. To work well, *li* must be subtle, the result of careful preparation and rule.

The Second Discourse departs from the essay format to record Confucius's dialogue with Duke Ai of Lu, who questions the importance of *li*. The literary convention of intellectual exchange with the duke creates a platform for Confucius pronouncements against the greedy, materialistic princes of his day. In the master's opinion, the height of civilization is a government that sets things right. The flow of civilizing principles moves through family, God's law, and love. In a dramatized summation, Confucius's rises from his seat to declare that following the natural law of things is the action of a great man.

The Third Discourse, which Tseyu may have recorded, envisions the ideal social order. The text begins with a personal encounter between Tseyu and the master, who sighs for the Golden Age, when the elderly, children, widows, orphans, and cripples received respect and care. He notes that this era—*Tat'ung*, the great commonwealth—produced no thieves and relegated men and women to a strict division of labor, a demarcation that forced women into subservience and home-centered seclusion. Because the Tao no longer prevails, deceit and war thrive. In place of Yu, T'ang, Wen, Wu, Ch'eng, and Duke Chou are a generation of flawed, unjust rulers lacking courtesy and respect for the people.

In pursuit of the harmony of long ago, Confucius visits the city of Chi to study ancient customs of the Hsia dynasty but finds little left. He journeys to Sung to observe remnants of the Shang dynasty and again is disappointed. All that he can unearth of past ritual appears in books, which detail burial customs of prehistoric Chinese. He determines that *li* must evolve from human nature, the yin-yang union of celestial and earthly forces. Humanity, he concludes, "is the heart of the universe, the upshot of the five elements, born to enjoy food and color and noise" (Yutang 1938, 235).

In the chapter on education, Confucius returns to essay form but retains the poetry and sagacity of the Analects. He declares, "A piece of jade cannot become an object of art without chiseling, and a man cannot come to know the moral law without education" (Yutang 1938, 241). When China had an elementary school in each village, a secondary school in each town, one academy per county, and a college in each state capital, educators controlled quality with a standardized testing program, beginning at the end of the third year. Discipline was stern; classroom procedure left ample time for students to solve problems on their own. Extracurricular activities taught stringed instruments, ritual, and archery and other physical activities to afford students "time to digest things, to cultivate things, to rest and to play" (Yutang 1938, 245).

To lead this enlightened form of classroom, the ideal teacher must follow the principles of preventing bad habits, teaching skills as students are ready to learn them, sequencing subject matter, and encouraging mutual stimulation among students. With confidence in his experience, Confucius sums up classroom procedure:

One who knows how to answer questions is like a group of
  bells.
When you strike the big bell, the big one rings,
  and when you strike the small bell, the small one rings.
It is important, however, to allow time for its tone gradually
  to die out [Yutang 1938, 249].

This summation of pacing is an experience-based observation no beginning teacher could make. He concludes

that a wise teacher must recognize the difference between source and outlet, for "to know this distinction is to know how to attend to the essentials" (Yutang 1938, 250).

Concerning music, Confucius declares that it "rises from the human heart when the human heart is touched by the external world" (Yutang 1938, 251). His intent is so fervent that he repeats the sentence at the beginning of the second paragraph and abridges it at the opening of paragraph four. He links music with *li* by stating that ancient kings instituted ritual and music "for teaching the people the right taste and the return to normality" (Yutang 1938, 255). Because music is built on mathematical harmony, it cannot survive in an era of strife and war. In harmonious times, three arts delight the individual:

The poem gives expression to our heart,
  the song gives expression to our voice,
  and the dance gives expression to our movements [Yutang
    1938, 261].

The resulting harmony of spirit creates a people incapable of deceit or pretense.

Mencius (or Meng-tze)

Mencius's writings, the conclusion of the Analects, contain an orthodox Confucianism that is the purest of post–Confucian philosophy. He appears to paraphrase the master when he urges individuals to study the inner self to understand idiosyncrasies. He declares, "There is nothing that is not destiny" (Bouquet 1954, 173). Following this pronouncement, he commands pupils to obey destiny and be faithful to personal principles. In characterizing the superior individual, Mencius lists benevolence, righteousness, propriety, and knowledge as the major qualities and adds that these four are so rooted in the heart that they emerge naturally, without pretense or forethought.

The text mimics the student-to-master presentation, with Mencius guiding his pupils through general glimpses of human nature. After careful development, Mencius concludes that the sage "first discovered what is common to men's souls," a delineation of the philosopher's role in society. To express the preservation of good qualities in humanity, Mencius returns to his teacher to quote a conundrum:

Keep it carefully and you will have it, let it go and you will
  lose it.
It appears and disappears from time to time
  in we do not know what direction [Yutang 1938, 283].

Mencius clarifies that Confucius used "it" to mean the soul.

Although Mencius preserves the style and flavor of the master, his adages lack terseness and wit. He produces an inferior cadencing and pedestrian imagery, for example, "Charity is in the heart of man, and righteousness is the path for men" (Yutang 1938, 286). Still, Mencius is not without quality, as shown by his reply to Kungtutse's questions about differences in men. Like Confucius, he resorts to antithesis: "Those who attend to their greater selves become great men, and those who attend to their smaller selves become small men" (Yutang 1938, 288). Developing the thought to the next level, Mencius adds, "One who cultivates his higher self will find that his lower self follows in accord. That is how a man becomes a great man."

The text of the Analects calls for mental discipline, reverence, and dedication to learning, three elements of humanistic education taught at China's prestigious learning center, the White Deer Grotto Academy in Kiangsi province. In 1175 at Goose Lake Temple, a contemporary, Lu Chiu-yüan, challenged Chu Hsi's curriculum. Lu declared the revived Confucian Way was fragmented and ineffectual, but detracted little from the reputation and authority of Chu, the great Chinese educator. Despite the disdain of Lu and other detractors, the *Four Books* continued to serve elementary classrooms; mature students studied the *Five Classics*. In North China, Confucianism dominated government and society in a unique system that paralleled the flowering of the Sung dynasty. At the reunification of China in 1279, Confucians rededicated themselves to the Tao. Educator Hsü Heng, president of the Imperial Academy, taught a scaled-down version of Chu Hsi's curriculum to Mongol nobility and produced a new cadre of Confucian scholars. The *Four Books* took precedence at the Yüan court and remained influential until 1905.

By preserving the master's teachings during eras of censorship and adulteration, Confucians spread them to Korea, Japan, the Ryukyu island chain, Indochina, the Americas, and Europe. Korea instituted a broad-based Confucianism during the Yi dynasty, which lasted from the end of the fourteenth century until 1910. An innovative interpreter, Yi T'oegye, author of *Discourse on the Ten Sagely Diagrams*, salvaged from China's Sun dynasty the best principles to suit sixteenth-century needs. This modernization of hard-line Confucianism entered Japan a century later with a merger of principles with Shintoism, which introduced the average person to the *Four Books*.

In the eighteenth century, the resurgence of Confucian monarchy during China's rule by Manchus distorted humanism into fascism. In 1773, compilation of an imperial manuscript collection resulted in the *Complete Library of the Four Treasures*, a bloated overview of scholarly contributions to the classics, literature, philosophy, and history. Over two decades, project leaders coordinated 15,000 copyists in the production of 36,000 volumes of commentary on 10,230 works. Syncretism in the 1800s gradually fused Confucianism with Shintoism, Taoism, and Buddhism as the master's tenets crept into other Asian ideologies. However, the long life of Confucianism met greater diffusion and skepticism as Asians embraced Western culture, technology, and ideals. After communism overran China's political and social systems in 1949, overt Confucianism ended, but old behaviors, attitudes, and commitment still permeated the cultural fiber. The burgeoning economies of Taiwan, Singapore, Japan, and South Korea after World War II swept the Pacific rim into heated market competition with Europe and the Americas, yet Confucianism flourished in the office, classroom, and home.

A bearer of the Analects to the New World, Thomas Hosuck Kang, became the West's first Confucian missionary. He was born in Milyang, Korea, on November 24, 1918, and prepared himself as a teacher. After settling in Seattle, Washington, in 1958, he earned a library science degree from the Catholic University of America and a Ph.D. from American University in Far Eastern and international studies. His command of English, Korean, Japanese, and Chinese prefaced U.S. citizenship in 1971 and classroom work in elementary and high schools in Japan and among United Nations forces' officers in Korea. To increase the availability of Eastern thought, he catalogued Korean and Japanese texts for the East Asia Collection of McKeldin Library at the University of Maryland and volunteered at the Library of Congress as senior East Asian expert on Oriental thought and calligraphy.

Kang's version of Confucianism is a form of humanism rather than theology or religion. At the beginning of the twenty-first century, to halt conflict, he promotes peace, cooperation, and duty as the essentials of community. To enhance the type of reform that Confucius advocated, he assists people toward health and service in positions that suit their talents and aims. He urges society's best-adjusted citizens to bolster the humble by sharing wealth and honoring civil rights. Essential to his teaching are courses in meditation and I Ching and private sessions in self-healing. He disseminates Confucius's philosophy through articles on principles, world religion, and peaceful global unification. From his Center for Tao-Confucianism, he offers a library of more than 5,000 works in Western languages, maintains an internet site introducing Confucianism in English and Korean, and intends to dispatch missionaries to introduce Confucius's teachings abroad.

See also **I Ching.**

SOURCES: Ballou 1944, Berry 1956, Bouquet 1954, Cavendish 1970, Confucius 1992, *Eerdmans' Handbook to the World's*

Religions 1982, Eliade 1967, Fingarette, Frost 1972, Hastings 1951, Hinnels 1984, Kang 1999, *New Catholic Encyclopedia* 1967, Pelikan 1992, Schwartz 1985, Sharma 1987, Smith 1958, 1995, Snodgrass 1995, 2001, Waley 1986, 1989, *World Literature* 1998, *World Religions* 1998, Yutang 1938.

Dasam Granth *see* Granth

Dead Sea Scrolls The Dead Sea Scrolls, a monument to Jewish outrage at sacrilege and willful obstruction of tyranny, survived from terrible times when Rome's indiscriminate boot crushed the holy lands. Miraculous in their longevity, these historic manuscripts from the desert frontier have multiplied current knowledge of the Bible, rabbinic Judaism, the evolution of Christianity, and Jewish and early Christian beliefs in a catastrophic end to the world. Because the cache lay outside Jericho on the far northwestern shore of the Dead Sea, these and subsequent cave discoveries earned the name Dead Sea Scrolls.

Ironically, after nearly 2,000 years of storage, it was an Arab teenager who found the writings. In the winter of 1946 in the Palestinian wilderness at Wadi Qumran near Ain Feskha, while searching for a lost goat in the brown limestone escarpment overlooking Secacah, Muhammad Ahmed el-Hamed, nicknamed adh-Dhib (The Wolf), a Bedouin shepherd of the Ta'amireh tribe, located some heavy pottery jars deep in a natural cleft. The discovery was accidental—Muhammad tossed a pebble into the cave overlooking the northwestern shore of the Dead Sea and smashed a cylindrical earthenware jar around twenty inches tall that was topped with a lid two inches high and seven inches in diameter. He fled in terror of demons. Eventually, the herder and his companion, Ahmed Muhammed, returned in search of treasure, but they found only jars filled with musty manuscripts in the form of ancient Hebrew and Aramaic scrolls, which they stashed in their camp until the spring of 1947, the date most authorities cite for the discovery.

The priceless cache was a deposit that hopeful survivors of a devastating colonial war had made for future generations. Protected from deterioration by the aridity of the low-lying shore 1,300 feet below sea level, which averages less than two inches of moisture per year, the scriptural treasury consisted of seven linen-wrapped manuscripts written in ink on tanned leather. One was so well wrapped that excavators pieced together surface embroidery denoting a schematic layout of a temple. The genres included in the find ranged from an apocalyptic scroll called the War Between the Children of Light and the Children of Darkness to Hymns of Thanksgiving, prophecies of Ezekiel and Daniel, a midrash or commentary, on the oracles of Habakkuk, a Manual of Discipline (or Rule of the Community), and the Apocalypse of Lamech,

an alternate edition of Genesis. Later finds added nineteen copies of the prophecies of Isaiah, twenty-five copies of Deuteronomy, thirty copies of the Psalms, unprecedented psalms of Joshua, the last words of Moses's father, Amram, and an array of scraps that scholars compared to existing texts. To the dismay of Christians, the writings are contemporaneous with Jesus, but make no mention of him, his disciples, or the origins of the Christian faith.

Translators did not immediately begin work. The scrolls passed to an antiquarian in Bethlehem before coming into the possession of scholars. One purchaser took out a classified ad in the *Wall Street Journal* on June 1, 1954, offering four scrolls for sale. As word spread of the implications for such a trove of writings, a year later, excitement within archaeological and religious circles mounted in response to articles published in the *Biblical Archaeologist* and *Bulletin of the American Schools for Oriental Research*. Further excavation was tedious and protracted:

- Within months of the discovery in 1947, Polish field archaeologist and coin expert Eliezer Lipa Sukenik, an associate of Hebrew University in Israel and director of the Museum of Jewish Antiquities, bought three scrolls—one of hymns, one containing the War Between the Children of Light and the Children of Darkness, and a partial text by the prophet Isaiah.
- In January 1949, Captain Philippe Lippens, a Belgian officer attached to the United Nations Armistice Observer Corps, and Major General Lash of Jordan's Arab Legion launched an expedition to Qumran after a political shift in the unstable Middle East had passed the territory to Jordan. The search yielded seven scrolls and hundreds of parchment fragments, which were retrieved by French Dominican Bible scholar and archaeologist Father Roland de Vaux, an expert in Aramaic and Arabic, and Englishman Gerald Lankester Harding of Jordan's Department of Antiquities.
- In October 1949, the Library of Congress in Washington, D.C., mounted a display of four of the Dead Sea Scrolls.
- In 1951 Ta'amireh tribesmen located parchment fragments in three caves at Wadi Murabba'at, eleven miles south of Qumran. Searchers also unearthed a similar jar and a coin from C.E. 10 at Khirbet Qumran, an ancient nonresidential community north of Wadi Qumran and excavated that same year by de Vaux and Harding.
- A similar mission to Murabba'at in 1952 produced biblical books, legal contracts, lists, and letters abandoned by fugitives from the armies of Simon (or Simeon) Bar Kokhba, leader of a Jewish insur-

rection against imperial Rome. With a force under Julius Serverus, the Emperor Hadrian had crushed a revolt at Bethar in August C.E. 135, where Bar Kokhba fell in battle. The Murabba'at site yielded a first-century C.E. Greek translation of the twelve minor prophets that corroborates the traditional Hebrew version. In addition, the cave contained biblical fragments and legal documents in Aramaic, Greek, and Nabataean, an ancient Arabic dialect of a desert people, which was used from 150 B.C.E. to C.E. 150. Of particular interest were fifty messages and two letters written by Bar Kokhba to his officers. Perusal of a cave in Nahal Ze'elim clarified the Bar Kokhba era and revealed more biblical fragments, letters, and documents.

The search for ancient manuscripts spread along the territory west of the Dead Sea into hiding places, cave dwellings, and *genizot*, the holy repositories for religious scrolls that had deteriorated or frayed beyond repair. A cave at Nahal Hever farther down the shore produced the remains of a Greek translation of the minor prophets plus human bone fragments. A Samarian cache found 8.5 miles north of Jericho held the deteriorated remains of forty legal documents from the mid–fourth century B.C.E. From Masada, an ancient hill fortress near the lower portion of the Dead Sea's western shore, archaeologists removed a copy of Ecclesiasticus in Hebrew, an Essene hymnal intended for use during the sabbath ritual, and fragments of Genesis, Leviticus, and Psalms.

The white chalk cliff and terraced marl of Qumran remain the center of archaeological inquiry. The complex, called the Fortress of the Pious, suggests a highly developed civilization thriving apart from the mayhem of Herodean control, widespread hedonism and profligacy, and ruinous taxation. It contains meeting rooms, a watchtower, a dining hall, a scriptorium, a pottery shop, and a cemetery with 1,100 graves yielding only male skeletons. Its history was one of turmoil, flight, and natural disaster. The community appears to have flourished from 130 to 27 B.C.E. and may have ended in 31 B.C.E. after an earthquake damaged the site. After a dormant period, new tenants lived in the area from 4 B.C.E. to the spring of 68 C.E., when Vespasian's troopers invaded the southern tip of the Jordan Valley. For reclusive Jews, it was armageddon, the beginning of the end prophesied in scripture. About the time of Titus's destruction of the Temple of Jerusalem and deterioration of the city, the community came to a violent end that included fighting and a fire that may have been set by the Roman Tenth Legion.

Archaeological detective work has answered basic questions about the occupants of Qumran. The absence of domiciles so far from the nearest town implies that residents slept in caves, huts, or tents. They were well supplied with water from a catchment system that channeled rain into reservoirs. In addition to a Herodean lamp, a stone measuring cup, plates, dozens of identical porringers, chalices, a vase, plaited baskets, rope and cording, fiber sandals, a bronze inkwell and table, a bowl carved of acacia wood, boxes, mirror frames, boxwood combs, a silver coin dating to 126 B.C.E. and depicting the profile of Demetrius II of Syria, another coin dating to 27 B.C.E. and marked with the Roman eagle, and pottery items for drinking, serving, and cooking, the literary discoveries from Qumran consist of carbon ink on hundreds of leather and papyrus documents. They survive in fragments and whole scrolls dating from 200 B.C.E. to C.E. 200 The best preserved is a scroll of forty-five Hebrew psalms. From the caves at Murabba'at and Engedi, excavators reclaimed an account of the second Jewish revolt against the Romans, a three-year conflict that ended in C.E. 135, which makes the events contemporaneous with the early foundations of Christianity.

After years of piecing together 15,000 fragments of Hebrew and Aramaic script and a few bits in Greek written in a neat *merubba'*, the typically square Hebrew penmanship, scholars from the Hebrew University of Jerusalem formed a clearer picture of the time period and the library's owners. Scholars established the time frame from archaeological evidence and carbon-14 dating plus epigraphy or inscription dating, pottery analysis, numismatics (coin assessment), and paleography (the study of ancient handwriting). Over time, they were able to confirm early findings with a more modern, less invasive technique, accelerator mass spectrometry. Additional evidence from the following five respected sources by three first-century authors substantiated their surmise:

- a geographical identification in *De Vita Contemplativa* (On the Contemplative Life) of Judeus Philo, a first-century C.E. Jewish philosopher among the Alexandrian literati
- Pliny the Elder's Latin encyclopedia, *Historia Naturalis* (Natural History) 5:17, 4 (C.E. 77)
- *De Bello Judaico* (The Jewish War) 2:119–120 (C.E. 75) and *De Antiquitate Judaica* (Jewish Antiquities) 15:371–379 (C.E. 94) by the Hebrew apologist and priest Josephus Flavius

These commentaries identified the 825–870 manuscripts as a scholarly book collection of the Essenes, a sect of semi-monastic Jewish *hasidim* (ascetics), descendants of the high priest Zadok.

Organized by an unnamed "teacher of righteousness," the mystical brotherhood, which flourished near Qumran from 150 B.C.E. to C.E. 68, consisted of fundamentalist dissidents—a company of disgruntled dropouts from the greater number of Palestinian Jews who became "volunteers for holiness" in a new world order described as the true Israel. They interpreted literally Isaiah 40:3, which commands, "In the desert prepare the way for the Lord; make straight in the wilderness a highway for our God." Obediently, they regrouped in the wilderness in a utopian theocracy or city of God in preparation for the coming of the messiah. Essential to Essene membership was a pledge or covenant with God. To remain free of Roman adulteration, they accepted self-exile from lax Jewish society, maintained sexual purity, and observed a scrupulous devotion to the outlook and actions demanded by the Torah. Only those who survived a two-year probation without expulsion for infractions became full-fledged Essene brothers. Those who backslid suffered demotions, reduced rations, confinement, and penance.

The commune consisted of laymen living under a rigid hierarchy. Officials ranked from a supervisor, bursar of funds, and a council of twelve men and three priests to a priest-governor, called the master or guardian, who organized annual events according to a 364-day solar calendar. Their activities called for separation from non–Essenes, celibacy for the devout, strict agricultural laws, and ritual cleanliness. Regularly, they ate and prayed together, then studied and discussed Torah and liturgy. The purpose of their community was to maintain a pious observance of God's law until the appearance of a second Moses as prophet, a second Aaron as anointed priest, and a second David as warrior-king, all in accordance with the prophecy of Isaiah.

The collection, the oldest biblical manuscripts in existence, survives in a fine, readable script, indicating that scribes copied with great care. It includes all the Hebrew books of the Old Testament except Esther along with parts of the Septuagint, the first Greek translation of the Torah; an Aramaic version of Job; a copy of Isaiah nearly a thousand years older than the earliest extant copy; bits of horoscopes; and apocryphal writings in Hebrew, Aramaic, and Greek. Many are untranslated texts written in their original languages. Additional manuscripts come from the Essenes themselves, explaining the philosophy and life of the community, the rules of membership, statutes governing daily life, prayers and hymns, and Bible commentary. Of particular worth is a set of directions for fighting the end-time war, when the good will fight the wicked for possession of the earth. In addition to manuscripts, the Qumran site yielded the earliest tefillin (phylacteries), folded leather straps worn by pious Jews on the arm or forehead. Each contained a compartment with a strip of parchment inscribed in minute handwriting with verses from the Torah: Exodus 13:1–10 and 13:11–16 and Deuteronomy 6:4–9 and 11:13–21.

A multinational consortium helped to bring the Dead Sea Scrolls to public attention. Najib Albina, a Jordanian photographer at the Rockefeller Museum, made infrared photographs of the scrolls and secured them during the 1956 Arab-Israeli War.

Archbishop Mar Athanasius Yeshue Samuel, head of the monastery of St. Mark in the old part of Jerusalem, championed the Dead Sea Scrolls for their contribution to biblical understanding. He presented four manuscripts to Jerusalem's American School of Oriental Research. Eliezer L. Sukenik identified the Qumran scrolls and wrote *The Dead Sea Scrolls of the Hebrew University* (1955).

In the first half of the 1960s, Israel's top archaeologist and professor at Hebrew University, Yigael Yadin, Sukenik's son, rose to the posts of general of the Israel Defense Force and deputy prime minister. He led an expedition to the Dead Sea caves and Masada and published *Hidden Scrolls from the Judaean Desert* (1948, 1949) and *The Message of the Scrolls* (1957, 1962). Parisian scholar André Dupont-Sommer, an orientalist at the Sorbonne, coordinated history with Essene philosophy in *The Essene Writings from Qumran* (1961).

In 1965, a Viennese sculptor and architect, Frederick John Kiesler, and architect Armand Bartos completed the Shrine of the Book, a repository for the Dead Sea Scrolls in the Israel Museum complex in Jerusalem. Other manuscripts reside in the scrollery of Jerusalem's Palestine Archaeological Museum, later renamed the Rockefeller Museum. The Copper Scroll is part of the Amman Museum collection in Amman, Jordan.

Publication of the scrolls themselves moved slowly. The most complete writings reached the public quickly, but the fragmented texts required a long period of intense cleaning, sorting, deciphering, identifying, and translating. The work progressed under protective light and hermetic conditions under the direction of de Vaux and his team of eight scholars:

- three Frenchmen, Abbé Josef T. Milik, a Polish-born priest and expert in Semitic languages at the Dominican École Biblique et Archéologique (School of Bible and Archaeology) in Jerusalem, author of *Ten Years of Discovery in the Wilderness of Judea* (1959); Abbé Jean Starcky, an Aramaic expert of the Centre Nationale de la Recherche Scientifique (National Center of Scientific Research) in Paris; and Abbé Maurice Baillet
- two Americans, Monsignor Patrick Skehan of Catholic University in Washington, director of the William F. Albright Institute for Archaeological Research, and Dr. Frank Moore Cross, professor of Hebrew and other Oriental languages at Harvard University

- a German, Dr. Claus-Hunno Hunzinger of Göttingen University
- two Englishmen, Oxford philologist John Marco Allegro, author of *The Mystery of the Dead Sea Scrolls Revealed* (1981), and John Strugnell, a Harvard graduate and doctoral candidate at Oxford, who headed the editorial process until his ouster in December 1990
- American James A. Sanders, working independently, issued a translation of the Psalms manuscript as *Discoveries in the Judaean Desert of Jordan, IV: The Psalms Scroll from Qumran Cave 11* (1965).

For a quarter century, problems with limited staff, elitism, and a rule of secrecy hindered progress. In 1988, John Strugnell published *A Preliminary Concordance to the Hebrew and Aramaic Fragments from Qumran Caves II to X*. In September 1991 Hebrew Union College in Cincinnati, Ohio, used an online concordance to reconfigure one of the unpublished works. Within weeks, the Huntington Library in San Marino, California, opened its vault and liberated a series of photographs of the Dead Sea Scrolls for public use. Archives at the Oxford Center for Postgraduate Hebrew Studies and at the Ancient Biblical Manuscript Center at Claremont opened to independent researchers. The Biblical Archaeology Society published *A Facsimile Edition of the Dead Sea Scrolls* (1991).

Under pressure from Hershel Shanks, editor of *Biblical Archaeology Review*, the Israel Antiquities Authority — which he nicknamed the Dead Sea Scrolls Prison — sanctioned its own catalogue and photographic display of the Dead Sea Scrolls. E. J. Brill and Professor Emanuel Tov of Hebrew University published the lot as *The Dead Sea Scrolls on Microfiche* (1993) in response to California State University professor Robert Eisenman and University of Chicago interpreter Michael Wise's *The Dead Sea Scrolls Uncovered* (1992), a diatribe against the coterie's secrecy and exclusion of the global academic community. In mid–October 1999, Daniel C. Peterson, director of the Center for the Preservation of Ancient Religious Texts, issued a searchable electronic database of the scrolls.

The discoveries known as the Dead Sea Scrolls yielded a mixed lot. The first cave contained the best-preserved works. The second cave housed only tatters. The third sheltered the Copper Scroll, an inventory of the hiding places of temple treasures. A fourth cave contained the preponderance of the Essene scroll collection, of which 100 were biblical writings and the remaining 400 were sectarian texts. The latter body includes the beginnings of a parable about a divine tree, a sectarian calendar offering a timetable of work days and feast and fasting days, a schedule of priestly duties, horoscopes and phases of the moon, songs for the sabbath sacrifice, "Words of the Heavenly Lights" to mark the days of the week, and "Register of Rebukes," the only document to name individuals. From cave nine, searchers located a third-century B.C.E. volume of Leviticus in ancient Hebrew, some unknown psalms, and canonical and apocryphal hymns. In 1967, scholars negotiated a purchase of the Temple Scroll, which describes how the ideal worship center should be constructed; Bedouins may have taken it from cave nine around 1957. Scroll versions of the Apocrypha, a body of noncanonical works cherished as supplements to the Bible, and the pseudepigrapha, noncanonical books composed under pen names, proved invaluable to biblical and historical knowledge.

Although it is not clear whether the Essenes composed or merely collected these writings, the valuable texts reveal data and cryptic hints about the historical period that separates the writing of the Old and New testaments, and they illuminate the origins of Christianity and Christian liturgy:

Genesis Apocryphon

A restatement of the first book of the Torah, the Genesis Apocryphon, which Yigael Yadin published in 1956, bears information about Abraham, Noah, Lamech, and his grandson Enoch. The segment on Noah is a lush text delighting in nature and blessing the Creator for making such splendors. Mention of Mount Ararat and the names of Shem, Ham, Japhet, and their sons precedes a dream of Abram, which he narrates to his wife Sarai before God renames the two Abraham and Sarah. An erotic encomium of Sarai by an Egyptian king lauds her fine hair, bright eyes, white skin, and shapely limbs, hands, and feet. The text declares her fairer than other women and adds:

> Yet together with all this grace,
> she possesses abundant wisdom,
> so that whatever she does is perfect [Silberman 1994, 56].

The verse alarms Abram, who fears the speaker has taken his wife from him for service in the royal harem. The book concludes in the tenth year of the departure from Haran with Abram's vision of God. Still bereft of sons, he fears he will die naked and childless with only Eliezer for an heir.

Book of Noah

Gleaned from fragments retrieved from the first, fourth, and sixth caves of Qumran, the Book of Noah offers a Hebrew version of the Noah story. Also called the Birth of Noah, the pseudepigraphic text enriches the canon biography of Noah, the perfect human and "elect of God" (Eisenman and Wise 1992, 34). Because of Noah's purity, he understands all nature, the "secrets of mankind," and celestial mysteries. He will receive a vision "while upon his knees" and will "reveal mysteries like the highest angels" (Eisenman and Wise 1992, 36).

Temple Scroll

At nearly twenty-eight feet, the Temple Scroll is the longest of the discoveries, but remains unpublished. It did not come to light until 1967, when a Christian cobbler and curio dealer at Bethlehem, Khalil "Kando" Iskandar Sahin, retrieved it from a shoebox. He and his partner, George Ishaya Shamoun, sold the manuscript for $105,000. Editing took another decade. Composed before 100 B.C.E., the Hebrew text describes the perfect temple and cult worship, which parallels information contained in the Book of Jubilees. The Essenes anticipated that the end-time would restore them to power in Jerusalem, where they would reconstruct the Temple in fulfillment of God's command.

Concerning funeral behavior, the manuscript warns that Jews are not to cut their flesh or hair, as did the Greeks and Romans to honor the dead. The author directs that burial should take place in a ritual cemetery with areas restricted for people who died of contagious diseases. Those handling corpses or defiled with blood should wash before evening. Additional prohibitions against earth-crawling creatures— weasel, mouse, lizard, gecko, or chameleon — require the washing of body and clothing. The warning concludes:

> For I, YHWH [God], abide among the children of Israel.
> You shall sanctify them and they shall be holy.
> They shall not render themselves abominable
> by anything that I have separated for them
> as unclean and they shall be holy [Vermes 1998, 208–209].

Book of Jubilees

The Book of Jubilees (also the Little Genesis), nationalistic Hebrew pseudepigrapha from Palestine composed before 100 B.C.E., is a miniature Genesis. Its compilation of legends enlarges on the first two books of the Torah up to Moses's residency on Mount Sinai. Composed in biblical Hebrew, it derives from a revelation that Moses receives from the Angel of the Face (or Angel of the Presence). It contains God's command to Abraham to look into the stars and count the sand of the seashore and dust of the earth as an exercise in numbering his descendants. The text describes Abraham's test, the journey up Mount Moriah to sacrifice Isaac according to God's instructions.

I Enoch

I Enoch (also Ethiopic Enoch, Liber Enoch, or Henoch) is a long-lived body of lore in Hebrew or Aramaic dating to 200 B.C.E. and accumulated over a lengthy period. In an Ethiopic translation from Greek, the book is an end-of-time composite of 108 chapters about Enoch, father of Methuselah, who was one of two people whom God enraptured into heaven. Chapters 1–36 of the rambling narrative cover the fall of angels that preceded the Great Flood, fantastic journeys into outer space, reports of giants and tongues of fire, and descriptions of Gehenna and paradise. Chapters 37–71, which appear to have originated in Hebrew, contain sermons predicting resurrection, punishment of the wicked in Sheol, rewards to the just, and the coming of a messiah, the son of man. The last two of these chapters, composed in the first century B.C.E., identify the son of man as Enoch.

Chapters 72–82, containing Aramaic fragments of an astronomy book called the Book of the Heavenly Luminaries, details star mysteries that the angel Uriel reveals to Enoch. Composed before 100 B.C.E., this treatise replicates the solar calendar that appears in the Book of Jubilees. Chapters 83–84 narrate flood lore and introduce the next six chapters, the Vision of Seventy Shepherds, a visionary history of humankind from Adam to the Jewish hero Judah Maccabee and the coming of the messiah.

Chapters 91–107, a moral sermon written at the end of the first century B.C.E., includes warnings to Enoch's family, a series of beatitudes or blessings, and an overview of the sufferings of the Jews. The first three of this section, chapters 91–93, contain the Apocalypse of Ten Weeks, a capsule life story of the good man divided into ten weeks, seven from the past and three from the future. Chapter 105 is an interpolation from Christian sources. The editor also appended segments of the Book of Noah and other passages of Enoch lore gleaned from past periods that reveal varied trends and beliefs.

Testaments of the Twelve Patriarchs

The Testaments of the Twelve Patriarchs is a compilation of the dying words of the patriarch Jacob's twelve sons, Reuben, Simeon, Levi, Judah, Issachar, Zebulun, Dan, Naphtali, Gad, Asher, Joseph, and Benjamin. The composite, which resembles a sheaf of twelve sermons, appears to have been written in Greek by a Jewish priest after 200 B.C.E., but contains obvious Christian interpolations. Each testament reveals personal regret and an appropriate didactic lesson to the man's heirs. All but Gad make predictions concerning the end-time.

The collection closes on expectation of a messiah from the Levites, who will serve as high priest and civil magistrate. Under his eternal rule, sin will give place to righteousness. Heaven's gates will open to Jews and gentile converts, who will eat the fruit of the tree of life. An Aramaic segment, the Testament of Levi, duplicates a fragment located in Cairo, Egypt, at the medieval Geniza, a synagogue storeroom. It repeats the standard biblical injunction to practice righteousness, honor wisdom, and teach biblical truths to the next generation.

A Hebrew fragment of the Testaments of Naphtali characterizes Jacob's extended family by Hannah, mother of Zilpah and Bilhah, who bore children sired by Jacob. In addition, searchers found bits of a Joseph Apocryphon and the Testament of Judah, both in Hebrew. The Testament of Asher advises hatred toward the wicked, a point of view absent from the other eleven, which proclaim the importance of love. This humanistic law of love was central to Christ's restatement of Jewish law, which reduced ten commandments to two—love God and love other people.

The Dead Sea Scrolls contain the source material from which the author composed the Testaments of the Twelve Patriarchs. These works provided motifs and a demon named Belial. An innovation in the testaments is a belief in good and bad inclination and in the resurrection of the body, but there is no mention of predestination, a doctrine cherished by the Qumran Essenes.

Pesharim

Pesharim (Commentaries), sectarian views on Genesis, II Samuel, Psalms, and the minor prophets, reveal the experience and philosophies of the Qumran sect. The commentary on Genesis stresses that the messiah will come from the Davidic line of succession, implying that the Hasmonean dynasty has no claim on the savior. Remarks on II Samuel, Psalms, Isaiah, Hosea, Micah, and Zephaniah are too fragmented to orient the average reader toward any useful insight.

Two of the Pesharim analyze the books of Habakkuk and Nahum in greater detail than the previous bits. The Nahum commentary was the first of the Dead Sea Scrolls to name historical figures, i.e., King Antiochus, who precedes the rulers of Kittim, and Demetrius, king of Greece. The author of the better-preserved Habakkuk commentary, first published in Millar Burrows's *The Dead Sea Scrolls of St. Mark's Monastery* (1950), moves passage by passage through the book, analyzing its meaning to the prophet's era and comparing it to his own time. The commentator reveals no names, but identifies the teacher of righteousness as founder of the sect and leader of the Essenes in the last days preceding the coming of a messiah.

Damascus Document

The Damascus Document (also the Zadokite Fragments) parallels earlier writings from two medieval copies discovered by Jewish scholar Solomon Schechter in 1896 and issued in 1910 as *Fragments of a Zadokite Work*. The

Damascus Document has raised a controversy over its application. It appears to derive from a less rigid community at Damascus. Another interpretation suggests that "Damascus" is another name for the ascetic community of Qumran.

The text, divided into exhortation and statutes, lists commune rules and sect history. The manuscript opens on a stern reminder that God condemns the waywardness of flesh and that he turned away from Israel because of the people's unrighteousness. The admonition extols a model of probity, Abraham, a friend of God who kept the commandments and avoided willfulness. The book closes on a reminder that God's followers can rid themselves of sin by confessing to God their iniquities. Their reward will be forgiveness and salvation.

The statutes list injunctions concerning oath breaking and profaning God's name and assigns to husbands the cancellation of pledges made by women. The text warns that vows of destruction bring the death penalty and that execution of law belongs to the authorities rather than to individuals. Strictures on the sabbath remind the reader not to aid the house staff or even assist in the birthing of animals. An enforced hierarchy requires that priests shall assemble before Levites, Israelites, and proselytes.

Tobit

Part of the Jewish apocrypha, Tobit is a patchy thirteen-line text in Aramaic and Hebrew from the first century B.C.E. The first-person testimony is rich in action verbs—informed, burying, killed, fled, owned, and empowered. The narrative accounts for the rise of Ahiqar, Tobit's nephew, to keeper of the royal signet ring, chief cup bearer, and comptroller of the kingdom of Sennacherib, the Assyrian king.

II Ezekiel

II Ezekiel, which connects two fragments into a questionable whole, opens on Ezekiel's vision of a radiant chariot and four dray animals. He witnesses the peculiar alliance of the faces of a lion, eagle, calf, and man. His experience of a series of conjoined wheels streaming fire repeat elements from the canon Book of Ezekiel. The prophet enjoys preferential treatment from God, who promises not to refuse Ezekiel.

The mystic sign of heavenly grace is the reconnection of bones, which God will cloak in sinew and flesh. After the foretelling of a great destruction against the wicked of Memphis and Babylon, the speaker predicts that gentiles will hold sway over Israel, which will labor in captivity without a deliverer in punishment for forgetting holy law.

Letter of Jeremiah

The Letter of Jeremiah (also VI Baruch or Pseudo-Jeremiah), a twenty-two-line segment of an Ezekiel apocryphon, is a barely readable Hebrew text describing the prophet's journey from Jerusalem to Babylon, the kingdom of Nebuchadnezzar. A clear emphasis from these disconnected phrases is the assertion that Jeremiah served as God's chosen spokesperson.

Pseudo-Daniel

A fifty-five-line tatter of disjointed phrases, Pseudo-Daniel reveals episodes between Daniel and King Belshazzar and summarizes biblical history, in particular, the Tower of Babel, the Flood, an exodus from Egypt, a Babylonian exile, four kingdoms, and the end-time, when Rome appears to colonize Israel. The text fades out into a list of biblical characters and a promise of the return of holy ones.

Book of Ordinances

The Book of Ordinances, prescriptive material on Essene membership published in 1951, is divided into three segments: the Manual of Discipline, the Rule of the Congregation, the Manual of Benedictions.

The first division, the sect's constitution, is one of the group's oldest documents. It legislates the criteria for membership, the rules that govern communal life, the beliefs held by the group, and sectarian hierarchy and organization. The volume contains an outline of officers and a treatise on sect theology, a legalistic statement of obedience to God's commands.

In reference to the headmaster's teachings, the author states that he would instruct "all the sons of light and shall teach them the nature of all the children of men according to the kind of spirit which they possess, the signs identifying their works during their lifetime, their visitation for chastisement, and the time of their reward" (Vermes 1998, 101). Specifically, the leader should inculcate humility, patience, charity, goodness, understanding, intelligence, wisdom, discernment, zeal, and loyalty. A list of behaviors to avoid includes greed, spiritual laxity, wickedness, lies, haughtiness, deceit, cruelty, bad temper, folly, insolence, lust, blasphemy, and other evidence of bad character. A poetic covenant asserts a series of parallel vows, which promises:

> I will praise Him before I go out or enter,
>   or sit or rise,
>   and whilst I lie on the couch of my bed.
> I will bless Him with the offering
>   of that which proceeds from my lips

> from the midst of the ranks of men,
> and before I lift my hands to eat
> of the pleasant fruits of the earth [Vermes 1998, 113].

The anthem closes with a series of four rhetorical questions reminding the singer that humanity can never duplicate God's wonderful deeds because life sprang from dust, a lowly source, and depended on the hand of the Creator for shape and direction.

The second book, the Rule of the Congregation (also the Messianic Rule) is a brief text published in 1955. It derives from the Community Rule Scroll and survives in tatters. The text predicts the end-time, when the Essenes will rise above less righteous people. A regimented marshaling of forces specifies who shall sit before Israel's messiah and in what order, based on reputation. A communal meal, blessed by the priest, consists of the first fruits of bread and wine. After the congregational blessing, an orderly procession advances to partake.

The last chapter, the Manual of Benedictions (or Blessings), which also survives in fragments, lists benedictions suitable for the future. The five-stage manuscript opens with blessings on the faithful and proceeds to bless the high priest and lesser priests. After an unattributed blessing, the fifth beatitude calls on the master to bless the prince of the congregation.

War Between the Children of Light and the Children of Darkness

The War Between the Children of Light and the Children of Darkness (also the War Scroll or the War Rule Scroll), a description of conflict marking the end of time, when the Essenes or sons of light battle non–Essene Jews and gentiles, was first issued in 1954. The exacting arrangement names a proclamation of war, forty-year program of combat, camp location and age of recruits, duties of priests, prayers and battle liturgy, individual commentary on trumpets and standards, strategy and weapons, infantry attack, and thanksgiving ceremony. The battle anthem proclaims:

> O Zion, rejoice greatly!
> O Jerusalem, show thyself amidst jubilation!
> Rejoice, all you cities of Judah;
>   keep your gates ever open
>   that the hosts of the nations
>   may be brought in! [Vermes 1998, 176].

According to sectarian beliefs, God ordered history exactly and knew how the world would end. The opposing armies, led by angels and Belial's demons, would fight for forty years until all the unrighteous were destroyed. The author adds prayers, ordinances, and military exhortations and anticipates the arrival of a prophet and the messiahs of Aaron and Israel.

Hodayot

Hodayot (Praises or Thanksgiving Psalms), a badly deteriorated collection of sectarian hymns and liturgy praising God and thanking him for his grace, was published in E. L. Sukenik's posthumous *The Dead Sea Scrolls of the Hebrew University* (1955). Possibly a composition of the teacher of righteousness, the songs ally the members with angels and contain a meal of bread and wine that suggests a pre–Christian communion. The song may have celebrated *therapeutae* (remediation) on the Feast of Pentecost.

Hymn 9 is a lengthy, graceful text extolling wisdom. The first-person speaker declares himself a clay figure molded in water and grounded in shame and pollution. In Hymn 14, the speaker compares his chaotic state to a sailor tossed on the deep. He cries for "calm in the whirlwind" (Vermes 1998, 273). Riddled with graphic images of self-abuse and propitiatory cries to a merciful rescuer, the anthems prefigure the apostle Paul's preoccupation with sins of the flesh.

Apocryphal Psalms

Apocryphal Psalms, a truncated scroll from the eleventh cave, consists of seven verses unknown in the canon Bible. One, which the Greek Psalter lists as Psalm 151, exists in a Syriac version. It opens with a bold hallelujah and glorifies the elevation of David the shepherd to smiter of Goliath and Israel's eventual king. The text stresses the fact that David superseded his brothers, who were more handsome but less valuable to God. The facile poetic images echo the beauties of the canonical Psalms both in grace and godly themes.

Bless, My Soul

A separate poem from the Thanksgiving Hymns, Bless, My Soul lauds God for his marvels, deliverance of the poor, kindness, and mercy. Another stanza advocates contrition and observance of the law. A final fragment returns to praise for God's shelter, protection, and comfort.

Seductress

Part of a collection of wisdom texts or proverbs that describe creation and righteous conduct, the Seductress applies the image of the strumpet to Sophia, the female personification of wisdom. The poet warns of oily words, flattery, and derision. The sensual picture of the Seductress depicts dark clothing, corrupt jewelry, and evil couches linked to night and destruction. Perched at the town gates, she flicks her gaze about and flirts with virtuous men to lead them astray. Another wisdom poem, which lacks a title, pairs with the Seductress by urging the wise to seek God's wisdom.

Songs of Righteousness

Another series of aphorisms, the Songs of Righteousness is a twenty-four-line text describing the fruitful man. The instructor warns about relying on deceitful and unstable role models and counsels against assigning responsibilities to the slacker. Other warnings alert the wary to the whiner, sneak, and coveter and advise against expecting too much from those who lack keen hearing, sight, and compassion.

Book of Mysteries

A brief fragment published by Father Josef T. Milik, the Book of Mysteries extends the theme of the triumph of righteousness over evil in what may be a sermon or prophecy.

Vision of Michael

Also called the Words of Michael, the Vision of Michael is an ecstatic fifteen-line statement that parallels Jacob's experience during the dream of a ladder to heaven with angels freely ascending and descending. In this vision, the archangel Michael climbs to heaven's heights and returns to lower climes to reveal his discoveries. He spies fiery troops, nine mountains, and the angel Gabriel. The Great One, a focus of Michael's vision, shall be celebrated with a new city. No one will commit evil in the Lord's presence.

Resurrection Fragment

A messianic apocalypse also called the Messiah of Heaven and Earth, the Resurrection Fragment predicts a *meshiach* (savior), a devout Jew who "will not turn aside from the commandment of the *kedoshim* (Holy Ones)" (Silberman 1994, 114). The lines of this affirmative fragment anticipate that the faithful will cling to the hope of rescue. Upon the messiah's arrival, the cosmos will heed him, and all people will obey the sacred commandments. The text, which parallels prophecies of Jesus's birth, earthly ministry, and wonder working, declares that the savior will liberate prisoners, give sight to the blind, and relieve the torment of cripples. Subsequent lines promise that he will heal wounds, resurrect the dead, open prison cells, and offer good news to the poor.

Messianic Leader

A parallel text on the coming of a rescuer, the Messianic Leader suggests the resurrection of the *nasi* (leader), who will survive catastrophic events. The shreds of this work refer to Isaiah, the prophet who predicted a leader arising from the Davidic dynasty: "A staff shall rise from the stem of Jesse and a shoot shall grow from his roots" (Eisenman and Wise 1992, 25). Among the lines reduced to phrases is a promise, "Wickedness will be smitten" (Eisenman and Wise 1992, 29). At issue is a puzzling series of words indicating that the leader will be executed or will execute someone else. The atmosphere of Levite rejoicing and the blowing of the ram's horn connect the lines to standard Jewish ceremonial practices.

Angels of Mastemoth and the Rule of Belial

A thirty-six-line fragmentary apocalypse written in the first person, the Angels of Mastemoth and the Rule of Belial relates to Daniel and Ezekiel and alludes to the prophet Hosea. The warnings to priests refer to an era of sacrilege, which may relate to the rule of the Maccabees or Herod the Great. As though speaking for an angry God, the writer declares, "And I will speak to them and send them commandments, and they will understand to what extent they have wandered astray, they and their forefathers" (Eisenman and Wise 1992, 56). God's wrath directs his displeasure at those who abandoned worship and who committed evils, notably enriching themselves from the misery of others.

Targums

Targums (Translations) include scraps of the canon books of Leviticus and Job in Aramaic. One eighteen-line messianic fragment, the Son of God, reveals a prophecy to Daniel of a time of warfare preceding the accession of a king of God's people. Called "the son of God" and "the most high," he will initiate a rule beset by international carnage "until the people of God arise and cause everyone to rest from the sword" (Eisenman and Wise 1992, 70). The end of widespread warfare will usher in an era of peace, when all people will propitiate the God of peace. Another Aramaic apocalypse, the Vision of the Four Kingdoms, is a first-person observation of a balsam tree representing Babylon. The vision continues with a series of talking trees and references to seizure and the flight of a king.

Heavenly Prince Melchizedek

The Heavenly Prince Melchizedek, a first-century B.C.E. fragment illuminating an unknown heavenly emblem of justice, was first published in 1965. Melchizedek, a godly deliverer, heads the sons of heaven and judges his demonic opponent, Belial, also called Melkiresha.

Prayer for King Jonathan

The Prayer for King Jonathan (also the Paean for King Jonathan) is an uncertain historical reference that appears to name the Hasmonean Alexander Jannaeus, king of Judea from 103 to 76 B.C.E. The eighteen-line text is an unusual blessing of a non–Davidic king and may indicate favor for a kindness to the Jews. The style replicates that of the canon book of Psalms.

New Jerusalem

The New Jerusalem, an Aramaic fragment envisioning Jerusalem in the messianic age, survived in five Qumran caves. Replete with unfamiliar vocabulary, it derives from the canon Book of Ezekiel and parallels lines from Revelation. The speaker observes an angel surveying the houses, streets, staircases, pillars, rooms, doors, and windows of an immense holy city guarded by 1,432 watchtowers. The manuscript refers to nine of twelve gates named for Levi, Simeon, Joseph, Reuben, Naphtali, Benjamin, Judah, Dan, and Asher, all members of the Twelve Tribes of Israel. Exacting measurements of blocks, a plaza, and roads paved with white stone and the use of marble and jasper indicate an architectural intensity, a common element among authors who expected to walk the streets of heaven after the long-predicted apocalypse.

Songs of the Sabbath Sacrifice

The Songs of the Sabbath Sacrifice, also called the Angelic Liturgy, a total of ten copies of a ritual hymnal from three archaeological sites, contain verses for the first thirteen sabbaths of the year. The style ranges from praise and description of priests to worship at a celestial temple.

Tree of Evil

A scrap of a fable that survives in twenty-one fragments, the Tree of Evil continues the apocalyptic elements of fire, swallowing up, harlots and pollution, lawlessness, angels, moon and stars. Opposite catastrophes to the uncircumcised stands the survival of the righteous, who "were justified and walked according to the laws" (Eisenman and Wise 1992, 48). The familiar description of a leader appears in the final phrase, "anointed with the oil of the kingship" (Eisenman and Wise 1992, 49).

Copper Scroll

The Copper Scroll, a mysterious inscription on metal provoking much speculation and treasure hunting, was at first too corroded to be unrolled. After Professor H. Wright Baker of Manchester College of Science and Technology in England reduced it to strips, J. M. Allegro published a translation, *The Treasure of the Copper Scroll* (1960). The text names sixty-four hiding places—under stairs, in a canal, between tamarisk trees, at a cave mouth, under a cairn, at a guard post, in a cistern, under a wall, in a pond, in a courtyard, in a hill, in a tomb—for offerings, scrolls, holy vessels, ritual garments, incense and aromatic herbs, money, and precise amounts of precious metals from the Temple of Jerusalem.

SOURCES: Barnstone 1984, Bowker 1997, "The Dead Sea Scrolls Project" 2000, "Dead Sea Scrolls Still a Puzzle after 50 Years" 1991, Eisenman and Wise 1992, Gabel and Wheeler 1990, Hinman 1996, Nell 1999, "The Orion Center for the Study of the Dead Sea Scrolls and Associated Literature," "Scrolls from the Dead Sea" (1996), Silberman 1994, Vermes 1998.

Dhammapada
Written in the west Indian dialect of Pali, the language of the Buddha, the Dhammapada (Words of Doctrine or Way of Truth) is the most cited and appreciated work of the Buddhist canon. The scripture for Buddhists of Sri Lanka and Southeast Asia, it is a succinct gnomic manuscript packed with the individual beliefs and counsel of Siddhartha Gautama, founder of Buddhism. The text derives from the Tipitaka (Three Baskets), a massive encyclopedic trilogy containing these major divisions and subsets:

Abhidhamma (or Abhidharma) Pitaka (Basket of Supplementary Doctrines)

This collection is an abstruse treatise in Sanskrit that eludicates metaphysical doctrine and philosophical theology abstracted, condensed, and systematized into books of lists and charts comprising 10,000 pages. The work dates from the third to first centuries B.C.E.

DHAMMASANGANI (RECITAL OF DHAMMAS)

One of the earliest chapters, which analyzes the tenets of Buddhism and names psychic elements.

DHATUKATHA (DISCOURSE ON THE ELEMENTS)

A supplement to the *Dhammasangani* and a perusal of psychological elements of the spiritually advanced Buddhist.

KATHAVATTHU (POINTS OF CONTROVERSY)

The most recent and most valuable, comments on the doctrines and schisms that produced the eighteen schools of Buddhism. It refutes 219 faulty teachings of schismatic monks.

PATTHANA (BOOK OF RELATIONS)

The longest volume in the Tipitaka, describes laws of conditionality and all possible permutations of Buddhist tenets.

PUGGALAPANNATI (THE DESIGNATION OF HUMAN TYPES)

Contains psychological definitions of personality types.

THE SAGE VAMAKA

A treatise on applied logic, systematizes analytic procedure in pairs.

Sutta (or Sutra) Pitaka (Basket of Discourses)

This is a fragmented body of sermons, parables, anecdotes, metaphors, and teachings divided into sub-texts called *Nikayas* (collections).

ANGUTTARA (OR EKOTTARA) NIKAYA

Some 2,300 fragmentary sermons and hymns by monks and nuns, arranged by the number of topics in each discourse.

DIGHA NIKAYA (ALSO DIRGHAGAMA; LONG COLLECTION)

A heavily repetitive body of teachings divided into three chapters comprising thirty-four narratives, including:

Ambattha, Sonadanda, and *Kutadanta,* a trio of refutations of Brahman elitism from the Buddhist point of view.

Brahmajala, a list of popular superstitions and pastimes of ancient India.

Mahanidana, exposition of the law of dependent origination or chain of causation.

Mahapadana, legends of six buddhas who preceded Gautama along with their parents' names and birthplaces.

Mahaparinibbana, the details of the last weeks of the Buddha's life, his cremation, and the building of *stupas* (or *thupas*; reliquaries) to house his remains.

Mahasatipatthana, discourse of the Buddha to monks on mindfulness and holy truths.

Samannaphala (Fruits of Monasticism), doctrines of six Buddhist teachers and the benefits of a monk's life.

Sigalovada, duties of parents, children, masters, slaves, teachers, and pupils.

KHUDDAKA NIKAYA

A collection of miscellaneous short prose texts that includes:

Apadana (Tales or Legends), stories of the previous lives of worthy monks and nuns.

Buddhavamsa (History of the Buddhas), the lineage of buddhas other than Gautama.

Cariya (or *Cariva*) *Pitaka* [Basket of Conduct], tales of the Buddha's former existence and the moral virtues that elucidate doctrine.

Dhammapada, a short collection of poetic aphorisms, the jewel of the Buddhist canon.

Itivuttaka (Thus It Is Said), miscellaneous moral verses introduced by the formulaic phrase "Thus it is said."

Jatakas (Incarnations or Birth Stories), six volumes of character-building folk stories, anecdotes, and fables illustrating Buddhist teachings about the Buddha's appearances on earth as a monkey, lion, tiger, hare, elephant, and other animals; also, stories that the Buddha told his son Rahula.

Khuddakapatha (Short Passages), miscellaneous moral rules, catechism questions and answers, and formulas used in Buddhist devotions.

Niddesa, a commentary on historical aspects of early Buddhism contained in the *Sutta Nipata*.

Patisambhida-magga (Way of Analysis), an analytic treatise on the application of the Eightfold Path.

Petavatthu (Stories of Spirits of the Dead), recount the fates of the departed who are not reborn.

Sutta Nipata (also *Vimanavatthu*; Stories of Heavenly Mansions), the earliest material on primitive Buddhism and the virtuous lifestyle of monks and hermits.

Theragatha (Hymns of the Elder Monks) and *Therigatha* (Hymns of the Elder Nuns), composed by 265 senior monks and nuns.

Udana (Inspired Utterances), eighty statements of the Buddha, each preceded by a suggestion of occasions on which they should be read.

Vimana Vatthu, eighty-three stories arranged in seven groups to describe the lives of heavenly beings enjoying rewards for benevolence.

MIJJHIMA (OR MADHYAMA) NIKAYA (MEDIUM-LENGTH SUTTAS)

A collection of 152 sermons and reminiscences of the Buddha's life and past existences.

SAMYUTTA (OR SAMYUKTA) NIKAYA

Comprises short sermons, parables, and dialogues arranged by topic.

Vinaya Pitaka (Basket of Rules or Discipline)

A three-part handbook that guides the neophyte on the path to blamelessness, virtue, and self-perfection before initiation into the Buddhist order.

KHANDHAKA (THE GROUPS)

Early history of the order:

Cullavagga (Lesser Chapter), a series of meeting rules on dress, robing, medicine, diet, residence, furniture, and holy days.

Mahavagga (Greater Chapter), a collection of instructions to the novice monk written in dialogue form between the Buddha and some beginners, including Sona and Siha.

PRATIMOKSA (ALSO PATIMOKKHA OR PATTIMOKKHA; MONASTIC RULES)

Composed of 227 rules for monks and 311 for nuns, systematized by 200 offenses in descending order of seriousness to be recited at monastic assemblies. Each variance requires confession and a suitable penalty.

VIBHANGA

Narrative rulings on offenses or faulty practices followed by the Buddha's opinion.

The Tipitaka is the Pali cornerstone of a vast library of scripture that evolved from the spread of Buddhism around the globe to practitioners from other language families. Three noncanonical addenda are worth mentioning:

Milindapanha

Written in the first century C.E., *Milindapanha* is a dialogue between King Milinda and the monk Nagasena on rebirth.

Visuddhimagga (Path to Purity)

A fifth-century manual of the Buddhist lifestyle covering conduct, concentration, and wisdom. It was written by Buddhaghosa, a Ceylonese monk-scholar.

Abhidhammatthasangaha (Summary of the Meaning of Scholasticism)

A popular primer or handbook composed by the prominent Sinhalese monk Anuruddha around the eleventh century.

In 423 stanzas arranged into twenty-six loosely organized chapters, the Dhammapada is an anthology of egalitarian aphorisms in the Pali language. As described by the *Digha Nikaya*, these verses were spoken by "the venerable Gautama ... [who] bids all men welcome, is congenial, conciliatory, not supercilious, accessible to all" (Smith 1958, 98). The wording of his teaching is a Prakrit peasant vernacular related to the Middle Indo-Aryan language tree and similar to Sanskrit. In flowing lyric comments, the text merges into a thin volume the ethical and moral teachings of the Buddha (Enlightened or Awakened One). Some are verses or stanzas; others, axioms and wise sayings. Some appear in the form of an extended parallel, for example,

> Health is the greatest of gifts;
>   Contentedness is the best of riches;
> Trust is the best of relationships;
>   Nirvana the highest happiness [Berry 1956, 42].

The poetic style of the original facilitates translation and yields a pleasantly rhythmic recitation.

Authorship of the Dhammapada is attributed to the founder himself. A legendary figure, miracle worker, and source of Buddhism, the Buddha is the honorific of Siddhartha Gautama or Gotama, also called *Bhagavan* (Blessed One). A contemporary of Lao-tzu, Pythagoras, Confucius, Aeschylus, and Thales, he was a master psychologist and mentor with piercing insight into human faults. In one of a series of incarnations, he appeared on earth as a member of the warrior class and a native of northern India's Shakya republic on the south-central border of Nepal. He lived probably from May 563 to May 483 B.C.E., although other scholars name dates before and after this span. According to the Pali Tipitaka, the earliest surviving biographical material, he was a Hindu aristocrat, just as Christ and St. Paul, founders of Christianity, were Jews by birth. The Buddha's parents, Queen Mahamaya and King Suddhodana (also described as a rajah or clan chieftain), resided in the capital city of Kapilavatthu.

According to the mythic pattern of a buddha's birth,

the spirits of the Blessed Ones wait in heaven until the time is right for their appearance on earth. As explained in the *Digha Nikaya*, "It is the rule that when a future Buddha descends into a mother's womb, no illness whatsoever befalls [her]" (Smith 1995, 131). Before the Buddha's birth, his mother dreamed that angels carried her to the Himalayas, where the gods' wives washed and robed her like a divine. At a royal palace, she conceived through her right side a silver-white elephant, which Brahmans interpreted as an omen of future greatness for her child.

After this mystic conception and a ten-month gestation marked by extreme abstinence and withdrawal to a tower, the queen gave birth among sal trees in the Lumbini gardens while on the way to visit with her parents in Devadaha. Pictorial evidence suggests that the boy was born by Caesarean section. In legend, she grasped a sal tree to ease her struggle and painlessly delivered the child to four angels, who received him on a golden net. The site, revered as Rummindei, became holy ground under Emperor Ashoka, who ruled India in the third century B.C.E.

King Suddhodana's adviser, Asita (also called Kaldevala or Kala Devala), examined the infant's body and found three signs of his destiny — elongated ear lobes, a lock of hair in the center of his forehead, and a bulge at the top of his skull. All have prevailed in artistic representations of the Buddha for 2,500 years. According to a Jataka story, Asita concluded that the child would become a buddha and predicted that he would retire from the world after observing four passing sights: an elderly man, a diseased man, a corpse, and a monk. From retirement, the boy would emerge into the military or ministry as either a world conqueror and unifier of India or a great redeemer of humankind. To ensure himself of many years with his son, the king declared that no such aged, diseased, deceased, or ascetic persons should come near the prince. To accomplish this feat, he locked the palace gates, posted guards, and had runners sweep the boy's path of all evidence of human frailty or austerity.

From infancy, the child was a *bodhisattva* (one destined for enlightenment). Royalty worshiped him; Brahmans predicted that he had to leave home to develop enlightenment. As required by the laws of a buddha, his mother could never have more children; thus, she died seven days after parturition and went straight to heaven to be reborn as a goddess. Named Siddhartha (or Siddhattha) Gautama of the Sakyas, at one week of age, the prince passed to the care of his mother's sister, Mahapajapati Gotami, who the king chose as a second wife. The boy grew straight and tall, with a broad chest, entrancing eyes, and a deep voice. During a harvest festival, he sat in the shade of a jambu or rose-apple tree like a yogi — cross-legged in a trance. The pose is the prototype of thousands of artistic representations of his first metaphysical transport.

To lavish the princeling in every respect, the king surrounded him with luxury and delicacies. The boy dressed in the best jackets, tunics, cloaks, and turbans. At his winter, summer, and monsoon palaces, he played among lotus ponds to the strains of native masters of the lute and cymbals. Royal tutors prepared him in languages, classics, military strategy, charioteering, foot racing, discus, and lance. At age sixteen, he took a wife, his cousin, the princess Yasodhara, who legend declares was born the same instant as he. Despite her loveliness and grace, he directed his mind from domesticity to universal wisdom.

Just as Asita had predicted, Siddhartha's abandonment of worldly aims and pleasures came in 534 B.C.E., while he traveled in his chariot. Upon seeing a man bent with age, he began contemplating the decline of humankind. On another jaunt, he saw a man cramped with illness and fouled with body excretions. A third encounter introduced him to pall bearers shouldering a corpse. He again directed his thinking to the limits of mortal life. A fourth observation of a yellow-robed *samana* (holy man) relieved the prince's concerns about monasticism because the monk went about his mission in peace.

The prince's introduction to the four signs made him pensive at the thought of earthly evanescence. According to the *Digha Nikaya*, he mourned:

Verily, this world has fallen upon trouble —
  one is born, and grows old, and dies,
  and falls from one state,
  and springs up in another.
And from the suffering, moreover, no one knows of any way
  of escape,
  even from decay and death.
O, when shall a way of escape from this suffering be made
  known? [Eliade 1967, 475].

On return to his family, Siddhartha received a newborn son, who he called Rahula (Fetter or Hindrance). Immediately, the prince renounced his title and, after looking one last time at his family, set out in the guise of a homeless ascetic wanderer.

On Kanthaka, his wise and noble white steed, Siddhartha departed into the night with his groom Channa for company. At the perimeter of the royal compound, the locked gate sprang open spontaneously, acknowledging the Buddha's future divinity. After crossing the Anoma River at sunrise, he presented Channa with his jewels and bid him return with Kanthaka to the palace. According to one legend, the horse was so brokenhearted that it wept, lay down, and gave up its life. On learning of her abandonment, his wife, Yasodhara, mourned:

Alas! the mind of that wise hero is terribly stern, —
  gentle as his beauty seems it is pitilessly cruel, —
who can desert of his own accord such an infant son
  with his inarticulate talk,
one who would charm even an enemy! [Ballou 1944, 102].

After exchanging clothing with a poor beggar, Siddhartha journeyed south to Rajagaha, now called Rajgir, and seated himself at the foot of an incline to think on the impermanence of life. A kinsman, King Bimbisara of Magadha, visited him and learned his identity and noble lineage. He offered the prince half of the realm, but Siddhartha declared that he was done with power and wealth. He desired only truth, whatever the cost.

On a constant search, Siddhartha studied under many sages. The *Mijjhima Nikaya* describes two — the mystic Alara Kalama, who received him as an equal, and Uddaka Ramaputta, who elevated him to the next level of perception through raja (or royal) yoga, a total withdrawal from worldliness through deep meditation. Siddhartha wandered on to Senanigama near modern Gaya, the location of a pleasant grove bounded by a river. As the sixth of a group of ascetics, he welcomed the Brahman Konañña, who had correctly predicted his greatness at birth.

Austerity severely tested Siddhartha. For six years, he rid himself of earthly desire and fasted so assiduously on rice, sesame seeds, and jujube fruit that he looked like a skeleton coated in filth. He wailed:

I have plucked out the hair of my head and the hair of my
  beard,
  have never quitted the upright for the sitting posture,
  have squatted and never risen up, ...
  having couched on thorns,
  have gone down to the water punctually thrice before nightfall
to wash away the evil within.
After this wise, in diverse fashions, have I lived to torment
  and to torture my body, to such a length in asceticism have I
  gone [Ch'en 1968, 21].

He concluded that extreme self-deprivation is a form of exhibitionism. After he abandoned austerity and returned to sensible diet and cleanliness, his five fellow hermits turned against him and left.

Living homeless and alone under a banyan tree in Bodh Gaya on the Nerañjara River, one May night at age thirty-five, Siddhartha entered the last phase of his awakening. He received a portion of rice gruel from Sujata, daughter of a local landowner. Anticipating enlightenment, he sat that day among sal trees; that night, he settled cross-legged under a ficus or pipal tree, later renamed the bodhi or bo tree, and plunged deep into meditation. He struggled against an evil lord of passion named Mara, a satanic figure common to temple art. Supported by the ten *paramitas* (virtues) he had acquired during past incarnations, he took strength from charity, morality, renunciation, wisdom, perseverance, patience, truth, resolution, love, and equanimity. He correctly identified Mara's ten cohorts as lust, low pursuits, body needs, yearning, laziness, fear, doubt, hypocrisy, glory seeking, and pride. Thus, countering the ten vices with the ten virtues, he quelled Lord Mara.

That night, Siddhartha continued meditating and tapped the wisdom of his former incarnations. As described in the *Samyutta Nikaya*, he intended to "work out the life that's holy ... the heart's the altar, the fire thereon, this is man's self, well-tamed" (Bouquet 1954, 141). Late in the night, he acquired divine vision, which enabled him to watch beings dying and being reborn in new forms. Before dawn, he learned the Four Noble Truths, which overpower impurity. As stated in chapter 5 of the *Samyutta Nikaya*, they appear as four simple statements:

- Birth, illness, and death cause grief.
- Grief is an outgrowth of desire.
- Control of desire will end grief.
- The best way to control desire is by living wisely.

From bliss, he awoke freed of ignorance and darkness and achieved transformation into an *arhat* (perfected one), the supreme Buddha, the first living human to attain nirvana.

As described in the *Mahavagga*, upon encountering Upaka the holy man, the Buddha identified his new glory:

I have overcome all foes; I am all-wise;
  I am free from stains in every way;
  I have left everything;
  and have obtained emancipation by the destruction of desire.
Having myself gained knowledge, whom should I call my
  master:
  I have no teacher; no one is equal to me;
  in the world of men and of gods no being is like me.
I am the holy one of this world, I am the highest teacher
  [Eliade 1967, 478].

Upaka was stunned at his claims and hesitantly replied, "It may be so, friend." Shaking his head in disbelief, he went his way by a separate path. The Buddha continued on his earthly mission, the preface to forty-five years of wandering. He sought annual respites from June to September, the rainy season, when he withdrew to a monastery that King Bimbisara built for his rest.

The metamorphosis preceded weeks of meditation on the doctrines later contained in the Dhammapada. Still seated under the banyan, he concluded that nothing is permanent — all earthly life is relative and interdependent, forever in a state of flux. He determined that he must enlighten humanity to the dangers of passion and the joy of truth. His four elementary truths formed a new gospel. For scripture, he turned to the Hindu Upanishads, but rejected much Brahmanic tradition and teaching, discarded ritual and the caste system, and discredited speculation and Vedic law. In place of liturgy, he lauded a therapeutic self-effort composed of moral living, salvation, and compassion. This concern with world suffering made Buddhism the third missionary religion, after Christianity and Islam.

According to the *Mijjhima Nikaya*, the Brahman Sahampati declared to the Buddha, "Beings there are whose vision is but little dimmed, who are perishing because they do not hear the doctrine — these will understand it!" (Eliade 1967, 479). Thus, he convinced the Buddha to accomplish his lofty aims by teaching and counseling. The Buddha returned to his five ascetic friends, who had settled in Isipatana near Benares (or Varanasi), and revealed the transformation that had exalted him to nirvana. The five accused him of reverting to luxury. In reply, he spoke his first sermon, the *Dhammacakkappavattana Sutta* (Text on Setting in Motion the Wheel of Truth), which taught them that the extremes of sybarism and austerity divert the seeker from the central path, the way to nirvana. He summarized this route as the Eightfold Path and identified its character-building traits:

- right belief, rid of delusion and superstition
- right aims, which are the elevated goals of blameless, intelligent, and benevolent seekers
- right speech, which combines discretion, kindness, and truth
- right conduct, composed of actions that are pure, honest, and peace loving
- right livelihood, which harms or injures no living being
- right effort, which leads to self-knowledge, self-guidance, and self-control
- right thought, derived from an active mind
- right rapture, a mystic search of earthly mystery through meditation, concentration, and contemplation.

As a course of treatment, the eight-part path leads to self-liberation. Of the height of this worthy attainment, he proclaimed an end to the cycle of reincarnation: "This is the last birth! There is now no more rebecoming" [Bouquet 1954, 144].

The Buddha enlisted the renunciates as his first *bhikkhus* (monks), who formed the first *sangha* (holy order). Days later, he delivered a second sermon, the *Anattalakkhana Sutta*, which elevated his monks to perfection. He urged them to live in unity, remain upright in behavior, and teach themselves his precepts. As he states in the *Tevigga Sutta*, a series of twelve dialogues on problems of right conduct:

The truth doth he proclaim both in its letter and in its spirit,
  lovely in its origin, lovely in its progress,
  lovely in its consummation:
  the higher life doth he make known,
  in all its purity and in all its perfectness [Frost 1972,143].

After three months, the Buddha had converted a sixth monk, Yasa, plus his father, stepmother, and wife. Yasa brought the total to thirteen by adding four friends to the disciples, who, in turn, enlisted fifty more. In all, the *sangha* grew to sixty members. As described in the *Mahavagga*, these original disciples lived plainly and learned to think and act in accordance with the Buddha's teachings. In the words of one brother, "Every five days, Lord, we spend a whole night, sitting together, in religious discourse. In this way, Lord, do we live in earnestness, zeal, and resolvedness" (Frost 1972, 139). The founder was pleased with the men's dedication and stated in the *Mahaparinibbana Sutta*, "So long as these conditions shall continue to exist among the brethren ... so long may the brethren be expected not to decline, but to prosper" (Frost 1972, 140).

The Buddha dispatched the monks one by one to spread peace, wisdom, and compassion by teaching goodness. According to the *Vinaya Pitaka*, he commissioned them personally to do good:

Go forth, disciples, and wander, to the salvation and joy of
  much people,
  out of compassion for the world,
  to the blessing, salvation, and joy of gods and men.
Go not two together on the same way.
Preach, disciples, the doctrine which is salutary in its beginning,
  in its course and in its consummation, in the spirit and in
  the letter;
  proclaim the pure way of holiness [Braden 1954, 124].

Living quietly at his hut and receiving all who came to hear his advice, he continued to draw people through word-of-mouth recommendation.

The Buddha converted three more ascetics, members of the Jatila clan named Uruvela Kassapa, Gaya Kassapa, and Nadi Kassapa. To these, he directed the *Aditta-pariyaya Sutta* (Fire Sermon), a text denouncing the passions of lust, hate, and delusion. In the *Saddharma Pundarika* (Lotus Sutra), he proclaimed to potential converts:

I am the Tathagata, O ye gods and men!
  the Arhat, the perfectly enlightened one;
  having reached the shore myself, I carry others to the shore;

being free, I make free;
being comforted, I comfort;
being perfectly at rest, I lead others to rest [Bouquet 1954,
  151].

In Rajagaha, the Buddha rejoined King Bimbisara and received more followers. Bimbisara converted Veluvana Park into a monastery and joined the lay monkhood. To a growing entourage, the Buddha added his royal family, son, and clan. At Shravasti, the financier Anathapinika built a second monastery, which became the order's headquarters.

From there, by word and example, the Buddha preached and taught all types and social levels of seekers and evolved an order of nuns. Chief of his teachings to them was the differentiation between the false and true, as stated in the *Anguttara Nikaya:*

Nowhere can any cover up his sin.
The self in thee, man, knows what's true or false.
Indeed, my friend, thou scorn'st the noble self,
Thinking to hide the evil self in thee
  from self who witnessed it [Bouquet 1954, 141].

On many miles of travel, he faced death threats. Once, his kinsman, the monk Devadatta, grew angry at the Buddha's refusal to give him control of the order. Devadatta sent an assassin, who stopped in the Buddha's presence, too overcome by his sanctity to harm him. A second incident was a stoning, which caused only a bruise to his foot. The third endangerment involved releasing a crazed elephant in his path. Like the would-be assassin, the animal saw only goodness in the Buddha and diverted his charge without harming him.

The Buddha's final journey north took him to Beluva, where, at age eighty, he collapsed from severe digestive upset. At Pava, he accepted the hospitality of Cunda the goldsmith and relaxed in a mango grove. Deathly ill and bleeding internally from eating tainted mushrooms, he journeyed on to Kusinara and lay down between sal trees to die. Before expiring, he sent a companion to thank Cunda for the glorious meal that would soon set him free from earth. To his weeping follower Ananda, the Buddha reminded, "Have I not always told you that all things dear and pleasant are subject to change, loss, instability? How else could it be here?" (Schumann 1973, 31). According to chapter 26 of the *Buddhacarita*, after three initial trances, he achieved *parinirvana* (entry into nirvana). The unprecedented event unleashed storms, fire from heaven, lightning, wind, and thick darkness.

The Buddha's disciples cremated his remains and divided the ashes among a series of *stupas* for veneration. They reunited at Rajagaha, where three monks — Kasyapa, Upali, and Ananda, the St. John of Buddhism — recited the Tipitaka, the earliest oral collection of precepts, which preceded the written tenets of Buddhism. Upali incorporated into the *Vinaya Pitaka* the Buddhist decalogue, the ten requirements of monks:

- Kill no living thing.
- Take nothing that belongs to another.
- Commit no adulteries.
- Tell no lies.
- Partake of no intoxicants.
- Eat nothing after midday.
- Abstain from drama, dance, and musical performance.
- Wear no personal adornment or perfume.
- Never sleep in a bed.
- Own no precious metals.

Ananda concluded the recitation with sermon material that resembles the Dhammapada in its brevity and self-evidence, for example, "If one man conquer in battle a thousand times ten thousand men, and another conquer himself, the latter is the greater victor" and "To him in whom love dwells, the whole world is but one family" (Berry 1956, 56; Ballou 1944, 106).

The Buddha's disciples displayed a lifelong devotion to their holy teacher and honored him at four shrines: Lumbini Grove, where he was born; Bodh Gaya, where he was transformed; Benares, where he first preached; and Kusinara, where he departed earth for nirvana. According to chapter 5 of the *Sutta Nipata*, one elderly follower declared his reverence in terms of a mental oneness with the Buddha:

I do not stay away from him even for a moment,
  from Gautama of great wisdom who taught me the
  Dhamma.
I see him in my mind and with my eye, vigilant night and
  day;
  worshipping I spend the night.
Therefore, I do not stay away from him.
As I am worn out and feeble my body does not go there,
  but in my thoughts I always go there, for my mind is joined
    to him [Braden 1954, 127].

New disciples joined the order by making a simple declaration that they took their refuge in the Buddha, the Dhamma, and the sangha.

Ultimately, Buddhism was revered like a religion, but its precepts name no deity or priestly hierarchy and require no sacrifice or ritual. The goal is the achievement of personal salvation solely by controlling the excesses of ego. The Buddha's followers in northern India collected his wise words into the Dhammapada, which reciters performed orally. The Council of Ashoka canonized the text in 240 B.C.E. and began spreading it through missions to India. The movement east to Bengal preceded a southeastern advance to Cambodia, Vietnam, and Malaysia; a northwestern advance to Kashmir and Parthia; a northeasterly movement to Tibet and central Asia; and thence to China, Korea, and Japan.

Over time, syncretism altered the Buddha to a god and nirvana to heaven. Disputes over canon split India and Nepal into two branches—northern Buddhism, called Mahayana, and southern Buddhism, the Hinayana sect. Other methods of dispersion altered the texture and application of Buddhism worldwide. Tibetan Buddhists acquired scripture translated from Indian dialects into Tibetan; Mongolian Buddhists revere translations of the Tibetan scripture. In Japan, Buddhism evolved into Shintoism. Japanese Buddhists, along with worshipers from China, Korea, and Vietnam, revere Chinese scripture and translations of Indian texts.

In China, Buddhism became Taoism and generated a half million pages of scripture, exegesis, and philosophy. A translated version of the Chinese text serves the Manchu. American Buddhism got its beginning in 1854 with the immigration of Chinese laborers in the Southwest. Only in Thailand, Sri Lanka, and Burma did Buddhism remain faithful to the Buddha's original teachings, as recorded in the Dhammapada.

After 200 years of oral transmission, the Dhammapada reached written form under the reign of Vattagamani Abhaya in Sri Lanka around 29 B.C.E., when scribes stenciled Sinhalese script on ola leaves, then treated the surface with oil. The original written version continues to serve as a textbook for monks and the laity. The tone is cheerful; the style is pithy, witty, and clear, like the pulpit homiletics of Buddhist preachers, for example, "Like the Himalayas, good men shine from afar" (Byrom 1976, 114). Themes center on nonviolence and self-restraint. Examples are as universal as the moon, as intriguing as fire and shadow, as unassuming as the mustard seed. Disciples find these profound principles uplifting and applicable to everyday life.

Early versions of the Dhammapada exist in numerous translations, in particular, Prakrit, Sanskrit, and Chinese. Nearly half of the text excerpts other writings. Its impact on Asian literature is considerable, particularly among Sri Lankan monks, who learn it verbatim as a manual of holiness. It also has had an impact on Theravada and Mahayana traditions of India, Burma, Cambodia, Laos, Thailand, and Vietnam with soulful wisdom promoting purity of body, mind, and heart, the source of joy and salvation on earth and in the afterlife.

The Buddha taught through pragmatism and a sublime simplicity that teased the listener with puzzling, illuminating axioms. He urged that the individual travel alone and carefree like an elephant in the forest or a king who has abdicated his throne. As stated in the translation by Thomas Byrom, the Buddha believed:

We are what we think.
All that we are arises with our thoughts.
With our thoughts we make the world.
Speak or act with an impure mind
  and trouble will follow you
  as the wheel follows the ox that draws the cart [Byrom 1976, 3].

Couched in rustic imagery, these liberating truisms have nurtured seekers for centuries. Above all, they urge a return to instinctive truth as revealed to the heart by a reflective mind.

Among the precepts of the Buddha are advisories to abandon gossip, spiteful words, hate, and vengeance. He taught that hate is self-perpetuating and, by extension, self-damning. His list of vices to avoid targets adultery, drunkenness, deceit, passion, enmity, folly, and recklessness. He urges sensible regimens that avoid too much food or sleep. Instead of self-indulgence, he advocates perseverance and moderation, the sources of strength and humility. He explains:

By watching and working
  the master makes for himself an island
  which the flood cannot overwhelm [Byrom 1976, 10].

Those who negate personal faults and act on holy words he honors with the yellow robe, the garment of the disciple.

As a moral text, the Dhammapada speaks directly to twenty topics. In advice on the mind, the Buddha compares a controlled mind to the fletcher's whittling of straight arrows and likens a careless mind to a fish thrashing and quivering on shore. Worse than an enemy, the Buddha declares, are unguarded minds. Also dangerous are distracted thoughts, which flit from topic to topic like a bee gathering nectar from individual blossoms. More lasting are virtues, which stay the course of human life by defeating the senses.

The Dhammapada specifically treats foolishness. The Buddha warns of mischief makers, whose bad company blunt the force of truth. In place of riotous living, he urges the seeker to cultivate serenity the way a farmer irrigates the land. Freed of desires for prestige, power, money, and "the dark places of the heart," the disciplined, detached mind becomes a well-watered parcel that survives adversity unscathed (Byrom 1976, 35). Liberated from the "soft fetters" of acquisitiveness, the mature individual, like a rose stripped of thorns, takes pleasure in abandoning yearning, a source of sorrow (Byrom 1976, 131). After foregoing unbridled wants, the wise give thanks for what they have, but prefer quiet to affluence.

The Buddha characterizes the master as one who moves effortlessly on earth like a bird in flight:

He wishes for nothing.
His food is knowledge.
He lives upon emptiness.
He has broken free [Byrom 1976, 37].

Like the charioteer taming horses, the master subdues pride and desire by removing impurities one by one. Thus, the master thinks and works effortlessly, becoming a truly free individual. The prudent disciple honors the model of purity, who has loosed the self from the thongs of previous strivings.

Crucial to the good life is inner peace, a victory over self. To achieve true calm, the Buddha recommends contemplation, reflection, and determination. He warns that failings eat away at virtue drop by drop. Like dust tossed at a gale, these small flaws blow back into the face, growing more harmful and dangerous. Violence, the subject of chapter 10, is a major failing that develops from harsh words, anger, and uncurbed ambition. To those who lash out at the innocent, the Buddha predicts a future wracked by torment, infirmity, madness, persecution, and loss.

Over negative traits that become a self-annihilating bondage, the Buddha counsels gently, almost as though speaking to children: "Be harmless, be blameless" (Byrom 1976, 53). He repeats the humble models of incremental self-improvement — the farmer irrigating the field, the fletcher whittling arrows, and the carpenter turning wood. He urges self-straightening as a bulwark against unavoidable sorrows, a topic outlined in the *Mahavagga*:

Birth is suffering, old age is suffering, illness is suffering,
  death is suffering;
grief, lamentation, pain, affliction and despair are suffering;
to be united with what is unloved,
to be separated from what is loved is suffering;
not to obtain what is longed for is suffering [Schumann 1973, 39].

This delineation of human woes derives from the Buddha's belief that any state, pleasant or wretched, is transitory and thus illusory.

To the fear of old age, the Buddha advocates reevaluating the body as a puppet or jointed toy, frail and insubstantial. He declares:

You are a house of bones,
  flesh and blood for plaster.
  pride lives in you,
  and hypocrisy, decay and death [Byrom 1976, 55].

A sensible outlook, according to the Dhammapada, is discovery of self and dedication to a life's work. However, the wise must realize that, whatever their success at a trade or profession, their earthly existence is a beguiling bubble that must burst. They achieve the right path by avoiding fear and seeking health, family, and contentment. By patiently cultivating goodness and self-control, the pure in heart seek a higher consciousness that prepares the way for a transcendent life beyond death.

Sources: Alexander and Alexander 1982, Ballou 1944, Berry 1956, Bouquet 1954, Bowker 1997, Braden 1954, Byrom 1976, Cavendish 1970, Ch'en 1968, Conze 1995, Eliade 1967, Frost 1972, Gard 1961, Gentz 1973, Hastings 1951, Hinnells 1984, Hirayanna 1932, Hoover 1980, Ling 1972, McArthur 1992, *New Catholic Encyclopedia* 1967, Schumann 1973, Sharma 1987, Smith 1958, Smith 1995, *World Religions* 1998.

Doctrine and Covenants *see* Book of Mormon

Egyptian Book of the Dead

The Egyptian Book of the Dead (1842), a general title for a compendium of spells or incantations that served as a passport for the dead, describes any collection or arrangement of some 200 magic formulas that priests of ancient Egypt may have intoned at funerals. From myth and sacred traditions, the Egyptians surmised that God's name was the source of his power and a charm against evil. Because kings were revered like gods, their names appear on rings, seals, and scarabs with an oval or cartouche that ends with a bar. This enclosure symbolizes a lariat around the name and a magical knowledge protecting the king from harm. Similarly, God could be exalted through veneration of his name or obliterated from earth by expunging his name. Likewise, the soul, to avoid oblivion, had to be remembered by name, which mourners cried out, inscribed on papyri, and carved into steles, walls, tomb furnishings, and art objects. By extension, to free the spirit from an underworld power, the deceased had to memorize the name correctly to circumvent a malevolent deity's will.

The Egyptian concept of the afterlife evolved over time. The Book of What Is in the Netherworld (ca. 1554 B.C.E., eighteenth dynasty), a painted scroll from the Valley of the Kings, describes the cosmic struggle between light and dark, a standard image from world scripture. The text speaks of a dark underground kingdom and one segment similar to the Roman Elysian Fields. It contains twelve regions or caverns connected by a great river, a replica of Egypt itself split by the River Nile. In the murky subterranean world, the deceased have to vindicate their worthiness at a tribunal held in the Hall of the Two Truths or Hall of Double Justice. Ferried down the waterway to be lodged within these caverns, spirits come under the control of individual deities. As depicted in chapter 110, Osiris appears to govern the sixth cavern, a flourishing farmland irrigated by canals, and to hold court on an island.

With the aid of magic formulas, litanies and hymns, lamentations and confessions of sin and misery, chants and prayers, mythic episodes, and powerful passwords uttered at their burial, Egyptians aspired to one of several hopes for the future: to return to earth, to devour or join the gods, or to travel the sky as stars. If they achieved life on earth, the daily existence of the dead followed a pattern. By day, spirits raised and threshed a grain crop or superintended farm laborers, much as they had in life. Each night, the boat of Ra left earth and traversed the underworld river to shed light and beneficence on its inhabitants. After a life-after-death cult supplanted the state veneration of the sun deity, the dead could aspire to reside in Osiris's realm.

According to E. C. Krupp's *In Search of Ancient Astronomies* (1977), pyramid texts anticipate the climb of the dead king from the tomb to the sky, where the constellation of Orion and the dog star, Sirius, show the way. The chamber ceiling was often inscribed with a map flecked with star itineraries. By allying with cosmic companions, the soul flees corruption and attains immortality in the heavens. As expressed in the text of King Pepi, the monarch ascends the stairway of heaven:

The roaring tempest drives him, it roars like Seth.
The guardians of heaven's parts open the doors of heaven for
  him.
Dawning as a falcon, he reaches the celestial realm of Ra
  on the "Imperishable Star"
  and is placed on the throne of Osiris.
His lifetime is eternity, its limit everlastingness ["The Nightmarish Underworld"].

The search for these circumpolar stars may account for air shafts from the King's Chamber in the Great Pyramid at Giza, which point upward to Orion and Sirius. The builder may have constructed these apertures as ramps or ejection tubes from which the king could access the upper world.

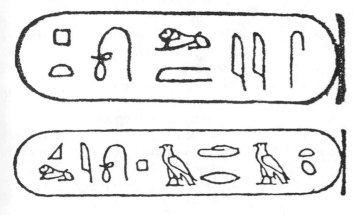

Top: Cartouche for Ptolemy. *Bottom:* Cartouche for Cleopatra.

The pyramid texts echo a tradition of funeral writings that picture a lighthearted union with Ra: "He flieth as a bird, and he settleth as a beetle on an empty seat that is in the ship of Ra" (Cavendish 1970, 306). A central purpose of burial writings was to preserve the body from corruption or dismemberment until it could reach a happy afterlife. As explained in Sir James George Frazer's *The Golden Bough* (1947), over time, the pharaoh's body, if properly mummified, converted into a silver skeleton covered in gilt flesh and topped with hair of lapis lazuli. To assure this metamorphosis into precious substances, attendants had to prepare the body to survive decay, which would guarantee an endless rule in the life beyond.

Segments of the Book of the Dead derive from two sources—pyramid texts and coffin texts. Artisans of the Old Kingdom, 2575–2130 B.C.E., inscribed pyramid texts on sarcophagi, coffins, steles, and papyri and on the walls of the pyramid's inner chambers housing the remains of pharaohs or their wives. These inscriptions are the earliest evidence of religious writings and are the first mention of an afterlife in world history. They derive from the Egyptian concept of duality, which pictured each person as a pair—the earthly form and the *ka*, a spirit twin. While living in the tomb, the *ka* fed on the provisions buried in the tomb chamber and subsequent foodstuffs left in the tomb chapel by mourners.

As represented in ritual drama, Osiris's regenerative power was a stabilizing force in Egyptian society. The annual Abydos passion play, a long-lived sacrifice and resurrection motif performed at the Temple of Osiris from the fourth to the twenty-seventh dynasties, ca. 2500 B.C.E.–550 B.C.E., reenacted Seth's slaying of his brother Osiris. As described by the actor I-kher-nefert in 1868 B.C.E., this fertility pageant was a blend of processional, drama, and festival celebrating the Nile's yearly overflow. The stage version appears to have incorporated a real human sacrifice and may have cast the pharaoh in the starring role of Horus, the savior. At the height of the spectacle, Seth dismembers his brother's corpse into fourteen pieces, which his wife/sister Isis carefully locates and reassembles. She conceives and gives birth to his son Horus, who defeats Seth and restores his father to life. Female dancers lifting their legs high as they accompany the coffin indicate how life oversteps death. Like a Christian passion play, the tableau struck terror in viewers and filled them with hope that the ever-renewing Osiris could rejuvenate them just as he himself was reborn in a mystic and holy metamorphosis.

Dating from 4000 B.C.E. to the Christian era, the anthologies of magic have appeared in three versions:

Heliopolitan Recension

The Heliopolitan Recension, which priests of the College of Anu or Heliopolis edited from texts, is now lost. The words were carved into chamber and corridor walls in the royal pyramids of Unas, Teta, Pepi I, Mehti-em-sa-f, and Pepi II during the fifth and seventh dynasties, 2494–2345 B.C.E. and 2181–2173 B.C.E. The French version, *Recueil de Travaux* (Selection of Works), was issued in Paris in 1893. A German version, *Pyramidentexte* (Pyramid Texts), was published in 1910.

Theban Recension

A pervasive hieroglyphic text, the Theban Recension was brushed onto papyri and painted on coffins in the eighteenth through twenty-second dynasties, which extended from 1570 to 730 B.C.E. It characterizes the principles of Egyptian religion with overlapping advice about successfully navigating the graphic pitfalls of the afterlife.

Chapter 1a	"Coming Forth by Day," the first praise hymn describing entry into the underworld
Chapter 1b	The spirit body's entrance into the Tuat, or dwat, a hellish twilight zone or heaven by night
Chapters 2–3	Coming forth by day and life after death
Chapter 4	Passing over earth
Chapter 5	Saving the soul for forced labor in the underworld
Chapter 6	Supplying *ushabti*, or *shawabti* (answerers), tomb figurines of servants who performed jobs assigned to the dead
Chapter 7	Eluding Apep (or Aapep) the serpent
Chapter 8	Passing through Amentet, the region where the deceased live off offerings from mourners
Chapter 9	Coming forth by day after passing through the grave
Chapter 10	Facing enemies
Chapter 11	Meeting enemies in the underworld
Chapter 12	Exiting the Tuat
Chapter 13	Entering and exiting Amentet
Chapter 14	Conquering shame
Chapter 15a	Praise to Ra (or Re), the sun god of Heliopolis, at morning and to Osiris, the slain corn spirit and chief civilizer of Egypt
Chapter 15b	Praise to Ra at setting
Chapter 15c	Passing secret places in Amentet

Chapter 16	A picture accompanying the litany to Ra	Chapter 62	Drinking water
		Chapter 63a	Avoiding fire
Chapter 17	Praise of passage through the beautiful region of Amenta and description of shape-shifting, gambling in Anubis's hall, and returning to earth as a living soul	Chapter 63b	Avoiding scalding
		Chapter 64	Coming forth by day
		Chapter 65	Mastering enemies
		Chapter 66	Coming forth by day
		Chapter 67	Opening the portals of the Tuat
Chapter 18	A picture of adoration of gods of cities that were centers of Osiris's cult	Chapters 68–71	Coming forth by day
		Chapter 72	Passing through Amhet (or Amehet), a region ruled by a worm god
Chapters 19–20	The victory crown		
Chapter 21	Giving a mouth to the soul and a priest opening the mouth	Chapter 73	Passing through the tomb
		Chapter 74	Giving legs to step onto earth
Chapters 22–23	Opening the mouth with the *ur-hekau*, a tool shaped like a serpent	Chapter 75	Receiving a throne in Anu
		Chapter 76	Changing into any form desired
Chapter 24	Offering magical words to the deceased	Chapter 77	Changing into a golden hawk
		Chapter 78	Changing into the divine hawk
Chapter 25	Remembering the name the deceased was called on earth	Chapter 79	Joining the gods and becoming a prince
Chapter 26	Offering a heart to the spirit	Chapter 80	Changing into a god and sending light into darkness
Chapters 27–30	Preserving the deceased's heart from theft		
		Chapter 81	Changing into a lily
Chapters 31–32	Repelling the crocodile who comes to steal the soul's magic words	Chapter 82	Changing into the cosmic god Ptah, enjoying cakes and ale, loosening the body, and living in Heliopolis
Chapter 33	Repelling serpents		
Chapter 34	Escaping snake bite	Chapter 83	Changing into the Benu bird (or phoenix), a symbol of Ra and Osiris
Chapter 35	Eluding flesh-eating worms		
Chapter 36	Repelling Apshai the insect	Chapter 84	Changing into a heron
Chapter 37	Repelling Isis and Nephthys, the Merti goddesses	Chapter 85	Changing into the soul and avoiding punishment
Chapter 38a	Living on air	Chapter 86	Changing into a swallow
Chapter 38b	Living on air and repelling the Merti goddesses	Chapter 87	Changing into the serpent Sa-ta, which has human legs and feet
Chapter 39	Repelling a serpent	Chapter 88	Changing into a crocodile
Chapter 40	Repelling the serpent that bites the neck of the ass	Chapter 89	Reuniting the heart soul with the body
Chapter 41	Avoiding underworld slaughter	Chapter 90	Forgetting evil thoughts
Chapter 42	Avoiding slaughter in Hensu (or Herakleopolis), the resting place of Ra	Chapter 91	Escaping being shut in
		Chapter 92	Opening the tomb so the deceased can use the legs
Chapter 43	Escaping decapitation		
Chapter 44	Escaping a second death	Chapter 93	Not sailing east into the underworld
Chapter 45	Avoiding corruption of the flesh	Chapter 94	Praying for ink and palette
Chapter 46	Living without decaying	Chapter 95	Standing before Thoth, the ape-headed god of order
Chapter 47	Retaining the underworld throne		
Chapters 48–49	Challenging enemies	Chapter 96	Standing near Thoth and glorifying the deceased
Chapter 50	Avoiding the chamber of the divine butcher's block		
		Chapter 97	Adoring Ra in his sun boat
Chapter 51	Avoiding tripping	Chapter 98	Bringing a boat to heaven
Chapter 52	Not eating filth	Chapter 99	Bringing a boat to the underworld
Chapter 53	Avoiding filth and polluted water	Chapter 100	Perfecting the spirit soul and entering Ra's boat with his divine followers
Chapters 54–55	Giving air to the deceased		
Chapter 56	Snuffing earth's air		
Chapters 57–60	Mastering waters of the underworld	Chapter 101	Protecting Ra's boat
Chapter 61	Retaining the heart's soul	Chapter 102	Entering Ra's boat

Saïte Recension

The Saïte Recension is composed of chapters predating the twenty-sixth dynasty, 664–525 B.C.E. It is found in hieroglyphic, hieratic, and demotic form on coffins and papyri. These texts, popular from 600 to 30 B.C.E., restate those of the Theban Recension in a particular order. Copies appear to be the work of scribes who did not understand or value them.

The earliest surviving example of pyramid texts was found in the necropolis of the ancient city of Memphis called Saqqarah (or Sakkara), now an Arab village fifteen miles southwest of Cairo, which contains pyramids of the fifth and sixth dynasties, 2494–2345 B.C.E. and 2345–2181 B.C.E. The oldest is a monument to King Unas, last monarch of the fifth dynasty, whose tomb set the example for later royal burial sites with 228 ritual segments. An introit envisions the king's arrival among the dead:

> Clouds darken the sky,
>   the stars rain down,
>   the Bows [a constellation] stagger,
>   the bones of the hell-hounds tremble,
>   the gatekeepers are silent
>   when they see king Unas
>   dawning as a soul [Hastings 1951, 3:93].

In imagery linking him with resurrection, one recitation states:

> Thy [Osiris's] body is the body of Unas.
> Thy bones are the bones of this Unas.
> If thou walkest, this Unas walks;
>   if this Unas walks, thou walkest [Cavendish 1970, 306].

Another proclaims:

Unas hath weighted his words with the hidden god who hath no name,
  on the day of hacking in pieces the firstborn.
Unas is the Lord of offerings, the untier of the knot,
  and he himself maketh abundant the offerings of meat and drink.
Unas devoureth men and liveth upon the gods,
  he is the Lord of envoys, whom he sendeth forth on his missions.
He who cutteth off hairy scalp, who dwelleth in the fields,
  tieth the gods with ropes ["The Nightmarish Underworld"].

Such scriptures reanimated each ruler and the family members, courtiers, and subjects whom the monarch chose to have buried nearby. In dangerous territory, the magic words protected the dead from mischief by ill-intentioned spirits.

Priests at the solar cult center of Heliopolis collected and arranged these incantations as part of their duty to the creator Ra. An example of their beauty comes from Amenhotep IV, who honored Ra with a Te Deum:

> How manifold are thy works
> They are hidden before men.
> Oh sole God, beside whom
>   there is no other.
> Thou didst create earth
>   according to thy heart ["The Nightmarish Underworld"].

The intent of these burial texts was to offer transportation for royal spirits aboard Ra's solar barque, which made a daily round through twelve districts—from the east, across the sky to the west, and, with the eclipsing of Ra's strength, into the underworld at night. In the eleventh district, the boat passed Sais, where Horus, wielding his magic boomerang, oversaw a fiery obliteration of the souls that menaced Ra. At the incineration of these enemies, Ra glided safely onward past the celestial waters of Nu in the twelfth district, home of the morning god Nut, and back to earth to complete another day's journey across the heavens. The beetle of Kehpera gave birth to a new sun to light the way; twelve goddesses towed the craft on its way through the great serpent Ankh-neteru as celestial and earthly voices sang paeans to Ra.

The reception of the pharaoh's soul allied him with the cyclical glories of Ra. According to text 572:

The gods who are in the sky are brought to you,
  the gods who are on earth assemble for you,
  they place their hands under you,
  they make a ladder for you
  that you may ascend on it into the sky,
  the doors of the sky are thrown open to you,
  the doors of the starry firmament are thrown open for you ["The Nightmarish Underworld"].

The assurance of these lines expresses the hope of Egyptians that death ended the pharaoh's tether to earth and freed his soul to wander the stars.

As described in Ninian Smart's *Religious Experience of Mankind* (1969), these idyllic depictions of the afterlife evolved into a nightmare called Tuat. A grim, murky region encircling Egypt and modeled on Sudan, it was a mixed terrain composed of scrub, trackless forest, and the desert home of the damned. Later pyramid texts picture this afterlife as perilous, beset by the serpent Apep and other phantasms and carnivores, and hindered by lakes of fire, twelve locked gates, and a fearful ferryman who responded only to a correctly worded magic password. The only safe passage for the disembodied over dark land and water was through a beneficent guide, who the deceased propitiated with powerful scriptural texts. With the right assistant, the sojourner could reach the Field of Offerings and penetrate the only oasis, the Field of Reeds, the city of god that was home to Osiris and his courtiers.

Artisans produced the text of the Book of the Dead in ornate calligraphy framed by fanciful borders in red or black ink on leather scrolls or papyri. The completed copy was a grand oratorio freighted with theatricality. Furled and bound, it accompanied the corpse into the sarcophagus as a protection from harm, whether natural or supernatural. The most popular religious text, chapter 17, parallels the Book of Genesis in its concept of creation by Ra:

The word came into being.
All things were mine when I was alone.
I was Re in [all] his first manifestations:
I was the great one who came into being of himself [Clark
    1978, 79].

Compiled orally and edited around 1570 B.C.E., these mortuary texts, in various combinations, equipped the deceased with a guidebook to the afterlife and an assurance that the body would survive intact.

In 1842, while cataloguing ancient archaeological finds to establish chronology, renowned German Egyptologist Karl Richard Lepsius, the first chair of Egyptology at the University of Berlin and curator of Egyptian artifacts at the Berlin Museum, entitled the collection *Totenbuch der Ägypter* (Egyptian Book of the Dead). His umbrella heading replaced an ancient title, *The Chapters of Pert em Hru* (Coming Forth by Day; ca. 3500 B.C.E.), the first anthology of burial texts. The original wording explains the purpose of these charms— to allow the dead to escape night, a metaphor for death, and to return to daylight, the realm of the living. Lepsius's student, Swiss scholar Henri Edouard Naville, professor at the University of Geneva and officer of the Egypt Exploration Society, published translations of the texts in the 1880s. Today, these 200 burial inscriptions serve as the main source of knowledge about ancient Egyptian theology and religious practice.

The British Museum houses the finest example of the Book of the Dead, a 78' × 15" copy from 1320 B.C.E., which was inscribed for Ani, a royal secretary at Thebes. The first notable translator was Sir Ernest Alfred Thompson Wallis Budge, keeper of Egyptian and Assyrian antiquities at the British Museum from 1894 to 1924, who aided digs in Egypt, Mesopotamia, and the Sudan and collected a library of Coptic, Greek, Arabic, Syriac, Ethiopian, and Egyptian papyri. In 1890 and 1894, he released facsimile editions of the papyri, the world's largest and most illuminated Egyptian funerary texts. The Ani collection opens with a sonorous hymn to Osiris. For banishing cannibalism and savagery he is known as

> Lord of eternity, King of the Gods,
>   whose names are manifold,
>   whose forms are holy [Budge 1993].

After appropriate invocations, the Chapters of the Coming Forth of Day humbly state the case of the deceased:

Permit thou not me to be judged according to the mouths of
    the multitude.
May my soul lift itself up before [Osiris]
    having been found to have been pure when on earth.
May I come into thy presence, O Lord of the gods;
    may I arrive at the [district of truth];
    may I rise up on my seat like a god endowed with life;
    may I give forth light like the Company of the Gods
    who dwell in heaven [Budge 1993].

In the Chapter of Giving a Heart to Osiris, a solemn plea asks that the heart accompany the body into eternity. Numerous prayers requesting new life forms, such as a lotus or heron, include a request for transformation into a divine hawk. The deceased asks, "Let me be in the company of Isis, the goddess, and let the gods keep me safe from him that would do an injury unto me" (Budge 1993).

Professional calligraphers at first wrote coffin inscriptions on bier lids, then copied, illustrated, and sold them on papyrus scrolls from 2341 to 1786 B.C.E. to be buried next to the body in anthropoid coffins. In the eighteenth dynasty, or New Kingdom, 1570–1200 B.C.E., Egypt underwent democratization. Its nobles and dignitaries and, eventually, commoners followed the royal example of anticipating and promoting life after death. Individuals saved all the wealth they could to pay burial attendants to cleanse and preserve their bodies with spices and balsam, anoint them with oils and embalming fluid, swathe them in linen strips, dress and adorn them with jewels and makeup, and seal them in protective coffins and sarcophagi, which reposed in hewn chambers. The last act of funeral professionals was to equip the deceased with food, protective amulets or talismans, weapons, and *ushabti.*

For this wider audience of departed souls, coffin texts

preserved formulaic chants that assured passage to a life after death. In a lyric first-person chant, the lines declare a divine presence that pre-dates creation:

I am that star which came forth from the two ... of Re,
  I am the space which came about in the waters,
  I came into being in them, I grew in them,
  but I was not consigned to the abode of darkness [Clark 1978, 44].

Another intones a similar grand statement of primeval being and purpose:

  I am the great Word,
    I am a redeemer—so shall I be redeemed,
    and I shall be redeemed from all evil [Clark 1978, 60].

As described by Barbara Watterson in *The Gods of Ancient Egypt* (1984), the right incantation at the right moment could protect the dead from afterlife wretchedness, for example, traveling upside down or having to eat excrement.

The cheapest coffin scrolls were a few feet of writing prepared in bulk and left blank to be filled in with the name of the deceased. The most expensive varied from sixty to a hundred feet in length and displayed 120–130 chapters of funerary verse. One model found at the cemetery of El-Bersheh from 2000 B.C.E. in the eleventh dynasty contains a map of the routes past monsters and around a fiery lake. A scroll from 1000 B.C.E. in the twenty-first dynasty illustrates ritual obeisance to Ra, symbolized by a stylized oculus on a sun disk. Such scrolls were either wrapped in linen strips like the mummified remains or concealed in a funerary statue of an Egyptian god, who interceded for the dead during judgment in the great netherworld court.

Most of the spells were written in linear hieroglyphs, the Egyptian pictographic writing, or in the cursive form of hieratic script, which appear in vertical columns. Only near the end of tomb writings did they conform to horizontal cursive writing. They vary in number and order according to the wishes of the departed or of family members who commissioned the artisan. From 322 to 30 B.C.E. in the Ptolemaic dynasty, burial inscription became standardized and continued into the period of Roman influence in the first century B.C.E. Publishers issued numbered texts, which anthologized over 200 spells. The use of burial scrolls ended with the decline of the Amen-Ra cult, when they were replaced with the *Shai-en-Sensen* (Book of Breathings), which omits hymns and addresses to deities.

The content is dramatic. Around 2000 B.C.E., funerary writings depict the soul pleading its case in a judicial hall before a formal assembly of divines. Segment 125 describes entrance to a future existence after judgment before Osiris, four lesser divinities, and a balance-beam scale on which the attendant weighs the heart against the feather of truth. If the deceased proved unworthy, Amemet (also Ammit or Ammut), a part-lion, part-hippo monster with a crocodile head, gobbled up the remains. The scene pictures forty-two *shenit* (divine personifications) including Clasper of Flame, Devourer of Shades, Crusher of Bones, Devourer of Blood, and Destroyer, one from each district of the land. These fearful beings ranged around the court and judged the deceased's repudiation of iniquity. At the center, Horus and the jackal-headed god, Anubis, oversaw the scale and checked its accuracy; Thoth recorded the result; and his dog-headed ape perched on the balance beam, the source of the second stage of judgment.

In search of *maat* (justice), the stylized court case followed a set pattern. In fear of cannibalism, individuals first kissed the threshold of the chamber, then presented themselves as suppliants to Osiris:

Praise be to thee, thou great god, thou Lord of the two truths!
I have come to thee, O my Lord, that I may behold thy
    beauty.
I know thee, and I know the names of the forty-two gods
  who are with thee in the Hall of the Two Truths,
  who live on the evil-doers,
  and who drink their blood each day of the reckoning before
    [thee].
I come to thee, and bring to thee truth, and chase away
    wrong-doing [Hastings 1951, 4:827].

The defendants pled their cases to Osiris by reciting chapter 125, a lengthy and specific negative confession, a thorough declaration of innocence of specific sins of character and behavior.

A forerunner of the code of Hammurabi and Moses's Ten Commandments, the defendant's declaration rejects the worst of Egyptian sins: oppression, fraud, murder, fornication, usurpation, cheating, slander, cruelty, theft, lying, assault, false testimony, blasphemy, pride, insolence, neglecting the poor, and impiety. Four commandments parallel four of the ten laws of Moses, found in Exodus 20:13–17:

- Not have I despised god. (Thou shalt not take the name of the Lord thy God in vain.)
- Not have I killed. (Thou shalt not kill.)
- Not have I fornicated. (Thou shalt not commit adultery.)
- Not have I borne false witness (Thou shalt not bear false witness.) ["The Nightmarish Underworld"].

The dead particularized their deeds one by one to the forty-two judges, whom the petitioner had to identify by their secret names. The final cry of "I am pure. I am pure" completed the deceased's statement of innocence (Hastings 1951, 4:828).

For ancient Egyptians, the search for justice was a solemn undertaking. As commanded by Ptah-hotep, fifth dynasty philosopher and author of the Prisse papyrus, the court must "take no word away, and add nothing thereto and put not one thing in the place of another" ("The Nightmarish Underworld"). In the last stage of the trial, the dead addressed their own hearts and begged them not to testify adversely:

> O my heart, my mother! O my heart, my mother!
> O my heart of my existence upon earth!
> May nought stand up to oppose me in judgment
>   in the presence of the Lords of the trial;
>   let it not be said of me and of that which I have done,
>   "He hath done evil against that which is right and true";
>   may nought be against me in the presence of the great god,
>   the Lord of Amentet!
> Homage to thee, O my heart!
> Homage to thee, O my heart!
> Homage to you, O my reins! [Hastings 1951, 4:827].

Those newly dead who attained the status of "true of voice" passed into the care of Maat (or Mayet), the goddess of truth, justice, and harmony, who decked them in feathers. Osiris's son Horus, the bailiff, presented the deceased to Osiris for assignment to a suitable chamber within the hall of the blessed.

Once the dead completed the obligatory trial, they underwent a ceremonial opening of the mouth and restoration of breath, which reinstated the spirit and restored the deceased to normal speech. They lived serenely in the style of earthly life with occasional visits to earth or journeys across the sky with Ra. These privileges accrued to the righteous, to those properly prepared for burial, and to those who knew the secret formulas admitting the chosen to the underworld. The only way to assure an easy passage into one of these life-after-death states was through burial of the Book of the Dead to prepare the way.

SOURCES: Alexander and Alexander 1982, "Ancient History Sourcebook: The Precepts of Ptah-Hotep, ca. 2200 B.C.E." 1998, "Archeology Explorer," Berry 1956, Book of the Dead, Bouquet 1954, Braden 1954, Brockett 1968, Budge 1929, 1959, 1960, 1993, Cavendish 1970, Clark 1978, Devereaux 1992, "E. A. Wallis Budge," Eliade 1967, Ellis 1998, Evans-Wentz 1960, Forbes 1995, Foster 1992, Frazer 1947, Hancock 1995, Hastings 1951, Hinnells 1984, Hope 1984, "How to Lose Your History" 1999, Ions 1968, "Karl Richard Lepsius," Krupp 1977, Lamy 1998, Lurker 1974, Malek 1986, Meyer 1987, Morenz 1973, "The Nightmarish Underworld," Patrick 1972, Roberts 1962, Smart 1969, Watterson 1984, Wechsler 1999, Zimansky 1999.

Ethiopian Book of the Dead   Composed around the sixteenth century, the Ethiopian Book of the

Dead, originally known as the *Lefafa Sedeq* (also *Lefafa Sedek* or *Lefaafa òsedeq* [The Bandlet of Righteousness]), is an anonymous native text derived from an era of change when Christianity confronted an age-old pantheon of indigenous deities. The Ethiopian text is the syncretic outgrowth of magic formulas that priests of ancient Egypt may have intoned at funerals. Few copies of the Ethiopian work survive; two are housed in the British Museum, another at Oxford, and one in Paris. Significant to the publication of the Ethiopian Book of the Dead was Sir Ernest Alfred Thompson Wallis Budge, keeper of Egyptian and Assyrian antiquities at the British Museum from 1894 to 1924, who aided and prepared guidebooks for digs in Egypt, Mesopotamia, and the Sudan and collected a library of Coptic, Greek, Arabic, Syriac, Ethiopian, and Egyptian papyri. He translated and named the Egyptian Book of the Dead, the world's largest and most illuminated Egyptian funerary text, and performed the same scholarly service for the Ethiopian codex in 1929, his last publication.

The version that Budge translated is a neat handwritten manuscript measuring 7" × 5" that arrived in England after its bestowal by trustees on missionaries in 1846. It is divided into two books: *Mashafa Haywat*, which contains magical spells composed in Ethiopic, and *Mashafa Terguame Fidal*, a text in Amharic summarizing the names of the members of the Trinity and other theological expressions. The juxtaposition of Christianity with exorcisms and pagan superstitions illustrates the psychological and religious ambivalence of a people converted to the Christian faith, yet unable to divorce themselves from a long and complex history. To accommodate past and present, they blended the two into their own version of orthodoxy.

A Syrian apostle from Tyre, St. Frumentius (also Abba Salama), brought Christianity to Abyssinia, the early name of Ethiopia. A trader nation on the Red Sea and Indian Ocean, Abyssinia lured world merchants with slaves, ivory, tortoise shell, rhinoceros horn, gold, silver, frankincense, and myrrh. On his return home from a journey to India in C.E. 340 with the philosopher Meropius, Frumentius and his brother Aedesius fell into the hands of Ethiopian slavers, who sold them to the royal family in the northern end of the kingdom. Frumentius acclimated well to his new home and rose to a position as courtier to King 'Ezana (or Ezanas), who was the first Christian convert from Middle Eastern paganism. Once Frumentius had baptized the king and his brother Sheazana, 'Ezana influenced his court to abandon idols and worship the Christian god, whom he made the state deity. His own preference for the crescent and star as royal symbols gave place to the Christian cross. At the king's death around 350, Frumentius took new posts as royal adviser to the queen regent and mentor of the crown prince.

Frumentius became the first bishop of Aksum (or Axxum), Ethiopia's ancient capital on the Tigray Plateau and an ally of Constantinople that combined Semitic-speaking peoples in Eritrea, Tigray, Gonder, Gojam, Shewa, and Welo. Under the commission of Athanasius, bishop of Alexandria, in C.E. 347, he began transliterating church texts into Ge'ez, a Semitic language. For his role in welcoming Abyssinians into Christian fellowship, they addressed their beloved "Feremenatos" as *Kasate Berhan* (Revealer of the Light) and as *Abuna* (Our Father), which became the official title of the patriarch of the Ethiopian Orthodox church.

During the next two centuries, until the fall of Abyssinia and the rise of Persia and Arabia, Christianity permeated the peasantry through the proselytizing of nine Syrian monks and their native-born colleagues. On the sites of ancient temples and shrines, they erected churches and opened monasteries. When Abyssinia waned as a coastal power, the Christian hegemony moved away from the sea and south to the agrarian stronghold. In C.E. 451, the Council of Chalcedon at Constantinople condemned the nation's religious beliefs. The Ethiopian church, headquartered in Addis Ababa, maintained independence from Roman, Orthodox, and Armenian doctrine and severed its relationship with the Coptic church in 1959.

According to Wallis Budge, the people to the south never completely abandoned paganism. By propitiating occult powers while simultaneously celebrating with Christian rites, they created a uniquely Ethiopian syncretic faith. Their reasoning reflected an animistic culture — applying incantations, magical words, and signs seemed more direct than entreating a faceless God to answer prayers. To the semi-pagan Abyssinian, the *Lefafa Sedeq* was a worthy composition because it collected powerful magic spells and incantations dating back centuries, perhaps to the Egyptians. It achieved its English title in 1929 when Budge allied its style and purpose with the Egyptian Book of the Dead, with which it shares a strong need to comfort the dead and return them to life through repetitions of magic charms.

Because Abyssinians evolved no structured mass for the dead, the strip that accompanied the deceased into the afterlife served as a passport through hell and an entree to heaven. According to the Book of Burial, the interment of a royal corpse began with an unspecified series of prayers for mercy on the deceased, for example, "Gather thou [him] together in a place of well-being, where living water is to be found, and in a Garden of Delights" (Budge 1929, 12). The prayer was intended to spare the dead from a sojourn in torment. Following this introit was a prayer of St. Athanasius, the chief monastic of eastern Catholicism. To obtain absolution of sins for the deceased, mourners prayed the penitential prayers that God divulged to St. Peter. The services followed with the Virgin Mary's prayers, an admonition to the dead, and a funeral sermon by St. Frumentius or Ya'kub al-Saruji (also Jacob of Serugh or Serug), a preacher and Syriac poet who wrote hundreds of religious poems, hymns, and homilies.

In contrast to the funeral service, the Ethiopian Book of the Dead was both scripture and a powerful amulet that required exact memorization. Its magic derives from the secret names that sustained the Christian Trinity and their servants on earth and in heaven. The codex takes its title from the Arabic *lifafah*, a linen, goatskin, or parchment strip or fillet that equalled the height of the subject benefiting from its magic. The width is not indicated, but may have been no more than three to six inches, like those mentioned in the Egyptian Book of the Dead and used in the Saite and Ptolemaic periods to swaddle corpses. The bandlet formed a shroud that contained inscriptions of a body of eight brief magical compositions and symbolic drawings of the cross. The purpose of the winding cloth was to protect the deceased from devils and serve as a token of free passage through obstacles on the way to heaven.

In this repetitious litany on God the Father and God the Son, the unique quality of its structure is the inclusion of name lore and mariology, which parallels the propitiation of Isis in the Egyptian Book of the Dead. Abyssinian Christians accepted God's creative power and eternity, but were curious about the secret of nature and godhood. They wished to apply this mystery to their own mortality as a guarantee of an afterlife. They concluded from both Egyptian and Christian sacred traditions that God's name was the source of his power and a verbal charm against evil. Thus God could be exalted through veneration of his name or obliterated from earth by expunging the name, an act that would unleash Satan and place evil in control.

Abyssinian Christians applied their typically Semitic thought to an understanding of God, Christ, and the Virgin Mary, a human endowed with a mystical language by which she could address her hallowed son in private. To protect his mother, Christ implored God the father to divulge secret names to impart the magic inscribed in a book that God composed at the dawn of time. Christ then revealed to the twelve disciples powerful holy names. Like the Celts, Copts, Gnostics, Hebrews, Arabs, and Egyptians, the Abyssinians carved these various names and attributes of God onto stones and amulets and intoned them with joy and solemnity in times of thanksgiving and need.

Each of the eight chapters of the Ethiopian Book of the Dead begins with a Christian mantra, "In the name of the Father, and the Son, and the Holy Ghost, one God" and concludes with drawings of crosses, which augment the magic of the words. Each segment maintains a particular focus on the nature of death. The first, *Salot Ba'enta Madkhanit* (Prayer for Redemption), contains God's magical orison composed before the conception of Jesus, which God later revealed to his son and the son to Mary. The purpose of the prayer is to shepherd the soul through the narrow gate and on to heaven. The text describes Mary's first viewing of paradise. She trembles at the sight of hell's torments and fears that the River of Fire will harm her family, whom she identifies as Joachim and Anne, her parents; three siblings, Samuel, Joseph, and Elizabeth; and her ancestor David. Jesus intercedes with his father, who promises to reveal all to her. God dictates the words to Jesus, who writes them with a gold pen.

Jesus offers the script to Mary with the injunction to show it only to the wise and godly. He promises with a formulaic command that echoes throughout the book:

Whosoever shall carry it, and whosoever shall attach [or hang] it
  to his neck (or body), his sins shall be remitted to him.
And if he repeateth it with his voice at the time of the offering [i.e., at the Eucharist], [his sins] shall be remitted to him, and he shall be cleansed from the pollution of sin [Budge 1929, 63].

This little drama precedes sixty-nine names that confer mercy. Abyssinians believed that these verbal charms protected the living body from disease, the fetus from a birth mishap, and the deceased from mutilation or torture in the afterlife. This copy of the book personalizes the text for the protection of two unidentified men, Stephen and Walda Mika'el.

The second section opens on another list of forty-four names compiled in Jesus's handwriting, which include the twenty-two letters of the Hebrew alphabet in order—*alif, bet, gamel, dalet, he, waw, zay, het, tet, yud, kaf, lamed, mim, non, samkit, 'e, pe, sade, kof, res, san,* and *taw*—and adds the seventy-two magic names that Jesus confided to Peter. Appended to the list of supernatural names is the Ethiopian version of a puzzling ancient twenty-five-letter Latin rebus in the form of a palindrome—Sator Arepo Tenet Opera Rotas. The use of such enigmatic spells for sorcery began with the ill-fated Sotades, the first palindromist, an early third-century Thracian from Maroneia. Because of his scurrilous iambics attacking Ptolemy Philadelphus (Ptolemy II) for an incestuous marriage to his sister Arsinoë, he was immured in a lead cask and hurled into the sea.

R. Heim's *Incantamenta Magica* (Magic Incantations) identifies the phrase as a truncated version of a Roman hymn, "Sat Orare Po(tenter) Et Opera(re rati)O

T(u)a S(it) [Let be sufficient your admonition to pray powerfully and to work]." Other explanations of the enigmatic five are these shortened anagrammatic phrases: Sa(lva)tor a Re(ge) P(ontifici)o (Savior by the Papal Monarch) or "Sator a R(erum) E(xtremarum) P(rincipio) O(mni) (Sower of All by the Prince of Final Things). The Sator Arepo acrostic has also been translated in a number of semi-satisfactory English versions: "Arepo the Sower holds the wheels at work," "The sower [i.e., God] in his field controls the workings of his tools [i.e., Christians], "The sower Arepo works with the help of a wheel," "The sower Arepo holds the wheels with care," "The sower Arepo works with the help of a wheel," "The sower Arepo holds his wheels with effort," "Arepo the farmer holds the works in motion," and an unlikely slang version, "The farmer Arepo keeps the world rolling."

The words—whether Christian, Mithraic, or otherwise—acquire added significance from the fact that they employ letters from Pater Noster (Our Father), the first two words of the Lord's Prayer, and stress *a* and *o*, derived from alpha and omega, the first and last letters of the Greek alphabet, which the gospels use as symbols of the divinity of Christ. The manuscript claims that the five words name Jesus's five wounds or the nails that held him on the cross.

Augmenting the potency of the phrase is its arrangement into a magic square, five letters on a side:

```
S A T O R
A R E P O
T E N E T
O P E R A
R O T A S
```

This two-dimensional presentation demonstrates the prominence of *a* and *o* on each side in alternating order, a stylistic touch found in magical incantations and verbal charms. Analysts note that the external square implies a four-sided wheel, possibly a reference to Ezekiel's fiery wheel in the Old Testament:

```
S A T O R
A       O
T       T
O       A
R O T A S
```

The whole unfolds from the square into two strings of "A Pater Noster O" at right angles, which form a cross with the *n* as the pivotal element with a square made up of two sets of *a* and *o*:

```
                    A
                    P
                    A
                    T
                    E
                    R
A   P A T E R N O S T E R   O
                    O
                    S
                    T
                    E
                    R

                    O
```

It has also been arranged with the square of *a* and *o* rotated beyond the cross:

```
A                   P                   O
                    A
                    T
                    E
                    R
    P A T E R N O S T E R
                    O
                    S
                    T
                    E
A                   R                   O
```

Another view places the *a* and *o* at a proportional distance from the central arm:

```
                    P
                    A
        A T O
                    E
                    R
    P A T E R N O S T E R
                    O
                    S
        A T O
                    E
                    R
```

Other proposals for the geometric talisman involve X shapes either capped by the *a* and *o* or framing them:

The acrostic allegedly could put out fires and dispel sorcerers. The Sator square appears on drinking cups and amulets, along a wall, in a house, and on a column in ancient Pompeii as well as in markings in Lugdunum (modern Lyons, France), the English town of Cirencester, and Herculaneum (modern Ercolano, Italy), within a pentagram on the seal of the Guild of Mercury, as a tattoo, on a stele in Glamorgan, Wales, and in bibles. It also adorns the façade of the thirteenth-century Church of Santa Lucia on Mount Velino, Italy, and on Saint Peter's Oratory in Capestrano. It has been touted as a cure for fever, dogbite, and colic, as a spell to win a love object, and as protection from plague and witchcraft. These multiple applications make the acrostic the most famous of ancient matrices.

The third section opens on a six-word rubric for carrying the corpse. The litany includes the legend of Gog and Magog, an image of King Nathaniel on horseback on judgment day, and a blackened sun and bloodied moon. This garbled line may be a scribe's error in naming Satan rather than Nathaniel. After an exchange between God and the angel Michael, God informs the angels of seven of his names, which include Kinya (Artificer), 'Imanu'el (Emmanuel), 'Iyasus (Jesus), Kerestos (Christ), and 'Egziabeher (Landlord). Seventy-nine more names for the deity appear. The section closes with a repeat of the five words of the magic square and a prayer for remembrance, the constant concern of the deceased, who does not want to be forgotten.

In the fourth section, the writer declares, "Hearken, O our brethren, and we will speak unto you. Peradventure ye will believe the word of Lefafa Sedek, which God gave to Mary as a covenant for the last day" (Budge 1929, 73). This list protected her womb like a helmet. She asks her son for the greatest of these names. Standing on a cloud, he appears in a flame and calls out three times each 'Elohe, 'Eran, and Rafon, which may represent Father, Son, and Holy Ghost. Stephen calls by name the eight archangels—Mika'el, Gabre'el, Surufel, Kirubel, Suryal, Rufa'el, 'Aya'el, and Saku'el and follows with the four beasts, the throne, city, heights, Mary, the four evangelists, fifteen prophets, twelve apostles, twenty-four priests, forty soldiers, seventy-two disciples, 500 friends, 318 fathers, and tens of thousands of angels. The section again concludes with the magic square.

The fifth section begs protection from Christ, Michael, Gabriel, and the Paraclete, a Greek designation of the Holy Spirit. To the seeker, who must make the long journey from life to heaven, God promises the standard rubric—that the person who wears the magic word on a sign about his neck "shall live at the last day, and on the day of judgment and punishment mercy shall be shown to them. And I will spare the fire of Gehenna," the Old Testament name for hell (Budge 1929, 77). The litany concludes with an invocation to Christ and the magic square.

In part six, the apostles proclaim the seventeen names Christ gave them, repeating them three times each and noting that the greatest are Demahihl, Beresbahil, and 'Akmahil. Jesus declares, "Of all the prayers which are written in this my book, there is no formula greater than this" (Budge 1929, 79). Jesus declares blessings on the reader of the prayer and the one who prays, who expels Satan and protects the body and soul from pain, weariness, and hunger. The prayer is so strong that it wards off thieves, guards the house and children, and calls down angels and blessings from the prophets, apostles, and Holy Spirit.

The next section narrates in threes the name-charms Christ told Andrew. Christ declares that only Mary has heard these magic names. He singles out a particularly powerful list: Geraden, Milos, Gaden, Satanawi, Katanawi, Tankaram, Katali, and Mahyawi. With the aid of spells that ward off the evil eye, Andrew frees Matthias from Cannibal City. The final section lists as protection against early death thirty-four more names. A chant beginning with the alpha and omega rejoices in eight more names and introduces a grand finale of 141 names that guarantee "that the foul spirits and the hosts of Diabolos [Satan] may not approach me on my right hand, or on my left hand, or before me, or behind me, wheresoever I may be" (Budge 1929, 87). Stephen closes with a humble claim to take refuge in God's names.

SOURCES: Atkinson 1951, Bowder 1982, Budge 1929, Cavendish 1970, "E. A. Wallis Budge," Ellis 1998, Ferguson 1970, Fishwick 1964, Hammond and Scullard 1992, Hastings 1951, Howatson 1991, "How to Lose Your History" 1999, Legg 1961, "Lfafe Sdq," Milburn 1988, *New Catholic Encyclopedia* 1967, Wechsler 1999, Zimansky 1999.

Gathas *see* Avesta

Gemara *see* Talmud

Granth (or Guru Granth)

A compendium of nearly 6,000 Sikh scriptures, the Granth, Punjabi for "first book," anthologizes instructive aphorisms, bardic verses, and hymns. The writers range from God-crazed Sufi mystics to profound preachers, missionaries, and saints. The earliest composers include Ramananda, Ravi Das, Kabir, Surdas, and Namdev.

Ramananda, founder of the Ramanandi sect, was a late fourteenth-century religious leader and missionary throughout India. He disdained the caste system and patriarchy. His disciples included women and Muslims. Ramananda's preaching was so moving that it produced a fervent revival of piety.

Ravi Das (also Ravidasa or Raidas), a poet and saint of the late fourteenth and early fifteenth centuries, began as a leather worker and disciple of Ramananda. Forty of Ravi Das's hymns appear in the Granth. His piety permeates one apostrophe to the most high:

> O Lord Ram, life of creation, do not forget me.
> I am your slave.
> Remove my calamity, bestow love on your servant.
> I do not let go your feet
>   though my body be consumed [Bowker 1997, 802].

Another of Ramananda's disciples, Kabir, a Hindu poet and saint who wrote devotional songs tinged with Sufism, was born in Benares in 1440. In a divided, sometimes hostile society, he concluded that Hinduism and Islam are essentially the same faith and developed an egalitarian outreach to all social classes. He expressed spiritual awareness of God through vernacular *bhajans* (stanzas) and mystic lyrics, some as short as a *doha* (couplet). Some 243 of his poems appear in the Granth. One paradoxical stanza poses an image of the search:

> Hari is like sugar spilled in the sand
>   that an elephant cannot pick up.
> Says Kabir: The Guru gave me the hint:
>   become an ant and eat it! [Bowker 1997, 520].

Kabir's writings returned to popularity when they were translated by twentieth-century Indian poet Rabindranath Tagore.

The most difficult to identify, Surdas was a blind poet and musician of an unknown era. A devotee of Krishna and a disciple of Vallabhacarya, he authored the *Sursagar*, which summarizes the Sikh God's childhood and dance.

Namdev, a Hindu lyricist from Maharastra and student of Visoba Khecar, lived from 1272 to 1350. He composed 2,000 Hindi poems, some of which appear in the Granth Sahib. His focus was the world's need of an abstract deity, who could liberate all from rebirth. In a religious ecstasy, he exclaimed, "Now all my days with joy I'll fill, full to the brim/With all my heart to Vitthal cling, and only Him" (Bouquet 1954, 243).

Sikhism developed through the contributions of ten orthodox gurus, whose lives encompassed truth:

Nanak	1469–1539
Angad	1504–1552
Amar Das	1479–1574
Ram Das	1534–1581
Arjan	1563–1606
Har Govind	1595–1644
Har Rai1	630–1661
Har Krishan	1656–1664
Tegh (or Teg) Bahadur	1621–1675
Gobind Singh	1666–1708

Like individual candles lit from their predecessors, they passed the holy flame. Each performed the service to God essential to that stage of evolving Sikh philosophy.

The heart of the Granth is by Nanak, the first Sikh guru. The most noteworthy poet, he was a Punjabi hymnologist and hybridizer of the Hindu and Muslim faiths. The son of Mehta Kalian Das, an accountant, he was born to the mercantile class on April 15, 1469, in Rai Bhoi di Talvani southwest of Lahore, India. He grew up dreamy-eyed and introspective and annoyed his parents by losing things. By age five, he could debate Vedic issues; he advanced to Persian and Arabic literature, then abandoned formal education to take up with fakirs and hermits. At age thirteen, he refused to be invested as a Hindu. A vi-

From the Granth.

sion commanding him to work in God's name, give alms, purify, worship, and remember ended his secular life.

After abandoning his wife, Sulakhni, his sons, Sri Chand and Lakhmi Das, and work at a granary, Nanak gave himself to the mystic All-Father and declared, "His love is infinitely inexpressible. O Father, how shall I write of it?" (Hastings 1951, 9:183). He became an itinerant bard and teacher in Assam, Tamil Nadu, Sri Lanka, Mecca, Medina, Basra, and Baghdad. His sermons reviled the sinner in verses:

> Covetousness is a dog, falsehood is a sweeper,
>   living by cheating is carrion.
> To defame another is to touch filth,
>   tale-bearing is fire,
>   wrath is an evil spirit [Hastings 1951, 9:183].

He turned his loathing inward and declared, "I am not chaste, nor truthful, nor learned; foolish and ignorant am I." He lauded the guru, the ladder by which the sinner seeks the heavenly pardoner. His text declares, "Without the guru there is darkness; without the word there is no understanding. Death comes not where the infinite word of the guru is" (Hastings 1951, 9:183).

Nanak took as traveling companion a Muslim musician named Mardana, a childhood friend. The minstrel performed on the stringed *rabab* during the master's sermons and recitations and contributed three couplets to the Granth. Mardana joined Nanak in extolling right thinking and spiritual unity with the one God. At Baghdad, the two aroused anger in the devout. Nanak responded:

There are worlds and more worlds below them
  and there are a hundred thousand skies over them.
No one has been able to find the limits and boundaries of
  God.
If there be any account of God, than alone the mortal can
  write the same;
  but God's account does not finish
  and the mortal himself dies while still writing.
Nanak says that one should call him great,
  and God himself knows his ownself ["The First Master"].

Such a challenge to established ritual and Muslim religious exhibitionism brought Nanak and Mardana into danger and earned them prison sentences for preaching blasphemy. Nanak's influence, however, won him a public monument, raised in Baghdad in 1520.

To prevent misunderstanding and violence, Nanak often spoke of the religious experience from his own point of view. One verse exclaims:

Me, the bard out of work, the Lord has applied to His service.
In the very beginning he gave me the order to sing his praises
  night and day.
The master summoned the minstrel to his true court.
He clothed me with the robe of his true honour and eulogy.
Since then the true name has become my ambrosial food.
They, who under the guru's instruction, eat this food to their
  satisfaction, obtain peace.
By singing the guru's hymns, I, the minstrel spread the lord's
  glory.
Nanak, by praising the true name I have obtained the perfect
  lord ["The First Master"].

Never boastful or judgmental, Nanak maintained humility in self-abasing verses, crying, "O, my lord, who knows thy qualities? My vices cannot be numbered" (Hastings 1951, 9:184). Because of the similarity of this text to the writings of Jeremiah and Ezekiel, historians conjecture that the two—Nanak and Mardana—may have encountered Christians, but there is no proof of a meeting.

Nanak spent his last twenty years at Kartarpur, where he established the Sikh faith. Through devotional hymns, the beloved Baba showed disciples and pilgrims how to apply meditation on God's name toward personal salvation. His pithy, thought-provoking psalms include this injunction: "Precious stones, jewels, and gems shall be treasured up in thy heart if thou hearken to even one word of the guru" (Bouquet 1954, 314). One female-centered hymn declares:

When a wife entertaineth great love for her spouse,
  he mercifully taketh delight in her and enjoyeth her.
Her bed is pleasant in the company of her beloved;
  her seven tanks are filled with nectar...
She who is dyed with God's love and prayeth to him,
  shall abide in happiness through his name [Bouquet 1954,
  316].

The *Janam-Sakhis* anthologizes hagiographical testimonies and anecdotes about Nanak's life, including his travels in the Arab world, Ceylon, China, and Rome.

Before Nanak died on September 22, 1539, he transferred spiritual authority to Lehana (or Lehna), a humble, obedient disciple, and renamed him Angad (Part of my Body). Angad became Nanak's successor and Sikhism's second guru. The originator of the Gurmukhi (Mouth of the Guru) sacred script, Punjabi's official alphabet, he assembled Nanak's hymns and added sixty-two of his own. Before his death in 1552, Angad passed over his own sons, Datu and Dasau, and awarded religious leadership to a devout Hindu, Amar Das, an elderly native of Basarke in Amritsar province and annual pilgrim to the sacred Ganges River. An egalitarian, he selected men and women as missionaries and angered Brahmans by ignoring caste distinctions. He is revered for establishing the communal kitchen, which served all seekers, regardless of social caste, race, or religious affiliation.

Angad composed rituals for births and funerals and collected and systematized the *Mohan Pothi* (also *Goindval Pothis*), two volumes of religious songs that were the source material for the Granth. In all, he composed 869 original hymns. The most famous, the "Anand Sahib" (Song of Bliss), is a favorite conclusion of the Karah Prasad ceremony, when Sikh worshipers distribute sweets to the congregation. In extreme old age, he returned the title of guru to Angad's son Datu and withdrew to his hometown.

Ram Das (God's servant), the fourth guru, assumed the post in 1574. He married Bibi Bhani, daughter of Amar Das, and sired a successor, Arjan (also Arjuna or Arjun) Dev, whom he trained in scripture. Ram Das founded the spiritual capital of Amritsar and organized spiritual agents to spread Sikh teachings. He created the Lavan, the Hindu marriage rite in which the couple walks clockwise around a sacred fire, and contributed 679 hymns to the Granth.

Composed in Punjabi and Hindi with traces of Arabic, Persian, Sindhi, Sanskrit, and Marathi, the Granth reached its current length in 1603 and 1604, when Arjan, the fifth Sikh guru, compiled two volumes of sacred texts. He dictated them to secretary and former missionary Gurdas Bhalla, who presented the work to Emperor Akbar. Born in Goindwal in northern India, Arjan was the producer of many firsts, including first temporal and spiritual leader and first Sikh martyr. He cultivated Sikh worship at Amritsar by erecting a pilgrimage center, the Harimandir, called the Golden Temple in the Pool of Immortality. His worship site became the center of Sikh commerce and headquarters for extensive missions. Arjan issued the whole Sikh scripture at Amritsar as the Adi Granth (First Volume or Original Book) or Gurbani (The

Guru's Words), a volume of thirty-three sections consisting of 1,430 pages in Gurmukhi script. Of the work, he proclaimed,

In this dish are placed three things: truth, harmony, and wisdom.
These are seasoned with the name of God
   which is the basis of all;
      whoever eats it and relishes it, shall be saved [Mansukhani 1977, v].

After the demise of Emperor Akbar, Jahangir, his successor, envied Arjan's popularity and held him under house arrest at Lahore. He persecuted Sikhs, fined Arjan 200,000 rupees, and ordered expunged all entries to the Adi Granth that disagreed with the Muslim Koran and Hindu Vedas. When Arjan refused, Muslims tortured him to death on May 30, 1606. The Sikh scripture passed to his grandson, guru Har Govind (also Dhir Mal). It was captured and awarded to Maharaj Ranjit Singh. In 1849, British colonizers found the manuscript in the Lahore treasury and restored it to Arjan's descendants.

In 1704, scholar and linguist Gobind Singh, the tenth and last guru, expanded the canon to include the hymns of his father, the ninth guru, Tegh Bahadur. A native of Patna in Bihar, India, and grandson of Guru Har Govind, Singh was born Gobind Rai in 1666 and came to power at age nine. He distinguished himself as a lawgiver, poet, and chivalric founder of the Khalsa, the Sikh military brotherhood. The militia got its start in 1699 from five volunteers known as the Five Beloved and fought Mughals and hill tribes, combat cost Singh his four sons at a skirmish near Ambala and his wife and parents in other battles. Revered as a soldier-saint, he dictated Sikh scripture to Mani Singh and added fifty-nine original hymns and couplets by his father.

Singh republished the canon as the Guru Granth Sahib (The First Book Personified or Lord Book), thus deifying the book itself as a living being and holy teacher. He chose texts for the canon hymns from seven of the ten Gurus, as well as from other members of the faith.

Contributing Guru	Number of Hymns
Amar	907
Angad	63
Arjan	2218
Gobind Singh	1
Nanak	974
Ram Das	679
Tegh Bahadur	116

Other Contributors	Number of Hymns
Bal	5
Beni	3
Bhikha	2
Bhikhan	2
Dhana	4
Farid	134
Gend	5
Harbans	2
Jai Dev	2
Jalup	4
Kabir	541
Kal	49
Kalsehar	4
Kas	14
Kirat	8
Mardana	3
Mathra	10
Nal	6
Namdev	60
Ravi Das	41
Sal	3
Sata and Balvanda	8
Sevak	7
Sundar	6
Surdas	2
Trilochan	4

There is also one each from Parmanand, Sain, Pipa, Sadna, Ramanand, Jal, Tal, Bahil, and Jalan. In Singh's words, the book is the ultimate guide: "After me you shall everywhere mind the book of the Granth as your guru. Whatever you shall ask, it shall show you" (Braden 1954, 110). He died in combat on October 7, 1708, at the hand of a Pashtun tribesman at Nanded, Maharashtra.

Singh's myths, fables, Krishna legends, praise to creation in *Akal Ustat*, the autobiographical *Bachitra Natak* (Wonderful Drama), and philosophy comprise the Dasam Granth (Tenth Volume). Also called the Dasven Padshah ka Granth (Book of the Tenth Emperor), it is a less sacred work than the Adi Granth and a challenge to the faithful because it is composed in Braj with some passages in Hindi, Persian, and Punjabi. Judging by its unusually broad selection, literary historians assume that some of the entries were composed by Singh's fifty-two court poets.

Like the Koran, the Granth opens with a fundamental prayer, the Mul Mantra, a paean to divine truth. It serves as an introit to the *Japji* (Recital), composed by Guru Nanak in old age. The invocation is Sikhism's most profound and beloved sacred recitation, which epitomizes the collection as it addresses the centrality of monotheism:

There is but one God, whose name is true,
  the creator, devoid of fear and enmity,
  immortal, unborn, self-existent....
The true one was in the beginning;
  the true one was in the primal age.
The true one is now also, O Nanak;
  the true one also shall be [Bouquet 1954, 313].

Meditation on oneness with the Almighty continues with the concept of shapelessness. The text declares the sublime abstractness of the divine: "If man should have thousands and hundreds of thousands of devices, even one would not assist him in obtaining God." The passage concludes that the only knowledge of God comes from following a preordained path of righteousness.

The *ragas* (hymns) appear in groups ordered by their meter and style:

Asa Ki War

Aphorisms by Nanak and a few stanzas by Angad, the *Asa Ki War* is used by worshipers as morning devotions. They feature the chants or minstrel performances of Nanak's writings and are composed in strict parallelisms, as with this twenty-six-line nature anthem:

Wonderful thy word, wonderful thy knowledge;
  wonderful thy creatures, wonderful their species;
  wonderful their forms, wonderful their colors;
  wonderful thy wind; wonderful thy water [Frost 1972, 361].

In similar themes and patterned modes, he exalts God's power as creator and controller of all nature:

By thy power were made the nether regions and the heavens;
  by thy power all creation.
By thy power were produced the Vedas, the Purans, the
    Muhammadan books,
  and by thy power all compositions.
By thy power we eat, drink, and clothe ourselves;
  by thy power springeth all affection [Frost 1972, 361].

Like the Hebrew Psalms 8 and 100, written by David to honor Jehovah, Nanak's praise reaches its climax in the final line: "Thou beholdest and pervadest all things subject to thy command: Thou art altogether unrivalled."

Rahiras (also Sodar Rahiras)

Even-songs and prayers repeated daily, these *Rahiras* include verses by Nanak, Ram Das, Arjan Dev, and Gobind Singh. Similar to Jesus's Sermon on the Mount and the Analects of Confucius, they speak to the heart of the individual. In "Rag Gujari," Arjan declares:

No one can rely on mother, father, friends, children, or wives,
  God provideth every one with his daily food;
  why, O man, art thou afraid? [Frost 1972, 365].

In Arjan's "Rag Asa," he declares to the individual seeker, "Since thou hast now obtained a human body, O man, it is time for thee to meet God" [Frost 1972, 365].

Sohilas

Late-night prayers that precede bedtime and a public reading for cremation ceremonies, these works were written by Nanak, Ram Das, and Arjan Dev. The most popular, the "Kirtan Sohila," reads:

God is only One, you reach him by the true master's grace
  and his word.
Does not matter, where you are led by thoughts and travel,
  with him you should meditate and praise him as lord.
Please praise my God, the fearless even here.
I sacrifice for the inner sound, which grants everlasting peace
    without fear.
God cares for all His beings and looks for them daily,
  if no one sees the worth of your gifts,
  is it not impossible to judge the giver, tell me?
Fixed is hour and minute of marriage with death,
  thus the friends should perform rites and not mourn.
Bless the bride, so that she can unite with her master and end
    this sojourn!
Such calls reach daily so many a house,
  Nanak reminds us: meditate on the one, as this day will
    arouse! ["Kirtan Sohila"].

Saloks

These are couplets that break up the expanses of longer poems. One popular verse was contributed by Tegh Bahadur (Hero of the Sword), the ninth guru and son of Guru Har Govind and Nanaki. He succeeded over twenty-two other claimants to the title. He traveled India with his wife, Gujari, mother of Guru Gobind Singh. After arrest in Agra, he and five other Sikhs were martyred at Delhi on November 11, 1675, when he was decapitated. While awaiting execution, he composed more than fifty hymns and saloks incorporated in the Granth canon. One of his famous maxims begins with a question: "Why do you go to the forest to find God?"

He lives in all and yet remains distinct.
He dwells in you as fragrance resides in a flower
  or the reflection in a mirror [Bowker 1997, 19].

Savayyes (also Swayyas)

These are panegyrics honoring the first five gurus, one of which exults:

As waves beating on the shingle,
  go back and in the ocean mingle.
So, from God come all things under the sun,
  and to God return, when their race is run ["Guru Gobind
  Singh"].

Throughout the Granth, the focus remains constant — praise and rejoicing in the oneness of God, the one true guru, whose name is the main thought and desire of the Sikh. One text, which describes the selfish individual as a frog immersed in mud, envisions God as an ocean and the disciple as a fish. The meeting of God and seeker is a powerful union capable of creativity and destruction:

Once it comes it is as though a lotus flower blossoms in the
  heart;
  it serves as a ship whereby we may cross the evil ocean of
    existence.
The one who is asleep is awakened,
  and he who was aflame with fever is cooled.
Once this experience comes no one will assert that he has deserved it.
It is as though the disciple has no purity of his own,
  but the Lord seizes his arm and washes him [Alexander and
    Alexander 1982, 214].

The passage concludes that the rescued being "ceases to be a puppet of *maya* [delusion]" and can freely serve God. In another stanza, the imagery ponders the small fry in deep waters:

    Lord, mighty river, all-knowing, all-seeing,
      and I like a little fish in your great waters,
      how shall I sound your depths?
    How shall I reach your shores?
    Wherever I go, I see you only,
      and snatched out of your waters
    I die of separation [Bowker 1997, 19].

These insightful meditations employ a variety of names for the one God — Allah, Brahma, Hari, Lakhshmi, Mohan, Ram, Sahib, Siv, Vishnu — but the abiding concept of God is ineffable truth, a revelation through grace of salvation from cyclical reincarnation.

As though venerating a divinity, Sikhs worship the Granth at *gurdwaras* (temples or shrines), where they ritualize the daily presentation of scripture in four stages: opening, reading, purifying with a sweep of the silver-handled *chauri* (whisk or fan), and storing of the text. Worship incorporates *kirtan* (hymn-singing), either unaccompanied or in combination with instrumental performance. On holy feasts, readers and temple caretakers called Granthis follow the conventions of their forerunner, Bhai Budha. At an *akhand path* (uninterrupted reading), they intone all passages. For more leisurely recitations, they bear the holy book in processions commemorating martyrs and gurus.

On lesser occasions, the Granth supplies devotions to be read at weddings, child namings, and searches for advice to human problems. Currently, Sikhs select at random a *hukam*, a passage to read aloud at breakfast and use as the day's directive. In addition, readers can search for particular passages on the internet or CD-ROM in multiple languages and can supplement canon liturgy with the stanzas of Bhai Gurdas, secretary of the fifth guru, and Ghai Nand Lal "Goya," court poet under Gobind Singh.

SOURCES: Alexander and Alexander 1982, Ballou 1944, Bouquet 1954, Bowker 1997, Braden 1954, Cavendish 1970, Eliade 1967, "The First Master," Frost 1972, "Guru Gobind Singh," "Guru Granth Sahib on CD-ROM" 1995, Hastings 1951, Hinnells 1984, "Kirtan Sohila," Mansukhani 1977, McArthur 1992, "The Siri Guru Granth Sahib," Smith 1958, Smith 1995, Steinberg 1953, *World Religion* 1987.

Homeric Hymns

Homeric Hymns   The Homeric Hymns, a splendid liturgical product of eighth- to sixth-century B.C.E. Greece, is a sampling of thirty-three *humnos* (religious poems), preludes, and one fragment composed in honor and celebration of the gods. Four major poems pay tribute to Demeter, Apollo, Hermes, and Aphrodite, with twenty-nine lesser paeans to Zeus, Hera, Poseidon, Athena, Artemis, Hephaestus, Ares, Hestia, Helios, Selene, Herakles, the Muses, Dioskouri, Asklepios, and the Earth Mother. The thirty-fourth honors the guest-friend.

The hymns survive in a corpus along with Orphic Hymns and the hymns of Callimachus and Proclus. Individual poems display qualities and topics of the archaic age, the beginning of lyric poetry sung or recited to the strum of a lyre or cithera. The collection itself is undatable. Verse structure is standardized — each begins with a formulaic call on the Muse, followed by variation in the midsection and a distinct closure at the end.

The name "Homeric" is misleading, referring to the era of the Homeridae (sons of Homer) rather than to the epicist Homer, author of the *Iliad* and *Odyssey*. Although the dactylic hexameter verses are composed in artistic epic style, one by a blind poet, varied mentions from the ancient world attest that they are not the work of Homer or of any one writer. Literary historians date the hymns over a period of years and attribute the work to a guild of *rhapsodes* of the Homeric school, a clannish brotherhood of itinerant minstrels and "stitchers of songs" who imitated Homer. They entertained and enlightened households and banquets with solo performances of verse and recited in competition at games and festivals.

The poems are valuable cultural cameos that may have been commissioned by priests as elements of ceremonial occasions. The collection consists of individual works marked by sincerity of purpose. They contain candid vignettes of personalities, such as the Ionians decamping at Delos for all-out fun at the festival honoring Apollo. The poems range in length from 580 lines, the size of a chapter of the *Odyssey*, to three lines, the succinct length of introits to epic recitation. They serve as invocations to the particular god celebrated at each festival. Their language is Homeric, including borrowings from Homer's phrasing and formulaic epithets. The poems have remained in favor, especially among poets. George Chapman translated them from Greek in 1616; Percy Shelley translated some of them as verse in 1818.

Hymn to Dionysus

The first hymn and the first of a trio honoring Dionysus survives in two fragments, one of which Diodorus Siculus quoted and attributed to Homer. The focus of these lines is the possible birthplaces of the deity. The poet hints at the god's unusual double gestation, first in his mother, Semele, then sewn into father Zeus's thigh, where the premature infant completed his growth. The poem closes with a reference to female ecstatics, who worshiped in mad frenzy and dance, a subject that Euripides describes in *Bacchae*.

Hymn to Demeter

Although mediocre in style and quality, the second Homeric Hymn, Hymn to Demeter, is a sacred history of the Great Mother that may have been composed near Eleusis around 675 B.C.E. Its solemn, noble narrative describes Hades' abduction of Persephone (or Kore) from the plain of Nysa to the underworld in a golden chariot. Drama and pathos pervade the corn goddess Demeter's grief, a nine-day search for her missing daughter, and their reunion. The text honors Triptolemos, founder of agriculture, and concludes with the establishment in Attica of the Eleusinian mystery cult, an eight-day religious holiday held in late September or early October. The cult is a holdover from the pre–Hellenic past that calls for fasting, purification, sacrifice of a piglet, torch bearing, repartee, and veiling and ceremonial costume. Details of the ritual drink, *kykeon*, list three ingredients—barley flour, peppermint, and water. Central to the mystery is the power of the sprouting grain, which shoots up with youthful vigor to be slain by harvesters.

The creation of mystic rites and sacred dramas is the work of Demeter, goddess of goddesses, who shifts her shape from an elderly mother figure to a shining countenance:

> Beauty spread round about her and a lovely fragrance
> was wafted from her sweet-smelling robes,
> and from the divine body of the goddess
> a light shone afar,
> while the golden tresses spread down over her shoulders,
> so that the strong house was filled with brightness
> as with lightning [Flaceliere 1962, 87].

The transformation reduces her companion to weak knees and speechlessness. The effect carries over to participants in the Eleusinian mysteries. Held fourteen miles west of Athens, these rituals require strict night-long performance of ritual and total secrecy. Anyone divulging them risks death. The poet addresses those blessed by the mysteries and warns:

> He who dies without fulfilling the holy things,
> and he who is without a share of them,
> has no claim ever on such blessings,
> even when departed down to the moldy darkness [Meyer 1987, 30].

Hymn to Apollo

The third work, *Prooemion Apollonos* (Hymn to Apollo), contains a two-stage honorarium to the god in his dual existence as Delian Apollo and Pythian Apollo. Although Thucydides and Aristophanes claim that Homer was the author, the poet identifies himself otherwise in lines 169–173:

> When a stranger asks of you: "Whom think ye, girls,
> is the sweetest singer that comes here,
> and in whom do you most delight?"
> then answer with one voice:
> "He is a blind man and dwells in rocky Chios:
> his lays are evermore supreme" [Flaceliere 1962, 68].

Hippostratus, a chronicler of the third century B.C.E., calls him Kynthaios (or Cynaethus), who first performed Homeric Hymns at Syracuse for the Olympiad of 504–501 B.C.E. The absence of details of the Delphic cult — the ecstatic Pythia priestess and annual games — suggests that the composition dates to around 690 B.C.E., the early days of Apollo worship.

The poem originates material about the rise of Apollo over earlier local deities at Delphi. The narrative describes the birth of the archer god and his twin, Artemis, to Leto at Delos, a small island north of Crete. Leto's parturition affects Delians as well as the cosmos: "So she cast her arms around a palm tree and kneeled on the soft meadow, while the earth laughed for joy beneath her. Then the child leapt forth into the light, and all the goddesses raised a cry" (Flaceliere 1962, 88). In tribute to their patron, Delians honor Apollo in *panegyria* (annual feasts), where

> The long-robed Ionians gather in your honor
> with their children and their shy wives,
> and delight you with their games,
> and with songs and dancing [Flaceliere 1962, 88].

Most memorable are the Delian handmaidens, a chorus of girlish voices praising the god and his sister and mother.

A vignette from Mount Olympus pictures Apollo strumming the lyre. A satiric touch depicts the bumptuous dancing of Ares and Hermes, an uncultured duo in contrast to the suave, intellectual Apollo. The second stage of the narrative accounts for the oracle at Delphi, the mystic heart of Greece. After killing the bloated she-serpent called Python, Pythian Apollo deliberately places his seat and sanctuary at the foot of Mount Parnassus and performs wonders, including shape-shifting into a dolphin that abducts a Cretan ship. At the harbor of Crisa, he selects the Cretan mariners as priests and commands:

Guard you my temple and receive the tribes of men
  that gather to this place and especially show mortal man my
    will,
  and do you keep righteousness in your heart.
But if any shall be disobedient and pay no heed to my warn-
    ing,
  or if there shall be any idle word or deed and outrage
  as is common among mortal men,
  then other men shall be your masters
  and with a strong hand shall make you subjects for ever
    [Hopper 1977, 215].

Apollo predicts that the sanctuary will accrue prestige and wealth equivalent to its holiness.

Shelley's verse translation, "Hymn of Apollo," stresses the self-control and assertiveness of the god of light and creativity. The poet declares:

I am the eye with which the Universe
  beholds itself and knows itself divine;
  all harmony of instrument or verse,
  all prophecy, all medicine are mine,
  all light of art or nature; — to my song,
  victory and praise in their own right belong [Norton and
    Rushton 1952, 48].

Hymn to Hermes

Although not written for ritual purpose, the fourth and most famous of the hymns highlights the beginnings of the Hermic cult, in particular, fasting, kindling a sacrificial fire from firesticks, and worship at a firepit. The narrative, composed with full knowledge of the Hymn to Apollo in Hipparchan Athens around 520 B.C.E., covers the Arcadian messenger god's birth and early childhood exploits. His adventures begin the day of his birth in a cave on Mount Cyllene as he is seen constructing a lyre by stretching cow gut over a turtle shell, singing of his conception and birth to the nymph Maia, stealing his brother Apollo's oxen from Pieria, and slipping back to his cradle with a pose of innocence. With a peal of laughter, the divine rapscallion counters Apollo's anger and Zeus's judgment between the two brothers and earns a touch of grace, a family reconciliation. For Hermes' offer of the lyre to Apollo, Zeus rewards Hermes with a messenger's uniform — a wide-brimmed traveler's hat, winged sandals, and a herald's staff, the serpent-twined *caduceus*.

Witty and humorous, the poem glitters with charm, zest, and immediacy as it details the child god's ingenuity and capriciousness. Like old Greek comedy, its vulgarisms and Aristophanic boisterousness appear to appeal to peasant listeners rather than to court sophisticates or intellectuals. Hermes' absorption in music ties the hymn to an early phase of his cult. The poet features him rapt in composition:

He sung how Jove and May of the bright sandal
  dallied in love not quite legitimate;
  and his own birth, still scoffing at the scandal,
  and naming his own name, did celebrate [Brown 1947, 133].

The song speaks to the human condition, which allots to each mortal a limited tenure on earth. As an antidote for sorrow, the poet lauds Hermes' music:

What skill! What Muse's art!
What salve for sorrow and despair!
It gives the choice of three blessings together all at once:
  joy and love and sweet sleep [Morford and Lenardon 1977,
    179].

The poet's rejoicing in the arts fleshes out the remaining lines and concludes with the sound of shepherd's pipes, which were invented by Hermes' son Pan.

Hymn to Aphrodite

The fifth hymn, a graceful work tinged with Ionic traits, dates to 675 B.C.E. It establishes the power of Aphrodite, patron of lovers, over all creation, humankind, and gods, except for Artemis, patron of virgins, and Hestia, goddess of the hearth. In an epic apostrophe to the Muse, the poet commands:

Tell me the deeds of golden Aphrodite the Cyprian, who stirs up sweet passion in the gods and subdues the tribes of mortal men, and birds that fly in the air, and all the many creatures that the dry land rears, and the sea. All these love the deeds of rich-crowned Cytherea [Flaceliere 1962, 89].

Throughout, the poet balances divine majesty with the perverse anthropomorphisms that mark the gods as flawed like humans.

The narrative relates how Zeus forces the love goddess to choose the mortal Anchises for a mate and to pursue him boldly on the slopes of Mount Ida. By causing the wayward goddess to fall in love with a shepherd prince, Zeus reclaims patriarchal control of his daughter and makes her suffer the mortal pangs that she blithely inflicts on earthlings. The poem concludes before Aeneas's birth. Its inside information about the wild creatures of Mount Ida, home of the Great Mother, suggests the poet's connection and possible membership among the Aeneadae of Troy.

A touching parallel to Aphrodite and her shepherd is the love of Eos for Tithonus. Eos avoids him when he begins graying:

But she kept him in her house and tended him,
giving him food, ambrosia, and lovely garments....
She laid him in a room and closed the shining doors [Morford and Lenardon 1977, 30].

The image suggests the tender care of the gods, even after the human frame is committed to the tomb.

Hymn to Aphrodite

The sixth hymn and the second of a pair to Aphrodite, the Hymn to Aphrodite celebrates in twenty-one lines her loveliness and birth on the island of Cyprus. To the poet, she is resplendent in the gold jewelry the Graces drape on her neck and limbs—a "quick-glancing, honey-sweet" divinity who inspires song (Shelmerdine 1995, 141).

Hymn to Dionysus

In fifty-nine lines, the seventh hymn and second paean to Dionysus lauds the elements of his cult— miracles, shape-shifting into bestial form, recompense to enemies, and compassion for the faithful. The text recounts how pirates apprehended the purple-robed god of wine and his punishment for their audacity. The poem concludes with Dionysus's miracles and features his crossing the sea in a boat that sprouts vines and leaves from the masts.

Significant to the hymn is a reminder of the god's power. He terrorizes the bold seamen by metamorphosing into a lion and overpowering the lead pirate. To worshipers, Dionysus exults in divine pedigree:

Be of good courage, you who have become dear to my heart.
I am loud-crying Dionysus, whom my mother,
  Semele, daughter of Cadmus,
  bore after uniting in love with Zeus [Morford and Lenardon 1977, 212].

Hymn to Ares

One of the later hymns, in seventeen lines, the Hymn to Ares, eighth of the collection, displays astrological knowledge of the Hellenistic era, which worshiped the *planetes* (wanderers), a metaphor for the sun, moon, Mer-cury, Venus, Mars, Jupiter, and Saturn. Poetic themes include strength, courage, and obedience to the god's command to avoid cruelty.

Hymn to Artemis

The ninth hymn, honoring Artemis, patron of the hunt, sings of her golden arrows and chastity. Extra devotion accrues to her for being the twin sister of Apollo, "the far-shooting pourer of arrows" (Shelmerdine 1995, 146).

Hymn to Aphrodite

Tenth in order is the third paean to the goddess of love. In only six lines, the poet establishes her virtue as a giver of "gentle gifts to mortals" (Shelmerdine 1995, 147). An appreciation for feminine beauty marks the third line, which praises her smiles and blooming good nature.

A series of brief poems propitiates additional divinities with allusion to their individual myths:

Hymn to Athena

The eleventh poem pairs Athena, goddess of war, with Ares, another belligerent Olympian. In the center of this five-line prelude, the poet manages to list combat, sacking of cities, battle cries, and the rescue of refugees, Athena's major contribution to civilization.

Hymn to Hera

Twelfth in order is a very late addition to the corpus, which pictures Hera, queen of heaven, on a gold throne. The poet stresses her serenity in contrast with the loud thunder of Zeus, her brother and consort.

Hymn to Demeter and
Her Daughter Persephone

The thirteenth hymn, only three lines long, is barely an invocation to the goddess of spring and grain and her daughter. The poet requests that Demeter "stand by this city," a reminder of the time when she deserted earth and left humans to fend for themselves (Shelmerdine 1995, 148).

Hymn to Mother of All Gods and Men

The fourteenth hymn, which extols the fertile mother of humanity and the gods, offers specifics of liturgical music from the archaic age. The poet speaks of "the sound of castanets and drums along with the piercing sound of flutes" (Shelmerdine 1995, 149). The feral nature of the Earth Mother summons the howls of wolves and lions, which echo about the mountain and woods.

Hymn to Herakles the Lion-Hearted

The fifteenth verse, singing honor to Herakles (or Hercules), invokes him for heroism after a life of toil. To the poet, the hero god is "by far the greatest of men on earth" (Morford and Lenardon 1977, 373). Ever the appreciator of attractive women, he deserves domestic bliss with Hebe, his wife of the fair ankles, at their home on Olympus.

Hymn to Asklepios

The sixteenth hymn, honoring Asklepios (or Asclepius), lauds his curative powers. The tone of this poem speaks to the personal relationship between the great healer and humankind, which has suffered "evil pains" (Shelmerdine 1995, 152).

Hymn to the Dioskouroi

The seventeenth hymn, to the Dioskouroi (or Dioscuri), Kastor and Polydeukes (also Castor and Polydeuces), requires five lines to extol the holy pair, whom Leda bore in secret. The poet concludes, "Farewell, Tyndaridai [sons of Tyndareus], riders of swift horses" (Shelmerdine 1995, 7).

Hymn to Hermes

The eighteenth hymn and second honoring of Hermes speaks of the secret birth in a shaded cave of the divine herald, "giver of joy, guide, giver of blessings" (Shelmerdine 1995, 153).

Hymn to Pan

Derived from cultic worship of central Greece, the nineteenth hymn honors the Arcadian goat god, the horned and hooved son of Hermes. In Shelley's version, the rustic Pan is self-confident in performance:

And all that did then attend and follow,
Were silent with love, as you know, Apollo,
With envy of my sweet pipings [Norton and Rushton 1952, 40].

The poet stresses the adjectival meaning of Pan as "all," a connection that spreads the god's influence over humankind.

Hymn to Hephaistos

The twentieth hymn, addressed to Hephaistos (or Hephaestus), god of artisans and crafters, honors invention. The poet credits Athena as teacher of "glorious crafts to men on the earth, who formerly used to live in caves on the mountains like wild animals" (Shelmerdine 1995, 155). This nod toward the civilizing influence of the gods is a humanistic touch for which the Greeks were noted.

Hymn to Apollo

Hymn twenty-one, the second addressed to Apollo, salutes singers, even the swan, who "sings of you in a clear tone to the beat of her wings" (Shelmerdine 1995, 156). Mention of Apollo as "first and last" parallels the biblical description of Jesus as alpha and omega, the beginning and the ending.

Hymn to Poseidon

In seven lines, the twenty-second verse, honoring Poseidon the earth shaker, horse tamer, and master of the seas, seeks safety for those who work and travel by water.

Hymn to Zeus

The twenty-third poem honors the lord of heaven and master of the Olympian gods. The poet, apparently lacking skill with imagery, falls back on superlatives— best, greatest, and most glorious.

Hymn to Hestia

In five lines, the twenty-fourth hymn praises Hestia, housekeeper of Apollo. The poet presents an unusual vision of Hestia as dripping olive oil from her hair. To protect the poet's residence, the fourth line asks that the goddess of the hearth "come to this house" (Shelmerdine 1995, 158).

Hymn to the Muses, Apollo, and Zeus

The twenty-fifth poem lauds Apollo and the Muses for producing songs for singers and citherists and honors Zeus for establishing earthly monarchies. In an indirect reflection on his own trade, the poet declares, "Blessed is the one whom the Muses love, for sweet speech flows from his mouth" (Shelmerdine 1995, 158).

Hymn to Dionysus

The third paean to the wine god, hymn twenty-six, appears to be an outtake from Hesiod's *Theogony* (ca.

eighth century B.C.E.). The poem describes the infant wonder worker's care under nymphs in his boyhood cave at Nysa. After growing to a gorgeous, irresistible male, he leads the nymphs. The poet invokes the god to allow annual rejoicing to "Dionysus, rich in grapes" (Shelmerdine 1995, 159).

Hymn to Artemis

Hymn twenty-seven links Artemis's work in the field among hunters with her off-duty service at Delphi, where she leads dancers in praise of Apollo, her twin. She delights in Delphi, Phoebus Apollo's home and shrine, where "she supervises the lovely dances of the Muses and the Graces" (Morford and Lenardon 1977, 133). In salute to the twin powers, the poet concludes with a standard hymn closure, "Hail children of Zeus and Leto of the lovely hair; I will remember you and another song too" (Morford and Lenardon 1977, 134).

Hymn to Athena

The second paean to Athena (or Athene), number twenty-eight, showers the goddess with honor for "bright eyes, quick mind, and inflexible heart, chaste and mighty virgin, protectress of the city, Tritogeneia" (Morford and Lenardon 1977, 98). The descriptors pile up beauty in detail—her gold armor, birth from her father, Zeus's, head, and the flash of her spear. She deserves fealty for protecting cities and holding at bay the cruel mischief makers of Olympus.

Hymn to Hestia

Flawed by the loss of a line, the twenty-ninth paean begs the aid of the goddess of the hearth and Hermes, the herald god. Distinctive to Hestia worship are the prologue and epilogue to banqueting, which begins and ends with a libation to the goddess of domesticity.

Hymn to Earth, Mother of All

The thirtieth hymn calls on the Earth Mother for sustenance from nature. The poet exults:

I will sing of well-founded Earth, mother of all, eldest of all
  beings.
She feeds all creatures that are in the world,
  all that go upon the goodly land,
  and all that are in the paths of the seas,
  and all that fly: all these are fed of her store.
Through you, O queen, men are blessed in their children
  and blessed in their harvests [Eliade 1967, 55].

The second half of this short paean lauds the worshiper of the Earth Mother, who harvests ample corn and fills his storehouse with good things. The poet links the devout with orderly rule, the love of fair women, wealth, strong offspring, and "bountiful spirit." To the writer, such praise "cheers the heart."

Hymn to Helios

The thirty-first song, also weakened by a missing line, exults in the sun god's daily chariot ride across the heavens, from which he sheds brightness and heat on the earth below. The poet connects the piercing glance of Helios with "delightful sustenance" and offers perpetual celebration (Shelmerdine 1995, 164).

Hymn to Selene

To the moon goddess, hymn thirty-two salutes her beauty and subdued light. In a graceful image of moonrise, the poet declares, "The air, unlit before, glistens with light from her golden crown, and her beams linger in the air" (Shelmerdine 1995, 164). The poem welcomes the cyclical nature of the moon's phases, which become a celestial sign on earth.

Hymn to the Dioskouroi

To Kastor and Polydeukes, the Dioskouroi, the thirty-third hymn offers praise for assistance to sailors during sea storms. The poet describes the ritual of propitiation: "The men on the ships call on the sons of great Zeus offering prayers with white lambs, as they mount the topmost points of the stern" (Shelmerdine 1995, 166).

Hymn to Guest-Friends

The final poem, an epigram that lies outside the realm of liturgy, lauds friendship, the relationship most praised by the Greeks. The obligations of guest and host were mutually binding: hosts welcomed strangers and visitors to share home, hearth, entertainment, and the protection of the villa; guests were equally obliged to take part in native fare, respect home and family, and maintain equanimity regardless of differences of political or personal opinion.

SOURCES: Brown 1947, Durant 1939, Eliade 1967, Feder 1986, Flaceliere 1962, Graves 1968, Hadas 1954, Hathorn 1966, Highet 1949, "Homeric Hymns," Hopper 1977, Howatson 1991, Kitto 1951, Lesky 1996, Meyer 1987, Morford and Lenardon 1977, Norton and Rushton 1952, Radice 1973, Shelmerdine 1995, Slater 1968, Snodgrass 1994, Starr 1991.

I Ching Over twenty-one centuries, the I Ching (also Yi Ching, Yee King, or Yi Jing; Classic of Changes or Book

The ruler is modest and therefore open to the counsel of able men. Thus he is surrounded by men who suggest to him the lines of action. This brings blessing, fame, and good fortune to him and all the people.

Six at the top means:
His house is in a state of abundance.
He screens off his family.
He peers through the gate
And no longer perceives anyone.
For three years he sees nothing.
Misfortune.

This describes a man who because of his arrogance and obstinacy attains the opposite of what he strives for. He seeks abundance and splendor for his dwelling. He wishes at all odds to be master in his house, which so alienates his family that in the end he finds himself completely isolated.

旅

56. Lü / The Wanderer

≡≡ *above* LI   THE CLINGING, FIRE
≡≡ *below* KÊN   KEEPING STILL, MOUNTAIN

The mountain, Kên, stands still; above it fire, Li, flames up and does not tarry. Therefore the two trigrams do not stay together. Strange lands and separation are the wanderer's lot.

THE JUDGMENT

THE WANDERER. Success through smallness.
Perseverance brings good fortune
To the wanderer.

When a man is a wanderer and stranger, he should not be gruff nor overbearing. He has no large circle of acquaintances, therefore he should not give himself airs. He must be cautious and reserved; in this way he protects himself from evil. If he is obliging toward others, he wins success.

A wanderer has no fixed abode; his home is the road. Therefore he must take care to remain upright and steadfast, so that he sojourns only in the proper places, associating only with good people. Then he has good fortune and can go his way unmolested.

THE IMAGE

Fire on the mountain:
The image of THE WANDERI R.
Thus the superior man
Is clear-minded and cautious
In imposing penalties,
And protracts no lawsuits.

When grass on a mountain takes fire, there is bright light. However, the fire does not linger in one place, but travels on to new fuel. It is a phenomenon of short duration. This is what penalties and lawsuits should be like. They should be a quickly passing matter, and must not be dragged out indefinitely. Prisons ought to be places where people are lodged only temporarily, as guests are. They must not become dwelling places.

THE LINES

Six at the beginning means:
If the wanderer busies himself with trivial things,
He draws down misfortune upon himself.

A wanderer should not demean himself or busy himself with inferior things he meets with along the way. The humbler and more defenseless his outward position, the more should he preserve his inner dignity. For a stranger is mistaken if he hopes to find a friendly reception through lending himself to jokes and buffoonery. The result will be only contempt and insulting treatment.

From the *I Ching*.

of Changes) has served the Chinese as sacred scripture, manual of metaphysics, and venerable book of counsel drawn from symbolic permutations. It is a source of strength and serenity in difficult times, but a study of its genius is no assurance of material success. Readers find in its disjointed correspondences to positions in the family, parts of the body, members of the animal kingdom, trees, colors, and minerals a hidden pattern of the universe — the hours, seasons, phases of human life, and celestial movements. An understanding of the workings of Shang Ti (God) allegedly offers a path to a pure, blameless life based on harmony with the environment rather than extrinsic reward.

The entire system got its beginning around 2800 B.C.E. in the musings of the first of the Five Sage Rulers, the semi-mythic emperor Fu Hsi, a nature-centered leader who was sensitive to patterns in sky and earth. He bears credit for domesticating animals, instituting marriage and sacrifice as worship, inventing trapping, writing the first symbols, and knitting patterns with string to make hunting nets and fishing seines.

The I Ching grew from his knowledge of yin and yang, the eternal opposites symbolized in two related symbols:

———— *Yang-Hsiao*, an unbroken line for yang or male
— —— *Yin-Hsiao*, a broken line for yin, the female

He observed these emblems in eight *pa kua* (trigrams), trios of three broken and unbroken lines, on a tortoise shell on the banks of the Hwang Ho River. From this God-given message, he formulated his octet of symbols to classify mental and spiritual operations and natural phenomena. Application of these oracles resembles interpretations of the signs of the zodiac:

Trigram	Name	Correspondence	Interpretation
———	Ch'ien (heaven)	sky, cold, horse, head, father, northwest, jade, metal, God's struggles, a time for action	lively, strong, firm, light, proper, creative, open, bright, active, advantageous, beneficent, untiring effort, the opposite of K'un
——	Tui (lake)	marsh, mist, rain, autumn, sheep, mouth, youngest daughter, west, sorceress, harvesting fruit, soil, salt, God's rejoicing, a time for rest and relaxation	joyful, pleasant, attractive, happy, blissful, elated, satisfying
——	Li (fire)	fire, lightning, summer, sun, pheasant, eye, second daughter, south, turtle, crab, mussel, God's processes, a time for human gatherings	bright, beautiful, clinging, intelligent, adhering, elegant, illuminated, tenacious, dry, dependent, catching
——	Chên (thunder)	thunder, spring, dragon, feet, eldest son, east, azure, highway, sedge, rushes, resurrection, God coming forth, a time for alteration and revolution	lively, moving, initiating, exciting, motivating, decisive, vehement, luxuriant, inspired, arousing
——	Sun (wind)	wood, fowl, thigh, eldest daughter, southeast, wind, plumb line, T-square, hair, white of the eye, God bringing processes to the full, a time of persuasion	gentle, penetrating, following, long, white, strong-scented, vacillating, pursuing gain, deciding, productive, pure, equality, yielding, flexible, advancing and receding
——	K'an (water)	cloud, pit, moon, winter, the deep, pig, ears, second son, north, channel, bow, wheel, God	enveloping, perilous, abysmal, increasingly active, distressful, lying in wait,

Trigram	Name	Correspondence	Interpretation
		comfortably resting, a time of venture and progress	alternately straight and crooked, deep, draining, hidden, precipitous
———	Kên (mountain)	thunder, dog, rat, hands, youngest son, northeast, path, small rock, gate, fruit and creeping plant, porter, ring finger, rat, God completing a year's work, a time for meditation and introspection	impassive, halting, immovable, resting, arresting, massive, quiet, perverse, still
——	K'un (earth)	heat, ox, belly, mother, southwest, earth, cloth, cauldron, lathe, heifer, wagon, multitude, handle or support, black soil, service to God, a time to withdraw and renew the self	receptive, responsive, weak, yielding, docile, parsimonious, devoted, variegated, dark, shaded, inactive, the opposite of Ch'ien

Fu Hsi's successor, Shen Nung, the second of the Five Sage Rulers, profited from the patterns. He organized weekly market days, devised the plow from bent wood, and taught farmers professional methods of managing the land and selling their produce. The next three emperors—Huang Ti, Yao, and Shun, the last three wise kings—initiated comfortable garments, oar-driven canoes, yoked beasts of burden, chariots, walled cities, security systems, mortars and pestles, bows and arrows, projecting eaves, coffin burial, and written characters. These transformations illustrate the good that Fu Hsi's pattern manipulations brought to China.

Composed around 1150 B.C.E. in a prison cell in Lu-li, the first written version of I Ching was the *T'uan* (Judgment or Decision), the work of Wen Wang (also Hsi Po or Xi Bo; King of the West), founder of the semi-barbaric Chou dynasty and resident magus. Writing from right to left, he gave the patterns their configurations and numbers. His son, the duke of Chou, expanded his father's notes into *Chou I* (Changes of Chou; ca. 1110 B.C.E.) or the *Yao*, which analyzes mystic lines and spaces. The text is a deliberately enigmatic handbook of magic based on shifts of yin and yang through geometric patterns, matrices, combinations of musical tones, and/or numbering schemes used for divination and wizardry. Around 480 B.C.E. , Confucius added *T'uan Chuan* (Commentary on the Decision), a supplement and dialogue on ethics, and may have composed the *Hsiang Chuan* (Commentary on the Images).

An abstruse element of Chinese Confucianism, the I Ching is the first of the Wu Ching (or Five Classics; 136 B.C.E.), China's long-lived textbook. Isolated statements from the I Ching tease and perplex, as with these examples:

> Guests come unurged to give their help, and if the subject of the line receive them respectfully, there will be good fortune in the end.
> Though there is sincerity in one's contention, he will yet meet with opposition and obstruction.
> A one-eyed man who thinks that he can see … a mere bravo acting the part of a great ruler [Waltham 1969, 129, 131, 143].

By applying the basic meaning of each trio and the interpretation of yin and yang, the opposing principles of light and dark, male and female mentioned in an appendix, the *Hsi tz'u* (Appended Explanations; ca. fourth century B.C.E.), the interpreter explains the interactions and changes of elements of nature:

One *Yin* and one *Yang* constitute what is called *Tao*.
That which is perpetuated by it is good.
That which is completed by it is the nature [of things]…
How prolific is its *Te* [power] and how great its achievement!
    [Legge 1964, xli].

The inclusion of the I Ching among books of history, philosophy, and morality violates Confucius's beliefs, which denigrated superstition, and thus appears to be the choice of his interpreters, perhaps in the third century B.C.E. Subsequent interpretation has produced wide variances and much disagreement about accuracy.

Unlike other compendia of witchcraft and necromancy, the I Ching is the only book of magic that has spawned scholarly interest. Psychologist Karl Jung surmised that the manipulation of symbols communicated with primordial susceptibilities in the unconscious mind. Vendors of the occult still display octagonal cards that order the eight trigrams clockwise (1, 7, 6, 4, 8, 2, 3, and 5) as a protection from harm. The mathematical principle of unity on these amulets is the recurrence of the number 9 by the addition of opposite hexagrams, e.g., 1 + 8, 7 + 2, 6 + 3, and 4 + 5. Soothsayers in China, Indochina, Japan, Korea, and the West still value the I Ching as a manual of fortune telling. In the mid-1600s, Japan's Confucian militarist Yamaga Soko educated the Samurai class into an awesome force with strategies he acquired from applying the I Ching to combat.

The work unites nature and humankind into a single cosmology that values chance above reason. Unique to its doctrine are sixty-four chapters, each representing a different hexagram. These sixty-four hexagrams can be manipulated to apply to human events, past, present, and future. To form these six-sided symbols, the student of the I Ching casts lots to pair vertically two of eight trigrams. According to the *Shuo Kua* (Discussion of the Trigrams), which antedates Wen Wang, the trigrams are a conduit of instruction from God.

To give a reading, augurers toss yarrow stalks to generate naturally occurring hexagrams that predict the future. The resulting shapes form pairs that are identified by a number limited to the square of eight or sixty-four.

	Ch'ien	Chên	K'an	Kên	K'un	Sun	Li	Tui
Ch'ien	1	34	5	26	11	9	14	43
Chên	25	51	3	27	24	42	21	17
K'an	6	40	29	4	7	59	64	47
Kên	33	62	39	52	15	53	56	31
K'un	12	16	8	23	2	20	35	45
Sun	44	32	48	18	46	57	50	28
Li	13	55	63	22	36	37	30	49
Tui	10	54	60	41	19	61	38	58

To identify the resulting hexagram, locate the first trigram by name on the top line and the second vertically at left. The number of the pair appears at the convergence of the perpendicular. For example, K'un on the top line paired with Tui on the left column produces hexagram 19.

In addition to numbers, the hexagrams used in divination have names and semi-transcendental interpretations that apply with mathematical precision to human life and destiny:

Number	Combination	Name	Interpretation for the Wise Individual
1.	Ch'ien + Ch'ien	Ch'ien (Heaven or Firmness)	develops power and endurance; connects the beginning and end in one endless revolution
2.	K'un + K'un	K'un (Earth or Submission)	sustains the world through subordination and produces unlimited goodness from the earth
3.	K'an + Chen	Chun (Initial Obstacles or Bursting)	establishes order; demonstrates the struggle of the disordered state to right itself
4.	Ken + K'an	Meng (Inexperienced Youth, Education, or Obscurity)	improves the self by being thorough; illustrates the undeveloped stripling

Number	Combination	Name	Interpretation for the Wise Individual
			and the promise contained in ignorance and inexperience
5.	K'an + Ch'ien	Hsu (Waiting or Anticipation)	eats well and is happy and optimistic; encourages the enjoyment of uneventful periods
6.	Ch'ien + K'an	Sung (Conflict or Contention)	assesses the beginning of a venture; encourages the wise to remain alert and to avoid danger
7.	K'un + K'an	Shih (Military Hosts or a Multitude)	sways people with consideration; advocates nourishing the state to assure a strong army
8.	K'an + K'un	Pi (Merging or Collaboration)	wins friends among the nobility; illustrates the value of benevolence
9.	Sun + Ch'ien	Hsiao Ch'u (Limiting by the Weak or Taming Force)	influences uncontrollable events; foresee vigor, progress, and success
10.	Ch'ien + Tui	Lu (Treading or Deliberate Action)	has a sense of place; urges duty and propriety as a means of preserving order
11.	K'un + Ch'ien	T'ai (Peace or Success)	controls the universe by division; symbolizes beginnings and ends as the natural state of life
12.	Ch'ien + K'un	P'i (Decadence or Failure)	retreats from promotions to avoid strife; teaches that decay is the antithesis of growth and progress
13.	Ch'ien + Li	T'ung Jen (Human Association or Community)	orders varying parts by diversity; illustrates how freedom from selfishness promotes unity
14.	Li + Ch'ien	Ta Yu	follows the way

Number	Combination	Name	Interpretation for the Wise Individual
		(Profuse Wealth or Abundance)	of goodness; celebrates greatness, progress, abundance, and success
15.	K'un + Kên	Ch'ien (Humility)	balances more with less; teaches that humility is the root of lasting greatness
16.	Chên + K'un	Yu (Enthusiasm)	propitiates gods and ancestors; lauds obedience and service to God
17.	Tui + Chen	Sui (Adjusting, Succession, or Contentment)	sleeps to restore the body; learns to suit action to the times and demands
18.	Kên + Sun	Ku (Removing Decay or Major Power)	inspires others; welcomes a natural process that restores and cleanses
19.	K'un + Tui	Lin (Drawing Near or Advancement)	educates and cares for others; applies authority by inspecting, comforting, and guiding
20.	Sun + K'un	Kuan (Contemplation)	observes and enlightens others; manifests authority by example
21.	Li + Chên	Shih Ho (Severing or Criminal Proceedings)	makes just laws; removes obstacles to unity
22.	Kên + Li	Pi (Elegance or a Model)	is delicate in minor matters; welcomes an opportunity to adorn and observe ritual
23.	Kên + K'un	Po (Overthrow or Dispersal)	maintains status through charity; acknowledges evil in the world
24.	K'un + Chên	Fu (Returning or Reversal)	halts for the winter solstice; acknowledges recovery and a return of goodness
25.	Ch'ien + Chên	Wu Wang (Innocence or Sincerity)	blesses humankind; recognizes honesty and correctness as essentials to power

Number	Combination	Name	Interpretation for the Wise Individual
26.	Kên + Ch'ien	Ta Ch'u (Accumulation or Taming Force)	learns from history; restrains the self and acquires virtue
27.	Kên + Chen	I (Sustenance or Nourishment)	is moderate in speech, food, and drink; prefers nourishment that is correct and harmonious
28.	Tui + Sun	Ta Kuo (Greatness, Difficulty, or Preponderance)	remains strong and avoids fear; chooses extraordinary means for unusual demands
29.	K'an + K'an	K'an (Pit, Sinking, or Danger)	is upright and unwavering; values faith, righteousness, and loyalty as defenses
30.	Li + Li	Lien (Sunlight, Adherence, Emptiness)	lightens the world; welcomes the chance to enhance brightness
31.	Tui + Kên	Hsien (Persuasion or Influence)	humbly accepts advice; advocates mutual influence as a wise practice
32.	Chên + Sun	Heng (Continuity or Perseverance)	is strong and flexible; embraces new methods and perseverance
33.	Ch'ien + Kên	Tun (Retiring or Regression)	avoids fools; seeks seclusion to sustain the inner self
34.	Chen + Ch'ien	Ta Chuang (Abundant Strength or Major Power)	avoids conflicts with the right path; subordinates right to harmony
35.	Li + K'un	Chin (Advancement or Progress)	illumines the self to teach others; uses force cautiously and wisely
36.	K'un + Li	Ming I (Repressed Intellect or Lack of Appreciation)	walks humbly with humankind; resists pomposity
37.	Sun + Li	Chia Jen (Family or Household)	is resolute and well-spoken; regulates the household
38.	Li + Tui	K'uei (Alienation or Opposition)	does not violate the true self; heals divisions, no matter how small
39.	K'an + Kên	Chien (Barrier, Obstacle, or Difficulty)	looks inward to perfect the self; advances with prudent caution
40.	Chên + K'an	Hsieh (or Chieh) (Liberation or Deliverance)	forgives and forgets; relieves by loosening bonds
41.	Kên + Tui	Sun (Reduction or Diminution)	controls passion and impulse; regulates expenditures to control debt
42.	Sun + Chên	I (Expansion, Addition, or Advantage)	corrects faults by emulating the good; shares benefits with all
43.	Tui + Ch'ien	Kuai (Outburst or Resolution)	keeps an open mind and is generous; removes obstacles
44.	Ch'ien + Sun	Kou (Confrontation or Session)	scatters commands abroad; meets with a variety of people
45.	Tui + K'un	Ts'ui (Congregating or a Collection)	protects against ambush; gathers with others to promote strength
46.	K'un + Sun	Sheng (Advancing or Surging Upward)	grows steadily; applies flexibility and obedience to advancement
47.	Tui + K'an	K'un (Restriction or Repression)	remains true to self; grows within self-ordained limits
48.	K'an + Sun	Ching (Cistern, Well, or Source)	maintains harmony; recognizes the unchanging source of nourishment
49.	Tui + Li	Ko (Overthrowing or Change)	organizes time; regulates change slowly and prudently
50.	Li + Sun	Ting (Cauldron, Cook Pot, or Feeding)	establishes a firm foundation; progresses through nourishment
51.	Chên + Chên	Chên (Advance-	harmonizes the self through

Number	Combination	Name	Interpretation for the Wise Individual
		ment or Arousing Power)	introspection; harnesses power
52.	Kên + Kên	Kên (Repose or Stability)	lives in the present; refuses to be distracted from principle
53.	Sun + Kên	Chien (Maturing or Gradually Progressing)	sets a mature example; maintains a sensible rate of advance
54.	Chên + Tui	Kuei Mei (Returning Home or Marriage)	separates the transient from the lasting; recognizes and avoids imprudence
55.	Chên + Li	Feng (Affluence or Prosperity)	avoids grief; applies intellect and motivation to development
56.	Li + Kên	Lu (Wayfarer or Wandering)	judges swiftly and wisely; is wary of the spread of evil
57.	Sun + Sun	Sun (Yielding or (Penetrating)	finishes projects; yields to the inevitable
58.	Tui + Tui	Tui (Pleasure or Satisfaction)	converses pleasantly; forgets fears of death
59.	Sun + K'an	Huan (Dispersing or Dissolution)	worships and gives back to God; remedies alienation
60.	K'an + Tui	Chieh (Law, Regulation, or Limitation)	studies the right path; promotes a strong framework of regulation and restraint
61.	Sun + Tui	Chung Fu (Truth of the Mean or Central Sincerity)	learns from criminals; establishes an inner sincerity
62.	Chen + Ken	Hsiao Kuo (Small Excesses or a Minor Preponderance)	is devout, sincere, and thrifty; advances humbly through small steps
63.	K'an + Li	Chi Chi (Accomplishment, Completion, or Consummation)	prepares to meet danger; does not overlook small details
64.	Li + K'an	Wei Chi (State of Transition or Anticipation of Completion)	keeps everything in its place; sustains the self through order

The enigmatic nature of the master's commentary has provoked centuries of comment and debate. Like the ramblings of the Pythia at the Delphic oracle of ancient Greece, these hexagrams generate cryptic phrases that tease the mind into widely variant readings. For example, Confucius says of the twelfth hexagram:

We see him who brings the distress and obstruction to a
    close,
    the great man and fortunate.
But let him say "We may perish! We may perish!"
So shall the state of things become firm,
    as if bound to a clump of bushy mulberry trees [Waltham 1969, 65].

The skillful interpreter of such readings requires years of study and trial and error to understand even the rudiments of its wisdom.

The I Ching is the source of an important world view that modern Chinese continue to read with understanding and reverence. The central doctrine, T'ai Chi (Great Ultimate or Absolute), the Chinese prime mover and fount of all, is the source of yin and yang, the opposing principles of passive and active, negative and positive, dark and light, receptive and creative, female and male. In art, the T'ai Chi, or yin-yang diagram, is one of the world's oldest patterns. As drawn by philosopher Chu Hsi (or Chicius) in the twelfth century, the mated pair of opposites, like nested tadpoles, are colored black and white with dots of the opposite colors in each, suggesting the seeds of duality. The pantomimed version of T'ai Chi is a stylized or ceremonial martial art, a series of continually moving gestures and stances that relieve tension and induce harmony to body and mind. Unlike Western directional concepts of north, south, east, and west, the Chinese add a fifth dimension, the center, the anchor that holds the individual to earth beneath an axis extending into heaven.

In the tenth century, the era that produced block printing, thinkers of the Sung dynasty applied T'ai Chi to *li* (the principle of social order), a focus of the Second Discourse in Confucius's Analects. They evolved a theory of earth science that *li* generates *ch'i* (matter), which yin and yang transform into the five elements, the building blocks of the universe. An eleventh-century Taoist philosopher, mystic, and mathematician, Shao Yung (also Shao K'ang-Chieh or Shao Yao-Fu), from Kung-ch'eng, China, influenced neo-Confucianism through his theories based on the I Ching. By applying numerology to natural elements, he generated a complex scientific theory of fours—the celestial elements (sun, moon, stars, constellations), the directions (north, south, east, west), the sense organs (eye, ear, nose, mouth), and the elements (fire, water, earth, stone). This natural unity substantiated the *yüan*, which Buddhists referred to as *kalpas* (recurring cycles).

The I Ching has provoked numerous commentaries. China's first book of alchemy, the *Chou-i ts'an t'ung ch'i* (Commentary on the I Ching), relates chemical manipulation of metals to the mystic math. At the beginning of the Han dynasty's cultural renaissance in the second century B.C.E., scholars replaced books that had been destroyed during the Great Interdiction, a mass book burning engineered by Shih Huang Ti of the Ch'in dynasty in 213 B.C.E. The revered "I," the familiar name for the I Ching, survived this radical event, as is noted in historian Pan Ku's *Ch'ien Han Shu* (History of the Former Han Dynasty; ca. C.E. 90): "During the Ch'in interdiction of learning, the *I*, being a book of divination, was the only work which had not been forbidden, and therefore its transmission was not interrupted" (Legge 1964, xxxiii). Emperor Wu Ti's prime minister, Tung Chung-Shu, compiler of the Wu Ching, issued an original work, *Ch'un-ch'iu fan-lu* (Luxuriant Gems of the Spring and Autumn Annals), a metaphysical handbook reflecting the influence of the I Ching. Withdrawn to his studio for three years, he analyzed the five elements — metal, wood, water, fire, and earth — and coordinated human elements with celestial numbers. He theorized the existence of sympathies between like things within a naturalistic cosmology. Combined with Confucian ethics, his scheme allowed Confucians to quantify the behaviors of their leaders.

In the same vein, Chou Tun-i (or Chou Lien-Hsi), philosopher and government minister from Ying-tao, China, reformulated and enlarged on the I Ching around 1070 in two metaphysical treatises — *T'ai-chi-t'u shuo* (Explanation of the Diagram of the Great Ultimate), a theory of relativity that bases all life on the Great Ultimate, and the *T'ung-shuo* (Explanatory Text), a resetting of Confucian moralism. His elevation of the I Ching influenced Confucian disciple Chu Hsi, the twelfth-century theologian and educator who wrote *Lessons on the I for the Young* (ca. 1177). He reconstituted tradition by reinterpreting scripture and recasting its tenets into neo–Confucianism. The I Ching flourished into the eighteenth century under Emperor K'ang Hsi of the Ch'ing dynasty, who commissioned extensive editing, compilation of scholarly citations from 200 B.C.E. to C.E. 1700, and issuance of an imperial K'ang Hsi version in 1715.

SOURCES: Albertson 1969, Ballou 1944, Berry 1956, Bouquet 1954, Cavendish 1970, Confucius 1992, *Eerdmans' Handbook to the World's Religions* 1982, Eliade 1967, Fingarette, Frost 1972, Hastings 1951, Hinnels 1984, Kang 1999, Legge 1964, *New Catholic Encyclopedia* 1967, Pelikan 1992, Schwartz 1985, Sharma 1987, Smith 1958, 1995, Snodgrass 1995, 2001, Waley 1986, Waltham 1969, 1989, *World Religions* 1998, Yutang 1938.

Juju Shinron *see* Tantra

Kabbala

A mystic sourcebook, Kabbala — also spelled Cabala, Cabbala, Cabbalah, Kabala, Kabbalah, and Kabballa — derives from the Hebrew *qabbalah* (acceptance or tradition) and delineates a pervasive inner stirring in Jews seeking more warmth and reassurance from their faith than mere two-dimensional rules to live by. Thus, Kabbalistic doctrine reflects an obscure and controversial branch of Judaism deviating from the formal, legalistic interpretation of scripture to inner longings and human suppositions about the nature and purpose of the unknowable divine, which Kabbalists call *en sof* (or *soph*; the infinite). The premise grew out of a simplistic if-then proposition: If humankind takes the shape and form of the Creator, then, by analogy, human beings can know the shape and form of God, the very essence of the divine.

Like astrology and the zodiac, Kabbala asks a web of humanistic questions:

- What is the nature of God? Is God male or female or a blend of both?
- Why is there evil and suffering? Are there spirits devoted solely to evil?
- What is the purpose of humanity?
- What complex, symbolic truths lie unexplored in the Torah?
- What value lies in dreams, visions, and revelations?
- Who and what are angels? How do they relate to humankind?
- What happens to mortals after death?
- Who is the messiah? Where and when will the savior appear?
- How will the messiah end evil?

Kabbala speculates on a direct, face-to-face experience with God, a hazardous undertaking in a supernatural realm consisting of seven palaces, each guarded by seven gates. It bases its probing into the secrets of the universe on the style and method of the apocalyptic books of Ezekiel and Daniel.

As a complement to rabbinic tradition rather than as a competitor, Kabbala imposes order on the ineffable mysteries, for example, by dividing the universe into four identifiable layers:

- *Asilus* (or *Asiluth*; Noblest or Most Sublime) at the top, the sublime realm of *sefirot* (sacred numbers)
- *Ber'iah* (Creating), God's throne in the subdivine sphere
- the angels in *Yesirah* (Forming), the realm of heavenly spheres
- humanity and the material world in *Asiyah* (Making), the sublunar universe and least stable region

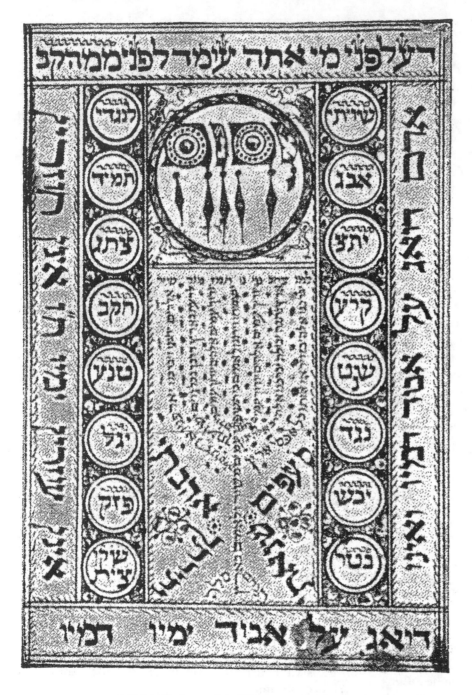

A Kabbalistic amulet of the seventeenth century.

peacemaker. In C.E. 905, he departed from his African *yeshiva* (school) to seek more learning and migrated from Palestine to Syria and Babylon. He served Babylon's Jewish community and as exilarch and principal at the school at Sura. His wide knowledge and publication preserved and strengthened Judaism. In particular, he composed commentary on mysticism, thus legitimizing a tradition that had lacked a scholarly champion. A formalized Kabbala appeared in print in the twelfth century, supplanting the *Sefer Yesira* (or *Yetsirah*; Book of Creation; C.E. 500s), the oldest Kabbalist writing. The updated text departed from simple number and letter combinations by introducing philosophies and practice along with warnings about the human misapplication of mystical experience, which draws on unwritten messages that God passed to Adam and Moses.

The era of unwritten Kabbala is known as *Merkava* (also *Merkabah*; chariot) mysticism, a reference to the vision of the prophet Ezekiel, who saw God seated on a flying throne surrounded by strange winged creatures. The apocalyptic passage so intrigued Palestinian mystics around the first century C.E. that they created a unique branch of speculation open to those who kept each commandment and freed the self from idolatry, sexual impurity, violence, slander and swearing, pride, and hatred. These early sky pilots named themselves the *Yorde ha-Merkavah* (Descenders to the Chariot). Their probings flourished into the seventh century, when the center of Merkavism resituated in Babylon and remained there for 400 years.

These and other categories serve as channels of the imagination and as terminology to enable philosophers and scholars to discuss divine mystery.

A product of oral folklore dating to the time of the birth of Christ, Jewish mysticism began in Egypt and Babylon. The conduit of Eastern lore to European Jewry was Aaron ben Samuel, a semi-legendary miracle worker who carried abstruse Babylonian speculation to Italy. The originator of mystic scholarship was a strict adherent to monotheism, Saadiah ben-Joseph (also Sa'adya or Sa'id ibn Yusuf Al-Fayyumi), a tenth-century scholar and

The Merkavans, under the influence of gnostic intellectuals, told of ecstatic dream states in which God revealed his throne or chariot encircled by ranks of angels. In the modern parlance of Kabbalist Gershom Gerhard Scholem, the excursion into the divine paralleled hypnotic states that turned the eye inward to the unrevealed self. Initiates readied themselves for the sublime face of the Almighty by fasting. To reach heaven, the seekers or riders of Merkava, aided by prayers, penitence, and asceticism, advanced through seven levels guarded by hosts of angels to union with perfection. Some practitioners used amulets or charms, such as parchment or metal strips inscribed with the hexagrammatic shield of David, the palm side of an open hand, or a circle.

Because Kabbalists depended on the word rather than signs, the only mutually accepted way to gain passage to heaven was the application of seals, magical incantations. A misstatement of the formula could call down a fiery retribution, madness, or death on the unwary. One early text, *Ma'aseh Merkavah*, collects the hymns that mystics composed, chanted, or heard on these magical ascensions to the presence of the Almighty.

According to the Talmud, only Rabbi Akiba (or Akiva) ben Joseph of Jerusalem, second-century C.E. systematizer of the law and martyr to Roman oppression, completed the appropriate spells and saw God. His experience is the subject of *Hékhalot Zutarté* (The Smaller Book of Celestial Palaces), one of the five major treatises of Jewish mysticism. An early history of the Kabbalists and Kabbalism is recorded in Akiba's writings and those of his contemporary, tannist Ishmael ben Elisha, and in two apocryphal texts, *Sefer Hékhalot* (The Hebrew Book of Enoch) and the *Shi'ur Qoma* (or *Komah* [Divine Dimensions]), which details an eyewitness glimpse of God. Ishmael's ascension to the divine is the focus of *Hékhalot Rabbati* (The Greater Book of Celestial Palaces), a source of information on ten legendary martyrs.

One handbook on cosmology and white magic, *Sefer Yetzira* (or *Yetzira* [Book of Creation]) written over a three-century period from C.E. 200 to 500, was erroneously called the *Otiyyot de Avraham Avinu* (Alphabet of Our Father Abraham). The book links creation with God's ten *sefirot* (or *sephirot* [sacred numbers or spheres]) and the twenty-two-letter Hebrew alphabet, which are the paths connecting the magic numbers and the routes by which Kabbalists travel. The sefirot fall into three levels of ten crowns worn by God or ten doors through which the truly devout, created in God's image, can understand sacred mystery:

- three mental manifestations of divine power, usually depicted as an isosceles triangle
  1. *Keter* (or *Kether*; Striving or Crown; also *Ayin* [Nothing] or *Keter Elyon* [Supreme Crown]) is the all-knowing God, the infinite and endless source of all. In the triangle, *Keter* is the apex.
  2. From *Keter* grows *Hokhmah* (Wisdom), a higher stage of hidden knowledge, which Kabbalists familiarized as *Reshith* (The Beginning) and Father Wisdom.
  3. *Binah* (Understanding or Intelligence) is the upper or heavenly portion of God's presence, also familiarized as Mother Intelligence. *Hokhmah* and *Binah* form the two base angles of the triangle.

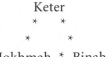

- a trio of moral virtues based on the duality of God, which form a second isosceles triangle
  4. *Hesed* (or *Gedullah*; Kindness or Grace) is the positive, merciful, or beneficent element of God.
  5. *Gevurah* (also *Gebhurah*; Energy; or *Din*; Self-discipline, Strength, or Judgment) is the godly power that punishes wrongdoing. *Hesed* and *Gevurah* form the base angles of the inverted triangle.
  6. *Tiferet* (also *Tifereth* or *Tiph'eret*; Beauty; or *Rahamin*; Mercy or Compassion) reconciles God's wrath with his beneficence. The apex of the inverted triangle, *Tiferet* stands below the other two points in glory at the hub of the tree of life.

- when power and virtue function harmoniously, they produce a third trio of natural elements, also depicted as an isosceles triangle
  7. *Nezah* (also *Netsah* or *Nesah*; Victory or Endurance) is the parent of Foundation, the eternal endurance of God.
  8. *Hod* (Splendor or Beauty) is the divine majesty, a product of Father Mercy and Mother Justice. *Nezah* and *Hod* are the base angles of the inverted triangle.
  9. *Yesod Olam* or *Saddiq* (also *Zaddik*; Foundation or Nature) is the ultimate source of all God's activities, in particular, life on earth. The inverted triangle climaxes in *Yesod*, the apex.

```
Nezah * Hod
  *        *

  *      *
    Yesod
```

- Standing alone, the tenth element, *Malkhut* (or *Malkhuth*; God's Rule or Kingdom), also called Israel, the bride of God, or *Shekhinah* (Divine Presence), sustains and assures the continuation of creation, in which the blessed glimpse God himself. This tenth sefirot is a two-way channel by which creation flows down to earth and by which humankind ascends to heaven. In erotic terms, *Malkhut*, a womb figure, becomes the bride and queen of *Tiferet*, the potent source and harmonizer

186

of power. This holy union, like the Chinese concept of yin-yang, is the unified divine. Disunity of the pair would produce calamity of universal proportions.

The completed arrangement yields a geometric view of the sefirot hierarchy:

Keter

*   *

*   *

Hokhmah * Binah

Hesed * Gevurah

*   *

*   *

Tiferet

Nezah * Hod

*   *

*   *

Yesod

Malkhut

The three to the left — Hokhmah, Hesed, and Nezah — are male entities; the three opposite — Binah, Gevurah, and Hod — are female. The four at center — Keter, Tiferet, Yesod, and Malkhut — are the balancing, unifying agents that sustain the tree of life.

The total of thirty-two symbols opened routes to the secret knowledge of how God made the universe through godly raw material, an externalization of divinity. The text classifies the first four magic numbers with the elements of air, water, fire, and holy spirit, producer of darkness, light, and wisdom. The last six magic numbers constitute directions — north, south, east, west, up, down. Another correspondence influencing human affairs was the application of the thirty-two ciphers to parts of the body, much as astrologers correlated them to the signs of the zodiac for the purposes of diagnosis, healing, and divination.

In the Middle Ages, German Hasidics associated magic formulas with the golem, a mythic monster created by magic incantation. The golem was a soulless body or zombie molded from clay just as God made Adam from the dust of the earth. In the Prague tradition, the golem is a harmless robot who populates stories from Germany, Austria, and Czechoslovakia and influences drama, film, opera, ballet, and symphonic music, notably Joseph Achron's orchestral *Golem Suite* (1932) and Francis Burt's ballet *Der Golem* (1962).

The second great era of Kabbalism occurred during the twelfth century in two parts of Europe — Ashkenazic Hasidism along the Rhine and the Kabbala school in southwestern Europe, around the Pyrenees and into Iberia. The Germanic branch of Jewry owes its nurturance to Worms and Speyer, specifically to Rabbi Samuel ben Kalonymus he-Hasid (the Pious) and his son, Judah ben-Samuel he-Hasid, a gifted writer who chose to issue anonymous works, including the *Sefer ha-Kavod* (Book of Glory), now lost, and *Sefer Hasidim* (Book of the Pious). The Book of Glory illustrates the lyric beauty of Kabbala:

I have not seen thee, yet I tell thy praise,
  nor known thee, yet I image forth thy ways,
  for by thy seers' and servants' mystic speech
  thou didst thy sov'ran splendour darkly teach.
And from the grandeur of thy work they drew
  the measure of thy inner greatness, too.
They told of thee, but not as thou must be,
  since from thy work they tried to body thee [Hastings 1951, 7:624].

In contemplation of sublimity, Judah honored the Creator for inventing out of divine matter ten categories of worldly material governed by seven types of quantity, six kinds of motion, three methods of prediction, three forms of time, and three dimensions, none of which existed before the formation of earth.

From Judah's seminary at Regensburg came a distinguished pupil, the ethicist and scientist Eleazar ben Judah (or Eleazar Roke'ah) of Worms, survivor of persecution during the Third Crusade, which cost him his wife, daughters, and son. His *Sodé Razayya* (Secrets of Secrets) compiles mystic tradition among pious Jewish Rhinelanders in multiple divisions: *Sod Ma'aseh Bereshit* (Secret of Genesis), *Sefer ha-Shem* (Book of the Holy Name), and *Hokhmat ha-Nefesh* (Psychology). He based his depiction of the true mystic on the attainment of saintliness, which is the only method of seeing God. For miracles, he applied mathematical spells composed of recombinations of known quantities.

In Provence, late in the 1100s, the *Sefer ha-bahir* (Book of Brightness), or simply *Bahir*, profoundly influenced Jewish mysticism. Although Kabbalists credited the work to a first-century C.E. rabbi, Nehunya ben Haqana (also Hakana or Hakkanah), and its interpolations to *tannaim* (Talmudic scholars) from C.E. 50 to 200 and *amoraim* (Talmudic interpreters) from C.E. 200 to 500, the actual composition is a twelfth-century compilation of Eastern lore. It is a puzzling, controversial text composed in chaotic, illogical lines of Hebrew and Aramaic with occasional Arabisms, and it draws on the ancient Arabic *Raza Rabba* (Great Mystery), a book of magic and angelology composed in Babylon. Through discourse and mystic parable, the *Bahir* explains how the thirty-two ciphers, both written and pronounced orally, initiated creation. From this twelfth-century compendium comes the concept of *gilgul* (metempsychosis or reincarnation), the transmigration of souls, and an extensive mystical tree or network of interpretation and application of God's creative urge. In section 99 of the *Bahir* appears God's reflection on his tree:

It is I who have planted this "tree" that the whole world may
  delight in it
and with it I have spanned the all,
called it "all," for on it depends the all
and from it emanates the all;
all things need it and look upon it and yearn for it,
and it is from it that all souls fly forth [Scholem 1987, 71].

The passage emphasizes that God alone made the tree, which was in place before the creation of angels. God delights in the fact that no one knows the secret because no being existed at the time of his rooting the tree in earth. In section 71, the text describes a human link between earth and heaven — a column founded on righteousness, the virtue that causes the world to prosper and survive.

A pair of late twelfth-century Kabbalists, Abraham ben David (also Rabad or Ravad) and his son Isaac the Blind, also called Isaac Saggi Nehor (Rich in Light), initiated a Jewish renaissance in Narbonne, France. In Posquières near Nîmes, Abraham headed a rabbinic academy for needy students and furthered the education of Iberian Jewry. For his glosses he earned the title of *ba'al hassagot* (top critic). His *yeshiva* (Jewish learning center) pioneered a scholarly, but secretive perusal of Kabbala, which was never intended to serve the average Jew. In addition to nurturing the French Kabbalism of Elhanan de Dampierre and Jacob de Corbeil into the early 1200s, Isaac and his pupil Azriel (or Ezra) ben-Menahem of Gerona were the impetus to a school of Kabbala at Toledo during a golden age of esoteric learning, which standardized Kabbalist terminology. Azriel's catechism of sefirot, *Sha'ar ha-Sho'el* (Gate of the Inquirer), carried an explanatory subtitle, *Perush 'Eser ha-Sephirot* (Explanation of the Ten Sefirot).

Later in the thirteenth century, an anonymous Hebrew text, the *Sefer ha-temuna* (Book of the Image; C.E. 1200s), probed the concept of cosmic *shemittot* (cycles or eons), each a key to one aspect of the Torah. Produced in Spain, the book freights each letter of the Hebrew alphabet with a magic value and refers to invisible writings of the Torah. The author allies the first three universal cycles with grace, judgment, and mercy. By classifying human history as a segment of the second cycle, the author accounted for his era's interpretation of Torah as laws and prohibitions and predicted a fuller understanding of the universe in the third stage, the era of mercy, when human understanding would move beyond legalism to pure emotion.

In the era of gnosticism or intellectualism, mystic philosophy focused on divine duality and the influence of evil, which proponents declared was a lefthand divine number outside the realm of God in the *Sitra Ahra* (or *Ahera*; The Other Side), a sphere equated with divine wrath and dominated by demons. Satanic power is the antithesis of *Shekhinah*, a hovering presence of God, which oversees the right sector. In the late thirteenth century, ascetic scholar and numerologist Abraham ben-Samuel Abulafia of Saragossa, Spain, founded an ecstatic movement employing Hebrew script itself as a means of union with God. His prophetic Kabbala, forty-eight manuals on mysticism and prophecy composed during a twelve-year tour of Italy, displays a worldly influence that separates his philosophy from the most devout Jewish philosophers. His self-promotion as the messiah annoyed both Judaic and Christian authorities. Because he attempted to convert Pope Nicholas II to Judaism in 1280, Abulafia spent a part of his last years as a prisoner and only escaped execution because of the pope's death.

Based on intuition, Sufism, and the work of monks known as the Byzantine Hesychasts, Abulafia's writings speculate on the sound and shape of Hebrew lettering. He proposed a scientific agent to achieve oneness with God and invented gematria (or grammateia), reductions of words to numbers. These permutations produced a form of mystic transformation akin to amulets, casting of lots, and magic spells. Derived from the Hebrew *gimatriyya* (numerology), gematria were the province of soothsayers in Greece, Assyria, and Babylon. The use of gematria is common in aphorisms, acrostics, omens, dream interpretations, and wedding toasts based on the number values of the bride's and groom's names. Current applications involve encoding in computer systems to determine a logical pattern of wisdom or revelation.

The height of Kabbalism is a Spanish text, *Sefer ha-zohar* (or Zohar [Book of Splendor or Illumination]; ca. 1286), the mystic Bible. This clever literary hoax of multiple authorship peruses the nature of evil, goodness, and the soul. The work is composed in stylized Aramaic with only one segment, *Midrash ha-Ne'lam* (Interpretation of What Is Hidden), in Hebrew. The Zohar, like the Talmud, collects wisdom from past generations of mystics to enlarge and energize the study of magical interpretation. The exegesis, commentary, and parables derived ostensibly from the writings of Simeon ben Yohai, a second-century C.E. Palestinian patriot and tannist, and his followers. The Zohar comprises five main volumes:

- The three most important volumes cover the Torah: book 1 on Genesis, book 2 on Exodus, and book 3 on Leviticus, Numbers, and Deuteronomy. Called the Zohar Proper, this trio illuminates the core meaning of Torah plus Ruth and the Song of Songs.

- Book 4 contains the anonymous fourteenth-century additions *Ra'aya Mehenna* (Loyal Shepherd) and *Tikkuné* (or *Tiqquné*) *ha-Zohar* (Corrections of Zohar). A fifth tome, *Zohar Hadash* (New Zohar), appends lost sections from the first four volumes. The five are so revered that the Zohar approaches the holiness of scripture.

Current evaluation credits Rabbi Moses ben Shem Tob de Leon, the famed moralist called Moses de Leon of Guadalajara, whose writings, including the *Midrash ha-Ne'lam*, comment on the Pentateuch and offer guidance and religious counsel. Although he claimed otherwise, at his death in 1305, his wife declared that her husband was the pseudepigraphist who had composed the Zohar. Influenced by the philosophies of Maimonides and by Palestinian mystic Isaac ben Samuel of Acre, de Leon's Zohar pretends to derive from Simeon, a semi-legendary journeyman doctor, who withdrew from Roman persecutors to a cave. There, over thirteen years of self-exile, he formulated an intuitive doctrine of God, nature, and humanity. With his son, Eliezar (or Eleazar) ben Simeon, he discussed universal issues while on their walk to Palestine and encountered *Sava* (Old Man) and *Yenuka* (Child), contrasting sources of celestial secrets. De Leon uses this contrived discourse as a survey of immorality and social upheaval. It reaches a culmination in Simeon's death-day speech, which discloses the heart of his mystic wisdom.

The Zohar reveals five elemental myths on cosmogony, divine emanations or outpourings, sexual symbolism, the struggle between good and evil, and the messiah. The first myth explains the derivation of ten godly powers from the divine Creator. The second myth accounts for a network of dynamic powers, particularly the interplay of *Din* (Justice) and *Hesed* (Mercy), which stream from the godhead. Sexuality dominates the third myth. Crucial to the fourth myth is the perpetual antagonism between divinity and evil, which resides beyond the earthly realm in a satanic counterpart. The final myth, which supplants the struggles and mysteries of the current cosmos, is the messianic era, a coming of perfection to earth through a redemptive new world order. The complexity of these five cosmological views provoked multiple variations and dissent as Kabbala developed in subsequent centuries.

Influenced by neo–Platonic thought and the *Ginnat Egoz* (Nut Orchard; 1615) of Joseph ben-Abraham Gikatilla (also Chiquatilla or Jikatilla) of Castile, Abulafia's follower, the Zohar is theosophic in that it views the divine through intuitive wisdom. The text expands on the ten divine numbers, which God used to create the world. The innovation of Moses de Leon is the question of why God allows evil and the purpose of prayer and good works. He appears to have composed his controversial homiletic text as a support for orthodoxy in an era of rationalist philosophy, which threatened to undermine the true faith. Still revered for divine revelation, the Zohar survives as a preservation of traditional explanations of creation and honors the priests and scholars who center the faith's orthodoxy. Echoing the four-phase Christian scripture, i.e., literal, moral, philosophical, and mystical, the Zohar accounts for the universe, humanity, history, and Judaism and justifies revelation, messianic tradition, and rabbinic scholarship.

In the initial stage of the Renaissance, Kabbalists produced two masterworks, *Peliah* and *Kanah*. A Saragossan rationalist, Bahya ben-Asher, employed Kabbalistic methods to interpret the Bible, a major leap from superstition to scholarship. After the Inquisition forced Jews from Iberia in 1492, despairing individuals turned to Kabbala and dreams of a messiah as they scattered about Europe, Byzantium, and Palestine. A major shaper of loose schools of mysticism, Moses Cordovero of Safed systematized lore into a logical framework called *Pardes Rimmonim* (Garden of Pomegranates; 1548). In part 30, chapter 8, he lists major styles of gematria: the total value of letters in one word equals the total value of letters in another; a squared number is valued by the sum of the squares of each letter; or an arithmetic series of numbers creates values for the letters of a word. Simultaneously, the Zohar underwent printings at Cremona and Mantua in 1560 and joined the Torah and Talmud as the Judaic triad of law, prophecy, and wisdom.

Around the mid–1500s, a hotbed of Kabbalism in Safed, Galilee, championed Isaac ben-Solomon Luria (or Ari), the innovative visionary and Kabbalist who taught Cordovero. Luria evolved the concept of *Tzimtzum* (also *Tsimsum* or *simsum*; withdrawal or contraction) of the divine light, God's deliberate self-limitation to reveal the primordial void. This revelation of the all-in-all into empty space overtaxed creation, causing a prehistoric catastrophe known as *Shevirath ha-kelim* (breaking of the vessels), a preface to divine sparks that activated the demonic powers below.

In this flawed universe, Adam, the first man, lived in the contracted realm, where God forced divine understanding from his being to suit him for life on earth. To Kabbalists, the great calamities that befell God's divine plan were the fall of Adam and Eve and the destruction of the Temple of Jerusalem. Both left humanity yearning for divine origins and salvation from evil. The Lurianic doctrine envisioned the coalescing of light into *qellipot* (or *keliphoth*; shells or scales) and the resultant *tikkun* (or *tiqqun*; cosmic restoration), the struggle to restore order on earth and the application of mysticism to conquer evil. Luria neared sainthood for promoting religious piety and the daily application of Kabbala as the means of suppressing evil and redeeming the chosen people, who would hasten a return to divine order.

Because Luria composed orally, his extensive system survives from the composition of his pupil, the alchemist Hayyim Vital, who produced *Es Hayyim* (Tree of Life) and *Sepher ha-Gilgulim* (Book on Transmigration of Souls). Another student of Luria, Israel Saruk, spread his master's teachings to Italy and Germany.

Luria's followers supported the messianic movement known as Shabbetaianism and influenced eighteenth-century Hasidism. The former, an outgrowth of the fanaticism of seventeenth-century Turkish Kabbalist and zealot Shabbetai Tzevi (or Sabbatai Zebi or Zevi), challenged orthodoxy across the eastern Mediterranean and Europe in the second half of the seventeenth century. Around the eastern Mediterranean rim, his ecstatic charisma drew disciples to an ersatz messiah, a contemporary hero who would redeem the Jews. His travels over Asia Minor, Africa, Rhodes, Greece, and the Balkans indicate a restless, energized, and probably mad propagandist:

1651   from his birthplace at Smyrna to Patras and Athens

1654   from Athens north to Salonika

1658   expelled from Salonika east to Constantinople, then expelled back to Smyrna

1662   from Smyrna to Jerusalem and south to the island of Rhodes and Cairo

1663   from Cairo east to Gaza, Jerusalem, and Hebron

1664   return to Cairo to marry Sarah of Podolia and rid himself of demonic states

1665   from Hebron a return to Jerusalem and northeast to Safed and Aleppo; back to Smyrna and withdrawal to his brother's house

1666   from Smyrna to Constantinople and, after arrest at sea, west in chains to Gallipoli, where he and Sarah converted to Islam; north to Adrianople and west to Salonika, then back to Adrianople

1672   return to Constantinople, where he was arrested and exiled to Ulcinj

1673   from Constantinople through Adrianople northwest to Ulcinj (Dulcigno), a Yugoslavian port city on the Adriatic, where he died unexpectedly at age fifty on September 17, 1676.

With the aid of the equally peripatetic prophet Nathan of Gaza, Shabbetai's philosophy forged into Italy, Germany, Holland, and England, carrying Kabbala to new territory. Shabbetarians attempted to pass off their leader's apostasy as a necessary next stage prefacing the messianic era and an end to disease, violence, war, and suffering.

The eighteenth century produced the Hasidim, a post–Lurianic sect founded in Poland and Galicia by Israel ben-Eliezer, called Ba'al Shem Tov or Besht. By reframing Lurian Kabbala from a grim asceticism to a burst of joy and ecstasy, Besht lifted mysticism to a place of authority in everyday life. His pupil Baer (or Dob) of Meseritz taught Hasidism until the death of Besht, whom he succeeded as Hasidic authority. During his last decades, he battled Talmudists, who eventually broke with the Hasids, relegating them to the realm of cultic fanatics.

See also Apocrypha.

SOURCES: Abrahams 1896, Armstrong 1994, Baer 1961, Cavendish 1970, Comay and Cohn-Sherbok 1995, Demaitre 1996, Dolan 1968, Harris 1924, Hastings 1951, Idel 1988, "The Jewish Controversy over Calendar Postponements," Léon 1997, "Letter of R. Isaac the Blind to the Kabbalists of Gerona," Lyons and Petrucelli 1987, Magill 1998, "Post-Talmudic Period," Potok 1978, Scholem 1978, 1987, Siraisi 1990, "Timeline: Principal Medieval Rabbinic Authorities," "The Toledano Tradition of Kabbalah" 2000, Wigoder 1989, Wilson 1996.

Koan

Koan   More mind teaser than scripture, the koan, derived from the Chinese legal term *kung-an* (establishment of precedent), is a literary genre unique to Zen Buddhism, a branch of Mahayana or liberal Buddhism. As a means of disciplining the thoughts of novice monks, the unsolvable riddles state a tidy paradox, enigmatic phrase, or question that focuses on a *wato* (key word), for example:

"What is the way?" [Conze et al. 1995, 3020].

"What is nothing?" "It is no 'what.'" "What then?"

"What is the body of space?" [Wood 1962, 67].

"There is a jewel in the sky; how can we get hold of it?"

"There is a piece of stone in my house. Sometimes it stands up and sometimes it lies down. Now, can it be carved into the image of Buddha?" [Hoover 1980, 99].

"Since all things return to one, where does this one return to?" [Hoover 1980, 106].

"A man is hanging over an abyss by his teeth. Someone asks him why Bodhidharma came to China. If he does not answer he fails. If he does answer he falls. What should he do?" [Wood 1962, 68].

"A cow passes by a window. Its head, horns, and the four legs all pass by. Why did not the tail pass by?" [Smith 1958, 146].

"What was your face before you were born?" [Gentz 1973, 587].

Solution or explanation, either by gesture or word, requires an abrupt breakthrough to a higher state of consciousness.

For good reason, the koan is called the "gateless barrier," for example, Wu-tsu Fa-yen's challenging question: "If you meet a man of Tao on the road, greet him with neither words nor silence: so then, how will you greet him?" (Bowker 1997, 553). The object of the koan is to throw the mind off track, break old and familiar habits, and transcend everyday logic by awakening illumination and innate wisdom. Each day, on hearing the bell, the novice approaches his master for a private consultation and rings twice. The master proposes a koan and listens to the student's response. The master either praises him for a correct solution, reproaches him for a faulty answer, or rechannels him toward another try. Another strike on the bell ends the session. In regular application, the student's continued reflection on the koan fosters tranquility, courage, wit, and spontaneity, all universal human capabilities.

Rendered as *Dhyan* in Sanskrit and *Ch'an* in Chinese, Zen means "meditation" and derives from the immanence of Buddha in every person. It appears to have originated in India before becoming a thriving philosophy in China and Japan. According to legend, the Indian monk Bodhidharma carried its tenets east in C.E. 520. After merging with Taoist mysticism, Zen thrived from the T'ang dynasty into the 1400s. During this golden era, master Ch'ing-Yüan proposed a conundrum as a definition of Zen:

Before you study Zen, mountains are mountains and rivers
  are rivers.
While you study Zen, mountains are no longer mountains
  and rivers no longer rivers.
When you have obtained enlightenment, mountains are again
  mountains,
  and rivers again rivers [Schumann 1973, 168].

The teaser was a preface to koan study.

The first koan is attributed to Nan-yüan Hui-yung around C.E. 920. These enigmas became a means to individualized instruction of Zen trainees. They serve as jolts to reality by short-circuiting ordinary thinking and shocking the mind out of self-suppression. Koans and student replies to them appeared in collection during the Sung dynasty and acquired a body of commentary and systematic study that served masters as textbooks. The teaching method based on the koan was the innovation of Ta-hui around 1130 in Anhwei province. He revolutionized the classroom method by abandoning the silent contemplation on which Buddhism was based. He advised the beginner:

Just steadily go on with your koan every moment of your life…. Whether walking or sitting, let your attention be fixed upon it without interruption. When you begin to find it entirely devoid of flavor, the final moment is approaching: do not let it slip out of your grasp. When all of a sudden something flashes out in your mind, its light will illumine the entire universe, and you will see the spiritual land of the Enlightened Ones [Hoover 1980, 179].

After opening a temple in Hangchow in 1137, he taught 2,000 disciples by his method of intellectual challenge.

Zen philosophy crossed the straits to Japan in 1191 through the travels of the aristocratic priest Eisai (also Myoan Yosai), who made two pilgrimages from Kyoto to China. In addition to introducing tea to Japan, he propagated Zen at Kyoto and used the koan as a springboard to sudden enlightenment. In the vacuum left by the collapse of the Japanese aristocracy, Zen and its intriguing koans filled the needs of the intellectual Buddhist and rising samurai class. During the Ashikaga shogunate, which began in 1338, Zen influenced art, writing, and noh theater. After lying dormant from the seventeenth century into the modern age, it returned to popularity after World War II, with the counterculture of the 1960s, and late in the twentieth century among New Agers. It thrives in male and female masters throughout Korea, Japan, and Vietnam.

Essentially, Zen is a radical version of Buddhism that abandons deity, scripture, good deeds, and ceremony. The goal moved from external practice through meditation and intuition to an individualized inward state of *wu* or *satori* (enlightenment), an indescribable internal process that supersedes logic. One mind-jogging definition of Zen reads like a koan:

When one looks at it, one cannot see it.
When one listens for it, one cannot hear it.
However, when one uses it,
  it is inexhaustible [Cavendish 1970, 3088].

Zen functions by reordering or restructuring the problem into an intelligible pattern. It requires a lifetime of dedication, as expressed in Hashida's *Shobo Genzo Shakui*:

To study the way of the Buddha is to study your own self.
To study your own self is to forget yourself.
To forget yourself is to have the objective world prevail in
  you.
To have the objective world prevail in you,
  is to let go of your own body and mind
  as well as the body and mind of others [Eliade 1967, 510].

Hashida concludes that the enlightenment thus attained is more than a sudden flash of recognition. Rather, it challenges the seeker to a long contemplation. By honing perceptive power, it appeals to intellectuals and artists.

Each koan grows out of a mundane experience or anecdote and falls into one of five categories:

hosshin-koan	awakens awareness of identity with the buddha within
kikan-koan	illuminates distinction within nondistinction
gonsen-koan	stresses depths in the masters' sayings
nanto-koan	offers the greatest challenge to the mind

go-i-koan   carries a former answer to a
                            higher level

The most famous koan is the command to listen to one
hand clapping. The puzzler can solve the koan by abandoning standard analysis and will and opening the mind
to a sudden flash of genius.

The first published koans derived from the writings
of Fen-yang Shan-chao and his successor, Shih-shuang,
and in the *Tensho Kotoroku* of Li Tsu-hsü. The body of
1,700 koans have been collected by a Chinese priest,
Yüan-wu K'o-ch'in, in his anthology *Pi-yen lu* (Blue Cliff
Records; 1125), a series of posers and commentaries translated into Japanese as *Hekigan-roku*. A third volume, *Wu-
men Kuan* or *Mumon-kan* (The Gateless Barrier; 1228),
draws from the Blue Cliff Records. Anthologized by Wu-
men Hui-k'ai, a Chinese priest, it consists of forty-eight
koans beginning with a question about the Buddha nature
of a dog. His epitaph applies koanist logic to the Buddhist concept of nothingness:

> Emptiness is not born.
> Emptiness does not pass away.
> When you know emptiness,
>   you are not other than it [Bowker 1997, 1047].

A contemporary, Wan-sung Hsing-hsiu, collected koans
in *Ts'ung-jung lu* (Book of Equanimity; ca. 1240), translated into Japanese as *Shoyoroku*.

A proponent of koan, the itinerant priest and writer
Hakuin Ekaku of Hara, Japan, revived Rinzai Zen Buddhism in Japan. While wandering Japan in the early 1700s,
he achieved enlightenment and launched a campaign
against sterile Buddhism. In a classroom treatise he
snorted:

> What's earth's foulest thing, from which all men recoil?
> Charcoal that crumbles? Firewood that's wet? Watered lamp
>   oil?
> A cartman? A boatman? A second wife? Skunks?
> Mosquitoes? Lice? Blue flies? Rats? Thieving monks!
> Ahh! Monks! Priests! You are thieving brigands, every one of
>   you.
> When I say brigand priest, I mean the "silent illumination
>   Zennists" who now infest the land [Webley 1988].

On return to Hara's Shoin Temple, he expounded a philosophy of truth that permeated all levels of society and
promoted a partnership between religion and morality. In
his seventies, he declared his vitality ten times what it was
at midlife and maintained that his mind and body were
strong because he continued to challenge himself to ponder, write, and teach students to think for themselves.

Hakuin's origination of the koan of one hand clapping popularized the strategy for developing the intellect.
For his brightest pupils, he published *Keiso Dokozui* (Poi-

sonous Stamens and Pistils of Thorns). His other writings
include *Hogo-roku* (Record of Talks on the Law) and practical wisdom in *Orategama* (The Embossed Tea Kettle)
and *Yasen Kanwa* (An Evening Chat on a Boat).

SOURCES: Aitken 1991, Alexander and Alexander 1982, Ballou 1944, Bowker 1997, Brown 1996, Cavendish 1970, Ch'en 1968,
Conze *et al.* 1995, Eliade 1967, Gard 1961, Gentz 1973, Griffith
1892, Hastings 1951, Hinnells 1984, Hoover 1980, Ling 1972, *New
Catholic Encyclopedia* 1967, Schumann 1973, Senior 1985, Smith
1958, Smith 1995, Snodgrass 2000, Webley 1988, Wood 1962,
World Literature 1998s, *World Religions* 1998.

Kojiki
The scripture of Shintoism, the Kojiki (or
Koji-ki [Records of Ancient Matters or Events]; C.E. 712)
is a valuable source of Japan's origins. Along with a later
text, the Nihon Shoki (or Nihon-Gi [Chronicle of Japan];
C.E. 720), a thirty-volume chronicle, it forms the nation's
earliest and most authentic written record. Compiled
from oral traditions of various *uji* (clans), the Kojiki syn-
chronizes Japanese genealogy, kingship, and imperial
court chronicles into a unified mythic-historical whole.
It offers the theological and sociological beginnings of ritual, customs, prophecy, and metaphysical practice from
ancient times, when *majinahi* (magic) superseded religion in importance. At one time, European critics dis-
missed the work as "a tissue of vulgar fables," but subsequent readings have unearthed fundamental threads of
sociology, anthropology, and religion (Steinberg 1953,
1:318).

The text, which may replace two earlier works that
did not survive, is a compilation of myth, legend, and
kyuji (or *honji*; song cycles) from prehistory to the reign
of Empress Suiko in the early seventh century C.E. The
variance of literary texture parallels the variety of island
topography, which ranges from sea and shore to rocky
tor, green valley, mountain crest, terraced hillside, and
inland plains. Analysis of the text's naturism influenced
the development of Shinto (or Shen-tao; Way of the
Gods), a theanthropic religion that merges the mystic and
the real. A political as well as religious document, the Kojiki legitimizes Japan's imperial rule as a divine right
willed by the gods.

The oral groundwork of the Kojiki dates to C.E. 400,
before Japan had a written language. Under the command
of Emperor Temmu, scribes recorded the original version
in *waka*, an alternating pattern of five- and seven-syllable lines in one of two verse lengths—*tanka*, containing
five lines, and *choka*, a longer poem ending in a seven-syllable couplet. To bolster the position of the Imbe clan of
Shinto priests, Temmu commissioned the work in C.E.
681 to correct inaccuracies in the oral tradition before it
was too late to eradicate false information, which had crept
in from Korean and Chinese sources. He also appointed

his nephew Prince Kawashima to compile a factual version of the imperial family tree and early records. In justification of this two-stage project, Temmu declared, "This is the framework of the state, the great foundation of the imperial influence" (Bowker 1997, 554).

Although composed to favor the Yamato dynasty, the Kojiki is more than propaganda. It demonstrates the humanism of the Nara period, an era of substantial literary growth influenced by Chinese civilization. In the first phase of the compilation, imperial storyteller Hiyeda no Are, who may have been a woman, memorized and recited at court the master text. In C.E. 712, a scribe, O no (or Ohono) Yasumaro, undertook the written version, which is Japan's oldest written document. His introduction states the Kojiki's importance to Japanese history:

Thus, though the primeval beginnings be distant and dim, yet by the
  ancient teachings do we know the time when the lands were conceived and the islands born;
Though the origins be vague and indistinct, yet by relying upon the
  sages of antiquity do we perceive the age when the deities were born
  and man were made to stand ["Quote of the Week"].

Working phonetically, the recorders applied *kanji* (Chinese ideographs) to represent Japanese sounds. Yasumaro presented the completed copy to Empress Gemmei (or Gemmio). The texts remained in the care of Shinto priests until 1664, when printing made them more accessible.

After centuries of neglect, in the mid–eighteenth century, the Kojiki returned to favor. The reintroduction was the work of Moto-ori Norinaga, a physician and Shinto scholar from Matsuzaka, Japan, who came under the influence of the *Kokugaku* (National Learning) movement, a nativist revival launched by Kada Azumamaro and Kamo no Mabuchi. Norinaga's intent was to substantiate Japan's beginnings before the nation came under Chinese influence. To return to the country's pure foundations, he compiled commentary on *The Tale of Genji* and reevaluated the Kojiki's moral, religious, and ethical precepts. His commentaries fill forty-nine volumes entitled *Annotation of the Kojiki* (1798), which was translated into English in 1882. According to his analysis, the Kojiki is the philosophical basis of modern Shintoism. He discovered from a study of classical Japanese myths that the national belief system owes more to indigenous writings, creationism, and ancient sacred tradition than to Buddhism and Confucianism.

The Kojiki connects the Japanese of the eighth century with their primordial forebears, an anthropomorphic pantheon that appears to derive in part from Poly-

nesian lore, Korean king myth, and Malay rice gods. The preface, based on Taoism, opens on a shapeless cosmos resembling an embryo:

[It] formed a chaotic mass like an egg,
  which was of obscurely defined limits,
  and contained germs.
The purer and clearer part was thinly diffused
  and formed Heaven,
  while the heavier and grosser element settled down
  and became earth.
The finer element easily became a united body,
  but the consolidation of the heavy and gross element
  was accomplished with difficulty.
Heaven was therefore formed first, and Earth established subsequently.
Thereafter divine beings were produced between them [Eliade 1967, 94].

As described in this most-quoted passage, cosmic matter divides the world into three tiers, which are stages for spectacular drama:

- *Amagahara* (Plain of High Heaven), home of the *ama tsu kami* (celestial deities)
- Earth, ruled by *Kuni tsu kami* (earthly deities), including humankind, plants, and animals
- *Yomi no kuni* (Underworld), residence of the dead

The three-part narrative describes how primordial chaos preceded the compartmentalization of earthly beings.

Book I is a compendium of Japanese myth, cosmogony, and theogony. It traces the global creation of Japan to Izanagi (He Who Invites) and Izanami (She Who Invites or Is Invited), the mythic parents of Japan. To create its eight islands and lesser deities:

The two deities, standing upon the Floating Bridge of Heaven,
  pushed down the jeweled spear and stirred with it,
  whereupon, when they had stirred the brine till it went curdlecurdle,
  and drew [the spear] up,
  the brine that dripped down from the end of the spear
  was piled up and became an island [Frost 1972, 350].

By this divine process performed from the rainbow's arc, the island of Onogoro or Onokoro (Self-coagulating) becomes the first land mass to coalesce on the planet.

The Kojiki links creation with bloody sacrifice, its prime ingredient. From Izanagi's spear, each drop of gore forms a *kami* (divinity), which the Kojiki names in lists. From the plane of heaven, three appeared spontaneously: Ame-no-mi-naka-nushi-no-kami (Deity Master of the August Center of Heaven), Taka-mi-musu-bi-no-kami (High August-Producing Wondrous Deity), and Kami-musu-bi-no-kami (Divine-Producing Wondrous Deity).

Produced among reeds on earth were two: Umashi-ashi-kabi-hiko-ji-no-kami (Pleasant Reed Shoot Prince Elder Deity) and Ame-no-toko-tachi-no-kami (Deity Standing Eternally in Heaven). Born separately were two: Kuni-no-toko-tachi-no-kami (Deity Standing Eternally on Earth) and Toyo-kumo-nu-no-kami (Luxuriant Integrating Master Deity). Next came nine siblings: U-hiji-ni-no-kami (Deity Mud Earth Lord), Su-hiji-ni-no-kami (Deity Mud Earth Lady), Tsunu-guhi-no-kami (Germ into Life Integrating Deity), Oho-to-no-ji-no-kami (Deity Elder of the Great Place), Oho-to-no-be-no-kami (Deity Elder Lady of the Great Place), Omo-daru-no-kami (Deity Perfect Exterior), Aya-kashiko-ne-no-kami (Deity Oh Awful or Venerable Lady), Izana-gi-no-kami (Deity the Male Who Invites), and Izana-mi-no-kami (Deity the Female Who Invites). The spiritual founders of Shinto, these *kami* (divine presences) inhabit rocks, mountains, and other natural wonders.

The workings of nature become the modus operandi of Kojiki. The parent gods, who are brother and sister like the Greek Zeus and Hera, descend to the first island and observe the coupling of a pair of wagtail waterbirds. Seized by marital passion, the divine pair procreate in earnest. Their first child, a weak leech-baby, is abandoned in a reed boat. The Kojiki accounts for the deformed offspring as the fault of the wife, who spoke first at the wedding ceremony, a violation of patriarchy. When primacy is restored to the male, through a process of evolution, they produce the tribe of nature divinities. The second child is the islet of Awa (Foam). In order come waterfalls, mountains, trees, herbs, meadows, and wind, who blows away the mist to reveal the island chain.

At a high point in Japanese mythic drama, the earth mother Izanami burns to death in the throes of bearing the fire *kami*, Kagu-tsuchi, who carries the taint of matricide. According to the text:

As she was dying, she gave birth to the earth goddess
  and the water goddess.
The god of fire married the goddess of the earth,
  and their daughter produced the mulberry tree
  and the silkworm from the hair on her head
  and five kinds of grain from her navel [Rosenberg 1992,
  403].

Mother Izanami, charred in childbed, descends below earth and becomes queen of the Yomi, the gloomy underworld. Like the Greek myth of Prometheus's sufferings to give fire to earthlings, the story bears the universal element of sacrifice for the good of humankind.

The separation of the first parents is excruciating to Izanagi. He weeps piteously and buries his mate on Mount Hiba. In a frenzy, he slices the fire god to bits with his sword, producing new divinities from the shreds:

The head of Kagu-tsuchi became "the lord of steepnesses,"
  his breast "the lord of the descent,"
  his belly "the lord of the innermost mountain,"
  his genital organs "the lord of the black mountain,"
  his left arm "the lord of the dense forests,"
  his right arm "the lord of the first slopes,"
  his left leg "the lord of the high meadows,"
  and his right leg "the lord of the mountain gates" [Hastings
  1951, 4:237].

The union between the lord of the mountains and the goddess of the lowlands produces another array of divine children: gods of the passes, gods of the boundaries of passes, gods of the dark gates, and princes of the valleys. From this primitive cosmogony, the Japanese deify all terrain and, by extension, staple crops of millet, rice, corn, and beans.

Like the Greek Orpheus following the shade of Eurydice, Izanagi travels to the underworld to retrieve Izanami. He arrives after she slips into the dark passageway, and he breaks off a tooth of his comb and lights it as a torch. Peering into the forbidden land of the dead, he finds her corpse already decomposing and riddled with maggots. His violation of taboo, like the Greek Pandora's opening of the fatal box of evils, unleashes death among earthlings. He recoils from the disgusting sight and resolves: "Having gone to Nay! a hideous and filthy place, it is meet that I should cleanse my body from its pollutions" (Bouquet 1954, 320). On his return to the earth's surface, he scrubs himself in preparation for completing creation. His ablution sets the example for Shinto's *misogi* (purification rite), the ceremony that precedes religious functions and events. As honor to the ancestral *kami*, it restores a pristine state by removing sin and earthly contaminants.

Izanagi's left eye becomes the deity of order, Amaterasu Omikami (Heavenly Illuminating Deity), the sun goddess, weaver, manager of heaven, initiator of rebirth, and progenitor of the imperial lineage. The text explains her role as great and beneficent mother goddess and declares that she "shed mercies on all things everywhere" (Bouquet 1954, 319). In a parallel birthing, Izanagi's right eye becomes her counterpart, Tsuki-yomi-no-kami, the moon deity, who poses back to back with Amaterasu and becomes her consort. Like sun to moon, he is a pale, inferior divinity in comparison with his glorious, life-sustaining sister/wife.

Izanagi's production of offspring becomes more problematic with a third deity, the impetuous, disorderly Susano-o (also Sosa-no-wo; Swift Impetuous Deity), the storm god. From his appearance, he rivals his sister Amaterasu for power. In a fit of baby-of-the-family willfulness, he tears up rice fields and terrorizes her into hiding in a cave. At the end of his labors, Izanagi stands back to admire the trio and proudly gloats, "I, begetting child after child, have at my final begetting gotten three illustrious children" (Hastings 1951, 4:1164).

The willful Susano-o, as god of the sea, resists control. Cropping up at will, he threatens earthly existence by disrupting planting seasons and polluting two focal ceremonies, the weaving ritual and the *Ninamesai* (Tasting First Fruits). He is given to fits of weeping, groaning, withering green swards, drying up rivers, and shaking the island cluster with tremors. He even attempts to assassinate the goddess who nurtures all living things. In response, father Izanagi upbraids him. According to the Kojiki, Amaterasu "endeavors to appease him with the most indulgent calmness; and the eclipse of the goddess at last takes place only when, disregarding her patient gentleness, he perpetrates the worst crimes" (Hastings 1951, 4:235). The most dreadful act for humankind is forcing Amaterasu to flee into hiding in a cave. The scenario, like Hades' kidnap of Persephone, terrorizes earthlings, who must temporarily dwell in darkness.

An ancient sun ritual requires the five clan heads to invoke Amaterasu from seclusion. In the ceremony, Ame no Uzzume no Mikoto, possessed by divine spirit, performs the *Ama-no-iwado-no-kagura* (play before the celestial gate) to propitiate the goddess and restore sunlight before it is too late to save earth. As described in the Nihon Shoki;

[She] took in her hand a spear wreathed with Eulalia grass
  and standing before the door of the Rock-cave of Heaven,
  skillfully performed a mimic dance.
She took, moreover, the true Sakaki tree of the Heavenly
  Mount Kagu,
  and made of it a headdress.
She took club moss and made of it braces.
She kindled fires.
She placed a tub bottom upwards,
  and gave forth a divinely inspired utterance [Eliade 1967,
  50].

The performance, which is the fount of Japanese drama, lures Amaterasu to peep around the rock slab over the cave mouth and see her reflection in a mirror hanging opposite in a sasaki tree. Taking advantage of this womanly curiosity and vanity, a male *kami* takes her hand and leads her forth, thus resurrecting light.

The episode of Amaterasu's self-exile and restoration is central to Japan's mythology. As a result, mirrors remain a part of Japanese court ritual and imperial regalia. The divine drama is the source of the nocturnal Daijōsai ritual, through which the spirit of the goddess departs from the deceased emperor and enters his successor. The episode also generated the every twenty-year re-erection of the Ise Shrine, which is sacred to Amaterasu.

Susano-o does not go unpunished. His erratic be-

havior results in *harai* (exorcism), plucking of his nails and hair, and banishment from heaven. On earth, he becomes a hero like the Greek Perseus or Theseus and defends a maiden, Kushi-nada-hime, from the eight-forked serpent, Koshi. The story, derived from a background of human sacrifice like the Greek youths fed to the Minotaur of Crete, turns on the demands of a ravenous beast that annually devours a chaste victim. As described by Kushi-nada-hime's weeping father:

Its eyes are like the winter-cherry;
  it has one body with eight heads and eight tails.
Moreover, on its body grows moss....
Its length extends over eight valleys and eight hills,
  and if one looks at its belly,
  it is all constantly bloody and inflamed [Hastings 1951,
  6:855].

Susano-o the hero is as resourceful as his earlier persona was obnoxious. After intoxicating the dragon on eight bowls of *sake* (rice wine), he slices off each of the eight heads. In fairytale style, he weds the girl and founds a family at Izumo on the island of Honshu, where his offspring Okuninushi founds a divine dynasty. His son, the harvest god Ohotoshi no Kami, begets the harvest gods Mi-toshi no Kami and Uka no mitama (Spirit of Food), who is venerated at the Temple of Inari.

Subsequent segments of the Kojiki depart from bloodier elements to a golden age. A separate heroic cycle tells of Oho-kuni-nushi (Master of the Great Land), who employs a dwarf magician to construct the rest of earth and complete the divine order. In balance to Susano-o's mischief, Amaterasu showers blessing on the land. From her comes a celestial grandson, Ninigi no Mikoto, ruler of Japan, who wears the sacred regalia as he leads the clan chieftains. To solidify control, he overthrows Izumi and houses him in a shrine. The struggle suggests a historic event that pacified and civilized prehistoric Japan.

Book II of the Kojiki continues chronologically from the Hohoderi interlude, a cycle of genealogical folktales, to the acts of Jimmu (or Jinmu) Tenno, Ninigi's great-grandson, the "Divine Warrior." An historical figure, he emerges from the era of legend to rule a clan confederacy from 660 to 585 B.C.E. He was a devout nature worshiper and the touchstone of Japan's historic first dynasty, which he settled in the Yamato region. Upon him, Amaterasu, the sun goddess, bestowed appropriate gifts:

one mirror of the offing, one mirror of the shore, one eight-hands-breadth sword, one jewel of birth, one jewel of return from death, one perfect jewel, one jewel road-returning, one serpent-scarf, one bee-scarf, and scarf of various things. She added: "In case of illness, shake these treasures and repeat to them the words '*Hi, fu, mi, yo, itsu, mu, nana, ya, kokono, tari*' and shake them *yura-yura*. If thou does so the dead will certainly return to life" [Hastings 1951, 8:299].

Common to world folklore, these talismans of light and regenerative power along with the magic incantation recur in Japanese ritual as symbols of national rejuvenation. The sacred mirror, jewel, and sword remain the symbols of imperial authority and validate claim to the throne.

Aided by Amaterasu, Jimmu establishes a "lasting great august reign over the Great-eight-island-country" of Japan and an imperial throne at Yamato, the center of the island cluster, at modern Kyoto. It remained there until 784, when it moved to Nara in Honshu; a decade later, it passed to Kyoto (Hastings 1951, 8:299). As Jimmu proceeds from Mount Takjachiho in Kyushu in search of the earth's center, he vanquishes evil by subduing rebellious gods. The ruling house takes shape with the aid of a white horse, a motif of purity common in mythology:

As this white horse plants his fore-hoofs and his hind-hoofs,
  so will the pillars of the Great Palace be set firmly on the
    upper rocks
  and frozen firmly on the lower rocks;
  the prickling up of his ears is a sign that your majesty will,
  with ears ever more erect, rule the Underheaven [Hastings
    1951, 10:372].

With the help of a great crow, Jimmu erects the grand imperial palace at the capital city. The narrative recounts details of the reigns of a list of fifteen legendary emperors:

Jimmu	660–585 B.C.E.
Suizei	581–549 B.C.E.
Annei	549–511 B.C.E.
Itoku	510–477 B.C.E.
Kosho	475–393 B.C.E.
Koan	392–291 B.C.E.
Korei	290–215 B.C.E.
Kogen	214–158 B.C.E.
Kaika	158–98 B.C.E.
Sujin	97–30 B.C.E.
Suinin	29 B.C.E.–C.E. 70
Keiko	71–130
Seimu	130–190
Chuai	ca. 192–200
Empress Jingo	201–269 (regent)

The text ends with Jingo's heir, the Emperor Ojin, a real figure, who ruled in the early C.E. 400s.

The Kojiki characterizes an early heroic tradition. The birth of Ojin figures in the legendary exploits of a mighty empress, Jingo (or Jingu Kogo), wife of the emperor Chuai. He died in C.E. 200 from an arrow wound during an insurrection at Kyushu, but the Kojiki altered his death to a peaceful demise while plucking on a stringed instrument. To carry out his plan to invade Korea, his consort equipped the imperial army and led the expedition to the Asian mainland. Of necessity, she stopped her birth canal with a stone and carried her unborn son Ojin three years until she had time to give birth on Japanese soil. Still subjugated in 285, the Korean faction sent a copy of Confucius's Analects to Japan, thus introducing to Japan two increments to its civilization—Chinese characters and Confucianism.

According to book II and to the *Hitachi Fudoki*, an eighth-century gazette, Japan claims a male hero, Yamato-takeru, who prefigures Britain's chivalric conventions. Born O-usu-no-mikato, he was a fearless warrior and the second son of the twelfth emperor, Keiko, Japan's first shogun. As the prototypical samurai, Prince Yamato demonstrates prowess in his mid-teens, when he slays a seditious older brother. Dressed in his aunt's clothing like Achilles before marching off to the Trojan War, he overcomes the chief of the troublesome Kumaso tribe by perching coyly at a royal banquet table and quickly stabbing his adversary with a dirk retrieved from his bodice. The dying Kumaso heir names the hero Yamato-takeru. Analysts compare this hero tale to the emergence of young Arthur, who retrieved a sword hidden in an altar stone as divine authorization of his succession to Britain's King Uther Pendragon.

Yamato-takeru also emulates the Arthur cycle in obtaining a magical sword, Mura-kumo (Assembled Clouds), which he receives from Yamato-hime, a mystic female. She, like the Lady of the Lake, invests him with the power to head a war band, cross the straits to the mainland, and overthrow multiple enemies. Just as Arthur is forced to return Excalibur to the Lady of the Lake, the Japanese hero falls to a god in the form of a giant white boar, whom he tries to strangle barehanded on Mount Ibaku. Pelted by a terrible hailstorm, Yamato-takeru expires after surrendering the supernatural sword.

Like the dying Arthur ferried to the mystic island of Avalon on a barge rowed by chaste maidens, Yamato-takeru shifts his shape for a similarly pure flight from earth: "From that place [the white bird] again soared through the heavens and flew away" (Littleton 1995). The Nihon Shoki adds, "At last it soared aloft to Heaven, and there was nothing buried but [Yamato-takeru's] clothing and official cap." For his he-man adventures, he remains a popular subject of Japanese opera and stagecraft.

Book III of the Kojiki continues the story of Japan's royal families. The narrative, which covers imperial reigns from Emperor Nintoku to Empress Suiko in C.E. 628, identifies the sixteenth to the thirty-third emperors:

Nintoku	313–399
Richu	400–405
Hanzei	406–410

Ingyo	412–453
Anko	453–456
Yuryaku	456–479
Seinei	480–484
Kenzo	485–487
Ninken	488–498
Buretsu	498–506
Keitai	507–531
Ankan	531–535
Senka	535–539
Kimmei	539–571
Bidatsu	572–585
Yomei	585–587
Sushun	587–592
Empress Suiko	592–628

The text is replete with hero worship, an element of Japanese iconography that was still active at the beginning of World War II.

SOURCES: Alexander and Alexander 1982, Ballou 1944, Bouquet 1954, Bowker 1997, Braden 1954, Eliade 1967, Frost 1972, Gall 1999, Habu and Fawcett 1999, Hastings 1951, "Japanese Creation Myth" 1998, Kato 1979, "Kojiki," Littleton 1995, *New Catholic Encyclopedia* 1967, Ohnuki-Tierney 1995, Perkins 1991, Piggott 1973, "Quote of the Week," Rosenberg 1992, "Shinto" 1999, Smith 1995, Steinberg 1953, *World Religions* 1998.

Koran

Islam's holy book, the Koran (also Coran, Kur'an, or al-Qur'an) is a remarkably static text — a physical and uncorrupted proof of the beneficence of Allah, an uncreated and eternal heavenly power who composed his teachings at the beginning of time. His agent presented the work verbatim to the prophet Muhammad bin 'Abdallah over a period of twenty-two years. In the first ten verses of surah 53, a commemorative poem recreates the drama of the Koran's transmission:

By the star when it setteth,
  your comrade erreth not, nor is deceived;
  nor doth he speak of [his own] desire.
It is naught save an inspiration that is inspired,
  which one of mighty powers hath taught him,
  one vigorous; and he grew clear to view
  when he was on the uppermost horizon.
Then he drew nigh and came down
  till he was [distant] two bows' length or even nearer,
  and he revealed unto his slave that which he revealed [Pickthall 1930].

Honored as *al kitab* (the Book), the compendium offers sacred commands, warnings of a day of judgment, and advice on such subjects as marriage and divorce, sanctioned intercourse and incest, giving birth and breastfeeding infants, alms, usury, contracts and inheritances, justice, war and treaties, emigration, vanity and sin, and prayer and fasting.

For the many Muslims scattered about the globe, the Koran is the supreme source of moral instruction and a guide to legal, historical, polemical, and religious issues. Unlike other scriptures, it lacks a simple outline. Instead, the text offers moral teachings in random order intermixed with commentary on creation, prophecy, and the Muslim worshiper's responsibility to Allah. A parallel to these esoteric 'ayat (tokens) or verses are the *hadith* (traditions), anthologies of Muhammad's biography and wisdom concerning specifics of religious practice and the human moral struggle. Additional religious elements derive from the *sunna*, or social and legal customs.

Koranic scripture, which children learn by rote in the *maktab* (religious school), establishes the duty of believers to impose justice on society and to respect the poor and vulnerable, for whom Muhammad had an abiding sympathy. The text overflows with honorifics for Allah, as with verses 23–24 of surah 59, which heaps on God the names sovereign lord, sacred name, peace giver, keeper of the faith, guardian, bold one, all-powerful, most high, exalted, creator, originator, and modeler. Other examples inscribed on talismans to protect Muslims are these favorites:

al-'Alim, the Knower	al-Muhaimin, the Protector
al-'Aziz, the Mighty	tor
al-Bari, the Maker	al-Musawwir, the Fashioner
al-Fattah, the Opener	ioner
al-Ghaffar, the Forgiver	al-Mutakabbir, the Great
al-Jabbar, the Repairer	al-Wahhab, the Bestower
al-Kabiz, the Restrainer	ar-Rahim, the Compassionate
al-Kahhar, the Dominant	sionate
al-Khalik, the Creator	ar-Rahman, the Merciful
al-Kuddus, the Holy One	ar-Razzak, the Provider
al-Malik, the King	as-Salam, the Peace
al-Mu'min, the Faithful	[Budge 1929, 9].

As Allah's gift to his people, the Koran is so sacred that early Muslims developed a protocol for handling their copies, which requires sobriety and clean hands. It is stored on a high shelf or above a door with nothing on top and no dust accumulating on its ornate covering. It is never dropped, never touched with the left hand, nor held below the waist. It remains out of reach of infidels and accompanies believers to school, into battle, and at all other significant human events between birth and death.

Because Muslim fundamentalists consider the text a divine revelation, the inspired word of Allah, the Islamic God, in its original language, Koranic scripture is perhaps the purest text to survive from ancient times. From its initial composition, the Koran went through a five-stage period of transmission to readers:

Two pages from a manuscript copy of the Koran written in North Africa, probably in the thirteenth century. (Saudi Aramco World/Peter Keen.)

- revelation from C.E. 610 to 632
- individual written texts from around C.E. 610 to around 635
- compilation of a canon codex from C.E. 635 to 655
- voweling and punctuating the Arabic C.E. 661–785
- translation into other languages, beginning with a Latin version in 1143 and continuing into the present

It remains perhaps the most cherished, most memorized of world scriptures.

The terse, forceful, often indecipherable style of the Koran presents an obstacle to converts living outside Middle Eastern cultures. It lacks the transition and standard chronological narrative found in other world scriptures and contains chapters made up of a mixture of revelations from early and late in Muhammad's service to Allah. The Koran's arcane language, unpunctuated and preserved in the original seventeen consonants of Arabic, and its unexpected shifts in subject, person, and style render it less available to the faithful worldwide. In the estimation of late eighteenth-century English historian Edward Gibbon:

The harmony and copiousness of style will not reach, in a version, the European infidel: he will peruse with impatience the endless incoherent rhapsody of fable, and precept, and declamation, which seldom excites a sentiment or an idea, which sometimes crawls in the dust, and is sometimes lost in the clouds [Arberry 1970, 11].

With more pointed disdain, nineteenth-century English critic Thomas Carlyle wrote of the Muslim scripture:

I must say, it is as toilsome reading as I ever undertook. A wearisome confused jumble, crude, incondite; endless iterations, long-windedness, entanglement; most crude, incondite; — insupportable stupidity, in short! Nothing but a sense of duty could carry any European through the Koran [Carlyle].

In contrast to the majority of forthright condemnation of their eras, Gibbon and Carlyle were surprisingly generous.

Yet, to Muslims, the holy book of Islam is the eternal scripture, an emotive work of genius and a miracle of God's handiwork. Under no circumstances can authors edit or mimic the holy scripture. Such a sacrilege is punishable by death, as demonstrated by a bounty of $1 million offered by the Ayatollah Ruhollah Khomeini of Iran to the killer of Salman Rushdie for writing *The Satanic*

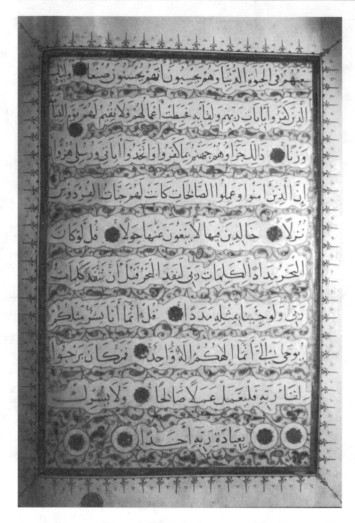

A page from an Ottoman manuscript copy of the Koran written in Istanbul or Damascus. (Saudi Aramco World/Peter Keen.)

Verses (1989), a fantasy novel that allegedly defames the Koran, Islam, and the prophet Muhammad.

Muslims believe that the angel Jibreel (Gabriel) dictated the Koran to Muhammad. This miraculous transmission allowed a humble man to recite fragmented phrases and sparks of enlightenment word for word and exalted him to Allah's supreme prophet. The sanctity of the language is unquestioned. As stated in surah 15:9, the Koran is meant to survive in the original: "Absolutely, we have revealed the reminder, and, absolutely, we will preserve it" (Khalifa 1999). Surah 75 declares in verses 17–18: "It is we who will collect it into Qur'an. Once we recite it, you shall follow such a Qur'an" (Khalifa 1999).

Although much of the Koran is strict and forbidding, there are tender passages that comfort and uplift, for example, surah 2:286:

Our Lord! Condemn us not if we forget, or miss the mark!
Our Lord! Lay not on us such a burden as thou didst lay on
    those before us!

Our Lord! Impose not on us that which we have not the
    strength to bear!
Pardon us, absolve us and have mercy on us, thou, our pro-
    tector,
  and give us victory over the disbelieving folk [Pickthall
    1930].

Because its 114 surahs of history, prophecy, and spiritual guidance remain in the classic state, subsequent generations have had to access the scripture in the original Arabic and have struggled to apply its occluded meanings to their lives.

In the tenets of Islam, worshipers approach Allah through an aural experience called *tajwid* or *tartil*, a highly refined oral recitation performed by professional *qurra'* (readers). For this reason, Muhammad entitled the work Koran, meaning "recitation," "lectionary," or "reading." For cantillation, the reader is typically seated on the ground bending over the book, which is held in the lap or placed on a low table. The skilled reciter sways the torso in an oval while articulating the hypnotic phrases in a chanted meditation comparable to yoga, Lakota vision quests, and Buddhist trance states. During recitation, spoken Islamic scripture creates a hallowed atmosphere uniting Allah with truth, the earth, and peace.

In response to hearing the Koran intoned aloud, the reverent Muslim falls silent, never yawns or lets the eyes wander, and studies the artful pronunciation of Arabic words read rhythmically at sixty beats per second, supposedly the same way that Allah recited them to Muhammad. The result is the *sakinah* (divine tranquility) and a feeling of nearness to Allah and his angels. This constant stream of scripture in holy buildings, places of business, courtrooms, and homes of the faithful permeates all levels of life and inspires personal choices, politics, law, the military, the arts, and education. The oracular style and sweep of the Koran became the foremost model of rhetoric and grammar and the standard by which critics judged secular Arabic literature.

Central to the Koran is an assurance of Allah's supremacy over human actions. For this reason, the faith is called Islam, meaning "submission" or "commitment." For Muslims (literally, submitters), discerning divine command and submission to Allah's will are the focuses of their existence. A strict form of monotheism, the worship of Allah prepares each seeker for death, judgment, and an afterlife of perpetual torment or eternal reward. As earthly guides and messengers, Allah dispatches prophets known to Jews and Christians—Adam, Enoch, Methuselah, Abraham, Lot, Ishmael, Ismail, Moses, Isaac, Jacob, the patriarchs, Job, Jonah, Aaron, Solomon, Zechariah, John the Baptist, Jesus, Alexander the Great, and Muhammad—and less well known Arabic figures including Hud, Luqman, Salih, and Shu'ayb—to restore the wayward to truth and orthodox behavior. On the subject of the prophets' miracles, the Koran parallels the Judeo-Christian scripture in honoring Noah, Abraham, Moses, and Jesus. Above their blameless lives, the text ennobles the life of Muhammad, whose receipt of Allah's word transcends earthly greatness.

The background of the Koran is one with the life and significance of Muhammad, a proponent of Abrahamic monotheism. The first *sira*, or biography, compiled by Muhammad ibn Ishaq in C.E. 750, reached print 120 years after the prophet's death and was followed by a second telling by ibn Hisham around C.E. 830. Another source is the *hadith*, anthologies of Muhammad's aphorisms and deeds originally compiled by six separate editors: Abu Dawud, al-Nisai, al-Tirmidhi, Bukhari, ibn Maja, and Muslim.

Also called Ahmad, the Apostle, Mahmud, Maho-met, Mohammed, and Mohammad, the prophet was born in C.E. 570 at Mecca (or Makkah), fifty miles from the Red Sea, to a respected couple, Amina, a high-strung mother, and 'Abdallah ibn Abd al-Muttalib, an Ishmaelite merchant of the Quaraysh tribe who died before his son was born. Muhammad spent his early childhood in the care of Halima, a foster mother. Bereft of his birth mother at age six, he came into the custody of his maternal grand-father, Abd al-Mutallib. At his grandsire's death, Muhammad passed to a paternal uncle, Abu Talib, who trained him to herd sheep and apprenticed him in the merchant trade.

After serving as a soldier in a tribal war at age twenty, Muhammad worked as a cameleer and manager for Kha-dijah bint Khuwaylid, a wealthy Arab trader and widow some twenty years his senior who plied lucrative trade routes between Mecca and Syria. She proposed to him in C.E. 604, after his successful caravan to Syria. Muham-mad's union with Khadijah, which lasted until her death, provided Islam with a model marriage based on love, honor, and mutual respect.

During their marriage, an ample income and newly acquired prestige allowed Muhammad the freedom to visit holy shrines. At night, he often withdrew from Mecca to a cave in a barren rock on nearby Mount Hira to practice *tahannuth* (devotional exercise). During med-itation, he experienced visions, voices, tremors, and swooning into episodes of catalepsy. As described by En-glish critic Thomas Carlyle in lecture 2, "The Hero as Prophet," in *Heroes and Hero Worship*, "this great fiery heart, seething, simmering like a great furnace of thoughts" reached out for divine solace (Carlyle). These heavenly visitations—erratic, disorienting, and unpre-dictable—naturally caused him alarm.

Khadijah aided her husband when he feared for his sanity and took him to a kinsman, Waraqa ibn Nawfal, a Christian scholar, for affirmation concerning Muham-mad's calling to serve Allah. According to *hadith*, Waraqa exclaimed:

> Surely by him in whose hand is Waraqa's soul, thou art the prophet of these people. There has come to thee the great-est *Namus*, who came to Moses. Thou wilt be called a liar, and they will use thee despitefully and cast thee out and fight against thee. Should I live to see that day, I will help God in such wise as he knoweth [Williams 1961, 62–63].

He introduced Muhammad to the *hanifs* (penitents), who secretly disdained paganism and worshiped only Allah. Although minimally educated, Muhammad gained confi-dence and thought of himself as an instrument of the most high. This conversion freed him of material con-cerns and turned his mind and heart to righteousness. He responded wholeheartedly with the familiar Islamic affirmation, "Allahu Akbar! La ilaha illa Allah! [God is great. There is no God but Allah.]" (Smith 1958, 221).

Khadijah became Muhammad's initial convert after his cave vision of the angel Jibreel in C.E. 610 in the holy month of Ramadan on the Night of Power. The appari-tion ordered him to read what was written on his heart. The Koran describes the event in surah 96, *al-'Alaq*, "The Embryo," verses 1–5:

> In the name of god, most gracious, most merciful
>   read, in the name of your lord, who created.
> He created man from an embryo.
> Read, and your lord, most exalted.
> He teaches by means of the pen.
> He teaches man what he never knew [Khalifa 1999].

Completely convinced of the holy nature of these visita-tions, Khadijah urged Muhammad to accept the challenge by becoming Allah's messenger and spokesman for the oppressed. Thus began his twenty-two years of commu-nion with the Almighty, which he achieved through reg-ular states of trance or ecstasy and through Jibreel's edu-cation in seven methods of recitation.

With Khadijah, Muhammad sired four daughters—Zaynab, Ruqayya, Umm Kulthum, and Fatima—and al-Qasim, al-Tayyib, and al-Tahir, three sons who died in childhood. His daughter Fatima, also called Al-Zahra (Shining One), was born in the second year of their union. She and her husband 'Ali ibn Abu Talib, Muhammad's nephew and lieutenant, produced sons Hassan and Hus-sein, noble heirs of Muhammad. One of the four perfect women lauded in the Koran, she was faithful to her father and nursed him during his last months. At her death from a wasting disease at age twenty-six, she was proclaimed one of the four perfect women of Islam. Shi'ite Muslims revere her descendants as the Fatimids, the prophet's true line.

During a period of expanded trade, Muhammad's evangelism soothed spiritual and intellectual unrest and aroused heathens to fervent spirituality. Some seekers insisted that he perform miracles, but he maintained that he was a simple preacher, not a wonder worker. Initially ignored by Jews and ridiculed by polytheists, he rejuvenated and energized Mecca's slaves and underclass freemen until the Quraysh hegemony saw him as a threat. They ousted him for defaming the goddesses Allat, Alozza, and Mana and for preaching unfamiliar and theologically unsettling concepts: resurrection of the dead and punishment in hell for the *kafir* (unbeliever). Their hostility also demonstrated a fear that Mecca would lose revenue from Bedouin pilgrims if they allowed Muhammad to overthrow a steady trade in idols and shrine visitation.

Like the prophet, early Muslims suffered disrespect, insults, stoning, and vilification. Some languished in prison; the first *muezzin*, who summoned Muslims to prayer, lay in the desert with a rock on his chest. At length, his tormentor gave up trying to force him to recant and sold him into slavery. On July 16, 622, an assassin made an attempt on the prophet's life. On September 16, Muhammad began the holy *hijra* (or *hegira*; migration). Over a roundabout route that took him south to a cave on Mount Thaur and west across the desert toward the Red Sea, he proceeded some 200 miles north to the agrarian community of Yathrib (later named Medina or Madinah), arriving around September 22 or 24. The event marks the birth of Islam and the first year of the Islamic calendar.

In new territory, Muhammad allowed his camel to choose the appropriate site for a mosque. He raised an army of Bedouin, agricultural, and merchant converts and, in March 624, successfully countered an overwhelming Meccan foe at the battle of Badr, the first decisive Islamic conflict. To his troops, he was outspoken, even militant. Surah 47 commands in verse 4:

If you encounter [in war] those who disbelieve,
  you may strike the necks.
If you take them as captives you may set them free or ransom
  them,
  until the war ends.
Had god willed, he could have granted you victory, without
  war,
  but he thus tests you by one another.
As for those who get killed in the cause of god,
  he will never put their sacrifice to waste [Khalifa 1999].

At a subsequent battle fought at Mount Uhut, Muhammad fell in combat from a javelin wound to the jaw. Shortly recovered, he marched on Mecca in C.E. 628 and made a triumphant entry to the city shrine on al-Kaswa, the same camel that had carried him out of the city six years before.

Ultimately, Muhammad and his army of 30,000 seized Arabia and forced an end to idol worship. To his soldiers, he awarded glory in the afterlife for fighting the cause of Allah; to all Muslims, he proclaimed a fraternity of believers that ended tribalism. After making Medina the "City of Cities" and Madinat an-Nabi, the "City of the Prophet," in C.E. 630, he became the first leader to unite clannish herders and tribal factions into a great empire under Islam. He broadcast the all-consuming nature of Allah:

Allah! There is no god save him, the alive, the eternal.
Neither slumber nor sleep overtaketh him.
Unto him belongeth whatsoever is in the heavens
  and whatsoever is in the earth.
Who is he that intercedeth with him save by his leave?
He knoweth that which is in front of them
  and that which is behind them,
  while they encompass nothing of his knowledge
  save what he will.
His throne includeth the heavens and the earth,
  and he is never weary of preserving them.
He is the sublime, the tremendous [Surah 2:255; Pickthall
  1930].

Muhammad's decision to make non–Muslims choose conversion, death, or a tax on infidels enriched the Muslim state, for large numbers chose the latter. Throughout these diplomatic and military exploits, he continued dictating scripture to his four secretaries, his nephew 'Ali ibn Abu Talib, Mu'awiyah ibn Abi Sufyan, 'Ubey ibn Ka'ab, and Zayd ibn Thabit.

In reaction against the Christian doctrine of celibacy, Muhammad embraced polygyny and married a total of twenty wives, thirteen of whom can be identified by name. They were a varied group and included a Jew and an Ethiopian Christian. One, Mary of Egypt (or Mary the Copt), bore his fourth son, named Ibrahim. At the infant's death, Muhammad buried him with his own hands. He followed the advice of a matchmaker and took a child bride, Ayesha (also A'iesha) bint abu-Bakr (or Bekr), third of his nine wives. Born in C.E. 613 to first caliph Abu Bakr, Muhammad's friend and adviser who accompanied him on the flight to Medina, she converted to Islam and entered a three-year period of betrothal at age seven. Before the age of ten, she married Muhammad and rose to the position of second wife after the death of Khadijah. Ayesha was present during his communion with the angel Jibreel. For her role in assisting Muhammad's revelations, she earned the titles of Prophetess, Mother of the Believers, and Mother of the Faithful.

In the midst of the army's attack on Medina, Ayesha strayed from the convoy to search for a missing necklace. In returning her to Muhammad, the handsome bodyguard Safwan incurred scandal that clouded the marriage.

At the urging of 'Ali, Muhammad sent her back to her family. The incident inspired Muhammad to compose surah 24. Verses 5–10 encode a sacred law governing punishment of adulterers with 100 lashes:

If they repent afterwards and reform, then god is forgiver,
    merciful.
As for those who accuse their own spouses,
  without any other witnesses, then the testimony may be ac-
    cepted
  if he swears by god four times that he is telling the truth.
The fifth oath shall be to incur god's condemnation upon
    him,
  if he was lying.
She shall be considered innocent if she swears by god four
    times
  that he is a liar.
The fifth oath shall incur god's wrath upon her if he was
    telling the truth.
This is god's grace and mercy towards you.
God is redeemer, most wise [Khalifa 1999].

The softening of the last verses suggests that Muhammad believed his wife's innocence.

In a final illness on June 8, 632, Muhammad asked to be carried to Ayesha's hut, where he laid his head in her lap. Before his death, he left his following in the charge of Abu Bakr, known as As-siddiq (the Upright), who conducted prayers for the dying prophet. When he expired, the *hadith* reports Ayesha's reaction: "The apostle died in my bosom. ... Then I laid his head on a pillow, and got up beating my breast and slapping my face" (Williams 1961, 75). The devout declared that he had gone straight to Allah without first dying a mortal death. Muhammad's body lies buried at the *Masjid al-Nabi* (Mosque of the Prophet) in Medina, near Fatima, his disciple 'Ali, and Ayesha's humble cottage.

The aftermath of Muhammad's death was a dynamic but troubled period that saw the spread of Arab power from Syria, Iraq, Persia, and Egypt to Central Asia, North Africa, and southern Europe. In awe of the prophet, followers memorize his revelations. They follow the five pillars of Islam:

- recitation of the creed "There is no God but Allah, and Muhammad is his prophet" (Smith 1958, 236).
- *salat* (daily prayer) in the *qiblah* position — that is, facing Mecca — at morning, noon, mid-afternoon, after sunset, and before bed
- *zakat* (charity) to uplift the poor
- annual observance of thirty days of Ramadan by abstaining from food and drink during daylight hours
- *hajj* (or *hadj*), a sacred once-in-a-lifetime ritual journey to Mecca conducted during *Dhu al-Hijja*, the month of pilgrimage

In addition, the faithful give up alcohol and gambling, receive no interest on their money and goods, and eat no pork. They limit sexual activity to marriage, abandon infanticide, defend the faith, and include daughters in inheritance. Other evidence of the civilizing effect of Islam includes pursuit of peace and fellowship with all Muslims, who are greeted with the traditional address "*Salam alakum* [Peace be upon you]" (Smith 1958, 250).

Because many of the several hundred *qurra'* died in C.E. May 633 at the battle of al-Yamamah at Najd, a rocky flat in central Arabia, adviser 'Umar (or Omar) ibn Al-Khattab urged Abu Bakr to secure the prophet's revelations, some of which may have perished on the battlefield. To the prophet's young scribe and foster son Zayd (or Zaid) ibn Thabit, Abu Bakr entrusted the job of collecting scriptural sayings and visions from oral accounts and from a jumble of writings on scraps of paper and parchment, stones, bark, palm leaves, splinters of boards, and dry shoulder blades and rib bones of camels and sheep. Zayd was overwhelmed by the importance of the task, which he compared to moving mountains.

Composed in an abbreviated form of Arabic writing, the lettering Zayd employed was more memory aid than formal written text. He admitted to misplacing one key segment, verse 23 from surah 33, which says, "Among the believers there are people who fulfill their pledges with God. Some of them died, while others stand ready, never wavering" (Khalifa 1999). For this oversight and others, some historians surmise that, owing to the fragility of scattered sources, Zayd may have had more influence on the completed *mushaf* (written codex) than orthodox Muslims are willing to admit.

Through repeated clashes with apostates, Abu Bakr successfully quelled opposition to Islam while bringing Arabia under control. At his death, 'Umar (or Omar) ibn Al-Khattab or 'Umar I, father of Muhammad's wife Hafsa, rose to a dual religio-political post — caliph and commander of the faithful — and established Islamic Arabia as a world power. He remained in the caliphate for a decade, until a slave murdered him. At his death, Hafsa took charge of the precious sheets that Zayd had copied. In the seclusion of widowhood, she hid the finished text under her bed.

Ironically, it was the third successor, the corrupt and much despised Caliph 'Uthman (or Othman) ibn Affan, who retrieved the copy from Hafsa. He had two reasons for his bold act: to disseminate Allah's revelations among Muslims in Medina, Mecca, Baara, Kufa, and Damascus and to undermine the power of Koranic scholars. At Medina in C.E. 652, twenty years after the prophet's death, he appointed four Islamic insiders — Zayd ibn Thabit, Abdullah ibn Al Zubayr, Saeed ibn Al-Aas, and Abdur-Rahman ibn Harith ibn Hisham — to a commission to issue the segments in the original Quraysh dialect.

At its completion in C.E. 651, the caliph entrusted the original codex to Hafsa, who housed it in the Medina mosque. To standardize the faith, he sent copies to Damascus, Basra, and Kufa, of which two allegedly survive, one in the Topkapi Museum in Istanbul and a second in Tashkent, Uzbekistan. To end sectarian disputes and challenges to authority, the caliph ordered the burning of any scriptural material that deviated from his. He targeted the scriptural collections of 'Ubey ibn Ka'ab, Abu Musa al-'Ash'ari, Miqdad ibn 'Amr, and, particularly, 'Abdallah ibn Mas'ud of Kufa, who had refused to give up his copy, which contained 100 surahs. Scholars and historians have reason to wonder about the manuscripts that perished in the fires that purged Islam of rival versions of Muhammad's revelations.

The committee's reordering of Muhammad's visions produced an arrangement now recognized as the true version. They positioned as the first surah, *al-fâtiha* (also *Fatihah* or *fatihat al-kitab*), "The Commencement" (also "The Exordium or Opening"), a beloved seven-verse devotional prayer dating to around C.E. 613. A monument to monotheism, it exalts Allah and the godly life:

> In the name of god, most gracious, most merciful.
> Praise be to god, lord of the universe,
>   most gracious, most merciful,
>   master of the day of judgment.
> You alone we worship; you alone we ask for help.
> Guide us in the right path:
>   the path of those whom you blessed;
>   not of those who have deserved wrath,
>   nor of the strayers [Khalifa 1999].

Similar in reverence and function to the Jewish *Sh'ma* and the Lord's Prayer in Christianity, this surah states the essence of doctrine. Muslims intone it daily during ritual prayers, by sickbeds, and at funerals and inscribe it on religious amulets to ward off the evil eye. Some even write verses in ink, which they dissolve in water and drink to strengthen and protect the body.

Rather than by chronology or genre, the organizing principle for the remaining 113 surahs is by chapter length — greatest to least or from 700 lines to three. The longest chapter is surah 2 with 286 verses, followed by a gradual decline in length to surahs 103, 106, and 108, containing three verses, and the final surah, composed of six verses. The quality of the Uthmanic text was irregular for two reasons: variances in dialect and inadequacy of Arabic script, which, at that time, lacked vowels.

When an assassin killed the controversial caliph, in June C.E. 656, he precipitated the first Islamic civil war. Ayesha's troops clashed with 'Ali's supporters at Basra, Iraq. Against the scolding of Umm Salama, another of Muhammad's wives, Ayesha refused to be silenced or accept a subservient female role. At the battle of the Camel

on December 13, 656, she joined an expedition of Shi'ites, or true successors of the prophet, to prevent 'Ali and his Sunnites from seizing the succession. Popular stories assert that seventy troopers died in the act of guarding her camel. 'Ali ordered her mount hacked to death and routed her army. Under his guard, she lived at Medina to her mid-sixties and recounted Muhammad's wishes and deeds.

Over some four decades, Islam became the first philosophy to abolish paganism and unite Arabs into one civilization. The faith took its current shape at Mecca, home of Muhammad and Khadijah and the location of the Kaaba (also Qa'bah or Ka'bah; cube), a small box-shaped shrine and sanctuary at the heart of the Great Mosque. Composed of marble and gray stone and covered much of the year in black velvet, which is shredded annually and distributed as holy relics, it rests on three columns and is lighted by hanging lamps. A paradigm of structure and order, it is situated so its corners mark north, east, south, and west. Oral tradition attributes its holiness to the Black Stone of Mecca, a foundation block that God gave Adam upon his expulsion from Eden. The patriarch Abraham and his first son, Ishmael, completed the shrine after it had crumbled following the Great Flood that only Noah and his family survived.

After abandoning a plan to dismantle the great cube, Muhammad sanctified the Kaaba as Holy of Holies by destroying the 360 idols on its premises, including likenesses of Jesus and the Virgin Mary, and cleansing the interior of pagan offerings. On one inner wall are ancient paintings that Muhammad spared because they depict the patriarch Abraham. Since that time, the shrine has served Muslims of all races and cultures as a focus for prayer and *hajj*. As commanded in surah 2:197, composed shortly after Muhammad's flight to Medina:

Whoever is minded to perform the pilgrimage
  therein [let him remember that]
  here is [to be] no lewdness nor abuse
  nor angry conversation on the pilgrimage.
And whatsoever good ye do, Allah knoweth it [Pickthall 1930].

Pilgrims follow severe injunctions to dress in a ritual cotton garment, cover their feet in special slippers, refrain from shaving or cutting nails, abandon hunting, halt all quarrels and trivial conversation, and separate men from women to assure the concentration of the godly. Seekers known as *hajji* (or *hadji*) humble themselves at the Kaaba during *Dhu al-Hijja*, when they walk the perimeter seven times and venerate the cornerstone with kisses. According to legend, the stone, once white, has blackened from contact with so many sinners and, after years of caresses, is held together with a silver band. A more scientific version identifies the stone as a meteorite. Adjacent to the Kaaba is the well called Zem-zem, a stream of holy water that flowed spontaneously in the desert to rescue Hagar and her son Ishmael from perishing.

For Muslims, who forbid architectural and sculptural likenesses of God, the Kaaba requires less veneration than the Koran, which is a source of permanence in a changing world. Islamic scripture comprises aphorisms, admonitions, legal prescriptions, prayers, paeans, formal addresses to Allah, fables, parables, polemics, lists of rituals, and graphic eschatology, a description of the end of time. The text falls into identifiable but abrupt and disjointed chapters on didactic topics. Seventy carry concrete titles; the rest appear under abstract headings, preserved in Arabic even in translation:

Surah 1, *al-Fatehah*, "The Key" or "The Opening"
Surah 2, *al-Baqarah*, "The Heifer" or "The Cow"
Surah 3, *Ali-'Imran*, "The Amramites," "The Family of Imran," or "The House of Imran"
Surah 4, *Al-Nesa'*, "The Women"
Surah 5, *al-Ma'edah*, "The Feast," "The Dinner Table," or "The Table"
Surah 6, *al-An'am*, "Livestock" or "Cattle"
Surah 7, *al-'Araf*, "Purgatory," "The Elevated Places," or "The Battlements"
Surah 8, *al-Anfal*, "Spoils of War"
Surah 9, *Bara'ah*, "Ultimatum," "Accessions," or "Repentance"
Surah 10, *Younus*, "Jonah"
Surah 11, *Hud*, "Hood" or "The Holy Prophet"
Surah 12, *Yousuf*, "Joseph"
Surah 13, *al-Ra'ad*, "Thunder"
Surah 14, *Ibrahim*, "Abraham"
Surah 15, *al-Hijr*, "Al-Hijr Valley," "The Rock," or "El-Hijr"
Surah 16, *al-Nahl*, "The Bee"
Surah 17, *Bani Israel*, "The Children of Israel" or "The Night Journey"
Surah 18, *al-Kahf*, "The Cave"
Surah 19, *Maryam*, "Marium," "Miriam," or "Mary"
Surah 20, *Ta-ha*, "Ta Ha"
Surah 21, *al-Anbya'*, "The Prophets"
Surah 22, *al-Hajj*, "The Pilgrimage"
Surah 23, *al-Mu'minun*, "The Believers"
Surah 24, *al-Noor*, "The Light"
Surah 25, *al-Furqan*, "The Statute Book," "The Distinction," or "Salvation"
Surah 26, *al-Shu'ara'*, "The Poets"
Surah 27, *al-Naml*, "The Ant"
Surah 28, *al-Qasas*, "History," "The Narrative," or "The Story"
Surah 29, *al-'Ankaboot*, "The Spider"

Surah 30, *al-Room* or *al-Rum*, "The Romans" or "The Greeks"
Surah 31, *Luqman*, "Luqman" or "Lokman"
Surah 32, *al-Sajdah,* "The Prostration" or "The Adoration"
Surah 33, *al-Ahzab*, "The Parties," "The Clans," or "The Confederates"
Surah 34, *Saba'*, "Sheba" or "The Saba"
Surah 35, *Faater* or *al-Mala'ika*, "The Initiator," "The Originator," or "The Angels"
Surah 36, *Ya-Sin*, "Ya Sin" or "Yasin"
Surah 37, *al-Saffat*, "The Arrangers" or "The Rangers"
Surah 38, *Saad*, "Sad" or "Suad"
Surah 39, *al-Zumar*, "The Throngs," "The Companions," or "The Companies"
Surah 40, *Ghafer*, "The Forgiver" or "The Believer"
Surah 41, *Fussilat*, "Detailed," "Ha Mim," or "Distinguished"
Surah 42, *al-Shoora*, "Consultation" or "Counsel"
Surah 43, *al-Zukhruf*, "Ornaments" or "Gold Ornaments"
Surah 44, *al-Dukhan*, "Smoke"
Surah 45, *al-Jatheyah*, "Kneeling" or "Hobbling"
Surah 46, *al-Ahqaf*, "The Dunes," "Sandhills," or "Sand Dunes"
Surah 47, *Muhammad*, "Muhammad"
Surah 48, *al-Fatt-h*, "Victory"
Surah 49, *al-Hujurat*, "The Walls," "The Chambers," or "Apartments"
Surah 50, *Qaf*, "Q"
Surah 51, *al-Dhareyat*, "Drivers of the Winds" or "The Scatterers"
Surah 52, *al-Toor*, "Mount Sinai" or "The Mountain"
Surah 53, *al-Najm*, "The Stars" or "The Star"
Surah 54, *al-Qamar*, "The Moon"
Surah 55, *al-Rahmaan*, "Most Gracious," "The Beneficent," or "The All-Merciful"
Surah 56, *al-Waaqe'ah*, "The Inevitable," "The Event," or "The Terror"
Surah 57, *al-Hadeed*, "Iron"
Surah 58, *al-Mujaadalah*, "The Debate," "She Who Pleaded," or "The Disputer"
Surah 59, *al-Hashr*, "Exodus," "Banishment," or "The Mustering"
Surah 60, *al-Mumtahanah*, "The Test," "The Examined One," or "The Woman Tested"
Surah 61, *al-Suff*, "The Column" or "The Ranks"
Surah 62, *al-Jumu'ah*, "Friday" or "Congregation"
Surah 63, *al-Munaafeqoon*, "The Hypocrites"
Surah 64, *al-Taghaabun*, "Mutual Blaming," "The Mutual Deceit," or "Mutual Fraud"

Surah 65, *al-Talaaq*, "Divorce"

Surah 66, *al-Tahreem*, "Prohibition" or "The Forbidding"

Surah 67, *al-Mulk*, "Kingship" or "The Kingdom"

Surah 68, *al-Qalam*, "The Pen"

Surah 69, *al-Haaqqah*, "Incontestable," "The Inevitable," or "The Indubitable"

Surah 70, *al-Ma'aarej*, "The Heights," "Ways of Ascent," or "The Stairways"

Surah 71, *Noah*, "Noah"

Surah 72, *al-Jinn*, "The Jinn"

Surah 73, *al-Muzzammil*, "Clocked" or "The Enwrapped One"

Surah 74, *al-Muddath-thir*, "The Hidden Secret," "The Wrapped Up," or "Shrouded"

Surah 75, *al-Qeyaamah* or *al-Kiyama*, "Resurrection"

Surah 76, *al-Insaan*, "The Human," "Time," or "Man"

Surah 77, *al-Mursalaat*, "Dispatched," "The Sent Forth," or "The Loosed Ones"

Surah 78, *al-Naba'*, "The Great Event" or "The Tiding"

Surah 79, *al-Naaze'aat*, "The Snatchers," "The Draggers," or "The Pluckers"

Surah 80, *'Abasa*, "He Frowned"

Surah 81, *al-Takweer*, "The Rolling," "The Folded Up," "The Overthrowing," or "The Darkening"

Surah 82, *al-Infitaar*, "The Shattering," "The Cleaving," or "The Splitting"

Surah 83, *al-Mutaffifee*n, "The Cheaters," "The Deceivers in Measuring," or "The Stinters"

Surah 84, *al-Inshiqaaq*, "The Rupture" or "The Rending Asunder"

Surah 85, *al-Burooj*, "The Galaxies," "The Celestial Stations," or "The Constellations"

Surah 86, *al-Taareq*, "The Bright Star," "The Nightly Visitant," or "The Night Star"

Surah 87, *al-A'alaa*, "The Most High"

Surah 88, *al-Ghaasheyah*, "The Overwhelming Calamity" or "The Enveloper"

Surah 89, *al-Fajr*, "The Dawn" or "The Daybreak"

Surah 90, *al-Balad*, "The Town," "The City," or "The Land"

Surah 91, *al-Shams*, "The Sun"

Surah 92, *al-Layl*, "The Night"

Surah 93, *al-Duhaa*, "The Forenoon" or "The Brightness"

Surah 94, *al-Sharrhh*, "Cooling the Temper" or "The Expansion"

Surah 95, *al-Teen*, "The Fig"

Surah 96, *al-'Alaq*, "The Embryo" or "The Blood Clot"

Surah 97, *al-Qadr*, "Destiny," "The Grandeur," or "Power"

Surah 98, *al-Bayyinah*, "Proof," "The Clear Evidence," or "The Clear Sign"

Surah 99, *al-Zalzalah*, "The Quaking" or "The Earthquake"

Surah 100, *al-'Aadeyaat*, "The Gallopers" or "The Chargers"

Surah 101, *al-Qaare'ah*, "The Shocker," "The Calamity," or "The Clatterer"

Surah 102, *al-Takaathur*, "Hoarding," "Vying in Abundance," or "Rivalry"

Surah 103, *al-'Asr*, "The Afternoon" or "The Age"

Surah 104, *al-Humazah*, "The Backbiter" or "The Slanderer"

Surah 105, *al-Feel*, "The Elephant"

Surah 106, *Quraish*, "The Qureaish Tribe" or "Koraish"

Surah 107, *al-Maa'oon*, "Charity" or "Alms"

Surah 108, *al-Kawthar*, "Bounty" or "The Abundance of Good"

Surah 109, *al-Kaaferoon*, "The Disbelievers" or "Unbelievers"

Surah 110, *al-Naasr*, "Triumph" or "Help"

Surah 111, *al-Masad*, "Thorns," "The Flame," or "Perish"

Surah 112, *al-Ikhlaas*, "Absoluteness," "Unity," or "Sincere Religion"

Surah 113, *al-Falaq*, "The Daybreak" or "The Dawn"

Surah 114, *al-Naas*, "People" or "Men"

Surahs open on a formulaic arrangement called the *basmalah*, a prescribed prayer or brief formal address to Allah, as with surah 79, which begins, "In the name of god, most gracious, most merciful" (Khalifa 1999). Early revelations produced short verses marked by *fasila* (assonance) that reflect the influence of the rhymed and cadenced utterances of seventh-century *kahana* (soothsayers), whose inspiration came from the *jinn* (genies). The result is an original, mystical, and subtly nuanced expression. For example, surah 112, the shortest of chapters, sums up Allah's being:

In the name of god, most gracious, most merciful,
 proclaim, "He is the one and only god, the absolute god."
Never did he beget.
Nor was he begotten.
None equals him [Khalifa 1999].

Later visions tend toward longer, more complex prosaic statements of Allah, who speaks as "we," the royal plural. Allusions imply a common body of lore and hagiography widely known in Muhammad's day, especially the battles by which the prophet established Islam and raised Allah above pagan gods.

The Koran instructs the faithful to memorize verses and practice the lessons of scripture. Among the more revered of the pious is the *hafiz* (custodian), an individual who has committed the entire Koran to memory. Ordinary worshipers learn as much text as possible and recite appropriate verses during the daily series of five prayers. For such special occasions as marriage, birth, and death, recitation of scriptural blessings links human endeavors with the divine. In the most devout countries, meetings and gatherings open with readings.

During Ramadan, the sacred ninth month of the year, daily fasting accompanies a reading of the entire Koran in thirty segments and concludes with the '*Id al-Fitr*, a joyful festival of charity and gift giving. The selection of this hallowed time follows the scriptural injunction in surah 2:185:

The month of Ramadan in which was revealed the Qur'an,
  a guidance for mankind, and clear proofs of the guidance,
  and the criterion [of right and wrong].
And whosoever of you is present, let him fast the month,
  and whosoever of you is sick or on a journey,
  [let him fast the same] number of other days.
Allah desireth for you ease; he desireth not hardship for you;
  and [he desireth] that ye should complete the period,
  and that ye should magnify Allah for having guided you,
  and that peradventure ye may be thankful [Pickthall 1930].

To express respect and admiration for the sacredness of scripture, artisans adorn copies of the Koran with calligraphy, illumination, mosaic, and ornate binding, and they inscribe on mausoleums, mosques, schools, and façades of government buildings names for Allah and key scriptural passages. One of the most famous is the lengthy conflated citation refuting Christianity in blue and gold glass mosaic, which Abd al-Malik inscribed in C.E. 692 around the inner and outer surfaces of the octagonal arcade at Jerusalem's Dome of the Rock.

To the seeker, the Koran offers solace and acceptance. The sonorous richness of surah 93, epitomizes Allah's goodness:

By the forenoon, by the night as it falls,
  your lord never abandoned you, nor did he forget.
The hereafter is far better for you than this first [life].
And your lord will give you enough; you will be pleased.
Did he not find you orphaned and he gave you a home?
He found you astray, and guided you.
He found you poor, and made you rich [Khalifa 1999].

This direct commentary speaks to the Muslim in general and to the orphaned Muhammad, whose childhood was filled with upheaval. Such personal reassurances permeate the text, reminding in this same surah:

With him are the keys to all secrets;
  none knows them except he.

He knows everything on land and in the sea.
Not a leaf falls without his knowledge.
Nor is there a grain in the depths of the soil.
Nor is there anything wet or dry,
  that is not recorded in a profound record [Khalifa 1999].

To intensify the image of the omniscient overseer, this hymnic surah declares that Allah knows the actions of all, day and night. He puts his people into the false death of sleep and reawakens them at morning in a miniature resurrection. He supervises all of life, "until your life span is fulfilled, then to him is your ultimate return. He will then inform you of everything you had done." This antithesis between preserving and ending life gives the Koran its stern yet loving authority.

In addition to Arabic philosophy, custom, and moral counsel, the Koran acknowledges the sacred scriptures of Palestine, found in the Torah, Psalms, and the Christian gospels. It contains biographies of Noah, Jonah, and Abraham and reflects the influence of older hallowed authorities, notably, the Torah, Talmud, and Zoroastrian lore. Surah 2 declares:

We believe in God, and in that which has been sent down on us
  and sent down on Abraham, Ishmael, Isaac and Jacob, and the tribes,
  and that which was given to Moses and Jesus and the Prophets, of their lord; we make no division between any of them and to him we surrender [Williams 1961, 28].

A long narrative, surah 12 recounts the life of Joseph, the beloved son of the patriarch Jacob, a life history more heavily detailed in Genesis 39–50. The story opens at a dramatic moment when Joseph reports to his father a vision of eleven planets, sun, and moon prostrating themselves before him. Jacob assures the boy that the revelation is proof of divine blessing on him and his offspring. This family favoritism causes Jacob's other sons to concoct a ruse in which they deposit Joseph in a well and present a bloody shirt as evidence he was savaged by a wolf.

After a caravan of traders sells Joseph into bondage in Egypt, his owner's wife accuses him of attempted rape, but the husband, who is governor of the land, recognizes the truth. To prevent subsequent seductions, Joseph asks for a prison sentence. Because of his skill at divination, he interprets the king's dream about seven fat cows and seven lean cows and is elevated to state treasurer.

The story provides an opportunity for vengeance when the evil brothers appear before Joseph but do not recognize him. Through trickery, he causes them to return with his younger brother and aged father. In verse 100, Joseph declares:

O my father, this is the fulfillment of my old dream.
My lord has made it come true.

He has blessed me, delivered me from the prison,
  and brought you from the desert,
    after the devil had driven a wedge between me and my
      brothers.
My lord is most kind towards whomever he wills.
He is the knower, the most wise [Khalifa 1999].

The story, interlaced with interpretation, concludes with a homily on faith and trust in Allah. In this and other lore paralleling Judaic tradition, words from Hebrew and Syriac—*iblis* (devil), *injil* (gospel), *taurat* (law), *amana* (believe), *salat* (prayer)—suggest that the Jewish version was an influential source.

The exemplum, a brief moral tale or anecdote common to religious texts, appears in verses 9–21 of surah 18. The action depicts two young men sealed in a cave for several years. When released into the light, they explain how they calculated the passage of time. Verse 17 offers one form of time measurement:

And thou mightest have seen the sun when it rose
  move away from their cave to the right,
  and when it set go past them on the left,
  and they were in the cleft thereof.
That was [one] of the portents of Allah.
He whom Allah guideth, he indeed is led aright,
  and he whom he sendeth astray,
    for him thou wilt not find a guiding friend [Pickthall 1930].

Filled with allegorical layering, this gnomic story has provoked various interpretations. One characterizes Allah's promise as a guarantee of resurrection of the body, the symbolic freeing of the men from the cave, which represents earthly life.

To Jews and Christians, Islam's religious rivals in the Middle East, the Koran speaks directly to the differences in their doctrines. Muslims abhor and construe as blasphemous the Holy Trinity, the Christian concept of Father, Son, and Holy Spirit. Surah 5, verse 18, declares:

The Jews and the Christians said, "We are God's children and
  his beloved."
Say, "Why then does he punish you for your sins?
  You are just humans like the other humans he created."
He forgives whomever he wills and punishes whomever he
  wills.
To God belongs the sovereignty of the heavens and the earth,
  and everything between them, and to him is the final des-
    tiny [Khalifa 1999].

The passage asserts that mockers, deceivers, and those who follow other scriptures are doomed for their sins. Verse 65 tempers this stern dictum with a promise, "If only the people of the scripture believe and lead a righteous life, we will then remit their sins, and admit them into gardens of bliss."

Of particular concern in this surah is the Christian elevation of Jesus to a god. The reasoning appears in verse 75, "The messiah, son of Mary, is no more than a messenger like the messengers before him, and his mother was a saint." The surah juxtaposes Christ worship with the sins of drinking intoxicants, gambling, and worshiping idols. Verses 116–119 supply an illuminating exchange between Allah and Jesus that justifies Koranic doctrine:

God will say, "O Jesus, son of Mary, did you say to the people,
  'Make me and my mother idols beside god?'"
He will say, "Be you glorified. I could not utter what was not
  right.
Had I said it, you already would have known it.
You know my thoughts, and I do not know your thoughts.
You know all the secrets.
I told them only what you commanded me to say, that:
  'You shall worship god, my lord and your lord.'
I was a witness among them for as long as I lived with them.
When you terminated my life on earth, you became the
  watcher over them.
You witness all things.
If you punish them, they are your constituents.
If you forgive them, you are the almighty, most wise."
God will proclaim, "This is a day when the truthful will be
  saved
  by their truthfulness."
They have deserved gardens with flowing streams.
They abide therein forever [Khalifa 1999].

The surah closes with Allah's delight in the righteous and the triumph of his salvation.

Surah 19 corroborates the Christian belief in Jesus's divine nativity. Verses 19–21 attest to the annunciation from a heavenly messenger to Mary and a gentle reassurance that her miraculous pregnancy was predestined by Allah. The dramatic birth described in verses 22–25 bears little connection with gospel accounts:

When she bore him, she isolated herself to a faraway place.
The birth process came to her by the trunk of a palm tree.
She said, "[I am so ashamed;]
  I wish I were dead before this happened, and completely for-
    gotten."
[The infant] called her from beneath her, saying,
  "Do not grieve.
  Your lord has provided you with a stream.
  If you shake the trunk of this palm tree, it will drop ripe
    dates for you" [Khalifa 1999].

In retort to New Testament accounts in Matthew and Luke, the Koran justifies the Islamic version in verse 35, "It does not befit god that he begets a son, be he glorified. To have anything done, he simply says to it, 'Be,' and it is." Also adverse to Christian doctrine, verses 4:157–158 deny the crucifixion by asserting that Allah received Jesus directly into heaven.

Integral to Islam in the twenty-first century is the place of women. Arab society has outgrown desert patriarchy, yet rejects what it considers the decline of Judeo-Christian morality. Muslims tend to lump together the faults of the West under the broad headings of sexual license, betrayal of faith, and the Western woman's abdication of duties to home and family. Significant to critics of Islam, who also tend to overgeneralize and oversimplify, is the fact that segregated worship, veiling, and immurement of women in harems—cultural requirements that Christians equate with misogyny—are not scriptural dictates. Rather, they evolved three generations after Muhammad's death. Even then, the covering of the face was limited to aristocratic women as a mark of elevation above the peasantry. The practice was first openly and widely challenged in the 1920s in imitation of the example of Hud Sha'rawi, an Egyptian feminist who discarded the veil following her attendance at an international women's conference.

According to tradition, at the suggestion of his wife Umm Salama, Muhammad attempted to overcome patriarchal practice by outlining the specifics of women's social and moral role. In contrast to Judeo-Christian dictates, Islamic marriage is a legal contract, not a sacrament. An inclusive statement of human morality, surah 4 is the heart of Koranic teachings on gender. Verses 3–4 justify polygyny as an act of compassion:

If you deem it best for orphans, you may marry their mothers—
　you may marry two, three, or four.
If you fear lest you become unfair, then you shall be content with only one,
　or with what you already have.
Additionally, you are thus more likely to avoid financial hardship.
You shall give the women their due dowries, equitably.
If they willingly forfeit anything, then you may accept it;
　it is rightfully yours [Khalifa 1999].

These lines suggest a pragmatic, altruistic arrangement intended as a public service to fatherless children and their widowed mothers. The basis for Muhammad's doctrine returns to his core intent to uplift oppressed minorities and other downtrodden people. However, the Koran does not provide a similar privilege to women, who may marry only one man, who must be a Muslim.

Additional admonitions in surah 4 protect women from unscrupulous or exploitive men. Verse 20 declares that women retain their possessions after divorce. Verse 23 lists women who are off limits: mothers, daughters, sisters, aunts, nieces, wet nurses, mothers-in-law, stepdaughters, and daughters-in-law. Also forbidden for courtship are the sisters of a man's wife and married women. To these injunctions against incest and home wrecking, the text adds in verse 25 Allah's permission to marry Muslim slave women. Such a union requires permission from their guardians, a dowry, and mercy should

they fall into fornication. A sage conclusion notes, "Marrying a slave shall be a last resort for those unable to wait. To be patient is better for you" (Khalifa 1999).

In reference to marital happiness, surah 4 advocates that men take responsibility for women, whom scripture characterizes as less able to care for themselves. Annoyed husbands should apply a three-stage punishment for rebellious wives, beginning with a lecture and abstinence from intercourse and advancing to beating as a last resort. Verse 128 recommends that troubled mates seek reconciliation rather than divorce. To the man seeking additional wives, verse 129 warns, "You can never be equitable in dealing with more than one wife, no matter how hard you try." The line suggests that Muhammad may have been speaking from personal experience.

Additional guidance regarding marital relationships are topics of surah 33, which speaks directly to Muhammad's wives. Verses 30 -31 note that, on account of their privilege of marriage to the prophet, these women were doubly punished for faults and twice rewarded for piety. Verse 32 gives permission for these paragons to violate Arabic custom by speaking up for righteousness in the presence of men. To set an example, the prophet's wives should perform prayer and charity, abstain from unholiness, and embrace purity. The next verse stresses the equality of all who keep Allah's commandments:

The submitting men, the submitting women, the believing men, the believing women, the obedient men, the obedient women, the truthful men, the truthful women, the steadfast men, the steadfast women, the reverent men, the reverent women, the charitable men, the charitable women, the fasting men, the fasting women, the chaste men, the chaste women, and the men who commemorate God frequently, and the commemorating women; God has prepared for them forgiveness and a great recompense [Khalifa 1999].

Verse 59 notes that demure women should lengthen their dress to "avoid being insulted." In recognition of women's inability to halt would-be rapists, the Koran declares that men who stalk or harass women deserve execution. The passage concludes with an uplifting promise, "God redeems the believing men and the believing women. God is forgiver, most merciful." Umm Salama adds in the *hadith* that women who die while in good stead with their husbands go directly to paradise.

A paean to Muhammad's followers faithful to the Muslim creed, both male and female, is the text of surah 23, which avows in verses 1–11:

Successful indeed are the believers;
　who are reverent during their contact prayers.
And they avoid vain talk.
And they give their obligatory charity.
And they maintain their chastity.
Only with their spouses, or those who are rightfully theirs,

do they have sexual relations; they are not to be blamed.
Those who transgress these limits are the transgressors.
When it comes to deposits entrusted to them,
 as well as any agreements they make, they are trustworthy.
And they observe their contact prayers regularly.
Such are the inheritors.
They will inherit paradise, wherein they abide forever [Khalifa 1999].

To those in *akhira* (the afterlife), Allah holds a place in paradise, as described in surah 48:5:

He will certainly admit the believing men and women
 into gardens with flowing streams, wherein they abide forever.
He will remit their sins.
This is, in the sight of god, a great triumph [Khalifa 1999].

For those who fail to live up to Koranic dictates, the end-time described in surah 18 is a misery that begins with an occluded sun, stars ripped from their courses, mountains atremble, and boiling seas. Much of the impact derives from the picture of a solemn day of judgment, a terrifying call to account for human choices. Scripture warns in surah 75, *al-Kiyama*, "Resurrection," of natural cataclysm, the preface to reckoning before Allah:

Does the human being think that we will not reconstruct his bones?
Yes indeed; we are able to reconstruct his finger tip.
But the human being tends to believe only what he sees in front of him.
He doubts the day of resurrection!
Once the vision is sharpened and the moon is eclipsed
 and the sun and the moon crash into one another.
The human being will say on that day, "Where is the escape?"
Absolutely, there is no escape.
To your lord, on that day, is the final destiny [Khalifa 1999].

At world's end, the dead will return to life to hear Allah's judgment of human behavior. Surah 100 contains a surreal vision of the end-time:

By the fast gallopers, igniting sparks, invading [the enemy] by morning,
 striking terror therein,
 penetrating to the heart of their territory,
 the human being is unappreciative of his lord.
He bears witness to this fact.
He loves material things excessively.
Does he not realize that the day will come when the graves are opened
 and all secrets are brought out?
They will find out, on that day,
 that their lord has been fully cognizant of them [Khalifa 1999].

Scripture describes the ingathering of souls as an assembly of "scattered moths" whose deeds Allah will weigh on a balance. Unlike those who earn eternal joy, the doomed will sink into flames at "the womb of the pit."

Because it states sacred revelation in a language dating to the ninth century, the Koran is a daunting task for the average reader. The Koran's chapters fall under two general headings—the *Makkiyah*, or those revelations received in Mecca, and the *Madaniyah*, or the later visions following the migration to Medina. For the sake of clarity, the text underwent redaction through three stages of repunctuation: by Abu Al-Aswad Al Doaly after C.E. 661; by Nasr ibn Asem and Hayy ibn Ya'amor after C.E. 685; and under the completed system of syntactical markings created by Al Khaleel ibn Ahmad Al Faraheedy around C.E. 785. The Uthmanic codex reached canon status by the tenth century, the end of the classical era, when Abu Bakr ibn Mujahid of Baghdad reduced some seven variant readings to one standard version.

These changes were anathema to hard-line Muslim zealots, who have traditionally demanded that nothing be altered in Allah's message to the prophet and that only the original Arabic be recited for ritual purposes. Nonetheless, translators wrestled with the vivid imagery, drama, and mesmerizing rhythm that made Arabic a global language. To serve the global spread of Islam, they issued several translated versions.

A Latin translation was commissioned in 1142 by Peter the Venerable, eighth abbot of the independent monastery at Cluny, and was completed by scholar Herman Dalmatin (also Hermannus Dalmata, Hermannus Sclavus, and Hermannus Secundus) and Deacon Robert of Ketton (also Robertus Retenensis). Theologian Theodor Bibliander (or Buchmann) of Zurich, father of biblical exegesis in Switzerland, published this Latin recension at Basel in 1543.

The first printing in Arabic at Rome was supervised by Dominican friar Santes Pagninus in 1530. A French version, *L'Alcoran de Mahomet* (The Koran of Muhammad), was completed in 1647 by André du Ryer, a trader in the Levant and French consul in Alexandria, Egypt. It is a flawed recension marred by errors, transpositions, omissions, and additions. The translator's desultory introduction indicates the extent of his prejudice:

Thou shalt find it of so rude, and incongruous a composure, so farced with contradictions, blasphemies, obscene speeches, and ridiculous fables, that some modest, and more rational *Mahometans* have thus excused it.... Nor are the vulgar permitted to read it, but live and die in an implicit faith of what their Priests deliver [Arberry 1970, 8].

He adds that Christians opposed its publication in French. Du Ryer persevered in the belief that a true Christian would remain "untainted of their follies" of believing in "this *Ignis Fatuus* [will-o-the-wisp] of the *Alcoran*." He further characterizes the scripture as "a poyson, that hath infected a very great, but most unsound part of the Universe."

In 1694, D. Abraham Hinckelmann, pastor of St. Katharinen, printed an Arabic text in Hamburg. A Latin version, *Alcorani Textus Universus* (The Universal Text of the Koran), was translated by Father Ludovico Maracci, confessor of Pope Innocent XI, and printed in Padua in 1698.

A respected English translation with introductory essay and commentary based on Maracci's version was completed in 1734 by attorney and orientalist George Sale, author of *Lives and Memorable Actions of Many Illustrious Persons of the Eastern Nations* (1739), who had lived a quarter century in Arabia and had studied local customs and language. Sale chose Hinckelmann's Arabic edition as his basis to supplant Alexander Ross's version of du Ryer's *Alcoran*. In the preface, Sale states his religious bias:

> The writers of the Romish communion, in particular, are so far from having done any service in their refutations of Mohammedanism, that by endeavouring to defend their idolatry and other superstitions, they have rather contributed to the increase of that aversion which the Mohammedans in general have to the Christian religion, and given them great advantages in the dispute. The Protestants alone are able to attack the Koran with success; and for them, I trust, Providence has reserved the glory of its overthrow [Arberry 1970, 11].

Versions of Sale's popular text were translated into Dutch in 1742, French in 1750, German in 1764, Russian in 1792, Swedish in 1814, and Bulgarian in 1902.

An 1861 version was translated by the Reverend J. M. Rodwell and published by J. M. Dent and Sons Ltd. In addition to imitating the versification and diction of the ancient Arabic, he reordered surahs and historical sequencing. Based on the text that Gustav Fluegel printed at Leipzig in 1841 and written in an era of scholarly orientalism, the work lacks the superiority, intolerance, and hostility of du Ryer's and Sale's translations. In 1909, the Rodwell translation, considered the standard English version, became a part of Everyman's Library. In deference to Muhammad, Rodwell declared:

> Muhammed was actuated by a sincere desire to deliver his countrymen from the grossness of its debasing idolatries—that he was urged on by an intense desire to proclaim that great truth of the Unity of the godhead which had taken full possession of his own soul—that the end to be attained justified to his mind the means he adopted in the production of his Suras—that he worked himself up into a belief that he had received a divine call—and that he was carried on by the force of circumstances, and by gradually increasing successes, to believe himself the accredited messenger of Heaven [Arberry 1970, 15].

On the surface open-minded, Rodwell's receptivity to the Koran lapses into a patronization of the prophet for "his mistakes and imperfections [which were] the result of circumstances, of temperament, and constitution."

A part of an Oxford University Press series entitled *Sacred Books of the East*, Edward Henry Palmer, a Cambridge scholar and translator of the verse of Egyptian poet Baha al-Din Zuhair issued another version in 1880. Oxford extended circulation of the text by including it in *The World's Classics*.

Muhammad Marmaduke Pickthall, an orientalist and lecturer, published the first version by an English Muslim, *The Meaning of the Glorious Koran* (1930) in London in a dated Elizabethan English that parallels the King James Bible. The translation received the encouragement of his employer, the Nizam of Hyderabad, India, and was reprinted in India, Pakistan, the British Empire, and the United States. Out of respect for Muhammad's scripture, Pickthall noted:

> The result is not the Glorious Koran, that inimitable symphony, the very sounds of which move men to tears and ecstasy. It is only an attempt to present the meaning of the Koran—and peradventure something of the charm—in English. It can never take the place of the Koran in Arabic, nor is it meant to do so [Arberry 1970, 21].

To assure the reader of an authorized version, Pickthall had an English-speaking Egyptian physician, Muhammad Ahmad al-Ghamrawi, scrutinize each word and revise his version with recourse to an authority, Mustafa al-Maraghi, Sheikh al-Azhar.

Richard Bell, reader of Arabic at the University of Edinburgh, published a 1939 edition in two volumes, in a meticulous piece of scholarship that reconstructed verses in tabular form.

Professor Arthur J. Arberry, Sir Thomas Adam Professor of Arabic at London University and author of *The Holy Koran: An Introduction with Selections* (1953), produced a celebrated 1955 translation from the original Arabic. The preface captures the wonder of a true aficionado who once sat through Ramadan nights at Gezira with a master reciter:

> It was then that I, the infidel, learnt to understand and react to the thrilling rhythms of the Koran, only to be apprehended when listened to at such a time and in such a place. In humble thankfulness I dedicate this all too imperfect essay in imitation to the memory of those magical Egyptian nights [Arberry 1970, 28].

Arberry's text rose to prominence, as did his ecumenical spirit of inclusion of the Koran among the world's great spiritual writings.

More onerous than translation from Arabic is analysis and exegesis. *Tafsir* (explanation), a strict science of paraphrasing pithy statements and explaining ambiguities in the Koran, began after the death of the prophet Muhammad and generated philology and lexicography in a necessary assessment of the vocabulary and rhetoric of pre-Islamic poetry. In the first third of the ninth century, under Caliph al-Ma'mun, orthodox Muslims accepted scripture as created over time, like the earth itself. One divergent school of exegetes, the Mu'tazilists, rejected questions of when and how the text came into being and accepted it simply as metaphor. At their eclipse late in the 900s, standard interpretation remained traditional and literal, as unvarying as the Protestant fundamentalist belief in biblical inerrancy.

To unravel the mysteries contained in the message of Allah, officially sanctioned commentators and professional exegetes must meet strict criteria, including knowledge of theological tenets; skill in Koranic sciences, grammar, rhetoric, and linguistics; and mastery of Islamic and scriptural history.

In the golden age of Arabic literature, around C.E. 900, the Iranian historian and scholar Abu Ja'far Muhammad ibn Jarir at-Tabari compiled a thirty-volume encyclopedia, *The Koran Commentary*, a compendium of traditional scholarship up to that time.

In 1972, discovery of a stack of discarded copies of the Koran between the inner and outer roofs at the Great Mosque of Sana'a in Yemen rewarded scriptural scholarship with fragments of the oldest Korans in existence. The cache, which yielded over 15,000 sheets from 1,000 volumes, has affected linguistic, religious, and paleographic study of the literature of the Arabic language and of the early centuries of Islam. A grant from the Getty Institute is underwriting a study of the bindings and illuminations; UNESCO is considering aiding the project as part of its interest in preserving ancient world scripture. Currently catalogued in Yemen's House of Manuscripts and restored with funds from the German government, the fragments have been compared to the Dead Sea Scrolls in their importance to theology and world literature.

Significant to those who examined and ordered these parchment bits from Sana'a are deviations from the canon text. According to Toby Jepson:

> There was still considerable textual modification since the time of Uthman. These manuscripts, possibly from the early eighth century, show significant variation from the text used today. Whole sections are missing and added in with a much later hand. Passages that today read "Say..." [a divine command to Muhammad] are seen to have once been "he said..." or "they said...," indicating a possible attributing of the words of humans to Allah. Over one thousand variants have been found within the first eighty-three surahs alone [Jepson 1997].

This unanticipated disclosure counters the Muslim belief that the Koran is the perfect, unaltered, and unchanging word of Allah.

In 1981, Gerd-R. Puin, a specialist in Arabic calligraphy and paleology at Saarland University in Saarbrücken, Germany, oversaw the vast project of restoring ancient bits from Sana'a. He noted rare spellings, embellishments, verses out of order, palimpsests or erasures of earlier writing, and other variations from the standard Koran. He concluded that, contrary to orthodox belief in a one-time revelation to a prophet, the Koran evolved over a lengthy period before reaching a canon text. Together with his assistant, H.-C. Graf von Bothmer, an Islamic-art historian at Saarland University, Puin has published scholarly articles on the project. In 1997, Bothmer finished taking 35,000 photos on microfilm, which will make the scriptural findings more portable and more accessible to European theologians and Islamicists.

Late twentieth-century scholarly surmise has produced some revisions of long-held suppositions, which disturb orthodox Muslims. Among these queries are several late twentieth-century revisions, including a lengthening of the time line of Islam and the Koran to show the early development of monotheism before Muhammad; another setting of Islam's founding to the northwest of Mecca; a migration of Muslims long after the prophet's death; and a later composition of the Koranic text and the institutionalization of Islam.

Puin concludes that "the Koran is a kind of cocktail of texts that were not all understood even at the time of Muhammad" (Lester 1999, 46). He adds that these concepts may pre-date Islam by a century. Andrew Rippin, professor of religious studies at the University of Calgary, Canada, claims that the Sana'a cache casts doubt on the Koran as a supreme religious authority. A theory proposed by N. A. Morozov suggests that Islam was a twin of Judaism until the Crusades, which began in 1096, when Arab religion developed individuality, in part through the mythic structure of Muhammad, his wars, and the caliphs who succeeded him.

A significant Western exegete, John S. Wansbrough, orientalist at the University of London, proposed in *Quranic Studies: Sources and Methods of Scriptural Interpretation* (1977) and *The Sectarian Milieu: Content and Composition of Islamic Salvation History* (1978) that the Koran was never standardized. Based on the absence of early evidence, he surmised that Islam evolved organically and came together in the tenth century, contemporaneously with Koranic commentary. To establish continuity, religious scholars "projected back in time" to give the faith validity (Lester 1999, 55). A sharp riposte from Muslim apologist S. Parvez Manzoor retorted that these studies produced "a project born of spite, bred in frustration, and nourished by vengeance" (Lester 1999, 48). He restated the orthodox belief that the Koran is historically authentic and morally unassailable.

See also **Mathnawi.**

SOURCES: Abid 1996, Al-Kadi, "Al-Mizan," Arberry 1970, Armstrong 2000, Berry 1956, Braden 1954, "A Brief History of Compilation of the Qur'an" 1997, Bouquet 1954, Burman 1998, Carlyle, Crone and Cook 1977, "The 850th Anniversary of the Scientific and Philosophic Work 'De Essentiis' by Herman Dalmatin," Eisele 1997, Eliade 1967, "Exploring Ancient World Cultures: Islam," Frost 1972, Geissinger 1999, Gentz 1973, Gibb 1963, "The Great Men of Croatian Science," "Herman Dalmata," "Holy Qur'an Sources on the Internet" 1999, Hornstein 1973, Ibrahim and Johnson-Davies n.d., Jepson 1997, Khalifa, M., Khalifa, R. 1999; Lester 1999, "Medieval Sourcebook: Hadith: Traditions of the Prophet" 1996, "Medieval Sourcebook: The Qur'an, 1, 47," Mervin and Prunhuber 1990, *New Catholic Encyclopedia* 1967, Oussani 1999, Pickthall 1930, 1997, Pike 1965, Raffee 1996, Reese 1998, Rifkin 1998, "Rushdie File," Sells 2000, Sharma 1987, Smith 1944, Smith 1958, Snodgrass 1999, 2001, Strayer 1983, Trager 1994, 1995, Turner 1993, Warraq 1998, Watt 1994, Whelan 1998, Williams 1961, *World Literature* 1998, *World Religions* 1998.

Lefafa Sedeq *see* Ethiopian Book of the Dead

Mathnawi

An encyclopedia of deformalized Islamic worship, Rumi's Mathnawi (also Masnavi-ye-Ma'navi [Spiritual Couplets]; ca. 1270) is a compendium of vigorous, euphoric scripture of the Sufi, mystic Muslim zealots. The Sufist order was named for the gray wool cone-topped hat and long-skirted garment that the Sufi wore to whirl in ecstatic gyration to facilitate worship. Fulsome lines violate the strict conservatism of Islam and seek Allah through exquisite sensual delight:

Wine, torch, and beauty are epiphanies of verity,
  for it is that which is revealed under all forms soever.
Wine and torch are the transport and light of the knower;
  behold the beauty, for it is hidden from none [Hastings 1951, 12:16].

Verse intoxicants urge the seeker to let the self die and free the spirit to rapturous delights of the primal soul.

Sufism (also Sufiism) is an alternative method of knowing God. Unlike strict ritual, conservative prayer, and meditation, the movement expresses divine truth, love, and union with the Almighty through dance and ecstatic gestures. Based on ancient practices in India and Europe, it took root in medieval Islamic ascetics who abandoned the materialism of urban Islam, perhaps in imitation of Christian hermits. The Sufist fled the legalism of conservative religious scholarship and obeyed Koranic laws by enlarging on the wonder and power of a personal relationship with Allah.

Sufism generated a hunger for fellowship. Late in the C.E. 700s, Rabi'ah al-'Adawiyah, a female Sufist from Basra, injected a controlling element of unconditional love of Allah. Like Pentecostalism, the faith advocated complete trust in a higher power. Around 850, al-Muhasibi phrased the search for oneness with Allah in terms of ridding the spirit of impurity; simultaneously, Nubian Sufist Dhu an-Nun characterized the *ma' rifah* (interior knowledge) as a juncture of the universe with divinity. In the C.E. 870s, Iranian Sufist Abu Yazid al-Bistami formulated the doctrine of *fana* (annihilation of self), which explained how individual worshipers purged themselves of ego. Around C.E. 900, theologian Junayd of Baghdad standardized Sufist theology, which spread to rulers, politicians, and artisans. Late in the century, Abu Talib Makki, Kalabadhi, and Sarraj issued manuals on Sufism that defended its orthodoxy. Abu Hamid al-Ghazali promoted a centrist view in the *Ihya' 'ulum ad-din* (Revival of Religious Science; ca. 1110), a treatise on moderate mysticism.

Following the rise of Islamic monasticism and the veneration of saints in the twelfth century, Sufism's golden era began in the 1200s and flourished under a theosophical belief in the unity of being and demonstrations of miracles in the name of Allah. Hagiography, didactic verses, letters, and anthologies of mystic aphorisms from the period reflect the social and political practices of the Muslim world. Egyptian poet Ibn al-Fari wrote mystical Arabic verse; in central Asia, Najmuddin Kubra systematized the emotional and intellectual initiation of the mystic through repentance, discipline, meditation, repetitions of a rosary, mastery of self, and patience while awaiting illumination. Indian Sufism had an impact on Hindu mystics, whose Indo-Muslim syncretisim valued the Muslim fakir's intuitive knowledge and evolving unity with Allah through prayer, music, dance, and poetry.

Composed at the height of Sufist religious versifying, Rumi's poems have produced dual strands of interest in the academic and popular realms. As mystic science, his poems are grounded in a whirling universe that shares much with Taoist cosmology and Zen reality. To fellow Muslims, whether scholar or laborer, he employed the imagery of the Koran and the *hajj* and exulted:

The heavens are like a dancing dervish-cloak,
  but the Sufi is hidden.
Oh Moslems, who ever has seen a cloak dance
  without a body within it?
The cloak dances because of the body,
  the body because of the spirit,
  and love for the Beloved
  has tied the spirit's neck to the end of a string [El-Zein 2000].

As literature, these extraordinary lines became the glory of Persian poesy.

Rumi's ecstatic poems returned to popularity in the 1990s through a series on National Public Radio, new translations of his verse, and CDs of love poems recorded by Pakistani singer Nusrat Ali Khan, Madonna, Rosa Parks, Goldie Hawn, Demi Moore, and Deepak Chopra. At the beginning of the twenty-first century, the Mathnawi, a bestseller on the charts of the *Christian Science Monitor,* has become the jewel of the elusive American spirituality called New Sufism. The movement springs from a New Age fascination with mysticism and a Whitmanesque wonder about the universe and humanity's relationship with the divine. To a new generation of readers, Rumi's poems are the ultimate upper, the antidote for despair.

The greatest Muslim poet to write in Persian, Rumi originally lived the predictable, circumscribed life of a man preparing to teach others. Born Muhammad Jalal ad-Din ar-Rumi in Balkh, Ghurid, in eastern Persia, now modern Afghanistan, on September 30, 1207, he was the son of unconventional theologian and professor of religious science Baha ad-Din Walad, author of *Ma'arif*, a volume of meditations. The family claimed descent from the first caliph, Abu Bakr, who followed Muhammad to power. In 1218, Rumi and his parents fled to Nishapur, Iran, in the pell-mell rush of refugees from Mongol insurgents.

Resettlement among Persian intelligentsia gave Rumi an opportunity to read the *Asrarnama* (Book of Secrets) of Farid al-Din al-'Attar, a gift from the aged odist who also produced *Mantiq ut-tayr* (Language of the Birds) and *Musibatnama* (Book of Affliction), a confessional of ascetic experiences during a forty-day period of seclusion. These sacred verses speak of a spiritual liberation, for example:

Virtually no hand but mine tied the infidel's girdle:
  and if it be loosed in acknowledgment of me,
  'twas my hand that loosed it.
And if the niche of a mosque is illuminated by the Qur'an,
  yet is no altar of a church made vain by the gospel:
Nor vain are the books of the Torah revealed to Moses for his
    people,
  whereby the rabbis converse with God every night [Bouquet
    1954, 308–309].

The sequence closes, "So this is not aimless sport," a motto to the Sufi, who were often castigated as heretic madmen. The poet proclaims otherwise: "The wisdom which endoweth essence with diverse attributes caused them to take that course in consequence of the divine decree." The verse is prophetic of Rumi's liberation from scholarship, a future that al-Attar predicted.

Rumi acquired a love of Sanskrit folklore and accepted his part in the mentoring tradition. The family made the obligatory pilgrimage to Mecca before stopping at the village of Rum near Laranda, Anatolia, ruled by Seljuq Turks. From the town came his name, Rumi, the "Roman" from Anatolia. He married twice, first to Gauhar Khatun, mother of two sons. Following his father's career pattern, he studied at Aleppo and Damascus. In 1227, he advanced to a position among scholars at the Madrasah, a religious academy. As Marlawi (also Maulana or Mawlana [Our Master]), he taught religion.

The scholar's life eventually palled on Rumi. At age twenty-five, he immersed himself in Iranian mysticism under the guidance of his father's pupil, Burhan al-Din Muhaqqiq. Dissatisfied with teaching and academic discipline, Rumi began visiting Syrian sufists, who followed Spanish Muslim philosopher Ibn al-'Arabi. When his father died, Rumi took his place and attracted pupils to the academy.

At age thirty-seven, Rumi underwent a midlife shift of thought through contact with itinerant dervish Shams ad-Din of Tabriz, a God-besotted illiterate and catalyst to innovative thought and visions. In the throes of love, the poet abandoned linear rationality and expressed his joy in vivid stanzas:

A call reached the lover from the world of his inmost mys-
    tery:
"Love is God's buraq, put it to the gallop!"
Mount upon love and think not about the way!
For the horse of love is very sure-footed.
Though the path be uneven, in a single bound
  it will take you to the waystation [El-Zein 2000].

Freed from intellectual shackles, Rumi formulated a divergent concept of God, declaring: "Love is the remedy for our pride and self-conceit, the physician of all our infirmities. Only he whose garment is rent by love becomes entirely unselfish" (Bowker 1997, 488). Rapt in soaring, semicoherent devotion, he called to Allah with the gladness of an ardent lover, "Thy face is there my sole delight: be not far, O be not far!" (Hastings 1951, 12:17).

For three months, Rumi entered the initiate's seclusion with his teacher and developed a personal relationship that appalled his family and students. Because they ejected Shams, Rumi fell into a decline that provoked the poet to cry:

Go comrades, fetch our beloved.
  Bring me a moment the runaway idol.
With sweet songs and on various pretexts
  fetch to the house the beautiful, comely face [Cavendish
    1970, 2439].

Rumi's eldest son, Sultan Walad, retrieved his father's mentor. In tribute to his liberator, Rumi declared, "I was a devout man. You made me a singer of songs" (Cavendish 1970, 2439). Their intense relationship continued for two years and ended suddenly when an unidentified assailant murdered the eccentric Shams. History places blame on either Rumi's sons or envious disciples.

A second soulmate, goldsmith Salah ad-Din Zarkub, introduced Rumi to rapturous dance. Like charismatics and glossolalists extolling God in unknown tongues, he thrilled to the rhythm of the master's hammer on metal and composed verse tributes to ecstasy. Through these spontaneous releases of the body to physical oneness with Allah, Rumi severed worship from scholarship and opened himself to a passion. It became his impetus for a shift from religion to mystic verse. Lyricism released him from human form to a stone, plant, animal, and angel. From there he transcended earthly times to "become what no man has seen, no thing, the Nothing" (Bowker 1997, 488).

Under the pen name Shams, Rumi produced *ruba'i-yat* (quatrains) that reveal his inner ache for a lost love. He proclaimed the mystic unveiling of Allah to the inner self:

Lo, for I to myself am unknown, now in God's name what
  must I do?
I adore not the cross nor the crescent,
  I am not a Giaour or a Jew.
East nor west, land nor sea is my home,
  I have kin nor with angel nor gnome.
I was born not in China afar, not in Saqsin,
  and not in Bulghhar:
Not in India, where the five rivers are,
  nor Iraq nor Khorasan I grew.
Nor from Eden and Rizwan I fell,
  not from Adam my lineage I drew.
In a place beyond uttermost place,
  in a tract without shadow of trace,
Soul and body transcending,
I live in the soul of my loved one anew [Bouquet 1954, 310].

Overall, his 30,000 verses set to drum and flute exalt nature, spirituality, and the mystic union with Allah through dance.

Rumi's text became not only a work of scripture, but also a classic component of world wisdom lore. Unlike the grim learned men who dominated Rumi's early life, the poet-philosopher opened himself to a childlike celebration of Allah:

He comes, a moon whose like the sky ne'er saw,
  awake or dreaming,
Crowned with eternal flame no flood can lay.
Lo, from the flagon of thy love, O Lord,
  my soul is swimming,
And ruined all my body's house of clay! [Hastings 1951, 12:16].

By abandoning the preacher's pulpit oration, Rumi sought the glowing heart that transcends theology by offering the self directly to the Almighty. In sacred intoxication, he ex-

ulted that "the giver of the grape my lonely heart befriended" (Hastings 1951, 12:16). His circle dance mimicked the controlled motion of the stars and planets and offered a tribute to cosmic love of all creation for Allah. He proclaimed himself "exempt from 'I' or 'Thou'-ness, and apart from all duality" (Hastings 1951, 12:16). The subtly textured narratives and precise poetic epiphanies of his rhyming couplets introduced inspiration, music, and dance into religious practice.

Rumi's jubilant diction and erotic dithyrambs fill *Divan-e Shams* (or Diwan-i-shams-Tabrizi; Collected Poems of Shams) with the poet's joy in *fana'*, *baqa'* (self-perpetuation with Allah), and *hulul* (oneness with Allah). Rewarded with peace and purity, he presses on through seven allegorical valleys:

The valley of search, or renunciation of earthly possessions
  and setting out on the pilgrimage.
The valley of love, or kindling with ardor for God the
  Beloved.
The valley of knowledge or illumination.
The valley of independence or detachment.
The valley of unity, or contemplation of the Divine Essence.
The valley of amazement, or torment at failure to achieve
  union.
The valley of the annihilation of self [Bouquet 1954, 305].

Like the Buddhist conquest of ego, the final release into total devotion and sanctity freed Rumi from the tyranny of academe to a life of writing allegories, discourses, and enigmatic rhymed fables.

Rumi's search for a new love led him to a disciple, Hasan Husam ad-Din Chelebi, whose beam of truth shone on the text of the Mathnawi, a six-volume anthology subtitled "The Principles of the Principles of the Principles of Religion Concerning the Unveiling of the Mysteries of Union and Certitude." Rumi organized the entries into seventy-one chapters of aphorisms, stories, fables, memoirs, and 26,000 *ghazals* (couplets) replete with the prophet Muhammad's motifs of circularity, momentum, solitude, wildness, and occasional savagery with images of wind, clouds, sand, stars, and champing steeds. In religious transport, he exclaims:

I am the slave of the Koran while I still have life.
I am the dust on the path of Muhammad, the chosen one.
If anyone interprets my words in any other way,
I deplore that person, and I deplore his words [El-Zein 2000].

The poet interprets his obsession with Allah in mystic identification. He declares, "I am not a Christian, I am not a Jew, I am not a Zoroastrian, and I am not even a Muslim" (El-Zein 2000).

Though disconnected and taxing to read, for its brilliance, the Mathnawi has been called the Koran in Persian. Rumi's hymns became the vehicle of Sufis at prayer.

His most famous stories, "The Caged Bird," "The Horseman and the Snake," and "The Blind Men and the Elephant," build on evocative imagery to link concrete objects like flutes, mountains, and lions to subconscious associations with majesty, zeal, and godhood. Interpretations produced a second layer of Rumi lore in fables that describe his influence on pupils. One, "The Merchant and the Christian Dervish" in Aflaki's *Munaqib el-Arifin*, depicts the poet as a sorcerer and clairvoyant.

After Rumi's death in 1273, his verse anthologies rejuvenated Islam from Mongol suppression. They reached seekers worldwide and influenced the *Gesta Romanorum* (Deeds of the Romans), William Shakespeare's dramas, and Hans Christian Andersen's stories. His letters, legends, parables, and collections of dialogues fill *Fihi Ma Fihi* (What Is Within Is Within), a prose complement to the Mathnawi that expresses more of classic Sufist symbolism, which is both erotic and bacchanalian. Ecstatic dancers and minstrels make pilgrimages to his tomb at the Green Dome, now a museum and *tekye* (shrine) to Sufism.

Chelebi and Sultan Walad founded the Mawlawiyah (or Mevlevi), commonly called whirling dervishes, a mystical brotherhood akin to Arabic fakirs, which remained openly active until the Turkish government disbanded them in 1927. Walad wrote his father's biography as well as the mystic poem "Rababnama," the earliest verse in West Turkish. As a result of the beautiful poems by Rumi and others, sacred music found a place in seven worship experiences: Islamic pilgrimages to stir enthusiasm for visiting a holy shrine, among soldiers preparing for combat, in battle, as personal regret for sins, at weddings and feasts, between lovers, and as an impetus for longing for Allah. In 1940, R. A. Nicholson completed a translation of Rumi's Sufist works in English.

SOURCES: Alexander and Alexander 1982, Bouquet 1954, Bowker 1997, Braden 1954, Burckhardt 1969, Cavendish 1970, El-Zein 2000, Gentz 1973, Ghazali 1964, Hastings 1951, McDermott 1997, *New Catholic Encyclopedia* 1967, Nicholson 1950, Renard 1997, Schimmel 1975, 1982, Shah 1975, Smith 1995, Snodgrass 1995, 1998, Waley 1993, *World Religions* 1998.

Nihon Shoki *see* Kojiki

Pearl of Great Price *see* Book of Mormon

Popul Vuh An authentic collection of sacred Quiché-Mayan scriptures, the Popul Vuh (or Popol Buj; Council Book), also called the Book of the Community, the Common Book of the People, the Sacred Book, the National Book of the Quiché, or the Book of Council is a Native American literary monument. Once treasured as a source of history and divination and called the Dawn of Life, it provides an invaluable source of knowledge of ancient Meso-American mythology and culture, which influenced southern Mexico. For good reason, 1967 Nobel-winning Mayanist Miguel Ángel Asturias, author of *Leyendas de Guatemala* (Legends of Guatemala; 1930) dubbed the Popol Vuh the first American novel. The text is based on indigenous thought patterns reflected in language, dramatic art, and oral histories. Beginning with the dawn of time, the scientific historiography focuses on a progression of identifiable beings: Vukup Cakix's family in the First Age; the Camé in the Second; Ixmucané, a day keeper or diviner in the Third Age; and the civilizer-hero in the Fourth.

Composed in the Spanish alphabet from Quiché, a hieroglyphic language of the Maya people of the Sierra Los Cuchematanesa Mountains in north-central Guatemala, the Popul Vuh is a cosmogony or creation theory composed by historian Diego Reynos, a proselytized Indian, between 1554 and 1558, thirty years after the area's conquest by Spanish expeditioners. The complex story chronicles the work of a godly creator, who places humankind on earth. Significant to place and time are the origin, mythos, and history of the Quiché people before the first sunrise and a chronology of Quichéan monarchs up to 1550. Although the original manuscript is lost, three copies of the original Popol Vuh exist, in Dresden, Madrid, and Paris; a fragment survives from the Spanish conquest of the New World. The discovery provoked a search for more manuscripts to cast light on Meso-American culture and religion.

Influenced by the Olmec, Gulf Coast forerunners of the Aztec, the Maya date to 1500 B.C.E., when their agrarian colonists formed the first villages and, using a slash-and-burn method, cultivated the three staples of the southwest diet, beans, maize, and squash, which flourished on irrigated terraces. By C.E. 250, they entered a classical period that survived for 650 years. In decline from outside aggression and depletion of farmland, they maintained the highland cities of Chichén Itzá, Mayapán, and Uxmal.

Before the Spanish conquest, the Maya had founded forty cities and occupied southern Mexico south to Guatemala and east into northern Belize in a great Native American civilization. They erected stone palaces and pyramid-shaped ceremonial centers, laid out plazas for markets, and played handball. They produced hieroglyphic writings on paper codices, formulated star maps and a calendar, advanced a mathematical system, and mastered stone sculpture, goldsmithing, and copper artistry. The Maya worshiped the sun, moon, rain, corn, and other nature gods. Their priests presided over an elaborate cycle of rites and ceremonies. Their ethos promoted aggression against rival cities and human bloodletting, torture, and sacrifice in propitiation of fertility gods.

The Quiché or Utlateca, highlanders of the Maya linguistic branch, were the principal aborigines of Guatemala and shared language roots with the Cakchiquel, Pokonchi, and Tzutnhil. The people originated from the north or northeast around C.E. 700 and spread from Quiche in the northwest south to Totonicapan and west to part of Quezaltenango. They linked their religion and resurrection lore with cave culture: the source of underground aquifers, stalactites dripping pure water, and dry storage for grain. They frequented limestone caverns formed when the rugged headwaters of the Caves Branch River coursed the Sibun Hills valley and joined the Sibun River. The flow passed through the Mountain Pine Ridge, a basalt and granite formation of the Paleozoic era. There, the Maya left petroglyphs on sacred walls that led to the underworld, Xibalba (scary place). To symbolize sacred mountains, the Maya built their first permanent worship centers, pyramid-shaped temples pierced by a cave mouth. At the Utatlan cave, the Quiché performed sacrifices and sought the gods' permission to plant maize or hunt animals for food. To cure the ill, whose souls wandered, seekers prayed in caves for the souls' return in exchange for a chicken. The Quiché also buried an infant's afterbirth to ally with a new generation of ancestors.

The end of the Popol Vuh coincides with the swift loss of Quichéan autonomy. In 1523, against the dictates of the Catholic pope, Pedro de Alvarado, conqueror of Mexico and Central America under the command of Hernán Cortés, began a four-year pacification of Guatemala. He set up as his capital Santiago de los Caballeros de Guatemala, now called Antigua, which he governed until 1534. He enforced native subjugation, slavery, and unbearable taxation. Two Dominican friars, Pontaz and de Torres, learned Quiché and taught and catechized the people in their native tongue. To quell pagan influence, authorities burned hieroglyphic texts, but the stories survived through oral passage.

In 1530, a Spanish priest, Francisco Marroquín, founded a Catholic church and the Colegio de Santo Tomás. After he rose to the post of bishop and protector of the Indians, he evangelized Tezulutlan. Father Bartolomé de Las Casas converted locals at the Dominican convent at Santiago, on the southern border of Quiché territory; in 1532, fathers Zambrano and Dardon of the Order of Mercy opened Santiago's second religious house; Franciscans arrived in 1541. Through their combined efforts, Mayans lost faith in indigenous beliefs, settled in towns, and rapidly shed native customs, although some pagan dances, meditations, and tenets permeated their domestic observance.

According to the present version of the Popol Vuh, creator Gugumatz (or Q'uk'umatz), the Plumed Serpent deity that resembles the self-martyred Aztec god Quetzalcoatl, shaped the first four males and four females, produced fire and light, rid earth of monsters, and founded religious sacrifice and rites. These progenitors preceded the Mayan race. After a three-century concealment from the intrusive white world, the manuscript resurfaced at El Calvario Church, at Chichicastenango, Guatemala, around 1722, when Archbishop Francisco Ximénez (or Jiménez), a Dominican scriptural scholar and Meso-American chronicler, received it.

As stated in his *Las Historias del Origen de los Indios de esta Provincia de Guatemala* (Histories of the Origin of the Indians of the Province of Guatemala; 1857), Ximénez rated the Mayan scripture a puerile legend on a par with children's tales. In *Historia de la Provincia de San Vicente de Chiapa y Guatemala* (History of the Province of St. Vincent in Chiapa and Guatemala; 1929–1931), he is quoted as declaring:

> [The Popul Vuh] was conserved among the Indians in complete secrecy, such secrecy that not even a written record of such a thing was made by its guardians of old; and, being in the parish of Chichicastenango and investigating that point, I found that it was the doctrine first imbibed with the mother's milk and that everyone knew it almost by heart [Girard 1979].

On a bark-paper folding book, he transcribed the codex in two columns: Quiché at left and Spanish to the right. His version passed to the control of the Dominican order until Guatemala obtained independence, when agents purchased it for the University of San Carlos in Guatemala City. Today, the handwritten text survives at Chicago's Newberry Library.

The discovery of the Popul Vuh remained unheralded until its rediscovery in the public archives of Guatemala City in the 1850s by interested parties, including Abbé Brasseur de Bourbourg. In 1861, he issued a more precise French recension based on the original text, which ethnographers and theologians exalted as an equal of Genesis and the Ramayana. Subsequent renderings include one in Italian and three more in Spanish. The University of Oklahoma Press published an English version in 1950, edited by Adrian Recinos.

In September 1997, workers under the direction of archaeologist Juan Yadeun uncovered a 1,500-year-old Mayan temple complex that validated the history and cosmology of the Popol Vuh. A bas relief found near the Acropolis, a 226-foot pyramid dominating Tonina in Chiapas, was an adornment of the Mayan empire's last capital. A square yard in size, the frieze's iconography depicts four Mayan governors, whom the Popol Vuh names as underworld lords. They dance in ritual headdresses as emblems of the four professions—war, agriculture, trade, and tribute. As a whole, the carving represents the classic Mayan concept of the universe. The discovery corroborated the theory of Ermilo Ebreu Gomez, a translator of the Popol Vuh, who believes the epic to be the writing of native converts to Catholicism who sought to preserve historical and religious lore passed orally or via Mayan hieroglyphs. In Gomez's translation, these lords were grandfathers who were authority figures at the Quichéan beginnings.

A late twentieth-century children's version of Quichéan scripture is a revered teaching tool for the Maya of southern California. Patricia Aldana, publisher of the Toronto-based Groundwood Books *I Ribros Tigrillo*, chose as writer Mayan teacher Victor Montejo, a refugee from torture during the Guatemalan turmoil of the 1980s, had fled the country and now serves as a member of the Peace Commission. Currently a professor of anthropology at the University of California at Davis, he composed *Popol Vuh: A Sacred Book of the Maya* (1999), a simplified version of the native mythos, to preserve the rituals and traditions that barely survived the ethnic cleansing of a million of his people. Even though some Catholic authorities castigate the Maya for witchcraft, in 2000, the Los Angeles archdiocese countenanced a procession honoring a patron saint, the Lord of Esquípulas, Guatemala's cultic Black Christ.

Still revered by the Maya, the Popol Vuh, like the biblical Genesis, Japanese Kojiki, and Navajo creation lore, expresses the spiritual reality of cultural values. The book is a single uninterrupted chronology beginning with *uxe* (the base or root) and covering the history of Quiché (or *k'iche*; many trees). The narrative perplexes modern readers with the oneness of all time, from mythohistory to the present. The narrative opens on creation by a Supreme Being. The text specifies him with a list of variations of the concept of creating: maker and modeler, bearer and begetter of all living things, heart of lake and sea, plate and bowl shaper, midwife and matchmaker, defender and protector. He is mother-father of life and humankind, breathgiver, heartgiver, upbringer of a lasting light, and knower of all, "whatever there is" (Tedlock 1996, 64).

In the first act of creation, the shaper Gugumatz looks out on a void that ripples, murmurs, sighs, and hums. The subsequent trinity of creators Tepew (or Tepeu; Sovereign), the water god; Juracán (Hurricane), the thunderer in the heart of the sky; and the fire god Gugumatz foresees the creation of the world:

And then the earth arose because of them,
  it was simply their word that brought it forth.
For the forming of the earth they said, "Earth."
It arose suddenly, just like a cloud, like a mist,
  now forming, unfolding....

By their genius alone, by their cutting edge alone
  they carried out the conception of the mountain-plain....
and the Plumed Serpent was pleased with this [Tedlock
  1996, 65–66].

They collaborate in the dark void on how to light the world and how to separate water from land. They choose a method of fertilizing seed and watering it with dew; they make animals and birds. After a pause, they proclaim the first creation complete.

In the First Age, the trio, called Grandfathers or Ancestors, decides that fertile land is useless without a gardener. As the right substance from which to mold humanity, the three gods select the Indian staff of life, maize, which they harvest at Split Place on the border between Guatemala and Mexico. They teach each species to speak the gods' names and to remember who created life. Because the animals reject harmony and ignore holy splendor, the gods condemn them to speak in different voices, to flee for their lives, and to cower in fear. Predators kill and devour the flesh of these heterogeneous lingual groups. Thus concludes the era.

The Second Age, contemporaneous with the end of hunting and gathering and the emergence of agriculture, begins with a plastic manipulation of mud, the archetype of the farmer's task. The gods propose: "Let's try to make a giver of praise, giver of respect, provider, nurturer" (Tedlock 1996, 68). In a parallel of the Peruvian creation myth, the uncouth Mayan creator god Aj bit (or Aj tzak) replaces animals with humankind formed of clay, a species that will worship the divine and harvest the earth's fruits. The faulty, fragile shape, toothless mouth, and blind eyes of the model discourage the gods. They complain that it cannot walk or multiply. The small image is lopsided, crumbly, soft, and easily dissolved in water, but it has a heavenly voice, a hint of the progress the gods are making. In spite of its defects, the trio order it to live, reproduce, and to improve its species.

A flash of lightning causes the Ancestors to try again. Working in coral wood from the *Erythrina corallodendron* tree to give the form stability, the trio improves on the clay model. As before, the experimental being is disappointing. It does not understand the cause and nature of life; it lacks reverence and emotion. It is limbless, bloodless, and lymphless. Jaguars rip the form apart; a hurricane and deluge overflow the earth. Again, the Ancestors make an improved model, this time molding males from maize and females from *espadana*, a tasseled grass that resembles corn. Still dissatisfied that the creatures do nothing for god, heaven turns against them. The Ancestors send the great bird Xecotcovah and the jaguar Cotzbalam to rend them with beak and claw. During a period of great darkness, small beings, grain, pots, jars, and other utensils rebel against the Ancestors. After their battle, survivors flee to forests, caves, and mountains. Those who flourish become monkeys. The earth returns to a primordial state. The god Macaw ruminates:

I am great.
My place is now higher than that of the human work,
  the human design.
I am their sun and I am their light, and I am also their
  months [Tedlock 1996, 73].

The Popol Vuh is the only Native American lore to account for the creation of a ball game and to place it in time alongside the evolution of solar worship. The heroes of the Quiché underworld introduced in part II are twins, Hunahpú (also Junajpu or Xjunajpu; One Blowgunner), the elder, and the second-born, Xpalanqué (also Xb'alanqué; Sun's Hidden Aspect). The first is the name of one of the twin volcanoes formed by the creator Zipacna, maker of the earth, who shaped Volcán de Acatenango and Volcán de Fuego southwest of Antigua Guatemala. The twins are sons of devotees of *tlachtli* or pok-a-tok, the onomatopoetic name for the Mayan handball game played on a court marked at each end with stone goals. Team members are helmeted with feathers and padded at the hips, wrists, and elbows. Using any part of the body except hands, they aim through a stone ring a rubber ball molded of tree resin, symbol of the day star (the sun). The boys' farewell to their mother, a significant episode in Mayan culture, represents a shift in family hierarchy from dominant male to dominant female parent, who offers a blessing.

On their own, the two athletes initiate a spirited match, a standard motif in Mayan bas relief, as found in the carved paneling of the *jom*, the great I-shaped ball court at Chichén Itzá and at Copán, and a profiled figure on the ball-court marker at La Esperanza, Chiapas. To halt their noisy competition, the twelve Lords of Death summon them to Xibalbá, the end of the sun's trajectory and its entry into the underworld, and invite them to bring their equipment. In a challenge match, the Lords win by cheating, then massacre the players. They bury one head under the ball court and hang the other in the fork of a calabash tree, a parallel of the position of Venus, the evening star. The symbol is meant to warn other obstreperous athletes that the Lords brook no irreverence. The head also causes the tree to bear the calabash, which the people venerate and use as a vessel for cacao drinks.

Like Pandora and Eve, Ixquic is the irrepressible daughter of Cuchumaquic (also Kuchuma kik' [Blood Gatherer]), a prestigious figure in Xibalbá. She grows curious about the suspended head and takes a closer look. Sweetly babbling, she asks, "What? Well! What's the fruit of this tree? Shouldn't this tree bear something sweet? They shouldn't die, they shouldn't be wasted. Should I pick one?" (Tedlock 1996, 98). In a mystic dream sequence, the head spits potent saliva, a divine seminal fluid, into the outstretched palm of her right hand, causing her to conceive. The text refers to a dual fatherhood by both martyrs.

Six months later, Cuchumaquic realizes his daughter's dishonor and seeks advice. The council advises him to get the seducer's name or sacrifice her. He demands the name of the father; still a virgin, she feels justified in claiming that there can be neither child nor sire. Cuchumaquic has the military keepers dispatch her to the sacrificial ground, where four executioners will perform the customary Quichéan excision of the heart with a stone knife and place it in a ritual cup.

Ixquic's dilemma reflects the development of a religious ritual central to Meso-American culture from human to symbolic ceremony. Using womanly wiles, she convinces her captors that execution is impious and offers a substitute. By having them collect a bloodlike resin from the fruit of the cochineal croton tree, which the Spanish call the *sangre de dragón* (dragon's blood), she replaces her real heart with a round crimson replica. When her father burns the pseudo-heart, it produces sweet smoke, the beginning of the use of incense and of the sacred cigar, which natives invented in prehistory.

Ixquic, renamed Blood Moon, follows the owl messenger through a hole leading to the surface of earth. In keeping with the matriarchal society, she visits her mother-in-law, Xmucane, and explains that the infant's sire is still alive. Nonetheless, the mother-in-law rejects her. To secure the children's acceptance, Ixquic agrees to perform a standard domestic task for her mother-in-law—to collect a netful of ripe corn. The episode puts the girl in the hands of Hun Bátz (or Jun B'atz) and Hun Chouén (or Jun Chuen), the creative but undisciplined monkeys and artisans who are jealous siblings of Ixquic's seducer. After following the duo to the garden, Ixquic finds only one hill of corn. Declaring herself both sinner and debtor, she prays to the grain deities:

Come on out, rise up now, come on out, stand up now:
  Thunder Woman, Yellow Woman,
  Cacao Woman and Cornmeal Woman,
  thou guardian of the food of One Monkey, One Artisan
    [Tedlock 1996, 103].

By confessing her weakness to the plant, Ixquic acquires the grain, which sprouts in profusion from only one stalk. Her action illustrates two aspects of Mayan culture—division of labor, which placed women in charge of field work, and the confession of sin to attain divine intervention in human predicaments. The abundance of sustenance from a single source also justifies loyalty to the ancient Mayan staff of nourishment and to faith. For Ixquic's embrace of the bases of Quichéan culture, the mother-in-law immediately accepts both the needy girl and her unborn children.

In native style, Ixquic seeks refuge in the wilds of the middle world, where she gives birth to the hero twins, Hunahpú and Xpalanqué, at dawn, symbolizing the emergence of the solar god. The twins are still outcasts in their grandmother's household among Hun Bátz and Hun Chouén, their older half brothers and sons of Egret Woman and One Hunahpú. Parallel to Romulus and Remus from Roman mythology, the ousted twins have to hunt for game to feed themselves and are forced to survive in the wild, first on an anthill, then on a spiny cactus. The use of self-sufficiency and natural punishments as proofs of manhood permeated native culture in the Western hemisphere, where children relied on their wits from early times for food and where enemies were often subjected to physical torment or trial by ordeal.

The invidious half brothers, who have already foreseen the twins' glorious future, are unrelenting in their spite, a parallel to the universal jealousy between laborers and artisans. In an act of self-preservation, the newcomers determine to end the stand-off, concluding:

> So be it, since they have caused us great suffering....
> Just as they wished us to be slaves here,
>   so we shall defeat them there [Tedlock 1996, 105].

With little effort, the twins trick their half brothers into following them at dawn to the forest and climbing a tree to retrieve the day's quarry of birds for dinner. When the tree begins growing and expanding, the brothers are trapped.

This complicated myth illustrates the inventiveness and humor of the Popol Vuh. The twins instruct the climbers to tie their pants around their waists and dangle their belts behind to make climbing easier. In frustration, the elder brothers leap and howl from limb to limb. When the tricksters drum, play the flute, and sing to lure the half brothers back to their grandmother's house, Hun Bátz and Hun Chouén look like howler monkeys with dangling tails and puckery lips. They cause the grandmother to titter. After four pretended attempts to lure them back home, the twins give up, blaming the grandmother for driving the climbers deep into the forest by shaming them with her laughter. The myth accounts for Mayan ridicule of the spider monkey, whose prehensile tail and ungainly scrotum rob it of dignity.

The twins, who symbolize the corn seed and sun, take over support of the women, attesting to a shift in Quichéan culture to male heads of family. The monkey brothers, who victimized their younger siblings, deserve their comeuppance. They remain in the trees, evolving into the patron gods of dancers, acrobats, musicians, humorists, and carvers. They symbolize creativity, fun, and lechery. With their skillful, lighthearted antics, they parallel performances of the *palo voladores* (pole fliers), the southwestern pole gymnasts and holy clowns of the Totonac, who banish evil and secure blessing for a full harvest.

The holy boys of the hero cycle know nothing of their paternity. After a life of labor with hoe, ax, and mattock defeating the devious four-footers and two-footers of the wild, they encounter a rat who knows their destiny to play ball. Instinctively, the brothers locate sports gear and learn the game. Like their elders, they annoy the Lords, who consider the matter of ballplaying ended long ago. When the grandmother learns that her grandsons must visit the Lords of Death, she sobs and relives the summons and deaths of the boys' fathers. A comic sequence describes how the grandmother sends the Lords' summons by a louse, who is swallowed by a toad, who is swallowed by a snake, who is the victim of a falcon. To retrieve the message, the boys have to reverse the order, like peeling an onion, layer by layer.

After traversing the cliff and canyons, the Pus River and Blood River, and the black, white, red, and green roads, the twin tricksters outwit the Lords. In the dank, drafty Dark House, a symbol of the grave probably named for a constellation, they keep lit a torch and two cigars through the night. Their method comes from nature — they put fireflies on the cigar ends and pass off a macaw tail as the torch flame. Cagily, they compete in a game against the Lords and deliberately lose. To stay alive, they continue performing tasks and tricking the lords in the Razor House, Cold House (or Rattling House), and Bat House (or Macaw House). In a final trial, they hide in blowguns from marauder bats. After a bat decapitates Hunahpú, Xpalanqué plays a new game with the head, then replaces it with a squash when it rolls into tall grass. Thus, the jolly duo sport and triumph over death.

Rejuvenation and shape-shifting dominate the myth. Enraged, the Lords of Death decide to immolate the twins in a great stone oven. The boys persuade two sages to advise the Lords to dispose of their bodies by grinding the bones and tossing the fragments into the river. Five days later, the twins come back to life with catfish faces. The next day, they return to human form as ragged vagabonds and travel Xibalba as magicians, stilt walkers, dancers, and sword swallowers. The twelve Lords invite them to perform at court. After destroying animals and resurrecting them, Xpalanqué sacrifices his twin. To the delight of the residents of the underworld:

One by one his legs, his arms were spread wide.
His head came off, rolled far away outside.
His heart, dug out, was smothered in a leaf [Tedlock 1996, 136].

Through self-transformation, the magicians, like the Greek sorceress Medea, lure the Lords into volunteering for the act. The twins dismember them, defeating death forever and earning lasting regard as saviors of humankind.

This pinnacle of Quichéan theology generates somber words from the holy twins. They identify themselves with their fathers' names and bring Xibalbans to their knees in anticipation of mass slaughter. All cry for pity and admit that the two ballplaying fathers were murdered and buried at the Place of the Ball Game Sacrifice. Relenting, the twins make a formal declaration that demotes the realm of death forever from its former supremacy and reduces sacrifices from human remains to "scabrous nodules of sap" (Tedlock 1996, 138–139). The twins declare that the only creatures worthy of sacrifice will be "the guilty, the violent, the wretched, the afflicted." The divine exhortation ends in a hymn degrading the Lords of Death as "makers of enemies," "inciters to wrongs and violence," and "masters of hidden intentions" (Tedlock 1996, 138–139). Afterward, souls arriving at Xibalba receive the greatest of gifts—an opportunity to return to earth once more. Like the Greek Thespis patterning the worship of the ancient wine god, Dionysus, the grandmother, crying and honoring the gods of plenty, becomes the progenitor of Quichéan worship by creating rituals to the annual corn cycle.

Central to the Popol Vuh is resurrection to new life. The twins reshape their fathers and restore them to life much as Isis, the Egyptian sister/wife, locates the parts of her dismembered brother/husband, Osiris, and accords him lasting life. The twins promise that the sacrificed fathers will receive prayers and solace at the Place of the Ball Game Sacrifice. Reverently, they pledge:

You will be the first resort,
  and you will be the first to have your day kept
  by those who will be born in the light, begotten in the light.
Your name will not be lost. So be it [Tedlock 1996, 141].

With that, the holy duo rises to the sky to merge with the sun and moon so that, at all times, one or the other smiles on the people below.

Part IV discloses the founding of theology as it applies to food staples and work. Following the lead of animals, the ancestors add cacao and tropical fruits to maize. The begetter's next attempt results in a thinking being of flesh and bone, whom he blesses with holy fragrance and night lights in the sky. The cat, vixen, parrot, cotorra, and crow welcome the new being and celebrate with a beverage of maize and water that will confer life on the four mother-fathers:

- Balam Quitzé (also B'alam k'itze; Jaguar Quitzé), husband of Kapa Paluma (also Cahapaluna; Red Sea Turtle), founders of the Cauec lineage

- Balam Acab (also B'alam aq'ab'; Jaguar Night), mate of Chomija (Prawn House) and sire of the Greathouse lineage
- Mahucutah (or Majukutaj; Not Right Now), husband of Tz'ununija' (also Tzununiha; Water Hummingbird) and fount of the Lord Quiché lineage
- Equi Balam (Ik'ib'alam; Dark Jaguar), paired with Kaqixaja (also Caquixaha; Macaw), the childless firstlings who establish no family tree.

Quichéan scripture lauds them for their human traits and skills, good looks, and understanding of all creation. In gratitude to the Creator for life, understanding, strength, and permanence, the four new humans sing a Te Deum of double and triple thanks to their grandsires. To keep the beings from penetrating the gods' mysteries and to rid them of the fatal sin of pride, the Creator limits their knowledge and faculties.

The text lists the resulting lineages and the thirteen original tribes, including the Rabinal from the northeast, frontier folk who built Spilt Water citadel and who speak Achí, a Quiché dialect; and the Cakchiquel from the south and east, who built Nettles Heights citadel and who also speak a Quiché dialect. Eleven of the tribes derive from the east:

- White Cornmeal, whose settlement grew into the town of Salcajá
- Lamac, whom the Spanish relocated at Sacapulas
- Serpent, whom the Spanish renamed the Coatecas and settled at Sacapulas
- Sweatbath House, also relegated to Sacapulas
- Talk House, also settled at Sacapulas
- Quiba House
- Yokes House, named for the yoke worn by ballplayers
- Acul, whose name today refers to a district of the Mayan town of Nebaj
- Jaguar House
- Guardians of the Spoils
- Jaguar Ropes.

In wonder at their vision, they multiply and lift eyes to heaven, even if they have no direction or home. Before they pray to *Che'ab'aj* (the Tree-Stone), a stele marked with classic Mayan inscriptions at Copán, the mountain people speak one language. To heaven, they direct a lyric prayer to the maker and modeler asking for guidance and a sign of a "greening path." As though fearful of what might lie ahead, they ask for steady light, level ground, and a "good life and beginning" (Tedlock 1996, 150). The focus of their prayer is the newly born sun in the east, the source of warmth and guidance of human work and design.

Back of stela at Copán. (From an engraving of Frederick Catherwood.)

The new ones spread over the land to Tulan, an eastern town bearing the bat emblem, and worship a pantheon of gods:

- Tohil (or Tojil) the fire maker and god of thunder, blood sacrifice, and rule, who Jaguar Quitzé bears in his backpack. In shape, he is the one-legged fire drill, worshiped at the Great Monument of Tohil, a temple and pyramid at Q'umaraq aj (Rotten Cane), a Quiché citadel now called Utatlán and lying in ruins three miles west of Santa Cruz del Quiché, which Pedro de Alvarado conquered in 1524.

- Auilix (also Awilix [Lord Swallow]), the patron god carried by Jaguar Night and established at Rotten Cane.
- Hacauitz (also Jakawitz [Bald Mountain]), Not Right Now's god, whom he bears to a mountain and places at the summit of a pyramid at the first Quiché citadel, which overlooks the first dawn.
- Middle of the Plain (or Nik'aj taq'aj), Dark Jaguar's deity received at Tulan.

The original unity ends as the people grow diverse and begin to dress differently.

This part of the scripture describes the beginnings of the Quiché from mountain and cave dwellers who migrated to Tulan in the north. During a great diaspora, the new people cross mountains, where they are cold and miserable. The first people generate fire in imitation of the first fire receivers, those at Tohil's shrine. In thanks, they say a simple prayer to their sustainer and watch intently toward the east for the morning star, which they call "the sun carrier," the focus of their rituals (Tedlock 1996, 150). When a storm douses their hearthside blaze, Balam Quitzé demands that Tohil give back fire. Tohil rubs his sandal to generate a spark. The pilgrims thrill to renewed life and warmth.

Newcomers cluster at the fireside and greet the pilgrims in a foreign tongue. Balam Quitzé casts them out for their strangeness, but Tohil's black, winged envoy chastises them for forgetting the gods' language. In propitiation of the gods, the new beings promise precious metal in exchange for fire. Tohil rejects ores and demands worship and "suckling," a euphemism for heart sacrifice. The people agree and give "their blood, their gore, their sides, their underarms" (Tedlock 1996, 156). Their reward is a "fiery splendor," the beginnings of sun worship, and greater knowledge, an intellectual growth paired with heavenly illumination similar to the Greek deification of Apollo as light bringer, oracle, healer, and lord of creativity.

At this point in Quiché history, the Popol Vuh stresses the goodness of God. Tohil rejects human sacrifice and sanctions a symbolic blood sacrifice — the bleeding of ears and elbows — and showers benevolence and love on his followers. Over smoky fissures in the earth, fetid waters, sharp stones, and hurricanes, the people migrate south to the lowlands on the coast. In Chi Pizah, jaguars and alligators eat many of them. With the aid of the gods, they brave these dangers until they reach the green mountain called Hacavitz and witness a good omen, the bright morning star. In thanks for deliverance, they burn copal, a fossilized resin of the *Bursera bipinnata*, which they value as incense. The rising of the sun brings the puma and jaguar, followed by a happy throng of great and small birds, who join the penitents and sacrificers as fellow suppliants. The sun dries and purifies and turns the three gods—Tohil, Auilix, and Hacauitz—into stone. The people realize their connection to Mexica, speakers of Nahua, and to the Mexican god Quetzalcoatl, the Plumed Serpent.

The narration shifts abruptly to the origin of Tohil's masking. He addresses them from on high about clean waters and a permanent bond with the Creator. He commands them to guard their thoughts, behave morally, and offer sacrifices of animals only. Thus, this exodus to a promised land marks the end of savagery and the foundation of a civilized society. Sunlight warms the earth and illuminated areas beyond the promised land. The people build white stone roads from plains to mountains to reach other tribes. They raise stone watchtowers and equip guards with snail shells and horns to warn of invasion. The elders refuse to be forced from their land. Instead, they feast on honey, venison, and turtle fat and drink from *cenotes* (natural wells) in the bedrock. From their contentment spring the original sins of selfishness and envy. Tohil commands that they cry so they will never die. By declaring tears worthy balm for body and soul, he expresses a valuable lesson in self-healing.

The old ones of Cavec, who practice dismemberment, apprehend and torture strangers to Hacauitz by twisting their limbs with wood forks, then abandoning them in the forest. Their victims decide to stalk these savages and destroy them. In battles against the old ones, they lose, but discover a fresh river they call the Bath of Tohil. The plains dwellers lure the old ones to the shores by stationing two beautiful girls, Lust Woman and Wailing Woman, to bathe and launder clothes. The old ones evade the lure and demand that the girls confess the plot. In payment, the old ones offer gifts of blankets for the elders, which scratch and bite the skin.

In this segment of the Popol Vuh, mythos gradually gives place to history. From the peaks, Balam Quitzé and the other Ancestors witness the brewing of war. The Hacauitzans cause their enemies to slumber, then confiscate their weapons and clothes, shave their beards, tie their feet, paint their cheeks, and urinate on them. The humiliated victims cloak themselves in banana leaves and flee. On the advice of Tohil and the other Ancestors, Hacauitzans dig a ditch concealed under a thin mud layer held up by a network of lianas and reeds. As guardians of the ditch, they place dummies dressed like soldiers. Before the next attack, Tohil promises his protection; the Ancestors attract flies and poisonous wasps to be held in readiness.

Scenes of war take on the drollery of Uncle Remus tales. Armed with shields, poisoned lances, blowpipes, and arrows, the plainsmen attack at dawn to the sound of drums, flutes, and whistles. The mountaineers open the boxes and release insects. The attackers drop their arms, roll on the ground from the pain of stings, and charge downhill. Balam Quitzé's people pursue and hack them with stone axes. The winners hold thanksgiving for victory over their enemies. Their contentment increases from knowledge of godly secrets, including farming and raising flocks. In honor of the heavenly aid, the mountaineers are faithful to the gods and revere their land and heritage. They pray to Juracan to strengthen the children in goodness and faith and to give them healthy sons and daughters to live united and devoid of arrogance.

Just as mythos withers and history grows strong, the firstlings age and die. Before expiring and disappearing, Jaguar Quitzé leaves his bundle of flames, a mysterious holy package similar to the Lakota medicine bundle mentioned in *Black Elk Speaks*. The wives and children leave it wrapped as a memorial to the first fathers and rejoice and burn offerings. The scripture closes this segment with a sober tribute to "the first people to come from beside the sea, from the east. They came here in ancient times. When they died they were old. They had a reputation for penitence and sacrifice" (Tedlock 1996, 175).

Part V connects generations by stating that the next Quichéan leaders—Noble Two, son of Jaguar Quitzé; Noble Acutec, son of Jaguar Night; and Noble Lord, son of Not Right Now—remember their history and their fathers' instructions. The trio crosses a lake on a pilgrimage to the east to receive lordship from Nacxit (Four Legs), lord of the eastern province in Yucatán. He confers on them emblems of authority—the canopy, throne, bone flute, bird whistle, yellow ocher, paws of the puma and jaguar, deer's head and hoof, snailshell rattle, tobacco gourd, and parrot and egret feathers. The trio returns to a period of stability on Hacauitz.

At the peak of their emergence from the primitive past, the Quichéans grow ambitious. They migrate to a citadel named Thorny Place, a town known today as Cauinal, which comprises four mountains north of the Sierra de Chuacús. From the summit, they look out on a distant slope that may contain the overflow of their population. Meanwhile, the aged pilgrims die. Their successors find Chi ismachi (Bearded Place), a mountain citadel where they begin new construction. Under two ministers, K'otuja (Noble Sweatbath) and Iztayul (Salty), the colonists enjoy a serene but modest period of advancement marked by the Shield Dance, a sign of sovereignty. This era of calm ends when Iztayul joins in an Iloc cabal to assassinate K'otuja and overthrow the Quiché. When the plot fails, the people sacrifice some of the Iloc to the gods and enslave others. Success magnifies Quiché lords as never before.

In the next migration five generations later, which

takes the people from Bearded Place north to Rotten Cane, the Quiché, now intermarried with the Cauec and Greathouse, enter another period of building. Lord Bishop Francisco Marroquín blesses the site in 1539, fifteen years after Pedro de Alvarado had conquered it and renamed it Santa Cruz (Holy Cross). Greatness precipitates quarrels and jealousy, which split the people into nine lineages and twenty-four great houses. They create nine Cauec titles—Keeper of the Mat, Keeper of the Reception House Mat, Keeper of Tohil, Keeper of the Plumed Serpent, Master of Ceremonies for the Cauecs, Councilor of the Stores, Quehnay Emissary, Councilor in the Ball Court, and Mother of the Reception House. The Greathouse branch produces a Lord Minister, Lord Herald, Minister of the Reception House, Chief of the Reception House, Mother of the Reception House, Lord Auilix, Yacolatam, and Chief Yeoltux Emissary. The Lord Quichés bear the titles the Herald, Lord Emissary, Lord Master of Ceremonies for the Lord Quichés, and Lord Hacauitz. Two lines of Zaquic lords follow the Lord Corntassel House and Minister for the Zaquics. Through a client relationship, these worthies build mansions and reciprocate to vassal laborers by granting petitions. For their prosperity, the people as a whole credit the Plumed Serpent, the supreme shape-shifter.

In the sixth generation, Quicab (K'iqab'), the patriarch who expands Quiché holdings, and Cauizimah, lord of the Cauecs, take control and quell the canyon people. In the words of the scripture:

Their citadels fell and they brought tribute to Quicab and
    Cauizimah.
Their lineages came to be bled, shot full of arrows at the
    stake.
Their day came to nothing, their heritage came to nothing
    [Tedlock 1996, 188].

A tense state of readiness grips the "makers of war." Their ritual includes fastings alternating with a vegetarian diet to build strength while occupying the temple for weeping, burnt offerings, and penance. The text cites a three-stave lamentation to the Heart of Sky calling for rain to nurture the soil and an end to deception and sorcery. In place of duplicity, the seekers plead for light and continuity.

The penalty of the canyon people is a heavy tribute in turquoise, metal, jade, gems, and feather work. This flow of riches elevates the Quiché. The author halts to name each series of lords from the firstlings to the fourteenth generation. The Quiché lords, beginning with Jaguar Quitzé, proceed to Noble Raiment, Jaguar Noble Rooftree, Noble Sweatbath and Iztayul, and Plumed Serpent and Noble Sweatbath in the fifth generation. The sixth, Tepepul and Iztayul, leads to Quicab and Cauizimah, Tepepul and Xtayub, Black Butterfly and Tepepul,

Eight Cord and Quicab, Seven Though and Cauatepech, Three Deer, and Nine Dog. The twelfth-generation lords were in power when the Spanish invaded and tortured them by suspending them from the wrists before burning them. From there, the tribute reverses, with thirteenth-generation lords Black Butterfly and Tepepul subjugated to Castile, followed by Don Juan de Rojas and Don Juan Cortés, their sons, who were in office at the time the Popol Vuh was compiled. The text concludes elegaically with the comment, "This is enough about the being of Quiché, given that there is no longer a place to see it" (Tedlock 1996, 198).

The world's awareness of the Popol Vuh emerged slowly in the second half of the twentieth century. The middle man who introduced the conceptual magnitude of the Quichéan scripture was Swiss-born ethnologist Raphael M. Girard. He came to the Western hemisphere in 1919 as head of a six-member French scientific mission to study aborigines of the Honduras forest. In 1924, he launched an archaeological and ethnological survey of Amerindian cultures from Patagonia to Canada. Applying mythology, ethnography, archaeology, and linguistics, he learned Mayan languages as an introduction to Mayan culture and represented the government of Guatemala at international Americanist consortiums. In 1977, he was nominated for a Nobel prize in literature; the next year, a half century of research and publication earned him the Organization of American States Diploma of Merit.

An analyst of the meaning of the Popol Vuh, Girard ranked the codex a key to unraveling the history, religion, and culture of the Quiché. He declared the text older than the Rig Veda, the Zend Avesta, and the law codes of Moses and Hammurabi. In his words, it "explains the first moment of the life of a religion, a society, an art, a language: of a culture coming to birth" (Girard 1979). A respected Americanist, he composed the first exegesis of the epic to clarify its meaning and illuminate the Quichéan sacred lifestyle. In a broad summary of myth and meaning, he particularized the epic as illustrating human immortality and an afterlife among the heavenly constellations.

After conferring with elders of the Chortí and Quiché-Maya tribes, native gnostics and guardians of sacred tradition, Girard concluded:

The native elders were never in error in the routine employment of their old symbols, and they adhered in every smallest detail to the teachings of the Popol Vuh. In all the cases where I doubted them, it was I who was in error for believing, as do the majority among ethnographers, that the Indian must unfailingly conform to our manner of thinking [Girard 1979].

Twenty years later, he compiled fundamental secret doctrines in an exposition, *Esoterismo del Popol Vuh* (1948), which was issued in French and Italian and by Theosophical University Press in English as *Esotericism of the Popol Vuh* (1979), translated by Blair A. Moffett. The scripture reveals aspects of astronomy, the calendar, and the symbolism of a prehistoric ritual cycle through four ages, from creation to the apotheosis of a solar deity dating from the Paleolithic age to European conquest.

Girard's unprecedented version of the codex clears up former misinterpretations that failed to elucidate the evolution of the Mayan civilization from its beginnings to a noble height. He demonstrates correspondences to Mexican and Andean cosmogonies and creation archetypes of other world civilizations. Girard characterizes the Mayan universe as a multilevel emanation of primeval forces. In native metaphysics, mythology allegorized their worlds according to numerous layers of divinity. The conceptual whole illuminates not just life in Meso-America, but the existence of humankind on earth — from hunter-gatherers to the matriarchal-horticultural cycle to the patriarchal-agrarian mindset. The fourth level, the emergence of the Quiché-Maya, lauds the spiritual linkage of natives with their creators through the semi-divine mediator, a Promethean demigod-redeemer, Hunahpú, who ordered and regulated life from planting to registering time. Comparable to the expulsion of Adam and Eve from the garden of Eden in punishment for their violation of God's injunction and their knowledge of good and evil, the episode parallels the Hindu scriptural record of *mânasaputras* (sons of mind) who descended from higher worlds to awaken human intellectual potential.

Prefiguring Charles Darwin's *Descent of Man*, the Popol Vuh accounts for the evolution of simians from early humanity, the obverse of human evolution from apes. The appearance of advanced man-gods echoes the Buddhist concept of the *bodhisattva* or compassionate buddha. Thus, Hunahpú represents a perfected, spiritually illumined human who sacrifices himself for all humankind. Girard identifies the character with the carved figure of the young maize god which adorned the facade of a limestone temple at Copán, a ruined Mayan city in Honduras at the center of the border separating it from Guatemala, which was discovered by New Jersey archaeologists John Lloyd Stephens and Frederick Catherwood in 1839 and reported in *Incidents of Travel in Central America, Chiapas, and Yucatan* (1841).

Girard's explanation challenges the prejudice that Native Americans, unlike Europeans, honored no history. By linking paleoanthropology with history, he captures the prehistoric Mayan aspiration toward perfection, as demonstrated in the religious sculpture of the maize god. He is crowned by a pointed corona of corn leaves, a pro-tuberance similar to the *ushnîsha* of the awakened Buddha. The hands, palm up, parallel the *mudrâ*, a classical teaching gesture of the *bodhisattva* in Asian iconography. By linking the epic codes with monuments, glyphs, symbols, and customs of the early Mayans, Girard offers insight into the ethos of present-day Maya. He explains that the chronology of events in the codex falls into four ages. Because cataclysms separate these stages of evolution, there are no human survivors of past eras of human development.

SOURCES: Fox 1995, Girard 1979, Hamann 1999, Howarth and Lamadrid 1999, Malatesta 1997, Martin 1969, Moffett 1979, *New Catholic Encyclopedia* 1967, "The Popul Vuh," "Popul Vuh — A Creation Story" 1999, "The Sacred Book of the Maya — Popol Vuh — Re-Creates a Tradition" 1999, Sharer 1996, "Stone Carving" 1997, Tedlock 1996.

Rig Veda *see* Vedas

The Sacred Pipe see *Black Elk Speaks*

Science and Health *see* Christian Science Writings

The Sixth Grandfather see *Black Elk Speaks*

Ssu Shu *see* I Ching

Talmud   Treasured by orthodox Jews as the supporting pillar of Judaism, the Talmud, Hebrew for "learning" or "teaching," is a sacred body of authoritative interpretation and legal commentary on its basic text, the Mishna (or Mishnah; repetition), the moral laws that govern all Jews. An example from Louis I. Newman and Samuel Spitz's quotation book, *The Talmud Anthology* (1945), expresses the commonsense wisdom of Jewish interpreters:

> God is continually working miracles without man's knowing it, in protecting him from unknown evils. But a man should not needlessly expose himself to peril in the expectation that God will miraculously deliver him. God may not do so; and, even if a miracle is wrought for him, the man earns demerit by his presumption [286].

Topics vary from homosexual practice and silence in the synagogue during prayer to the vulgar display of wealth, breeding of pigs, bigamy, extortion, forced conversion from Judaism, snooping in other people's mail, excommunication of informers, and ransom of captives. Just as in biblical times, Talmudic study is still required of all devout male Jews, both rabbis and the laity, from childhood and throughout adulthood, and is extending into communities of interested females.

Authority over interpretation of God's holy word has varied over time from holy figures to temple bureaucracy. After the waning of priestly power in Judea, regulation of Jewish life passed to two classes of officials, scribes and Pharisees. The professional scribe was a scriptural expert and copyist who, like Ezra in the Book of Ezra 7:6, secured biblical scrolls. The Pharisee, a more powerful authority figure, was a strict jurist of the seventy-one-member Sanhedrin, the Jewish supreme court. Pharisees ruled on such community and temple issues as tithing, cleanliness, and observance of the sabbath. At the heart of their service to the pious was the need for sensible application of laws and regulations to real-life situations.

The Talmud is an exhaustive, ongoing study of biblical meaning as it applies to every phase of human existence. According to tradition, Talmudic scholarship requires of the scholar fourteen character traits: correct behavior, humility, prudence, open-mindedness, wisdom, receptiveness, memory, service, faithful attendance, a questioning mind, obedience to rule, originality, readiness to travel, and the ability to learn, teach, and practice. For obvious reasons, Talmudic style is realistic: the text applies a general statute to actual cases and discusses the legalities of, for example, a prohibition against remarriage to a woman abandoned for infidelity and the trying of infractions in Jewish courts, which hand down punishments and methods of rectifying injustice. The Talmud comments on Jewish oral *halakha* (laws or statutes) governing ritual, doctrine, and social law as contained in the second–fifth books of the Torah: Exodus, Leviticus, Numbers, and Deuteronomy. An example of Talmudic wisdom in social dealings is the inclusion of non–Jews in the distribution of harvest portions to the poor. It derives from two sources—written law found in the Torah (or scripture) and the Mishnah, an organization of oral laws. Talmud also rules on *haggada* or *haggadah* (narrative), a minor segment dealing with the nonlegal or narrative actions and themes in scripture that serve as sermon topics.

Two independent groups produced Talmuds in the form of dialectic, which examines one issue from a variety of points of view. These consortiums conferred over long periods, yet issued different annotations separated by a century. The first, known as the Talmud Yerushalmi (also Palestinian or Jerusalem Talmud), was the work of Palestinian *amoraim* (scholars). They worked apart at the Jewish academies in Caesarea on the Samarian coast and at Sepphoris and Tiberias in northern Israel, but gave no details of their system of editing. Partially compiled in Caesarea around C.E. 350 and finished in Tiberias in C.E. 400, the work was composed in western Aramaic and reflects a strict biblical interpretation. After years of oral application, the Jerusalem Talmud entered print in Venice in 1524 in 5,500 folios and was later translated into French.

The leader of the compilation was Johanan bar Nappaha, a revered scholar and teacher from Sepphoris and a redoubtable anti–Roman. He was well connected to other authorities on Torah and mastered major sources of discussion and interpretation. He displayed humility in the simple wisdom of his sayings, such as "Where there's life, there's hope," "A person's table is his altar," "God gave Torah to all nations, but only Israel accepted it," and "A smile to a neighbor is more valuable than an offer of a drink." His respect for truth is evident in the adage "Since the destruction of the Temple, prophecy is the province of fools and children." Hopeful of the future, he declared that God would one day make Jerusalem the world's metropolis.

The second Talmud, known as the Talmud Bavli (Babylonian Talmud), was the compilation of an independent group of Babylonian experts whose working method is unknown. Completed by *gaon* (academy principal) Rav Ashi of Sura and Rabina (or Ravina) II and issued around C.E. 500 in eastern Aramaic, it is three times the size of the Jerusalem Talmud and contains nonbiblical influences from Persian culture. Because the Babylonian collaborators had the Jerusalem Talmud to work

A page from the "Codex Babylonicus Petropolitanus" (C.E. 916), oldest dated Bible manuscript, with the Masorah Parva in the margins.

from, they completed a thorough, more valuable work, later translated into German and English. The complete Babylonian Talmud reached print in Guadalajara, Spain, around 1482 and was standardized in Vilna in 1886 in a page layout juxtaposing laws with commentaries and references. In 1581, an edition of the Babylonian Talmud published in Basel by a church censor replaced the title of Talmud with Gemara (or Gemarah [Completion]), a more exact heading. Both terms survive and remain in use as virtual synonyms.

Because new challenges continually require judgment, Talmudic scholarship is an unending process. As an aid to the rabbinate in governing agriculture and the professions, weddings and festivals, civil laws, temple services, and ritual purity, the growing body of legality supplements scriptural law by ruling on needs and conceptualizing issues that have arisen since biblical times. To meet worship demands, a scholarly assembly added opening and closing benedictions and settled the issue of required and optional prayer times. The first category, introits, includes the *Avot* (Fathers), praising the faith of the patriarchs; the *Gevurot* (Power), glorifying God; and the *Kedushah*, exalting God's holiness. The latter type, final benedictions, offers *Avodah* (Worship), requesting restoration of worship in the temple; *Hoda'ah* (Thanksgiving), a blessing on life and goodness; and *Shalom* (Peace), a plea for nonviolence. Thirteen additional benedictions request knowledge, repentance, forgiveness, redemption, healing, good harvest, return of exiles, true judgment, punishment of evil, reward of piety, rebuilding of Jerusalem, restoration of the Davidic rule, and divine response to prayers. A standard feature of temple worship, the *Sh'ma Yisrael* (Hear, O Israel), a public affirmation of faith, remains central to the Jewish expression of belief in monotheism. The wise sayings compiled in the *Avot* are a favorite, which editors bound into prayer books and translated into numerous languages. Among the adages of the *Avot* are the seven characteristics of the boorish and courteous man, four types of charitable people, and honor to the Torah as the tree of life.

Over time, encyclopedic rulings branched out to particularize and clarify issues and ramifications involving architecture and building, astronomy, divination and interpretation of dreams, fables and folklore, history and legend, and metaphysics and natural science. To pious Jews, the Talmud keeps religious questions open and meaningful and engages the finest minds in active pursuit of truth as revealed by God's word. To Christians and reformed Jews, fastidious points of law and tortuous debates appear to enclose orthodox Judaism in an unrealistic legalism more suited to medieval thought and practice. Such narrow-mindedness inhibits ecumenism and the political coalitions necessary to solve multicultural world issues, in particular, the fate of the Palestinians.

As Jews spread about the Mediterranean world, lack of an official encyclopedia of laws hampered orthodoxy. Late in the first century B.C.E., the sage Hillel ha-Zaken of Babylon, a good-hearted thinker who headed the Jerusalem Sanhedrin, and his rival, the grumpy teacher Shammai ha-Zaken, attempted to organize loose segments of the Mishnah and commentary. Although the Sanhedrin sanctioned a version of the Mishnah after C.E. 135, the tedious, exacting work continued for over three centuries. The first written copy of the Mishnah was the work of Rabbi Judah ha-Nasi, a Palestinian patriarch and president of the Sanhedrin known as Judah the Prince, who compiled the Mishnah, the Tosefta (Additions), and laws omitted from the main text in biblical Hebrew around C.E. 200. He redacted the Mishnah's sixty-three *masskot* (tractates) into six *seders* (orders or categories). The modern version of Talmud totals 517 chapters under sixty-three headings, some chosen from the first word of the text rather than for applicability to the topic.

Seder Zera'im (Seeds)

Also called *Seder Emunah* (Faith), this eleven-part section covers a variety of issues concerning piety and charity.

Order	Chapters	Babylonian Pages	Jerusalem Pages	Topic
Berakhot (benedictions)	9	64	68	reading the *sh'ma*; timing and reciting the daily *adimah* prayer, saying grace before and after meals; special benedictions after thunder, lightning, earthquake, or upon receiving disturbing news
		Example: "Grow not angry, and ye shall not sin; grow not drunk, and ye shall not offend" (Newman and Spitz 1945, 9).		
Pe'ah (corner)	8	—	37	gleaning fields, orchards, or vineyards; distributing charity, abandoned sheaves, or windfalls; tithes of the poor; gossip
		Example: "I ... have laid up treasure for Above: a place where no force prevails—treasures bearing fruit;		

Order	Chapters	Babylonian Pages	Jerusalem Pages	Topic
				treasures for souls, treasures which I, myself, will enjoy; treasures of value in the World-to-Come" (Newman and Spitz 1945, 58).
Demai (suspected tithes)	7	—	34	questionable or improper tithes, offering suspect food to the poor or to Jewish soldiers, over working plow animals

Example: "If even a laborer in a profane occupation may not fast, how much the less may one engaged in a holy profession?" (Newman and Spitz 1945, 1).

Order	Chapters	Babylonian Pages	Jerusalem Pages	Topic
Kilayim (mixed species)	9	—	44	varieties of animals, seeds, and trees grown in Palestine; mixed seeds in a field or vineyard; harnessing unlike animals; cross-breeding; mixing garments of different materials
Shevi'it (sabbatical year)	10	—	31	the sabbatical year; leaving land fallow in the seventh year; prohibition of sowing, pruning, reaping, harvesting, or selling reseeded produce; forgiving debts

Example: "A Jew need not give up his life to avoid transgressing any law, except incest, murder and idolatry" (Newman and Spitz 1945, 214).

Order	Chapters	Babylonian Pages	Jerusalem Pages	Topic
Terumot (heave offering)	11	—	59	distribution of a share of harvest to priests before the remaining food is eaten, the consumption of priest's food by laypersons, misuse of tithes

Example: "The Torah tells us to give to the dogs carcasses of dead beasts" (Newman and Spitz 1945, 233).

Order	Chapters	Babylonian Pages	Jerusalem Pages	Topic
Ma'aserot (tithes)	5	—	26	contributions for the poor and the Levites, types of produce to be tithed, dates for tithes, consumption of produce by laborers, first and second tithes, tithes of the poor
Ma'aser Sheni (second tithe)	5	—	33	presenting a second tithe in Jerusalem of one-tenth of produce from which the first tithe has been removed, replacing goods with money, marking unharvested produce for use as a tithe
Halah (ascent)	4	—	28	making an offering of dough to priests
Orlah (uncircumcised)	3	—	20	protecting trees from harvest before the fifth year, exempting trees, mixing licit and illicit fruits among tithes, making dye or cooking over burning peelings
Bikkurim (first fruits)	3	—	13	temple offering of first fruits from Israel's seven species, qualities of first fruits, proceeding to Jerusalem with offerings, ritual impurity of the hermaphrodite

Seder Mo'ed (Season or Festival)

Consisting of twelve parts, this section comments on ceremonies, sacred holidays, and temple offerings.

Order	Chapters	Babylonian Pages	Jerusalem Pages	Topic
Sabbath (seventh day)	24	157	92	laws governing observance of the sabbath, special sabbaths, prohibition of labor, meals, prayers, recitation at the end of the sabbath

Example: "Food is better for a man up to the age of forty; after forty drink is better" (Newman and Spitz, 1945, 101).

Order	Chapters	Babylonian Pages	Jerusalem Pages	Topic
Iruvin or *Erubin* (mingling)	10	105	65	limits of sabbath observance

Example: "He who eats a tenth of an Ephah at a meal is healthy and blessed. He who eats more betrays his greedy character; he who eats less will be afflicted by ills" (Newman and Spitz, 1945, 101).

Order	Chapters	Babylonian Pages	Jerusalem Pages	Topic
Pesahim (paschal sacrifice)	10	121	71	leavened and unleavened bread, the lamb as paschal sacrifice, evening seder meal, stylized questions reflecting the history of the Exodus

Example: "Reside not in a town, the mayor of which is the community physician. He will be too busy to attend thee in thy illness" (Newman and Spitz 1945, 319).

Order	Chapters	Babylonian Pages	Jerusalem Pages	Topic
Shekalim (annual tax)	8	—	33	temple dues of a half shekel, ceremony of presenting the tribute, substituting gold coins, purchasing temple offerings, surplus funds, officers overseeing the temple, disposing of meat or coins found in the temple or on temple grounds
Yoma (the day)	8	88	42	fasting and sacrifice for Yom Kippur, special duties of the high priest, Holy of Holies ritual, bathing and clothing for the observance, abstinence from sexual intercourse

Example: "'And thou shalt love the Lord'—namely, thou shalt make the Lord beloved" (Newman and Spitz 1945, 156).

Order	Chapters	Babylonian Pages	Jerusalem Pages	Topic
Sukkah (booth)	5	56	26	erecting the sukkah and observing Succoth for seven days, eating bread, exemptions for women and inclement weather, blessings and prayers

Example: "Happy is our old age if it atones for our youth" (Newman and Spitz 1945, 182).

Order	Chapters	Babylonian Pages	Jerusalem Pages	Topic
Betsah (also *Betzah*; egg; or *Yom Tov*; Festival Day)	5	40	22	work during festivals, food preparation, compassion

Example: "A man's income is decreed on Rosh Ha-Shanah for the coming year, except that which he spends for the Sabbath, the Yom Tob, and for tuition. If he spends less than it was contemplated on high, they deduct it from his income. If he spends more, they add to it" (Newman and Spitz 1945, 399).

Order	Chapters	Babylonian Pages	Jerusalem Pages	Topic
Rosh Ha-Shanah (beginning of the year)	4	35	22	ordering the calendar, sounding the shofar [ram's horn], specific prayers for the new year, self-examination of conscience, blessings

Example: "God revealed the earth in His wisdom, and He prepared the world for his congregation" (Newman and Spitz 1945, 83).

Order	Chapters	Babylonian Pages	Jerusalem Pages	Topic
Taanit (fast day)	4	31	26	public declaration of fasting during drought, epidemic, or enemy invasion; fixed dates of fasting

Examples: "Great is the period of rain. Even the penny in the purse is blessed by it" and "Sunshine after a rainfall does as much good as two rains" (Newman and Spitz 1945, 366).

Order	Chapters	Babylonian Pages	Jerusalem Pages	Topic
Megillah (scroll)	4	32	34	feasting and celebrating on Purim, donating to the poor in honor of Queen Esther, reading scripture

Example: "Why was Hadassah called Esther [Star]? Because the nations declared her to be as beautiful as a star" (Newman and Spitz 1945, 28).

Order	Chapters	Babylonian Pages	Jerusalem Pages	Topic
Moed Katan (minor festival; also *Mashkin*; permission to irrigate)	3	29	19	intermediate festival days, forbidding work, exemptions for mourning

Example: "'I rule over man,' says God. 'Who rules over Me? The Zaddik [righteous man]. I decree and he annuls'" (Newman and Spitz 1945, 562).

Order	Chapters	Babylonian Pages	Jerusalem Pages	Topic
Hagigah (sacrifice)	3	27	22	rules governing required pilgrimage to Jerusalem for males during Passover, Shavuoth, and Succoth; donations, tithes, sacrifice, and ceremonial vessels; ritual purity of celebrants

Example: "If miracles are to be performed, God alone will perform them. The Messiah's advent will not change the course of nature" (Newman and Spitz 1945, 277).

Seder Nashim [Women]

This is a seven-stage ruling on aspects of betrothal, marriage, and family life.

Order	Chapters	Babylonian Pages	Jerusalem Pages	Topic
Yevamot (Levite marriage)	16	122	85	marriage of Levites, testimony concerning a husband's death, marriage of a man to the wife of his dead brother, exemption from marriage to a brother's widow, forbidden unions to minors and non–Jews; rape and seduction, remarriage of woman whose husband was erroneously reported as dead.

Example: "A man should not marry a woman with the thought in mind that he may divorce her" (Newman and Spitz 1945, 271).

Order	Chapters	Babylonian Pages	Jerusalem Pages	Topic
Ketubbot (marriage contract)	13	112	72	premarital contracts and agreements, a husband's obligations, dowry, marriage ceremony, punishment for rape and seduction, grounds for divorce, inheritance, moving of a wife and children, exemption for residents of Jerusalem

Example: "Rabbi Abba would lose a kerchief with coins among the poor. He was careful, however, to chase away rogues" (Newman and Spitz 1945, 56).

| Nedarim (vows) | 11 | 91 | 40 | voluntary vows, dedication, consecration, in validating oaths, abstinence from food, cancelling vows, annulment of the vows of a bride or betrothed woman |

Example: "Let those who hate me, rejoice, and God will turn away His anger from me. Those who love me will pray in my behalf" (Newman and Spitz 1945, 430).

| Nazir (Nazirite) | 9 | 66 | 47 | prohibitions governing Nazirites, who dedicate themselves to holy purpose; prohibitions on Nazirites, breaking vows, contamination of a Nazirite |

Example: "One who causes himself pain by abstinence from something he desires is called a sinner" (Newman and Spitz 1945, 1).

| Sotah (suspected adulteress) | 9 | 49 | 47 | war, murder by an unknown assailant, adultery; forcing a suspect to drink holy water with dirt from the temple floor, unbinding of hair, blessings and oaths, military exemption |

Example: "Even when thy left hand repulses, thy right hand should still draw sinners near" (Newman and Spitz 1945, 441).

| Gittin (bills of divorcement) | 9 | 90 | 54 | divorce and strictures on the bill of divorcement, delivery by husband to his wife, witnesses, canceling a bill of divorcement, alimony, divorcing a minor, divorce from an insane husband |

Example: "There is no remedy for a fool" (Newman and Spitz 1945, 129).

| Kiddushin (sanctification) | 4 | 82 | 48 | betrothal, marriage, family relationships, proxy marriage, intermarriage between classes, social conduct, nullification of a marriage ceremony |

Example: "If knowledge and wisdom are desirable things, their possessors surely deserve honor at our hands" (Newman and Spitz 1945, 408).

Seder Neziqin (or Nezikin; Damages; also called Seder Yeshuot; Rescues)

A ten-section civil and criminal law code, this part contains numerous court anecdotes and models.

Order	Chapters	Babylonian Pages	Jerusalem Pages	Topic
Bava Kamma (first gate)	10	119	44	intended and unintended damage, public and private harm, negligence, theft, violence, robbery

Order	Chapters	Babylonian Pages	Jerusalem Pages	Topic
Example: "The law of the land is law" (Newman and Spitz 1945, 179).				
Bava Mets'ia (middle gate)	10	119	37	property loss, usury, hiring, labor contracts, buying and transferring real estate, lost and found, interest, joint owners
Example: "If two men claim thy help, and one is thy enemy, help him first" (Newman and Spitz 1945, 184).				
Bava Batra (last gate)	10	176	34	partnership, selling, lending, inheritance, transfer of real estate, ownership, deeds and legal documents, fair weights and measures
Example: "Come and let us take stock of the accounts of the world: the loss caused through a Mitzvah [blessing] versus the gain, and the gain through a sin versus the loss" (Newman and Spitz 1945, 137).				
Sanhedrin (council)	11	113	57	the court system, sages and judges, felonies, faith
Example: "Seven laws are binding on the descendants of Noah [gentiles]: establishment of courts of justice; blasphemy prohibition; prohibition of the worship of other gods, of murder, of incest and adultery, of theft and robbery, and of eating the flesh of a living animal before it dies" (Newman and Spitz 1945, 303).				
Makkot (lashing)	3	24	9	court-ordered flagellation, false witness, manslaughter, flight, taking refuge
Shevu'ot (oaths)	8	49	44	swearing an oath, public and private oaths, defiling ritual, sacrificial atonement, trustees, deposits
Example: "What difference does it make if the plaintiff is a scholar? Can I decide the law otherwise if he is an unlearned man?" (Newman and Spitz, 233).				
Eduyyot (testimony)	8	—	—	testimony, menstruation, ritual bath, priest's portion of dough, Levite purity, a priest's dues, tithes, marriage
Example: "A court cannot reverse another court unless it is greater in learning and numbers" (Newman and Spitz 1945, 220).				
Avodah Zarah (idolatry)	5	76	37	avoiding idolatry and idol worshipers, business dealings with idolators, wine sold by idolators
Example: "He who studies the law, but does no works of love, lives without God" (Newman and Spitz 1945, 239).				
Avot (fathers)	5	—	—	ethics and personal conduct, moral aphorisms, traditions, ideals
Example: "Judge not thy neighbor until thou hast put thyself in his place; judge all men charitably" (Newman and Spitz 1945, 226).				
Horayot (court errors)	3	14	19	rectifying faulty court decisions
Example: "He who loves his neighbors and lends money to the needy in his need, concerning him it is written: 'Thou shalt call and I shall answer'" (Newman and Spitz 1945, 240).				

Seder Qodashim (also Kodashim; The Sacred or Holy)

This consists of eleven sections covering types and purposes of offerings and food.

Order	Chapters	Babylonian Pages	Jerusalem Pages	Topic
Zevahim (sacrifices)	14	120	—	sacrificial slaughter of four-footed animals and birds, sprinkling blood at the temple, offering a priestly portion, removing blood from clothes and vessels
Menahot (meal offerings)	13	110	—	gifts of food, prayer shawls, and written scripture bound to the body; sanctuary offerings,

Order	Chapters	Babylonian Pages	Jerusalem Pages	Topic
				both valid and invalid; gifts of drink; substitute offerings from the poor

Example: "Israel will never cease to exist" (Newman and Spitz 1945, 209).

Order	Chapters	Babylonian Pages	Jerusalem Pages	Topic
Hullin (unhallowed things)	12	142	—	dietary laws, food prohibitions, ritual slaughter, avoidance of blood and unclean meat, mixing meat and dairy foods

Example: "A single kernel of grain suffices for [the ant's] meal and it is easily obtained. Great is the charity which God has displayed to this tiny insect" (Newman and Spitz 1945, 13).

Order	Chapters	Babylonian Pages	Jerusalem Pages	Topic
Bekhorot (first-born)	9	61	—	first offspring of animals and humans, animals unsuitable for sacrifice, locating blemishes, redemption and rights of the first born
Arakhin (evaluation)	9	34	—	soil, worth of temple offerings, holy items, transacting in hallowed real estate, the jubilee year

Examples: "What is service with joy? Song" and "The books of life and death are open before [God] on Rosh ha-Shanah" (Newman and Spitz 1945, 295, 392).

Order	Chapters	Babylonian Pages	Jerusalem Pages	Topic
Temurah (exchange)	7	34	—	substitute offerings, faulty dedication, sin offerings, parturient animals, individual and congregational gifts, altar presentation, use of animals for temple maintenance

Example: "The congregation is immortal" (Newman and Spitz 1945, 359).

Order	Chapters	Babylonian Pages	Jerusalem Pages	Topic
Keritot (excommunication)	6	28	—	types of sacrifice for differing levels of sin, premature death, sin offering, childbirth pledges, guilt, violations of pure food, restrictions on the sabbath and intercourse

Example: "A great scholar, on whose legal teaching people rely, is forbidden to teach his pupils while drunk, for this teaching is like giving decisions" (Finkelman 1998).

Order	Chapters	Babylonian Pages	Jerusalem Pages	Topic
Me'ilah (profanation of sacred property)	6	22	—	temple sacrilege, atonement, unintentional sin, altar sacrifice, restitution, sacrilege through a third party
Tamid (continuous offering)	6	8	—	basic temple sacrifice, clearing ash from the altar, arranging logs, allotment of priestly duties, slaughtering lambs for the altar, morning prayers, hymns for sacrifice, incense, cleaning candelabra

Example: "Who is wise? He who foresees what will transpire" (Newman and Spitz 1945, 133).

Order	Chapters	Babylonian Pages	Jerusalem Pages	Topic
Middot (measurements)	5	—	—	temple shape and dimensions; placement of gates, walls, railings, steps, doors, inner courts; fitness of priests for duty
Kinnim (bird offerings)	3	—	—	mixed sacrifices, voluntary and obligatory offering, sprinkling blood, sin offering

The law imposed a hierarchy of priests, elders, and trainees and set up a temple staff of two overseers, seven administrators, and thirteen treasurers, who held keys to the strongbox.

Example: "The unlearned lose the power of clear thinking as they grow old, but scholars gain in it as their years advance" (Newman and Spitz 1945, 6).

Seder Tohorot (also Toharot; Purification)

This twelve-stage compilation of laws affects rituals and purity.

Order	Chapters	Babylonian Pages	Jerusalem Pages	Topic
Kelim (vessels)	30	—	—	maintaining purity in dishes and utensils,

Order	Chapters	Babylonian Pages	Jerusalem Pages	Topic
				sources of contamination, levels of impurity, cleaning ovens and hearths, the ashes of the red heifer, uses for ritual cleansing
Oholot (tents)	18	—	—	handling of corpses, entering a residence containing the dead, spread of contamination, still born children, crossing an unmarked grave, ritual bath, sprinkling holy water and ash of the red heifer
Nega'im (marks of the leper)	14	—	—	avoiding lepers, infection, treatment, kinds of leprosy, diagnosis, hair and tissue of lepers, spread of leprosy, isolating lepers, ritual cleansing of lepers
Parah (cow)	12	—	—	preparing ashes and decontamination after touching a corpse
Tohorot (cleanness)	10	—	—	types of ritual cleansing after childbirth or menstruation, unclean food and drink, contact with lepers, removal of corpses or dead animals
Mikva'ot (ritual baths)	10	—	—	ritual bathing; water from sea, river, rain, ice, snow, or blended sources; depth; mode of bath in flowing or still waters; pool walls of stone, cement, or clay; prohibition of metal pools; emptying of waters covered; discharge of water by gravity or human servants dipping out the contents; purity of brides, women ending their menses, mothers of newborn infants, converts to Judaism; purification on the sabbath or at Yom Kippur
Niddah (separation)	10	73	13	ritual cleansing for women after menstruation, contact with a husband, prohibition from the temple and food, expiation offerings, gonorrhea, abnormal discharge, impure sperm, touching a contaminated bed or chair, stains, irregular blood flow

Example: "God has endowed women with a special sense of wisdom which man lacks" (Newman and Spitz 1945, 545).

Order	Chapters	Babylonian Pages	Jerusalem Pages	Topic
Makhshirin (liquid contaminants)	6	—	—	types of pollution, unclean food, public bathing, non–Jewish impurity, clean liquids, transferring liquid between vessels
Zavim (discharge)	5	—	—	venereal disease and cleansing in male and female, clean days, ritual immersion, sin offering, burnt offering, impurity of an animal corpse
Tevul Yom (a person purified by bathing)	4	—	—	ritual contamination, timing of ritual baths, degree of impurity, entry into the temple after ritual bathing
Yadayim (hands)	4	—	—	cleansing the hands, degree of impurity, water and vessels for washing hands, rinsing, invalid offering, Jewish tithes outside Israel, disputes about purity
Uktsin (fruit stems)	3	—	—	items that are easily contaminated, stalks, nut shells, peelings, pits, egg shells, purpose of eating

Because the biblical injunction to use ash from the red heifer for ritual cleansing was incomprehensible in Solomon's time, the law is classed as beyond human comprehension.

The detailed laws clarified in the Talmud demonstrate Judaism's high level of civilization. Appended to the Babylonian Talmud are two monographs on *Derekh Eretz* (or *Erez* [Correct Behavior or Way of the Land]), the

code of conduct that characterizes proper Jewish deportment in all phases of marital and family relations, friendship, and professional life. The code obligates individuals to tend to their own needs rather than burden others, to educate and prepare their children for adulthood, and to respect the well-being of others. On a simpler level, *Derekh Eretz* specifies daily conduct — felicity of speech, common sense, table etiquette, and a pervasive dignity.

Study and clarification of divine law have resulted in

a complicated labyrinth of interpretations, each built on the work of predecessors. The linkage begins with the early *tannaim* (teachers), who interpreted law between Old Testament times and C.E. 200, including the organizer Rabban Gamaliel I (or Gamaliel the Elder), Hillel's grandson and consultant to Agrippa I. Gamaliel I elevated the status of women by protecting divorcees and easing the burden of proof at the death of a husband.

- The next teacher was Johanan ben Zakkai, who led the Pharisees and helped to restore the Temple of Jerusalem. As head of the Sanhedrin, he established pivotal statutes and clarified controversies.
- Johanan's successor was the strict jurist Gamaliel II of Yavneh, who presided over the temple restoration. His writings on law, ritual, and ethics were the groundwork of the Mishnah.
- Gamaliel II's brother-in-law Eliezer ben Hyrcanus (or Eliezer the Great), Johanan's pupil and rescuer, was known for a photographic memory. He smoothed over the chaos that followed the fall of the second Temple by supporting the Yavneh academy. A strict literalist and severe misogynist, he is known for exalting common labor and parenthood and for according honor to all people who appeared in court, whether pious or impious. His most famous prayer asked for serenity in the face of divine will.
- Eleazar ben Azariah, a child prodigy and successor of Gamaliel II, was a scriptural and Talmudic expert who preferred literal interpretation of the Torah.
- Gamaliel II's rival, Joshua ben Hananiah, a humble blacksmith and eminent scholar, was a student of Johanan ben Zakkai. A temple chorister and preacher, Hananiah uplifted spirits after the destruction of the Temple and inveighed against strict application of the law, including the prohibition of marriage to aliens.
- A moderate, Ishmael ben-Elisha the exegete, helped to consolidate the rabbinate. He defended the interpretation of Torah as idiomatic language. He pioneered Midrash (Exposition), a thirteen-rule method of exegesis, and founded a scholarly consortium that produced the *Mekhilta de-Rabbi Ishmael*, a commentary on Exodus. The purpose of Midrash was tricky territory — the reconciliation of scriptural contradictions through new interpretations, the grounding of new laws in ancient scripture, and the enrichment of Bible study with contemporary meaning and application.
- Tarphon (or Tarfon) was a reviler of Christianity and a strong proponent of Torah study. He is best known for commenting that no one must single-

handedly perfect the world, but neither is the individual allowed to stop trying. A favorite story about the rabbi describes him arguing with the Jewish elite until students summoned him to morning prayer.
- The patriot Akiba (also Aqiba or Akiva) ben-Joseph, systematizer of the law and martyr to Roman oppression, learned to read in adulthood through the assistance of his wife, Rachel. He is best known for extolling her with the comment: "What man has wealth? He who has a virtuous wife." Other sayings of his display his humanity: "Tradition is the fence of Torah" and "Man is beloved because he was made in God's image."
- Akiba's pupil and successor, Rabbi Meir, deputy to the Sanhedrin, rose to prominence during the Hadrianic persecution. His adages include a warning to keep prayers short and to spend more time at Torah than at business. He described Adam as a universal figure made from dust gathered around the globe.
- The court head and judicial reformer Simeon ben Gamaliel II was a revered disciplinarian and legislator, whose decisions influenced interpretive texts. A pragmatist and peacemaker, he disdained onerous restrictions and opted to follow folk customs.
- Jose ben Halaphta, who established legal chronology, provided detailed explanations of obscure examples from the Bible.
- The Galilean Judah ben Ilai (also Judah bar Ilai and Rabbi Judah), a student of Akiba and a court reformer, was both an editor and founder of an academy. He helped restructure the Sanhedrin and delivered hundreds of legal decisions, which yielded 3,000 Talmudic adages.
- The roll call concludes with Simeon's son, Judah ha-Nasi, and Judah's colleagues, the last of five generations of expositors.

As the Jews emigrated farther from Judea, legal commentary changed to suit their needs. After C.E. 200, Talmudic expounders were known as *amoraim* (interpreters), a vast scholarly brotherhood spread over academies at Tiberias and Sepphoris, Caesarea, Nehardea at the confluence of the Euphrates River and the Nahr Malka (Royal Canal), Sura in Babylon on the Euphrates River, and Pumbeditha (also Pumbedita or Pumpedita) on the Euphrates River at the site of modern Baghdad. In the 600s, after centuries of commentary and law codes, scholars originated the *responsum* method of discussion by letter. *Responsa* were a series of written replies to religious and legal questions from Jews of the Diaspora living outside academic centers. These letters took the place of local rabbis and schools in remote corners where Jews were a distinct minority. Of the tens of thousands of interpretive letters issued to individuals and isolated communities, only a fraction survive, many in fragments.

Individual scholars continued refining collections of opinions in the Gaonic period, from C.E. 650 to 1050. This era saw the publication of two major codes of rabbinic law in defiance of pervasive heresy and skepticism. In the second half of the eighth century, Yehudai Gaon, an unknown Babylonian jurist, compiled the *Halakhot Pesuqot* (or *Pesukot* [Decided Laws]; ca. C.E. 760), an Aramaic text issued in Hebrew as the *Hilkhot Re'u*. At the Babylonian academy at Sura, Simeon Kiyyara used Gaon's compilation as a basis for the *Halakhot Gedolot* ([Great or Large Laws]; ca. C.E. 825), later translated into French and German and printed in Venice in 1584. Both these revisions maintain Talmudic style and language, but deviate from dialectical presentation.

The need for recension in other Mediterranean languages was the impetus to linguistic scholarship. In northern Africa, Arabic grammarian and prolific exegete Sa'adi ben-Joseph (or Saadiah Gaon), an Egyptian, defended Judaism against skeptics and heretics and compiled a Hebrew-Arabic dictionary, *Safer ha-Agron*. At Sura, he composed *Kitab al-amanat wa al-i'tiqadat* (rendered in Hebrew as *Sefer ha-Emunot ve-ha-De'ot*; Book of Beliefs and Opinions; 935) and he translated the Old Testament into Arabic. To systematize religious law, he compiled a shelf of Jewish reference works in Arabic: *Kitab al-mawarith* (Book on the Laws of Inheritance), *Ahkam al-wadi'ah* (Laws on Deposits), *Kitab ash-shahadah wa al-watha'iq* (Book Concerning Testimony and Documents), *Kitab at-terefot* (Book Concerning Forbidden Meats), and *Siddur*, a collection of prayers, ancient and original, with commentary on each. Maimonides credited Sa'adi with rescuing the Torah from permanent loss.

Late in the tenth century and into the eleventh, Hai (or Hay) ben Sherira (also called Sherira Gaon) strengthened Jewish scholarship. A respected *gaon* of Pumbeditha, he composed nearly a thousand responsa and dispatched them to queriers in Spain, Italy, Tunisia, and Egypt. To clarify points for distant communities, he matched each with the language of the question, which was either Hebrew, Aramaic, or Arabic. To differentiate between biblical mysticism and superstition, he validated the mysticism of Kabbala except in instances of magic through linguistic manipulation of God's name, a technique he considered spurious and blasphemous. His letters were prized throughout Jewry and surfaced in French and Spanish translations.

Also bridging the tenth and eleventh centuries, revered Rhineland rabbi Gershom ben Judah, called Rabbenu or *Me'or ha-Golah* (Light of the Exile), advanced biblical scholarship and the social position of women and introduced Palestinian and Babylonian Talmudic commentary to Western Europe. As the leader of European Jewry, he wrote responsa to hundreds of queries and introduced a new form of exegesis famous for its clarity. He is best known as an editor for revising and collating the expanding Talmudic text, ridding it of accumulated transcription errors and variant readings. After uniting the European rabbinate, he convened synods to discuss ethics and settle disputes and held courts to grant divorces and halt polygamy. In addition to his poems and prayers, his anthology of commentaries by varied interpreters is a valuable resource on the evolution of Talmudic style. In his honor, Rashi proclaimed later generations the disciples of Gershom's disciples.

Freed of domination by Middle Easterners, the Talmud became more universal in the late Middle Ages. The eleventh-century Talmudic scholar and judge Rabbi Shlomo ben-Isaac (also known as Shlomo Yitzhaqi or Yitshaki or Rashi) of Troyes, France, became northern Europe's first respected authority on Judaism and an influence on Martin Luther and other Reformation leaders. He published a religious manual of eclectic commentary on the Torah and on the Babylonian Talmud that served Jewish students as a standard textbook. In Reggio, Italy, in 1475, his work became the first book printed in Hebrew. Rashi's grandsons Isaac, Jacob, and Samuel ben Meir (also called Rashbam) conceived *tosafot* (glossing), an interpretive method that standardized European biblical annotation as either commentary, analysis, or expansion. The outstanding family tosafists were Jacob ben Meir, called Rabbenu Tam, and Isaac ben Samuel of Dampierre, Tam's nephew.

Late in the eleventh century, Algerian jurist Isaac ben Jacob Alfasi (also Rif or Al-Phasi), a Tunisian-trained expert on the Torah and Talmud, composed in Arabic his "Little Talmud," the *Sefer ha-Halachot* (Book of Legal Decisions or Rulings; ca. 1050). He fled anti–Semitism in Fez, Morocco, in 1088 and resettled in Andalusia, where he opened a school and center of Talmudic study and answered stacks of queries from the Jewish world. The impetus to a Spanish renaissance in Talmudic scholarship, his updating of the Talmud reduced emphases on Palestinian practice and coordinated early treatises with medieval rulings on civil, criminal, and religious law.

Single chapters on issues appeared during the late Middle Ages. The classic interpreter, Rabbi Moses ben Maimon, a Cordoban court physician also known as Maimonides or Rambam, stood out from other interpreters and redactors. He sought to rid the Talmud of ambiguity by compiling a monumental work, *Mishneh Torah* (Review of the Torah; also called the *Yad ha-Hazakah* [Mighty Hand]; or the *Second Torah*; ca. 1180), which he

Two pages from Maimonides' "Mishneh Torah," printed in 1490 at Soncino, Italy, by Gerson ben Moses Soncino.

rendered in the style of Rashi. The work categorizes all religious matters under fourteen headings: knowledge, love, seasons, women, holiness, oaths, seeds, temple service, sacrifices, purity, acquisition, damages, law, and judges.

A strong critic of magic and superstition, Maimonides insisted that readers know God's love through discipline, serenity, and clear thinking. It was Maimonides' belief, as he stated in the introduction to *Moreh Nevukhim* (The Guide for the Puzzled; 1190), that the only route to spiritual perfection was through the didactic method, with the local rabbi teaching his congregants precepts of the Torah. The guiding principle of his style was to connect the Torah to an understandable level of language. A prime example of his pragmatism lies in the "Eight Degrees of Charity," to which he referred as a golden ladder. He advised:

> Anticipate charity by preventing poverty; assist the reduced fellowman, either by a considerable gift, or a sum of money, or by teaching him a trade, or by putting him in the way of business, so that he may earn an honest livelihood, and not be forced to the dreadful alternative of holding out his hand for charity [Bartlett 1992, 122].

Such sensible commentary benefited the ordinary practitioner of Jewish oral law.

European Jews continued to dominate the Talmudic endeavor. Thirteenth-century German law authority and liturgical poet Rabbi Meir ben Baruch of Rothenburg, known as Maharam, produced 1,500 responsa on law and ritual. His work, valued by the Ashkenazim, preserves medieval German community norms and customs. In mid-century, an aristocratic mystic and tosafist from Gerona, Spain, Nahmanides or Ramban (also called Nachmanides or Moses ben Nahman Gerondi), consented to debate a Christian apologist, Pablo Christiani, in

Barcelona. The success of Nahmanides's logic caused envious Dominicans to oust him from Spain. An emigrant to Israel at age seventy, he wrote *Sefer ha-Vikuach* (Book of the Debate), an abstract on his public disputation, and a revered compendium on the Torah greatly at odds with the rationalist opinions of Maimonides. Of the centrality of the Talmud, Nahmanides observes, "Everything we do today is according to the Talmud, and according to the custom and practice which we have observed in the Sages of the Talmud from the day it was composed until now" (Cantor 1994, 245).

In the early 1300s, German theologian Jacob ben Asher (also Rosh or Asher ben Jehiel), rose to the post of leader of German Jewry. He had to emigrate in 1303 because of government coercion and threat of seizure. As a refugee in Spain, he lived first in Barcelona, then Toledo, where he served as rabbi and authority on Spanish Jewry. He codified the *Piské Halakhot* (Decisions on the Laws; also *Piske ha-Rosh* [Decisions of Rosh]; 1313), a standard work printed with the Bomberg Talmud (1520) under the aegis of the Renaissance Pope Leo X. As a result of Rabbi Asher's emphasis on the Talmud, he revived religious study among Iberian Jews, who read his *Hanhagat ha-Rosh* as a source of moral enlightenment.

As liberal Renaissance inquiry further challenged conservative Judaism, commentators turned from strict biblical interpretation to outright attacks on orthodoxy. In the mid–fourteenth century, a Nicomedian theologian, Aaron ben Elijah Alfasi of Constantinople, compiled *Etz Hayyim* (Tree of Life; 1346), a summary of Karaism or scripturalism, a Babylonian movement that questioned the authority of Jewish oral tradition and the Talmud, which Karaists claimed the rabbis invented for political gain. Influenced by Maimonides' *Moreh Nevukhim*, Alfasi's *Gan Eden* (Garden of Eden; 1354) and *Keter Torah* (Crown of Law; 1362) were companion works justifying Karaism and commenting on the Torah. In 1490, Elijah Bashyatchi further negated Talmudic method by summarizing the ten principles of Karaism: belief in God's creation of the world, the existence of a divine Creator, the unity and spirituality of God, the superiority of Moses' prophecy, the perfection of Torah, the obligation to learn Hebrew, the mission of the prophets who followed Moses, resurrection of the dead, divine providence, and the coming of a messiah.

The sixteenth century continued the debate over the liberal versus conservative slant of commentary. Mystic Joseph ben-Ephraim Karo (or Caro or Qaro), also known as Maran (master), of Toledo, Spain, distinguished himself in Talmudic commentary. Forced into exile, he emigrated to Safed, Palestine, where he came under the guidance of the mystic spirit of the Midrash and attempted to standardize religious practice. He systematized the last authoritative law code, the *Bet Yosef* (House of Joseph;

1522), a masterwork that traces every law through centuries of debate. As a student aid, he abridged the book into a digest, the *Shulhan 'arukh* (or *Aruch* [The Readied, or Prepared, Table]; 1563), a compilation of Sephardic tradition, which details the religious practices of Spain, North Africa, and the Middle East. Although it was a significant Sephardic reference work, it lacked a balance of Ashkenazic traditions.

Later in the sixteenth century, Polish Rabbi Moses ben Israel Isserles or Rema, an Ashkenazi or German codifier in Cracow, established a rabbinical college that is still in existence. He reprised Karo's work in a northern European style, creating a volume accepted globally. To round out the commentary, he replaced Sephardic-centered interpretation with *Ha-Mappa* (also *Mappah* or *Mapah* [The Tablecloth]; 1571), a broader interpretation suited to both Sephardim and Ashkenazim, which organized the laws by topic and omitted obsolete statutes. His interpretation became the norm for all Jews. In his honor, his tomb carries the inscription: "From Moses to Moses there has arisen no one like Moses," a reference to the linkage between Moses Maimonides and Moses Isserles, both named for the great lawgiver chosen by God.

SOURCES: Agler 1999, Alexander and Alexander 1982, Alexy 1993, Anderson 1966, Armstrong 1993, Asimov 1981, Bartlett 1992, Bonchek 1996, Cantor 1994, Chwat 1999, Cohn-Sherbok 1998, Comay and Cohn-Sherbok 1995, "The Commentary of Rabbenu Gershom," Curtius 1953, Dolan 1968, Eckstrom 1995, "Fez," Finkelman 1998, Gentz 1973, "Golden Age of Muslim Spain," Greenspan 1994, Haberfield 1998, Harris 1924, Hastings 1951, Heer 1961, Hodges 1999, "The Jewish Controversy over Calendar Postponements," Lazare, May, and Metzger 1962, Mays 1988, "Medieval Sourcebook: Reciting the Grace after Meals" 1998, Metzger and Coogan 1993, *New Catholic Encyclopedia* 1967, Newman and Spitz 1945, "A Page from the Babylonian Talmud," Perry 1987, "Post-Talmudic Period," Potok 1978, Price 1925, "Rashi's Commentary on the Talmud," Roth and Wigoder 1977, "Significant Events in Jewish and World History," Smith, Mahlon, 1999, Snodgrass 1998, 2001, Steinsaltz 1976, Strayer 1983, Telushkin 1991, 1994, "Timeline: Principal Medieval Rabbinic Authorities," Wigoder 1989.

Tantra

Tantra, derived from the Sanskrit for "weaving" or "loom," names a massive encyclopedia of special directions for religious fulfillment through ritual. The term Tantrism has been tentatively defined as a thriving theo-anthropocosmic synthesis of God, humankind, and world. It arose among unfulfilled Brahmans in post–Vedic India during the Middle Ages. Tantric practice overturns the conservative philosophy of suppressing desire for meat and fish, alcohol, aphrodisiacs, and sex by putting forbidden yearnings to work. The purpose of Tantrism is twofold—to enhance the pleasures of earthly life and to liberate the individual from fear and enslavement to karma. In addition to religious indulgence, Tantrism contains elements of folk divination, witchcraft, and therapy. Thus, the application of Tantra's radical and highly stylized rituals frees the practitioner through the enjoyment of worldly and supernatural delights. Unlike hedonism, its philosophies enhance spiritual development through sacramental actions, which must be sincere, unselfish, and directed by a guru or master.

Tantrism's history is murky, in part because of the ambiguous role of Tantra in religious practice and also because much of the canon remains untranslated into modern tongues. Tantrism flourished under the Pala dynasty of Bengal from C.E. 800 to 1050, when conservative Hinduism took on new life and shifted direction from asceticism to indulgence. As the Kularnava Tantra (ca. C.E. 1000) declares, religious scholarship and piety lack ties with the real world:

> Ignorant of the truth within himself, the fool is infatuated with books, like the dull-witted shepherd who searches for a goat in the well when it is in its enclosure. Verbal knowledge is of no use for overcoming the delusions of the world, just as darkness does not cease to exist merely by talking about a lamp [Feuerstein 1996].

Because of its concreteness and immediacy, Tantrism regularly finds new and willing adherents, as in the American counterculture of the 1960s, and continues to generate written commentary and speculation.

The tantric canon is a highly syncretic, heterogeneous body of nonsectarian texts covering a massive variety of practices among Hindus, Buddhists, Jainists, and New Agers. The original manuscripts belong to the Sanskrit writings of Bengal, Assam, and Kashmir in northern India. Organized in the seventh century C.E., these popular handbooks, which overlap the Vedic Sutras, were composed at an earlier time from oral tradition. Their influence spread to Nepal, Tibet, Bhutan, Cambodia, and China.

The mysticism of Tantra, as summarized by the *Hevajra Tantra*, expresses a true liberation from the world:

> There is no bodily form, neither object nor subject,
>   neither flesh nor blood, neither dung nor urine,
>   no sickness, no delusion, no purification,
>   no passion, no wrath, no delusion, no envy,
>   no malignity, no conceit of self, no visible object,
>   nothing mentally produced and no producer,
>   no friend is there, no enemy,
>   calm is the innate and undifferentiated ["Selections from Mahayana Texts"].

The text also emphasizes the necessity for a one-on-one learning experience: "By no one may ... be explained, in no place may be found, it is known of itself by merit, and by due attendance on one's master" (Conze et al. 1995, 255).

Tantric manuscripts anthologize religious literature under three large categories of genre and purpose: literary, which encompasses myths, legends, parables, fables, and dialogues between gods and goddesses; public worship, including theology and disputation, yoga, temple and religious art, and *stotras* (hymns); private practice through ritual, symbolism, incantations, practical magic, and spells in "twilight language" steeped in an occult verbiage that borders on paganism (Schumann 9173, 157).

The largest of the three categories covers abstract philosophy as well as equipment. Paraphernalia for tantric ceremony extends to sorcerer's wands, incense, bells, candles, and magic circles. One compendium, the Devirahasya Tantra, lists names for the summoning and propitiation of deities; another, the *Saddharma Pundarika* (Lotus of the True Law), features an entire chapter on talismanic words, invocations, and litanies to a female divinity.

Tantras build on a divine polarity derived from the union of male and female elements. On the physical level, a mutually satisfying copulation is the supreme realization of human life; on the ethical level, satisfaction results from a balance of activity, called the Father Tantra, with appreciation, the Mother Tantra. Philosophically, Tantrism merges reality with an individual's mastery of compassion. As the *Cittavisuddhiprakarana* teaches:

Ordinary folk are afflicted with the poison of fear
  as though with poison itself,
  but he who has identified himself with compassion
  should uproot it completely and go his way [Conze et al.
  1995, 221].

Additional spheres of interest enable the well-rounded seeker to take pleasure in all forms of physical, mental, and emotional growth.

Tantric literature on yoga defines the human embodiment of Shakti as the *kundalini* (energy) housed in the lower end of the spine and activated by yogic exercise. The paradigm envisions the element of water in the genitals, fire in the umbilicus, air in the heart, space at the throat, and mind between the eyes. Tantras emphasize the application of visual aids to spiritual attainment.

Cakra

Any center of psychic power in the body, cakras are notably in the fontanel, forehead, throat, heart, navel, spine, and genitals. Study of esoteric anatomy, purification, and manipulation of these centers stimulates body awareness, healing, and rejuvenating power and promotes a state of health and well-being.

Yantra

A cosmogram, permutation, or mystic diagram that forms sacred art and geometry, yantras range in complexity from the cross, triangle, square, circle, star, and lotus patterns to mergers of several or all of these in concentric or contiguous alliance. Whether in art object, jewelry, fabric design, tattoo, or poster, the purpose of these visual aids to meditation is to express hidden models of universal or divine order.

Mandala

Like blueprints of the spiritual world, the ritual diagrams, meditation circles, or sacred polygon of mandalas represent cosmic and spiritual relationships. Within an artificial perimeter, they encompass holy space while shutting out external intrusion, as found in this depiction of the elements of the universe.

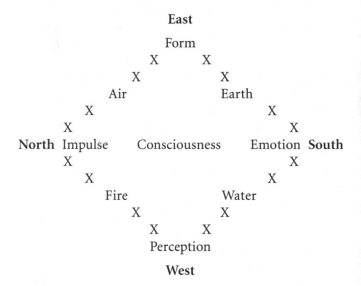

SOURCE: Conze et al. 1995, 247

Concentration on these and other geometrics and symbols leads thought from the body and earth to the divine.

To attain awareness from the mandala, the seeker follows a seven-stage ritual outlined in the *Guhyasmaja Tantra* (Treatise on the Sum Total of Mysteries), also known as *Tathagataguhyaka* (The Mystery of Buddhahood):

- site ritual, an ordering of the place and elimination of external distractions and obstructions
- preparation, which involves laying the boundaries in chalk, calling on deities, and readying the disciple for holy work
- ceremony, the actual construction of the mandala out of five colored threads, one for each of the five buddhas, followed by shading in the areas and inviting divinities to reside in the matrix
- initiation, which draws the preparer into the matrix
- offering, a series of gifts to the gods and the disciple's master

- permission, a granting of the disciple's right to call on the gods
- conclusion, the release of divinity and presentation of a burnt offering to overcome enemies or worldliness (Eliade 1987, 480).

Mantra

A mystic utterance, chant, or holy formula that internalizes the power of the divinity through magic language, a mantra, as explained in the *Advayavajrasamgraha*, may consist of one syllable, such as *om*, *tam*, or *hum*, or a string of meaningless sounds as in "Om ghuru ghuru ghudu ghudu ghata ghata ghotaya ghotaya ka" (Ch'en 1968, 82). In protracted recitation, a mantra carries consciousness beyond thought to a universal plane. The mantra can also be written on strips of paper and wound into a prayer wheel. The user, who may find a wheel along a high road or path, cranks out powerful energy as it is rotated, either by hand or wind power. The *Guhyasamaja Tantra* declares, "Even those who are considered poor wretches succeed by means of this recitation of mantras ... in this complete perfection of body, speech and mind" (Conze et al. 1995, 224).

The vision of shapes in harmony and balance and its reverence for the human form are not the cause of Tantrism's negative reputation. Beyond patterns and symbols, it extends to such "left-hand" practices as consumption of wine, ritual intercourse, and group orgies, as described in the Kularnava Tantra (ca. C.E. 1000); temple practice in the Kulachudamani Tantra (ca. seventh century); metaphysics and Kali worship in the Yoginihrdaya (ca. C.E. 1000); and magic in the Sharadatilaka Tantra (ca. 11th century). To the detriment of Tantrism, the blatantly carnal shapes and embraces found in carvings and drawings throughout the Indian subcontinent have confused the Western world, which tends to overgeneralize the underlying philosophy as unbridled eroticism or sexual license rather than sublime appreciation.

Actually, Tantrism helped to rescue the Asian woman by revolutionizing attitudes toward male supremacy. As stated in the Chandamaharoshana Tantra:

One should honor women.
Women are heaven, women are truth.
Women are the supreme fire of transformation.
Women are Buddha, women are the religious community.
Women are the perfection of wisdom ["Selections from
    Mahayana Texts"].

The Laksmi Tantra stresses that abusing women with patriarchal thoughts, words, or acts is a sacrilege. The text reasons that women bear elements of the goddess. To honor the divine, the male yogi should rejoice at the sight of women and revere the holiness they embody.

Because of the centrality of feminine traits in goddess worship, Tantrism overthrew primitive notions about the subservience of women and condemned the *sati* or *suttee*, a ritual burning of widows on their husbands' funeral pyres. Tantrists welcomed more women to roles of authority than either orthodox Hindus or Buddhists. As lay *siddhas* (religious practitioners) or sorcerers, women could elude traditional gender restrictions and follow unique careers in teaching and practice. Socially, they could eat meat, drink wine, and apply sexual energies toward salvation. In the third century in southern India, Master Aryadeva the Lotus-Born, a pupil of Nagarjuna and proponent of liberal Buddhism, advised:

Lust is to be crushed by lust.... Do strenuously that which is condemned by fools, united with your chosen deity, intent upon the purification of thought. Women stirred with the poisonous fire of love provide their lovers, ascetics of pure mind, with all the fruit of love ... Enjoy all the pleasures of love without fear. Do not fear; you do not sin [Hastings 1951, 12:196].

Equally free of restraint, their male counterparts practiced tantric copulation with wives, prostitutes and street women, and temple dancers. By gratifying the self, each worshiper honored the goddess within. In tantric terms, "The body glows, the mind is crystal clear, the spirit in harmony with heaven" (Cavendish 1970, 2783). The extremism of these tantric writings repelled many, who disliked overt sexuality and ecstatic practice and disdained the philosophy as degenerate.

Hindus who embrace Shaktism, especially those of Assam and Bengal, apply Tantra to the search for spirituality as well as satisfaction of worldly yearning. They propitiate Shakti, the goddess of energy and creativity, who is the complement and mate of Shiva or Siva, the most powerful Hindu god. In many manifestations—Ambika, Devi, Laksmi, Parvati, and Uma—her powers range from the divine mother and wife of Vishnu to the vicious Kali, goddess of death and destruction. Hindus differentiate reality into Shiva's male energy and Shakti's female realm—like yang and yin, one is conscious and active, the other transcendent and passive. Within the body, the dual energies derive from the central nervous system, which separates into a triad—spinal cord, nerves on the right side, and nerves on the left side.

To energize Shakti, the Tantrist arouses and channels the energy that lies in readiness at the base of the human spine like a coiled snake. When the two complementary forces of male and female merge and balance, they lose their duality in an ecstasy of supreme unity that courses the body from coccyx to cranium. Usually in secret, practitioners of Shaktism purify the body and harness physiological and psychological energy to attain the highest truth through worship, ritual, and magic.

As literature, the Tantras form a poetic, metaphoric canon that expresses the daily aspects of Buddhism. An illustrative parable from the *Yogacara Bhumi Sutra* (C.E. 284) characterizing sectarian disputes describes the arguing parties as children squabbling over individual sand castles. At nightfall, a metaphor for death, they abandon their precious play castles and return home. Tantras are both symbolic and secret and require expert interpretation, for example, the meaning of the red eight-petaled lotus in "An Evocation of Prajnaparamita" in the Sadhanamala. The text creates a poem as it moves, petal by petal, from the eastern point clockwise a full 360 degrees:

on the eastern petal	homage
on the southeastern petal	to the lady
on the southern petal	Prajnaparamita
on the southwestern petal	whose virtue is immortality
on the western petal	who responds to loving devotion
on the northwestern petal	who is replete with the knowledge of all (embodiments of the Buddha)
on the northern petal	who is loving towards all
on the northeastern petal	Om Dhih (Conze et al. 1995, 253).

The master advises, "Having thus set out these mantra-words, one should recite them and meditate upon them — for a day, or for a week, for six months or a year. Thereby one becomes possessed of wisdom" (Conze et al. 1995, 254).

The golden age of Buddhist Tantra, which arose in the seventh century, evolved at a period of decline for Buddhism in India. Tantric scripture began with the compilation of the *Guhyasamaja Tantra*, written by Indian sage Asanga, a philosopher, pietist, and yogi idealist of the fourth century C.E., who explained the esoteric terms of Tantra. A native of Purusapura, he was the son of a Brahman court priest. Asanga and his two younger brothers joined the Sarvastivada order; one brother, Vasubandhu, became a force in the spread of Mahayana, a liberal form of Buddhism.

Of the brothers, Asanga was the more prolific writer and definer of religious experience. In the *Guhyasamaja Tantra*, he explains emptiness in these terms:

Everything from the crown of the head to the feet dissolves
    into the heart;
    you engage in the perfect yoga....
All sentient beings and all other phenomena dissolve into
    clear light
    and then dissolve into you;
    then you yourself, as the deity, dissolve into your heart....

Just as mist on a mirror fades toward the center and disappears,
    so does everything — the net of illusory manifestation —
    dissolve into the clear light of emptiness.
Just as fish are easily seen in clear water,
    so does everything — the net of illusory manifestation —
    emerge from the clear light of emptiness ["Selections from
    Mahayana Texts"].

Asanga originated the Yogacara, or "mind-only" doctrine, of conscious imagery and extended his definition of conscious emptiness in the *Mahayana-samgraha* (Compendium of the Mahayana or Great Vehicle).

Although many tantric works were lost over time, particularly after the Islamic slaughter of Buddhists and destruction of libraries between C.E. 712 and 1250, their influence on Indrabhuti's *Jñanasiddhi* (Attainment of Knowledge; ca. C.E. 715) and Anangavajra's *Prajñopaya-vinishcayasiddhi* (The Realization of the Certitude of Appreciative Awareness and Ethical Action; ca. C.E. 750) as well as on the songs of poet Saraha, Bengali teacher Naropa, Krishnacharya, and other of the eighty-four *mahasiddhas* (saints or miracle workers) preserve the spirit of the original canon in the Vajrayanan tradition, the Buddhist version of Tantrism. Composed in Apabhramsa, a dialect of eastern India, they survive in corrupt form. Interpreters must depend on the Tibetan translation for fullness and clarity.

The starring bard of Vajrayana and challenger of the religious status quo is Saraha, a legendary Indian arrow maker. He is said to have lost himself in a trance for twelve years, then gave up his craft to become a monk. Imbued with assurance, his 280 stanzas in the *Dohakosha* (Treasury of Songs; ca. 790) open with a couplet maintaining that "Brahmans who do not know the truth, vainly recite the *Vedas* four" (Conze et al. 1995, 224). Individual quatrains rebuke pompous religious figures and sneer:

Vainly is the world enslaved by their vanity...
They adopt a posture and fix their eyes,
    whispering in ears and deceiving folk,
    teaching widows and bald-headed nuns and such like,
    initiating them as they take their fee [Conze et al. 1995,
    224–225].

The mockery also demeans ascetics who appear in public naked with disheveled hair and eat whatever they find in their paths. In place of these off-putting behaviors, Saraha honors the glorious aspects of humanity: "By means of that same essence by which one is born and lives and dies, by means of that one gains the highest bliss" (Conze et al. 1995, 227).

The mysticism of Saraha's verses seems simple on the surface, yet they tease the seeker out of mind. For example, verse 27 claims, "Here there is no beginning, no middle, no end.... There is neither self nor other" (Conze et al. 1995, 228). Couplet 32 offers a simple, formless image: "Know your own thought completely, O Yogin! Like water meeting with water" (Conze et al. 1995, 228). At the height of religious sentiment, stanza 26 epitomizes the body itself as the Lord's temple:

When the mind goes to rest
  and the bonds of the body are destroyed,
  then the one flavor of the innate pours forth
  and there is neither outcast nor Brahman [Conze et al. 1995, 230].

In celebration of the body as a cosmos, like Walt Whitman "singing the body electric," the poet exclaims, "I have visited in my wanderings shrines and other places of pilgrimage, but I have not seen another shrine blissful like my own body" (Conze et al. 1995, 230).

For method, Saraha retreats from fusty exegesis and religious disputation and exhorts the seeker to rely on the senses:

Look and listen, touch and eat,
  smell, wander, sit and stand,
  renounce the vanity of discussion,
  abandon thought and be not moved from singleness [Conze et al. 1995, 231].

Just as Jesus instructed his followers to become like children, Saraha offers the same advice to retreat into wonder and naivete. He identifies the essence of God obliquely as "devoid of names and other qualities … [unknowable] by discussion" (Conze et al. 1995, 232). He predicts that understanding will come "Even as the moon makes light in black darkness" (Conze et al. 1995, 237).

Two centuries after Saraha's lyric ecstasies, a late Sanskrit text from Central Asia, the Kalacakra-tantra (Wheel of Time Tantra; 966), expressed primeval buddhahood. It became the bible of adherents in northwestern India and the height of Indian tantric Buddhism. It expresses the coital pleasures of the god Kalacakra and his mate, Vishvamatr (Mother of the Universe), along with amplification of 250 divines and interpretation of a complex matrix of squares and circles. Unique to this obscure text is an introduction to religious astrology and the ritual observation of planets and constellations. Two centuries later, these Buddhist works spread from India to the north and east through Tibetan and Chinese translations from Sanskrit.

Tibetan Buddhism, an outgrowth of dynamic Indian Vajrayanan Buddhism, takes the form of Rnying-ma-pa. It derives from the teachings of Padma Sambhava (also Guru Rimpoche), an eighth-century miracle worker, instructor, and mystic from Udyana, Pakistan, who introduced Tantrism in Tibet. Invited to Samye by King Thisrong-detsan, in C.E. 747, he established its first monastery two years later. Padmasambhava's philosophy applies the

wisdom of Tantra from works he had translated for the library. These manuscripts he had buried during a repressive era in Tibet. Rediscovered in 1125, they fall into multiple categories:

- Kriyatantra, systematizing ceremony and ritual practice, for example, the *Manjusrinamasamgiti* (Collection of the Names of Manjusri)
- Caryatantra (or Charyatantra), displaying types of self-discipline and personal codes of behavior, as found in the *Bhadracharipranidhana* (Resolution of Pious Conduct)
- Upayoga, covering truths and the incarnations of buddhas
- Yogatantra, explaining the self's identification with God through mental exertion and meditation on mandalas
- Mahayoga, introducing meditation and conscious states
- Anuyoga, revealing secret admission to the divine through meditation that rids the mind of worldliness
- Atiyoga, describing meditation on the sexual union of gods
- Auttarayoga, expressing the supreme union, the crown of Tantrism.

Buddhist Tantrists produced an ample shelf of original and translated scripture. The teachings of Atisha (or Atisa), an eleventh-century Indian monk resettled in Tibet, filled the *Bka'-gdams gces-bsdus* (Collection of the Sayings of the Bka'-gdams-pa Saints; 1000s) with lyric maxims. A follower, Tsong Khapa, a scholar and monastic reformer at Radreng, produced a directive to Tantra, the *Lam-rim chen-mo* (The Great Gradual Path).

The school of the late eleventh-century Indian Buddhist master Tilopa preserved *A Hundred Thousand Songs,* a collection of lyrics composed by Milarepa (also Milaraspa) as well as his biography. A disciple, Sgam-po-pa, systematized methods of attaining enlightenment in the *Thar-rgyan* (The Jewel Ornament of Liberation; ca. 1180).

A Tibetan scholar and advocate of the Rnying-ma-pa tradition, Klong-chen rab-'byams-pa (also Longchenpa), withdrew from political unrest to Bhutan. At peace, he wrote a profound, lucid text, the *Klong-chen-mdzod-bdun* (Seven Treasures of Klong-chen; ca. 1350), which synopsizes essential liberal tantric practice and introduces Vajrayana.

Tantrism moved beyond continental Asia to the Pacific rim to become the Japanese Shingon (True Word), a pantheistic sect that worships the solar god Vairocana (or Dainichi). The philosophy entered Japan around C.E.

816, when the monk Kukai (or Kobo Daishi) returned from a study tour of China to spread Chinese Chen Yen (True Word), which he had mastered from C.E. 804 to 806 In C.E. 816, he erected a meditation center on Mount Koya in Wakjayama, which grew into the Japanese tantric center. Under the protection of Emperor Saga, Kukai replaced the abbot at the great state temple in Kyoto in 822. His contributions to Japanese tantric practice include mandalas, diamond and circle patterns, and other religious matrices. At the height of his meditative powers, in C.E. 835, he had himself buried alive while lost in a trance.

Kukai composed the *Juju Shinron* (Ten Stages of Religious Consciousness; C.E. 822), a ten-volume encyclopedia of spirituality through ten gradations, from base desire to moralism, mysticism, and enlightenment. His summary of a wide range of religious concepts expresses a lyric view of variant schools of thought:

- In the Confucian view, the mind is like a goat or animal in its desires, infantile but temperate.
- Under Brahmanism or Taoism, the mind is childish but hopeful, like a calf following its dam.
- In the orthodox Buddhist view, the mind recognizes only the outside world but not the self.
- From the Mahayana or liberal view, the mind brings about salvation of others.
- As the followers of Shingon describe it, the mind is filled with the splendor of the cosmic Buddha after esoteric teaching has cleared away the dust and displayed true and secret treasures (Bowker 1997, 561).

Redactors summarized the tenets of the *Juju Shinron* in the *Hizoboyaku* (Jewel Key to the Mysteries). Shingon reveres the mantra as a magic formula in addition to *manas* (thoughts) and *mudras* (gestures or hand signals). The trio functions as one in any religious action. To characterize the universe, as an aid to meditation on sacred symbols, they create womb and diamond mandalas around a core image of God as a means of transferring power to the practitioner.

SOURCES: Achaya 1998, Alexander and Alexander 1982, Ballou 1944, Berry 1954, Bhaskarananda 1994, Bouquet 1954, Bowker 1997, Braden 1954, Brown 1996, Burger 1998, Cavendish 1970, Ch'en 1968, Conze et al. 1995, Coulter and Turner 2000, Eliade 1967, 1987, Feuerstein 1996, Fischer 1954, Frost 1972, Gard 1961, Gentz 1973, Griffith 1892, Hastings 1951, "Hinduism" 1999, Hinnells 1984, Hoover 1980, Kosambi 1975, Kumar 1994, Ling 1972, *New Catholic Encyclopedia* 1967, Panikkar 1996, Renou 1961, Schumann 1973, "Selections from Mahayana Texts," Senior 1985, Sharma 1987, Sinha 1995, Smith 1958, Smith 1995, Snodgrass 2001, White 1996, *World Literature* 1998, *World Religions* 1998.

Tao-te Ching   An elusive, mind-teasing volume, the Tao-te Ching (Classic of the Way of Power) is the fount of Taoism, a paradoxical lifestyle based on the idealized Tao (Way). According to Chinese scripture, the Tao is the invisible, formless source of primordial power:

How quiet it is!
How spiritual it is!
It stands alone and it does not change.
It moves around and around, but does not on this account
    suffer.
All life comes from it.
It wraps everything with its love as in a garment, and yet it
    claims no honor,
    it does not demand to be lord.
I do not know its name, and so I call it *Tao*, the Way,
    and I rejoice in its power [Smith 1958, 215].

At the command of the limitless Tao, *wu* (a void or nothingness) supplied matter, form, and animation for *yu* (the universe).

Second only to the Analects of Confucius in spiritual influence among the Chinese, the Tao-te Ching is the culmination of centuries of folk beliefs and occultism dating to Huang Ti, the legendary Yellow Emperor of the twenty-fifth century B.C.E. The book was formerly called the Lao-tzu, the name of at least one of its authors, also Lao-tse or Lao Zi, and dates to 300 B.C.E. The purpose of the text was to revive serenity and harmony in China during a period of upheaval in part through nonaction, a noninterventionist philosophy of letting order restore on its own through reversion from extremes. Ensuing generations have puzzled over the Tao-te Ching, producing 350 early Chinese interpretations, 250 in Japanese, and some fifty English translations, which remain a stock item of book stores and the internet.

A questionable biography identifies the elusive Lao-tzu with two other figures—the Taoist Lao-Lai-tzu and Tan the astrologer. China's first definitive history, the *Shiki* (Historical Record; ca. 85 B.C.E.) of astronomer, calendar reformer, and archivist Szema (or Ssu-ma) Ch'ien, gives a more substantial picture of the patriarch. The legendary *shih* (historian) and scriptural archivist to the Chou dynasty, Lao-tzu was a court librarian and scholar of divination and astrology known as Master Lao for his wisdom and learning. He was conceived by a comet and born Li Tan or Li Erh, already a white-haired old man in infancy, in the hamlet of Ch'ü-jen, Hu, in the state of Ch'u of central China about 605 B.C.E. Similar farfetched legends declare that he lived 150–200 years. This convention was standard to the Chinese, who equated great wisdom with long life. At the royal library at Lo-yang, Lao-tzu appears to have been a closeted contemplative who avoided the society of his day. In 517 B.C.E., the young Confucius visited him to consult on mourning ritual. As though addressing an underling, Lao-tzu called him Ch'iu, his familiar name.

In flight from the deterioration of his homeland, Lao-tzu journeyed by water buffalo west across the central plains into the Gobi Desert to the Hsien-ku pass in the state of Ch'in. Before he pressed on into oblivion, the boundary warden, Yin Hsi, asked him to write a book of wisdom. In three days, Lao-tzu produced eighty-one enigmatic segments in two succinct parchment scrolls— the Tao and the Te. The speed of composition suggests that the philosophy of the Tao was already well developed in Lao-tzu's time.

In only 5,000 characters, Lao-tzu's mystic aphorisms on the universe illuminate the nature and purpose of change and the evidence of perfection in the individual:

He is cautious, like one who crosses a stream in winter.
He is hesitating, like one who fears his neighbors.
He is modest, like one who is a guest.
He is yielding, like ice that is going to melt.
He is simple, like wood that is not yet wrought.
He is vacant, like valleys that are hollow.
He is dim, like water that is turbid [Ballou 1944, 544].

Within four centuries, some sixty commentaries expanded on his brief writings; in another 600 years, the weight of commentary had risen to 4,500 volumes. From Taoist philosophy of patience and resilience came a parallel school of art, the poetry of Li Po, secret black art societies, banditry, and influence on Zen Buddhism, medical practice, and pharmacopoeia, which survives in the *Pen-ts'aokang-mu* (Great Pharmacopoeia) of the sixteenth century.

Less patriarchal than Confucius's Analects, the Tao-te Ching recommends an androgynous passivity suited to men and women practitioners. Its utopian form of happiness reflects simple village life, where residents live close to nature with no urge to stray, even to a neighboring hamlet. Written in hymns of praise and short, depersonalized statements, the text is a brief, highly condensed handbook filled with cryptic advice:

- to stay put rather than rove
- to learn the Tao without leaving home
- to learn more by seeking less
- to prefer silence to speech
- to move well and leave no footprint
- to remain in the background, yet at the vanguard of action
- to lead without standing out from the mass
- to beware of sensual desires
- to subtract rather than add to the self
- to value less as more.

These insights are intended to guide a king toward a social ideal — the ways of passionless, unobtrusive rule. By ridding the self of the world's artificialities, the Taoist removes the conscious state that obscures inward illumination. By suppressing the will and ambition, the Taoist monarch harbors a natural peace devoid of family squabbles, political maneuverings, and state rebellions. As the text indicates, the holy ruler overcomes strivings for primacy by keeping the people physically satisfied and strong. To assure the rarity of war, the wise king renounces the honors of victory and mourns those killed on the battlefield.

Lao-Tzu's connection with the primary text of Taoism earned him reverence as a god and as the savior Lao-chün (Lord Lao), revealer of the sacred Tao. In C.E. 165, Emperor Huan authorized sacrifices to Lao-tzu at the imperial palace and at *T'ai-ch'ing Kung* (Palace of the Grand Clarity), a shrine at Lu-i, the patriarch's birthplace. A court worthy, Hsiang K'ai, in C.E. 166 formalized the liturgy, which implies that Lao-tzu, after his disappearance in the west, took on the form and sublimity of the Buddha. Like the Buddha, Lao-tzu allegedly returned to earth in varying incarnations as a counselor to rulers, evangelist for the Tao, and savior of humankind. One commentary, *Lao-tzu Hua-hu Ching* (Lao-tzu's Conversion of the Barbarians; C.E. 200s) identifies him as the Buddha.

Hagiographies written six centuries after his birth cite the unusual conception and birth of Lao-Tzu under a plum tree of the Li (Plum) family and offer clues to the evolution of the Taoist religion. The *Lao-tzu Pien-hua* (Book of the Transformations of Lao-tzu), a scroll hidden in a desert library at Tun-huang, expanded on his mediation between heaven and earth and advanced Lao-tzu to godhood by declaring him the Creator, a form of *tzu-jan* (spontaneity), who is all-present and all-knowing. During the T'ang dynasty, he received veneration as an imperial ancestor; the Tao-te Ching was inscribed on stone tablets in every provincial capital. The devout reported visitations of the Lord Lao, who answered prayers for celestial aid and comfort, such as a prayer of exorcism in 1215 that called down Lord Lao to heal a sufferer infested with demons.

Taoism owes the doctrine of equality to Chuang Tzu (also Kwant-tze or Chuang Chou; Master Chuang). An anti-Confucian philosopher and lesser official at Ch'i-yüan, Ming province, in the early third century B.C.E., he claimed to be a student of the long-lived Lao-Tzu. His manuscript, known as the *Chuang Tzu* (or *Nan-hua Chenching* [The Pure Classic of Nan-hua]; ca. 288 B.C.E.), the second sacred Taoist text, comprises thirty-three books divided into three parts: seven books in the *Nei* (Inner), fifteen books in the *Wai* (Outer), and the remaining eleven books in the *Ta* (Miscellaneous). Of these, the first seven are the core tenets of Chuang's philosophy.

The *Chuang Tzu* deviates from the Tao-te Ching by contributing historical commentary from the Warring States period, 475–221 B.C.E., and more comprehensive philosophy of relativity and the unity of all things as they apply to private life. Written in loosely joined fables, dialogues, allegories, anecdotes, personal reflections, and commentaries, the work bears little resemblance to the sparse, compressed style of the *Tao-te Ching*. One passage remarks on death:

> There is the globe,
>   the foundation of my bodily existence.
> It wears me out with work and duties,
>   it gives me rest in old age,
>   it gives me peace in death.
> For the one who supplied me with what I needed in life
>   will also give me what I need in death [Reichelt 1954, 102].

No authentic copy of the *Chuang Tzu* survives; current versions appear to contain spurious additions and apocrypha.

Taoism, China's secondary religious system, coexists with Confucianism, the state religion, and supplements and enhances both Confucianism and Buddhism with a naturalistic monism. Central to Taoism are beliefs in nature's solidarity and the interaction between humankind and the outward world. Each element of the Taoist universe, including the human body, is a lesser version of the whole. Thus, to know anatomy is to understand all creation. Outside the dictates of civilization, Taoists acquiesce to the cyclical nature of existence, empty themselves of volition, and make no overt move toward orthodoxy, which violates the imperceptibility of the Tao:

> It is close at hand, stands indeed at our very side;
>   yet is intangible, a thing that by reaching for cannot be got.
> Remote it seems as the furthest limits of the infinite.
> Yet it is not far off; every day we use its power....
> It fills our whole frames, yet man cannot keep track of it.
> It goes, yet has not departed.
> It comes, yet is not here [Smith 1958, 202].

The Taoist saint is therefore recognized for the absence of religiosity and for a clarified energy, nonconformity, and simplicity of lifestyle that in no way set apart the individual from society.

As a source of inspiration and ethical standards, Taoism has enriched Chinese life with patience, serenity, forbearance, and reverence for nature. At the core of the faith is the indefinable Tao, a form of creativity that fuels all life, and the doctrine of *wu-wei* (passivity or acquiescence), an uninvolvement with events that leaves their outcome to chance. Taoists accept the end of life and ensuing merger with the great Tao as a return to the beginning, the ultimate unity. In explaining the effects of death, followers differentiate between the Tao and absence of being. Freed of mortal restrictions, the spirit released from life can join the unseen Tao, absorb its mystery, and comprehend its boundaries. By shedding anxieties about death and prosperity, Taoists cast off worldly responsibility, roam the internal mindscape in joyous ecstasy, and seek a state of pure energy. They cultivate a childlike appreciation for serendipity, the events that come their way. The resulting character traits of humility, gentleness, and nonviolence ennoble and uplift the Taoist as a model of harmony with all life.

Collective Taoism, like augmented visions of other world faiths, has passed through a series of transformations and resurgences. Around 400 B.C.E., the anti–Confucian philosopher-hermit Yang Chu taught that the individual should value the self over society, wealth, or prestige. Sometimes misconstrued as a hedonist, Yang Chu was a naturalist who advocated living in total harmony with nature.

A century later, around 300 B.C.E., philosopher Tsou Yen produced naturalistic formulas that served the *fang-shih* (prescription masters) of coastal China, occultists and mediums who circulated prophecy and apocryphal writings that vitiated pure Taoism. Central to their influence was a promise of direct communication with immortal beings and eventual transformation into immortality.

In the first century B.C.E., followers referred to Taoism as the Way of Huang-Lao, referring to the mythic Emperor Huangti, a patron saint of the faith who reputedly attained immortality in 2700 B.C.E. His mediation between earth and heaven prefigures the later evolution of Taoism into an immortality cult. Around 100 B.C.E., Emperor Han Wu applied Taoism to extend his reign and attempted to develop alchemy as an assurance of long life.

In Szechuan around C.E. 143, Chang Tao-ling, called T'ien Shih (Heavenly Teacher), allegedly experienced a vision of the *T'ai-shang Lao-tzu* (Divine Lao-tzu), who issued a sacred commission. The charismatic founder of a formalized Taoist religion, Chang revived widespread study of the Tao-te ching. He organized followers into a secret society of healers, the *Wu-tou-mi Tao* (Way of Five Bushels of Rice), which names his fee for membership. The title passed to later religious leaders until the death of the Taiwanese T'ien Shih in 1969. A rival Taoist society, the *T'ai-p'ing Tao* (Way of Perfect Peace), elevated cultist Chang Chiao, leader of the Yellow Turbans. He demanded of them written confessions and promises of expiatory deeds to obliterate sin. His army fueled a misguided rebellion in C.E. 184 that climaxed in a bloodbath.

The bifurcated religion produced second-century

C.E. cultists seeking immortality by harmonizing the body through meditation, breath control, absorbing exhalations of the stars and planets, ingesting edible gold, herbalism, physical and sexual manipulation, a seasonally balanced diet of the "five flavors," and ritual ablution. Led by Wei Po-yang, they studied his *Ts'an-t'ung-ch'i* (The Three Ways Unified and Harmonized; ca. C.E. 160), a synthesis of the search for immortality with divination from the ancient I Ching (The Book of Changes; 1150 B.C.E.).

In C.E. 221, Chang Lu acquired status in the northern Wei dynasty, founded by the Han general Ts'ao Ts'ao. Chang Lu's Taoist sect, composed of powerful families, violated pure Taoism by exonerating Ts'ao Ts'ao for overturning the Han dynasty and promoting compromise as a modus operandi.

Around C.E. 245, Wang Pi (226–249), founder of the school of Dark Learning, issued an influential commentary on the Tao-te Ching that remained in vogue into the fourth century.

About C.E. 312, Kuo Hsiang annotated the *Chuang Tzu*, a work of neo–Taoism that channeled the unemotional life into the operation of the state.

A second major cult, which the alchemist Ko Hung stimulated in the fourth century C.E., blended Confucian ideals with Taoist mysticism. According to his *Pao-p'u Tzu* (The Master Who Embraces Simplicity; ca. C.E. 317), he combined Taoist occultism with Confucian ethics. Thus, disciples seeking longevity earned extra days of life by the quality of their behavior. Eventually, this strand of Taoism rejected the "days for deeds" system in favor of a life of health and contentment on earth and a promised afterlife in paradise. Ko Hung's doctrine of long life introduced a number of aberrations in simple Taoism — charms and spells, vegetarianism, contemplation of mirror images, sexual continence, holding the breath, and longevity elixirs.

Another Taoist scripture, the *Lingpao Ching* (Classic of the Sacred Jewel; ca. C.E. 397), was the work of the visionary Ko Ch'ao-fu, who linked personal salvation with that of ancestors. The book outlined specific cathartic rituals to ward off disease and methods of confession to avoid punishment.

An early fifth-century Taoist movement in the north, led by K'ou Ch'ien-chih, favored *Ti'en-shih Tao* (Way of the Heavenly Teacher), a formal faith borrowed from Buddhism. In C.E. 415, responding to a revelation from Lao-chün, K'ou Ch'ien-chih became a *ti'en-shih* (celestial master) and radically reordered Taoism to remove such flaws as taxation to support priests, erotic ritual and sexual mysticism, breath retention, sectarianism, and opportunistic creeds founded on isolated phrases. Under the northern Emperor T'ai Wu Ti, K'ou Ch'ien-chih superintended religion and focused on a pantheon of deities,

temple worship on fixed holy days, monasticism, geomancy and amulets, and legalistic theology based on heaven and hell. By ousting Buddhists, he established Taoism as the official faith, with the emperor serving as *T'ai-p'ing Chen-chün* (Perfect Lord of the Great Peace) or the god Lao-tzu's deputy on earth. The rule of Taoism lasted until shortly after the emperor's demise in C.E. 448. The movement split into the magic-based School of True Unity to the south and the School of Complete Unity in the north, where practitioners withdrew to temples and practiced vegetarianism, herbalism, and medical intervention to assure longevity.

In the fifth century, Lu Hsiu-ching, abbot of the Ch'ung-hsü Kuan abbey, codified liturgies for use at Lu Shan, a Buddhist-Taoist center. Celebrants observed ritual and provided divination for the Liu-Sung dynasty, which lasted from C.E. 420 to 479.

After C.E. 530, master T'ao Hung-ching, a poet and the venerable Taoist of his day, retired to celibacy at the famed Mao Shan hermitage with an assistant, Chou Tzu-liang, to organize and annotate scripture and to refine ceremony to its original state. T'ao Hung-ching compiled and annotated the *Chen-kao* (Revelations of Immortals), a compendium of writings of the Mao Shan school of Taoism, revealed to the visionary Yang Hsi. T'ao Hung-ching's familiarity with both Taoism and Buddhism resulted in mutual respect among practitioners of both faiths. Followers honored him at a Taoist-Buddhist funeral service with priests of both faiths officiating.

Around 570, academicians compiled the first Taoist encyclopedia, a valuable source for religious leaders seeking continuity for the fragmented faith. The Chinese honored Taoism as the state religion in the fifth–sixth centuries and again from C.E. 618 to 906, during the T'ang dynasty. When the divided kingdom unified under the T'angs, Taoism gained a supporter in the dynastic founder, Li Yüan, who declared himself a descendant of Lao-tzu. The priests of Mao Shan supported his claim and greeted him as a messiah and the emperor as *sheng* (sage), under whom served worthies in high government posts. During this resurgence of Taoism, Lao-tzu's birthday became a national holiday. The faithful unearthed scriptural texts from caves at Tun-huang in Kansu province. From this western outpost, Taoists sent copies of the Tao-te Ching to Tibet and Kashmir, where translators rendered it in Sanskrit. Simultaneously, the theocracy dispatched Taoist texts and commentary to Japan. It survived as a folk religion and continues to find followers in Taiwan and Hong Kong, but has declined in China with the introduction of literacy.

Valuable religious writings owe their survival to the publication of the Tao canon, the *Tao-tsang*, in 1016, containing revelations, geographical treatises, obtuse manuals of observation and ritual, commentaries, and literary titles based on the faith, as well as the issuance of the *Yün-chi ch'i-ch'ien* (Seven Slips from the Bookbag of the Clouds; ca. 1022). By the time of the first printing of the *Tao-tsang* in 1120, the text consisted of 5,400 scrolls. A second edition published in 1244 survived until 1281, when Kublai Khan had it burned. Only what survived in separate printings remains today in the Ming *Tao-tsang*, a compendium of 1,120 volumes and 1,476 titles. Scholars divide the manuscripts into three sections: the *Shang Ch'ing* (Cavern of Realization), composed of liturgy and meditations of the Mao Shan sect; the Lino-pao scriptures and talismans in *Tung Hsuan* (Cavern of Mystery); the *San-huang Wen* (Three Sovereigns) and *Meng Wei Ching Lu* (Auspicious Alliance Canonical Registers), the main text of the Cavern of Deities. There are also four addenda: the *T'ai Hsuan* (Supreme Mystery), containing the Tao-te Ching; the *T'ai Ping Ching* (Classic of Great Peace), containing the *T'ai Ping* (Great Harmony), a utopian vision of a golden age grounded on world peace for all who experience and internalize theTao; the *T'ai Ch'ing* (Supreme Clarity), source of alchemical and philosophical Taoism; and the *Cheng I* (Upright Unity), titles derived from the sect of the Heavenly Master.

In this era, Taoism had become a marginalized faith. During perilous times, the devout Sung Emperor Hui Tsung summoned Chang Chi-hsien to offer Taoist counsel. Chang rejuvenated the Cheng-i Tao (Way of Orthodox Unity), an ancient sect, and introduced the ritual of the *wu-lei* (five thunders) to liturgy. This period of religious reclamation also saw the formation of three sects: the T'ai-i (Supreme Unity), Chen-ta Tao (Perfect and Great Tao), and the Ch'üan-chen (Perfect Realization). The third sect, led by Wang Ch'ung-yang, formally syncretized Taoism with Buddhism and Confucianism by teaching a triad of scripture — the Tao-te Ching, Hsiao Ching (Classic of Filial Piety), and the Buddhist Pan-jo Ching. Followers, impressed by the group's asceticism and refutation of magic, formed a strong brotherhood. One advocate, Ch'iu Ch-ang-ch'un, journeyed north to evangelize the Mongol leader Genghis Khan, who sought enlightenment as a source of immortality.

In 1131, Ho Chen-kung inspired a syncretic sect, the Ching-ming Chung-hsiao Tao (Pure and Luminous Way of Loyalty and Filial Obedience), an amalgamation of Taoism with Confucian virtues. As stated in the Book of Recompense, these virtues demand goodness:

Advance in all that is in harmony with good;
  retreat from all that is opposed to it.
Walk not in the paths of depravity,
  nor deceive yourselves by sinning in the dark where none
    can see you.
Accumulate virtue, and store up merit;

treat all with love and gentleness; be loyal; be dutiful;
be respectful to your elders and kind to your juniors;
be upright yourselves in order that you may reform others
  [Berry 1956, 51].

The passage continues with orders to pity orphans and widows, reverence the old, cherish children, and injure nothing living in nature. Like Jesus's Sermon on the Mount, the scripture demands that no one seek revenge, but rather return good for evil.

Central to the preservation of hagiography, the *Mao Shan Chih* (Treatise on Mao Shan; 1329) collected history, biographies of saints and patriarchs, historical and topographical data, and a millennium of literary witness to the evolution of Taoism. Taoism survives into the current age, but lost most of its mystique in 1930, when Mao's Red Army swept into its sanctums and destroyed the remains of a nonviolent faith dating to prehistory.

See also **Confucius's Analects; I Ching.**

SOURCES: Ballou 1944, Berry 1956, Bouquet 1954, Cavendish 1970, Confucius 1992, *Eerdmans' Handbook to the World's Religions* 1982, Eliade 1967, Fingarette, Frost 1972, Hastings 1951, Hinnels 1984, Kang 1999, *New Catholic Encyclopedia* 1967, Pelikan 1992, Reichelt 1954, Schwartz 1985, Sharma 1987, Smith 1958, 1995, Snodgrass 1995, 2001, "Tao Te Ching" 1995, Waley 1986, 1989, *World Literature* 1998, *World Religions* 1998, Yutang 1938.

Tibetan Book of the Dead

Composed in Sanskrit around C.E. 775, when Nepalese and Chinese Buddhism first flourished in Tibet, the Tibetan Book of the Dead — originally called Bardo Thödol (The Book of Liberation Through Understanding in the Between or The Great Liberation upon Hearing in the Intermediate State) — is a compendium of practical wisdom to be recited to the dying. It is part of a great literary tradition on the art of dying, which practitioners approached through yoga and meditation, quiescent states that calm and prepare the person for transformation. In the Tibetan philosophy, death is found in every newborn and struggles constantly with life forces throughout earthly existence. The body reaches its end from one of three causes: approaching the end of the lifespan, exhausting meritorious energy, or meeting with an accident, violence, or natural cataclysm.

In Buddhist thinking, the moment of death offers a great opportunity for self-purification. During the process of expiring, physiological changes accompany mental changes in which the base mind states disintegrate, giving place to subtler stages of consciousness. Thus, death offers a unique window on spirituality and personal integration. At the moment of death, the mind reaches perfect clarity. The purpose of the Tibetan Book of the Dead is to make the most of the mind's revelations and to aid the spirit in seeking unity with the divine.

The Dalai Lama wrote in 1992, "We [Tibetans] think of our systematic study and analysis of the human death process as a cautious and practical preparation for the inevitable" (Thurman 1994, xvii). He describes the book as a manual of useful instructions for the dying, for those facing wasting diseases, and for their next of kin. It offers a preparation for death, a means of dying with the least trauma, and an acceptance of what comes after life. The result is a method of dealing with life's impermanence skillfully, compassionately, and humanely. He concludes, "It is not considered morbid to contemplate it, but rather liberating from fear, and even beneficial to the health of the living."

The Tibetan Book of the Dead derives from the time of Master Padma Sambhava, whose name means "born from a lotus." The image characterizes his miraculous birth in a lake in Udiyana, an Indio-Afghan border region once visited by Alexander the Great. An alternate legend of his birth claims that he was the son of wisdom and truth and took shape as an iridescent meteor that struck earth and generated a giant lotus. Because of Sambhava's incipient holiness, skill at yoga, and ability to work wonders, the king adopted him and tried to turn him into crown prince, but Sambhava preferred the life of the wandering mystic and teacher. Called the Precious Afghan Guru, he was professor of yoga at the Buddhist University of Nalanda, India, and founder of the Nyingma-pa Buddhist order with its distinct Tibetan language and learning. In C.E. 747, he accepted an invitation from King Thi-Srong-Detsan (or Trisong Detsen) to come to Samye, near Lhasa, Tibet, to exorcise demons causing epidemics, flooding, and other natural disasters that were plaguing the country. In competition with the Bon-pos, shamans of Tibet's aboriginal animistic religion, the guru drove out evil from the kingdom's walls and established his authority and that of Buddhist doctrine, which became the state religion.

Under the aegis of Abbot Santaraksita (or Shantarakshita), a Buddhist text author and Indian saint living in Tibet, Sambhava began his three most important contributions to the nation: erection of a royal monastery at Samye in C.E. 749; organization of the nation's first community of lamas; the collection, translation, and protection of Buddhist scripture. He offered a liberal curriculum to students taught by scholars from Persia, India, and China. Revered as Amitabha, the Buddha of Infinite Light, Sambhava also earned the title of Guru Rinpoche, or Precious Spiritual Mentor. He spent most of his career studying and practicing Vajrayana or esoteric Buddhism, a continuation of the Mahayana doctrine with stress on psychic experiences of the present over distant goals. To assure the future of Tibetan Buddhism, he educated twenty-five notable disciples of the faith. According to

legend, at the end of a long life, Sambhava changed into a pure light and disappeared toward the west to the Glorious Copper-colored Mountain, a mystic buddha-field, where he resides in harmony with the divine.

In addition to translating sixty-five volumes of tantric books from Sanskrit into Tibetan, the sacred guru dictated to his Tibetan consort, the yogini Yeshe Tsogyal, the Bardo Thödol, an apocryphal sacred text, dating from the first centuries of lamaism and from the teachings of eight Indian gurus, designed to be whispered or read aloud to the corpse. An alternative account states that the monks recovered the text from ancient sources. This mystic revelation, printed in sacred block script and treasured as the Buddha's holy word, is a source of Mahayana doctrine, a universally appealing school of Buddhism that concentrates on compassion and goal setting.

The Tibetan Book of the Dead remained hidden from the world until Lama Jey Tsong Khapa, a revered scholar, initiated a spiritual renaissance in Tibet, founded the Ganden Monastic University, and taught the first Dalai Lama. In this resurgence of Buddhism, the book passed to Ridzin Karma Lingpa, a clairvoyant regarded as an emanation of Sambhava himself. Nicknamed the "Treasure Finder," Lingpa is said to have unearthed the text in central Tibet at the summit of Mount Gampodar around 1365, a time of political upheaval and persecution when Sambhava anticipated the world would need direction in facing death. Since that time, Vajrayana Buddhists have revered the text, practiced its teachings, and shared it with others.

The guru's writings address the faults of all humankind. According to this concept of life's end, death is another stage in perpetual change and the passage of time. During the forty-nine days that follow death, a lama or a mourner reads these words aloud at Tibetan Buddhist funerals as scripture. Whether facing the corpse itself, a picture, or an effigy, the reader addresses the disembodied spirit, who is still nearby in a between-time, a transitory realm known as bardo. Gautama Buddha expressed the nature and purpose of bardo:

There is, disciples, an unbecome, unborn, unmade, unformed;
  if there were not this unbecome, unborn, unmade, unformed,
  there would be no way out
  for that which is become, born, made, and formed;
  but since there is an unbecome, unborn, unmade, unformed,
  there is escape for that which is become, born, made, and formed [Evans-Wentz 1960, 68].

It is this escape, which the Buddha termed "the ending of sorrow," that is the focus of the Tibetan Book of the Dead.

Commentary and corroboration have revised and

restated the original book in numerous forms, including amulet and icon texts, mantra anthologies, soul-transmission manuals, and imitations of the original. The most common offshoot is a body of literature concerning near-death experiences, including *Death Rituals of the Tibetan Bon-pos* (ca. 1075) by Khu tsha zla Îod, an overview of the rituals accompanying dying, bardo, and rebirth.

The Visionary Account of Lingza Chökyiâ's Return from Death (1500s) is a retelling of the death of a woman who experiences turmoil on a great sea and fiery torments, overpowering roars, and prancing demons. She navigates the land of bardo and hears the Lord of Death list her wrongs. He returns her to the world to prepare others for death. Her experience echoes that of *The After-Death Visions of Lama Jampa Delek* (1977), an account of the sudden illness and death of Delek in 1596, including a vision of a shimmery light and the approach of a woman who guides him through bardo and helps him overcome sin.

The Mirror of Mindfulness (ca. 1650), by theologian Tse-le Natsok Rangdröl, is a tantric commentary on bardo and *tulku* (incarnation), the Tibetan concept of a spiritual personality that benefits a certain group of people. After studying with practitioners of the Kagyu and Nyingma orders, he wrote this practical instructional manual on the cycle of living, dying, the postmortem state, and rebirth plus advice on meditation and ritual.

The Peaceful and Wrathful Deities: A Collection of Visionary Revelations (ca. 1750) was written by Ridzin Kundröl Drakpa and based on visions of Dampa Rangdröl, writer of the *Bon-po Book of the Dead* (ca. 1190). The concept of a mystic doctrine concealed in one mind until its revelation in another accounts for the recurrence of esoteric theology. The work accounts for the harmony between the philosophies of Bon-po and Buddhist bardo teachings.

The Story of Karma Wangzinâ's Return from Death (ca. 1750) is the story of a popular near-death experience of a righteous Buddhist woman. Similar to Longwa Adrung's biography, *A Message from the Lord of Death* (1533), the narrative relates how she envisions Sambhava, founder of Tibetan Buddhism, and, a year later, undergoes a near-death experience and sojourn in bardo. She revives and becomes a Buddhist teacher and advocate of joy in the afterlife.

The full text of the Tibetan Book of the Dead did not reach English speakers until the twentieth century. Walter Yeeling Evans-Wentz, a native of New Jersey educated at Stanford University, University of Rennes in France, and Jesus College, Oxford, acquired the translation completed in 1919 by Lama Kazi Dawa-Samdup, interpreter for the British government in Sikkim and headmaster of the Gangtok academy. With the translator's collaboration, Evans-Wentz lodged in Gangtok, Sikkim, in 1927 while he edited and annotated this profoundly humanistic text. The work aroused controversy among Tibetologists and readers as to its meaning and application. He produced additional significant works on Tibetan tradition: *Tibet's Great Yogi, Milarepa* (1928), *Tibetan Yoga and Secret Doctrines* (1935), and *The Tibetan Book of the Great Liberation* (1954). Much of his last thirty years were spent at San Diego studying Tibetan Buddhism. He willed mineral rights from some 5,000 acres to found a chair of Oriental philosophy, religion, and ethics at Stanford University and left funds to build the Maha Bodhi Society in Calcutta, India. His manuscripts remain at the Bodleian Library at Oxford.

Among the proponents of the Evans-Wentz edition were Mahayana Buddhists and Karl Jung, Swiss psychoanalyst, who treasured the work's critical insights into the primitive fundamentals of human personality. Jung's 1938 essay made available the wisdom of Tibetan thanatology to anthropologists, philosophers, and psychologists. In his commentary, which became a standard element of the Evans-Wentz text in 1957, he declared, "We, as readers of the *Bardo Thödol*, shall be able to put ourselves without difficulty in the position of the dead man, and shall consider attentively the teaching set forth in the opening section" (Evans-Wentz 1960, xxxviii).

Later developments have made the book more accessible to modern Westerners in their quest to understand the afterlife. During the hippie counterculture movement of the 1960s, Timothy Leary, Harvard professor and self-promoting visionary, published *The Psychedelic Experience: A Manual Based on the Tibetan Book of the Dead*, which perverted the scriptural content by applying it to stages of experimentation with LSD, a psychedelic drug. From that same antiauthoritarian mindset, artist and mystic Eugene Jeffrey Gold wrote and illustrated *The Original American Book of the Dead* (1974), a forerunner of New Age postdeath experience literature.

To circumvent the romanticism of the Evans-Wentz recension, Tibetan teacher Chögyam Trungpa published a more readable edition in 1975. That same year, German Tibetologist and scholar of comparative religion Detlef Lauf published *Secret Doctrines of the Tibetan Books of the Dead*, which elucidates the symbolic complexities of Tibetan theology and compares it to the god views of ancient Egypt, Persia, Greece, and Rome.

Per Kvaerne, professor of the history of religions and Tibetology at the University of Oslo, published *Tibet Bon Religion: A Death Ritual of the Tibetan Bonpos* (1985), based on an Indian death ritual.

The last of the twentieth century saw a resurgence in interest in Tibetan Buddhism and in the original, unadulterated Tibetan Book of the Dead. In 1992, Sogyal Rinpoche wrote *The Tibetan Book of Living and Dying,* a practical self-help manual in the style of modern thanatology, which trains the individual to maintain composure in the face of annihilation. In 1994, Robert Alexander Farrar Thurman, Jey Tsong Khapa Professor in Indo-Tibetan Studies at Columbia University, the first endowed chair of Buddhism in the West, and president of Tibet House in New York City, produced an updated translation preceded by a relaxed, informative introduction. He prepared for the task with three decades of study with the Dalai Lama. In 1995, at the Orgyen Dorje Den Buddhist center in San Francisco, California, the venerable Gyatrul Rinpoche of eastern Tibet, the senior lama of the Payul lineage of the Nyingma order, began instructing Buddhists and non-Buddhists in the book's style of meditation and beliefs about death. In 1999, Stephen Hodge, a Buddhist scholar and Shingon monk, with the aid of Martin Boord, a practitioner of Tibetan Buddhism, produced *The Illustrated Tibetan Book of the Dead,* a lyric, unencumbered text that allies scripture and commentary with ethereal photography of Tibetan life.

The text of the Tibetan Book of the Dead offers salvation or altruistic enlightenment to protect the deceased from continual rebirth into earthly suffering. This phenomenal intermediate state falls into three stages:

- days 1–4, when the spirit may obtain immediate liberation
- days 5–19, when the soul confronts the peaceful and wrathful deities that represent the forces of karma and may voluntarily surrender desire and fear
- days 20–49, the most tenuous stage, when the opportunity for reform lessens as images of the six realms of rebirth — god, demigod, human, animal, hungry ghost, or hell being — precede return to the womb for another birth in a cycle of lives and rebirths known as *samsara.* Still capable of making fruitful decisions, the spirit has an opportunity to shed habits that entangle the individual in a benighted existence or can cling to tendencies toward selfishness and aggression, which precipitate another reincarnation on earth. This brief moment of clarity can release the soul into perfection.

As a guide to insightful living, the text functions as a psychological document. It speaks to the mourners' innermost minds and offers advice on seeking refuge from personal terrors derived from emotional habits or mental poisons during transformation to the spirit world. Through fantasy and symbolism, its passages address various personality types and cite thumbnail sketches of desire, sloth, envy, anger, jealousy, pride, and violence, as embodied in Tibetan deities and demons, manifestations of psychological states that reflect human selves. Self-recognition is instructive. By glimpsing faults as illusions, the individual can jettison egocentrism and faulty attitudes, improve psychic health and ethical actions, and enjoy a fuller, more liberated, and mature life on earth.

The book typifies consciousness as experience. In the bardo state, the individual observes clear light or reality for the first time. In this sinless vacuum, the uncluttered mind recognizes separation from earthly ties and begins its odyssey toward a new state of being. To clarify this in-between status, the "Root Verses of the Six Bardos" characterize six states of consciousness:

- *Skyes-gnas* or *Kye-nay Bardo,* normal or wakeful consciousness
- *Rmi-lam Bardo,* dream consciousness
- *Bsam-gtan Bardo,* which is meditative or trance consciousness
- *Chikhai* or *Hci-khahi Bardo,* the premortem conscious state as the body experiences death and recognizes the pure light of reality
- *Chönyid* or *Chos-nyid Bardo,* the state of immediately experiencing reality
- *Sidpa* or *Srid-pahi Bardo,* birth instinct or rebirth consciousness of a new animal existence on earth.

Book 1, the Chikhai Bardo, introduces the "great deliverance by hearing," a redemptive phenomenon that allows the newly dead to continue listening and learning in the days preceding a final, irrevocable state (Evans-Wentz 1960, 83). Before the text is read aloud, the reader sits either near the corpse, on a favorite bed or seat, or before a portrait or *jangbu* (ritual drawing). After summoning the spirit, the reader halts the weeping and wailing of mourners to enhance the spirit's hearing. In preparation, the reader stoops near the ear of the deceased without touching the body and begins the reading.

During the Chikhai Bardo, as the deceased realizes transition from a living body, the spirit has an opportunity to ascend the Great Perpendicular Path, which leads from initial faith to illumination, certainty, and emancipation from human life. The best guide is the guru who led the person in the past, an invaluable guide in the confusing passage. Lesser choices are a lama or learned Buddhist or, as a last choice, anyone who can read distinctly and correctly. As respiration ceases, the reader intones the opening passage, which calls the deceased by name:

O nobly-born [the deceased's name],
  the time hath now come for thee to seek the path [in reality].
Thy breathing is about to cease.

Thy guru hath set thee face to face before with the clear light;
  and now thou art about to experience it in its reality in the
  bardo state,
  wherein all things are like the void and cloudless sky,
  and the naked, spotless intellect is like unto a transparent
  vacuum
without circumference or centre.
At this moment, know thou thyself;
  and abide in that state.
I, too, at this time, am setting thee face to face [Evans-Wentz
  1960, 91].

In the updated text of Stephen Hodge, this terrifying but joyful reality is as undifferentiated as space, a "primordial mind, unsullied and unadorned, devoid of center and boundaries, in its emptiness and radiance" (Hodge 1999, 30). The reader turns the body on its side, compresses blood vessels of the neck, and repeats the injunction many times to impress the dying with the importance of the moment.

The text acknowledges that no one knows how long the swooning state lasts or how much time the soul requires for its passage from the body. It is thought to last up to seven days. In Hodge's description, the signs of death appear in an eight-stage sequence resembling a mirage as earth dissolves into water. He calls attention to smoke, then "glowing fireflies," followed by a candle flicker, bright moonlight, sunny red sky, dark night, and a twilight that signals attainment and dissolves into radiance (Hodge 1999, 32).

When the transitional state ends and death is complete, the reader acknowledges it aloud and urges the spirit to take advantage of death to reach the "illimitable expanse of the heavens, as to obtain Perfect Buddhahood, by resolving on love and compassion towards … the Sole Perfection" (Evans-Wentz 1960, 94). The reader exhorts the spirit to recall the devotional practice learned on earth and to experience the clear, effulgent light ahead for as long as possible. The reality, called the "All-Good," is pure intellect, which the text describes as "unobstructed, shining, thrilling, and blissful" (Evans-Wentz 1960, 96). The reader instructs the soul to identify the true self and grasp the opportunity to unite with the divine.

In the second stage of the Chikhai Bardo, the spirit enters an out-of-body state, but perceives earthly beings and hears mourners. As yet free of the terrors of death, the soul, still contained in a shining illusory body, can make a significant choice:

Do not be distracted.
Earnestly concentrate thy mind upon thy tutelary deity.
Meditate upon him as if he were the reflection of the moon in
  water,
  apparent yet inexistent.
Meditate upon him as if he were a being with a physical body
  [Evans-Wentz 1960, 99].

Part 2, the Chönyid Bardo, is a fearful stage when the deceased realizes the termination of life. Still wandering, the unliberated soul receives its most essential advice:

Do not cling, in fondness and weakness, to this life.
Even though thou clingest out of weakness,
thou hast not the power to remain here.
Thou wilt gain nothing more than wandering….
Be not attached [to this world]; be not weak [Evans-Wentz
  1960, 103].

The reader warns that postmortem sightings are merely hallucinations, "subtle, dazzling visions, vividly experienced, naturally frightening and worrisome, shimmering like a mirage on the plains in autumn" (Thurman 1994, 132). The reader urges the deceased to identify them as illusions of the mind. Hodge characterizes these end-stage visions as "meditational experiences of masters of great spiritual accomplishment" (Hodge 1999, 42). Repeatedly, the reader urges the soul not to fear these apparitions, for they are the natural, unavoidable phantasms of every expiring life.

On the fourth day of the readings, the soul should control the mind stream and channel psychic energy to identify the Buddha, a red figure carrying a lotus and sitting on a peacock throne in the embrace of the divine mother. Instruction intensifies the next three days as the soul studies the colored rays ahead. The steadying voice reminds, "Do not be attached to them! Do not be terrified of them! Relax in the experience of nonconceptualization" (Thurman 1994, 144). After guiding the soul through visions of fearful, blood-drinking demons, revealed one by one in a circular mandala pattern, the reader advocates a humble and sincere prayer, which will dispel fear and win perfect buddhahood.

Book 2, the Sidpa Bardo (Bardo of Becoming), urges the spirit to reject the flesh or desire-body and look out with pure celestial eyes. The reader acknowledges that whatever human faults once pertained — deafness, blindness, crippling — the new body is sense perfect:

Thou canst instantaneously arrive in whatever place thou
  wishest;
  thou hast the power of reaching there within the time
  which a man taketh to bend, or to stretch forth his hand
    [Evans-Wentz 1960, 159].

The reader urges prayer and faith as the deceased separates from earthly relationships. An injunction against the precipices of anger, lust, and stupidity guides the soul onward toward a crucial recounting of good and evil deeds.

In similar form to the Egyptian Book of the Dead, the Tibetan text describes the end-of-life accounting, when the Lord of Death consults the Mirror of Karma. The torments seem terrible—furies garrote and drag the body, decapitate it, yank out intestines, devour the brain, suck blood, chew flesh, and gnaw bones. Insentient, the soul feels no pain, even though the sight of the tortured body dismays. In Hodge's translation, "You will be liberated the moment you recognize them for what they are" (Hodge 1999, 94). The reader advises prayer and meditation as bulwarks against terror and loneliness. In Thurman's version, the prayer is simple and childlike: "I am wandering lost in the between—be my savior! For compassion's sake, do not let me go!" (Thurman 1994, 164).

In part 2, the process of transformation rewards the righteous with symptoms of rebirth. At this point, the spirit witnesses future parents in sexual union. In avoiding the womb, the soul now expresses earnestness and love while meditating on past teachings. Holding fast to good while quelling disruptive thoughts, the spirit can control the outcome—either escaping rebirth and entering the state of blessedness or choosing a womb door devoid of repulsive states. The text closes with "the profound heart-drops of the bardo doctrine," which liberate the dying to a positive destiny (Evans-Wentz 1960, 196). At this point, the guru burns the *jangbu* in the flame of a lamp, thereby releasing the soul from past sins and sending the purified spirit on its way.

The appendix is a collection of supplemental prayers and meditations for the spiritual mentor to memorize and recite to the dying. They begin with a formal "Prayer Requesting Assistance from the Buddhas and Bodhisattvas [Enlightened Ones]" or "Prayer for Help," a sincere request to all compassionate divines—the Lord of Compassion or the Goddess of Miracles—to comfort the dying or those in stages of bardo. In Thurman's translation, the mentor declares:

She has great suffering, no refuge, no protector, and no allies.
Her perception of this life is declining....
May you compassionate ones please give refuge to this help-
    less one [Thurman 1994, 106].

The prayer stresses that traveling in the between state, friendless and alone, places the journeying soul in a dark passageway where the terrors of the unknown increase her vulnerability.

The second stave, "The Path of Good Wishes for Saving from the Dangerous Narrow Passageway of the Bardo" or "Prayer for Deliverance from the Straits of the Between," enumerates the negative aspects of life—delusion, anger, pride, passion, jealousy, and ignorance—and asks the help of divinities as the spirit evaluates the illusions of bardo. The mentor pleads that the soul recognize sound and light as emanations from the mind rather than realities. In the Evans-Wentz translation, the prayer concludes, "May it come that all the radiances will be known as one's own radiances" and asks that the deceased pass safely through all final bardos to perfect buddhahood (Evans-Wentz 1960, 202).

In the third stave, "The Root Verses of the Six Bardos," the poet summarizes the instructions to the spirit to rid it of dread. Each verse calls for the abandonment of a fault: verse 1, laziness; verse 2, delusion; verse 3, distracting errors; verse 4, self-absorption; and verse 5, hallucination. Verse 6 asserts that the mind will focus on positive evolution. The final verse speaks to procrastinators, who devote themselves to useless things, earthly forms of waste, and who mistakenly ignore the search for holiness. In the Evans-Wentz translation, the poet asks, "Wilt thou not devote thyself to the Holy Dharma [Reality] even now?" The epilogue warns that those who ignore the guru's teachings are self-deceivers, traitors to themselves.

The fourth stave, "The Path of Good Wishes Which Protecteth from Fear in the Bardo" or "The Prayer for Refuge from All Terrors of the Between," speaks in the first person of the wanderings in the between world and asks that the soul recognize the apparitions of the mind. Thurman translates the fierce night sounds that turn the soul to meditation:

When wild beasts of prey roar savagely,
  may it become the dharma sound—
  Om Mani Padme Hum!
When I am driven by snow, rain, wind, and darkness,
  may I find the divine vision of brilliant wisdom [Thurman
  1994, 113].

Tibetan prayer wheel and writing.

The seeker prays that "whatsoever be wished for be fulfilled here and now" (Evans-Wentz 1960, 208). The author concludes his breviary with the Colophon, an inscription wishing that "virtue and goodness be perfect in every way" (Evans-Wentz 1960, 209).

See also Egyptian Book of the Dead and Ethiopian Book of the Dead.

SOURCES: "Center for Buddhist Studies, Columbia University," Ch'en 1968, Evans-Wentz 1960, Garraty and Carnes 1999, Gentz 1973, Gethin 1997, Hodge 1999, Lee 1996, Ling 1972, Mehta 2000, Morrell, Noss, and Noss 1984, "The Nyingma Lineage," "The Nyingma Tradition" 1997, Powers 1995, Rinpoche, Samdhong 1992, Rinpoche, Sogyal 1990, Schumann 1973, "Selections from Tibetan Buddhist Texts," "Self-Liberation Through Seeing with Naked Awareness," Tat 1997, Thurman 1994, "Tibetan Buddhism" 1997, "Tibetan Religion and the Western Imagination," Wallace 1997, Wicks 1997.

Torah *see* Bible: Old Testament

Upanishads *see* Vedas

Vedas

The four Vedas, from the Sanskrit meaning "sacred knowledge," are India's and the world's oldest scripture. The Vedas contain 10,552 verses in ten books or cycles intended for the use of sages, priests, and seers. Their teachings created tenets that evolved into modern Hinduism: belief in karma, the law of accountability for deeds; belief in the transmigration of the soul; pessimism that life is not perfectible and the desire for metaphysical release; regard for asceticism; regard for passive virtues; reverence for Vedic tradition; respect for pantheism; esteem for righteous living; and acceptance of the caste system. The Vedas comprise a fount of indigenous wisdom that has also influenced other world faiths, notably Buddhism.

Considered *apaurusheya* (superhuman) or revealed by the gods, the Vedas required no human scribe or editor such as Confucius or Muhammad to capture the words of God from the beginning of time. The Brihadaranyaka Upanishad enumerates the interlinking elements of Hindu sacred writings, beginning with the Rig Veda, Yajur Veda, and Soma Veda and continuing the tradition of learning in Itahasa (Legends), Purana (Cosmogonies), Vidya (Knowledge), the Upanishads (or Upanisads; Sacred Knowledge or Sacred Utterances), Slokas (Verse), Sutras (Rules), Anuvyakhyanas (Glosses), and Vyakhyanas (Commentary).

The totality of Vedic literature was deemed too sacred for recording on parchment or stone. Beginning about 2100 B.C.E., Brahmans, ascetic priests revered as India's walking encyclopedias, stored in their memories the precious texts, which remained unwritten for three millennia until around C.E. 900. The most ancient Vedas are the earliest record of the Aryan pantheon of gods at a time when vedistic polytheism was a living force and shaped Hinduism, which evolved from 500 to 100 B.C.E., after the later Vedas were composed. The faithful revere the Vedas as God's eternal words *sruti* (revealed) to seers to be recited skillfully and prayerfully.

Each hymnal, called a Veda, expresses the timeless points of view of the ruling class. Early students of the Vedas, who were mostly male, regarded scriptural language, a classical or archaic Sanskrit, as the perfect vehicle of expression. They parsed its rich array of grammatical forms, including numerous subjunctive verbs and twelve types of infinitives. The entire collection encompasses a theism that dates to the Persian veneration of three entities: Yima, the first man; *haoma*, the fermented hallucinogen made from juice pressed from twigs of a sacred bush; and Mithra (or Mitra), the bull representing a fertility or sun god, revered especially by soldiers. Performances of scripture incorporated dance and vocal and instrumental accompaniment on flute, drums, cymbals, *vina* (bow harp), zither, and other instruments.

By studying the Vedic authors, the modern world can experience the transformation of Hindu worship over time from veneration of natural phenomena through polytheism to monism, a belief that the individual soul merges with the divine Atman (Oversoul), a unique entity from which all spirit derives. The composers were Aryan insurgents from Iran to India's northwest who invaded, then subsumed the urban Harappan civilization. Primarily pastoral and agrarian, the Vedic peoples settled the banks of the Indus River, the lost Ghaggra-Hakra (or Sarasvati) River, and the adjacent Punjab around 1500 B.C.E. and migrated east to the Ganges Valley. The Aryan bard-priests drew on indigenous Dravidian beliefs in many gods to compose praises to the one God who is one with the self. They performed the most venerable Vedic material orally as early as 1700 B.C.E. in hopes of assuring power over enemies, a large number of male children, and the health of family and herds.

The Vedic collection, also called the Amnaya, forms a compendium of invocations and praise anthems propitiating the gods. They were India's first literature and the foundation of a complex religious system called Brahmanism, which based its faith on the worship of Brahman, the Great One and Lord of all. The Vedic corpus consists of four *samhitas* (collections) of hymns and rituals accompanying the central Brahman rite, the sacrifice of animals.

A night school at the Jade Buddhist Temple in Houston, Texas, relies on a library of sutras, including this copy of the Diamond Sutra (fourth century C.E.), said to be the world's oldest book. (Courtesy Texas Buddhist Association, Inc.)

Rig Veda

The oldest and most revered, the Rig Veda (or Rg Veda [Praise Stanzas]; ca. 1700–1400 B.C.E.) is the grand Indian bible, a liturgical handbook of 1,028 entries. It pulses with great beauty and mystery, as with this description of night:

Darkness—palpable, black, and painted—has come upon me.
  O Dawn, banish it like a debt.
I have driven this hymn to you as the herdsman drives cows.
Choose and accept it, O Night, daughter of the sky,
  like a song of praise to a conqueror [*World Literature* 1998, 456].

Like the Bible, it grew organically from oral verses composed in the Sapta Sindhu region of northern India. The hymns express the civilizing forces that acclimated the nomadic Aryans to a pastoral-agrarian existence on the Indian subcontinent. Significant to prosperity was the priestly offering, which assured the chief and clan protector continued victory over adversaries. In an era that saw monarchy replace the clan system, some hymns sin-gled out the Dasas, a dark-skinned race of cattle herders speaking an alien language and worshiping unknown gods. Other verses mention the Panis, a hostile race of rustlers.

Arranged in cycles or books, the Rig Veda anthologizes poems by generations of writers or seers. Each of books 2–7 is dedicated to a single family, for example, book 3 to the Vishvamitra, book 4 to the Vamadeva, book 5 to the Vasishtha. Books 1, 8, and 10 anthologize the work of numerous contributors. Organized by subject, book 11 contains 114 hymns concerning the sacrifice of *soma* and honoring its powers to heal, bestow wealth, and propitiate the god Indra to combat enemies. In terms of age, books 2 and 7 are the oldest; the tenth book is of the most recent origin.

Hindu sacrifice dominates much of the scriptures. In blind faith without temples or images, lay officials or priests conducted daily or monthly ceremonies in open spaces consecrated anew for each worship service. The first hymn of the Rig Veda uplifts an invocation to Agni, the fire god, who is the life force of nature and restorer of energy: "Agni I pray to, the household priest who is the god of the sacrifice, the one who chants and invokes and brings most treasure" (Bowker 1997, 815). The *vedi* (altar) at which priests spoke these calls to worship was a rectangle on the ground hollowed out for the *agnyadheya* (installation of the fire). At each, sacrificers conducted a *grhya* (domestic) or *srauta* (public) ritual by pouring the sacrifice over the flame while calling: "May that Agni who is to be extolled by ancient and modern seers, conduct the gods here" (Alexander and Alexander 1982, 174). The ceremonies marked human mileposts, which ranged from conception to burial and included the passage of seasons and the new moon. A royal occasion such as a coronation or celebration of victory required more elaborate oblations conducted by multiple officials at several sacred hearths.

To guarantee prosperity and health, a central ceremony presented a sacred beverage, the golden-hued hallucinogen *soma*, a multiform deity that operates on numerous levels— heavenly bull, bird, giant, and embryo. In addition to a divine, strength-giving ambrosia, it was the blood of sacrificial beasts and the sap that coursed through plants. In the mind, it was inspiration and poesy, ecstasy and dream state. In the sky, it flowed from the chalice-shaped moon and offered permanent residence for the departed. Worldwide, *soma* countered evil and assured immortality. In Hindu worship, it filled a dual purpose as a ritual offering to the gods and a spiritual drink for priests.

Akin to the Iranian stimulant drink *haoma*, *soma* was an exudate of an unspecified plant that grew in the mountains. History suggests several possibilities:

- the leafless shrub *Sarcostemma acidum*, a common Indian medicinal plant
- the toxic milkweed *Asclepias acida*
- the agaric mushroom *Amanita muscarita*
- the bhang or hemp plant *Cannabis sativa*
- the stimulant *Ephedra gerardiana*, *Ephedra vulgaris*, or *Ephedra major*.

In the absence of the holy plant, priests substituted adara, arjuna, or putika.

After the consecration of the sacrificer and altar recitations and chants, the official sprinkled the holy plant with water and positioned it between two grinding stones pierced with holes. He pressed the tawny juice three times, caught the runoff on a cowhide, and strained it through cloth woven of sheep's wool. After mixing it with milk, curds, melted butter, or flour, he offered some of the liquid to the fire, along with a slaughtered ram, and served another quantity of juice to the priests. Variants on liquid sacrifice included *ashvamedha* (horse sacrifice), described in the 162d hymn of the Rig Veda, and *purusa-*

medha (human sacrifice), which appears to have avoided actual human slaughter by substituting symbolic dismemberment of the mythic giant Purusa, father of the four castes: Brahman or priestly, the most intellectual Hindus; Rajanya or Kshatriya, the warrior class; Vaisya, a composite of farmers, artisans, and tradespeople; and Sudra, the lowly serf class. Similar procedures honored gifts of meat from horses, bulls, buffaloes, sheep, and goats as well as dairy foods and barley cake. In all cases, sacrifice of food was the basis of Vedic healing and wellness.

Like the Hebrew Proverbs, many of the Rig Veda's entries uplift and encourage, as with the hymn to faith in chapter 10:

> Man winneth faith by yearnings of the heart,
>   and opulence by faith.
> Faith in the early morning,
>   faith at noonday will we invoke,
>   faith at the setting of the sun.
> O Faith, endow us with belief [Frost 1972, 16].

The uncomplicated point of view assists even the lowliest and least educated Hindus in making spiritual choices and reassures those weak in commitment that the answers to their quandaries lie in the heart.

The anthology is replete with wonder and humility at creation and asks the age-old riddles that reduce seekers to the state of children:

> What covered in, and where?
> And what gave shelter?
> Was water there?
> What was above it then, and what below it?
> Who verily knows whence it was born,
>   and whence comes this creation?
> He, the first origin, he verily knows it,
>   or perhaps he knows not [Ballou 1944, 20].

To these openhearted seekers, natural phenomena were manifestations of a deity that may or may not fit the prevailing notion of godhood.

A major aspect of the Rig Veda is its moral guidance. Chapter 10 is a homily on generosity. It begins with a warning that hunger is an unholy state that Brahman never intended. Rather than being god-made, it stems from an imbalance in earthly wealth. Two verses chastise the tight-fisted rich man for ignoring the impoverished:

> The man with food in store who, when the needy comes
>   in miserable case begging for bread to eat,
> hardens his heart against him —
> even when of old he did him service —
> finds not one to comfort him [Frost 1972, 15].

Wisely, the verse reminds that "Riches come now to one, now to another, and like the wheels of carts are ever rolling," a prediction that everyone needs assistance at some time.

Around 1000 B.C.E., when the corpus of oral material grew unwieldy, priests canonized the Rig Veda as a manual for the *hotri* (chief sacrificer or reciter), the religious aristocrat and custodian of scripture. Generations of specialists committed the life-affirming verses to memory to assure correct recitation as a summons to the gods and as an introit to fire ceremonies. Written in seven common and eight unique meters, these priestly songs range from one to fifty-eight stanzas and cover varied topics, including the gods' deeds and battle chants; ceremonial mantras and pleas for recognition of sacrifices; requests for blessings at weddings and funerals; funeral and cremation rites; secular verses on the gambler's ruin of his family; genealogy; a poet's thanks for gifts; recognition of the skills of the wheelwright, tanner, metalsmith, seamstress, and weaver; augury; warnings about poisonous vermin; and riddles on the identities of deities and the meanings of symbols, for example, the twelve-spoke wheel, which represents the twelve-month cycle. The most common image is the cow, named 700 times. The most militant cycle synopsizes a war precipitated by a confederacy of ten *rajac* (chiefs or kings) of the Puru, Yadu, Turvashas, Anu, and Druhyu. They opposed the Bharatas of southern Punjab because of King Sudas's selection of a new priest.

Some 500 poems focus on the fire god Agni and the bountiful Indra, god of war, weather, and creativity, the opponent of Vrtra (drought). The following heroic verse extols Indra:

I will declare the manly deeds of Indra, the first that he
    achieved,
  the thunderwielder.
He slew the dragon, then disclosed the waters,
  and cleft the channels of the mountain torrents.
He slew the dragon lying on the mountain:
  his heavenly bolt of thunder Twashtar fashioned.
Like lowing cows in rapid flow descending the waters glided
  downward to the ocean.
Impetuous as a bull, he chose the Soma,
  and quaffed in threefold sacrifice the juices [Griffiths 1892,
  n.p.].

Other Vedic mythic verses cover a pantheon of deities, with twenty surpassingly lovely verses honoring Ushas (also Uma or Usas), goddess of the dawn. They also extol more divines:

- *soma*, the subject of all the hymns in book 9, which priests sang during the clarification of the sacred juice
- the twin Ashins (also Ashwins or Ashvins), sons of the sun and heroic horsemen who protect humankind

- the weather gods— Parjanya, the rain god or a beneficent cow; Vayu, the temperamental wind god; the unstable, unpredictable storm god, Rudra the terrible, bringer of disease and peril; and the sun gods Surya, symbolized by the swastika, an emblem of energy and supply, and Savitr (or Savitri), who commands the sun to rise and set and who assures order and peace
- Pushan, protector of roads and herds, guide of souls and of the sun's daily journey
- the parental pair— Aditi (or Adyita), the gods' mother, and Dyauspitr, father of heaven
- Prajapati, path of the gods and demons and maker of all creatures
- the paired sky gods— Mitr, the god of honor, and his counterpart, Varuna, the punisher and reward bringer, who wears the golden mantle.

To Varuna, the most ethical, god of divine authority over moral law and upholder of cosmic order, book 1 of the Rig Veda claims:

Whatever law of thine, O god,
  O Varuna, as we are men,
  day after day we violate,
  give us not as prey to death,
  to be destroyed by thee in wrath,
  to thy fierce anger when displeased.
  to gain thy mercy, Varuna.
With hymns we bind thy heart
  as binds the charioteer his tether horse [Eliade 1967, 310].

The seventh and eighth lines, like the psalms of David, depict Varuna as knowing the paths of birds in the sky, fish in the sea, and the moon in the heavens. Book 4 continues obeisance to Varuna and Indra with the worshiper's declaration that "lauds and Soma-juice have made me joyful" (Eliade 1967, 34).

Soma Veda

A post–Rig Veda anthology, the Soma (or Sama) Veda (Chant Lore) is a unified songbook that standardizes melodies intended for liturgical purposes. It collects 1,549 *samans* (stanzas) and musical notation of tone and pitch to accompany litanies sung by *udgatri* (chanters) for the pressing and sacrifice of soma. Historically, it displays alterations to the original hymns through repetition, pauses, prolonged syllables, phonetic shifts, and the addition of syllables serving as magic charms. Because 1,475 of the verses replicate hymns and anthems from books 8 and 9 of the Rig Veda, this liturgical compendium is the least important of the four Vedas.

Yajur Veda

Also borrowed from the Rig Veda, the Yajur Veda (Liturgical Formulas or Sacrificial Prayers) is a later rule-book for the *adhvaryu* (assistant) who aids the chief sacrificer. Contemporaneous with the Soma Veda, it consists of some 2,000 varied ritual *yajus* (prayers), hymns, and formulas arranged in 109 sections to accompany a wide range of ceremonies for the full moon, new moon, *soma* sacrifice, and fire ceremony. It is divided into two books:

WHITE VEDAS

Also called Vajasaneya Samhita, the White Vedas consist of forty chapters of 2,000 mantric chants attributed to the philosopher Yagnavalkya Vajasaneya, who received a revelation of the sun god. These formulaic statements prefigure propitiatory prayer. At a sacrifice of soma, the priest intones, "Thou art the body of *Soma*, thee I offer to Vishnu." Before taking hold of a sacred implement, he declares, "At the stimulation of god Savitr I grasp thee with the arms of the Asvins, with the hands of Pusan" (Hastings 51, 7:57). Among the entries is a recommendation that hosts sacrifice oxen or goats for special guests, who ranked with parents and teachers as honored figures. At the conclusion of some of the mantras, the congregation exclaimed the syllable *om*, an onomatopoetic tone that suggests the Hebrew *amen*.

BLACK VEDAS

Dating to 600 B.C.E., this section contains hymns for ritual sacrifice and prose theological interpretations rich in myth and mysticism. One example, a prayer for food, offers an encyclopedic list of the Vedic diet and other desirable items.

> May for me prosper, through the sacrifice, milk, sap, ghee, honey, eating and drinking at the common table, plowing, rains, conquest, victory, wealth, riches. May for me prosper, through the sacrifice, low-grade food, freedom from hunger, rice, barley, sesame, kidney beans, vetches, wheat, lentils, millet, panicum grain, and wild rice. May for me prosper, through the sacrifice, trees, plants, that which grows in plowed land, and that which grows in unplowed land [Kosambi 1956, 85].

There are also prose passages offering advice about correct sacrificial procedure to assure response from Brahman.

Atharva Veda

A later collection and the last to achieve canon status, the Atharva Veda ([Lore of the Fire Priests; also called Artharvahgirasah; Artharvans and Fire-priests]) is a normative handbook that dates to the Atharvan, a *rishi* (sage), who was a medium of scripture transmitted from God. Completely different from the first three Vedas, the Atharva Veda originated from the folklore of indigenous tribes in pre-Aryan India. Attributed to the mythic Dhanvantari, the first physician and teacher of healing, around 800 B.C.E., the written version consists of twenty books of 731 hymns in widely varying meters.

The text comprises 6,000 verses detailing the private life of the Hindu, for example, the charm against fear, a simplistic, repetitive verse that reassures in singsong parallelism:

> As heaven and earth are not afraid,
>   and never suffer loss or harm,
> Even so, my spirit, fear not thou.
> As day and night are not afraid,
>   nor ever suffer loss or harm,
>   even so, my spirit, fear not thou,
>   as sun and moon are not afraid,
>   nor ever suffer loss or harm,
>   even so, my spirit, fear not thou [Balou 1944, 36].

Written over a long period of time dating back to the Indo-European period, the collection covers secular topics common to private lives:

- prayer, charms to lure a potential mate, and love incantations
- sorcery, curses on rivals and enemies, and spells to protect travelers
- expiation of sin and purification
- hymns to creation and exaltations of royalty
- blessings and prayers for newlyweds and children, including a prayer for cutting teeth
- agrarian matters, including land fallowing, crop rotation, seasonal planting, and the collection of animal dung to fertilize plowed land
- diet and herbs to stop bleeding and treat fractures, abrasions, wounds, and numerous diseases—jaundice, fever, scrofula, leprosy, dropsy, cough, baldness, eye ailments, impotence, poisoning, and snakebite.

A prayer asking Agni to drive away fever speaks directly to the disease:

> Thou that makest all men sallow,
>   inflaming them like a searing fire,
>   even now, O Fever,
>   thou shalt become void of strength:

do thou now go away down, aye, into the depths! [Renou 1961, 73].

The prayer begs the healing plant to clear spots from the skin. It describes the alternation of cold with hot, delirium, cough, and relapse.

A hymn to the pearl amulet speculates on the source of its loveliness, which appears in the atmosphere as though formed of lightning and light. The speaker lauds the shell as a universal remedy:

> Born in the heavens, born in the sea,
>   brought on from the river,
>   this shell, born of gold,
>   is our life-prolonging amulet [Renou 1961, 74].

As a charm, it graces the chariot and the quiver. The devout believe, "That do I fasten upon thee unto life, luster, strength, longevity, unto a life lasting a hundred autumns. May the amulet of pearl protect thee!" (Renou 1961, 74).

An amorous verse, the charm to arouse passion in a woman, pictures a universal symbol, the arrow piercing the heart:

> The arrow, winged with longing, barbed with love,
>   whose shaft is undeviating desire,
>   with that, well-aimed,
>   Kama shall pierce thee in the heart [Renou 1961, 75].

The poet predicts the symptoms of a consuming ardor — parched mouth, burning passion, loss of will power, sweet speech, and devotion. As though working a magic spell, the speaker declares, "I drive thee with a goad from thy mother and thy father, so that thou shalt be in my power, shalt come up to my wish."

The fourth book honors Varuna as guardian, keeper of earth, and concludes, "May all thy fateful toils which, seven by seven, threefold, lie spread out, ensnare him that speaks falsehood; him that speaks the truth they shall let go!" (Eliade 1967, 33). Book 12, a paean to the Earth Mother, builds up to a winsome coda, "O mother earth, kindly set me down upon a well-founded place. With father heaven cooperating, O thou wise one, do thou place me into happiness and prosperity" (Eliade 1967, 40). The latest addition, book 20, repeats praises to Indra found in the Rig Veda.

The complete body of Hindu scripture supplies each Veda with three major ancillary books of interpretation — Brahmanas, Aryanakas, and Upanishads. These commentaries cover three focuses: Karma-Kanda (sacrificial or ritual worship), the most public veneration of Brahman; Upasana-Kanda (meditational worship), private individual worship; and Jnana-Kanda, revelation of the highest knowledge of Brahman.

Brahmanas

Brahmanas (Godly Discussions), the texts of Karma-Kanda composed from 900 to 600 B.C.E., are ceremonial handbooks. As guides, they became necessary over the centuries as Vedic ritual grew more complex. Failure to perform duties correctly was inauspicious to priest and laity and could precipitate a catastrophe by slighting the Vedas, which were revered as the Pilot of the Universe.

The Brahmanas consist of prose explanations of the mythic origins and meaning of sacrifices to thirty-three Hindu gods. A favorite, the famed creation story of the golden egg, provides a metaphor of evolution. After the egg floats on the liquid universe for a year, it pops open, producing a man named Prajapati. The shell divides into sky above and earth below. According to the Satapatha Brahmana, Prajapati produced gods and demons: he exhaled breath that rose to the heaven to form *devas* (deities) and he expelled intestinal gases that permeated the soil to form the *asuras* (evil spirits of darkness). In response to these beings, he exclaimed, "Verily, I have created a veil for myself, since, after creating, there has come to be, as it were, darkness for me" (Ballou 1944, 38). From deities and demons, he balanced earth time into day and night.

A speculative text, the Satapatha Brahmana muses on death and the gods. In a lyric summary of age, it comments:

The year, doubtless, is the same as death,
  for Father Time it is who, by means of day and night,
  destroys the life of mortal beings, and then they die.
Therefore the year is the same as death;
  and whosoever knows this year to be death,
  his life that year does not destroy, by day and night,
  before old age, and he attains his full extent of life [Renou 1961, 82].

Acknowledging the endless cycle of reincarnation for mortals, the treatise concludes with a prophecy that the pious die to immortal life and the impious "come to life again when they die, and they become the food of death time after time."

Each sacrifice mentioned in the Brahmanas honored a *yajamana* (sacrificer), who paid for the event. One conundrum from chapter 11 of the Satapatha Brahmana explains an ineffable mystery: "The sacrifice becomes the sacrificer's self in yonder world" (Smith 1995, 1117). By forming miniatures of the universe through ritual, the priest displayed to Hindu worshipers his understanding of both the earth and the realm of the deities.

Aryanakas

Aranyakas (Forest Treatises), books of Upasana-Kanda compiled around 600 B.C.E., are appendices describing the meditations of forest hermits that precede sacrifice. These treatises evolved from speculation about harmony and correspondence between local events and the universe. Thus, they move from objective study of the act of sacrifice to symbolic interpretation and application to the individual human life.

A major passage of the Brihadaryanaka is the creation of earth from the soul. An allegory, it pictures Soul as the main character, who lived alone and evolved the first pronoun, "I." His joy in creation is marred by loneliness:

Verily, he had no delight. Therefore one alone has no delight.
He desired a second.
He was, indeed, as large as a woman and a man closely embraced.
He caused that self to fall into two pieces.
Therefrom arose a husband and a wife [Renou 1961, 90].

From sexual union springs humankind. The couple become shape-shifters and produce cattle, goats, sheep, and other animals "even down to the ants." The straightforward account takes a mystic turn to explain the creation of the self. Its uniqueness acquires human overtones:

When breathing, he becomes breath by name;
   when speaking, the voice; when seeing, the eye;
   when hearing, the ear; when thinking, the mind.
These are the names of his acts [Renou 1961, 91].

Upanishads

Based on *upasana*, a traditional form of meditation and introspection, the Upanishads, also called the Vedanta (Conclusion to the Veda or Goal of the Veda), are 108 texts named for the act of sitting at the feet of a guru in search of truth found in the inner self. As expressed in the Brihadaranyaka Upanishad:

Whoever has found and understood the self
   that has entered into this patched-together hiding place,
   he indeed is the creator, for he is the maker of everything,
   his is the world, and he is the world itself....
If a man clearly beholds this self as god,
   and as the lord of all that is and will be,
   then he is no more afraid [Frost 1972, 29].

The most metaphysical of Vedic literature, the Upanishads are profound, sublime, and mystical. Of their power, German philosopher Arthur Schopenhauer wrote, "In the whole world there is no study so beautiful and so elevating as that of the *Upanishads*. It has been the solace of my life, it will be the solace of my death" (Smith 1958, 15).

Originated as teaching texts during an unsettled, questing period of dissatisfaction with polytheism, the Upanishads are the work of wandering ascetics and forest hermits who educated young seekers through discussion, disputation, and debate. The holy ones pondered universal humanistic concerns—the nature of God and humanity, the purpose of the soul, the human role in the world, the meaning of life and suffering, and the source of true salvation through belief in a single, omnipotent deity. In recent times, the Upanishads have included the Christopanishad and the Allopanishad, which acknowledge the wisdom of Jesus and Muhammad.

The Upanishads are a literary as well as spiritual and ethical triumph. Individual entries appear in identifiable literary modes.

DIALOGUE

Whether between seeker and guru or human and allegorical figure, these dialogues illuminate. For example, six questions are asked about matter, prayer, and dreams of the sage Pippalada in the Prasna Upanishad. The Chandogya Upanishad contains a discussion between Uddalaka Aruni and Svetaketu, his son, on creation, the universe, and the soul's destiny. One line from chapter 7 reads like an aphorism:

Verily if there were no speech, neither right nor wrong would
   be known,
   neither true nor false, neither good nor bad,
   neither pleasant nor unpleasant.
Speech indeed makes all this known [Bouquet 1954, 119].

Similarly pithy is the description of the bridge leading to the afterlife: "All evils turn back therefrom, for that Brahma-world is freed from evil" (Bouquet 1954, 119).

The purpose of Vedic dialogue is to guide thoughts from one handhold to another in the climb to holy, unchanging truth. The Chandogya Upanishad states:

The essence of all beings is the earth, the essence of the earth is water, the essence of water the plants, the essence of plants man, the essence of man speech, the essence of speech the Rig Veda, the essence of the Rig Veda the Soma Veda, the essence of the Soma Veda the *udgitha* [ultimate song], which is om [Frost 1972, 30].

By progressing from the outward signs of nature to the inward workings of human thought and faith, the scripture assures the worshiper that the simple chant of *om* to Brahman summarizes the grandeur of creation as it characterizes faith.

FORMAL DISCOURSE

The type of inwardization and spiritualization found in an address to Narayana on hymnology in the Mahanarayaniya Upanishad and the ethical discourse or "convocation address" on the self in the Taittiriya Upanishad, these complex treatises study monism and the ultimate reality "from which, verily, these beings are born, by which, when born, they live, and into which, when departing, they enter" (*World Religions* 1998, 697).

A scripture that is key to the understanding of Hinduism is the Svetasvatara Upanishad, which separates the concept of self from Atman, the personified universal soul in which all spirits have their being. The explanation opens with perennial questions:

Whence are we born? Whereby do we live, and whither do we
  go?
O ye who know Brahman, tell us at whose command we
  abide,
  whether in pain or in pleasure.
Should time, or nature, or necessity, or chance,
  or the elements be considered as the cause,
  or he who is called the person? [Frost 1972, 39].

In grappling with the essence of human nature and godhood, the scripture applies the metaphor of the wheel traveling multiple paths and advocates knowing Brahman through meditation. When union with the divine occurs, a restructuring of priorities overcomes the devout:

When that god is known, all fetters fall off,
  sufferings are destroyed, and birth and death cease.
From meditating on him, from joining him,
  from becoming one with him
  there is further cessation of all illusion in the end [Frost
  1972, 39].

Expository Essay

The Brihadaranyaka Upanishad comprises six chapters of philosophical speculation on nature, world origin, life after death, rebirth, and Atman, the absolute self. The four states of consciousness are discussed in the Mandukya Upanishad. A profound theological study of divinity is the Svetasvatara Upanishad, which depicts the self-sourced God as covered in gossamer threads of primary matter. The Aitareya Upanishad, a series of three chapters on creation, reflects the standard humanistic questions shared universally. The self asks:

If, without me, speech is uttered, breath is drawn, eye sees,
  ear hears, skin feels, mind thinks, sex organs procreate,
  then what am I? [*Adventures in World Literature* 1970,
  244–245].

The treatise concludes:

This self, who is pure consciousness, is Brahman.
He is God, all gods; the five elements — earth air, fire, water,
  ether;
  all beings great or small [*Adventures in World Literature*
  1970, 244–245].

The author determines that individual self is ongoing and, after its earthly existence, it returns to God, the fount of all life.

A discussion of yearning to become one with Brahman in the Kena Upanishad (also Talavakara Upanishad) summarizes the heart of the transition of death:

That which is the heart of the earth, the thought of the mind,
  the voice of speech, is also the breathing of the breath,
  and the sight of the eye!
Past these escaping, the wise on departing from this world,
  become immortal [Bouquet 1954, 123].

The next stanza notes that the soul, upon leaving the body, does not carry eye, tongue, or mind along on the journey to the afterlife.

In a stanza expressing the godly power behind each activity of humankind and nature, translators Swami Prabhavanada and Frederick Manchester render the original in lines linked by repetition:

May quietness descend upon my limbs,
  my speech, my breath, my eyes, my ears.
May all my senses wax clear and strong.
May Brahman show himself unto me [*Adventures in World
  Literature* 1970, 240].

The passage concludes with a prayer to remember Brahman as an ineffable part of human makeup and to strive to know the unity of the individual with godliness.

One essay, "What Is Joy?" expressed in an English translation by Irish poet and dramatist W. B. Yeats, concludes:

He who knows [joy] cries goodbye to the world;
  goes beyond elemental self, living self, thinking self,
  knowing self, joyous self.
Here is my authority: He who knows the spiritual joy mind
  cannot grasp nor tongue speak, fears nothing [Cavendish
  1970, 2934].

Another example, the Mindaha Upanishad, merges philosophy and poesy to declare:

The self is all-knowing, it is all-understanding,
  and to it belongs all glory.
It is pure consciousness, dwelling in the heart of all,
  in the divine citadel of Brahman.
There is no space it does not fill [Alexander and Alexander
  1982, 179].

Poem

Metrical, rhythmic statements of truth, the poems include the three interpretations of thunder in the Brihadaranyaka Upanishad as *damyata* (self-control), *data* (charity), and *dayadhwam* (compassion); the discussion of types of knowledge and the condemnation of ritual sacrifice in the Mundaka Upanishad; and the musing on nature in the Isha (also Isavasya or Isa) Upanishad, which prefaces its text with:

At the heart of this phenomenal world,
  within all its changing forms,
  dwells the unchanging lord.
So, go beyond the changing,
  and enjoying the inner,
  cease to take for yourself
  what to others are riches [Alexander and Alexander 1982,
    179].

The stanza closes with a general petition to Agni, the restorer, to keep the faithful from "crooked-going sin."

In a series of parallels, the text expresses the universality of scripture in terms of sensual and intuitive impressions:

As all waters find their center in the sea,
  all touches in the skin,
  all tastes in the tongue,
  all smells in the nose,
  all colors in the eye,
  all sounds in the ear,
  all precepts in the mind,
  all knowledge in the heart,
  all actions in the hands,
  all movements in the feet,
  and all the Vedas in speech [Frost 1972, 23].

The next verse compares the omnipresence of divinity to the dispersal of a lump of salt dissolved in water and remarks that "this great Being, endless, unlimited, consisting of nothing but knowledge, rise from out [of] these elements, and vanish again in them."

A prayerful model of poetry comes from the Shivatashvatara Upanishad, which intones to the Almighty:

Thou art the Eternal among eternals,
  the consciousness within all minds,
  the unity in diversity,
  the end of all desiring.
Understanding and experience of thee
  dissolve all limitations [Alexander and Alexander 19872,
    179].

The soothing, calming tone of these lines demonstrates the focus of the Upanishads, which turn the eye and mind from the material world to the wealth of godliness in the soul.

HYMN

In the Prasna Upanishad in honor of the life force, the purifying flame that is both being and nonbeing and therefore immortal, the thirteenth stanza swells to a reassuring summation:

This whole world is in the control of life —
E'en what is established in the third heaven!
As a mother her son, do thou protect us!
Grant to us prosperity and wisdom [Bouquet 1954, 127].

By appealing to a universal parental relationship, the verse makes the connection between divinity and humanity and guarantees that a great power protects humankind.

NARRATIVE

Two examples are the story of Svetaku in the Chandogya Upanishad and the interpretation of dreams in the Kausitaki Upanishad. The second chapter recreates a dying father's bestowal of powers on his son. This rigid ceremony follows a mechanical pattern of call and response:

FATHER: "My speech in you I would place!"
SON: "Your speech in me I take."
FATHER: "My breath in you I would place!"
SON: "Your breath in me I take" [Renou 1961, 100–101].

The patriarchal, man-to-man exchange proceeds through eye, ear, taste, deeds, pleasure and pain, bliss and procreation, actions, mind, and intelligence. The dialogue ends, "So let them furnish him as he ought to be furnished."

As in other parts of the Upanishads, many lines stand alone as maxims or didactic aphorisms. In chapter 3 of the Katha Upanishad, Yama instructs the boy Nachiketa (or Naciketas) to free himself from fear and passion. The boy learns about the immutability of the self, which springs from nothing and never dies. Neither great nor small, it lies hidden in the heart of creation. A single instructive line warns of the trap of cyclical reincarnation:

He who has not understanding,
  who is unmindful and ever impure,
  reaches not the goal from which he is born no more [Bouquet 1954, 121].

APHORISM

A series of *mahavakya* (wise sayings), the aphorisms include:

That thou art.
I am Brahman.
All this indeed is Brahman.
This self is Brahman.
Pure consciousness is Brahman [Renou 1961, 51].

The revealed philosophy of the Upanishads is a vehicle of enlightenment that consists of metaphysical dialogues speculating about Atman, the individual soul, and

Brahman, the world soul. Compiled from 1000 to 500 B.C.E., the Upanishads form a general compendium on Hindu philosophy and religion. These metaphysical texts question assumptions about the sacred and attempt to define Brahman less as a god than as a guide to the individual spirit.

The treatise on the nature of God and self in the Maitri Upanishad illustrates the pragmatism of Hindu scripture in the remark, "If men thought of God as much as they think of the world, who would not attain *nirvana* [liberation]?" (Alexander and Alexander 1982, 179). The text includes a Te Deum called "Kutsayana's Hymn of Praise," which rejoices in the knowledge that

Thou art all.
Yea, thou art the unshaken one....
　unthinkable, unlimited, beginningless and endless too!
　[Bouquet 1954, 136–137].

There are numerous collections of Upanishads, many of which are sectarian in nature. The oldest contain spiritual, life-transforming teachings and investigations into Indian philosophy. The eleven Upanishads that the philosopher Shankara (also Sankara, Sankaracarya, or Shankaracharya; Master Shankara) analyzed around C.E. 750 achieved special status.

Sutras

A fourth type of ancillary, written from 800 to 350 B.C.E., are the Sutras (Threads, Rules, or Clues), a collection of lesser importance. These explications of scriptural revelation attempt to organize, systematize, clarify, and apply ambiguous philosophies to common human situations, for example, marriage and child rearing. The texts consist of flashes of inspiration in the form of aphorisms, disciplines, and practical rules concerning metrics and grammar, astronomy, astrology, and everyday domestic activities, such as water filtration. The books follow a strict arrangement by topic:

- A major example is the Brahmasutra, which summarizes teachings on Brahman and reality.
- The Kamasutra, compiled by the ascetic monk Vatsyayana about 450 B.C.E., is an encyclopedic sex manual covering multiple aspects of male-female intercourse.
- The Dharmasutra is a series of normative aphorisms that control judgment, character, asceticism, and legalities.
- The three-part Kalpasutras contain the Srautasutras for public sacrifice, Sharmasutras for priestly duty, and Grhyasutras for household ceremony.

In the latter, one chapter of the Asvalayana describes betrothal and marriage, departure to a new home, and a recipe for producing an illustrious son after lighting of the nuptial fire and a sacrifice of curds:

From that time they should eat no saline food,
　they should be chaste, wear ornaments,
　sleep on the ground three nights or twelve nights;
　or one year, according to some teachers;
　thus, they say a seer will be born as their son [Renou 1962,
　　108].

Among the injunctions of the Sutras is the condemnation of drunkenness from imbibing *sura*, a wild paddy- or barley-based liquor. The Vasistha lists alcoholic consumption second among the five mortal sins, which appear in this order: violating a guru's bed; drinking sura; slaying a learning Brahman; stealing the gold of a Brahman; and associating with outcasts, by entering either into spiritual or matrimonial connection with them (Renou 1962, 113).

Although worship condoned *soma* as an introit to revelation, sura exceeded the bounds of propriety. Instead, the text urges the faithful to select wine or liquors made of honey, jaggery, or mahua blossoms.

The Sutras have a legalistic tone that is absent from the more sacred parts of the canon. The Gautama particularizes the monarch's duties, which begin and end with holy acts and speech and include education in theology and logic and control of sensual desires. A similar set of rules for the ascetic in the Baudhayana declares:

> Diligently standing in the daytime, keeping silence, sitting at night with crossed legs, bathing three times a day, and eating at the fourth, sixth, or eighth mealtime only, he shall subsist entirely on rice grains, oil cake, food prepared from barley, sour milk, and milk [Renou 1962, 111].

Other behaviors that set him apart from ordinary people is the absence of a home and hearth and a protector. Another proscriptive series is the Apastamba, which defines initiation of a consecrated person and a warning that "intercourse, eating, and intermarriage with [the uninitiated] should be avoided" (Renou 1962, 110).

SOURCES: Achaya 1998, Alexander and Alexander 1982, "Ancient Indus: Introduction" 1996, Ballou 1944, Berry 1954, Bhaskarananda 1994, Bouquet 1954, Bowker 1997, Braden 1954, Brown 1996, Burger 1998, Cavendish 1970, Coulter and Turner 2000, Eliade 1967, Fischer 1954, Frost 1972, Gentz 1973, Griffith 1892, Hastings 1951, Hinnells 1984, Kosambi 1975, Kumar 1994, *New Catholic Encyclopedia* 1967, Panikkar 1996, Renou 1961, Senior 1985, Sharma 1987, Smith 1958, Smith 1995, Snodgrass 2001, *World Literature* 1998, *World Religions* 1998.

When the Tree Flowered see Black Elk Speaks

The White Roots of Peace   Originally published in 1946, *The White Roots of Peace* is a written history based on Iroquois oral tradition. It explains how an obscure Indian tribe moved to a strategic position, achieved major social reform, and influenced peaceful negotiation and coexistence during the first two centuries of North American colonial history. Under a binding accord, the Iroquois, an agrarian nation based between the Hudson and Niagara rivers, settled their own animosities and joined with five other tribes in an organized, effective forerunner of the United Nations. Their system of checks and balances based on supreme law — the *Kainerekowa* (Great Law of Peace) — unified native tribes reaching from Maine to Illinois, north to the Ottawa River, and south to the Chesapeake Bay. During the founding of the United States, the league's constitution influenced both the Articles of Confederation and the U.S. Constitution.

Although their total population never exceeded 15,000, league members dominated the woodland tribes of the northeastern United States and lived amicably with Europeans. In retrospect, inventor Benjamin Franklin, founder of the Albany Plan of Union (1754), mused:

> It would be a strange thing if Six Nations of ignorant savages should be capable of forming a scheme for such a union, and be able to execute it in such a manner as that it has subsisted ages and appears indissoluble; and yet that a like union should be impracticable for ten or a dozen English colonies to whom it is more necessary and must be more advantageous, and who cannot be supposed to want an equal understanding of their interests [Wallace 1986, 3].

Devoid of the prevalent discounting of Indian rationality, the text of *The White Roots of Peace* summarizes the philosophy of the Iroquois and explains how it became a touchstone of North American political philosophy. Set on the north shore of Lake Ontario, the history accounts for the emergence of a mystic peacemaker, Deganawida, a legendary shaman and prophet of the Iroquois and founder of the Iroquois League.

The White Roots of Peace is the work of a meticulous scholar, Paul Anthony Wallace, who was eminently suited to the task of preserving Iroquois documents. Born October 31, 1891, to Johanna Wilson and Francis Huston Wallace, a professor at the University of Toronto, he attended his father's alma mater and emulated his scholarship. After two years as a dispatch rider for the Canadian Expeditionary Force, Wallace taught English at the University of Alberta. He sought similar classroom work at the University of Toronto and Lebanon Valley College, where he chaired the English department for nearly a quarter century. From 1951 to 1957, he edited *Pennsylvania History*, the quarterly journal of the Pennsylvania Historical Association, and advised the Pennsylvania Historical and Museum Commission.

Wallace's writings include a biography of patriot Conrad Weiser, *The Muhlenbergs of Pennsylvania* (1950), *Indians in Pennsylvania* (1961), and *Indian Paths of Pennsylvania* (1966). His papers, research notes on Daniel Boone and the Revolutionary War, maps, photos, and correspondence reside at the Pennsylvania Historical Museum. For his fairness to the Iroquois, they named him Toriwawakon and embraced him as a brother. For an illustrator of their history, Wallace chose a native, John Kahionhes Fadden, a Mohawk and member of the Turtle Clan. Fadden is an educator retired from the Saranac Central School District in New York and a respected artist exhibited in the United States, Canada, and Europe.

A scriptural text to the Iroquois, *The White Roots of Peace* opens with acknowledgments of three sources crucial to the composite narrative. The Gibson Version (1899) was dictated by Chief John Arthur Gibson of the Six Nations Reserve to J. N. B. Hewiss of the Smithsonian Institution. Chiefs John Buck, Sr., Joshua Buck, and Abram Charles revised the original. In 1941, William N. Fenton of the Bureau of American Ethnology, aided by Chief Simeon Gibson, translated the Gibson Version into English.

The Chiefs' Version (1900) is the compilation of leaders of the Six Nations Council on the Six Nations Reserve in Ontario and appears in Duncan C. Scott's *Traditional History of the Confederacy of the Six Nations*, published in 1911 by the Royal Society of Canada.

Three centuries after the institution of the Iroquois League, a Canadian Mohawk author, Seth Newhouse, committed to paper the oral constitution governing the confederacy. The 1916 edition, the Newhouse Version, was a revision by Albert Cusick, a New York Onandaga-Tuscarora. Editor Arthur C. Parker, archaeologist of the Rochester Museum and the New York State Musem at Albany, published it as *The Constitution of the Five Nations, or the Iroquois Book of the Great Law*.

The White Roots of Peace opens with a mythography of the semi-legendary figure of Deganawida (also Deganawidah, Dekanawidah, or Degandawida). A visionary statesman and constitutional genius born, according to astronomical data, around 1100 in Tkahaánaya, a Huron village near Kingston, Ontario, he was a renowned rationalist and peacemaker among Native Americans of the eastern United States. According to his maternal grandmother, a prenatal message from the Great Spirit declared that he would be born to her daughter, a virgin. The messenger proclaimed him Deganawida, which means Master of Things, and predicted that he would be a powerful ambassador and peacemaker.

Deganawida came of age in the traditions that Indians shared with the European pioneer. These core Native American concepts established basic principles: that working with nature is the only way to survive in the wilderness; that kings have no divine rights; and that skepticism is more fruitful than thoughtless faith. In childhood, he battled a speech impediment and suffered rejection by the Huron for his radical political musings. According to legend, he hollowed a canoe from stone and guided it east across Lake Ontario to the Mohawk, the People of Flint, who, at that time, lived by the rule of divination and vengeance. Skillfully building on native creation myth, he introduced concepts of humanism and mediation through a trifold message of *gáiwoh* (righteousness), *skénon* (health), and *gashasdénshaa* (power) and established a council in the *Kanonsiónni* (Longhouse), the first council chamber of nations. His first convert was a local woman he passed on the way. She welcomed him to her home and offered him food. In payment, he named her Jigónhsasee (New Face) and proclaimed her Mother of Nations.

The first confrontation between savagery and civilization occurred at the home of a cannibal who lived along the trail. When the man sat at his kettle, he stared at the reflection of Deganawida, who lay on the roof of his hut and gazed down through the smoke hole. The sight of a true and righteous face filled with inner strength caused the cannibal to dump the human contents of his pot outdoors and to swear off eating human flesh. Speaking like a sage, Deganawida said:

The new mind has come to thee, namely righteousness
  and health and power.
And thou art miserable because
  the new mind does not live at ease with old memories.
Heal thy memories by working to make justice prevail.
Bring peace to those places where thou hast done injury to
  man [Wallace 1986, 18].

Deganawida killed a deer as a substitute for the unspeakable stew in the pot. Together, the two men shared a meal of venison and discussed the creation of the Longhouse, a league, and the Great Peace or Great Law. In token of the cannibal's change of heart and his intent to subdue Atotarho, a snaky-haired wizard, Deganawida named him Hiawatha (or Aionwantha; He Who Combs).

The story continues with trial by ordeal, a standard element of Native American lore. To prove his merit, Deganawida climbed a tree near a cliff and allowed the Mohawk to chop through the trunk. When the tree toppled over the precipice, the tribe waited to see if the seer would survive. The next morning, he sat calmly before his fire. The Mohawk chief decided that Deganawida had greatness in him. Thus, the Mohawk became his first converted tribe and the founders of the Iroquois League. One by one, he added the next four member nations: the Oneida, the People of Stone or Granite People; the Onandaga, the

People on the Hill and the "name bearers" who kept the wampum belt history of the league; the Cayuga, the People at the Mucky Land; and the Seneca, the Great Hill People. To establish leadership, Deganawida crowned their chiefs with antlers as symbols of authority.

The historical account of Deganawida's campaign is less imaginative than the myth. As a believer in the life force, he expounded his views on peaceful interaction, brotherhood, and righteousness. A legend of his manipulation of a solar eclipse as proof of his power sets the incident in 1451. Because of his pronounced stutter, he mentored and chose as a spokesman a fellow Mohawk adoptee, Hiawatha, an Onandaga teacher, medicine man, and orator from New York state, who was recovering from the loss of his three daughters during an epidemic. Deganawida sought him out and spoke a cherished litany:

I wipe away the tears from thy face … using the white fawn-
  skin of pity.
I make it daylight for thee…. I beautify the sky.
Now shalt thou do thy thinking in peace when thine eyes rest
  on the sky,
  which the perfector of our faculties, the master of all things,
  intended should be a source of happiness to man. (Wallace
  1986, 25)

By consoling Hiawatha and restoring him to hope, Deganawida retrieved the sanity of a fellow negotiator and turned it to good purpose.

The incident served as a precedent for the formal Condolence Ceremony, an element of the peace process that survived both men. The somber litany accompanying a death became a treasured entry in the Iroquois Constitution:

Now then we say to you,
  "Persevere onward to the place where the Creator dwells in
  peace.
Let not the things of the earth hinder you.
Let nothing that transpired while yet you lived hinder you.
In hunting you once took delight;
  in the game of Lacrosse you once took delight
  and in the feasts and pleasant occasions your mind was
  amused,
  but now do not allow thoughts of these things [to] give you
  trouble.
Let not your relatives hinder you and also
  let not your friends and associates trouble your mind.
Regard none of these things" ["The Iroquois Constitution"].

This passage characterizes the dual nature of the Iroquois Constitution as both government document and religious prayer book. Additional litanies honor the passing of matrons, lower-ranking females, warriors, children, and stillborn infants.

Supernatural elements interweave the story of Deganawida and the Iroquois League. A half century before the arrival of Christopher Columbus to the New World, he foresaw a huge spruce with five roots, a typically animistic dream symbolizing five distinct Indian nations linked to one emblem of strength. In his interpretation, the dream prophesied the coming of peace. He and Hiawatha wove a wampum belt, which was made of one new string for each item of law they codified. Deganawida spread his doctrine of demilitarization and nonviolent negotiation to the Oneida and Onandaga. To assure the reality of his dream, he formally chartered the Hodesaunee or Iroquois League, a confederacy that bears the names of a major language group—an advanced nation of forest Indians, the first to arm themselves with rifles and renowned proponents of interclan blood feuds against the Algonquin and Mohawk.

Wallace describes the Iroquois as, above all, practical. After abandoning their penchant for feuds, they evolved the same word to mean "peace," "nobility," and "law" and recognized nonviolence as essential to a balanced life. The pacifism they embraced produced benefits—wisdom, soundness of reason, good health, hospitality, authority, and justice based on a system of law. The great peace equated with the great good, a slogan characterizing an ideal commonwealth. By 1570, they completed a constitution of 114 wampums and lauded it in history, legend, song, and ritual. It consisted of these divisions:

- rights, duties, and qualifications of sachems
- election of chiefs
- names, duties, and rights of war chiefs
- definition of clans and consanguinity
- official symbolism
- laws of adoption
- laws of emigration
- rights of foreign nations
- rights and powers of war
- treason or secession of a nation
- rights of the people of the Five Nations
- religious ceremony
- installation song
- protection of the house
- funeral addresses.

Under these statutes, they formed a cohesive alliance, the Hodinoshone (or *Haudenoshaunee* [People of the Longhouse]), which was as strong and binding a union as an extended family.

The Longhouse became the center of religious worship, based on the teachings of Handsome Lake, an eighteenth-century Seneca shaman-seer. It also served as a command post and center of government operations. In the event of an emergency, the constitution stated:

A messenger shall be dispatched either to Adodarhoh, Hononwirehtonh, or Skanawatih, Fire Keepers, or to their War Chiefs with a full statement of the case desired to be considered. Then shall Adodarhoh call his cousin [associate] Lords together and consider whether or not the case is of sufficient importance to demand the attention of the Confederate Council. If so, Adodarhoh shall dispatch messengers to summon all the Confederate Lords to assemble beneath the Tree of the Long Leaves.

A fail-safe was the matrons' selection of war chiefs on the basis of family, experience, and ability. These authorities, like temporary dictators, took control of tribal affairs only during war.

After Deganawida pacified and civilized the Iroquois, they did not enter war lightly. The declaration of war required the intoning of a solemn league hymn:

Now I am greatly surprised
  and, therefore I shall use it—
  the power of my war song.

I am of the Five Nations
  and I shall make supplication
  to the almighty creator.
He has furnished this army.
My warriors shall be mighty
  in the strength of the creator.
Between him and my song they are
  for it was he who gave the song,
  this war song that I sing! ["The Iroquois Constitution"].

It was the duty of war chiefs to continue singing the song as confrontation drew near. The words indicate the sacred nature of peace to the Iroquois and the "surprise" of having to violate the mores of peacelovers, summon an army, and fight with others.

The commonwealth of codified law is the linchpin of the *pax iroquoia*. Deganawida joined with Hiawatha to end constant warring between his adopted tribe and the Cayuga, Oneida, Onandaga, and Seneca. His intent was to apply the sanction of law to halt territorial squabbles, protect freedom, and settle internal differences without hostility or bloodshed. The league enjoyed two centuries of success and kept peace among the members, but did nothing to stem warfare outside the commonwealth against the Pequot, Mahican, Algonquin, Montagnais, Wyandot, Potawatomi, and Pocumtuc, tribes that lay outside the confederacy's jurisdiction. Another limitation of the league was its inability to persuade powerful southern nations—Chickasaw, Creek, Cherokee, Catawba, and Choctaw—to join the alliance.

The Iroquois Constitution provided a ritual to welcome children born into membership of the Five Nations. After the naming ceremony at the Midwinter Festival or at the Ripe Corn Festival, a cousin serving as speaker announced the child's name and identified the clan of the mother. The constitution states:

The uncle of the child shall then take the child in his arms and walking up and down the room shall sing: "My head is firm, I am of the Confederacy." As he sings the opposite cousinhood shall respond by chanting ... until the song is ended ["The Iroquois Constitution"].

Thus, the league provided belonging for individuals and cited tribal union as a proof of reason, a virtue honored from the cradle to the grave.

A singular contribution to Iroquois constitutional law was freedom of religion. The constitution states: "The rites and festivals of each nation shall remain undisturbed and shall continue as before because they were given by the people of old times as useful and necessary for the good of men" ("The Iroquois Constitution"). The sachems conferred on placing the Midwinter Thanksgiving on the calendar, arranged its rituals, and notified all of the time to convene, which was officially "five days after the moon of Dis-ko-nah is new." At the assembly in the Longhouse, the sachems bore responsibility for delivering a thanksgiving address and for acknowledging the Maple or Sugar-making Thanksgiving, Raspberry Thanksgiving, Strawberry Thanksgiving, Corn-planting Thanksgiving, Corn-hoeing Thanksgiving, Little Festival of Green Corn, Great Festival of Ripe Corn, and the grand Thanksgiving for the Harvest. Another sacred task was the appointment of religious instructors. According to law:

Whenever any man proves himself by his good life
  and his knowledge of good things,
    naturally fitted as a teacher of good things,
  he shall be recognized by the lords as a teacher of peace and
    religion
  and the people shall hear him ["The Iroquois Constitution"].

To affirm peace, Deganawida advocated courage, patience, and honesty as requisites to lawmaking. The constitution honored women, who kept fires burning in the event of an emergency council session, and singled out clan matrons by allowing them to serve the traditional communal bowl of cooked beaver tail to the assembled sachems. (Note that law forbade the use of utensils lest one man should injure another at mealtime and cause a fight.) The league's honored women bore a lifelong title: "The women heirs of the Confederated Lordship titles shall be called Royaneh [Noble] for all time to come" (The Iroquois Constitution"). It was the duty of the Royaneh to admonish chiefs who failed to live up to the demands of sachemhood. When the council honored a deceased chief woman in the Five Nations' Confederacy, the litany paralleled that of a sachem or male warrior with this addition:

Looking after your family was a sacred duty and you were
  faithful.
You were one of the many joint heirs of the lordship titles.
Feastings were yours and you had pleasant occasions ["The
  Iroquois Constitution"].

In many aspects, the Iroquois Constitution served as a moral compass to natives of the Five Nations. In regard to personal faults, Deganawida declared to the leaders:

Carry no anger and hold no grudges.
Think not forever of yourselves, O chiefs, nor of our own
  generation.
Think of continuing generations of our families,
  think of our grandchildren and of those yet unborn,
  whose faces are coming from beneath the ground [Wallace
  1986, 43].

The league established firm rules of compliance and expelled those chiefs who defaulted, disobeyed, lost their faculties through disease or accident, or acted incompetently. Thus, lifelong membership became a testimony to sturdiness and good character. One of the most prominent league members, Ely S. Parker (Donehogawa), was a Mohawk representative to the league, personal secretary to General Ulysses S. Grant at the surrender at Appomattox Courthouse, and commissioner of Indian affairs to Grant during his presidency.

A model to such league members, Deganawida was a man of moral energy and foresight. As a symbol of his vision of peaceful coexistence and power in unity, he planted a peace tree in central New York on Lake Onandaga:

- The trunk of this pine was an emblem of permanence.
- The branches symbolized the sovereignty of common law that sheltered and protected member tribes.
- The roots demonstrated how law could spread and ingather other peoples.
- At top he placed the eagle that sees afar to watch over all tribes and to serve as an alarm at the approach of danger.

After uprooting the pine, he pointed out a subterranean stream, where he cast hatchets and war clubs. At this dramatic moment, he pledged:

I, Deganawida, and the Confederated Chiefs,
  now uproot the tallest pine tree,
  and into the cavity thereby made we cast all weapons of war.
Into the depths of the earth,
  deep down into the under-earth currents of water
  flowing to unknown regions,

we cast all weapons of strife.
We bury them from sight and we plant again the tree.
Thus shall the great peace be established [Patterson and Snod-
  grass 1994, 63].

The league, which held its grand council fire in Syracuse,
New York, adopted a simplified symbol, a cluster of five
arrows bound with deer sinew to represent the binding
of five nations in union, power, honor, and dominion.

The league prefigured the concept of upper and
lower houses. Its governing council consisted of fifty
chiefs—ten Cayuga, nine Mohawk, fourteen Onandaga,
nine Oneida, and eight Seneca—but the Great Council al-
lotted only one vote to each nation. Its unity formed a living structure that Deganawida called "one body, one head,
and one heart" (Wallace 1986, 37). The Mohawk, who
were models of self-control and empathy, headed the
league. Onandaga firekeepers or hosts maintained protocol, prepared agendas, and provided a moderator. In
council, they invoked the Great Spirit, opened sessions,
and reported proceedings, over which they had the power
of veto. The Mohawk, Onandaga, and Seneca were the
"elder brothers" or "uncles" of foreign affairs. In token of
their position on the extremes of the territory, the Mohawk oversaw the eastern door and the Seneca the western door. The Oneida and Cayuga, later joined by the
Tuscarora, the Shirt-Wearing People, and Tutelo, were
called "younger brothers" or "nephews." In 1677, the
league signed its first treaty as the original Five Nations
and ceased negotiating as individual tribes.

The fifty sachems, elected for life by clan matrons,
assembled in the Longhouse around a line of five fires
representing member nations. As a sacred convocation,
each meeting opened with a thanksgiving prayer to the
Creator, the source of life and health, and the singing of
Jo-hah, a founder's hymn. Members, who dressed in
buckskin overslung with blankets in the style of Roman
togas, spoke one at a time and soberly weighed each issue.
The group's decisions had to be unanimous.

In place of paperwork, the league used symbolic
tableaus formed on two-dimensional strips of beadwork
constructed of white and purple whelk shells. Strings of
wampum tallied the number of issues covered in each session and established the authority of any message. The
belts also served as currency, invitations, condolence messages, treaty settlements, pledges and peace covenants,
and ritual badges. For somber occasions, such as the death
of a chief, the league sang "Hai! Hai!" also known as "The
Peace Hymn," and held an installation ritual to admit a
new member.

The league constitution established distinct categories of laws, which embody Indian responses to the
hardships they endured during the seventeenth and eighteenth centuries. At a time when whole tribes suffered

displacement as whites stole their lands or treaties moved
them farther west, wars decimated native peoples, and
others died out from smallpox, scarlet fever, measles, and
other European diseases, remnants of tribes accepted
membership as adoptees. These epidemics, wars, and
adoptions altered the balance of power by rapidly raising
or lowering the population of member nations. Another
factor affecting political stability was the decision of outlying tribes to join the alliance.

To the detriment of the league, these newcomers—
the Mahican, Delaware, Algonquin, and Sioux tribes—
entered the "covenant chain," but never earned full league
membership. Because the Iroquois considered themselves
ongwi honwi (superior people), subsequent members remained in the inferior position of disenfranchised or second-class citizens. As such, they received trade and military concessions, but no representation on the council.
This failing of the league to welcome outsiders and incorporate new blood caused the Mingo to defect and re-
settle in Ohio, the Caughnawaga to flee to Canada, and
others to drop out of active participation or ally with the
French of the St. Lawrence Valley.

With an eye to the future, Deganawida took change
into consideration. Before he mysteriously vanished from
sight, he promised that, should chiefs grow indifferent to
the confederacy, he would return once more to address the
league. However, it was not indifference that undermined
the league. Spread of his precepts brought to the original
member nations the Nanticoke of Maryland, the
Delaware, and the Tutelo of Virginia. Wars produced allies of the Neutrals, Erie, and Huron, all members of the
northern Iroquoian language group, but the league was
never able to trust the Hurons' commitment to peace.

By 1650, the league had destroyed the Huron confederacy and terrorized New France with skillful raids,
thus halting the advance of French colonization south of
the St. Lawrence. Still autonomous, it had survived confrontations with the French, English, and Dutch over a
century and a half when a Jesuit missionary, Father Milet,
encountered the Five Nations in 1691. In 1710, the Tuscarora of North Carolina, who also belonged to the Iroquoian language group, joined the union as the sixth sovereign member of the Iroquois League. After this point,
members referred to themselves as the Six Nations. As
white power began to subsume native sovereignty, the
league weathered a major threat to its survival. The
Philadelphia meeting of 1736 between the Onandaga
Council and Thomas Penn surprised Pennsylvanians, who
were not accustomed to granting Indians a role in citizen
meetings. In token of the league's sophistication in matters of negotiation and diplomacy, Joseph Brant, Mohawk
war chief and ambassador, observed that the native legal
system was superior to that of whites: "Among us we have

no prisons, we have no pompous parade of courts; we have no written laws" (Pastron 1993, 19). His older sister, Molly Brant, joined him in easing the animosities of the French and Indian War.

As a model of probity, self-restraint, and wisdom, the league served white colonial spokesmen as a touchstone for the U.S. government's representative democracy. Ironically, the founding of the nation followed the withdrawal of the league from U.S. territory. After surviving the French and Indian War, the league foundered during the American Revolution, when it continued to support the losing side, the English monarchy. After a rupture of the Great Peace in 1777 and defeat by Major General John Sullivan in 1779, the confederacy suffered irreparable harm. Joseph Brant attempted a reorganization, but league members, sapped by epidemics, acculturation by Jesuit missionaries, and retreat from white settlements, ultimately withdrew from the thirteen colonies and established council headquarters at Ohswéken, Ontario, where it still survives under the league flag that supplanted Hiawatha's wampum belt. The Indian Removal Act of 1830 added the coup de grace by forcing the Iroquois from New York. Under the 1838 Treaty of Buffalo Creek, they settled in southeastern Kansas.

The spirit of the Iroquois League revived during Native American protests in the last quarter of the twentieth century. In 1973, when the American Indian Movement organized antigovernment demonstrations at Wounded Knee, South Dakota, the Grand Council of the Six Nations added its support to tribes and alliances nationwide. On arrival at the site of council leaders Oren Lyons and Billy Lazore, the gathering cheered as some thirty members walked around federal roadblocks and joined peaceful delegations in nursing and first aid, cooking, sewing, and negotiation with federal authorities. On May 5, the Grand Council offered to represent protesters in Washington and, within three days' time, visited most of the one hundred U.S. senators. When federal marshals attempted to arrest activist Dennis Banks for his role in the protest, he sought sanctuary with the Onandaga, who welcomed and sheltered him in the peaceful tradition of Deganawida.

SOURCES: Chase 1903, Collins 1947, Hooker 1996, "The Iroquois Constitution" 1999, Johansen and Grinde 1998, "Modern History Sourcebook: The Constitution of the Iroquois Confederacy," Pastron 1993, Patterson and Snodgrass 1994, "Paul A. W. Wallace Papers," "Society: Iroquois," Wallace 1986, "Welcome to the AkweKon Virtual Tour."

Win Ching *see* I Ching

Zand-Avesta or Zend-Avesta *see* Avesta

Glossary

agnyadheya [ag' nyah . day' ah] in Hindu worship, the installation of the fire.

agrapha [uh . gra' fuh] citations of Jesus not contained within the canon Bible.

akhand path [ahk' hahnd pahth] in Zoroastrianism, uninterrupted reading of the Granth.

akhira [ah . kee' rah] the Islamic concept of the afterlife.

alpha and omega [al' fah; oh . may' gah] the first and final letters of the Greek alphabet, which the Book of Revelation applies as symbols of the beginning and end of time.

Amagahara [ah . mah . gah . hah' rah] in Japanese myth, the heavenly realm.

Amentet [ah' mehn . teht] in Egyptian tomb lore, the region where the deceased live off offerings from mourners.

amoraim [ah . moh' rah . eem] Talmudic interpreters.

apocalypse [uh . pah' koh . lihps] a revelation or disclosure of divine mystery; also, a literary genre predicting world cataclysm.

Apocrypha [uh . pah' krih . fuh] a body of scripture included in the Septuagint and Vulgate but omitted from Jewish and Protestant canons of the Old Testament.

Aramaic [a . rah . may' ihk] a Semitic language of Persians and Jews dating from the ninth century B.C.E. and used in place of Hebrew for scripture.

asceticism [a . seh' tih . sihzm] deliberate self-denial, mortification of flesh, or limitation or renunciation of physical desire and pleasure as a fulfillment of divine will.

Ashkenazi [ahsh . keh . nah' zee] adj. **Ashkenazic** Eastern European Judaism, as opposed to the Sephardic or Iberian strand.

Asilus/Asiluth [ah' see . loos/ah' see . looth] the Kabbalistic concept of the sublime realm.

asiyah [ah' see . yah] the Kabbalistic concept of making.

Atman [aht' mahn] the Hindu personification of the oversoul.

aubade [oh' bahd] a morning hymn or recitation.

avatar [a' vuh . tahr] an earthly incarnation of the god Vishnu.

baqa' [bah . kah'] the Sufist concept of self-perpetuation with Allah.

bardo [bahr' doh] in Tibetan Buddhism, the swooning state that precedes the soul's passage from the body.

basmalah [bahs . mah' lah] a prescribed prayer or brief formal address to Allah.

ber'iah [bayr' yah] the Kabbalistic concept of creating.

bhakti [bahk' tee] the Sanskrit term for devotion to the divine.

binah [bee' nah] in Kabbala, understanding or intelligence that accompanies acquisition of wisdom.

bodhisattva [boh. dee . saht' vah] in Buddhism, one destined for enlightenment.

cakra [kak' rah] in Tantrism, a center of psychic power in the body.

caliph [cah . leef'] among Sunnite Muslims, the political leader and defender of Islam.

canon [ka' nuhn] any writings accepted as holy scripture.

charismatic [ka . rihz . ma' tihk] a compellingly charming preaching or evangelism enhanced by a persuasive personality and magnetic speech.

chauri [chow' ree] in Zoroastrianism, a ritual whisk or fan.

ch'i [chee] the Chinese principle of matter.

Chikhai Bardo [chee' ky bahr' doh] in Tibetan Buddhism, the postdeath period when the spirit enters an out-of-body state, but perceives earthly beings and hears mourners.

choka [choh' kah] a long Japanese poem ending in a seven-syllable couplet.

Chönyid Bardo [chahn' yihd bahr' doh] in Tibetan Buddhism, a fearful postdeath stage when the deceased realizes termination of life.

chrism [krihzm] a consecrated oil that confers blessing

and grace during baptism, chrismation, confirmation, and ordination.

Daijôsai [dy' joh . sy] a ritual through which the spirit of the goddess departs from the deceased Japanese emperor and enters his successor.

damyata [dahm . yaht' tah] the Hindu concept of self-control.

data [dah' tah] the Hindu concept of charity.

dayadhwam [dah . yahd' wahm] the Hindu concept of compassion.

deuterocanonical [dyoo . tuh . roh . ka . nah' nih . k'l] referring to a substratum of honored writings that do not merit the designation of God-inspired scripture.

dhamma/dharma [dah' mah/dahr' mah] the Hindu concept of universal order.

Dhu al-Hijja [doo' ahl . heej' jah] the Islamic month of pilgrimage.

diaspora [dy . as' poh . ruh] the forced scattering of Jews outside Palestine following the Babylonian exile, Native Americans from their homelands, and Mormons from their headquarters to Utah.

din [deen] in Kabbala, self-discipline, strength, or judgment.

ecclesiastical [ehk . klee . zee . as' tih . k'l] referring to holy books.

en sof/en soph [ehn . sahf'] Kabbalistic concept of the infinite.

Essene [ehs . seen'] a tightly structured separatist order of Jewish hermits who retreated to the wilderness.

ethnarch [eth' . nahrk] the leader of a people or nation.

exegesis [ehk . sih . jee' sihs] textual interpretation.

fana' [fah . nah'] the Sufist concept of annihilation of self.

fundamentalism [fuhn . duh . mihn' tuh . lihzm] literal interpretation of a scripture.

gaon [gah' ohn] scholar-principal of a Jewish academy.

gebhurah/gevurah [gay . boo' rah] in Kabbala, energy.

Gemara/Gemarah [gih . mah' rah] a later and more exact title for the Talmud.

ghazal [gah . zahl'] the couplet used in Sufist verse.

Ghost Dance a ritual of the Plains Indians performed in costume thought to restore free-roaming buffalo and Indian spirits to earth and to make performers impervious to bullets.

gilgul [geel' gool] in Kabbala, metempsychosis, reincarnation, or the transmigration of souls.

giveaway among Native Americans, a tribal redistribution of wealth through exchange of gifts.

glossolalia [glahs . soh . lay' lyuh] a rapturous, incoherent utterance bursting out spontaneously during worship.

gnostic [nahs' tihk] relating to private knowledge and practice essential to salvation among an elite company of Christian cultists.

golem [goh' laym] in Kabbala, a soulless body or zombie molded from clay just as God made Adam.

Great Spirit Supreme God in the Native American faith.

grhya [gryah] domestic Hindu worship.

guru [goo' roo] a Hindu master or teacher who guides the progress of beginners.

hadith [hah . deeth'] Islamic tradition.

hadj/hajj [hahj] a Muslim's obligatory pilgrimage to the shrine at Mecca.

hafiz [hah . feez'] an individual who has committed the entire Koran to memory.

haggada/haggadah [hahg' gah . dah] A minor segment of Talmudic narrative dealing with the nonlegal or narrative actions and themes in scripture.

haoma [hay . oh' muh] in Zoroastrianism, a hallowed alcoholic drink and healing potion.

Hasidim [hah' see . deem] Jewish ascetics.

Hellenized [hehl' lih . nyzd] influenced by Greek culture.

hesed [hay' says] in Kabbala, kindness or grace.

heyoka [hay . yoh' kah] a Native American who has experienced a vision of thunder and direct communication with spirits who guard warriors.

hieroglyph [hyr' oh . glihf] a graphic character that serves as an element of a pictographic writing system.

hijra [heej' rah] Muhammad's migration in C.E. 622.

hinayana [hee . nah . yah' nah] the philosophy of detachment from self that distinguishes Buddhists in Sri Lanka and Southeast Asia.

hod [hohd] in Kabbala, splendor or beauty.

Hodesaunee [hoh . day . saw' nee] the Iroquois League.

Hodinoshone [hoh . dih . noh . shoh' nee] the people of the Longhouse.

hokhmah [hohk' mah] in Kabbala, attainment of wisdom.

hotri [hoh' tree] the chief sacrificer or reciter in Hindu ritual.

hulul [hoo . lool'] the Sufist concept of oneness with Allah.

humnos [hoom' nohs] ancient Greek religious poems.

'Id al-Fitr [eed' ahl . feet'r] an Islamic ceremony of gift giving and charity.

jangbu [jang' boo] in Tibetan Buddhism, a ritual drawing.

jataka [jah . tah' kah] character-building folk stories, anecdotes, and fables illustrating Buddhist teachings about the Buddha's appearance on earth.

Kaaba [kah' bah] the Islamic Holy of Holies, a cube-shaped shrine at the Great Mosque at Mecca.

Kaddish [kah' dihsh] a traditional Hebrew call to worship or prayer for peace recited at graveside, during memorial services, and on the anniversaries of a death.

Kainerekowa [kah . ee' neh . re. koh' wah] the Iroquois Great Law of Peace.

kalpas [kahl' pahs] the Buddhist concept of recurrent cycles.

kami [kah' mee] nature spirits venerated in Shintoism.

Karaism [kah' rah . izm] Jewish scripturalism, a Babylonian movement that questioned the authority of Jewish oral tradition and the Talmud.

karma [kahr' mah] the evaluation of a life based on actions.

karma yogi [kahr' muh yoh' gee] the Indian term for a saintly Hindu.

keter [kay' tayr] in Kabbala, striving for wisdom.

khu [koo] in Egyptian lore, the shining spirit-soul.

kinnikinnik [kihn . nih' kihn . nihk] ritual tobacco made of the dried inner bark of red alder or red dogwood.

kirtan [keer' tahn] Zoroastrian hymn singing.

koan [koh' ahn] an ancient Chinese or Japanese riddle or proverb that requires nonrational solution or contemplation.

Kuni tsu kami [koo' nee zoo kah' mee] in Japanese myth, the earthly realm.

kykeon [ky' kee . ohn] a ritual drink at the Eleusinian Mysteries.

kyuji [kyoo' gee] Japanese song cycles.

li [lee] the Chinese principle of social order.

Madaniyah [mah . dah . nee' yah] in reference to revelations Muhammad received after his migration.

mahasiddha [mah . hah . seed' dah] a Hindu saint or miracle worker.

mahavakya [mah . hah . vahk' yah] wise Hindu sayings or aphorisms.

Makkiyah [mahk' kee . yah] in reference to revelations Muhammad received before his migration.

maktab [mahk . tahb'] an Islamic religious school.

malkhut/malkhuth [mahl' koot] in Kabbala, God's rule or kingdom.

mandala [man' duh . luh] a matrix or graphic symbol used as a vehicle of worship.

Manichaean [ma . nih . kee' uhn] referring to a syncretic faith originating in Persia and based on the release of the spirit through self-denial.

manthras [man' thrahs] sacred Zoroastrian words or prayers.

mantra [man' trah] a spoken or intoned syllable, sacred name, word, or phrase that enhances meditation and worship.

ma'rifah [mah . ree' fah] the Sufist concept of interior knowledge.

maya [mah' yah] in Zoroastrianisim, the concept of earthly delusion.

Midrash [mihd' rash] interpretation of the Torah to disclose deeper meaning.

Mishnah [mihsh' nuh] a collection of Jewish traditions compiled around C.E. 200 as part of the Talmud.

misogi [mee . soh' gee] a Shinto purification rite.

moksha/moksa [mohk' shah] the Hindu and Sikh concept of release from cyclical reincarnation.

muezzin [moo . eh' z'n] a crier who summons Muslims to prayer.

nezah [nay' zah] in Kabbala, victory or endurance.

Ninamesai [nee . nah . may' sy] the Shinto ceremony called Tasting First Fruits.

nirvana [nuhr . vah' nah] in Buddhist theology, a sublime mental state of total enlightenment.

oral tradition a preliterate method of preserving narrative by memorizing it and passing it to succeeding generations.

orthodoxy [ohr' thoh . dahk . see] official opinions and beliefs of a religious group.

pa kua [pah . kwah'] trigrams or trios of three broken and unbroken lines used in Chinese divination.

parinirvana [pah . ree . nihr . vah' nah] in Buddhism, entry into nirvana.

Pentateuch [pehn' tah . took] the first five books of Old Testament scripture, consisting of Genesis, Exodus, Leviticus, Numbers, and Deuteronomy.

Pharisee [fa' rih. see] a strict jurist of the Jewish supreme court.

psalm [sahlm] a sacred song, hymn, or poem used in worship.

pseudepigrapha [soo' duh . pee' grah. fah] anonymous religious writings, including texts attributed to biblical characters.

pythia [pih' thyuh] title of the priestess divining in service to Apollo at Delphi.

qiblah [keeb' lah] a prayerful position facing Mecca at morning, noon, midafternoon, after sunset, and before bed.

qurra' [koor' rah] professional readers and reciters of the Koran.

rahamin [rah' hah . meen] in Kabbala, mercy or compassion.

reshith [ray' sheeth] in Kabbala, the beginning of wisdom.

responsum (pl. **responsa**) [reh . spohn' soom] a method of discussing Talmudic issues by letter.

rishi [ree' shee] a Hindu sage.

ruba'iyat [roo' bay . aht] quatrains used in Sufist verse.

sachem [sa' chihm] a chief or leader of the Iroquois League.

sakinah [sah' kee . nah] the Islamic concept of divine tranquility.

salat [sah . laht] for Muslims, daily prayer facing Mecca.

samadhi [sah' mah . dee] the Hindu concept of full consciousness of God.

saman [sah' mahn] a Vedic stanza.

sati/suttee [sah' tee/soo . tee'] the ritual burning of a Hindu widow on her deceased husband's funeral pyre.

satori [sah . toh' ree] the Zen Buddhist concept of a sudden intuition or insight.

scripture [skrihp' choor] writings that address the relationships between deity and humanity.

sefirot/sephirot [say' fee . roht] sacred numbers or spheres of Kabbala.

Septuagint [sehp' too . ah . jihnt] the Greek version of the Old Testament and Apocrypha, translated into vernacular in the third to second centuries B.C.E.

shaman [shah' man] a priest, diviner, or practitioner of magic.

shekhinah [shay' kee . nah] in Kabbala, the divine presence.

Shingon [sheen' gahn] a sect of Japanese pantheists.

siddha [seed' dah] a lay religious practitioner of Tantrism.

smudging for Native Americans, a ritual cleansing with the smoke of sweet grass.

soma [soh' mah] a hallucinogen used in Hindu worship.

srauta [srow' tah] public Hindu ritual.

stupa [stoo' pah] Buddhist reliquaries.

Sufi [soo' fee] a Muslim mystic monk, also called a whirling dervish.

sutra [soo' trah] a synopsis of Vedic teaching.

sweat lodge a temporary domed dwelling shaped of willow lathes and used during Native American purification ritual.

tafsir [tahf' seer] a strict science of explaining or paraphrasing the Koran.

tahannuth [tah . hahn' nooth] Islamic devotional exercise.

tajwid [tahj . weed'] a highly refined oral recitation performed by professional readers.

Talmud [tahl' mood] Jewish law and oral tradition of the fourth and fifth centuries C.E. that supplements scriptural law.

tanka [tahn' kah] Japanese verse containing five lines.

tannaim [tan' nah . eem] Jewish scholars of oral law.

tao [dow] the Chinese concept of the way or path.

Targum [tahr' guhm] translations of Hebrew scripture into Aramaic.

te [tay] in the I Ching, the concept of power.

tekye [tehk' yeh] a Sufist shrine.

tepew/tepeu [teh' poo] the Quiché sovereign.

Theravada [thay . rah . vah' dah] the original form of Buddhism drawn from Gautama's teachings.

t'ien-shih [tyehn . shee'] a celestial master of Taoism.

tiferet/tifereth/tiph'eret [tee' fay . rayth] in Kabbala, beauty.

tikkun/tiqqun [teek' koon] in Kabbala, cosmic restoration, the struggle to restore order on earth, and the application of mysticism to conquer evil.

tosafot [toh' sah . foht] Talmudic glossing, an interpretive method that standardized European biblical annotation as either commentary, analysis, or expansion.

tuat [twaht] in ancient Egypt, a hellish twilight zone in the afterlife.

tzimtzum [tseem' tsoom] in Kabbala, the withdrawal or contraction of the divine light, God's deliberate self-limitation to reveal the primordial void.

tzu-jan [zoo . chahn'] the Taoist concept of spontaneity, omnipresence, and omniscience.

udgatri [ood . gaht' ree] chanters of Vedic scripture.

Urim and Thummim [oo' rihm; thoom' mihm] magic stones that served Joseph Smith in decoding revealed scripture.

ushabti [oo . shahb' tee] answerers; Egyptian tomb figurines of servants who perform jobs assigned to the dead.

Veda [vay' dah] sacred Hindu writings.

Vedanta [vay . dahn' tah] Hindu theology derived from the ancient Vedas.

vedi [vay' dee] a Hindu altar.

vision quest the Plains Indians' spiritual search for a guardian spirit during initiation into adulthood.

waka [wah' kah] Japanese verse with an alternating pattern of five- and seven-syllable lines in one of two verse lengths.

Wakan Tanka [swah' kahn tahn' kah] the Sioux God, called the Great Spirit.

wampum [wahm' puhm] beaded strips used by Native Americans as money, messages, or badges.

wato [wah . toh] in Zen Buddhism, the key word in a koan; a word puzzle.

wu [woo] the Chinese concept of enlightenment.

yajamana [yah . jah . mah' nah] a Hindu sacrificer.

yantra [yan' trah] in Tantrism, a cosmogram, permutation, or mystic diagram that forms sacred art and geometry.

yeshiva [yay . shee' vah] a Jewish learning center or academy.

yesirah [yay' see . rah] the Kabbalistic concept of forming.

yesod olam [yay' sohd oh . lahm] in Kabbala, the foundation or source of God's activity on earth.

yin and yang the Chinese concept of vital, interrelated powers that parallel universal dynamism.

yoga [yoh' gah] the Hindu concept of enlightenment.

yogi [yoh' gee] an enlightened Hindu.

Yomi no kuni [yoh' mee noh koo' ni] in Japanese myth, the underworld, the land of the dead.

yüan [ywahn] the Chinese concept of recurrent cycles.

yuwipi [yoo . wee' pee] a Lakota conjuring ritual.

zakat [zah' kaht] Islamic charity to uplift the poor.

Time Line of World Scriptures

The dating of ancient texts is, at best, chancy. The following list is intended to provide a sense of chronological order in which writers received revelation and scriptures were composed, written down, translated, and discussed. Selection of uncertain dates and historical periods follows individual entries in the text. Where events range over a period of times, the date at left represents the earliest choice.

2800 B.C.E.	The I Ching is begun under the semi-mythic Emperor Fu Hsi.
2357 B.C.E.	Historians begin compiling the Shu Ching.
2100 B.C.E.	Brahmans, ascetic priests, memorize Vedic texts.
1766 B.C.E.	Poets write the first verse anthologized in China's first poetry anthology, the Shih Ching.
1700–1400 B.C.E.	The Rig Veda is composed.
1570 B.C.E.	The Egyptian Book of the Dead is compiled.
1554 B.C.E.	The Book of What Is in the Netherworld is painted on a scroll in the Valley of the Kings.
1500 B.C.E.	Vedic peoples settle the banks of the Indus River.
1200–100 B.C.E.	The Tanakh or Old Testament is composed.
1150 B.C.E.	Wen Wang composes the T'uan, the first written version of the I Ching.
1110 B.C.E.	The duke of Chou composes the Chou I, which analyzes mystic lines and spaces.
950 B.C.E.	A Judean writer organizes historic events into a Hebrew epic.
900–600 B.C.E.	The Brahmanas are composed as ceremonial handbooks.
800 B.C.E.	Dhanvantari, the first physician and teacher of healing, compiles the Atharva Veda.
800–350 B.C.E.	The Sutras are written.
750–250 B.C.E.	The Ketuvin, the final segment of Hebraic scripture, is composed.
700s B.C.E.	The first of the Homeric Hymns is composed.
600s–300s B.C.E.	Apocryphal books appear after the age of Ezra.
621 B.C.E.	The high priest Hilkiah, father of the prophet Jeremiah, discovers the Book of Deuteronomy.
609 B.C.E.	Jewish scripture groups Deuteronomy with Joshua, Judges, Samuel, and Kings.
600 B.C.E.	The Aranyakas are compiled.
	The Black Vedas anthologize interpretations of myth and mysticism and hymns for ritual sacrifice.
	The Saïte Recension of the Egyptian Book of the Dead is in wide use.
563 B.C.E.	Siddhartha Gautama is born in northern India.
550 B.C.E.	Zoroaster lives during the conquest by Cyrus the Great.
536 B.C.E.	The Book of Kings is completed.
534 B.C.E.	Siddhartha Gautama abandons worldliness.

529 B.C.E.	Siddhartha Gautama achieves enlightenment as the Buddha.
500–100 B.C.E.	Hinduism evolves.
483 B.C.E.	Confucius compiles the Book of Songs.
	Siddhartha Gautama dies.
481 B.C.E.	Confucius's annotated chronicle, the Ch'un-ch'iu, is China's first chronological history.
480 B.C.E.	Confucius adds to the I Ching the T'uan Chuan and possibly the Hsiang Chuan.
475 B.C.E.	Confucius writes the Li Chi.
458 B.C.E.	Moses' laws, which Ezra transport from Babylon, become the soul of Judaism.
400 B.C.E.	The Pentateuch is canonized.
	The Book of Job is completed.
300s B.C.E.	The I Ching acquires an appendix, the Hsi tz'u.
350 B.C.E.	Essenes stash forty legal documents in a cave near the Dead Sea.
	Priests of Artaxerxes I evolve a world-year calendar.
330 B.C.E.	Alexander the Great burns sacred works when he destroys Persepolis.
322–30 B.C.E.	Egyptian priests standardize burial inscriptions.
300 B.C.E.	The Letter of Jeremiah is written in Hebrew.
200s B.C.E.	Interpreters add the I Ching to books of history, philosophy, and morality.
250 B.C.E.	The Greek language supersedes Aramaic.
250 B.C.E.–C.E. 200	The pseudepigrapha are completed.
240 B.C.E.	The Council of Ashoka canonizes the Dhammapada.
213 B.C.E.	Shih Huang Ti burns Confucius's teachings in a mass book burning.
200 B.C.E.	A Jewish priest composes Testaments of the Twelve Patriarchs.
	I Enoch is composed in Hebrew or Aramaic.
	The Bhagavad Gita is written.
	The Nevi'im (prophets) enters the Hebrew canon.

100s B.C.E.	The Book of Jubilees and Bel and the Dragon are written in Palestine.
	The Book of Judith is composed.
	The Jewish Sibylline Oracles is composed in Alexandria.
	In the Han dynasty's cultural renaissance, scholars replace books destroyed during the Great Interdiction.
	The Temple Scroll is composed in Hebrew.
185 B.C.E.	Szema compiles *Shiki*, a biography of Confucius.
180 B.C.E.	Ben Sirach composes Ecclesiasticus, one of the oldest apocryphal writings.
175 B.C.E.	Tobit is written in Hebrew or Aramaic.
150 B.C.E.	The Greek Septuagint is translated.
	A Palestinian Jew writes I and II Maccabees.
136 B.C.E.	Confucianism becomes the state cult and the master's Analects a state-mandated textbook.
	Tung Chung-Shu compiles the Wu Ching, China's first book of scripture and long-lived textbook.
130 B.C.E.	The Letter of Aristeas is composed at Alexandria.
114 B.C.E.	Lysimachus, an Egyptian Jew, translates the Hebrew text into Greek.
48 B.C.E.	A single Hebrew poet writes the Psalms of Solomon.
29 B.C.E.	The Dhammapada reaches written form.
25 B.C.E.	Baruch is composed in Hebrew in Babylon.
30	A Palestinian Jew composes the Assumption of Moses.
44	The letter to James, a five-chapter harangue, is written.
	Zoroastrian fire cult vanishes.
	Paul composes his earliest letter,"I Thessalonians.
51	Paul follows with II Thessalonians.

53	Paul addresses the Philippians and writes I Corinthians.		Palestinian mystics create a unique branch of Jewish speculation.
54	Paul follows with II Corinthians and writes letters to the Romans and Galatians.	100s–300s	The New Testament Apocrypha are written.
61	Paul writes the Colossians.	100	The Gospel of the Hebrews is composed in Hebrew in Egyptian tradition.
62	From Rome's Mamartine Prison, Paul writes II Timothy, the letter to the Ephesians, and another to Philemon, a Colossian in Phrygia.		Josephus corroborates three separate categories of Hebrew scripture in book 1 of *Contra Apion*.
63	I Peter is a letter from Rome to churches in northern Asia Minor; II Peter is a sequel.	110	A Semite writes the Gospel of the Nazarenes.
64	Paul writes to Titus and composes I Timothy from Laodicea.	114	Peter the Venerable translates the Koran into Latin.
66	Paul sends a letter to the Hebrews.	115	The Apocalypse of Baruch is written.
67	Acts becomes the fifth New Testament book.	130	III Baruch is written.
70	The Jewish canon closes officially after the destruction of the Temple.	150	A gentile composes *Protevangelium Jacobi* in Greek.
	A Hellenized Jew composed IV Maccabees in learned Greek.		The Apocalypse of Peter is written in Greek.
75	Josephus writes *De Bello Judaico*.		The Apocryphon of James is composed.
77	Pliny the Elder completes a Latin encyclopedia, *Historia Naturalis*.		The Christian Sibyllines are written.
79	The Book of Jude appears to be written by Jesus's brother.		The Epistle of the Apostles is composed in the eastern Mediterranean.
80	Matthew, a tax agent, composes the Gospel of Matthew.		The Thomas Gospel of the Infancy is written.
90	Dr. Luke composes the Gospel of Luke.	170	Melito, a Lydian bishop, separates Apocrypha from the biblical canon and coins the term "Old Testament."
	John composes the Gospel of John; I, II, and III John become the most recent of New Testament books.	175	The Gospel of Truth, perhaps by Valentinus, is composed in Greek.
94	Josephus writes *De Antiquitate Judaica*.		A state-approved version of Confucius's Analects is inscribed on stone tablets as scripture.
95	A Jew composes IV Esdras.	180	The Acts of John is written.
	Revelation is prison literature written near the end of the reign of Domitian.	200	The Letter of Peter to Philip is composed.
100s	The Gospel of the Ebionites is written in Greek.		The Roman centurion Quintus Tertullian of Carthage coins the term "New Testament."
	Rabbi Akiba ben Joseph of Jerusalem completes mystic spells and sees God.	226	Tansar restores the native Iranian faith.
	Philip writes *De Vita Contemplativa*.	250	The Gospel of Philip is composed.
			Koreans send a copy of Confucius's Analects to Japan.

	Roman troops control territory between the Euphrates and Tigris.
300s	The History of Joseph the Carpenter is composed in Greek.
347	St. Frumentius transliterates church texts into Ge'ez and introduces Christianity into Abyssinia.
367	Athanasius refers to the New Testament.
380	The Correspondence of Paul and Seneca is composed.
388	The Apocalypse of Paul is written in Greek.
397	Augustine of Hippo issues *De Doctrina Christiana*, which maintains that the Apocrypha belong in the Latin Vulgate.
400	Talmud Yerushalmi is finished in Tiberias.
	The oral groundwork of the Kojiki begins before Japan has a written language.
	The New Testament canon receives unofficial acceptance.
500s	The *Sefer Yesira*, the oldest Kabbalist writing, is composed.
500	The Apocalypse of John is written in Greek.
	The Talmud Bavli (Babylonian Talmud) is completed.
	The Indian monk Bodhidharma carries Zen to eastern Asia.
	Dionysius Exiguus sets the birth of Jesus in December as A.D. 1.
	Khosrow promotes Mazdaism as the state faith.
	Muhammad is born at Mecca.
	Muhammad receives his first revelation from Allah.
613	Muhammad composes the Koran's first surah, *al-fâtiha*.
	Muhammad flees to Medina.
	Muhammad's forces win the first decisive Islamic conflict.
628	Muhammad marches on Mecca.
632	Muhammad dies.

652	Caliph 'Uthman commissions the standardized Koran and entrusts the original to Hafsa.
656	At the battle of the Camel, Ayesha's Shi'ites fall to 'Ali and his Sunnites.
661	Abu al-Aswad Al Doaly begins repunctuating the Koran.
670	Caedmon paraphrases Genesis, the first of a series of Bible poems in Anglo-Saxon verse.
681	Emperor Temmu commissions the Kojiki, written by O no Yasumaro.
685	Nasr ibn Asem and Hayy ibn Ya'amor repunctuate the Koran.
692	Abd al-Malik inscribes Koranic scripture at Jerusalem's Dome of the Rock.
700	Aldhelm translates the Psalms from Latin to Old English.
712	The Kojiki collects myths from Japan's origins.
720	The Nihon Shoki supplements the Kojiki.
735	The Venerable Bede translates the Gospel of John into Anglo-Saxon.
750	Muhammad ibn Ishaq compiles a biography of Muhammad.
760	The *Halakhot Pesuqot* is written.
775	The Tibetan Book of the Dead is composed in Sanskrit.
	Al Khaleel ibn Ahmad Al Faraheedy completes new syntactic markings for the Koran.
790s	Rabi'ah al-'Adawiyah, a female Sufist from Basra, evolves the Sufist doctrine of the unconditional love of Allah.
800	The Infancy Gospel of Pseudo-Matthew is written in Latin.
825	The *Halakhot Gedolot* is completed.
830	An unknown writer translates the gospels into Gothic in Hesse.
	Ibn Hisham compiles the second biography of Muhammad.
863	Cyril and Methodius translate part of the Bible into Slavonic.

890s	Alfred the Great produces an Anglo-Saxon psalter.
900s	The Masoretic Torah is completed.
	Abu Ja'far Muhammad ibn Jarir at-Tabari compiles the Koran Commentary.
	Theologian Junayd of Baghdad standardizes Sufist theology.
	The Vedas are written down.
905	Saadiah ben-Joseph's commentary legitimizes Jewish mysticism.
920	Nan-yüan Hui-yung creates the first koan to individualize instruction of Zen trainees.
935	Sa'adi ben-Joseph composes *Sefer ha-Emunot ve-ha-De'ot.*
1005	Aelfric Grammaticus produces the Heptateuch as an aid to priests.
1050	Isaac ben-Jacob Alfasi composes the *Sefer ha-Halachot.*
1070	Chou Tun-i reformulates and enlarges the I Ching in two metaphysical treatises—*T'ai-chi-t'u shuo* and the *T'ung-shuo.*
1075	Khu tsha zla Iod summarizes ceremony in Death Rituals of the Tibetan Bon-pos.
1110	Abu Hamid al-Ghazali issues the *Ihya' 'ulum ad-din,* a treatise on moderate mysticism.
1125	Yüan-wu K'o-ch'in collects 1,700 koans in *Pi-yen lu.*
1130	Ta-hui bases a teaching method on the koan.
1177	Chu Hsi writes *Lessons on the I for the Young,* reinterpreting the I Ching by the tenets of neo–Confucianism.
1180	Rabbi Moses ben Maimon rids Talmud of ambiguity with the Mishneh Torah.
1190s	Abraham ben David and his son Isaac the Blind initiate a Jewish renaissance in Narbonne, France.
1190	Dampa Rangdröl writes the Bon-po Book of the Dead.
1191	Zen reaches Japan.
	The *Sefer ha-bahir* influences Jewish mysticism.
1200s	*Sator Arepo Tenet Opera Rotas* adorns the church of Santa Lucia on Mount Velino, Italy.
1210	Isaac the Blind and Azriel influence a golden age of esoteric learning, which standardizes Kabbalist terminology.
1225	The *Sefer ha-temuna* probes the concept of cosmic cycles.
1228	*Wu-men Kuan* or *Mumon-kan* anthologizes forty-eight koans.
1240	Wan-sung Hsing-hsiu collects koans in the *Ts'ung-jung lu.*
1244	Hugh of Saint-Cher divides the Bible into chapters.
1270	Rumi compiles ecstatic sacred couplets in the Mathnawi.
1279	Confucians rededicate themselves to the Tao.
1280	Abraham ben-Samuel Abulafia of Saragossa founds an ecstatic movement employing Hebrew script as a means of union with God.
1286	The height of Kabbalism is the *Sefer ha-zohar,* the mystic Bible, written by Moses de Leon of Guadalajara.
1313	Jacob ben Asher codifies the *Piské Halakhot.*
1325	Namdev composes 2,000 Hindi poems, some of which appear in the Granth Sahib.
1346	Aaron ben Elijah Alfasi compiles *Etz Hayyim.*
1350	William of Shoreham completes a prose version of the Psalms.
1360	The Zohar is printed at Cremona and Mantua.
1365	Ridzin Karma Lingpa unearths the Tibetan Book of the Dead on Mount Gampodar.
1370	Ramananda founds the Ramanandi sect.
1382	John Wycliffe publishes a vernacular Middle English Bible.
1390s	Korea institutes a broad-based Confucianism.

1400	The Bible is available in Asian and African languages.		Martin Luther places Apocrypha in an addendum printed between Old and New Testaments.
1409	The Tibetan Book of the Dead reaches the outside world after Jey Tsong Khapa initiates a spiritual renaissance in Tibet.	1535	Miles Coverdale produces a vernacular Bible translation.
1410	Ravi Das writes hymns that appear in the Granth.		William Tyndale produces a scholarly New Testament and portions of the Old Testament.
1456	Johann Gutenberg publishes the first machine-produced Bible.	1539	Miles Coverdale issues the Great Bible.
1475	Kabir, a Hindu poet-saint, writes devotional songs that appear in the Granth.		Richard Taverner completes the Matthew Bible, begun by John Rogers in 1537.
	Shlomo ben-Isaac's writings become the first book printed in Hebrew.	1540	Angad composes Hindu rituals for births and funerals and systematizes the Mohan Pothi, which is source material for the Granth.
1482	The complete Babylonian Talmud reaches print in Spain.	1543	Theologian Theodor Bibliander publishes the Koran in Latin.
	Elijah Bashyatchi summarizes the ten principles of Karaism.	1548	Moses Cordovero systematizes Jewish mysticism into a logical framework called *Pardes Rimmonim*.
1492	The Inquisition forces Jews from Iberia.	1549	The Book of Common Prayer is published.
1500s	The Ethiopian Book of the Dead is composed.	1550s	Isaac ben-Solomon Luria evolves the concept of *Tzimtzum*, God's deliberate self-limitation.
1516	Erasmus issues a New Testament in Latin translation.	1551	Robert Estienne separates chapters of the French New Testament into verses.
1517	Francisco Ximénez de Cisneros publishes the first Polyglot Bible.	1554	Historian Diego Reynos composes the Popol Vuh.
1520	The people of Baghdad raise a public monument to Nanak.	1560	The Geneva Bible is the first English Bible to number verses and chapters.
	Sikhism's line of beloved gurus begins with hymnologist Nanak, hybridizer of the Hindu and Muslim faiths.	1568	The Bishop's Bible is the first to carry the imprimatur of the English church.
1522	Joseph ben-Ephraim Karo systematizes the last authoritative Jewish law code, the Bet Yosef.	1570	The Iroquois League completes a constitution of 114 wampums.
1523	Catholic authorities in Central America burn hieroglyphic texts.	1571	Moses ben-Israel Isserles replaces Sephardic-centered interpretation with *Ha-Mappa*.
1524	The Jerusalem Talmud enters print in Venice.	1575	Ram Das founds the Hindu spiritual capital of Amritsar.
1528	Santes Pagninus divides the Old Testament chapters into verses.		
1530	Santes Pagninus prints the Koran in Arabic at Rome.		
1534	Erasmus translates the Bible into German.	1581	The Babylonian Talmud published in Basel takes the title Gemara.

1584	The *Halakhot Gedolot* is printed in Venice.
1593	Moravians publish the modern language Old and New Testament in the vernacular.
1595	Arjan issues the whole Sikh scripture as the Adi Granth.
1604	The Granth reaches its current length.
1605	Jahangir persecutes Sikhs and orders expunged all entries to the Adi Granth that disagree with the Muslim Koran and Hindu Vedas.
1606	Muslims torture and murder the Hindu martyr Arjan.
1610	Gregory Martin completes the Rheims-Douai Bible.
1611	The Apocrypha appear between the Old and New Testaments of the King James Bible.
1613	The Bible is available in Japanese.
1616	Jacob ben Isaac Ashkenazi converts Hebrew scripture into the Yiddish *Tz'enah u-Re'na*.
1647	André du Ryer completes a French version of the Koran.
1650	Tse-le Natsok Rangdröl summarizes bardo in *The Mirror of Mindfulness*.
	Japan's Confucian militarist Yamaga Soko educates samurai with strategies from the I Ching.
1661	John Eliot produces a Native American Bible.
1664	The Kojiki is first printed.
1675	Tegh Bahadur and five other Sikhs are martyred at Delhi.
1704	Gobind Singh expands the Hindu canon to include the hymns of Tegh Bahadur and republishes the canon as the *Guru Granth Sahib*.
1708	Sikhism's last beloved guru, Gobind Singh, dies.
1715	Bartholomäus Ziegenbalg issues a Bible in Tamil.
	Emperor K'ang Hsi issues an imperial version of the I Ching.

1722	The Popol Vuh resurfaces in Guatemala.
1734	George Sale translates the Koran into English.
1742	The Koran is translated into Dutch.
1748	English composer Georg Friedrich Handel captures the life of Susanna in an oratorio.
1750	*The Story of Karma Wangzinâ's Return from Death* relates the near-death experience of a righteous Buddhist woman.
1755	John Wesley, the father of Methodism, issues a New Testament.
1764	The Koran is translated into German.
1773	Chinese compilers finish *The Complete Library of the Four Treasures*.
1782	Robert Aitken publishes the King James Bible in Philadelphia.
1792	The Koran is translated into Russian.
1798	Moto-ori Norinaga reevaluates the Kojiki's moral, religious, and ethical precepts in the *Annotation of the Kojiki*.
1804	The British and Foreign Bible Society distributes inexpensive Bibles worldwide.
1814	The Koran is translated into Swedish.
1816	The American Bible Society spreads Bibles to the frontier.
1823	William Milne publishes a Chinese Bible in Canton.
1829	Oceania receives a Bible.
1830	Joseph Smith completes the Book of Mormon.
1833	The Chippewa version of the New Testament is completed.
1834	Adoniram Judson issues a Burmese Bible.
1835	Missionaries distribute a Hawaiian New Testament.
1837	Gotthold Salomon produces the Torah in high German.
1842	The Egyptian Book of the Dead is published in English.

1845	Isaac Leeser renders the Torah in English and Hebrew on facing pages.	1898	Mary Baker Eddy establishes the *Christian Science Quarterly, Christian Science versus Pantheism*, and the weekly *Christian Science Sentinel*.
1848	Elizabeth Cady Stanton organizes a committee of five women to compile the Woman's Bible.	1899	Chief John Arthur Gibson of the Six Nations Reserve dictates the origins of the Iroquois League to J. N. B. Hewiss of the Smithsonian Institution.
1849	British colonizers find the Granth manuscript in the Lahore treasury and restore it to Arjan's descendants.		
1850	Samuel Adjai Crowther produces a book of the New Testament in Yoruba.	1900	Leaders of the Six Nations Council on the Six Nations Reserve in Ontario compile the Chiefs' Version of the Iroquois League's Constitution.
1853	Rabbi Isaac Leeser publishes the standard American Jewish Bible.	1901	The American Standard Version is published.
	American Buddhism begins among Chinese laborers in the Southwest.	1902	The Koran is translated into Bulgarian.
1858	Thomas Hosuck Kang becomes the West's first Confucian missionary.	1908	Mary Baker Eddy launches the *Christian Science Monitor*.
1871	An Eskimo Bible reaches print in Labrador.	1917	Max L. Margolis edits *The Holy Scriptures According to the Masoretic Text*.
1875	Mary Baker Eddy publishes *Science and Health*.		Reformed Jews publish a bible based on the Masoretic original.
1876	Mary Baker Eddy publishes *The Science of Man*.	1924	Raphael M. Girard introduces the conceptual magnitude of Quichéan scripture.
1879	The Dakota Bible is completed.		
1883	Mary Baker Eddy founds the monthly *Christian Science Journal*.	1927	Walter Yeeling Evans-Wentz edits and annotates the Tibetan Book of the Dead.
1885	The English Revised Version of the Bible is completed.		The Turkish government disbands the Sufis.
1886	Mary Baker Eddy publishes *Christian Healing* and *The People's Idea of God*.	1929	Wallis Budge names the Ethiopian Book of the Dead.
	The Babylonian Talmud is standardized in Vilna.	1930	An English Muslim, Muhammad Marmaduke Pickthall, publishes *The Meaning of the Glorious Koran*.
1887	Mary Baker Eddy publishes *Unity of Good*.		
1891	Mary Baker Eddy publishes *Retrospection and Introspection, No and Yes*, and *Pulpit and Press, Rudimental Divine Science*.	1932	*Black Elk Speaks: The Life Story of a Holy Man of the Oglala* becomes the first written work of Lakota scripture.
1893	Mary Baker Eddy publishes *Christ and Christmas*.	1939	Richard Bell reconstructs verses of the Koran in tabular form.
1894	Mary Baker Eddy completes *Poems*.	1941	William N. Fenton of the Bureau of American Ethnology, aided by Chief Simeon Gibson, translates the Gibson Version of the Iroquois League's Constitution into English.
1895	Mary Baker Eddy issues *The Manual of the Mother Church*.		
1896	Mary Baker Eddy finishes *The First Church of Christ, Scientist*.		

1946	Paul Anthony Wilson publishes *The White Roots of Peace.*
	The Dead Sea Scrolls are discovered at Wadi Qumran.
1947	Eliezer Lipa Sukenik purchases the scroll of The War between the Children of Light and the Children of Darkness.
1948	Esotericism of the Popol Vuh reveals aspects of astronomy, the calendar, and symbolism.
	Joseph Epes Brown issues Lakota scripture in *The Sacred Pipe.*
1949	Captain Philippe Lippens launches an expedition to Qumran.
	Yigael Yadin publishes *Hidden Scrolls from the Judaean Desert.*
1951	John Neihardt publishes memoirs of Black Elk in *When the Tree Flowered.*
	Ta'amireh tribesmen locate more of the Dead Sea Scrolls.
	The Book of Ordinances is published.
1952	An expedition to Murabba'at yields more of the Dead Sea Scrolls.
1953	Arthur J. Arberry translates the Koran from the original Arabic.
1954	The Dead Sea Scrolls are offered for sale in the *Wall Street Journal.*
1955	Eliezer L. Sukenik publishes *The Dead Sea Scrolls of the Hebrew University.*
1956	Najib Albina secures photos of the Dead Sea Scrolls during the Arab-Israeli War.
1959	Josef T. Milik publishes *Ten Years of Discovery in the Wilderness of Judea* (1959).
	The Ethiopian church severs its relationship with the Coptic church.
1960	J. M. Allegro publishes *The Treasure of the Copper Scroll.*
1961	André Dupont-Sommer coordinates Essene history and philosophy in *The Essene Writings from Qumran.*
1962	The Jewish Publication Society issues the Torah in simplified language.

	Yigael Yadin publishes *The Message of the Scrolls.*
1965	Frederick John Kiesler and Armand Bartos complete the Shrine of the Book in Jerusalem.
	James A. Sanders publishes *Discoveries in the Judaean Desert of Jordan, IV: The Psalms Scroll from Qumran Cave 11.*
1972	Ancient copies of the Koran are found in Yemen.
1974	Eugene Jeffrey Gold writes and illustrates *The Original American Book of the Dead.*
1975	Detlef Lauf issues *Secret Doctrines of the Tibetan Books of the Dead,* which elucidates Tibetan theology.
1981	John Marco Allegro publishes *The Mystery of the Dead Sea Scrolls Revealed.*
	Gerd-R. Puin oversees restoration of the ancient Koran texts.
1984	Raymond J. DeMallie reconstructs Enid Neihardt's notes on Black Elk as *The Sixth Grandfather.*
1985	A vernacular Hebrew Bible, Tanakh: The Holy Scriptures, employs idiomatic English.
1988	John Strugnell publishes *A Preliminary Concordance to the Hebrew and Aramaic Fragments from Qumran Caves II to X.*
1989	The Ayatollah Ruhollah Khomeini condemns Salman Rushdie for writing *The Satanic Verses,* which allegedly defames the Koran, Islam, and the prophet Muhammad.
1991	The Biblical Archaeology Society publishes *A Facsimile Edition of the Dead Sea Scrolls.*
	The Huntington Library liberates a series of photographs of the Dead Sea Scrolls for public use.
	Hebrew Union College reconfigures one of the unpublished Dead Sea Scrolls.
1992	Sogyal Rinpoche issues *The Tibetan Book of Living and Dying.*

1993   E. J. Brill and Emanuel Tov publish *The Dead Sea Scrolls on Microfiche.*

Michael F. Steltenkamp publishes a definitive biography, *Black Elk: Holy Man of the Oglala.*

1995   Hilda Neihardt's memoir, *Black Elk and Flaming Rainbow,* describes the Native American hoop-and-spear game.

1997   H.-C. Graf von Bothmer makes 35,000 photos on microfilm of ancient Koranic texts.

1999   Stephen Hodge produces *The Illustrated Tibetan Book of the Dead.*

Victor Montejo composes *Popol Vuh: A Sacred Book of the Maya,* a simplified version of native myth.

Bibliography

Abbott, Walter M., et al. *The Bible Reader.* New York: Bruce, 1969.

Abid, Abdelazia. "Memory of the World: Preserving Our Documentary Heritage," *UNESCO*, February 1996.

Abrahams, Israel. *Jewish Life in the Middle Ages.* Philadelphia: Jewish Publication Society of America, 1896.

"Achaemenid Royal Inscriptions." http://www-oi.uchicago.edu/OI/PROJ/ARI/ARI.html, 1998.

Achaya, K. T. *Indian Food: A Historical Companion.* Calcutta: Oxford University Press, 1998.

Adamson, Stephen, ed. *Mother Earth, Father Sky: Native American Myth.* London: Duncan Baird, 1997.

Adventures in World Literature. New York: Harcourt, Brace & World, 1970.

Agarwal, Satya P. "Review: The Social Role of the Gita: How and Why," *Journal of Asian Studies*, November 1, 1996, 1024.

Agler, Richard D. "Today's Disputations." http://uahc.org/congs/fl/fl002/rda/990326.html, 1999.

Ahlstrom, Sydney E. *A Religious History of the American People.* New Haven, Conn.: Yale University Press, 1972.

Aitken, Robert. "On Zen Teaching," *Diamond Sangha Newsletter*, July 1991, 1–2.

Albertson, Edward. *I Ching for the Millions.* Los Angeles: Sherbourne Press, 1969.

Alexander, David, and Pat Alexander, eds. *Eerdmans' Handbook to the World's Religions.* Grand Rapids, Mich.: William B. Eerdmans Publishing, 1982.

Alexy, Trudi. *The Mezuzah in the Madonna's Foot.* New York: Simon & Schuster, 1993.

Al-Kadi, Ahmed. "The Prophet's Marriage to Khadijah." http://www.jannah.org/sisters/khadija.html.

"Al-Mizan." http://www.almizan.org.

Alsberg, Henry G., ed. *The American Guide.* New York: Hastings, 1949.

American Decades (CD-ROM). Detroit: Gale Research, 1998.

"Ancient History Sourcebook: The Precepts of Ptah-Hotep, ca. 2200 B. C." http://www. fordham.edu/halsall/ancient/ptahhotep.html, 1998.

"Ancient Indus: Introduction." http://www.harappa.com/har/harrigveda1.html, 1996.

Anderson, Bernhard W. *Understanding the Old Testament.* Englewood Cliffs, N.J.: Prentice-Hall, 1966.

Anderson, Vern. "A Challenge to Origins of the Book of Mormon," *Los Angeles Times*, June 19, 1993.

The Apocrypha of the Old Testament. New York: American Bible Society, n.d.

Arberry, Arthur J., trans. *The Koran Interpreted.* New York: Macmillan, 1970.

"Archaeology Explorer." http://www.iversonsoftware.com/business/archaeologyLepsius.htm.

Armstrong, Karen. *A History of God.* New York: Alfred A. Knopf, 1993.

Asimov, Isaac. *Asimov's Guide to the Bible.* New York: Wings Books, 1981.

Atkinson, Donald. "The Origin and Date of the 'Sator' Word Square," *Journal of Ecclesiastical History*, January–April 1951, 1–18.

Augustine. *The Confessions of St. Augustine.* Chicago: Moody, 1981.

"Avesta — Zoroastrian Archives." http://www.avesta.org/avesta.html.

Baer, Yitzhak. *A History of the Jews in Christian Spain.* Philadelphia: Jewish Publication Society of America, 1961.

Ball, Ann. *A Handbook of Catholic Sacramentals.* Manassas, Va.: Trinity Communications, 1994.

Ballou, Robert O., ed. *World Bible.* New York: Viking, 1944.

Barnstone, Willis, ed. *The Other Bible.* San Francisco: HarperCollins, 1984.

Bartlett, John, ed. *Familiar Quotations.* Boston: Little, Brown, 1992.

"Battle of Wounded Me," *New York Times*, July 10, 1994.

Baugh, Albert C. *A History of the English Language.* New York: Appleton-Century-Crofts, 1957.

_____. *A Literary History of England.* New York: Appleton-Century-Crofts, 1948.

Bawer, Bruce. *Stealing Jesus: How Fundamentalism Betrays Christianity.* New York: Crown, 1997.

Bellafante, G. "Broken Peace," *Time*, July 31, 1995, 62.

Bentley, James. *A Calendar of Saints.* London: Little, Brown, 1993.

Berry, Gerald L. *Religions of the World.* New York: Barnes & Noble, 1956.

"Bhagavad Gita." http://www.bhagavad-gita.org, 1998.

"Bhagavad Gita: The Kingdom of God." http://www.geocities.com/Athens/2108/download.htm.

Bhaskarananda, Swami. *The Essentials of Hinduism.* Seattle: Viveka, 1994.

Biblia Sacra: Vulgatae Editionis. Roma: Editiones Paulinae, 1957.

"Biblical Canons." http://gbgm-umc.org/umw/bible/canon.stm.

"Biography Resource Center." http://galenet.com, 1999.

Bishop, Peter, and Michael Darton. *The Encyclopedia of World Faiths: An Illustrated Survey of the World's Living Religions.* London: MacDonald, 1987.

Black Elk, Wallace, and William S. Lyon. *Black Elk: The Sacred Ways of a Lakota.* San Francisco: HarperCollins, 1990.

"Black Elk, Holy Man of the Oglala Sioux." http://www.indians.org/prayer/blackelk.html.

"Black Elk's Prayer." http://www.geocities.com/Athens/Olympus/3025/blkelkp.htm.

"Black Elk: The Family Speaks." http://hometown.aol.com/Kels3984/Elk.html.

Bogan, Mary Inez. *Vocabulary and Style of the Soliloquies and Dialogues of St. Augustine.* Cleveland, Ohio: Zubal, 1984.

Bonchek, Avigdor. *Studying the Torah: A Guide to In-Depth Interpretation.* Northvale, N.J.: Jason Aronson, 1996.

Bono. Introduction to *Selections from the Book of Psalms.* New York: Grove, 1999.

"The Book of Abraham Revisited." http://www.xmission.com/~research/about/abraham.htm.

The Book of Mormon. Salt Lake City, Utah: Church of Jesus Christ of Latter-day Saints, 1981.

"The Book of the Dead." http://rmc.library.cornell.edu/Paper-exhibit/paper2.html.

Boorstin, Daniel J. *The Discoverers: A History of Man's Search to Know His World and Himself.* New York: Vintage, 1983.

Bouquet, A. C. *Sacred Books of the World.* London: Cassell, 1954.

Bowder, Diana, ed. *Who's Who in the Greek World.* New York: Washington Square Press, 1982.

_____. *Who's Who in the Roman World.* New York: Washington Square Press, 1980.

Bowker, John, ed. *The Oxford Dictionary of World Religions.* Oxford: Oxford University Press, 1997.

Braden, Charles S. *The World's Religions.* Nashville, Tenn.: Abingdon, 1954.

Bradley, S. A. J., ed. *Anglo-Saxon Poetry.* London: J. M. Dent, 1995.

"A Brief History of Compilation of the Qur'an." *Perspectives,* August–September 1997.

Brockett, Oscar G. *History of the Theatre.* Boston: Allyn & Bacon, 1968.

Broderick, Robert C., ed. *The Catholic Encyclopedia.* Nashville, Tenn.: Thomas Nelson, 1987.

Broderick, Robert C. *Historic Churches of the United States.* New York: Wilfred Funk, 1958.

Brooke, Barbara. *The Sioux.* Vero Beach, Fla.: Rourke, 1989.

Brown, Alban. *Lives of the Saints.* New York: Barnes & Noble, 1997.

Brown, Dee. *Bury My Heart at Wounded Knee.* New York: Henry Holt, 1970.

Brown, Joseph Epes. *The Sacred Pipe.* Norman: University of Oklahoma Press, 1989.

Brown, Norman O. *Hermes the Thief: The Evolution of a Myth.* New York: Vintage, 1947.

Brown, P. R. F. "The Rig Veda." http://www.magna.com.au/~prfbrown/rig_veda.html, 1996.

Bryant, Arthur. *The Medieval Foundation of England.* Garden City, N.Y.: Doubleday, 1967.

Buchanan, Paul D. *Historic Places of Worship.* Jefferson, N.C.: McFarland, 1999.

Budge, E. A. Wallis. *The Bandlet of Righteousness: An Ethiopian Book of the Dead.* London: Luzac, 1929.

_____. Introduction to *The Book of the Dead. The Hieroglyphic Transcript and English Translation of the Papyrus of Ani.* Avenel, N.J.: Gramercy, 1960.

_____. *Egyptian Religion.* Avenel, N.J.: Gramercy, 1959.

Budge, E. A. Wallis, trans. "Papyrus of Ani: Egyptian Book of the Dead." http://www.sas.upenn.edu/African_Studies/Books/Papyrus_Ani.html, 1993.

Burckhardt, Titus, trans. *Letters of a Sufi Master.* Middlesex, England: Perennial, 1969.

Burger, Bruce. *Esoteric Anatomy: The Body as Consciousness.* Berkeley, Calif.: North Atlantic Books, 1998.

Burke, Vernon J. *Wisdom from St. Augustine.* South Bend, Ind.: University of Notre Dame, 1984.

Burman, Thomas. "Tafsir and Translation: Traditional Arabic Qur'an Exegesis and the Latin Qur'ans of Robert of Ketton and Mark of Toledo," *Speculum* 73, 1998.

Butler, Alban. *Lives of the Saints.* New York: Barnes & Noble, 1997.

Buttrick, George Arthur, ed. *The Interpreter's Dictionary of the Bible.* New York: Abingdon, 1962.

Byrom, Thomas. *The Dhammapada: The Sayings of the Buddha.* New York: Alfred A. Knopf, 1976.

Cahill, Thomas. Introduction to *The Gospel According to Luke.* New York: Grove, 1999.

Cantor, George. *North American Indian Landmarks: A Traveler's Guide.* Detroit: Gale Research, 1993.

Cantor, Norman F., ed. *The Civilization of the Middle Ages.* New York: Harper Perennial, 1993.

_____. *The Jewish Experience.* New York: HarperCollins, 1996.

_____. *The Medieval Reader.* New York: HarperCollins, 1994.

Carlyle, Thomas. "Heroes and Hero Worship." http://library.thinkquest.org/19300/data/Etexts/heroes.htm.

Carmody, Denise Lardner, and John Tully Carmody. *Native American Religions: An Introduction.* New York: Paulist Press, 1993.

Carpenter, Gilbert C., Sr., and Gilbert C. Carpenter, Jr. *Mary Baker Eddy: Her Spiritual Footsteps.* Santa Clarita, Calif.: Pasadena Press, 1985.

"The Catholic Encyclopedia." http://www.csn.net/advent/cathen/12493a.htm, 1997.

"Catholic Online Saints." http://www.catholiconline.com/saints.html, 1997.

Catlin, George. *North American Indians.* New York: Viking-Penguin 1989.

Cavendish, Richard, ed. *Man, Myth & Magic.* New York: Marshall Cavendish, 1970.

"Center for Buddhist Studies, Columbia University." http://www.cc.columbia.edu/cu/religion/cbshistory.html.

Chaliand, Gérard, and Jean-Pierre Rageau. *The Penguin Atlas of Diasporas.* New York: Viking, 1995.

Champagne, Duane, ed. *Chronology of Native North American History.* Detroit: Gale Research, 1994.

_____. *Native North American Almanac.* Detroit: Gale Research, 1998.

Charles, Eleanor. "Seasonal Songs of Many Faiths," *New York Times,* December 12, 1999.

Chase, Franklin H. "Chronological Index of Onondaga History," *Syracuse Journal,* March 2, 1903.

Ch'en, Kenneth K. S. *Buddhism: The Light of Asia.* Woodbury, N.Y.: Barron's, 1968.

Chwat, Ezra. "Great Rabbis of the Muslim Empire." http://www.israel.org/mfa/go.asp?MFAH01vt0, 1999.

Clark, Peter. *Zoroastrianism: An Introduction to an Ancient Faith.* London: Sussex, 1998.

Clark, R. T. Rundle. *Myth and Symbol in Ancient Egypt.* London: Thames & Hudson, 1978.

Clifton, Chas S. *Encyclopedia of Heresies and Heretics.* Santa Barbara, Calif.: ABC-Clio, 1992.

Coates, Eyler Robert. "The Jefferson Bible." http://www. angelfire.com/co/JeffersonBible, 1999.

Cohn-Sherbok, Lavinia. *Who's Who in Christianity*. Chicago: Routledge, 1998.

Collier, John. *Indians of the Americas*. New York: New American Library, 1947.

Collins, John James. *Native American Religions: A Geographical Survey*. Lewiston, Dyfed, Wales: Edwin Mellen Press, 1991.

Comay, Joan, and Lavinia Cohn-Sherbok. *Who's Who in Jewish History*. London: Routledge, 1995.

"The Commentary of Rabbenu Gershom." http://www.acs. ucalgary.ca/~elsegal/TalmudMap/OtherComs.html#Gershom.

Confucius. *The Analects of Confucius*. New York: HarperCollins, 1992.

Contemporary Heroes and Heroines. Detroit: Gale Research, 1998.

Conze, Edward, I. B. Horner, David Snellgrove, and Arthur Waley, trans. and eds. *Buddhist Texts through the Ages*. Oxford: Oneworld, 1995.

Cooper, J. C., ed. *Dictionary of Christianity*. Chicago: Fitzroy Dearborn, 1996.

Coulter, Charles Russell, and Patricia Turner. *Encyclopedia of Ancient Deities*. Jefferson, N.C.: McFarland, 2000.

Crone, Patricia, and Michael Cook. *Hagarism: The Making of the Islamic World*. Cambridge: Cambridge University Press, 1977.

Crystal, David. *The Cambridge Encyclopedia of the English Language*. Cambridge: Cambridge University Press, 1995.

Cummings, Patricia J. "Preserving Sacred Sites," *Earth Island Journal*, Spring 1993, 28.

Cunningham, Lawrence S. "Preferred Providers: How the Church Chooses Its Doctors," *U.S. Catholic*, April 1998, 17–23.

Curtis, Edward S. *Chiefs and Warriors*. Boston: Bulfinch, 1996.

_____. *The North American Indian*. Boston: Bulfinch, 1997.

_____. *Native Family*. Boston: Bulfinch, 1996.

Curtius, Ernst Robert. *European Literature and the Latin Middle Ages*. Princeton, N.J.: Princeton University Press, 1953.

"Czech Bible of Kralice." http://www.fee.vutbr.cz/UIVT/ homes/michal/kr, 1998.

Dakin, Edwin F. *Mrs. Eddy: The Biography of a Virginal Mind*. Magnolia, Mass.: Peter Smith, 1990.

Darmesteter, James. "Vendidad: Book of Law." http://www. primenet.com/~subru/Zoroastrianism.html#anchor 365316, 1998.

"The Dead Sea Scrolls Project." http://www-oi.uchicago.edu/ OI/PROJ/SCR/Scrolls.html, 2000.

"Dead Sea Scrolls Still a Puzzle after 50 Years," *CNN News*, July 26, 1997.

Delehaye, Hippolyte. *The Legends of the Saints*. Dublin: Four Courts Press, 1955.

Deloria, Vine, Jr. *The Metaphysics of Modern Existence*. New York: Harper & Row, 1979.

Demaitre, Luke. "The Relevance of Futility: Jordanus de Turre (fl. 1313–1335) on the Treatment of Leprosy," *Bulletin on the History of Medicine*, 1996.

DeMallie, Raymond J., ed. *The Sixth Grandfather: Black Elk's Teachings Given to John G. Neihardt*. Lincoln: University of Nebraska Press, 1984.

Demke, Jared. "Davidic Chiasmus and Parallelisms." http:// www.geocities.com/CapitolHill/3500/davbom.html, 2000.

Deur, Lynne. *Indian Chiefs*. Minneapolis, Minn.: Lerner, 1972.

Devereaux, Paul. *Secrets of Ancient and Sacred Places*. London: Blandford, 1992.

Dhabar, Ervad Bamanji Nusserwanji. *The Persian Rivayats of Hormazyar Framarz*. Bombay: K. R. Cama Oriental Institute, 1932.

Dolan, Josephine A. *History of Nursing*. Philadelphia: W. B. Saunders, 1968.

Dobie, J. Frank. "Guide to Life and Literature of the Southwest," http://www.islandmm.com/llsw/llswp.htm, 1996.

Doctorow, E. L. Introduction to *The First Book of Moses, Called Genesis*. New York: Grove, 1999.

Durant, Will. *The Life of Greece*. New York: Simon & Schuster, 1939.

"Early Bilingual Lexica." http://www.epas.utoronto.ca:8080/ ~wulfric/edicta/shaw/a_n.htm#note23.

"E. A. Wallis Budge." http://emuseum.mankato.msus.edu/information/biography/abcde/budge_eawallis.html.

Eck, Diana L. *On Common Ground: Columbia University Press* (CD-ROM). New York: Columbia University Press, 1994.

Eddy, Mary Baker. *Miscellaneous Writings, 1883–1896*. Boston: n.p., 1924.

_____. *Science and Health with Key to the Scriptures*. Boston: n.p., 1934.

_____. *Science and Health with Key to the Scriptures*. Boston: First Church of Christ, Scientist, 1994.

"The 850th Anniversary of the Scientific and Philosophic Work 'De Essentiis' by Herman Dalmatin." http://www.tel.hr/ marke1/83.html.

Eisele, John C. "Modern Arabic," *Journal of the American Oriental Society*, April 15, 1997.

Eisenman, Robert, and Michael Wise. *The Dead Sea Scrolls Uncovered*. Shaftesbury, Dorset, England: Element Books, 1992.

Ekstrom, Reynolds R. *The New Concise Catholic Dictionary*. Mystic, Conn.: Twenty-Third Publications, 1995.

Eliade, Mircea, ed. *The Encyclopedia of Religion*. New York: Macmillan, 1987.

_____. *Essential Sacred Writings from Around the World*. San Francisco: HarperCollins, 1967.

Ellis, Normandi. "Kheperi, Ra, Atum: The Light Forms of Birth, Death, and Rebirth," *Parabola*, November 1998, 6–13.

El-Zein, Amira. "Spiritual Consumption in the United States: The Rumi Phenomenon," *Islam and Christian-Muslim Relations*, March 1, 2000, 71.

Encyclopedia Americana (CD-ROM). Danbury, Conn.: Grolier, 1999.

Encyclopedia Britannica, http://www.eb.com.

Encyclopedia of World Biography. Detroit: Gale Research, 1998.

Evans-Wentz, W. Y. *The Tibetan Book of the Dead*. New York: Oxford University Press, 1960.

"Exploring Ancient World Cultures: Islam." http://eawc.evansville.edu/ispage.htm.

Farmer, David Hugh. *The Oxford Dictionary of Saints*. New York: Oxford University Press, 1992.

Feder, Lillian. *The Meridian Handbook of Classical Literature*. New York: New American Library, 1986.

Ferguson, John. *The Religions of the Roman Empire*. Ithaca, N.Y.: Cornell University, 1970.

Feuerstein, Georg. "Tantrism and Neotantrism," *Moksha Journal*, 1996.

"Fez." http://www.ort.org/edu/rolnik/halacha/fez.htm.

Fine, John V. A., Jr. *The Late Medieval Balkans*. Ann Arbor: University of Michigan, 1994.

Fingarette, Herbert. "Who Is Confucius." http://www.wam. umd.edu/~tkangwho.html.

Finkelman, Eliezer. "Shemini: Jewish Law Allows Modest

Drinking of Wine." http://www.shamash.org/jb/bk 980424/torah.htm, 1998.

"The First Church of Christ, Scientist." http://www.tfccs.com/GV/TMC/TMCMain.html, 1999.

"The First Master." http://www.sikhs.org/guru1.htm.

Fischer, Louis. *Gandhi — His Life and Message for the World*. New York: Mentor, 1954.

Fishwick, D. "On the Origin of the Rotas-Sator Square," *Harvard Theological Review* 57, 1964.

Flaceliere, Robert. *A Literary History of Greece*. New York: New American Library, 1962.

Forbes, Dennis C. "Giants of Egyptology," *KMT: A Modern Journal of Ancient Egypt,* Summer 1995.

Foss, Michael. *People of the First Crusade*. New York: Arcade, 1997.

Foster, John L., trans. *Echoes of Egyptian Voices: An Anthology of Ancient Egyptian Poetry*. Norman: University of Oklahoma Press, 1992.

Fox, James A. "Maya Mythology and Multimedia: Using Each to Teach the Other," *Technological Horizons in Education Journal*, December 1995, 64–66.

Frazer, James George. *The Golden Bough*. New York: Macmillan, 1947.

Frazier, David. Introduction to *The Book of Job*. New York: Grove, 1999.

Freeman, David Noel, ed. *The Anchor Bible Dictionary*. New York: Doubleday, 1992.

Frost, S. E., Jr., ed. *The Sacred Writings of the World's Great Religions*. New York: McGraw-Hill, 1972.

Frye, Richard N. *The Heritage of Persia*. Costa Mesa, Calif.: Mazda, 1993.

Gabel, John B., and Charles B. Wheeler. *The Bible as Literature*. New York: Oxford University Press, 1990.

Gall, Robert S. "Kami and Daimon: A Cross-Cultural Reflection on What Is Divine," *Philosophy East and West*, January 1999, 63.

Gard, Richard A. *Buddhism*. New York: George Braziller, 1961.

Garraty, John A., and Mark C. Carnes, eds. *American National Biography*. New York: Oxford University Press, 1999.

Geissinger, Aiesha. "Orientalists Plot against the Qur'an under the Guise of Academic Study and Archive Preservation," *Muslimedia*, May 16–31, 1999.

Gentz, William H., ed. *The Dictionary of Bible and Religion*. Nashville, Tenn.: Abingdon, 1973.

George, Leonard. *The Encyclopedia of Heresies and Heretics*. London: Robson, 1995.

Gethin, Rupert. "Cosmology and Meditation: From the Agganna-Sutta to the Mahayana," *History of Religions*, February 1997, 183–217.

Ghazali. *The Alchemy of Happiness*. New York: Orientalia, 1964.

Gibb, H. A. R. *Arabic Literature: An Introduction*. Oxford: Oxford University Press, 1963.

Gibson, Clare. *Sacred Symbols*. Rowayton, Conn.: Saraband, 1998.

Gilson, Etienne. *The Christian Philosophy of St. Augustine*. New York: Hippocrene, 1983.

Girard, Raphael. *Esotericism of the Popol Vuh*. Wheaton, Ill.: Theosophical University Press, 1979. www.theosociety.org/pasadena/popolvuh/pv-hp.htm

"The Gita as It Is." *Hinduism Today*, August 31, 1997, 54.

Goeringer, Conrad. "Sun, Sand, Water — The Ecstasy of the Beach," *American Atheist*, July 1998.

"Golden Age of Muslim Spain." http://www.jewishgates.org/history/jewhis/gold.stm.

Goldman, Francisco. Introduction to *The Gospel According to Matthew*. New York: Grove, 1999.

Goring, Rosemary, ed. *Larousse Dictionary of Writers*. New York: Larousse, 1994.

Grant, Robert M. *Gnosticism*. New York: Harper & Brothers, 1961.

Graves, Robert. Introduction to *New Larousse Encyclopedia of Mythology*. Paris: Prometheus, 1968.

"The Great Men of Croatian Science." http://jagor.srce.hr/zuh/English/velik_e.htm.

"The Great Transcendentalist, Henry David Thoreau." http://www.gosai.com/chaitanya/saranagati/html/nmj_articles/east_west/east_west_2.html.

Greenspan, Karen. *The Timetables of Women's History*. New York: Touchstone, 1994.

Gregory, Sophfronia Scott. "Saints Preserve Us," *Time*, June 13, 1994.

Griffith, Ralph T. H., trans. *The Hymns of the Rig Veda*. Benares: E. J. Lazarus, 1892.

Grinnell, George Bird. *Cheyenne Campfire*. Lincoln: University of Nebraska Press 1971.

Groothuis, Douglas. "The Gnostic Gospels: Are They Authentic?" *Christian Research Journal*, Winter 1991, 15ff.

Grossman, David. Introduction to *The Second Book of Moses, Called Exodus*. New York: Grove, 1999.

"Guru Gobind Singh." http://www.alphalink.com.au/~harry/Intro/103.htm

"Guru Granth Sahib on CD-ROM," *India Currents*, November 30, 1995.

Gutiérriez, Ramón A., and Geneviève Fabre. *Feasts and Celebrations in North American Ethnic Communities*. Albuquerque: University of New Mexico Press, 1995.

Gutjahr, Paul. "The Golden Bible in the Bible's Golden Age: The Book of Mormon and Antebellum Print Culture," *American Transcendental Quarterly*, December 1, 1998, 275ff.

Haberfield, Shulie. "Jerusalem Day: Roving through the Rova," *Jerusalem Post*, September 29, 1998.

Habu, Junko, and Clare Fawcett. "Jomon Archaeology and the Representation of Japanese Origins," *Antiquity*, September 1999, 587.

Hadas, Moses. *Ancilla to Classical Reading*. New York: Columbia University Press, 1954.

Hallam, Elizabeth, ed. *Saints: Who They Are and How They Help You*. New York: Simon & Schuster, 1994.

Hamann, Byron. "Myths of Ancient Mexico," *Hispanic American Historical Review*, November 1, 1999, 740–741.

Hammond, N. G. L., and H. H. Scullard, eds. *The Oxford Classical Dictionary*. Oxford: Clarendon, 1992.

Hancock, Graham. *Fingerprints of the Gods*. New York: Crown, 1995.

"Handel's Oratorio Susanna." http://bruichladdich.dcs.st-and.ac.uk/HandelWWW/Oratorios/HWV66Susanna/ActIII.html.

Hannah, Barry. Introduction to *The Gospel According to Mark*. New York: Grove, 1999.

Harpur, James. *Revelations: The Medieval World*. New York: Henry Holt, 1995.

Harris, Maurice H. *History of the Mediaeval Jews*. New York: Bloch, 1924.

Harrod, Howard. *Renewing the World: Plains Indian Religion and Morality*. Tucson: University of Arizona Press, 1987.

Hartshorn, Chris B. *A Commentary on the Book of Mormon*. Independence, Mo.: Herald, 1966.

Hastings, James, ed. *Encyclopedia of Religion and Ethics*. New York: Charles Scribner's Sons, 1951.

Hathorn, Richmond Y. *Tragedy, Myth and Mystery*. Bloomington: Indiana University Press, 1966.

Heer, Friedrich. *The Medieval World*. New York: Mentor, 1961.

Heffernan, Thomas J. *Sacred Biography: Saints and Their Biographers in the Middle Ages*. Oxford: Oxford University Press, 1988.

Heinerman, John. *Spiritual Wisdom of the Native Americans*. San Rafael, Calif.: Cassandra, 1989.

"Herman Dalmata." http://www.studiacroatica.com/revistas/125/1250300.htm.

Highet, Gilbert. *The Classical Tradition*. Oxford: Clarendon, 1949.

Hindmarsh, D. Bruce. "The Moravian Church in England, 1728–1760," *Church History*, June 1, 1999, 471.

"Hinduism," *Canada and the World Backgrounder*, December 1, 1999, 40–43.

Hinman, Al. "Dead Sea Scrolls Alive on Computer," *CNN News*, April 18, 1996.

Hinnells, John R., ed. *The Penguin Dictionary of Religions*. London: Penguin, 1984.

Hiriyanna, M. *Outlines of Indian Philosophy*. London: George Allen & Unwin, 1932.

Historic World Leaders. Detroit: Gale Research, 1994.

Hodge, Stephen. *The Illustrated Tibetan Book of the Dead*. New York: Sterling, 1999.

Hodges, Miles. "Philosophers, Scientists, and Theologians of the Middle Ages." http://www2.cybernex.net/~mhodges/reference/middle-ages.htm, 1999.

Holler, Clyde. *Black Elk's Religion: The Sun Dance and Lakota Catholicism*. Syracuse, N.Y.: Syracuse University Press, 1995.

Hollister, C. Warren. *Medieval Europe: A Short History*. New York: McGraw-Hill, 1994.

Holmes, George, ed. *The Oxford Illustrated History of Medieval Europe*. Oxford: Oxford University Press, 1988.

The Holy Bible (King James Version). Iowa Falls, Iowa: World Bible Publishers, 1986.

"Holy Qur'an Sources on the Internet." http://www.quran.org.uk, 1999.

"Homeric Hymns." http://classics.mit.edu.

Hooker, Richard. "The Iroquois League." http://www.wsu.edu/~dee/CULAMRCA/IRLEAGUE.HTM, 1996.

Hoover, Thomas. *The Zen Experience*. New York: New American Library, 1980.

Hope, Murray. *Practical Egyptian Magic*. New York: St. Martin's, 1984.

Hopper, R. J. *The Early Greeks*. New York: Harper & Row, 1977.

Hornstein, Lillian, et al., eds. *The Reader's Companion to World Literature*. New York: New American Library, 1973.

Howarth, Sam, and Enrique R. Lamadrid. *Pilgrimage to Chimayó*. Santa Fe: Museum of New Mexico Press, 1999.

Howatson, M. C., ed. *The Oxford Companion to Classical Literature*. Oxford: Oxford University Press, 1991.

"How to Lose Your History," *Africa News Service*, April 9, 1999.

Hultkrantz, Ake. *Native Religions of North America: The Power of Visions and Fertility*. Prospect Heights, Ill.: Waveland, 1987.

Hunt, Tony. *Teaching and Learning Latin in Thirteenth-Century England*. Woodbridge, Suffolk, England: D. S. Brewer, 1991.

The Hymnal of the United Church of Christ. Philadelphia: United Church Press, 1974.

Ibrahim, Ezzedin, and Denys Johnson-Davies, eds. *Forty Hadith*. Jakarta: Dar al-ilm, n.d.

Idel, Moshe. "Language, Torah, and Hermeneutics." http://www.sunypress.edu/sunyp/backads/html/idellanguage.html, 1988.

Ions, Veronica. *Egyptian Mythology*. London: Hamlyn, 1968.

"The Iroquois Constitution." http://www.law.ou.edu/hist/iroquois.html, 1999.

"Islamic References." http://www.sijpa.org/references.htm.

Jackson, Samuel Macauley, ed. *The New Schaff-Herzog Encyclopedia of Religious Knowledge*. Grand Rapids, Mich.: Baker Book House, 1969.

"Japanese Creation Myth." http://www.wsu.edu:8080/~wldciv/world_civ_reader/world_civ_reader_1/kojiki.html, 1998.

Jeffrey, David Lyle, ed. *A Dictionary of Biblical Tradition in English Literature*. Grand Rapids, Mich.: William B. Eerdmans, 1992.

Jepson, Toby. "Does the Bible or the Qur'an Have Stronger Historical Corroboration?" http://debate.org.uk/topics/history/qur_hist.htm.

"The Jewish Controversy over Calendar Postponements." http://www.abcog.org/saadia.htm.

Johansen, Bruce E., and Donald A. Grinde, eds. *The Encyclopedia of Native American Biography*. New York: Da Capo, 1998.

John, De Witt. *The Christian Science Way of Life*. Boston: Christian Science Publishing Society, 1962.

Johnson, Allen, and Dumas Malone, eds. *Dictionary of American Biography*. New York: Charles Scribner's Sons, 1930.

Johnson, Charles. Introduction to *Proverbs*. New York: Grove, 1999.

Johnson, J. W., ed. *Utopian Literature: A Selection*. New York: Modern Library, 1968.

Johnson, Kevin Orlin. *Expressions of the Catholic Faith*. New York: Ballantine, 1994.

Josephus: Complete Works. Grand Rapids, Mich.: Kregel, 1960.

"Judaism." http://www.religioustolerance.org.

Kaltenbach, Chris. "The Gospel According to Smith," *Baltimore Sun*, November 26, 1999.

Kang, Thomas Hosuck. "Confucianism." http://www.wam.umd.edu/~tkang, 1999.

"Karl Richard Lepsius." http://www.kv5.com/html/index_lepsius.html.

Kato, Shuichi. *A History of Japanese Literature: The Years of Isolation*. New York: Kodansha International, 1979.

Kee, Howard Clark, Franklin W. Young, and Karlfried Froehlich. *Understanding the New Testament*. Englewood Cliffs, N.J.: Prentice-Hall, 1965.

"Keepers of the Sacred Traditions of Pipemakers." http://www.bnd.net/pipemakers.

Kemp, Peter, ed. *The Oxford Companion to Ships and the Sea*. Oxford: Oxford University Press, 1988.

Ketchum, Richard M. *The American Heritage Book of Great Historic Places*. New York: American Heritage, 1957.

Khalifa, Mohammad. "Translation — Tried and True?" http://users.erols.com/ameen/translate.htm.

Khalifa, Rashad. "The Authorized English Translation of the Quran." http://www.submission.org/suras/sura_table.htm, 1999.

Khan, Roni K. "Universalism and All That," *Jam-e-Jamshed Weekly* (Bombay), 1995. http://members.ozemail.com.au/~zarathus/roni33b.html

Kieckhefer, Richard. *Magic in the Middle Ages*. Cambridge: Cambridge University Press, 1989.

"Kirtan Sohila." http://home.t-online.de/home/practical-religion/kirtanso.htm.

Kitto, H. D. F. *The Greeks*. London: Penguin, 1951.

"Kojiki." http://www.harapan.co.jp.

Komroff, Manuel, ed. *The Apocrypha or Non-Canonical Books of the Bible*. New York: Tudor, 1937.

Kosambi, D. D. *An Introduction to the Study of Indian History*. Bombay: Popular Prakashan, 1975.

"Krishna Today." http://www.trancenet.org/krishna.

Krupp, E. C. *In Search of Ancient Astronomies*. Garden City, N.Y.: Doubleday, 1977.

Kumar, Arvind. "Women and the Vedas: Limiting Women Limits All of Society," *India Currents*, September 30, 1994.

Kunitz, Stanley J., and Howard Haycraft, eds. *American Authors 1600–1900*. New York: H. W. Wilson, 1938.

Lamsa, George M., trans. *Holy Bible from the Ancient Eastern Text*. San Francisco: Harper & Row, n.d.

Lamy, Lucy. *Egyptian Mysteries*. London: Cygnus, 1998.

Larue, Gerald A. *Old Testament Life and Literature*. Boston: Allyn & Bacon, 1968.

Lawless, George P. *Augustine of Hippo and His Monastic Rule*. New York: Oxford University Press, 1987.

Lazare, Bernard. "Antisemitism: Its History and Causes." http://www.abbc.com/aaargh/engl/BLantisem3.html.

Lee, Tae Seung. "A Study on J. N. Yaanagarbha's Theory of Satyadvaya," *Journal of Indian Philosophy*, 6, 1996, 135–174.

Leeming, David Adams. *The World of Myth*. Oxford: Oxford University Press, 1992.

Legg, L. G. Wickham, ed. *Dictionary of National Biography*. London: Oxford University Press, 1961.

Legge, James, trans. *I Ching: Book of Changes*. New York: Bantam, 1964.

Lehn, Cornelia. *Peace Be with You*. Newton, Kans.: Faith and Life Press, 1980.

Lesky, Albin. *A History of Greek Literature*. London: Gerald Duckworth, 1996.

Lessing, Doris. Introduction to *Ecclesiastes, or the Preacher*. New York: Grove, 1999.

Lester, Toby. "What Is the Koran," *Atlantic Monthly*, January 1999, 43–56.

"Letter of R. Isaac the Blind to the Kabbalists of Gerona." http://www2.trincoll.edu/~kiener/RELG208_saggine-horltr.html.

Leyser, Conrad. "Cities of the Plain," *Romantic Review*, March 1995, 191–212.

"Lfafe Sdq." http://anes235-1.ff.cuni.cz/projects/semitic/ethiopian/books/LS/contents_no-frames.htm.

Ling, T. O. *A Dictionary of Buddhism*. New York: Charles Scribner's Sons, 1972.

Littleton, C. Scott. "Yamato-takeru: An 'Arthurian' Hero in Japanese Tradition," *Asian Folklore Studies*, October 1995, 259–275.

Lopez, Robert S. *The Birth of Europe*. New York: M. Evans, 1967.

Lurker, Manfred. *The Gods and Symbols of Ancient Egypt*. London: Thames & Hudson, 1974.

Lyons, Albert S., and R. Joseph Petrucelli. *Medicine: An Illustrated History*. New York: Harry N. Abrams, 1987.

Maccabees. Garden City, N. Y.: Doubleday, 1976.

II Maccabees. Garden City, N. Y.: Doubleday, 1983.

MacDonald, Margaret Read, ed. *The Folklore of World Holidays*. Detroit: Gale Research, 1992.

Magill, Frank N., ed. *Cyclopedia of World Authors*. New York: Harper & Brothers, 1958.

_____. *Dictionary of World Biography*. Chicago: Fitzroy Dearborn, 1998.

Magnusson, Magnus, ed. *Cambridge Biographical Dictionary*. Cambridge: Cambridge University Press, 1990.

Malatesta, Parisina. "Reinterpreting the Icons," *Americas*, September 10, 1997, 20–21.

Malek, Jaromir. *In the Shadow of the Pyramids*. Norman: University of Oklahoma Press, 1986.

Mansukhani, Gobind Singh. *Sacred Literature*. New Delhi: Helmkunt, 1977.

Mantinband, James H. *Dictionary of Latin Literature*. New York: Philosophical Library, 1956.

Marquardt, H. Michael, and Wesley P. Walters. *Inventing Mormonism: Tradition and the Historical Record*. San Francisco: Smith Research, 1998.

Marriott, Alice, and Carol K. Rachlin. *Plains Indian Mythology*. New York: Meridian, 1975.

Martin, Bob. "Sanctuário de Chimayó," *New Mexico Magazine*, April 1969.

May, Herbert G., and Bruce M. Metzger, eds. *The Oxford Annotated Bible* (Revised Standard Version). New York: Oxford University Press, 1962.

Maynor, Malinda, and Toby McLeod. "America's First People Still Seek Religious Freedom," *Earth Island Journal*, Summer 1999.

Mays, James L., ed. *Harper's Bible Commentary*. San Francisco: Harper & Row, 1988.

McArthur, Tom, ed. *The Oxford Companion to the English Language*. Oxford: Oxford University Press, 1992.

McCall, Andrew. *The Medieval Underworld*. New York: Dorset, 1979.

McCluskey, Sally. "'Black Elk Speaks': And So Does John Neihardt," *Western American Literature*, Winter 1972, 231–242.

McConkie, Joseph Fielding, and Robert L. Millet. *Doctrinal Commentary on the Book of Mormon*. Salt Lake City, Utah: Bookcraft, 1987.

McCrum, Robert, William Cran, and Robert MacNeil. *The Story of English*. New York: Viking, 1986.

McDermott, Tom. "The Caged Bird," *Storytelling*, May 1997, 28–29.

McHenry, Robert, ed. *Liberty's Women*. Springfield, Mass.: G. C. Merriam, 1980.

McMurtry, Jo. *Understanding Shakespeare's England*. Hamden, Conn.: Archon, 1989.

"Medieval Sourcebook: Hadith: Traditions of the Prophet." http://www.fordham.edu/halsall/source/misc-hadith.html, 1996.

"Medieval Sourcebook: Reciting the Grace after Meals: The Status of Jewish Women, from Berakhot, Chap. 7." http://www.fordham.edu/halsall/source/jewishwomen-grace.html, 1998.

"Medieval Sourcebook: The Qur'an, 1, 47." http://www.fordham.edu/halsall/source/koran-sel.html.

Mehta, Julia. "Lessons from Tibetan Buddhism," *Nation*, February 15, 2000.

Melton, J. Gordon. *Encyclopedic Handbook of Cults in America*. New York: Garland, 1992.

Mervin, Sabrina, and Carol Prunhuber. *Women Around the World and Through the Ages*. Wilmington, Del.: Atomium, 1990.

Metzger, Bruce M. *The Apocrypha of the Old Testament*. New York: Oxford University Press, 1965.

Metzger, Bruce M., and Michael D. Coogan, eds. *The Oxford Companion to the Bible*. New York: Oxford University Press, 1993.

Meyer, Marvin, trans. and ed. *The Gospel of Thomas: The Hidden Sayings of Jesus*. San Francisco: HarperCollins, 1992.

_____. *The Secret Teachings of Jesus: Four Gnostic Gospels*. New York: Random House, 1984.

Meyer, Marvin W., ed. *The Ancient Mysteries: A Sourcebook*. San Francisco: HarperCollins, 1987.

McGuire, Anne, trans. "Thunder: Perfect Mind." http://www.uky.edu/ArtsSciences/Classics/thunder.html, 1996.

Milburn, Robert. *Early Christian Art and Architecture*. Berkeley: University of California Press, 1988.

Miller, Robert J. *The Complete Gospels*. Santa Rosa, Calif.: Polebridge, 1994.

Milne, Courtney. *Sacred Places in North America: A Journey into the Medicine Wheel*. New York: Stewart, Tabori & Chang, 1995.

"Modern History Sourcebook: The Constitution of the Iroquois Confederacy." http://www. fordham.edu/halsall/mod/iroquois.html.

Moffett, Blair A. "Ancient American Theosophy," *Sunrise*, October 1979.

Momaday, N. Scott. *The Way to Rainy Mountain*. Albuquerque: University of New Mexico Press, 1969.

"Mondino de Luzzi." http://www.astro.virginia.edu/~eww6n/bios/MondinodeLuzzi.html.

Morenz, Siegfried. *Egyptian Religion*. Ithaca, N.Y.: Cornell University Press, 1973.

Morford, Mark P. O., and Robert J. Lenardon. *Classical Mythology*. New York: Longman, 1977.

"Mormonism — No. II," *Tiffany's Monthly*, August 1859, 163–170.

Morrell, Peter. "Je Tsong Khapa." http://www.ajm.ch/pm_Tsong.html.

Murray, Peter, and Linda Murray. *The Oxford Companion to Christian Art and Architecture*. London: Oxford University Press, 1996.

Mutrux, Robert. *Great New England Churches: 65 Houses of Worship That Changed Our Lives*. Chester, Conn.: Globe Pequot, 1982.

"The Nag Hammadi Library." http://www.gnosis.org/naghamm/nhl.html, 1998.

"Native American Religion." http://cti.itc.virginia.edu/~jkh8x/soc257/nrms/naspirit.html.

Neihardt, Hilda. *Black Elk and Flaming Rainbow*. Lincoln: University of Nebraska Press, 1995.

Neihardt, John G. *Black Elk Speaks*. Lincoln: University of Nebraska Press, 1979.

_____. *When the Tree Flowered*. Lincoln: University of Nebraska Press, 1951.

Nell, Latricia, "Dead Sea Scrolls to Be Published on Compact Disc," *Daily Universe*, October 11, 1999.

New Catholic Encyclopedia. Washington, D.C.: Catholic University of America, 1967.

The New English Bible. Oxford: Oxford University Press, 1961.

Newman, Louis I., and Samuel Spitz, eds. *The Talmudic Anthology*. West Orange, N.J.: Behrman House, 1945.

Nicholson, R. A. *Rumi: Poet and Mystic*. London: George Allen & Unwin, 1950.

"The Nightmarish Underworld." http://www.fireplug.net/~rshand/streams/scriptsduat.html.

Norris, Kathleen. Introduction to *Revelation*. New York: Grove Press, 1999.

Norton, Dan S. *Classical Myths in English Literature*. New York: Rinehard, 1952.

Noss, David S., and John B. Noss. *Man's Religions*. New York: Macmillan, 1984.

Notable Asian Americans. Detroit: Gale Research, 1995.

"The Nyingma Lineage." http://www.palyulcanada.org/nyingma.html.

"The Nyingma Tradition." http://www.tibet.com/Buddhism/nyingma.html, 1997.

O'Daly, Gerard. *Augustine's Philosophy of the Mind*. Berkeley: University of California Press, 1987.

"The Odes of Solomon Annotated." http://www.piney.com/ApocOdeSolo.html.

Ohnuki-Tierney, Emiko. "Structure, Event and Historical Metaphor: Rice and Identities in Japanese History," *Journal of the Royal Anthropological Institute*, June 1995, 227–254.

"The Orion Center for the Study of the Dead Sea Scrolls and Associated Literature," http://orion.mscc.huji.ac.il.

Orr, James. *The International Standard Bible Encyclopedia*. Chicago: Howard-Severance, 1925.

Oussani, Gabriel. "Koran," in *Catholic Encyclopedia*, http://www.newadvent.org/cathen/08692a.htm, 1999.

"A Page from the Babylonian Talmud." http://www.acs.ucalgary.ca/~elsegal/TalmudPage.html.

Pagels, Elaine. *The Gnostic Gospels*. New York: Vintage, 1989.

Palmer, Martin J. "Adam: Ancient Sources," in *Encyclopedia of Mormonism*. New York: Macmillan, 1992.

Panikkar, Raimon. "The Vedic Experience: An Anthology of the Vedas for Modern Man," *Hinduism Today*, January 31, 1996, 10.

Parker, Michael St. John. *Britain's Kings and Queens*. Andover, Hants, England: Pitkin, 1994.

Parrinder, Geoffrey. *Religions of the Modern World: From Primitive Beliefs to Modern Faiths*. New York: Hamlyn, 1971.

Parry, Melanie, ed. *Larousse Dictionary of Women*. New York: Larousse Kingfisher Chambers, 1994.

Pastron, Allen. *Great Indian Chiefs*. Santa Barbara, Calif.: Bellerophon, 1993.

Patrick, Richard. *Egyptian Mythology*. London: Octopus, 1972.

Patterson, Lotsee, and Mary Ellen Snodgrass. *Indian Terms of the Americas*. Englewood, Colo.: Libraries Unlimited, 1994.

"Paul A. W. Wallace Papers." http://www.phmc.state.pa.us/PA_Exec/Historical_Museum/DAM/mg/mg192.htm, 2000.

Pelikan, Jaroslav. *On Searching the Scriptures — Your Own or Someone Else's*. New York: Quality Paperback Club, 1992.

Perkins, Dorothy. *Encyclopedia of Japan*. New York: Facts on File, 1991.

Perry, T. A. *The Moral Proverbs of Santob de Carrión: Jewish Wisdom in Christian Spain*. Princeton, N.J.: Princeton University Press, 1987.

Phillips, J. B. *The New Testament in Modern English*. New York: Macmillan, 1972.

Pickthall, Marmaduke. *The Meaning of the Glorious Koran*. New York: Dorset, 1930. www.quraan.com/Pickthall/Default.asp.

Pickthall, Muhammad Marmaduke. "Tolerance in Islam." http://salam.muslimsonline.com/~azahoor/toleran1.html, 1997.

Piggott, Juliet. *Japanese Mythology*. London: Paul Hamlyn, 1973.

Pike, E. Royston. *Mohammed: Prophet of the Religion of Islam*. New York: Frederick A. Praeger, 1965.

"The Popul Vuh." http://www.geocities.com/Athens/Academy/3088/popol.html.

"Post-Talmudic Period." http://miso.wwa.com/~curadist/ReferenceLibrary/Christianity/UCG/Contribs/caljchu2.htm.

Potok, Chaim. *Wanderings: Chaim Potok's History of the Jews*. New York: Alfred A. Knopf, 1978.

Powell, Lyman P. *Mary Baker Eddy: A Life Size Portrait*. Boston: Christian Science Publishing Society, 1950.

Powell, Peter. *Sweet Medicine: The Continuing Role of the Sacred Arrow, the Sun Dance, and the Sacred Buffalo Hat in Northern Cheyenne History*. Norman: University of Oklahoma Press, 1969.

Powers, John. *Introduction to Tibetan Buddhism*. New York: Snow Lion, 1995.

Powers, William K. *Oglala Religion*. Lincoln: University of Nebraska Press, 1977.

Prabhupada, A. C. Bhaktivedanta. *Bhagavad-Gita as It Is*. Los Angeles: Bhaktivedanta Book Trust, 1981.

Prabhavananda, Swami, and Christopher Isherwood, trans. *The Song of God: Bhagavad-Gita*. New York: New American Library, 1951.

Price, Ira Maurice. *The Monuments and the Old Testament*. Philadelphia: Judson Press, 1925.

"Quote of the Week." http://archaeology.about.com/education/archaeology/blquote97.htm.

Raby, F. J. E., ed. *A History of Christian-Latin Poetry*. Oxford: Clarendon, 1953.

_____. *The Oxford Book of Medieval Latin Verse*. Oxford: Clarendon, 1959.

Radice, Betty. *Who's Who in the Ancient World*. Middlesex, England: Penguin, 1973.

Radin, Paul. *The Story of the American Indian*. Garden City, N.Y.: Garden City Publishing, 1927.

Raffee, Shabier. "An Experience for the Soul." *Islamic Herald*, February 1996.

"Rashi's Commentary on the Talmud." http://www.acs.ucalgary.ca/~elsegal/TalmudMap/Rashi.html.

Reese, Lyn. *Women in the Muslim World*. Berkeley, Calif.: Women in World History Curriculum, 1998.

Reeves, Marjorie. "Review of *Liber Secretorum Eventuum*," *Catholic Historical Review*, July 1995, 435–439.

Reichelt, K. L. *Meditation and Piety in the Far East*. New York: Harper & Brothers, 1954.

Religious Leaders of America. Farmington Hills, Mich.: Gale Group, 1999.

Renard, John. "Poetry and Mysticism in Islam: The Heritage of Rumi," *Journal of the American Oriental Society*, January 3, 1997, 185–187.

Renou, Louis, ed. *Hinduism*. New York: George Braziller, 1961.

Reynolds, George, and Janne M. Sjodahl. *Commentary on the Book of Mormon*. Salt Lake City, Utah: Philip C. Reynolds, 1955.

Rice, David Talbot, ed. *The Dawn of European Civilization: The Dark Ages*. New York: McGraw-Hill, 1965.

Rice, Edward. *American Saints and Seers: American-Born Religions and the Genius Behind Them*. New York: Four Winds Press, 1982.

Rifkin, Ira, "Complexities of the Koran Make Mastery a Challenge," *Washington Post*, January 20, 1998.

Rinpoche, Samdhong. "Tibetan Culture: Nature and Process," *Common Voice* 2, 1992.

Rinpoche, Sogyal. "The Spiritual Heart of Tibetan Medicine: Its Contribution to the Modern World," *Alternative Therapies*, May 1999, 70–72.

Roberts, Vera Mowry. *On Stage: A History of Theatre*. New York: Harper & Row, 1962.

Robinson, James M. *The Nag Hammadi Library*. San Francisco: HarperCollins, 1990.

Rosenberg, Donna. *World Mythology*. Lincolnwood, Ill.: Passport Books, 1992.

Roth, Cecil, and Geoffrey Wigoder, eds. *The New Standard Jewish Encyclopedia*, 5th ed. Garden City, N. Y.: Doubleday, 1977.

"Rushdie File." http://www.pen.org/freedom/mideast/rushdie/rushdie4.html.

"The Sacred Book of the Maya — Popol Vuh — Re-Creates a Tradition," *Los Angeles Times*, September 25, 1999.

Schimmel, Annemarie. *Mystical Dimensions of Islam*. Chapel Hill: University of North Carolina Press, 1975.

_____. *As Through a Veil: Mystical Poetry in Islam*. New York: Columbia University, 1982.

Scholem, Gershom. *Kabbalah*. New York: Meridian, 1978.

_____. *Origins of the Kabbalah*. Princeton, N.J.: Princeton University Press, 1987.

Schumann, Hans Wolfgang. *Buddhism: An Outline of Its Teachings and Schools*. Wheaton, Ill.: Theosophical Publishing House, 1973.

Schwartz, Benjamin I. *The World of Thought in Ancient China*. Cambridge, Mass.: Harvard University Press, 1985.

"The Scientific Struggle for Anatomy." http://www.physics.wisc.edu/~shalizi/White/medicine/anatomy.html.

"The Scott and White Medical Moulage Collection." http://ww-moulages.htm, 1997.

"Scrolls from the Dead Sea." Library of Congress, http://lcweb.loc.gov/exhibits/scrolls/toc.html, 1996.

"Selections from Mahayana Texts." http://online.anu.edu.au/asianstudies/buddhism/maha.html.

"Selections from Tibetan Buddhist Texts." http://www.anu.edu.au/asianstudies/buddhism/tib.html.

"Self-Liberation Through Seeing with Naked Awareness." http://bands.hive.net/catawampus/self25.html.

Sells, Michael. *Approaching the Qur'án: The Early Revelations*. Ashland, Oreg.: White Cloud Press, 2000.

Senior, Michael. *The Illustrated Who's Who in Mythology*. New York: Macmillan, 1985.

Shah, Amina. *Folk Tales of Central Asia*. London: Octagon, 1975.

Sharer, Robert J. *Daily Life in Maya Civilization*. Westport, Conn.: Greenwood, 1996.

Shariari, Shariar. "Ahuna Vairya." http://www.zarathushtra.com/article/ahunavar.htm, 1998.

Sharma, Arvind, ed. *Women in World Religions*. Albany: State University of New York Press, 1987.

Shelmerdine, Susan C. *The Homeric Hymns*. Newburyport, Mass.: Focus, 1995.

Sherr, Lynn, and Jurate Kazickas. *Susan B. Anthony Slept Here: A Guide to American Women's Landmarks*. New York: Times Books, 1994.

"Shinto," *Canada and the World Backgrounder*, December 1, 1999, 63–64.

"Significant Events in Jewish and World History." http://www.jewishamerica.com/Time Line/rashi2ex.htm.Goldstein, Jonathan A.

Silberman, Neil Asher. *The Hidden Scrolls*. New York: G. P. Putnam's Sons, 1994.

Sinha, Indra. "The Five-fold Sacrament," *Parabola*, December 1, 1995.

Siraisi, Nancy G. *Medieval and Early Renaissance Medicine*. Chicago: University of Chicago Press, 1990.

Sircar, Jayanta L. "The Vedanta Society of New York: A Review of the First Century," *Bulletin of the Sri Ramakrishna Institute of Culture*, Calcutta, n. d.

"The Siri Guru Granth Sahib." http://www.sikhnet.com/s/GuruGranthSahib.

Skafte, Dianne. *Listening to the Oracle*. San Francisco: Harper, 1997.

Slater, Philip E. *The Glory of Hera: Greek Mythology and the Greek Family*. Boston: Beacon, 1968.

Smart, Ninian. *The Religious Experience of Mankind.* New York: Charles Scribner's Sons, 1969.

Smaus, Jewel Spangler. *Mary Baker Eddy: The Golden Days.* Boston: Christian Science Publishing Society, 1966.

Smith, G. E. Kidder. *The Beacon Guide to New England Houses of Worship.* Boston: Beacon, 1989.

Smith, Huston. *The Illustrated World's Religions.* San Francisco: HarperCollins, 1994.

_____. *The Religions of Man.* New York: Harper & Row, 1958.

Smith, Jane I. *Islam in America.* New York: Columbia University Press, 1999.

Smith, Jonathan Z., ed. *The HarperCollins Dictionary of Religion.* San Francisco: HarperSan Francisco, 1995.

Smith, Mahlon. "Persona in Rabbinic Tradition," http://www.rci.rutgers.edu/~religion/iho/rabbis.html, 1999.

Snodgrass, Mary Ellen. *Crossing Barriers: People Who Overcame.* Englewood, Colo.: Libraries Unlimited, 1993.

_____. *The Encyclopedia of Fable.* Santa Barbara, Calif.: ABC-Clio, 1998.

_____. *The Encyclopedia of Frontier Literature.* Santa Barbara, Calif.: ABC-Clio, 1997.

_____. *The Encyclopedia of Utopian Literature.* Santa Barbara, Calif.: ABC-Clio, 1995.

_____. *Religious Sites in America.* Santa Barbara, Calif.: ABC-Clio, 2000.

_____. *Roman Classics.* Lincoln, Nebr.: Cliffs Notes, 1988.

_____. *Voyages in Classical Mythology.* Santa Barbara, Calif.: ABC-Clio, 1994.

_____. *Who's Who in the Middle Ages.* Jefferson, N.C.: McFarland, 2001.

"Society: Iroquois." http://lucy.ukc.ac.uk/EthnoAtlas/Hmar/Cult_dir/Culture.7849.

Spaugh, Herbert. "A Short Introduction to the History, Customs and Practices of the Moravian Church," in *Everyday Counselor.* Winston-Salem, N.C.: New Philadelphia Moravian Church, 1999.

Starr, Chester G. *A History of the Ancient World.* Oxford: Oxford University Press, 1991.

"A Statement from Dr. Arvol Looking Horse." http://www.wintercount.org/people/lakota.web.

Steiger, Brad. *Medicine Power.* Garden City, N.Y.: Doubleday, 1974.

Steinberg, S. H., ed. *Cassell's Encyclopedia of World Literature.* New York: Funk & Wagnalls, 1953.

Steinke, Darcey. Introduction to *The Gospel According to John.* New York: Grove, 1999.

Steinmetz, Paul B. *The Sacred Pipe: An Archetypal Theology.* Syracuse, N.Y.: Syracuse University Press, 1998.

Steinsaltz, Adin. *The Essential Talmud.* New York: Basic, 1976.

Steltenkamp, Michael F. *Black Elk, Holy Man of the Oglala.* Norman: University of Oklahoma Press, 1993.

_____. *The Sacred Vision: Native American Religion and Its Practice Today.* New York: Paulist Press, 1982.

Stockman, Robert H. "The American Bahá'i Community in the Nineties," in *America's Alternative Religions.* Albany: State University of New York Press, 1995.

"Stone Carving May Validate Mayan Book: Discovery Matches the Historical Account," *Dallas Morning News,* November 17, 1997.

Stow, Kenneth R. *Alienated Minority: The Jews of Medieval Latin Europe.* Cambridge, Mass.: Harvard University Press, 1992.

Strayer, Joseph R., ed. *Dictionary of the Middle Ages.* New York: Charles Scribner's Sons, 1983.

Suzuki, Daisetz Teitaro. *An Introduction to Zen Buddhism.* New York: Causeway, 1974.

Szarmach, Paul E., et al., eds. *Medieval England.* New York: Garland, 1998.

"Tao Te Ching." http://rhino.harvard.edu/elwin/pJoy/taoteching.html, 1995.

Tat, Mark. "Contributions on Tibetan Language, History and Culture: Contributions on Tibetan and Buddhist Religion and Philosophy," *Journal of the American Oriental Society,* July–September 1997, 576–577.

Tedlock, Dennis, trans. *Popol Vuh: The Mayan Book of the Dawn of Life.* New York: Touchstone, 1996.

Telushkin, Rabbi Joseph. *Jewish Literacy.* New York: William Morrow, 1991.

_____. *Jewish Wisdom.* New York: William Morrow, 1994.

"Temple Square." *Utah Encyclopedia.* http://eddy.media.utah.edu/ucme/t/TEMPLESQUARE.html.

"Theravada Buddhism." http://www.buddhanet.net/burma.htm.

Thompson, Oscar, ed. *The International Cyclopedia of Music and Musicians.* New York: Dodd, Mead, 1975.

Thoreau, Henry David. *Walden and Other Writings.* New York: Bantam, 1982

Thurman, Robert A. F., trans. *The Tibetan Book of the Dead: Liberation Through Understanding in the Between.* London: HarperCollins, 1994.

"Tibetan Buddhism." http://www.zip.com.au/~cee_gee/tibet.html, 1997.

"Tibetan Religion and the Western Imagination." http://www.lib.virginia.edu/exhibits/dead/western.html.

Tickle, Phyllis A. *God-Talk in America.* New York: Crossroad, 1997.

"Timeline: Principal Medieval Rabbinic Authorities." http://www.acs.ucalgary.ca/~elsegal/RelS_365/Rabbis_timeline.html.

"The Toledano Tradition of Kabbalah." http://www.kabbalah-society.org, 2000.

Trager, James. *The People's Chronology.* New York: Henry Holt, 1992.

_____. *The Women's Chronology.* New York: Henry Holt, 1995.

"Translation or Divination?" http://www.irr.org/mit/divination.html, 1999.

Tsumuro, Yukihiko. "Purpose of Tsubaki America." http://www.csuchico.edu/~georgew/tsa/purpose.html, 1988.

Turner, Alice. *The History of Hell.* New York: Harcourt Brace, 1993.

Turner, Darrell. "Fifth Gospel Throws Light on Sayings of Jesus," *Religious News Service,* December 27, 1991.

"The Unbound Bible." http://unbound.biola.edu.

"A Valentinian Exposition." http://www.gnosis.org/naghamm/valex.html.

"Vedanta, Ramakrishna, and Vivekananda." http://www.silcom.com/~origin/sbcr/sbcr084.

Vermes, Geza. *The Complete Dead Sea Scrolls in English.* New York: Penguin, 1998.

Vogel, Howard J. "Bear Butte, Black Hills," http://web.hamline.edu/law/lawrelign/sacred/bearb.html, 1998.

Vu, Harriet. "Foundations of Mahayana Buddhism." http://www.geocities.com/Athens/8916/index2.html.

Waldman, Carl. *Who Was Who in Native American History: Indians and Non-Indians from Early Contacts Through 1900.* New York: Facts on File, 1990.

Waley, Arthur, trans. *Confucianism: The Analects of Confucius.* New York: Continuum, 1986.

_____. *The Analects of Confucius.* New York: Vintage, 1989.

Waley, M. I. *Sufism: The Alchemy of the Heart.* San Francisco, Calif.: Chronicle, 1993.

Walker, Barbara G. *The Woman's Encyclopedia of Myths and Secrets*. Edison, N.J.: Castle, 1996.

Walking Turtle, Eagle. *Indian America*, 3d ed. Santa Fe, N.M.: J. Muir, 1993.

Wallace, B. Alan, trans. "Natural Liberation: Padmasambhava's Teachings on the Six Bardos." http://vs1.channel1.com/users/wisdom/books/natlib.html, 1997.

Wallace, Paul A. W. *The White Roots of Peace*. Philadelphia: University of Pennsylvania Press, 1986.

Walters, Wesley P. "The Book of Mormon Today." http://www.irr.org/mit/bomtoday.html, 1999.

Waltham, Clae. *I Ching: The Chinese Book of Changes*. New York: Ace, 1969.

Warraq, Ibn, ed. *The Origins of the Koran: Classic Essays on Islam's Holy Book*. Amherst, N.Y.: Prometheus, 1998.

Watt, William Montgomery. *Companion to the Qur'an*. Oxford: One World, 1994.

Watterson, Barbara. *The Gods of Ancient Egypt*. London: Batsford, 1984.

Webley, Don. "Nirvana Is Openly Shown to Our Eyes: The Life of the Zen Master Hakuin," *Crazy Wisdom*, July–October 1988.

Webster, Douglas O. "The Good Book: Reading the Bible with Mind and Heart," *Christianity Today*, April 7, 1997, 42–45.

Webster, Hutton. *Early European History*. New York: D. C. Heath, 1924.

Wechsler, Shoshana. "A Matter of Fact and Vision: The Objectivity Question and Muriel Rukeyser's 'The Book of the Dead,'" *Twentieth Century Literature*, January 1999, 121.

Weddell, James R. "The Black Hills Are Not for Sale." http://users.skynet.be/kola/bhills.htm.

"Welcome to the AkweKon Virtual Tour." http://www.campuslife.cornell.edu/main/SSL/Akwekon/virt7.html.

Weldon, Fay. Introduction to *The Epistles of Paul the Apostle to the Corinthians*. New York: Grove, 1999.

Whelan, Estelle. "Forgotten Witness: Evidence for the Early Codification of the Qur'an," *Journal of the American Oriental Society*, January 12, 1998.

White, David Gordon. "The Rise of the Goddess in the Hindu Tradition," *Journal of the American Oriental Society*, April 15, 1996.

Whittaker, David J. "Danites" in *The Encyclopedia of Mormonism*. http://www.mormons.org/response/history/danites_eom.htm, 1992.

"Who Are Moravians?" *Lutheran*, August 1, 1999, 43.

"Who Is a Hindu?" *Hinduism Today*, October 1999, 8.

Wicks, Robert. "The Therapeutic Psychology of 'The Tibetan Book of the Dead,'" *Philosophy East and West*, 1997, 479–494.

Wiget, Andrew. *Handbook of Native American Literature*. New York: Garland, 1996.

Wigoder, Geoffrey. *The Encyclopedia of Judaism*. New York: Macmillan, 1989.

Williams, John A. *Islam*. New York: George Braziller, 1961.

Wilson, Terry. *Lakota: Seeking the Great Spirit*. London: Labyrinth, 1994.

"The Woman's Bible." http://henry.huntington.org/vfw/orgpub/womensbible.html.

Wood, Ernest. *Zen Dictionary*. New York: Citadel, 1962.

Wood, Wilford C. "Memorandum of John H. Gilbert," in *Joseph Smith Begins His Work*. Salt Lake City, Utah: Deseret News Press, 1958.

World Literature. New York: Holt, Rinehart & Winston, 1998.

World Religions. New York: Macmillan Reference USA, 1998.

Yamamoto, Yukitaka. *The Way of the Kami*. Stockton, Calif.: Tsubaki America, 1999.

Yutang, Lin, ed. and trans. *The Wisdom of Confucius*. New York: Modern Library, 1938.

Zacharias, Paul B. *Swedenborgians See It This Way* (brochure). Newton, Mass.: J. Appleseed, n. d.

Zeinert, Karen. *Cults*. Springfield, N.J.: Enslow, 1997.

Zimansky, Paul. "The Conquest of Assyria: Excavations in an Antique Land," *Bulletin of the American Schools of Oriental Research*, February 1, 1999, 92.

"Zoroastrianism." http://www.religioustolerance.org/zoroastr.htm.

"Zoroastrianism Page." http://coulomb.ecn.purdue.edu/~bulsara/ZOROASTRIAN/zoroastrian.html.

Zweig, Stefan. *Mental Healers: Franz Anton Mesmer, Mary Baker Eddy, Sigmund Freud*. New York: Frederick Ungar, 1990.

Index

Main entries are in boldface; illustrations are bracketed

French and Indian War 265
French New Testament 100
Frost, Robert 65
Frumentius 162–163
Fu Hsi 177, 178

Gabriel 22, 70, 145, 198
Gad 16, 44, 51, 71, 72, 142
Gahs 34
Galatians 89–90, 125
Gamaliel I 232
Gamaliel II 232
Gan Eden 234
Gandhi, Mohandas 39, 82, 129
gaon 224, 232–233
Gaon, Yehudai 232–233
Gatha Days 28
Gathas 30–31
Gebhurah see *Gevurah*
Gedullah see *Hesed*
Gemara 225
gematria 187, 188
Gemmei, Empress 192
genealogy 114, 115, 191, 194, 253
Genesis 16, 21, 40, 42–44, 48, 78,
 98, 120, 124, 138, 139, 142, 143,
 160, 187, 205, 215, 216
Genesis Apocryphon 141
Geneva Bible 100
Genghis Khan 244
genocide 69
Gentileschi, Artemisia 9, 10
geomancy 133
German Bible 12
German Requiem 62, 64
Gerondi, Moses ben Nahman *see*
 Nahmanides
Gershom ben Judah 233
Gesta Romanorum 214
Gettysburg Address 99
gevurah 185
Gevurot 225
Ghai Nand Lal 171
ghazal 213
Ghost Dance 104, 107, 113–114
ghosts 128
Gibbon, Edward 197
Gibson, John Arthur 260
Gibson, Simeon 260
Gibson Version 260
Gideon 49, 50
Gikatilla, Joseph ben-Abraham
 188
gilgul 186
Ginnat Egoz 188
Giotto 17
Girard, Raphael M. 222–223
The Gita As It Is 40
gnosticism 5, 17, 18, 21, 24, 96,
 184, 187, 222
Gobind Singh 167, 169, 170, 171
go-i-koan 191
Goindval Pothis see *Mothan
 Pothi*
Gold, Eugene Jeffrey 246
Golden Age 32, 42–43, 128, 130,
 135, 187, 194, 244
The Golden Bough 156
golden mean 134
Golden Rule 9, 79, 129, 135
golem 186
Der Golem 186
Golem Suite 186
Goliath 40, 51–52

Gomer 58
Gomez, Ermilo Ebreu 216
gonsen-koan 191
The Good Earth 132
Good News Bible 103
Good Samaritan 82
Good Shepherd 63, 84
Goodspeed, Edgar J. 102
Gordian III 29
Gorgias 10
gospel 74
The Gospel According to the
 Egyptians 18
The Gospel of Bartholomew 18
The Gospel of Gamaliel 23
Gospel of James 17
Gospel of John 23, 39
The Gospel of Nicodemus 18,
 22–23
The Gospel of Peter 23
The Gospel of Philip 19
The Gospel of the Ebionites 18
Gospel of the Essenes *see* The
 Gospel of the Nazarenes
The Gospel of the Hebrews 17
The Gospel of the Nazarenes 18
The Gospel of the Twelve *see*
 The Gospel of the Ebionites
The Gospel of Thomas 17, 18–19
The Gospel of Truth 21
gospels, Christian 74–85, 121,
 205
Gothic 99
grammateia *see* gematria
Grandin, E. B. 115
Granth 166–[167]–171
Great Awakening 115
Great Bible 100
Great Mosque at Mecca 202
Great Mosque of Sana'a 210
Great Mother 172, 173; *see also*
 Demeter
Great Spirit 105, 106, 108, 109,
 110, 111, 112, 260–261, 264
Great Way 132
The Greater Bundahishen 34
Greathouse lineage 219
Greek Bible of Alexandria 5–6
Green Dome 214
Grhyasutra 259
Gründler, Johann Ernst 101
Guatemala 214–223
Guercino, Giovanni 9
Gugumatz 215, 216
Guhyasmaja Tantra 236, 237
Gurbani see *Adi Granth*
Gurmukhi 168
Guru Granth Sahib 167, 169
Guru Granth see *Granth*
Gutenberg, Johann 74, 99

Habakkuk 9, 49, 55, 57, 60, 138,
 143
Hadhoxt Nask 33
hadith 199, 201, 207
hadj see *hajj*
Hadrian 139, 232
hafiz 205
Hafsa 201–202
Hagar 43, 203
haggada 224
Haggai 49, 57, 60–61, 71
hagiography 40, 61, 168, 204, 211,
 241, 244

hajj 201, 202, 211
Hakana *see* Nehunya ben
 Haqana
Hakuin Ekaku 191
halakha 224
Halakhot Gedolot 233
Halakhot Pesuqot 232–233
Halaphta, Jose ben 232
Hale, Emma 115
Hall of the Two Truths 155
Haman 8, 68–69
Ha-Mappa 235
Hamlet 9
Hammurabi 46, 161, 222
Han Yü 133
Hananiah, Joshua ben 232
ha-Nasi, Judah 225, 232
Hanblecheyapi ritual 110
Handel, Georg Friedrich 8–9, 11,
 51, 68
Hanhagat ha-Rosh 234
hanifs 199
Hannah 11, 51
Hanukkah 11, 61, 73
haoma 29, 30, 34, 250, 252
Haqana, Nehunya ben 186
Harding, Gerald Lankester 138
Harimandir 168
Harkavy, Abraham 74
harmony 132, 136, 240, 242, 244;
 see also Tao-te Ching, yin-yang
 cosmogony
Harris, Martin 115, 116
Hashida 190
hasidim 139, 186, 189
Hasmoneans 10–11, 143
Haudenoshaunee see *Hodi-
 noshone*
Hawaiian New Testament 102
Hayy ibn Ya'amor 208
Heavenly Prince Melchizedek
 146
Hebbel, Friedrich 10
Hebrews (book) 74–75, 87,
 93–94
Hebrews (people) 40–58, 73, 75,
 77
Hecataeus of Abdera 26
Hegel, Georg 123
hegira see *hijra*
he-Hasid, Judah ben-Samuel 186
he-Hasid, Samuel ben Kalonymus
 186
Hékhalot Rabbati 185
Hékhalot Zutarté 185
Hekigan-roku 191
Helaman 117, 119, 120
Helaman (book) 120–121
Helaman (son of Helaman) 120
Helen of Troy 20
Heliopolitan Recension 156
Helios 176
Hellenism 5–6, 7, 13, 14, 15, 28,
 41, 73
Hellmouth 60
Henry VIII 100
Hera 174, 193
Heraclius 34
Herakles 175
Herald of Christian Science 125
herbalism 242–243
Herman Dalmatin 208
Hermes 20, 28, 173, 176
Hermic cult 173

hero tale 50, 59, 69–70, 195–196
Herod the Great 17, 73, 78, 79,
 82, 86, 139, 146
Heroes and Hero Worship 199
Hesed 185, 188
Hesiod 132, 175–176
Hestia 173, 175, 176
Hesychasts 187
Hevajratantra 235
Hewiss, J. N. B. 260
Hexapla 98
Hexateuch 48, 49
Heyoka ceremony 114
Hezekiah 14, 55, 64, 65, 72, 73
Hiawatha 261
Hicks, Edward 16
*Hidden Scrolls from the Judaean
 Desert* 140
hieroglyphics 155–162, 215, 216
hijra 200
Hilkiah 47, 54, 55, 73
Hillel 98, 225, 232
Hinayana Buddhism 153
Hinckelmann, D. Abraham 209
Hinduism 35–40, 149, 166, 167,
 235, 237, 250–259
Hippolytus 74
Hippostratus 172
*Historia de Conceptione Beatae
 Maria* 17
*Historia de la Provincia de San Vi-
 cente de Chiapa y Guatemala*
 215
Historia Naturalis 139
*Historia Religionis Veterum Per-
 sarum* 35
*Las Historias del Origen de los In-
 dios de esta Provincia de
 Guatemala* 215
historiography 214
history: Chinese 32–133; Jewish
 225; Quichéan 221–223
*The History of Joseph the Car-
 penter* 22
*The History of the Blessed Virgin
 Mary* 23
Hitachi Fudoki 195
Hiyeda no Are 192
Hizoboyaku 240
Ho Chen-kung 244
Hod 185
Hoda'ah 225
Hodayot 16, 145
Hodesaunee see Iroquois League
Hodge, Stephen 247, 248
Hodinoshone 262
Hogo-roku 191
Hokhmah 185
Hokhmat ha-Nefesh 186
Holofernes 9–10
*The Holy Koran: An Introduction
 with Selections* 209
Holy of Holies (Jewish) 13, 45,
 227
Holy of Holies (Muslim) 202
*Holy Scriptures According to the
 Masoretic Text* 74
Holy Spirit 77, 85, 86, 87, 88, 118
Homer 25, 171
Homeric Hymns 171–176
honji see *kyuji*
Horace 68
Hohoderi interlude 194
Horse Dance 106